Franco Montanari
History of Ancient Greek Literature

Franco Montanari

History of Ancient Greek Literature

Volume 2: The Hellenistic Age
and the Roman Imperial Period

With the collaboration of
Fausto Montana

Translated from the Italian original
by Orla Mulholland

DE GRUYTER

Italian original: Franco Montanari, Storia della letteratura greca, con la collaborazione
di Fausto Montana: nuova edizione Roma, Edizioni di Storia e Letteratura, 2022.

ISBN 978-3-11-041992-4
e-ISBN (PDF) 978-3-11-042632-8
e-ISBN (EPUB) 978-3-11-042634-2

Library of Congress Control Number: 2022935008

Bibliographic information published by the Deutsche Nationalbibliothek
The Deutsche Nationalbibliothek lists this publication in the Deutsche Nationalbibliografie;
detailed bibliographic data are available on the Internet at http://dnb.dnb.de.

© 2022 Walter de Gruyter GmbH, Berlin/Boston

Cover image: Young girl reading. Roman bronze statuette after a Hellenistic model. From Rome.
Bibliothèque nationale de France, Cabinet des Médailles, Caylus Collection
© Marie-Lan Nguyen / Wikimedia commons
(https://commons.wikimedia.org/wiki/File:Bronze_young_girl_reading_CdM_Paris.jpg)

Printing and binding: CPI books GmbH, Leck

www.degruyter.com

Contents

The Hellenistic Age

I   The Period —— 737
1   The Hellenistic Age —— 737
2   Greece during the Hellenistic Age —— 738
3   The diffusion of Greek culture: the new centres —— 741
4   The literary genres in the Hellenistic Age —— 743

II   Theatre —— 750
1   The New Comedy and Menander —— 750
1.1   Hellenistic society and New Comedy —— 750
1.2   The authors of New Comedy —— 751
1.3   Menander: historical context and biographical notices —— 752
1.3.1   The transmission of the comedies —— 753
1.3.2   Menander's dramaturgy —— 755
1.3.3   The better-preserved comedies —— 758
1.3.4   The poetic and moral world of Menander —— 761
1.3.5   Language and style —— 762
1.3.6   Reception —— 762
2   Tragedy and phlyax —— 763
2.1   Tragedy between heritage and new developments —— 763
2.2   The tragic output of the Hellenistic Age —— 764
2.3   Phlyax or hilarotragedy —— 765
2.4   Rhinthon —— 766

III   Philology, Grammar, Erudition —— 767
1   The literature of erudition —— 767
1.1   Philology, grammar and the transmission and interpretation of texts —— 767
1.2   Textual philology and scholiography —— 768
1.3   Lexicography —— 771
1.4   Grammar —— 772
1.5   Paroemiography —— 773
1.6   Biography —— 774
2   Philology in Alexandria and Pergamum —— 774
2.1   Pre-Alexandrian exegesis —— 774
2.2   Alexandrian philology: from Zenodotus to Aristarchus —— 776
2.3   Philology at Pergamum —— 780
2.4   From Aristarchus to the Augustan Age —— 783

IV	**Poetry in the Hellenistic Age** —— 787	
1	Scholar poets and the mixing of genres —— 787	
1.1	A radically new poetic consciousness —— 787	
1.2	The poetic genres —— 789	
2	Elegy and epigram —— 791	
2.1	Elegy —— 791	
2.1.1	Narrative elegy: myth and love —— 791	
2.1.2	Philitas of Cos —— 792	
2.1.3	Hermesianax of Colophon —— 793	
2.1.4	Phanocles —— 793	
2.1.5	Simmias (or Simias) of Rhodes —— 794	
2.1.6	Alexander the Aetolian —— 794	
2.1.7	Parthenius of Nicaea —— 794	
2.2	Epigram —— 795	
2.2.1	The origins of epigrammatic poetry —— 795	
2.2.2	The epigram in the Classical Age —— 796	
2.2.3	The Hellenistic epigram and the epigrammatic "schools" —— 796	
2.2.4	The "Peloponnesian school" —— 798	
2.2.5	The "Ionian-Alexandrian school" —— 798	
2.2.6	The "Phoenician school" —— 800	
2.2.7	The tradition of anthologies of Greek epigrams —— 802	
3	Callimachus: new poetics and philology —— 803	
3.1	Life —— 803	
3.2	The works —— 804	
3.2.1	The lost works —— 804	
3.2.2	The surviving and fragmentary works —— 805	
3.3	The *Hymns* —— 806	
3.4	The *Aetia* —— 808	
3.5	The *Iambi* —— 811	
3.6	The *Epigrams* —— 813	
3.7	*Hecale* —— 814	
3.8	Callimachean poetics —— 815	
3.9	Language and style —— 817	
3.10	The reception of the works —— 818	
4	Didactic poetry —— 818	
4.1	Following in the footsteps of the hexameter tradition —— 818	
4.2	Aratus of Soli: astronomy in verse —— 820	
4.3	Nicander of Colophon —— 821	
5	Hellenistic epic and Apollonius Rhodius —— 823	
5.1	Epic in the Hellenistic Age —— 823	
5.1.1	Evolution of the genre —— 823	
5.1.2	The lost epic output —— 823	

5.2   Apollonius Rhodius — 824
5.2.1   Life — 824
5.2.2   The works — 826
5.2.3   The *Argonautica* — 826
5.2.4   Epic model and Hellenistic poetics — 829
5.2.5   Language and style — 833
5.2.6   Later reception — 833
6   Theocritus and bucolic poetry — 833
6.1   Bucolic-pastoral poetry and Hellenistic poetry — 833
6.2   Theocritus of Syracuse — 834
6.2.1   Biographical notices — 834
6.2.2   The works — 835
6.2.3   The bucolic idylls — 836
6.2.4   The other "idylls" — 838
6.2.5   The *Epigrams* — 840
6.2.6   Theocritean poetics — 840
6.2.7   Language and style — 841
6.3   The bucolic corpus: Moschus, Bion and the "figured" poems — 841
7   Ancient genres and new poetics — 842
7.1   Selection and preservation — 842
7.2   Lycophron of Chalcis — 843
7.3   Euphorion of Chalcis — 844
7.4   Sotades — 845
7.5   Iambographi: Phoenix and Cercidas — 846
7.6   Melinno — 846
8   Mime and Herodas — 847
8.1   Mime: a dramatic genre of popular origin — 847
8.2   The *Mimiambi* of Herodas — 848

V   The Hellenistic Philosophies — 852
1   The primacy of ethics and the problem of happiness — 852
1.1   General characteristics — 852
1.2   The philosophical schools in the Hellenistic world — 853
2   Scepticism — 855
2.1   *Skepsis* in Greek thought — 855
2.2   Pyrrhon and Scepticism — 855
2.3   Scepticism and the Academy — 857
3   Epicureanism — 858
3.1   Optimism without hope — 858
3.2   Life and works of Epicurus — 858
3.3   The doctrines — 859
3.4   The school after Epicurus — 862

4	Stoicism —— **862**	
4.1	A rational response to the problem of happiness —— **862**	
4.2	Zeno and the Early Stoa —— **863**	
4.3	The doctrines of early Stoicism —— **864**	
4.4	The Middle Stoa —— **866**	
VI	**The Sciences —— 868**	
1	Mathematics, astronomy, mechanics —— **868**	
1.1	The centrality of Alexandrian scientific culture —— **868**	
1.2	Astronomy —— **870**	
1.3	Mathematics and mechanics —— **871**	
2	Medicine —— **875**	
2.1	Medicine at Alexandria: "dogmatists" and "empiricists" —— **875**	
2.2	The Methodist school —— **878**	
2.3	The Pneumatist school —— **879**	
VII	**Oratory and Rhetoric —— 881**	
1	The triumph of *technē* —— **881**	
1.1	A scarcely documented output —— **881**	
1.2	The interest in technique —— **882**	
2	The schools of rhetoric —— **883**	
2.1	Hegesias of Magnesia and Asianism —— **883**	
2.2	Atticism —— **884**	
2.3	The Schools of Rhodes —— **885**	
2.4	Hermagoras of Temnos —— **886**	
VIII	**Historiography —— 887**	
1	Problems and tendencies in Hellenistic historiography —— **887**	
1.1	Loss of texts and problems of reconstruction —— **887**	
1.2	The panorama of Hellenistic historiography —— **887**	
1.3	The Alexander Historians —— **889**	
1.3.1	The birth of a genre —— **889**	
1.3.2	Authors and works contemporary to Alexander —— **890**	
1.3.3	Authors later than Alexander —— **895**	
1.4	Forms of historiography in the age of the Diadochi —— **897**	
1.4.1	Histories of the Diadochi: Hieronymus of Cardia, Duris, Philarchus —— **897**	
1.4.2	Local history —— **900**	
1.4.3	Sicilian historiography: Timaeus of Tauromenium —— **901**	
1.4.4	Historians and polymaths —— **903**	
2	Polybius —— **904**	
2.1	A Greek at Rome —— **904**	

2.2	The minor works —— **906**	
2.3	The *Histories* —— **906**	
2.4	Polybius' sources —— **910**	
2.5	Polybius' conception of history and historiography —— **910**	
2.6	Language and style —— **915**	
3	Historiography after Polybius —— **915**	
3.1	Posidonius of Apamea —— **915**	
3.2	Diodorus Siculus —— **916**	
3.3	Nicolaus of Damascus —— **920**	
3.4	Castor of Rhodes —— **921**	
3.5	Anti-Roman historiography —— **921**	

IX	**Judaeo-Hellenistic Literature —— 923**	
1	The Jews of Alexandria and the *Septuagint* —— **923**	
1.1	The *Bible*, the fundamental text of Jewish culture —— **923**	
1.2	The *Septuagint* in the ancient sources. The *Letter of Aristeas* —— **923**	
1.3	Alexandria and Judaeo-Hellenistic culture —— **924**	
1.4	Other Greek translations of the *Bible* —— **926**	
2	Jewish literature in Greek —— **926**	
2.1	Aristobulus and biblical exegesis —— **926**	
2.2	The *Exagōgē* of Ezekiel —— **926**	
2.3	*Joseph and Aseneth*: the novel —— **927**	

The Roman Imperial Period

I	**The Period —— 931**	
1	The Roman Imperial Period —— **931**	
2	The fortunes of Greece in the Imperial Period —— **932**	
3	The bilingual empire: integration and resistance —— **935**	
4	Classicism, Atticism and the Second Sophistic —— **937**	
5	The literary genres in the Imperial Period —— **939**	

II	**Rhetoric and Literary Criticism —— 943**	
1	Rhetorical tendencies in the Rome of Augustus —— **943**	
1.1	The establishment of Greek rhetoric at Rome —— **943**	
1.2	Apollodorus of Pergamum and Theodorus of Gadara —— **944**	
2	Dionysius of Halicarnassus —— **945**	
2.1	A key figure —— **945**	
2.2	The works —— **945**	
3	The rhetorical and stylistic debate —— **948**	
3.1	Caecilius of Caleacte —— **948**	

3.2	The treatise *On the Sublime* —— 948
3.3	Demetrius —— 950
4	The spread of rhetoric in the Imperial Period —— 950
5	Hermogenes of Tarsus —— 952
III	**Historiography** —— **954**
1	Historiography in the Augustan and Imperial Periods —— 954
1.1	A Romanocentric historiography —— 954
1.1.1	The legacy of Hellenistic historiography —— 954
1.1.2	The establishment of a universal culture —— 955
1.2	Dionysius of Halicarnassus —— 956
1.2.1	Rhetor and historian —— 956
1.2.2	The historiographical work —— 956
1.3	Greek historians of the Imperial Period —— 958
1.3.1	Appian of Alexandria —— 958
1.3.2	Arrian of Nicomedia —— 959
1.3.3	Cassius Dio —— 962
1.3.4	Herodian —— 965
1.3.5	Dexippus —— 966
1.3.6	Military treatises: Polyaenus —— 966
2	Historiography in the Late Antique Period —— 966
2.1	Historiography and Christianity —— 966
2.2	Eusebius of Caesarea and ecclesiastical historiography —— 967
2.3	Zosimus —— 968
2.4	Procopius of Caesarea —— 970
2.4.1	Biographical notices —— 970
2.4.2	The works —— 971
2.4.3	Aspects of Procopius' historiography —— 974
2.5	Other historians of the Late Antique Period —— 976
IV	**Geographical and Periegetic Literature** —— **977**
1	Authors and literary forms —— 977
2	Strabo —— 978
2.1	Biographical notices —— 978
2.2	The lost historical work —— 979
2.3	The *Geography* —— 980
3	Pausanias —— 982
3.1	Biographical details —— 982
3.2	The *Description of Greece* —— 983
3.3	The *Description of Greece* and the Greek historiographical tradition —— 985
3.4	Reception —— 986

4	Claudius Ptolemaeus —— 987	
4.1	An encyclopaedic scientist —— 987	
4.2	Biographical notices and principal works —— 987	
V	**Plutarch of Chaeronea —— 988**	
1	Plutarch and Graeco-Latin culture —— 988	
2	Life —— 988	
3	The Plutarchan corpus —— 989	
4	The *Lives* —— 990	
4.1	Plutarch's *Lives* and the relation between biography and historiography —— 992	
4.2	Peripatetic influences on Plutarch's *Lives* —— 994	
5	*Moralia* —— 994	
5.1	Philosophical and pedagogical writings —— 995	
5.2	Ethical and political writings —— 997	
5.3	Treatises on miscellaneous themes —— 997	
5.4	The primacy of ethics —— 999	
6	Language and style —— 1000	
7	Reception —— 1000	
VI	**Jewish and Christian Literature —— 1001**	
1	Jewish literature in the Greek language —— 1001	
1.1	Philo of Alexandria —— 1001	
1.1.1	Philo and the Alexandrian setting —— 1001	
1.1.2	Philo and the *Bible*: allegorical interpretation —— 1002	
1.1.3	Philo's thought —— 1003	
1.2	Flavius Josephus —— 1004	
1.2.1	A witness of the first rank —— 1004	
1.2.2	Life —— 1004	
1.2.3	Chronology and general character of the works —— 1006	
1.2.4	The historical works —— 1006	
1.2.5	Reception of the historical works —— 1008	
1.2.6	Language and style —— 1008	
2	The first centuries of Christian literature: the *New Testament* —— 1008	
2.1	Christianity and literature —— 1008	
2.2	The writings of the *New Testament* —— 1009	
2.3	The *Letters* of Paul of Tarsus —— 1010	
2.4	The narrative texts: the *Gospels* and the *Acts of the Apostles* —— 1013	
2.4.1	The *Gospel of Matthew* —— 1014	
2.4.2	The *Gospel of Mark* —— 1015	
2.4.3	The *Gospel of Luke* and *Acts of the Apostles* —— 1016	
2.4.4	The *Gospel of John* —— 1017	

2.5   The *Letters* of John —— **1019**
2.6   The *Apocalypse* —— **1019**
2.7   The *Letters* of James, Peter and Jude —— **1021**

VII   **Philosophical and Scientific Literature —— 1022**
1   Philosophical literature —— **1022**
1.1   General characteristics of philosophical thought —— **1022**
1.1.1   Under the sign of continuity —— **1022**
1.1.2   Philosophy, rhetoric and literature —— **1023**
1.2   The Academy and the Peripatos —— **1024**
1.2.1   The Academy: Middle Platonism —— **1024**
1.2.2   The Peripatetic school —— **1025**
1.3   Other philosophical schools —— **1025**
1.3.1   Scepticism —— **1025**
1.3.2   Cynicism —— **1026**
1.3.3   Stoicism —— **1026**
1.3.4   Epicureanism —— **1028**
1.3.5   Neopythagoreanism and mystical currents —— **1028**
1.4   Neoplatonism —— **1029**
1.4.1   The twilight of Greek philosophy —— **1029**
1.4.2   Ammonius Saccas —— **1029**
1.4.3   Plotinus and the School of Rome —— **1030**
1.4.4   Porphyry —— **1032**
1.4.5   Iamblichus and theurgy —— **1033**
1.4.6   The School of Athens: the epigoni of Neoplatonism —— **1033**
1.4.7   The School of Alexandria —— **1034**
2   Scientific literature —— **1035**
2.1   Scientific culture in the Imperial Period —— **1035**
2.2   Medicine and Galen —— **1036**
2.3   "Parascientific" literature —— **1038**
2.3.1   The *Corpus Hermeticum* —— **1038**
2.3.2   Artemidorus and the interpretation of dreams —— **1039**

VIII   **The Second Sophistic and Lucian —— 1040**
1   The Second Sophistic —— **1040**
1.1   Character of the Second Sophistic —— **1040**
1.1.1   The primacy of rhetoric —— **1040**
1.1.2   Star orators and intellectuals —— **1041**
1.2   The "rhetor-philosophers" —— **1042**
1.2.1   Philosophy and eloquence —— **1042**
1.2.2   Dio of Prusa (or Dio Cocceianus), called Chrysostom —— **1042**
1.2.3   Maximus of Tyre —— **1044**

1.2.4   Favorinus of Arles —— **1045**
1.2.5   Herodes Atticus —— **1046**
1.2.6   Aelius Aristides —— **1046**
1.2.7   Aelian —— **1048**
1.2.8   The Philostrati —— **1049**
2   Lucian of Samosata —— **1050**
2.1   A free spirit —— **1050**
2.2   Life —— **1051**
2.3   The Lucianic corpus —— **1052**
2.3.1   The dialogues —— **1053**
2.3.2   *A True Story* —— **1054**
2.2.3   *Lucius or The Ass* —— **1054**
2.4   Style —— **1055**

IX   **Narrative Literature —— 1056**
1   The Greek novel —— **1056**
1.1   Origins and characteristics of the novel —— **1056**
1.1.1   A "new" genre —— **1056**
1.1.2   The origins of the novel —— **1056**
1.1.3   The themes of the novel —— **1057**
1.2   *Callirhoe* by Chariton of Aphrodisias —— **1059**
1.2.1   A nearly unknown author —— **1059**
1.2.2   The plot —— **1060**
1.2.3   The historical background —— **1060**
1.2.4   The protagonists —— **1061**
1.2.5   The spectacular in the narrative —— **1062**
1.2.6   The presence of the Homeric model —— **1062**
1.3   *Anthia and Habrocomes* of Xenophon of Ephesus (also known as *The Ephesian Story*) —— **1063**
1.3.1   The author and the work —— **1063**
1.3.2   The plot —— **1064**
1.3.3   A dry narrative —— **1064**
1.3.4   The religion of *Anthia and Habrocomes* —— **1064**
1.4   *Leucippe and Clitophon* by Achilles Tatius —— **1065**
1.4.1   A hit novel —— **1065**
1.4.2   The plot —— **1066**
1.4.3   A complex and artificial plot —— **1067**
1.4.4   The first-person narrator —— **1067**
1.5   *Daphnis and Chloe* by Longus —— **1068**
1.5.1   A pastoral novel set on Lesbos —— **1068**
1.5.2   The plot —— **1069**
1.5.3   An original formula —— **1069**

1.5.4	The importance of Eros —— 1070	
1.5.5	Reception —— 1070	
1.6	The *Aethiopica* of Heliodorus of Emesa —— 1071	
1.6.1	A different climate —— 1071	
1.6.2	The plot —— 1071	
1.6.3	A flashback construction —— 1072	
1.6.4	The triumph of virginity —— 1072	
1.7	Fragmentary and lost novels —— 1073	
1.7.1	Riches to be discovered —— 1073	
1.7.2	The *Ninus Novel* —— 1073	
1.7.3	*Metiochus and Parthenope* —— 1074	
1.7.4	The *Novel of Chione* —— 1074	
1.7.5	Antonius Diogenes and *The Incredible Things Beyond Thule* —— 1075	
1.7.6	Iamblichus —— 1076	
1.7.7	Lollianus —— 1076	
1.7.8	Other novels —— 1076	
2	The novella, the fable, epistolary literature —— 1078	
2.1	The novella —— 1078	
2.2	The fable —— 1078	
2.3	Letter collections of the Imperial Period —— 1079	
X	Grammar, Scholarship, Compilation —— 1081	
1	The study of grammar —— 1081	
1.1	The culmination of a tradition —— 1081	
1.2	Apollonius Dyscolus —— 1081	
1.3	Aelius Herodianus —— 1083	
2	The interpretation of texts and lexicography —— 1084	
2.1	Philological exegesis —— 1084	
2.2	Lexicography —— 1085	
2.3	Paroemiography —— 1087	
3	Late Antique and Byzantine erudition —— 1087	
4	Metrical and musical studies —— 1088	
4.1	Metrical studies and Hephaestion —— 1088	
4.2	Aristides Quintilianus and musical studies —— 1089	
5	Miscellanies, compilations, anthologies —— 1089	
5.1	Useful and precious compilations —— 1089	
5.2	Athenaeus of Naucratis —— 1090	
5.3	Diogenes Laertius —— 1090	
5.4	The *Anthologion* of John of Stobi —— 1091	

XI	**Oratory and Rhetoric in Late Antiquity** — 1092	
1	The revival of rhetoric — 1092	
2	Himerius of Prusa — 1093	
3	Themistius — 1093	
4	Libanius of Antioch — 1094	
5	Emperor Julian and the pagan restoration — 1095	
6	Eunapius of Sardis — 1098	
7	Synesius of Cyrene — 1098	
8	The School of Gaza — 1099	

XII	**Poetry in the Imperial Period** — 1101	
1	Epigram — 1101	
1.1	A flourishing genre — 1101	
1.2	The epigrammatic poets of the Imperial Period — 1101	
2	Hymnography — 1103	
2.1	The forms of the hymn — 1103	
2.2	The *Orphic Hymns* — 1104	
2.3	The *Magical Hymns* — 1105	
3	Oracular literature — 1105	
4	Epic and didactic poetry — 1107	
4.1	Diffusion of the genre of epic — 1107	
4.2	Narrative epic in the Homeric tradition — 1107	
4.3	Nonnus of Panopolis — 1109	
4.4	The romance epic of Musaeus — 1110	
4.5	Historical and encomiastic epic — 1112	
4.6	Didactic epic — 1112	

XIII	**Christian Literature in Greek** — 1114	
1	Christian literature before Constantine — 1114	
1.1	Under the sign of continuity and difference — 1114	
1.2	The Apostolic Fathers — 1116	
1.2.1	Clement of Rome — 1116	
1.2.2	Ignatius of Antioch — 1116	
1.2.3	Polycarp of Smyrna — 1117	
1.2.4	Pseudo-Barnabas — 1117	
1.2.5	The *Didachē* — 1118	
1.2.6	Papias of Hierapolis — 1118	
1.2.7	The *Shepherd* of Hermas — 1118	
1.2.8	Early Christian poetry — 1119	
1.2.9	The origins of homiletic writing — 1119	
1.3	Christians and pagans: the apologetic writers — 1120	
1.3.1	The time of persecutions — 1120	

1.3.2	The authors and works —— 1121	
1.4	Acts and Passions of the Martyrs —— 1123	
1.4.1	Dying for the faith —— 1123	
1.4.2	The *Acts of Justin* and the *Martyrdom of Polycarp* —— 1124	
1.5	Internal polemic: the struggle against heresy —— 1125	
1.5.1	Heresy and heresiarchs —— 1125	
1.5.2	Gnosticism —— 1125	
1.5.3	Writers against heresy —— 1126	
1.6	The school of Alexandria —— 1128	
1.6.1	The rational study of revelation —— 1128	
1.6.2	Clement of Alexandria —— 1128	
1.6.3	Origen of Alexandria —— 1129	
1.6.4	*Cohortatio ad gentiles* —— 1131	
2	Christian literature after Constantine —— 1132	
2.1	Christianity as the religion of the empire —— 1132	
2.2	The Alexandrian area: the Arian controversy —— 1133	
2.2.1	Arianism —— 1133	
2.2.2	Athanasius of Alexandria —— 1133	
2.3	Eusebius of Caesarea —— 1135	
2.4	Authors from the Syrian-Palestinian area —— 1136	
2.4.1	Cyril of Jerusalem —— 1136	
2.4.2	Epiphanius —— 1137	
2.4.3	Apollinaris of Laodicea —— 1137	
2.5	The Cappadocian Fathers —— 1138	
2.5.1	Saints at the frontier —— 1138	
2.5.2	Basil of Caesarea —— 1138	
2.5.3	Gregory of Nazianzus —— 1140	
2.5.4	Gregory of Nyssa —— 1142	
2.6	The school of Antioch —— 1144	
2.6.1	Historical and literal biblical exegesis —— 1144	
2.6.2	John Chrysostom —— 1144	
2.6.3	Theodoret of Cyrrhus and the Christological controversy —— 1146	
2.7	Africa: the end of the Alexandrian school —— 1147	
2.7.1	Cyril of Alexandria —— 1147	
2.7.2	Synesius of Cyrene —— 1148	

Bibliography of Translations (by Elena Squeri) —— 1151
Index of Authors (by Elena Squeri) —— 1159

The Hellenistic Age

I The Period

1 The Hellenistic Age

With the death of Alexander the Great in 323 B.C. and the disintegration of his empire, a phase began in Greek cultural history which gradually – since historical transformations are never sharp or sudden – acquired different connotations from those of the preceding Classical Period. The era subsequent to the death of Alexander is termed "the Hellenistic Age," conventionally understood as continuing until the Roman conquest of the Hellenistic kingdom of Egypt that followed the battle of Actium in 31 B.C. when Octavian (the future Augustus) defeated Antony and Cleopatra and subjected Egypt to Rome. A little less conventionally, one may talk more broadly of the period as including the third to the first century B.C., a time characterised by a substantial historical change in the Greek world: in this period the civilisation of the *poleis* gave way to that of the Hellenistic kingdoms, a new landscape that took shape at start of the third century; by the end of the first century the Hellenistic kingdoms had all been absorbed by Rome, which by then held absolute dominance over the scene. Another term sometimes used is "the Alexandrian Age," in reference to the special importance assumed by the city of Alexandria, capital of the Hellenistic kingdom of Egypt. However, the two names should not be understood as interchangeable. The term "Hellenistic Age" is preferable, since it conveys a general concept, whereas one may talk of Alexandrian literature, poetry, philology or science when referring specifically to the extraordinary cultural flourishing that occurred in this city on the Nile delta, as we shall frequently have reason to note.

It was a nineteenth-century German scholar, Johann Gustav Droysen, who introduced the terms "Hellenism" and "Hellenistic" in a historical and cultural sense to define the period between the death of Alexander and the Roman conquest of Egypt. He took his cue from a passage of the *Old Testament* (2 *Maccabees* 4, 13) and two passages of the *Acts of the Apostles* (6, 1 and 9, 29), where we find, respectively, the terms Ἑλληνισμός (*Hellēnismos*, traditionally used to refer to correct use of Greek and linguistic propriety) and Ἑλληνιστής (*Hellēnistēs*) to indicate the adoption of the Greek language and Greek cultural habits by Hebrews. Droysen noted the use of these terms for the adoption of elements of Greek culture, primarily of course the language, by non-Greek and non-Greek-speaking peoples. On that basis he used "Hellenism" and "Hellenistic" to distinguish the period in which, after the conquests of Alexander, Greek culture was diffused across vast areas in the eastern territories, mingling with the different countries' local cultures and so giving rise to forms of syncretistic civilisation with their own distinctive characteristics, in which Greek was the common language of the cultivated elites.

https://doi.org/10.1515/9783110426328-021

2 Greece during the Hellenistic Age

From a historical point of view it is a useful convention to distinguish between an "Early Hellenistic Period" from the death of Alexander the Great through the whole third century B.C., which saw the establishment of the principal ruling dynasties in the territorial kingdoms, and a "Late Hellenistic Period" consisting of the second and first century B.C., which encompasses Rome's entry onto the eastern Mediterranean scene and the final subjection of all the Hellenistic kingdoms, when even Egypt became part of the Roman realm.

The earlier period is marked by the turbulent and uneasy formation of the Hellenistic kingdoms by Alexander's generals (the Diadochi, literally "successors") and their followers after the dismemberment of the Macedonian empire. In the course of just thirty years or so, from Philip of Macedon's first meddlings in the relations between the Greek cities in the 350s B.C. down to the subjection of Greece at the battle of Chaeronea (338 B.C.) and the resounding conquests of Alexander the Great between 336 and 324, Greece's political reality and cultural horizon were transformed radically and expanded to a whole different scale. The Macedonian hegemony over Greece favoured the establishment of a form of political dominion that was new to the Greek world: the galaxy of independent, sovereign *poleis*, which corresponded to a centuries-old understanding of state as a community in the Greek lands, was forcibly replaced by the concept of the vast territorial state subjected to the central power of an absolute monarch and equipped with a capital city. In the first decades after the death of Alexander in 323 and during the struggles of the Diadochi to divide up his empire, some Greek cities nurtured the illusion that they would be able to win back their lost liberty, but the rebellions against Macedonian rule incurred swift and harsh repression; there were indeed some significant instances of partial political autonomy, but only in transient and ephemeral episodes.

One of these brief interludes began at Athens in 317. On the death of the Diadochus Antipater (319), ruler of Macedonia and Greece, the city once again chose the path of rebellion, which was promptly suppressed by Antipater's son and successor Cassander. He entrusted the government of the city to Demetrius of Phaleron, a man of culture trained in the Peripatos, Aristotle's school, who held power for a decade (317–307) and launched a political programme of developing the city and consolidating its middle class, considered in the Aristotelian view to be the element of society that guaranteed peace and stability. In 307, during the struggles among the second generation of Diadochi for control of Greece, Athens was stormed by Demetrius Poliorcetes, son of Antigonus Monophthalmos, forcing Demetrius of Phaleron to abandon the city. He fled to Thebes, then to Macedonia and finally he went to Alexandria to the court of Ptolemy. For Athens this prompted a new search for political autonomy. In 302 Demetrius Poliorcetes was able to reconstruct the Hellenic League (or "League of Corinth"): the Greeks swore an oath not to fight among themselves and to ally with the Antigonids. But in the battle of Ipsus (301 B.C.), fought deep inside Anatolia, Demetrius Poliorcetes was defeated along with his father. The Hellenic League broke up and Athens seized the opportunity to rebel and proclaim its independence, but Demetrius Poliorcetes besieged it a second time and managed to storm it in 294; and so he came to control almost the whole of Greece.

In the Greek and Macedonian area and the other regions that had been part of Alexander's empire, genuinely royal dynasties were coming into existence. After the battle of Ipsus in 301, which marked the definitive collapse of Antigonus Monophthalmos' attempt to unite the entire Macedonian empire under his rule, in the early third century B.C. the partition of most of the empire crystallised into three large kingdoms under the three dynasties that had emerged victorious: in Egypt the Lagids or Ptolemies (descendants of Ptolemy, son of Lagus); in the kingdom of Syria, including the Middle East and part of Asia Minor, the Seleucids (descendants of Seleucus); and in the kingdom of Macedonia, which included Greece, the Antigonids (descendants of Antigonus Monophthalmos). In addition to these three most important monarchical states, there were some others of smaller size: the kingdoms of Thrace, Epirus, Bithynia, Pontus, the Parthian kingdom and the kingdom of Pergamum in Asia Minor, which had special importance as a cultural centre under the Attalid dynasty. In the course of the century the three principal kingdoms were embroiled in numerous conflicts, such as the repeated wars between the Ptolemies and Seleucids for control of parts of the Syrian region. In the meantime within the borders of the different kingdoms new cities were founded and important and prosperous urban centres developed, some of which would become fundamental points of reference for the culture of the period.

The experience of the eastern Greeks of the Hellenistic monarchies should also be considered alongside, in the western context, the activities of Agathocles of Syracuse, a bold cavalry officer who was able to gain prominence following the hostilities of his *polis* with Carthage, and ultimately (316 B.C.) to achieve personal power, which he did not hesitate to present as royal in character, including by establishing family connections with the dynasties that had arisen out of the dissolution of the empire of Alexander the Great. Agathocles revived the old hegemonic policy of the Deinomenids over Sicily and continued the conflict against Carthaginian power. But the renaissance of Syracuse was tied to Agathocles' own forceful charisma and from the moment of his death (289 B.C.) this Sicilian city began a decline that would ultimately end with its definitive submission to Rome in the course of the First Punic War (264–241 B.C.).

Alongside these deep changes in Greece's internal political arrangements, another change of enormous historical significance occurred. Alexander the Great's ventures in the East had opened up new and unexplored geographical, cultural and intellectual horizons, and as a result the Greeks' fundamental framework of the thought, mentality and cultural consciousness widened beyond previous imagining. Greek civilisation found itself facing, and in direct relation to, other cultures, living together with them and merging with them: the world of Greek-speakers became vast and included within it a large number of non-Greeks. The circumscribed and self-sufficient universe of the *polis*, which had kept its autonomy intact from the Archaic Period down to the end of the Classical Era, little by little came to be dissolved in the broad spatial and cultural perspectives that were flung open by the conquest: gradually but profoundly, mentality, intellectual attitude, points of reference and perspectives changed. Yet, while underlining these differences in politico-social structure we should not imagine any sudden ruptures nor overlook elements of continuity. The city-state had lost many of its characteristic features, but the Macedonian conquest had not dismantled the centuries-old reality of the *poleis*. Although diminished and demoted, social life at city-level continued to exist, putting up a tenacious struggle among the larger state organisms; and the cities of Greece continued to pursue their relatively autonomous political life of alliances and alignments (one need think only of the existence of the Aetolian Confederacy and Achaean Confederacy, which fought in the so-called Social War of 220–217 B.C.). Nonetheless, parallel to the vanishing of their full freedom and self-determined political life, so also their temper and outlook, intellectual attitude and points of reference changed too: at various speeds, their minds and consciousnesses, ideas and conception of the world altered.

Beginning from the end of the third century, after the Tarentine War (280–272 B.C.) and the First and Second Punic Wars (264–241 and 218–202 B.C.), by which the rising power of Rome secured control over Magna Graecia, Sicily and parts of the Iberian peninsula and expanded its own sphere of influence in the Mediterranean, Rome turned directly to the affairs of Greece. The opportunity was presented in 215 by the anti-Roman alliance of the Carthaginian Hannibal with Philip V, the Antigonid who was at that time monarch of Macedonia, during the Second Punic War. For a decade, until 205 B.C., Rome maintained an active military front in the Adriatic (the First Macedonian War) and shortly afterward adopted the programmatic role and image of champion of the liberty of Greece against Macedonian domination: in this way Rome ensured support from the Greek cities and that of many politicians and intellectuals and was met with sincere and spontaneous agreement.

Events took a decisive turn at the end of the Third Macedonian War (171–168 B.C.) when the Macedonian king Perseus (successor to Philip V) was defeated by the Romans under the leadership of the consul L. Aemilius Paullus at the battle of Pydna in 168. Macedonia was divided into four republics and in the Greek cities the pro-Roman factions were dominant, convinced that in Rome they had a defender of their own ancient liberty. Yet after just a few years this situation collapsed and the Romans' hegemonic intentions became clear. In 147 an attempt to restore the Macedonian kingdom was harshly suppressed and Macedonia reduced to a province. The same fate befell the rest of Greece a little later: when the Achaean Confederacy, spearheaded by Corinth, attempted a military response to Roman domination, Corinth was conquered and destroyed. It was 146 B.C., the same year as the destruction of Carthage at the end of the Third Punic War.

From then on the Greek peninsula was a site of destruction and plunder for the Roman commanders and armies: together with the rich booty of precious objects, works of art, statues and treasures of every kind, ships also brought to Italy men of culture and forms of thought, taste, tradition and intellectual and aesthetic sensibility, in sum – all the various expressions of Greece's magnificent cultural heritage. The conqueror Rome thus assumed, along with its empire, the prestigious and weighty responsibility of accepting and securing the immense legacy of Greek civilisation. A little over a century later, this historic role became even more apparent and, as it were, definitive, when the whole Greek and Hellenised world was in a certain sense reunified within the vast Roman empire. For Greek culture, the Imperial Age began at a time when its relation to Rome was already a couple of centuries old.

3 The diffusion of Greek culture: the new centres

The political and cultural geography of the Hellenistic Age is hence characterised by various kingdoms that emerged from the dismemberment of Alexander the Great's conquests. The area of diffusion of Greek language and culture expanded enormously and literature too revealed a rich and varied polycentrism that encompassed vast territories beyond the traditional areas (viz. continental Greece and the islands, the Ionian coasts and Greek regions in the West). The diffusion of Greek civilisation and its integration with other cultures, in different zones of the East, was a patchwork phenomenon. In a certain sense one can talk of a new colonisation but unlike the archaic colonies, which had been pursued separately by different cities, this new colonisation at first occurred with a unitary character conferred on it by the venture of Alexander and his armies. However, this initial unity very soon broke up and came to differ in the various territorial kingdoms: the shared Greek surface could not belie the cultural differences of the different territories (which had known deeply rooted civilisations of great antiquity, such as in Egypt and the Middle East), which are admittedly harder to grasp only from what was written in Greek.

There is no doubt that language represented a powerful unifying factor. The form of Greek called κοινὴ διάλεκτος (*koinē dialektos*, "common language"), based principally on the Attic dialect, was diffused throughout the Mediterranean basin and across vast zones of the Middle East (in parallel to local languages, which continued to live their own lives) and in those areas it became the principal literary language of the Hellenistic Age. The written *koinē* was a kind of ideal common language of educated people who expressed themselves in Greek, at first in the Greek kingdoms and then in the Graeco-Latin bilingual world of the Roman empire. It was normally used in literary prose and it is therefore the form of Greek for which we have the most extensive documentation, through a large number of preserved texts. Two cases of special historical significance are the Greek translation of the *Bible* called the *Septuagint* (begun in the third century B.C. with the translation of the *Torah* or *Pentateuch*, and written in a literary *koinē* laced with Hebraisms: cf. *The Hellenistic Age* IX 1) and the *New Testament*, whose authors were addressing their Christian preaching to less educated people too and so preserve elements that are closer to the spoken language.

The polycentrism of Hellenistic cultural geography is due to the emergence of new centres of culture, a development favoured also by the numerous foundations of cities carried out in the period of Alexander and the Diadochi. That is absolutely not to say that the ancient centres of continental Greece, the Aegean, Asia Minor and the West (above all Syracuse and Tarentum) had lost their importance. Athens continued to maintain a major role and great prestige: Menander pursued his theatrical activity there, the philosophical schools of the Academy and the Peripatos flourished, Epicurus and Zeno carried out their teachings, giving rise to Epicureanism and Stoicism. Yet, alongside the traditional ones, new centres of development and of cultural attraction emerged in various regions of the Mediterranean, both in areas that had always been Greek but were previously cast in the shade by the predominance of Athens, and in areas recently "Hellenised." In this, Alexandria stands out, a city founded by Alexander the Great in 332, which rose under the Ptolemies to a cultural centre of the first importance in numerous cultural spheres, to the extent that, as mentioned already in the opening section above, we speak of "Alexandrian literature." But there was no shortage of other cities that vied with each other in their artistic and cultural brilliance: from Cyrene and Carthage to Pergamum, which was for a time the rival of Alexandria; then Antioch (which had an important library, where towards the end of the third century B.C. the poet Euphorion of Chalcis was appointed director), Pella, Rhodes, Jerusalem and others, until Rome appeared on the scene and swiftly became the principal cultural pole of attraction. During the Hellenistic Age, in the cultural context of the Mediterranean, Latin literature emerged and soon rose to the greatest heights.

An important factor in the proliferation of cultural centres and institutions was a distinctive attitude by rulers which is conventionally called euergetism (from εὐεργέτης, *euergetēs*, meaning "one who does good, benefactor"). All dynasties and all sovereigns invested huge resources to celebrating themselves, their city and their kingdom by means of projects of every kind in city-planning, construction, art and culture, summoning craftsmen, artists and men of culture in order to promote their own prestige in rivalry with others. What the Ptolemies in Alexandria and the Attalids in Pergamum did are well known and striking examples, but the phenomenon was quite widespread in the Hellenistic courts. From this munificence the sciences, arts and letters derived great benefits, including the creation of suitable cultural institutions (not only libraries, but for example the Museum of Alexandria).

We have already stressed how concepts such as the widening of cultural horizons and polycentrism characterised the Hellenistic Age; this context also makes comprehensible what is generally classed as the final phase of the classical *polis* experience. Yet one must take care not to slip into the erroneous habit of thinking that the final phase of any experience – the change in position and climate and new social and intellectual framework – simply means decadence. That was not the case at all: in the Hellenistic Age the Greek cities continued to be generally prosperous and lively centres (Athens especially). Yet it is clear that the new situations did not permit the cities a political and civil life of the kind typical of the Classical Age, nor one guided by the same framework, namely direct and active participation by all the citizens in a socio-cultural universe that, in its small scale, could be dominated by single individuals. An author such as the comic playwright Menander (342–291 B.C.) already belonged to the Hellenistic world, if for no other reason than that his work appears remote from the classical *polis* experience and does not exhibit an explicit participation in the social-political events that his city, Athens, was undergoing (cf. *The Hellenistic Age* II 1). His theatre is a clear and immediate example of the change in atmosphere and sensibility, but we will see that other genres offer material for similar observations: no literary form is able to take the entire community as its immediate public, as had once been the case with epic recitations, theatre and oratory. Literature and thought reflect, on the one hand, the tendency towards individualism, in which each person feels and speaks as an individual, rather than speaking in the name and for the sake of a community, and is addressing groups of individuals rather than a community. On the other hand they reflect a cosmopolitan vision through which intellectuals reflect the creation of a continuous exchange around the widened horizons of their Greek-speaking culture. The intellectual and the citizen of a community are no longer two sides of the same individual.

4 The literary genres in the Hellenistic Age

The intellectuals of the Hellenistic Age have a clear awareness of being heirs to a grand tradition of art and thought, which forms the invaluable heritage of their παιδεία (*paideia*), their civil and cultural identity. Aristotle and his school made a decisive contribution to the formation of this awareness: with reflections on rhetoric and poetics, based on the idea of an evolution that had reached the highest levels; with a wide-ranging interest in literary works and authors; with work in the exegesis of texts, which turned the past into an object of study and research. In the field of literature, the awareness of this imposing heritage resulted in various phenomena in the Hellenistic Era which, with inevitable simplifications, we can define as follows: on the one hand the urge to preserve, interpret and understand the texts hallowed by tradition, with the help of a weighty apparatus of erudite instruments and materials; on the other hand an attitude of competitive emulation towards the models of the past, a rivalry with them in the search for brilliant and sophisticated novelties, the value of which derives from its relation to the tradition, which was to be grasped in its full significance. The phenomenon of learned poetry, characteristic of the

Hellenistic Age and, as far as our knowledge of it goes, concentrated essentially in the surviving Alexandrian poetry, is an organic synthesis of these two aspects: with the resources of intellectual and erudite instruments that were more effective and shrewd than ever, the poet-philologist interpreted the great figures of the past, while out of his philological hermeneutics he drew sustenance and stimulation for compositions that vied with the ancient, authoritative model. Callimachus and Apollonius Rhodius stand out as two of the major examples of this way of creating poetry, but it was shared also by many other poets.

Typical of the period is the transformation and combination of literary genres, a phenomenon that fits perfectly into the framework of a culture that studies the past and compares itself to it in a critical and competitive way in the search for its own originality. The system of traditional literary genres could count on an established ensemble of compositional rules for structure, language and metre as well as par-atext, which were linked to the occasions to which each genre corresponded. In the Archaic and Classical Periods, the weight of a tradition that was accepted as an unarguable authority supported a series of norms by which genres were identified, namely epic, the various genres of lyric, tragedy and comedy, historiography and oratory. The disappearance, or rather the substantial alteration, of the occasions for which in the past poetic-literary works had been produced (one may think here, as well as of the situations of epic and the lyric genres, also of theatre and oratory in the changed socio-political conditions of the Hellenistic kingdoms), but also the taste, outlined above, for demonstrating a brilliant competitiveness in rivalry with the past but based on a sound knowledge of it, meant that especially in the Hellenis-tic Age, and above all on the part of poets, the traditional genres were profoundly transformed and sometimes mixed together to create new and original solutions. The old genres became structures that were open to experiments and innovations.

The set of characteristics outlined here matches well with the fact that it was in the Hellenistic Period that a book-based civilisation became definitively established. In the Archaic Period and part of the Classical Period a lot of literature, especially poetry, had been enjoyed primarily through recitation or public performance in the various occasions and contexts for which the different genres were intended. The practice of reading began to spread in the Classical Period (one need think only of Isocrates and the work of Aristotle), but by the Hellenistic Period literary communi-cation was based primarily on individual reading. The civilisation of the book also ushered in the fact that literature addressed a restricted and elite public. This might be, as was often the case, the court of a ruler or a small group of specialists, but certainly no longer a whole community in all its elements. And so a "high" culture is differentiated from a popular culture which continued to develop along its own paths, including traditional forms such as reciters of epic songs and travelling play-ers. In the Hellenistic Period an important step was taken towards the separation between the culture of the learned and that of the rest of the populace. Society be-came ever more divided into two strata: a wealthy and privileged class which had the means to participate in the life of society and to access refined culture, and a middle and lower-middle class, which was often weak economically and at the margins of socio-political and cultural life.

In Greek literature of the Hellenistic Period too the losses have been massive. The majority of the poetry preserved is of the third century B.C. (or at most the first part of the second century) and was written in Alexandria or, if not, with links to Alexandria. On the other hand, we unfortunately have very little of the poetry written from the mid-second to the first century, which had a major influence on Latin poetry. With the end of the great classical tragedy, theatre is represented by the last great comic playwright, Menander, in comic forms that are already far removed from Old Comedy. As regards poetry, this is the period that sees the great flourishing of elegy and epigram (a poetic genre that changes radically in its purpose and enjoys its greatest literary period at this time), the learned, refined poetry of Callimachus, the new epic of Apollonius Rhodius, the bucolic poetry of Theocritus, the dramatic monody of Lycophron and the didactic poetry of Aratus and Nicander.

One of the most significant and novel phenomena is that of Alexandrian philology, which in the three centuries of the Hellenistic Period enjoyed its extraordinary heyday. As well as what we can define as learned poetry, in the sphere of prose a notable amount is represented by the work in the field of historiography: despite severe losses, we can observe the important phenomenon of the historiography about Alexander; then we meet the names of Polybius and Diodorus, and also those of Timaeus and Posidonius, a philosopher as well as a historian. The sciences enjoyed an important phase, again primarily in Alexandria: astronomy, mathematics, mechanics and medicine are the disciplines that achieve the greatests results. As regards oratory and rhetoric, we must lament the near-total loss of the Hellenistic output. Philosophy is illustrated by the continuation of the traditional schools but also by the foundation at Athens, by Epicurus and Zeno, of the schools that gave birth to the two major post-Aristotelian philosophies, Epicureanism and Stoicism. In the face of this magnificent productivity and the enormous influence that it exerted on late Republican and Imperial Roman civilisation, the size of the losses caused by the disappearance of the majority of Hellenistic literary culture cannot but leave a bitter taste.

Tab. 1: Chronological Table of Principal Historical Events (all dates are B.C.).

323	Death of Alexander the Great: struggles break out among the Diadochi
323–322	Rebellion of the Greeks against Macedonia: the Lamian War
322 (summer)	Athenians defeated at Amorgos and Crannon; death of Hyperides and Demosthenes; death of Aristotle
321–316	Second period of struggles among the Diadochi
319	Death of Antipater: Polyperchon "regent of the kingdom" and "*stratēgos* of Europe"

318	Decree of Polyperchon on the liberty of the Greeks; democratic interlude at Athens (death of Phocion)
317	At Athens the government of Demetrius of Phaleron begins (317–307)
316	Death of Olympias; Cassander founds Cassandria and rebuilds Thebes; death of Eumenes Agathocles is *stratēgos autokrator* ("general with full powers") at Syracuse
315	At Tyre, Antigonus is proclaimed "regent of the kingdom": repetition of the proclamation of Polyperchon on the liberty of the Greeks and counter-proclamation by Ptolemy
315–311	Third War of the Diadochi
311	Peace accord between Antigonus, Cassander and Lysimachus
310/09	Alexander IV and Roxane are assassinated by Cassander
310	The Carthaginians defeat Agathocles at Ecnomum; Agathocles sails to Africa
309/8	Seleucus assumes the title "king of Babylonia"
307	Demetrius Poliorcetes at Athens: end of the governement of Demetrius of Phaleron
307–304	"Four Years' War" between Cassander and Demetrius Poliorcetes
306	Antigonus and Demetrius Poliorcetes assume the title of *basileus*; peace between Carthage and Agathocles
305/4	Ptolemy, Cassander, Lysimachus and Seleucus likewise assume the title of *basileus*; Demetrius Poliorcetes besieges Rhodes
301 (summer)	Battle of Ipsus and death of Antigonus
298/7	Death of Cassander
294	Demetrius gains control over almost the whole of Greece, Macedonia and Thessaly
289	Death of Agathocles at Syracuse; the Mamertines treacherously seize Messina
288	Pyrrhus and Lysimachus divide up Macedonia
286/5 (winter)	Surrender of Demetrius to Seleucus I
285	Ptolemy I Soter associates his son Ptolemy, later II Philadelphus, with himself on the throne
284	Lysimachus takes possession of the whole of Macedonia and strengthens his position in Greece
283	Death of Demetrius Poliorcetes and Ptolemy I
281	Battle of Corupedium and death of Lysimachus
280–275	Military campaign of Pyrrhus, king of Epirus, in defence of Tarentum and in Sicily against the Romans
280	Death of Seleucus I at the hand of Ptolemy Ceraunus; Ptolemy defeats Antigonus Gonatas, securing his domination of Macedonia
279	Invasion of the Celts: Ptolemy Ceraunus dies fighting them

	Victory of Pyrrhus at Ascoli Satriano
278	The Celts present in central Greece
277	Antigonus Gonatas defeats the rearguard of the Celts at Lysimachia
277 or 276	Antigonus Gonatas ascends the throne of Macedonia
275	At Maleventum the Romans defeat Pyrrhus, who returns to Greece
	Hieron II *stratēgos* with full powers at Syracuse
ca. 275/4	Battle of the Elephants: Antiochus I defeats the Celts, who settle in the interior of Phrygia (Galatia)
274–270	First Syrian War: Ptolemy II against Antiochus I
272	Death of Pyrrhus; Roman capture of Tarentum
269 or 265/4	Success over the Mamertines by Hieron II, who assumes the title of *basileus* (until his death in 215)
267–262 (?)	Cremonidean War: Ptolemy II, Athens and Sparta against Antigonus Gonatas
264–241	First Punic War: Rome against Carthage
260–253	Second Syrian War: Ptolemy II against Antiochus II and Antigonus Gonatas
253 (or 252)	Rebellion of Alexander, son of Craterus, against Antigonus Gonatas, in whose name he had been governing Greece
246–241	Third Syrian War or War of Laodice: Ptolemy III against Seleucus II
239	Death of Antigonus Gonatas
239–229	Demetrius II king of Macedonia
229	Restoration of democracy at Athens promoted by Aratus and maintained by the Ptolemies
229–228	Rome's First Illyrian War
227	Sicily becomes a Roman province
223	Antiochus III the Great ascends the throne (until 187)
222 (or 223)	battle of Sellasia
222/1	Antigonus Doson dies fighting the Illyrians; he is succeeded by Philip V (until 179)
220–217	Social War (between the Aetolian Federation and the Achaean Federation)
219	Second Illyrian War
	Death of Cleomenes III at Alexandria
219–217	Fourth Syrian War: Antiochus III against Ptolemy IV
218–201	Second Punic War
217	Victory of the Ptolemies over the Seleucids at Raphia
	Peace of Naupactus
215	Philip V allies with Hannibal in war against Rome
215–205	First Macedonian War (Rome against Macedonia)
206	Separate peace between Philip V and the Aetolians
205	Peace of Phoenice between Philip V and the Romans and their respective allies

203/202	Secret pact between Antiochus III and Philip V to divide up the possessions of Ptolemies
202–200	Fifth Syrian War: Antiochus III against Ptolemy V
201	Naval victory of a coalition led by Attalus I of Pergamum against Philip V at Chios
200–196	Second Macedonian War
197	Battle of Cynoscephalae
196	At the Isthmian Games Titus Quinctius Flamininus proclaims the autonomy of the Greeks who were hitherto subject to Macedonia
192–188	Roman–Syrian War
192/1	Expedition to Greece by Antiochus III (defeated at Thermopylae by Marcus Acilius Glabrio in the first months of 191)
190/89	Roman victory over Antiochus III at Magnesia ad Sipylum
189	Marcus Fulvius Nobilior conquers Ambracia (peace between Rome and the Aetolians in the winter of 189/188)
188	Peace of Apamea
179	Perseus king of Macedonia (to 168)
171–168	Third Macedonian War
170–168	Sixth Syrian War: Antiochus IV against Ptolemy VI
168	Battle of Pydna: Macedonia, defeated by Rome, is divided into four republics
ca. 167–151	Around a thousand Achaean politicians (including Polybius) are handed over as hostages to Rome
167–164	Antiochus IV prohibits the cult of Yahweh and introduces to the Temple in Jerusalem the cult of Olympian Zeus: Jewish revolt led by Judas Maccabeus
164–163	Antiochus IV dies at Gabae; Ptolemy VI (king of Egypt from 180) is expelled from Egypt
163	Partition of the Ptolemaic kingdom: Ptolemy VI and Cleopatra II receive Egypt and Cyprus, Ptolemy VIII receives Cyrene
149–146	Third Punic War
149–148	Revolt of Andriscus: Fourth Macedonian War
147 ca.	Macedonia reduced to a Roman province along with Illyria and Epirus; in 146 also the rest of Greece, except the cities *liberae* and *immunes*
147/6	Achaean War and destruction of Corinth (shortly after that of Carthage) in 146
145	Ptolemy VI dies fighting Alexander Balas
145–116	Ptolemy VIII Euergetes II king of Egypt (forced to abandon Alexandria from 131 to 127)
141	Mithradates I, king of the Parthians, annexes Media, conquers Seleucia on the Tigris and advances to Mesopotamia
134	Antiochus VII Sidetes reconquers Jerusalem

133	Attalus III, king of Pergamum from 138, bequeaths the kingdom to the Romans: revolt of Andronicus (put down in 129)
129	Antiochus VII dies in Media fighting the Parthians: beginning of the final decline of the Seleucid kingdom
	Creation of the province of Asia
121–63	Mithradates VI Eupator king of Pontus
96	Ptolemy Apion bequeaths Cyrenaica to the Romans (who do not annex it until 74)
89–85	First Mithradatic War
88	Massacre of Italians at Ephesus and in other cities of Asia Minor
86	Sulla defeats Archelaus, general of Mithradates, at both Chaeronea and Orchomenus: sack of Athens, Olympia and Delphi, confiscations at Epidaurus
85	Peace of Dardanus between Sulla and Mithradates
83	Tigranes I of Armenia governs Syria (to 69)
80	Ptolemy XII Auletes king of Egypt (to 51)
67	Pompey reorganises the province of Cilicia (constituted already in ca. 100)
63	Creation of the province of Syria by Pompey
58	Cyprus annexed to the province of Cilicia
48	Battle of Pharsalus: Pompey flees to Egypt, where he is killed by Ptolemy XIII
48/7	"Alexandrian" War of Gaius Julius Caesar
44	Corinth refounded as a Roman colony (*Laus Iulia Corinthiensis*)
34	Antony in Alexandria: partition of the territories among the members of the royal family
31 (2 September)	Battle of Actium: the Roman fleet defeats the Egyptian fleet
30	Death of Antony and Cleopatra; Egypt becomes a Roman province

II Theatre

1 The New Comedy and Menander

1.1 Hellenistic society and New Comedy

The characteristic features of comic theatre in the Hellenistic Age, which was called "New" Comedy (*nea*) already by the Alexandrian grammarians, were shaped by important political and cultural phenomena distinctive to the period. These included the consequences that arose when the centuries-old setting of the Greek *poleis* was profoundly altered first by the establishment of Macedonian power and then, especially, by its dismemberment into the Hellenistic kingdoms, with their very different state-formations. The centre of theatrical production and performance remained Athens, but the expansion of the form of the state from city to kingdom favoured the expansion also of theatre well beyond Attica and the strictly Greek region. On the other hand, when the ancient autonomy typical of the Greek city-states disappeared, sacrificed to the logic of the much larger territorial state with its centralisation of political and decision-making power in the hands of a monarch and a consequent drastic reduction of freedom of expression and criticism, comic playwrights and their audiences lost a near-inexhaustible resource: the topics and inspirations provided by a busy day-to-day city life and fierce civic polemics, which had given Old Comedy its irresistible force and its direct connection to current affairs. And that is even before we reckon with the fact that the dissolution of citizen sovereignty, in particular in those *poleis* that had been governed by democratic regimes, ended a characteristic component of their theatre, namely collective participation in the productions and performances, the most emblematic expression of which was the composition of the dramatic chorus out of popular and non-professional performers. Now the chorus lost its importance and was reduced to a corps of dancers engaged to "fill" the intervals between acts of the dramas.

The ventures of Alexander in the East opened up geographical and cultural horizons that had previously been unthinkable and this brought a significant change in the fundamental coordinates of the collective imagination: man, society, economy, politics, all ceased to be identified with the familiar, limited space of the *polis* and its *chōra* and gradually took on the associations – none too clear nor entirely controllable – of a much larger and less familiar world with different and less predictable features. In consequence, traditional systems of value and established certainties came to be debated and compared, due to the increased variety of cultural experiences that could now be encountered. While the citizens' horizons now spanned a generally more cosmopolitan world, this was counterbalanced by a greater individualism, the sense that the individual spoke for himself and not for a community, that the addressees of his message were other individuals, rather than a community as a whole.

https://doi.org/10.1515/9783110426328-022

These reflections are very relevant to Menander, whose theatrical career began in 321, just two years after the death of Alexander, but who is already a good example of the changed atmosphere and sensibility: his work reveals a personality far removed from the experience of the classical *polis* which had nourished the theatre of Aristophanes and he displays no – or at least very limited – involvement in the political and social events that his city was undergoing.

The comic playwrights active in this period adopted and brought to maturity deep changes in themes and dramaturgy, the roots of which can be identified already in the last surviving works of Aristophanes himself (who died around 385 B.C.) and which were developed in the Middle Comedy (cf. *The Classical Age* VI 2.3). Typical characteristics are: a preference for plots inspired by private life, introducing characters drawn from the world of the middle or lower social classes (country people, artisans, slaves, *hetairai*), alongside the mythological motifs that continued to appear, often as parody; and a tendency towards fixed characters in masks that were to some degree stereotyped, using conventional traits to represent human types from various spheres of social life, such as trades and professions. The comic hero, who had been enough in himself to fill Aristophanes' theatre, is dissolved into a series of characters drawn from everyday life and presented in the private sphere of family and individual bonds. The stories concern everyday facts, as people fend off the blows of fate, moved by a sense of human solidarity. For that reason it has been called, more or less aptly, "bourgeois comedy." These aspects are echoed in the contemporary literary theories of Aristotle and his pupils, as μίμησις φαυλοτέρων, that is, "imitation of modest situations (or persons)," and in the Aristotelian definition of comedy in the *Poetics* (5, 1449a 32). The interest in human types and the ethical characterisation of individuals that forms the basis of the characters in comedy is echoed in the collection of *Characters* by Theophrastus, a pupil of Aristotle and his successor as the leader of the Peripatetic school (cf. *The Classical Age* XIII 3.8).

1.2 The authors of New Comedy

Compared to Middle Comedy, of which we know only some fragments of limited size, in the case of the *nea* (νέα) we are in a much better position. As well as numerous short fragments, preserved for the most part in quotations by later authors, some fortunate papyrus discoveries have made it possible to recover large parts of the comedies of Menander, which are hence known to us through a quite ancient direct tradition, as will be discussed in the next section. Fate has not been as kind (so far at least) to the other comic playwrights contemporary to or a little later than Menander. Their works are known only in a fragmentary form that makes it impossible to gain a clear sense of them. The habit of calling them "minor" should hence be understood as describing the limits of our knowledge and not as a reductive assessment of their work. Here more than ever it is the accident of papyrus finds that determines the limits of our knowledge: no author of Middle or New Comedy survived the medieval period to be transmitted through the Byzantine manuscripts. Playwrights earlier than Menander include Philemon and Diphilus, later than him were Apollodorus of Carystus and Machon.

Born perhaps at Syracuse but established as an active comic playwright at Athens, Philemon (360–263 B.C. ca.) composed around a hundred plays, with a chronology that places some of them as still part of Middle Comedy. Some of his plays were used as models by the Latin playwright Plautus: *Emporos* (*The Merchant*) as model for the Latin homonym *Mercator*, *Phasma* (*The Apparition*) for *Mostellaria* (*The Ghost*), *Thesauros* (*Treasure*) for *Trinummus* (*Three coins*).

A contemporary of Philemon, and like him the author of comedies used as models by Plautus, was Diphilus, originally from Sinope on the Black Sea. He too lived for a long period at Athens, then moved to Asia Minor, where he died in the early years of the third century B.C. Among the roughly one hundred titles attributed to him, many reflect the choices of the poets of Middle Comedy: as well as mythological themes, what stands out are the plays inspired by "types" and stylised figures from the professional world, such as the merchant.

From the generation after Menander, Apollodorus, born at Carystus on the island of Euboea, composed comedies that provided inspiration for the Latin comic playwright Terence: *Epidikazomenos* (*Claimant*) was the model for Terence's *Phormio*, while his *Hecyra* (*Mother-in-law*) was model for the play of that name by Terence.

We should briefly note Machon, a native of Corinth or Sicyon who lived in the third century B.C. and who, unlike the authors considered so far, worked at Alexandria, bringing to the Ptolemaic capital the forms and themes of New Comedy. It is said that he turned the attention of the Alexandrian grammarian Aristophanes of Byzantium towards the study of comedy (cf. *The Hellenistic Age* III 2.2).

1.3 Menander: historical context and biographical notices

There are few records of Menander's life. He was born into a noble family at Athens (in the deme of Cephisia) and lived in the troubled years when the city lost its political autonomy through the establishment of Macedonian domination and when profound social and political upheavals permanently changed the character of the city from that of the Classical Era. A few years after Menander's birth, which occurred in 342 or 341 (depending on the source), the famous battle of Chaeronea took place (in 338), at which Philip of Macedonia in reality took control of Greece, despite allowing the cities a semblance of autonomy. For a while the regime led by the orator Lycurgus (338–326) attempted to resurrect Athens' fortunes, but when, at the death of Alexander the Great (323), the Athenians attempted an open rebellion against Macedonia and were defeated, the domination of Antipater, general and successor of Alexander in Macedonia, became more oppressive and more obvious.

According to an ancient report, Alexis, a comic playwright of Middle Comedy (cf. *The Classical Age* VI 2.4), was Menander's teacher. Menander himself began his career at the Lenaea contest in 321 with a comedy entitled *Anger*, which won the prize; he was victorious again at the Lenaea in 316 with *Dyskolos* (*The Peevish Fellow*); his first victory at the Dionysia was in 315, but we do not know what the play was in that case. In total, he was victorious in the competitions only eight times.

After the death of Antipater in 319 Athens rebelled against the regent of Macedonia and Greece, but the revolt was put down very swiftly by Antipater's successor, his son Cassander, who entrusted the government of the city to Demetrius of Phaleron, a cultivated and scholarly man who had trained in the Peripatetic school. Demetrius established an oligarchic regime and based his political activity (317–307) on support for and consolidation of the middle class, which Aristotelian political thought identified as a stabilising element. The sources report that Menander too was trained in the Peripatos, at the time when it was directed by Theophrastus (but this report is not certain), and that he enjoyed the friendship of Demetrius. Some sources speak of a friendship between him and Epicurus, who was his exact contemporary (born in 341) and who settled in Athens around 307.

When in 307 Athens was stormed by Demetrius Poliorcetes (the son of Antigonus Monophthalmos), Demetrius of Phaleron fled and a political trial was launched against Menander, but he managed to avoid condemnation, apparently thanks to the intervention of a friend who was related to Poliorcetes. In 301 Antigonus Monophthalmos and Demetrius Poliorcetes were confronted and defeated in battle at Ipsus by the army led by the Macedonians. Athens seized the chance to rebel again, but Poliorcetes managed to storm the city and overpower it in 294. Menander died around 290, a little over 50 years of age. In what survives of his plays, there is no hint (or very scarce and hidden) of the eventful political developments in his city which he witnessed and in which he was involved, if only indirectly: Attic comedy was already striking out on paths quite different from the Aristophanic immersion in political events.

1.3.1 The transmission of the comedies

Despite being the author of over a hundred comedies (105 or 109, according to the sources), Menander managed to be successful in the dramatic contests only eight times. Yet his theatrical works enjoyed a significant and fertile success among the Romans (the greatest Latin comic playwrights Plautus and especially Terence drew on his plots) and up to the beginning of the Middle Ages they enjoyed great favour among the reading public: after Homer, Menander is the author for whom we have the greatest number of surviving papyri, a sign of the wide circulation of copies of his works. Strangely, however, his plays did not make it through the selection made in the Byzantine Era. They stopped being copied and were forgotten, and so until just a few decades ago we had no more than the meagre fragments that have been transmitted through the indirect tradition. Aside from these, all that has been transmitted through the manuscripts is a collection of 877 maxims in iambic trimeters, each of a single verse and therefore known as γνῶμαι μονόστιχοι (*gnōmai monostichoi*, "single-line maxims"). The collection was assembled in the Roman period by excerpting single lines from the comedies of Menander and, in part, from other dramatic poets, following criteria of anthologisation that aimed to extract the moral pith of an author's work.

Our knowledge of Menander's plays, which is by now quite good, thus does not depend on the testimony of medieval manuscripts, aside from a recent discovery. In a Syriac manuscript of the ninth century, preserved at the Vatican Library (*Vat. sir.* 623), some palimpsest folios have been identified that originally belonged to an older Greek manuscript (fourth century A.D.), in which many lines of the *Dyskolos* can be read and of another, otherwise unknown comedy, which may be identifiable as *Titthē*, "the wetnurse" (in 2021 the text is still in the process of publication). Aside from this exceptional case, the works of Menander, too, as in the case of Bacchylides, Aristotle's *Athenian Constitution* and many other authors, offer a dazzling example of the successes that can be achieved by papyrological research, which recovered and identified large parts of several comedies and many fragments of others in the course of the twentieth century. Recent discoveries have recovered and continue to recover large sections of text, which have been established thanks to four major finds:

Parts of five comedies are preserved in the pages of a papyrus codex of the latter part of the fifth century A.D., found in 1905 in Cairo and published two years later (*P. Cair.* 43227): *Herōs* (*The Guardian Spirit*, around a hundred of the opening lines), *Epitrepontes* (*Men at Arbitration*, more than 700 lines), *Perikeiromenē* (*The Girl with Her Hair Cut Short*, around 320 lines), *Samia* (*The Woman from Samos*, around 350 lines); and 64 lines from a fifth comedy of unknown title.

- The papyrus leaves of a codex of the third or fourth century A.D., part of the private collection of the Swiss collector Bodmer and published in 1959 and 1969, have allowed us to expand our knowledge of *Samia* (*P. Bodmer* XXV), from which 737 lines are so far known (the play will have included in total of around 900 lines), and have restored almost the whole of *Dyskolos* (*The Peevish Fellow*, *P. Bodmer* IV) and in fragmentary form *Aspis* (*The Shield*, *P. Bodmer* XXVI), of which part of the prologue was already known (though it had not been identified as such) thanks to a parchment preserved in Florence (*Comoedia Florentina*, PSI 126).

- The *cartonnage* of an Egyptian mummy (that is, the outer cover of the mummy, which was made out of sheets of papyrus pressed together, like *papier maché*) found in a village in the Fayum, treated and partly unravelled in 1906 and then again in 1962–1963, provides us with around half of the *Sicyōnios* (*The Sicyonian*, 470 lines); the papyrus fragments are dated to the second half of the third century B.C., and so to a period quite close to that of the author.

– Finally, a papyrus from Oxyrhynchus of the fourth century A.D., published in 1968 (*P. Oxy.* 2656), has restored around 300 lines of the comedy *Misoumenos* (*The Hated Man*); a roughly similar number of lines from this play are also known from a group of other, smaller fragments.

Thus in the past century thousands of lines once lost have come to light again and have enormously enriched the meagre testimonies from the indirect tradition. The play *Dyskolos* (which is also the earliest among the surviving comedies and the only one for which we know the date of its performance: 316 B.C.) is completely known; of *Epitrepontes* we have more than 900 lines and more than 700 from the *Samia* have re-emerged from the desert sands.

Of other comedies we have a number of lines that is not negligeable but insufficient to reconstruct their plot adequately or to fully evaluate their dramatic characteristics. We have around 196 lines of a comedy that can be identified as the *Titthē* (*Wetnurse*, see above), in which we read of a "young woman" (νύμφη), a "child" (παιδίον) and an "old woman" (γραῦς) in reference to a childbirth, perhaps connected to a violent episode; 150 lines of *Geōrgos* (*The Farmer*), around 120 of *Colax* (*The Fawner*), around a hundred each from *Dis exapatōn* (*Twice a Swindler*), *Phasma* (*The Apparition*) and *Citharistēs* (*The Lyre Player*); about fifty lines each remain of *Carchēdonios* (*The Man from Carthage*) and *Theophoroumenē* (*The Demoniac Girl*). More often we must be content with little more than the title, though from that alone it is possible to derive some useful information on the repertoire of themes and characters represented. Among the known titles, we may note those based on a dramatic character-type (such as *The Misogynist* and *The Superstitious Man*), those drawn from the world of the professions (such as *The Porter*, *The Fisherman*, *The Helmsman*), those that mention stage-characters (*Women drinking hemlock*; or *Thais*, *Glykera*, names of well-known prostitutes) or an object (such as *The Necklace*) that must have been at the heart of the action. Also typical are titles that express family relations (for example *The Brothers*, *Cousins*, *The Twins*) or a character's geographical origin (*Woman from Andros*, *The Girl from Perinthus*, *Locrians*, and others).

1.3.2 Menander's dramaturgy

This striking increase in the available witnesses makes it possible to give a fairly well documented outline of the distinctive characteristics of Menander's theatre.

At the level of dramaturgical structure, we find some significant differences from Attic "Old" Comedy. A different function is assigned to the prologue, which is sometimes placed after the presentation of the characters or even after the first scene (in the *Aspis*). As had already happened in some of Euripides' tragedies, the prologue ceases to be a true act of the drama, that is, one characterised by action, and becomes fixed in the function of providing scene-setting information and presenting the characters. The spectators are told of the crucial issue in the events presented and, not infrequently, they are put in a position to guess what will happen and how the plot will be resolved. The role of the chorus has been scaled down emphatically: there are no longer any choral sections, which in Old Comedy had featured text, music and dance; the episodes (the number of which seems to have settled at five) are separated by intermezzi of pure entertainment, signalled in the manuscripts by the stage-direction χοροῦ (*scil.* μέρος: "(part) of the chorus," "choral intermezzo"), of which nothing at all survives.

At the level of the system of characters and the plot, as has already been noted, "New" Comedy favours themes inspired by recurring, everyday situations from society and private and family life, though at times with problematic conflicts. The plots are realistic in type, as was emphasised already in antiquity (as attested by the comment attributed to the grammarian Aristophanes of Byzantium: ὦ Μένανδρε καὶ βίε, πότερος ἄρ' ὑμῶν πότερον ἀπεμιμήσατο; "O Menander, o life: which of you two imitated the other?"). The characters are drawn from the real world, from the middle class of artisans and country people of modest position (but not the lowest social class), within their social environment, which included slaves and *hetairai*, and they carry out roles that are essentially conventional, adopting the traits of fairly fixed "types" or "characters": the young man in love, the young woman seduced, the clever slave, the stingy and cantankerous old man, and so on.

The central nucleus as well as secondary parts of the plot quite often concern a situation of flawed love: a young woman has been raped and has given birth to a child without knowing the father; two lovers want to marry but encounter obstacles that seem insuperable; an old man crushes the dreams of a young woman by aiming to marry her. The resolution of the events is always happy and reaches its fulfilment thanks to a *coup de théâtre* (generally a "recognition," ἀναγνωρισμός, *anagnōrismos*) that makes it possible to re-establish a balance that meets fair and appropriate aspirations: the raped woman discovers the identity of the supposed and repentant rapist, identifying him with someone with whom she was already in love, and marries him willingly and gladly; the two parted lovers can finally meet and be united in marriage; the old man in love backs off from his rash marriage proposals and permits the young woman to realise her own dreams of love. The drama often concludes with the celebration of a marriage party or the return of family harmony and peaceable relations between people.

Behind this frequent recurrence of themes concerning the family one can easily discern the strong desire for normality that must have characterised Athenian society, which was pervaded by a crisis in family relations (signalled also indirectly by the situations in which two characters tied by bonds of blood or shared experience are unaware of that fact, making necessary a recognition scene). Sociological studies on this topic have been made, which identified the root of this recurring choice of theme in the dramatic social phenomenon of single mothers – their guardianship was evidently problematic due to the subaltern role of women – and, further, in the exposure of infants, often the result of extra-marital relations. These two phenomena profoundly altered the social system supporting the weaker groups in society (women and children, in particular), a system that had been guaranteed by the nuclear family.

A strong sense of the decisive importance of chance (τύχη, *tychē*) in human affairs is likewise symptomatic of the atmosphere of insecurity that characterised Menander's times, given the succession of political troubles that we have noted. The irrational sequences of events and actions driven by chance, often inscrutable and beyond the range of the limited human capacity for foresight, are a source of confusions and misunderstandings of every kind, until it produces unexpected results and sudden turns of events, sometimes fortunate, sometimes disastrous. The individual seeks support and friendship in other individuals: the world of Menander is pervaded by the sense of human solidarity. The fact that life is a plaything of an unfathomable fate favours the idea of the impossibility of correctly interpreting events and of the vanity of any attempt to discern their significance, foresee their result or influence them. What seems like a stroke of luck may be transformed into a misfortune, just as an apparent disgrace may be revealed to be a source of happiness. Similarly, an action taken for a good purpose often generates an effect opposite to the intention, while a wicked action may turn out well in an unhoped-for way.

One of the typical situations that expresses this lack of faith in the possibility of reading reality correctly at the moment it is occurring – postponing the cognitive act to the "afterwards" and so qualifying it as "recognition" – is the circumstance by which a young man and young woman, linked by a dramatic personal experience (often a rape perpetrated by the young man during an encounter at night), end up meeting by accident and, not recognising each other, fall in love and get married. Only a chance circumstance leads to their reciprocal recognition (ἀναγνωρισμός) and to forgiveness for the crime.

The typical ending with a marriage celebration, then, is notably different from the κῶμος (*kōmos*) of Old Comedy. In the latter case the festive and enjoyable procession fulfils the function (a ritual one, in a certain sense) of giving a final outlet to the many different comic tensions expressed by the quick succession of jokes and *coups de théâtre*. In Menander's comedy, weddings occur as a coherent result of the parted lovers' story, whose meeting again is the worthy and inescapable happy end of the drama that has been presented, the expression of the proper social order's reconstitution.

In conclusion, the distance of Menandrean comedy from that of Aristophanes and from Old Comedy in general is clear. Times had changed, and the biting and mocking aggression with which the author, through the protagonists on the stage and thanks to the sharp jokes, turns his barbs on contemporary society, evoking uncontrollable laughter from the spectators, had passed away. The theatre of Menander has a more uniform approach and a more reflective character. It suggests and mirrors back a precise ethical vision of the world, in the face of which a certain melancholy outweighs laughter and presumptuous self-assurance. Politics and the grand themes of existence are remote, while friendship, understanding and human solidarity are the deep values that sustain the drama.

1.3.3 The better-preserved comedies

In reconstructing the plot of the more lacunose among the better preserved plays, we are helped by the indirect tradition, the known prologues of the comedies themselves and, in the case of the *Herōs*, from a *hypothesis* that precedes the text of the comedy in the papyrus that transmits the beginning of the play.

Dyskolos or Misanthrōpos. Literally the title *Dyskolos* means "difficult, intractable (in character)" (whence the translation *The Peevish Fellow*), referring to the protagonist, an old man who stands in the way of the love for his daughter felt by Sostratos. Only an unexpected moment of need will make him aware of the value of disinterested human relations and emotions and will transform him into a less gruff and more understanding person. This is the only comedy that we possess in its entirety. It was performed in 316 and is the earliest of those that are better preserved.

> Sostratos has fallen in love with a country woman whom he saw during a hunting party and he aims to win her, but all his attempts are thwarted by Knemon, the elderly and cantankerous (*dyskolos*) father of the girl, whom he is unable to get close to despite the help of Gorgias, Knemon's stepson. Knemon has sent away his wife and lives alone with his daughter and her nurse. The old man demonstrates his own rough temper when the mother of Sostratos arrives for a sacrifice near a little temple of Pan located close to his house. The cooks employed for the ritual meal call on him to ask to borrow a pot and are rudely chased away. The turning-point occurs when the old man, in the attempt to recover an amphora that has dropped into a well, falls down the well himself and, in order not to drown, has to ask for help from Gorgias and Sostratos, who pull him to safety. Reformed thanks to this episode, the old man shows his change of heart and his gratitude to the two young men: he gives his possessions to Gorgias, entrusts to him the task of finding a husband for his daughter, and shuts himself up in solitude. Gorgias gains the hand of Sostratos' sister and Sostratos can finally marry Knemon's daughter. Knemon himself is tricked into taking part in the marriage.

Perikeiromenē. The title, *The Girl with Her Hair Cut Short*, alludes to a specific situation and character in the play: the young Glykera, whose head is shorn by a jealous lover (*perikeiromenē* means "shaved down to nothing") as an exemplary punishment for a cheating kiss. On the basis of a supposed historical allusion, the play is thought to be later than 314, but this is far from certain. There are major lacunae in what survives, but the plot can easily be reconstructed.

> As we learn from the prologue, recited by Agnoia (the personification of Ignorance), an old woman had found two exposed newborn infants, Moschion and Glykera. She kept the girl in her own home and entrusted the boy to Myrrhine, a rich lady who is her neighbour. When Glykera grew old enough, the old woman told her the circumstances in which she and her brother were found. Then, before she dies, she entrusts her to the soldier Polemon. One evening, Moschion, drunk, came up to the girl and, unaware that he was her brother, kissed her. In order not to offend the young man, she did not withdraw from the kiss. Polemon, seized by jealousy,

punishes Glykera by cutting off her hair. The girl seeks refuge in the house of Myrrhine, and Polemon aims to force her to return with him. A mutual friend, Pataikos, offers to mediate between the two. During the negotiations, which are heading for failure, out of the house are thrown the objects with which the two siblings had been exposed as infants, and so Pataikos recognises the two young people as his children. Moschion, learning that Glykera is his sister, renounces a love that would be unnatural. The play concludes with the reconciliation of Polemon and Glykera, while Pataikos promises a new fiancée for Moschion.

Aspis. We do not know the date of performance of the play entitled *The Shield*. It is certainly later than *Dyskolos* and is close to *Perikeiromenē*, which is believed to date after 314. In *The Shield* the ineluctable and unfathomable action of personified Tyche (Chance) forms a framework for the motif of love pursued by two young people but thwarted by the intentions of a rapacious old man; this is opposed by the scheming of a loyal slave who promotes the well-being and interests of his own master. Tyche causes it to be believed that Kleostratos has fallen in battle, making it attractive for the old man Smikrines to seek marriage to Kleostratos' sister. This intricate web of human actions and intrigues is frustrated when, in the finale, Kleostratos returns to the scene alive and well, demonstrating how it rested on illusory and deceitful assumptions.

> The slave Daos comes home from the war with a rich booty but without his master Kleostratos, whose shield he brings back: he had found it beside a disfigured corpse, which he believed must have been that of his master. At this point Tyche enters the scene, and we learn from her that in reality it was not the body of Kleostratos, who was taken captive and is destined to return. Tyche then presents the characters of the play and introduces the development of the action. When setting off for the war, Kleostratos had entrusted his sister to their uncle Chairestratos, who is now thinking of giving her in marriage to his stepson Chaireas; but the elder brother of Chairestratos, the mean old man Smikrines, wishing to gain possession of the wealthy booty brought back by Daos, makes the proposal that he, rather than Chaireas, should marry the young woman instead. The loyal Daos, understanding the intentions of the old miser, suggests to Chairestratos that he pretend to die, so that Smikrines, attracted by his brother's wealth, will redirect his marriage interests towards his niece, Chairestratos' daughter: in this way, once the marriage between Chaireas and the sister of Kleostratos is concluded, the reappearance of Chairestratos will cock a snook at Smikrines. In the finale, the slave's plan succeeds, and to the wedding of Chaireas is now added the wedding of the returned Kleostratos to the daughter of Chairestratos.

Samia. The plot of this comedy is based on an unexpected pregnancy and on the misunderstandings that follow from it. The title, *Woman from Samos*, refers to the active protagonist of the action: her initiative, based on good intentions, is unexpectedly the cause of a misunderstanding, to the point that she, though entirely blameless, is treated as a vile adulteress and is chased out of the house. There are two views on the chronological position of the play: some believe it to be a juvenile work, others see in it a level of dramatic skill that indicates the playwright's maturity.

The young man Moschion is the adoptive son of the old man Demeas, who lives with a concubine who originally came from Samos, the prostitute Chrysis. During Demeas' absence, Moschion has seduced the girl Plangon, daughter of the nextdoor neighbour, and has had a son, but he has said nothing about it to his father. To deflect Demeas' anger at Moschion, Chrysis pretends that the little boy is her child and the old man receives this news with ill temper, since he is afraid he will have to marry her. Although Demeas agrees with the neighbour that Moschion and Plangon will marry, he is seized by the suspicion that the father of the child is Moschion, becomes convinced that Chrysis has cheated on him with his son and chases her out of the house. When Demeas finally discovers the whole truth, the misunderstandings and confusions come to an end: Chrysis returns to Demeas, Moschion can marry his beloved Plangon and reclaim his son.

Epitrepontes. This play is traditionally assigned a date later than 304, i.e. the period of Menander's maturity. It takes its title (literally, "appellants," normally rendered as *Men at Arbitration*) from the two characters who appeal to the judgment of a third character, so that he may decide who shall keep the tokens that were found alongside an exposed newborn infant. Skilful combinations characterise the complex plot of this play, in which chance meetings and accidental circumstances (alongside all the typical elements of the repertoire: violence, rape, marriage, infant exposure, misreadings, recognition, repentance and forgiveness) strew with misunderstandings the tortuous path of the protagonists towards their reciprocal recognition and reconciliation.

Charisios raped Pamphile during a nocturnal festival. At the moment of the attack, the young woman tore a ring from his finger. Some time later the two of them, without recognising each other, marry each other. When the young man is away for a while, Pamphile gives birth to the child conceived by the rape and has it exposed along with some symbolic tokens, including the ring. The slave Onesimus informs Charisios of this event, and the latter, believing that his wife has cheated on him, leaves her and, in order to forget her, abandons himself to dissolute living in the company of the *hetaira* Habrotonon. The child, in the meantime, has been found by a shepherd, who passed it on to a charcoal-burner. However, the two of them quarrel over who should keep the tokens. While they are discussing this, they happen to pass in front of the house of Charisios and run into the father of Pamphile, who has come to find his son-in-law. They ask him to be the judge of the question and he decides that the tokens should go to whoever takes the child. Onesimus, the slave of Charisios, meets the charcoal-burner and recognises the ring. He persuades him to lend him it and wants to show it to his master, but is too scared. When the charcoal-burner asks for the return of the ring, the *hetaira* Habrotonon, who has been present during this scene, guesses what has happened. When the *hetaira* realises that Pamphile is the young woman raped by Charisios, it becomes clear that the child is the son born out of this relation. Charisios, who even before the recognition had repented of his abandonment of Pamphile, is now very happy to restore unity to the family.

Herōs. The title of the comedy – which can be rendered as *The Guardian Spirit* – most probably derives from the guardian genius of the two young co-protagonists, who was probably given the part of reciting the prologue. As well as around a hundred lines of the text, we are helped in the reconstruction by a metrical *hypothesis* in twelve line of iambic verse. Violence against women, exposure of newborn infants and a resolution in a recognition scene are the stock ingredients of the play.

> A young man, Laches, has raped Myrrhine, who has then given birth to a twin son and daughter, Gorgias and Plangon. The girl entrusted the twins to a herdsman and, some time later, married Laches, without knowing that it is he who made her pregnant. On the death of the herdsman, in order to settle a debt of his, Gorgias and Plangon, by now youths, go into service in Laches' house. Plangon is raped by a neighbour and becomes pregnant; she is to become the wife of a slave who wants to take her, until Laches recognises the two youths as his children. The marriage of Plangon with the man who raped her concludes the play.

Sicyōnios or *Sicyōnioi*. The theme of the disappearance of beloved persons, whose return takes place in the finale (this too a kind of "recognition" at the symbolic level) recurs also in *The Sicyonian* or, according to more recent studies, *The Sycionians*. The young daughter and a loyal slave of the old man Kichesias are kidnapped from him and sold in Caria to a wealthy soldier from Sicyon. After various reversals, in the finale the old man rediscovers his daughter and the play concludes with a wedding between the girl and the soldier.

Misoumenos. The title, *The Hated Man*, alludes to the play's protagonist, who is in love with a girl who hates him. The soldier Thrasonides is in love with the girl who belongs to him, perhaps because she is his prisoner; but his love is not returned, since she hates him (hence the title of the play). Despite this, he does not disrespect her. In the finale the young woman rediscovers her father and probably marries Thrasonides.

1.3.4 The poetic and moral world of Menander

By reconstructing the plots of Menander's works, we can see how political comedy was transformed into an ethical drama centred on family themes. With the fading of the lively social outlook of the *polis*, which in its political and economic self-sufficiency could be identified with the world itself, the playwright's goal has dropped in depth, focusing on more intimate and private realities. Family, the smallest unit placed at the basis of society, is a microcosm open to the risks of dissolution. A preoccupation that emerges with urgency is how to maintain this small world, a task that requires sincere and constructive attitudes on the part of individuals. In Menander's comedy there are no characters that are intimately or definitively compromised by wickedness or who cannot be redeemed into a positive role. The moral evolution of the *dyskolos* – "peevish" – old man, a genuinely existential journey of "conversion," can stand for this idea of the role of individuals in society, which is expressed also through the positively connoted efforts of characters commonly confined to the margins of traditional ethics and excluded from paradigmatically positive roles: the *hetaira* Habrotonon, whose disinterested generosity gives rise to the happy ending of events in *Epitrepontes*; the woman from Samos, a foreigner and a prostitute, who is ready to take a risk herself to cover up for the profligate son of Demeas; the slave

Daos, who in *Aspis* does not flag in his determined pursuit of the well-being of his master, even though he believes him to be dead; the slave Onesimos, again in *Epitrepontes*, torn between the desire to tell his master that the infant is his son and the thought of the additional suffering that will afflict the unfortunate Pamphile.

The characters' readiness to be constructive and show solidarity is confirmed in attitudes of trust/distrust. Although often the action begins from the disappearance of a relation of trust between a couple (*Epitrepontes*, *Samia*, *Perikeiromenē*), this occurs through false evidence of guilt. As soon as the belief prompted by appearances dissolves when the truth is revealed, the person thought to have been offended is quick to restore the balance that had been disrupted. In fact often – and in a way quite significant for the constructive attitude assigned to the characters – the person who thought he was offended changes his interior attitude to a state of comprehensive forgiveness and readiness to pardon and reconcile, even before the truth has been discovered (such as Charisios in *Epitrepontes* and Polemon in *Perikeiromenē*). The initial trust that had been breached by the misleading appearance of the facts is reconstituted, with the help of the unknowable intervention of Tyche, when the real situation is discovered to be less serious than had been feared and, even before this, through the ethical gain of comprehensive forgiveness for the errors of those held dear. Love, friendship and solidarity are the main ethical values of the Menandrean world. Appearance and reality, distrust and trust, misunderstanding and understanding, resentment and reconciliation are the extreme poles from which the dramatic plots take their form, plots that the characters face with the reasonable good sense of the common man, the non-hero.

1.3.5 Language and style

In Menander's language we see in action the progressive simplification of the Attic dialect, at both the morphological level (with the ever rarer use of the optative and disappearance of the dual) and the lexical level (semantic variations and neologisms). These changes, favoured by the expansion of the Greek language in the Mediterranean area, would come to define the form of the *koinē dialektos* (cf. *The Hellenistic Age* I 3). The style is kept consistently at a medium tone, without ever indulging in either colloquial forms or poetic echoes. In this way very different from Old Comedy, the New Comedy thus reflects the values of the middle class also in its chosen form of expression, being neither over-elaborate nor excessive or shouted.

1.3.6 Reception

As happened with other authors of New Comedy, the plays of Menander too were models for Latin comedies. Plautus drew on them for plays including *Stichus*, *Bacchides* (*The Two Bacchises*, which we can compare to the roughly hundred lines that survive from *Twice a Swindler*), *Cistellaria* (*The Casket Comedy*) and *Aulularia* (*The Pot of Gold*, which has points of contact with *Dyskolos*). Terence, with his characteristic procedure of combining episodes and situations inspired by different plays by Greek authors, took ideas, for example, from *Epitrepontes* for *Hecyra* and from other comedies for *Heautontimoroumenos* (*The Self-Tormentor*), *Eunuchus* (*The Eunuch*), *Adelphoe* (*The Brothers*) and *Andria* (*The Woman of Andros*). As we have noted, the large number of papyri found attest that the comedies of Menander enjoyed a certain success with readers throughout the whole of antiquity, up to the beginning of the Middle Ages, when they met their fate of falling into obscurity. They emerged from it only around the middle of the last century, the moment of the most important discoveries.

2 Tragedy and phlyax

2.1 Tragedy between heritage and new developments

In the course of the Hellenistic Age tragic drama was affected by transformations even more profound than those met by comedy. The context changed for commissioning, producing and performing tragedies and now they received particular support from rulers and tyrants keen to add lustre to their own names and courts. A distinctive aspect of this period was the practice of staging re-runs of the fifth-century tragic repertoire. Everywhere, productions flourished of the plays of Euripides, especially, but also those of Aeschylus and Sophocles, which were recognised as the masterpieces of the era of Athens' greatest brilliance. Yet this included interventions – often grave ones – to modify the text with solutions to the staging or direction prompted by the pursuit of spectacular effects. There was a deep change, compared to classical tragedy, in the aesthetic taste of the performances: the pedagogical and intellectual values that tragedy had held in Athenian society of the fifth and fourth centuries were lost and it became a genre of mere entertainment, in which the public sought and found an occasion for astonishment and wonder.

For this reason, the text and the message that the author entrusted to it both lost importance; what was favoured instead was the staging, performance and virtuoso skills of the actors, on whose bravura the success of the whole show depended. A similar aspect is the accentuation of pathos and the emotional stimulation of the spectators, which took precedence over the narrative and problem-focused aspects that are equally present in the tragic texts themselves. This emphasis on effects of pathos, to the detriment of the play's action, is expressed clearly in the type of interventions generally made on the texts of the classical repertoire. Entire scenes were cut, the choral parts were suppressed, the recitative was transposed into sung parts with musical accompaniment and songs were introduced, as solos or duets, and performed to music by the actors. All this ultimately combined to induce strong emotions in the spectators and to make an impression on their senses through a kind of expressive intensification by theatrical means.

2.2 The tragic output of the Hellenistic Age

These remarks on the tragic repertoire of the Classical Age should not suggest that there was any lack of original tragedies produced during the Hellenistic Age. To the contrary, from the end of the fourth and in the third century B.C. there was a flourishing output of new works. This was favoured by demand for performances and commissions that came primarily from rulers and tyrants, as we have noted, as patrons who sought to raise their own prestige. This explains the encomiastic character of this theatre. By the representation of mythical episodes or historical events in the remote or recent past, the author was often addressing an elegant eulogy to his prestigious sponsor and exalting his gifts and achievements. The theme selected, be it mythological or historical, often in fact fulfilled this encomiastic function.

As regards dramatic technique, the newly composed tragedies exhibited the same characteristics that were sought and heightened in performances of the classical repertoire even at the cost of doing violence to it, namely a prevalence of emotive and pathetic elements over narrative ones, accentuating histrionic aspects by ostentatiously displaying the actors' personal talents, reducing the choral parts in favour of solo execution with musical accompaniment and, in general, a search for spectacular effect at the level of scenography and direction.

The greatness of the three fifth-century tragedians obscured the Hellenistic authors' output in the later tradition. Although some of their names and the titles of their tragedies have survived, only a meagre set of fragments have been preserved, along with some records of their theatrical activity in the erudite tradition and the epigraphic sources. Yet the importance accorded in antiquity to the Hellenistic tragedians' own work is attested by the interest shown in them by later grammarians and scholars. In particular, we owe to the Greek erudite tradition the term "the poets of the Pleiad," evoking the constellation with seven bright stars, a title given to the main authors of tragedy active in Alexandria at the court of Ptolemy II Philadelphus. These authors worked in the fertile and multifaceted culture of Alexandria which, from the end of the fourth century to the Roman period, constituted the innovative centre of greatest importance for the preservation and transmission of ancient literature, as we will see more fully in the section on Hellenistic philology (cf. *The Hellenistic Age* III 2.2).

Of the seven poets of the "Pleiad" some are better known for reasons other than their tragic output. Alexander the Aetolian pursued philological work at the Library of Alexandria and made efforts to collect and order tragedies and satire plays. From Lycophron of Chalcis we have the poem *Alexandra*. We know that he was also the author of a tragedy entitled *Cassandreis*, on the topic of Cassander, son of the *diadochos* Antipater and king of Macedonia in the late fourth and early third century B.C. (i.e. it was a play on a historical theme). Of the other poets who formed the "Pleiad" we know very little. Certainly part of the group were Homerus of Byzantium, Philicus of Corcyra and Sositheus; as for the other two members, the sources disagree on the names, varying between, on the one hand, Sosiphanes of Syracuse and Aeantides, or else Dionysiades of Mallus and Euphronius of Chersonesus.

A short fragment in iambic trimeters preserved in a papyrus from Oxyrhynchus (*P. Oxy.* 2382) is considered to be part of a tragedy with a historical background which presented a stage adaptation of the story of Candaules and Gyges, matching the account of Herodotus. The historian relates (*Histories* I 8–14) that the Lydian king Candaules had shown Gyges how he could secretly admire the queen while she undressed in her own chamber, but she noticed him and informed Gyges that he must either kill himself or kill her husband Candaules. Gyges killed the king and took his place, marrying the queen and becoming ruler of Lydia. The first column of the papyrus text presents a very lacunose scrap of dialogue between the queen of the Lydians and the chorus, which is presumed to have been composed of loyal slaves. In the second column, which is better preserved, the protagonist recalls the trick played by Candaules and the shameful night: it is supposed that here the queen is revealing to her interlocutor what happened and organising the revenge on Candaules. It cannot be excluded that the third column, which is very fragmentary, reports snippets of the meeting with Gyges, in the course of which the woman gives the man her ultimatum. Scholars debate the period when this tragedy was composed. In the past, on account of its historical theme, it was considered to be archaic and was attributed to Phrynichus; others have preferred instead to ascribe it to Ion of Chios (cf. *The Classical Age* III 2.1.2 and V 3.1); an alternative idea is to interpret the fragment as a novella in iambic trimeters of the Hellenistic period. This latter hypothesis should be rejected as far as the fragment's genre is concerned, but the dating to the Hellenistic Age seems acceptable, above all considering the characteristics of its metre, language and style, as well as some Sophoclean influences.

2.3 Phlyax or hilarotragedy

The term phlyax (in Greek φλύαξ) refers to a particular theatrical genre, parodic in character, that developed in southern Italy between Middle and New Comedy, the "inventor" of which was identified by the ancients as Rhinthon (see below). Phlyax is properly the name of a grotesque divinity or demon associated with the cult of Dionysus which presided over fertility and the blooming of vegetation. This figure was the protagonist of brief and basic mime scenes of popular character, namely phlyax farce. As well as having close connections to successive forms of farce diffused within Italic cultures and later known also at Rome (Oscan and Atellan farce), phlyax should perhaps be connected to the complex process by which Attic comedy was formed. The parodic nature of this performance genre is recalled by the term hilarotragedy (ἰλαροτραγῳδία, "amusing tragedy"), which refers to the literary form of phlyax perfected by Rhinthon: this consisted of stagings that generally parody mythological subjects familiar from Attic tragedy.

2.4 Rhinthon

The poet Nossis (cf. *The Hellenistic Age* IV 2.2.4) composed a fictive funerary epigram on Rhinthon, in which she calls him a Syracusan, whereas the later scholarly tradition (the *Suda* lexicon and Stephanus of Byzantium) believes him to be from Tarentum. However that may be, it was at Tarentum that the poet probably spent most of his life, pursuing a busy theatrical career. His date is placed by the sources between the late fourth and early third century B.C., during the reign of Ptolemy I Soter in Egypt (305–282 B.C.).

As we have said, the ancient tradition considers Rhinthon to be the inventor of phlyax farce. As in other similar cases, we should understand this report as meaning that Rhinthon perfected for the theatre a farcical form of mime that was widespread in the popular culture of the Italic communities, giving it literary form and standing. The sources ascribe to him thirty-eight dramatic works, but only nine titles have survived: *Amphitrion, Eunobatai* (*Those who get into bed*), *Heracles, Iphigenia in Aulis, Iphigenia in Tauris, Meleager the slave, Medea, Orestes* and *Telephus*. From the few, brief fragments it emerges that the metre used was the iambic trimeter of tragedy, but the genre must have admitted some mixture of metres for parodic purposes, given that one fragment has preserved for us a choliambus imitating Hipponax. The scarcity of the evidence prevents us from taking any further the discussion of the characteristics of Rhinthon's farce, yet from the surviving titles it is clear that his parody was directed above all at the theatre of Euripides.

III Philology, Grammar, Erudition

1 The literature of erudition

1.1 Philology, grammar and the transmission and interpretation of texts

After epic, lyric, drama, historiography, oratory and philosophical and scientific literature, philology and grammar too made their appearance in the patrimony of Greek literary civilisation. People began to see clearly, and to try to solve, the problem of the correctness and accuracy of the texts of the ancient authors that had been passed down. In a broad and systematic manner, they faced up to the need to interpret those works in the most complete and appropriate way, with the most refined and nuanced tools and methods, using approaches that were genuinely philological and historical. Reflections on language, which were at first linked to the sphere of rhetorical and philosophical thought, would later be broadened and advanced by the observation of phenomena that were in a true sense grammatical, until a rich and vigorous science of grammar took root. Various spheres of research were developed and the activities of constituting the text and interpreting and commenting on the classical authors gave rise to a vast and varied production of erudite work, bringing into being whole new literary genres. An important chapter of Greek culture in the Hellenistic and Imperial Periods is formed by everything connected to philology, grammar, lexicography, paroemiography, biography, repertoires of materials, antiquarian and doxographic collections, compendia and miscellaneous compilations – all of which we summarise by the term "the literature of erudition." The whole vast domain of erudition appears to have aimed to deepen by every means both the interpretation of the great authors of the past and their works and the understanding of the culture of which they were thought to be the repository. It was a literature that embodied the trends of an era devoted to assiduously and tenaciously studying, collecting, summarising and preserving treasures of doctrine, which formed a glorious, centuries-old intellectual inheritance, and to delineating and fixing a cultural identity that deserved to be kept alive.

Finally we should recall another aspect that researchers have now brought to light in its full significance. In the transmission of the works of Greek literature, an important first selection was made in the Hellenistic Period by the Alexandrian philologists (roughly third to first century B.C.), whose choice of "canonical" authors marked a decisive moment not only for interpretive approaches and the establishment of a philological and exegetical toolkit, but also for the preservation and loss of the ancient works themselves.

The most creative phase of philology and textual exegesis was, above all, the Hellenistic Age, along with the first two centuries of the Imperial Period. After the second century A.D. one could say that the very creative phase was over, though for many

https://doi.org/10.1515/9783110426328-023

centuries scholarly work continued to fulfil its important function. By then it was devoted primarily to preserving texts and creating epitomes, collections and compendia, a focus that determined the selection of material. Most of the works produced in this field in the Hellenistic and Imperial Ages have been lost. Usually, what is available to us is large collections compiled much later, particularly in the Byzantine Period, from which we can glean fragments of information that are sometimes quite extensive, sometimes very meagre. Since most of our knowledge of the Hellenistic material is owed to these collections and since they are the filter and main channel through which our image of this activity and its productions has been formed, we need to begin by considering these literary genres and then work back from them to their ultimate sources.

1.2 Textual philology and scholiography

Many of the Greek authors have come down to us in manuscripts equipped with an amalgam of ancient comments present as marginal notes, sometimes very brief, sometimes of considerable length, known as scholia (Greek σχόλια, Latin *scholia*: the original meaning of the word is "little lesson, short teaching," which evolved into "short note, brief explanation"). The interest and quantity of these notes varies across the collections of *scholia* to different authors. Their value differs depending on the sources on which they drew and, by and large, they offer material of greater value whenever the critical-exegetical world of the scholars of the Hellenistic and Imperial Periods forms their distant starting point. In general, the scholiographic literature is the main place where we find the remains of interpretive and exegetical work on literature by the ancient grammarians in various phases and eras. By different routes, the scholiasts were heirs to the works of exegesis typical of the Alexandrian Age, namely: *hypomnēmata* (ὑπομνήματα), i.e. commentaries that accompanied the text passage by passage; *syngrammata* (συγγράμματα), treatises on single problems, usually in monographic form; and lexicographical collections (from *lexeis*, i.e. "words"), in which terms and phrases that were found problematic, in literary works above all, were given a brief grammatical, lexical or antiquarian explanation.

While the commentary, *hypomnēma*, can in some sense be considered the most characteristic and important product of the Alexandrians' work of scholarly exegesis, another typical result of the Alexandrian grammarians' work was the *ekdosis* (ἔκδοσις), that is, the edition of texts. To produce a new edition of a work involved both the task of emending, i.e. correcting any errors produced in the transmission of the received text and brought to light by the philologist, and also the selection between variants found in different copies; for such "corrective" interventions is used the term *diorthōsis* (διόρθωσις), literally "correction." Although there has been some scepticism, at the current stage of research it seems very hard, not to say impossible, to deny that the grammarians of the Hellenistic Age did indeed address this problem of the correctness of a text and sought to equip themselves with the tools needed to recover the "genuine" text, freeing it from errors and corruption caused by transmission via the successive copying of so many exemplars. Of course, their methods and results are characterised by all the weaknesses to be expected in the embryonic phase of any discipline, but this does not detract from the fact that they genuinely did lay the first foundations for what later became philology, a historic development.

There has been much debate over what specifically Alexandrian *ekdosis* was. When a grammarian was the author of an edition of Homer or Pindar or Herodotus, what did he actually do, and what precisely was produced? One alternative is that result of the activity consisted in the very drafting of a new copy that presented *his* text, i.e. the complete literary text in the form that the philologist regarded as correct. The other possibility is that he worked on a carefully chosen existing copy and made his interventions on this text, writing them in the margins or discussing them in the commentary. In recent studies the more significant and well-founded arguments have favoured the latter hypothesis, which allows a better understanding of how the philologists worked in practice and a better explanation of many problems posed by the available testimonia, and also of the meeting of the term *diorthōsis*.

The link between the text and the commentary was established by critical signs, which were placed beside the text and indicated the type of textual intervention or exegetical problem that was the subject of discussion, such as deletion (i.e. the elimination of a word or part of the text), transposition of parts, difficulties of interpretation, readings of a predecessor that were open to criticism or changes in the linguistic forms. The system of critical signs came to be perfected and adapted to the different types of text and was a technical advance of great importance in work on transmission and interpretation of texts. From the material available to us, it is clear, further, that exegetical questions as well as textual problems were discussed not only in commentaries but also in monographic treatises (the *syngrammata*) or lexicographical collections, where it was the *lexis*, a keyword used as a lemma, that provided the link to the text and so indicated the problem to be discussed (etymology, meaning, linguistic-grammatical difficulty, and so on).

It is the papyrus finds, ranging across a time-span from, in its broadest definition, the third century B.C. to the seventh century A.D. (though the majority of finds belong to the first three centuries A.D.), that have introduced us to significant remains of this type of work. These include copies of texts with marginal variants and annotations of varying quantity, snippets of *hypomnēmata* and of *syngrammata* and remains of lexica of various genres produced from the Hellenistic and Imperial Periods to the Late Antique Period. We thus have in our hands fragments of various size and of quite varied interest and content, from simple glossographic explanation of single words to discussions of problems philological, exegetical, antiquarian and mythographic, matters of linguistic usage, lexicon, rhetorical figures, stylistic observations, proverbs, anecdotes, biographical questions, down to aesthetic and moral judgements.

The fragments recovered in the papyri are just sorry remnants of the works of the grammarians of the Hellenistic and Imperial Periods, which are for the most part lost. Yet much of this varied mass of erudite materials has been transmitted across the centuries by a different route, by being combined into collections compiled out of heterogeneous sources, epitomised into more or less meagre annotations, enriched over time by new additions, reworked in revised forms, reduced or expanded according to convenience – an evolution that continued into the collections or corpora of scholia, which were copied in the margins of the manuscripts to form a true commentary on the work. The value of the various corpora of scholia is quite unequal. They were usually first put together at the end of the Late Antique Period and the beginning of the so-called Byzantine Renaissance of the ninth century, and their value differs depending both on the sources they used and on the quantity and quality of their preservation.

The papyri offer remnants of exegetical material for many authors who had no Byzantine transmission and for whom, therefore, we do not have a scholiographic corpus. Without the fragments of *hypomnēmata* and *syngrammata* restored by the papyri we would know a lot less about ancient philological activity, for example on lyric poets other than Pindar, who is the only one for whom we have a corpus of scholia in the manuscripts. Nonetheless, a significant number of collections of scholia have reached us through the Byzantine manuscripts, usually copied in the margins. As concerns poetic works, the greatest quantity of scholia are those to the *Iliad* and *Odyssey*, offering what is probably the richest trove of information on the philological and hermeneutic activity of the Alexandrians, together with materials from different periods and other proveniences. After the Homeric corpus, the largest corpora are the scholia to Aristophanes and Pindar; those to the three great tragedians Aeschylus, Sophocles and Euripides; and then those to Hesiod. Of the major Hellenistic poets, we have sizable collections of scholia to Lycophron, Theocritus and Apollonius Rhodius; and there is a little trove of scholia to the *Hymns* of Callimachus preserved in the medieval manuscript tradition. Finally, there is a considerable group of scholia to certain didactic poets, above all to Aratus, but also to the two surviving poems of Nicander, to Dionysius Periegetes and to Oppian. The scholia to works of prose are on the whole less rich. There are just a handful of scholia to Herodotus, though the scholiographic corpus to Thucydides is more substantial; we also have a slim set of scholia to each of Xenophon, Strabo and Plutarch. In the sphere of oratory, the most studied seems to have been Demosthenes, whose ancient exegesis was substantial, although the scholia preserved in the manuscripts must be considered poor by comparison. Altogether scanty are the few surviving scholia to Aeschines and Isocrates. For the later prose authors we have collections of scholia to Lucian, Aelius Aristides, Hephaestion and Hermogenes. A special case is the substantial and quite interesting corpus of grammatical scholia to the *Technē grammatikē* attributed to Dionysius Thrax.

1.3 Lexicography

As well as from the *hypomnēmata* and *syngrammata*, the collections of scholia drew material also from the lexicographical works of scholars of the Hellenistic-Roman Period. The roots of lexicography go back to at least the fifth century B.C., when school education made use of explanations of single difficult words in poetic texts (ones that were foreign to the everyday language, obsolete, dialectal or technical). This primarily concerned the principal, obligatory educational text, namely Homer, but it occurred also, for example, with the difficult phrasing of early laws, such as those of Solon. The phenomenon certainly had older origins and continued without interruption. Glosses and paraphrases are documented for the Hellenistic and Imperial Ages and on into the production of paraphrases in the Late Antique and Byzantine Periods.

To explain the meaning of individual words was an activity at first linked, on the one hand, specifically to school education and to the explication of texts needed in that sphere, and on the other hand to reflections on language primarily made by the poets themselves and then by philosophers such as Democritus, Gorgias and the Sophists, not to mention the interest in the true signification of words attested in Plato's *Cratylus*. With the Alexandrian Age, it passed also into the hands of learned philologists, acquiring different aspects and content and continually widening its range. The result of this work was a set of critical material comprising *glōssai* (γλῶσσαι), that is "difficult words" found in the authors and in need of an interpretation tied to the precise passage in which each had been found (a concept codified by Aristotle in the *Poetics* 21, 22 and 25), and *lexeis* (λέξεις), "words," which provided a motive or hook for treating a topic that might be linguistic, lexical, philological or antiquarian in any way and which functioned as a lemma for collections that were at first largely thematic but later arranged ever more strictly in alphabetic order. Lexicography then became an exegetical and erudite activity that was scientifically autonomous and was practised and beloved by the Alexandrian philologists.

Lexicographical activity did not cease its development in the work of later grammarians and the output was enormous: lexica of dialect, synonyms, etymologies, of single authors or genres, onomastics, compilations on particular topics, epimerisms (the term refers to the division into single words of the text being analysed and their classification according to the parts of speech, to which might be added other grammatical notices on accentuation, spelling and other matters, including observations on examples of the word's usage). New collections of *lexeis* were compiled, which increasingly tended to gather the results of the previous centuries' labours. Part of this substantial heritage flowed into the lexicon of Hesychius of Alexandria (fifth to sixth century A.D.), which has survived in an incomplete and considerably interpolated form; with over 50,000 lemmata, it is one of our richest mines of erudite notices. In this case too, as for scholiography, a large part of what was produced in the Alexandrian Age and Imperial Period has been lost. Our possibilities for gaining information lie once again in the great Late Antique and Byzantine collections, which inherited and compiled the materials of the earlier tradition, often accumulating various notices at a single lemma with encyclopaedic aims and ambitions. These are, above all, the *Glossary* known as that of Cyril (going back to the fifth century A.D. and then expanded in various ways), the *Lexicon* of the patriarch Photius (ninth century), the *Suda* lexicon (tenth century), the lexicon of Pseudo-Zonaras (late twelfth century), four large *Etymologica* and numerous other similar texts of smaller bulk.

1.4 Grammar

The advance of Hellenistic grammatical studies proceeded in parallel and in cooperation with the evolution of exegetical and text-critical studies. Beginning from the Roman Period and especially at the height of the Imperial Period, the task of systematising and consolidating grammatical thought and norms was undertaken.

Interest in problems of language by philosophers such as Democritus, Gorgias, the Sophists and Plato also stands at the origins of the metalinguistic reflection that is grammatical science. In the philosophical sphere, debate began on questions such as the relation between words and things, or observations on homonyms and synonyms, or posing the problem of the correctness of language. In Aristotle's *Poetics* (20, 1456b 20 ff.) we find a series of considerations on the concepts of letter, syllable, conjunction, noun and verb and on inflection. After that it was within the framework of Stoicism (cf. *The Hellenistic Age* V 4) that grammar acquired its first foundation as a science. Studies and definitions were made of many aspects of the doctrine of inflection and tenses; elements of terminology were fixed and then remained in use; investigations were made of topics such as vowels and consonants, the parts of speech, the ambiguity of language and the relation between the linguistic form and the concept. For the Stoic Chrysippus, "anomaly" indicated the discrepancy between signified and signifier, though subsequently in the linguistic sphere the term came to mean a conception of language based rather on the free usage of speakers (in Greek *sunētheia*, in Latin *consuetudo*) than on the application of formal rules, and consequently it was seen as opposed to analogy, which was based on a predefined normative system. In reality there was a mutual exchange and interaction between the philosophical, the rhetorical and the linguistic-philological sides, and this led to the birth of the normative grammar of the Greek language. While the Stoics set the accent on linguistic anomaly and on the primary role of usage in defining correctness in language, the Alexandrian grammarians, on the other hand, concentrated on the observation of regular phenomena in morphology, inflection and the formation of words and they privileged the principle of analogy.

There has been much research and debate on whether a normative system of grammatical rules had been defined already in the first half of the second century or only in the first century B.C., i.e. on the moment at which the autonomous scientific status of the discipline was fully recognised, when it definitively became a *technē* independent of its philosophical roots. It is likely that an embryonic system of rules of normative grammar was created and defined by the Alexandrian grammarians of the third to second centuries B.C., especially Aristophanes of Byzantium and Aristarchus (from whom we have numerous linguistic and grammatical observations), which then received a systematic treatment in the work of Dionysius Thrax (ca. 170–90 B.C.), a student of Aristarchus. On the basis of the information we possess, we can certainly ascribe to Dionysius a treatise that was grammatical in nature and content, but probably not much of it coincides with the *Technē grammatikē* preserved under his name and which raises serious doubts about authenticity (cf. *The Hellenistic Age* III 2.4). When reflection on linguistic phenomena moved from the sphere of rhetoric and philosophy to that of the philologists, its fundamental organic bond was with the interpretation of texts. The foundations of grammar were laid in the context of literary exegesis, on the basis of an ever broader and deeper observation of linguistic phenomena in the authors that were the subject of editorial and exegetical attention. The following generations of grammatical scholars continued on the path marked out by the Alexandrian grammarians.

1.5 Paroemiography

The roots of paroemiography probably lie in the earliest collections of sayings, aphorisms and proverbial wisdom attributed to persons of charismatic authority. The presence of this kind of *gnōmai* (γνῶμαι) in literary works and the function assigned to them by the poets would have stimulated interest in their interpretation and also in collecting them. In truth the definition of what was included in the paroemiographic collections does not ever seem to have been rigidly codified but was, rather, very elastic. They found room, without distinction, for traditional sayings and saws, wisdom maxims, popular proverbs and turns of phrase. In the collections we find apophthegms of the Seven Sages (cf. *The Archaic Age* IV 1.5) and lines from the poets, together with sayings that seem to have a genuinely popular character.

    In a philosophical setting, the traditional maxims were seen as the remains of an ancient wisdom, the first steps of thought, which was worth recovering and analysing. An explicit interest in proverbs is found in Aristotle, who wrote a work, unfortunately now lost, with the title *Proverbs*; on this path the master was followed in the Peripatetic sphere by Theophrastus, Clearchus of Soli and Chamaeleon. The Stoic Chrysippus, too, wrote a work *On proverbs*, of which some fragments survive. Almost contemporary with Aristotle was the Attic historian Demon, he too author of a work *On proverbs*. In all probability interest in this whole tradition was raised within the sphere of the Peripatos, not only for the sake of a "history of philosophy" but also with an erudite-antiquarian perspective, which created an opening for the philologists to take an interest and then for autonomous work in paroemiography.

In the sphere of Alexandrian philology, Aristophanes of Byzantium studied this material under scientific criteria and from the perspective of the interpreter of texts. We have some fragments of two of his collections, one dedicated to metrical proverbs and one to non-metrical ones. The link with philology and the exegesis of authors was emphasised and strongly applied, a path that was well trodden. The next stage of major importance was represented by Didymus (first century B.C.), who devoted to proverbs a large collection of thirteen books, in which, it seems, a lot of material from comedy was present. This approach was then channelled into the large collection of Zenobius (second century A.D.), which has survived in reworkings, in which we can recognise a series of proverbs arranged by the different literary genres from which they are taken. In the case of paroemiography, too, our main source of information is formed by much later collections that were composed in the period from the Imperial to the Byzantine Age and have been preserved. In these large paroemiographic collections, the proverbs are arranged in alphabetic order.

1.6 Biography

Among the genres of erudite literature, we should also remember biography, at least insofar as it reconstructed the lives of the poets and writers on the basis of notices derived from interpreting passages of their works. The Hellenistic Age was an era of major development in biographical research on the people involved in poetry and literature in general, in direct connection to the demand for exegesis of their texts. By interpreting hints in the works, it was possible – or it was believed possible – to reconstruct moments in the author's biography while, on the other hand and in the opposite direction, the author's biography was an essential component among the tools that aided comprehension of a work.

2 Philology in Alexandria and Pergamum

2.1 Pre-Alexandrian exegesis

The earliest testimonies to the activity of explaining literary texts principally concern (Homeric) epic poetry: they go back to at least the sixth to fifth century B.C., much earlier than the development of Hellenistic philology, and they take an interest in two quite specific areas. On the one hand there is the explanation of single words and expressions, which is usually termed glossography and which essentially aims for the literal understanding of the poetic text, explaining its difficult points in easily comprehensible terms. On the other hand, there is the interpretation of myths, aiming above all at discovering and describing the meaning of the epic mythological story;

this approach is mostly represented by various forms of allegoresis, i.e. of attributing an allegorical meaning to the literal content of the texts.

The earliest allegorical interpretations known to us are those on Homer by Theagenes of Rhegium in the sixth century B.C. Subsequently this approach was pursued by the philosopher Anaxagoras and his followers and later picked up again in Stoic circles and by the critics in Pergamum. It then had a large place in Late Antique philosophical currents (especially in the context of Neoplatonism) and in the mainstream of Christian culture. Plato too was very familiar with this use of allegory and refers to it in the *Ion*, *Phaedrus* and *Republic*. Aristotle, in a fragment of the lost *Homeric Problems*, explains the meaning of the seven cattle herds of the sun in the *Odyssey*, each formed by fifty cows, as being analogous to the number of days in the lunar year, and so being a genuine allegory.

It seems to be quite well established now that the first people to provide interpretations of epic poetry were the rhapsodes who recited it, when the text and audience provided the opportunity. In this sense, the interpretation of poetry was born and took its first steps in the sphere of poetry itself. After those earliest forms of exegesis, the activities of interpreting poetry and reflecting on language were usually practised by sophists and philosophers such as Protagoras, Prodicus, Democritus and Plato. And it is again a poet, the comedian Aristophanes, who intervenes directly in the ethical-political and cultural debate of the fifth century B.C. with observations on poets that show him to be a true precursor of literary criticism. The poet Antimachus of Colophon (fifth to fourth century B.C.) not only studied the language of epic but, long before the Alexandrian philologists, also produced an "edition" of Homer, which we find cited in the scholia (though it is not clear what exactly it was that he did). There are doubts about the tradition that claims Aristotle made a *diorthōsis* of the Homeric text to produce the famous copy of the *Iliad* that Alexander the Great – his pupil – used to carry with him, but it is significant that this tradition existed at all and that it used such a technical term as *diorthōsis*.

In the first decades of the third century B.C. the name γραμματικός (*grammatikos*, "grammarian") seems already to have become specialised as the name for a philologist who is an exegete of poetry. Previously, in classical Greek, the term referred to the elementary schoolteacher who taught reading and writing. The change in meaning was noticed already in the ancient world, and the question of who was the first to be given the epithet in the new sense was a topic of inquiry. One tradition identified this figure as the Peripatetic Praxiphanes, a student of Theophrastus. That notice may be connected to another that speaks of Aristotle as the initiator of *grammatikē* (*scil. technē*), in the sense of "erudite study of literature," making him the ideal master of the Alexandrian *grammatikoi*. Aristotle and the Peripatetics, with their interests in the literary history of the poets viewed biographically and in their works (for example the practice of monographic treatmens of *problēmata*, that is, questions of various kinds raised by the texts), should be acknowledged as the true predecessors and inspirers of Alexandrian philology. The decisive creative contribution was that of the Aristotelians and Peripatetics.

A pupil of Theophrastus, Demetrius of Phaleron, moved to Alexandria around 295 B.C., perhaps at the invitation of Ptolemy I. We find this Peripatetic, the author of Homeric treatises exactly in the style of the Peripatetic school, present in Alexandria at the time of the foundation, under Ptolemy I Soter (305–283 B.C.), and the dazzling completion, under Ptolemy II Philadelphus (283–246 B.C.), of the great institution encompassing the Library and the Museum. These were sites that brought together the precious heritage of books and the activity of scholars. In the Museum scholars and scientists could study, discuss and teach with full independence and free from all material burdens or worries, which led to an extraordinary scientific and cultural flourishing. Ptolemy I had previously invited another Peripatetic, Straton of Lampsacus, to tutor his son in the scientific disciplines. Unfortunately we have almost no explicit records about their activity or their cultural influence, but the presence in Alexandria in this period of two Peripatetics such as Demetrius and Straton is a connecting link that cannot be downplayed (on these two figures cf. *The Classical Age* XIII 3.8.2 and *The Hellenistic Age* V 1.2).

2.2 Alexandrian philology: from Zenodotus to Aristarchus

Philitas of Cos. The exquisite poet and *kritikos* Philitas of Cos (cf. *The Hellenistic Age* IV 2.1.2) lived in the fourth to third century. His role in the history of philology is based above all on the fact that he composed a collection of difficult expressions drawn from the works of the poets, under the title Ἄτακτοι γλῶσσαι (*Ataktoi Glōssai*) or simply Ἄτακτα (*Atakta*, meaning, it seems, "unordered words," i.e. not in alphabetic order), that was characterised by a new critical and exegetical depth compared to the elementary glossography of the previous era.

Zenodotus of Ephesus. The most important student of Philitas was Zenodotus of Ephesus (330 ca.–260 ca.), the true founder of the line of Alexandrian philologists. He was both tutor to the royal household and the first to obtain the position of librarian, at the head of the important new institution founded by the Ptolemies. He compiled a collection of *Glosses* arranged alphabetically (unlike those of Philitas) and studied Homer, Hesiod, Pindar and perhaps Anacreon. All that remains of this is a few fragments, but we are far better informed about his work on Homer, which was the main testing ground for his philology (as was the case for almost all his successors too). In the presence of copies that diverged from each other, in some cases quite considerably, Zenodotus posed the critical problem of the authenticity and correctness of the transmitted text. It seems that he did not give much credence to the "wild" copies, which are full of lines that are today termed "additional." He also judged many lines to be inauthentic on the basis of internal criteria (repetitions, inconsistencies, improprieties), doing this in two ways: either eliminating them altogether, or leaving them in the text but with a mark of deletion (or "athetesis"), indicated by the *obelos* (a horizontal bar placed in the margin, to the left of the line in question), the first of the critical signs introduced by the Alexandrian philologists. The adoption of the *obelos* as a critical sign must be seen as an intellectual advance of real historical importance: it introduces the idea of proposing a textual doubt while leaving the reader the possibility of forming an opinion on it, since the doubtful reading is left in the text and not eliminated (the signs to mark a deletion in modern critical editions are based on the same principle). Zenodotus' interventions in the text must be the result of two procedures: on the one hand, the collation of various exemplars, making choices between readings; and on the other hand, a frequent recourse to conjectures of his own (including those made on the basis of notions such as propriety and decency). The totality of this work on the text was called *diorthōsis*, the product of which was *ekdosis*, of which we have already spoken. It is certain that Zenodotus did not write extended commentaries that set out his reasonings and the motives behind his positions. Part of the material can be found in the *Glosses*, but much depends on transmission through the school, which understandably gives rise to uncertainties. There is no secure proof that he was responsible for the division of the Homeric poems into twenty-four books, but it is well attested that he devoted a study to calculating how many days passed in the action of the *Iliad*.

Alexander the Aetolian and Lycophron. Zenodotus did not work on dramatic poetry, which was instead the field of two of his contemporaries, themselves both poets and philologists: Alexander the Aetolian and Lycophron. The former studied tragedy, the latter comedy, but we know very little about their work on this topic, since almost nothing has survived.

Rhianus of Bene. We know something of the Homeric edition by the epic poet Rhianus of Bene (on Crete), who was active in the second half of the third century B.C. As a philologist he was certainly influenced by Zenodotus, and his Homeric *diorthōsis* could not have existed without the foundations laid by his illustrious predecessor. Yet it is significant that over forty textual readings by Rhianus are preserved among the Homeric scholia, attesting that he enjoyed a certain esteem.

Callimachus and Apollonius Rhodius. In the chapter on poetry we will discuss at length Callimachus and Apollonius Rhodius, who were at once great poets and great philologists, roles united in an exemplary way, forming the figure of the poet-philologist. Callimachus of Cyrene (310 ca.–240 ca.) should be noted in the present context above all for his work *Pinakes*, a sort of expanded catalogue of the patrimony of books collected in the Library of Alexandria, which certainly had the status of an independent work while also in some way constituting an annotated bibliography of Greek literature. The authors were in alphabetical order, with a biography; for the works it gave the title, incipit and length, with some other notices occasionally added. Callimachus also wrote numerous scholarly and antiquarian monographs and works of literary criticism, such as *Against Praxiphanes*. Moreover, he demonstrates his intensive philological activity in his poetic works.

The successor to Zenodotus as head of the Library, Apollonius Rhodius (300 ca.–220 ca.) demonstrates in his poem *The Argonautica* his important philological activity, if only through the rich yield of Homeric interpretations, on a sound scholarly basis, that can be found throughout his poetry. He treated problems of Homeric exegesis in *Against Zenodotus*, in which he evidently criticised his predecessor: it is an interesting testimony to the first polemics to emerge within the school. He also took an interest in Hesiod and Antimachus and wrote a monograph on Archilochus (Περὶ Ἀρχιλόχου).

Eratosthenes. The position of librarian next passed to Eratosthenes of Cyrene (295–215 or 275–195 B.C. ca.), an extraordinary figure who was a grammarian, philologist, scientist and, more marginally, poet. His scientific research was prodigious, in which we may note here his chronological and geographical works. As we will see also in the section on historiography (cf. *The Hellenistic Age* VIII 1.4.4), he was an influential pioneer in the field of chronology. In his *Chronographiai*, which refined earlier materials, he fixed key dates such as the Fall of Troy in 1184 B.C., the *akmē* of Homer a hundred years later, the view that Hesiod was of later date than Homer, and the first Olympiad in 776, with his list continuing down to the death of Alexander the Great in 323. He also wrote a work on the victors at the Olympic games (*Olympionikai*) and made the series of Olympiads the basis of his chronological system. In the *Geographica* he began his history of geography with Homer, but held that the setting of the poem was for the most part imaginary, since poetry ought to delight rather than teach. He was the first to apply systematically a mathematical method in cartography (he drew the first map based on a network of meridians and parallels) and in the measurement of the earth's circumference, in which his calculation was out by only 300 km. A more strictly literary topic was treated in the major work *On Old Comedy*, in at least twelve books. The few fragments that remain of this reveal an interest in the language of the comic playwrights and in problems of performance. He carried out lexicographical research, took an interest in lyric poets, and more besides. His works on these subjects are, however, almost entirely lost.

Aristophanes of Byzantium. The highpoint of Alexandrian philology is marked by Aristophanes and Aristarchus. Aristophanes of Byzantium (265 ca.–190 ca.) in his turn became head of the Library of Alexandria. His edition of Homer is distinguished from that of Zenodotus by greater caution. Rather than the drastic choice of "not writing" the lines that were contested, he preferred simply to propose their cancellation, marked by the *obelos*, and in this way many of the lines that had been eliminated completely by Zenodotus were accepted back into the text, though marked with the sign of athetesis (*obelos*). It seems that Aristophanes founded his *ekdosis* on an expanded documentary base by consulting a larger number of copies in order to make a choice among their readings and treating the text with less boldness. He increased the number of critical signs, by adding to the Zenodotean *obelos* also the *asteriskos* for repeated lines and the pair *sigma–antisigma* for two consecutive lines with the same content. He achieved major advances in the notation of the accents and in the enrichment of the system of punctuation signs. This technical progress led him to produce critical editions of great importance. As well as Homer, he also worked on Hesiod and he achieved innovative developments especially in the field of lyric and dramatic poetry. His classification of the poems of Pindar into seventeen books is famous, for which he made use of further critical signs: a *corōnis* (the stylised image of a crow, drawn in the left margin) divided the poems from each other, while *paragraphoi* (horizontal strokes placed to the left of the text, between the lines) distinguished the strophes. All lyric poetry was divided into rhythmic *cōla*, which formed a decisive advance in the analysis of the metrical structure of the poems. Critical work by Aristophanes of Byzantium on the text of Sophocles and Euripides is also attested: his *hypotheseis* to the plays are well known, giving for each theatrical work the main records about the occasion of first performance, the setting, characters and finally the plot. It is certain that he worked on comedy, but the only aspect securely attested is that he produced an edition of Aristophanes' comedies. It seems that he too did not write true *hypomnēmata*, but we have already noted his lexicographical work, the *Lexeis*, and his grammatical observations, in particular on certain regularities in inflection.

Apollonius eidographos. The Library was then directed by a certain Apollonius known as the *eidographos* (that is "the classifier"), a grammarian who escapes us almost entirely, though the few existing testimonia allow us to glimpse a classification of works by literary genre, the importance of which we have already noted.

Aristarchus. Then came the turn of Aristarchus of Samothrace (215–144 ca.). His role stands out, among other reasons, because he wrote a significant number of *hypomnēmata*, the major commentaries with which he gave greatest prominence to the interpretation of texts. Further, in numerous *syngrammata* he treated various topics monographically, sometimes with a polemical aim; we have various titles and fragments, for the most part on Homeric topics. There are differing views on the form taken by his philological activity on the text of Homer, namely whether he produced the *ekdosis* and *hypomnēma* in one or more redactions, or just a *hypomnēma* which also contained his opinion on the constitution of the text. The use and number of critical signs was expanded even further than Aristophanes: characteristic were the *diplē* (for miscellaneous exegetical observations and learned notes) and the *diplē periestigmenē* (to signal passages where he disagreed with Zenodotus).

The principle that an author is his own best interpreter, and that hence comparisons should be made primarily and principally within his own oeuvre, was applied to the analysis of Homeric language and also in general to the contents of Homer. For Aristarchus Homer was the author of both the *Iliad* and the *Odyssey* and he pursued polemics against the *Chōrizontes*, grammarians who instead distinguished two different authors of the works and attributed to Homer only the *Iliad*. His unitarian analysis, both of language and of the historical elements, habits and customs, led him to define that which was specifically Homeric (τὸ Ὁμηρικόν) as distinct from that which was cyclic or neoteric (or also Hesiodic), i.e. later material. Thus a principle of internal and analogical criticism, which could work both at the level of form and of content, led him to the conception of an organic historical and literary vision. His philology was generally characterised by a circumspection based on the examination of manuscript witnesses, but he certainly did not refrain from making conjectural interventions or from drawing on the interpretive resources of an attention to detail that became proverbial.

Sound method and breadth of knowledge led Aristarchus to accomplish rich and wide-ranging work on classical texts. Aside from Homer, we know most about his work on the text of the lyric poets. This concerned primarily Pindar (it is likely that he wrote a commentary on the whole of Pindar's oeuvre, soundly based on the path pioneered by Aristophanes of Byzantium), but we know that he also worked on Bacchylides, whose works he must have commented upon. Also attested are commentaries on Hesiod, Archilochus and Alcman and it is certain that he produced an edition of Alcaeus and perhaps one of Anacreon; there are also traces of interventions on Hipponax, Semonides and perhaps Mimnermus. In Attic drama we know that he worked on Aeschylus and Sophocles, but we have less information concerning Euripides; the sources allow us to conclude that he commented on at least eight comedies of Aristophanes, but we do not have enough data to suppose that he wrote a commentary on the entire surviving corpus. He is the first figure who we know for certain worked on prose authors, as we have a secure fragment of his *hypomnēma* on Herodotus.

In Aristarchus' editorial and exegetical work, Aristophanes of Byzantium was an important model. They must often have been in agreement, with the result that much less material is preserved for Aristophanes, since whoever made selections from their work saw no point in citing Aristophanes in cases where Aristarchus held the same position. The latter took his predecessor's observations further in the field of grammar too, giving a more thorough formulation to the principle of linguistic and grammatical analogy. This aspect and the refusal of allegorical interpretations (at least for Homer) were the two fundamental elements of his divergences and polemic with the philologists of Pergamum.

2.3 Philology at Pergamum

At Pergamum there was no tradition like the Alexandrian one and no school formed with the richness and long duration of that of Alexandria. Erudite antiquarian studies became established under King Attalus I (241–197) with Antigonus of Carystus, from whom we know of a work on painters and sculptors, a collection of paradoxography and the biographies of the philosophers; and with Polemon of Ilium, who wrote an important antiquarian *periēgēsis* (a geographical description), which is notable above all for the fact that he made use of inscriptions. Mainly in the field of Homeric topography he was surpassed by Demetrius of Scepsis, who lived perhaps a generation later and was author of a large commentary to the *Catalogue of Trojan Forces* (*Iliad* II 816–877), written around the mid-second century B.C. (most likely on the model of the Alexandrian *hypomnēma*). Scepsis was a city not far from Ilium, some kilometres inland in Asia Minor along the river Scamander, and it seems that Demetrius always lived there. Given the rather reclusive life that he led, his links to Pergamum as a centre were not in fact particularly strong. This was in the reign of Eumenes II (197–159), a king of notable character who founded a rich library and welcomed many scholars, and so almost miraculously turned Pergamum into a cultural centre to rival Alexandria.

The reign of Eumenes, contemporary with the career of Aristarchus (who died probably after 145 B.C.), was a highpoint. Summoned and supported by the king in the capital, the most important Pergamene philologist, Crates of Mallus, pursued his studies there. We know two titles of treatises of his, *Diorthotica* and *Homerica*, and numerous fragments, mostly connected with Homeric matters. It is conventional to state that Crates was trained as a Stoic philosopher and that he transferred his philosophical positions to the analysis of literary texts. In reality Crates' Stoic training and especially his actual membership of the Stoic school are debated points and today they tend to be played down, since they are based on only a few testimonies that are themselves problematic. The hypothesis that he was a pupil of Diogenes of Babylon is in fact wholly hypothetical, based mostly on the idea that Crates was a Stoic philosopher, with an obvious risk of circular reasoning. And, against this, some aspects of Crates' cosmology differ substantially from Stoic cosmology.

What is certain is that Crates differed from the Alexandrian *grammatikos* by assuming the designation *kritikos*, which was meant to stress the value of an approach to literature that was more broadly cultural, and also philosophical, than one that limited interest to questions of language, form and *Realien*. The ancient allegorical interpretation, which continued to be practised in philosophical circles and was adopted above all by the Stoics in order to explain myths, seems to have been accepted in Crates' exegetical method for poetic texts. Yet, in truth, even this *communis opinio* is quite contested. To summarise, one may talk of true allegory in the case of Crates only in a fragment in which the shield of Agamemnon is interpreted as μίμημα τοῦ κόσμου ("imitation of the cosmos"). The fragment is transmitted by Eustathius, who cites οἱ περὶ τὸν Κράτητα ("those around Crates"), but in the exegetical scholion that is unanimously acknowledged to be Eustathius' source the name is Ξενοκράτης (Xenocrates), to whom the fragment should probably be ascribed. And so even this is not beyond doubt. The attribution to Crates of an interpretation of the shield of Achilles as an "imitation of the cosmos" is based on the parallel of the shield of Agamemnon, whereas it is anonymous in all the testimonia apart from Eustathius, who ascribes it to a mysterious Demo.

In sum, we here have a case where the *communis opinio* that has become established in the research literature and among scholars ought to be reviewed completely. The exegetical method for poetry was certainly a reason for diverging from the

Alexandrians (and notably from Aristarchus), but, on this too, more precision is needed and absolute, generalising views should be avoided. So far as we can tell, it seems that Crates and his followers believed, as noted above, that they could use an exegetical method that was open to various approaches drawn from philosophical thought, including the use of allegoresis, to find the true significance of a poetic text. To the Alexandrians, the applicability of this method, in its various realisations, depended in the first place on the poetic intention of the author whether or not to use allegory as an expressive mode. In other words, it would be permissible to interpret a text allegorically only if its author chose to express himself by means of allegories; Homer did not use allegory and hence his poetry could not be interpreted allegorically.

The other area of polemic was theory of language, on which again a fairly widespread schematic dichotomy exists, which goes back essentially to how the different positions were outlined by the Latin scholar Marcus Terentius Varro (first century B.C.), though with a further hardening of positions among modern scholars. This scheme presents the issue as follows: at Alexandria Aristophanes and Aristarchus pursued their investigations on the basis of analogy, but Crates, to the contrary, principally adopted from Chrysippus the Stoic concept of anomaly (literally "irregularity, discrepancy, incoherence," on which see above), using a concept of language in which the *ratio* of normative analogy is opposed to the freer development described by *consuetudo*. In reality the situation is rather more nuanced. Reflections on the role of usage by speakers are not lacking among the Alexandrians, even according to Varro, Aristarchus applied rules of similarity in the derivation of words "within the limits permitted by usage". Yet in the passages of Varro in which Crates and Aristarchus are presented as counterpoints what does seem to emerge is a discussion of the criteria and limits of application of linguistic-grammatical analogy.

As well as Homer, Crates worked on Hesiod (we have information on this from the scholia), on authors of lyric and drama and also on the didactic poem *Phaenomena* by the Hellenistic poet Aratus. His influence on the Greco-Roman world was notable, his lengthy visit to Rome in 168 B.C. contributing to this.

Allegoresis, above all in the field of Homeric studies, enjoyed a broad following in the Roman Imperial Period, a success that is the origin of its prominent presence in the margins of manuscripts, containing all kinds of comments on the poems. We may note above all the *Homeric problems* attributed to a certain Heraclitus, dated to the start of the Imperial Period, as well as the extracts from works of Homeric exegesis by Porphyry (third century A.D.). Yet even in a work of literary criticism such as the anonymous work *On the Sublime*, commenting on the divinities of Homer and their actions, we read: "they are utterly irreligious and breach the canons of propriety, unless one takes them allegorically" (IX 7). This is an idea with deep roots and which already had many centuries behind it. It was supported by a basic structure of thought that was in its essence extremely clear, and which set up an opposition between a literal sense that was bad, and a profound but hidden – good – sense on the other.

The legacy of this method, with its liberties and arbitrary interpretations, was transmitted to the later pagan philosophers, and then the Christians turned it into a precious means of appropriating the authoritative patrimony of the ancient world, a tool to dominate it and to provide foundations for an idea of continuity from the ancient to the Christian world.

As we have said, it is not possible to speak of a Pergamene "school," since we cannot document a regular series of masters and pupils as we can at Alexandria. However, the followers of Crates continued to pursue polemics with those of Aristarchus on the topics we have noted, even if there were not infrequently points where they were close to each other, for example in the field of grammar. Here Pergamum played host to another interesting character, namely Telephus, who lived in the second century A.D. and so contemporary with Galen, Pergamum's most outstanding cultural figure, whom we shall meet in due course.

2.4 From Aristarchus to the Augustan Age

Aristarchus is justly famous also for his band of disciples, but their works have often survived only in a few fragments and for the most part we will pass over them here. The most significant were certainly Apollodorus of Athens and Dionysius Thrax. They were both involved in the political crisis of 145–144, which was connected to Ptolemy VIII's ascent to the throne, which forced Aristarchus and many other scholars to flee Alexandria. The philological and grammatical activity of the Alexandrian school continued in a significant way down to the Augustan Age, with a tradition of study of literature and language that continued to yield important fruit and determined the first stages of preservation of the materials produced in the Hellenistic Era.

Apollodorus of Athens (180–115 ca.) stands out for the singular richness of his lived experience: first a student in Athens of the Stoic philosopher Diogenes of Babylon, then pupil and collaborator of Aristarchus in Alexandria, it seems that he subsequently fled to Pergamum and finally returned to Athens, where he died between 120 and 110. He was the real successor of Eratosthenes in the field of chronology (as we will see also in the section on historiography, cf. *The Hellenistic Age* VIII 1.4.4): the *Chronica*, from the Fall of Troy to his own times, were written in iambic trimeters, a choice that was clearly intended to aid memorisation. It was based, naturally, on the work of his predecessor, but he introduced notable changes and sought to establish many dates more effectively. This work also made notable advances in the chronological framework on which literary history was based. The major treatise *On the Gods* examined the figures of religion with an in-depth analysis of their epithets, drawing on etymology (he also wrote a treatise on etymology, and it is hard not to see Stoic influence at work in this, given his training); the basis was formed primarily by the study of epic poetry and its representations of the gods. He produced a weighty piece of exegesis in the work *On the Catalogue of Ships* in Book II of the *Iliad*, which made productive use of the studies of Eratosthenes and Demetrius of Scepsis, and of Aristarchus' philology. The geography of Homeric times was here the fundamental problem in both a historical-scientific and a literary perspective, in which general questions and innumerable problems were linked to the interpretation of single names. And, finally, he did important research on Doric comedy, studying Epicharmus and the mimes of Sophron. Known titles are: *On the Athenian Hetairai*, *On Epicharmus*, *On Sophron*, *Glosses* and *Etymologies*.

The mythological manual called *The Library*, attributed to Apollodorus in the tradition, is generally considered to be a work of the first century A.D. or even the second. It starts with a theogony and treats various myths and legends, but then interrupts them with the mythical genealogy of Attica. For the rest, of which we get an idea from the epitome preserved in the manuscript *Vat. gr.* 950 and other fragments found in 1887 in Jerusalem, it follows Homer and the Epic Cycle. There is debate on what its relation to Apollodorus may be, whether it is entirely independent or used some material of his.

Dionysius Thrax (170–90 B.C. ca.), despite his name (meaning "Thracian," but taken from his father), was from Alexandria and was educated during Aristarchus' final teaching years. He dedicated himself primarily to Homer and, following his teacher's example, he produced *hypomnēmata* and monographs (a polemic *Against Crates*). He also worked on Hesiod and perhaps Alcman. Some fragments survive of writings on grammatical topics. But in this field Dionysius Thrax is famous above all for the problem of the *Technē grammatikē* attributed to him (see above), which would be the first work of an Alexandrian grammarian to be transmitted more or less entire, if the surviving text were indeed genuine. In reality the testimonia allow us to say with certainty that he did write a grammatical treatise, but in all probability it is not the one that survives, at least not in its entirety. The ancient testimonia confirm that the opening paragraph of the preserved *Technē* certainly goes back to Dionysius (which proves that he did write a treatise of this kind), but there are differing scholarly positions on the paragraphs that immediately follow it: paragraphs 2–4 may go back to Dionysius, since in content they are connected to the first one and paragraph 3 seems to be secured by a quotation by Varro, but the rest of the preserved *Technē* is later.

After fleeing from Alexandria, perhaps in 144 B.C. (in connection with the political events in the city and at court), Dionysius Thrax kept a school at Rhodes. One of his pupils there was Tyrannio, who lived at Rome from 71 B.C., where he had the luck to be the first to study the writings of Aristotle that Sulla had brought from Athens. They were edited in full a generation later by Andronicus of Rhodes (as we saw in the chapter on Aristotle: cf. *The Classical Age* XIII 3.3). A short treatise on the language of the Romans was written by either Tyrannio or his contemporary Philoxenus. The latter played an important role in the field of grammar, being noted for his treatment of the monosyllabic verbal root, a taste for etymology and the attention he gave to the principle of analogy. His works also include some comments on Homer.

An important figure is Asclepiades of Myrlea in Bithynia (second half of the second century B.C. to first century B.C.; it is not certain if he was a pupil Crates, nor of Dionysius Thrax), a grammarian and philologist active also at Rome and then in Spain. In his exegetical works on Homer, Pergamene influence can be detected and notably that of Crates; he also worked on Pindar, Theocritus and perhaps Apollonius Rhodius and Aratus. In addition, he wrote a book *On the grammarians* and one *On grammar*, which contained a definition of the *technē grammatikē* and a description of its parts (a treatise that enjoyed some diffusion in later times, given that it was used by Sextus Empiricus). The two works must have had some connection, at least in concept: it has been hypothesised that they represented two sections of a larger monograph, perhaps with the title *Grammatica* (Γραμματικά), devoted to a consideration of erudite research as a whole. He was finally the author of a treatise regarding the astrological representation of the sky according to barbarian traditions, and two works of local history, respectively on Bithynia and Turdetania.

In the sphere of grammatical studies we should also recall: Tryphon of Alexandria, who lived in the Augustan Period; Alexion, active in the first century A.D.; and Ptolemaeus of Ascalon, whose dating is uncertain. This is the line that leads to the grand systematisation of Greek grammatical learning carried out in the second century A.D. by Apollonius Dyscolus and Aelius Herodianus, whose work survives in substantial part and whom we will treat later (cf. *Roman Imperial Period* X 1.2 and 3).

The Augustan Period also offered important figures, who collected and compiled the fruits of earlier researches. Through generations of pupils of Aristarchus, the tradition of studies in textual criticism, exegesis and scholarship culminated in the colossal output of Didymus, who was active in the second half of the first century B.C. at Alexandria and was famous already in the ancient world for the vast bulk of his monographs and commentaries on a great number of authors, which gave him the nickname Chalcenterus, or "guts of bronze," for his capacity to "ingest" every type of erudite information. His works taken as a whole constitute a true reservoir that collected and compiled the results of the previous centuries and transmitted them to many later collections and then to various corpora of scholia, perhaps (as is often repeated, but further study is necessary) with little originality but with great and scrupulous erudition.

Almost contemporary with Didymus was Aristonicus, who dedicated much effort to setting out detailed explanations of Aristarchus' critical signs to the text of Homer, and so became a mediator of material that went back to the master (much of this work has passed into the scholia to Homer), and he also worked on Hesiod and Pindar and wrote some monographs. The same decades saw the *akmē* of Theon of Alexandria, who commented not only on the canonical classical authors, but also on Alexandrian poets such as Callimachus, Theocritus, Apollonius Rhodius and Nicander. Today we know that he was not the first to do this (he had been preceded by Asclepiades of Myrlea, for example), but it is clear that with him this area of philology was greatly enriched. Linked to traditional exegesis, there is also the Homeric lexicography of

Apion and Apollonius Sophista (active respectively in the first and second half of the first century A.D.), which drew on the Aristarchean school.

IV Poetry in the Hellenistic Age

1 Scholar poets and the mixing of genres

1.1 A radically new poetic consciousness

The last decades of the fourth and the early third century B.C. saw the fulfilment of certain aspects of the evolution in the conception of poetry that had been signalled clearly and explicitly already at the end of the Classical Age. The spaces and occasions in which poetry took place were remodelled in relation to the broadened cultural horizons and altered institutional and social conditions, privileging the restricted, private sphere of refined and cultured circles, in many cases at the courts of the Hellenistic monarchs. These new contexts began a successful rivalry with the great public festivals that had formed the natural setting of spectacles of music and poetry and of dance in the Classical Era. What we now see is a marked dichotomy between a public and popular poetic culture, on the one hand, and a learned and elitist one on the other. Music had been acquiring an ever more marked autonomy from the fourth century onwards, favouring spectacular performance to the disadvantage of the literary text. This was the context of the so-called New Dithyramb, which accentuated the elements of musical and vocal virtuosity (cf. *The Classical Age* VII 2.3). During the Hellenistic Age, in the more elevated poetic culture, the execution of the text became ever more detached from the musical accompaniment. The enjoyment of poetry (as also with other literary genres) through declamation or private reading by individuals or small groups became established and, passing via the Latin world, has remained the most common way of enjoying poetry ever since.

As we have already noted (cf. *The Hellenistic Age* I 4 and III 2), from the early third century B.C. onward we observe a new phenomenon that is absolutely typical of the Hellenistic Age, namely the fact that many literary figures were at the same time scholars and interpreters of literature and poetry writers: we use the term poet-philologists. In the past it was sometimes maintained that in these authors' works the philological erudition had ultimately overwhelmed the genuine poetic inspiration. This judgement is entirely false and depends, consciously or not, on an idea of poetry that has deep roots in the romantic vision of art as an "instinctive" creation, the direct and immediate expression of feelings and movements of the spirit. This is a conception that is not only very different from that accepted in the Hellenistic Age and other eras, but is unsustainable in general too, for the good reason that there is no poetry without study and education, rules and precedents, cultural traditions and other poetry that provide it with nourishment. Yet it remains a real fact that Hellenistic poetry is an extremely learned type of poetry, in the sense that it tends to establish a subtle and refined web of allusions and references to the literary code in which it inscribes itself, which is the centuries-old Greek cultural tradition of the Archaic and Classical

https://doi.org/10.1515/9783110426328-024

Ages. This was the first time that, to such a wide and deep degree, literature lost its effective link to a specific real or existential occasion and tended to become a purely artistic production, a creation that, already in the intention of its author, enclosed in itself its own raison d'être. For the first time in the history of Western literature we are confronted with the idea of *l'art pour l'art*.

The deep culture and literary consciousness of the protagonists of Hellenistic poetry explain the importance that they ascribed also to the elaboration of a poetic theory, which would be reflected in their specific compositional choices. It is possible to identify some constants in the ideas expressed by the various poets, different though they certainly were. One of these common elements emerges from what has just been said, namely the need for a cultivated poetry, that is, one that arises from a deep knowledge of past literature and the models it offers and from an intellectual background of broad and varied erudition, and one that knowingly displays this learning by weaving a web of hidden allusions and references that are hard to catch, but intended to be understood. The convergence of these two aspects – erudite creation and creative erudition – is well attested by the fact that now the poet for the first time became, in a systematic and programmatic way, the editor and publisher of his own poetry collections, a philologist of himself. These are characteristics that we will meet many times in the poets of this period. This poetry, so rich in direct and indirect meanings, was subjected to formal attention that was extreme, almost obsessive, in the search for expressive effects that were ever more refined in style and content. Another general aspect of Hellenistic poetry, linked to the idea of refined poetry, is the need to present creations inspired by originality, i.e. ones that would avoid repeating the models but would draw new and unheard-of forms and solutions from the tradition. This standard of originality is the source of a seam of experimentalism that can be found in Hellenistic poetry. Its more significant expressions involve the mixture of different poetic forms and stylistic registers, the crossing of genres, and the departure from tradition when associating metrical forms with particular poetic genres.

The Hellenistic poets' attachment to a theorised poetics also explains why the tradition records fierce disputes and literary polemics. A consciousness of possessing the interpretative keys to the literature of the past and of the difference of present conditions from those of the past put these learned poets in the position to adopt and maintain precise and clearly argued positions at the theoretical level, which were sometimes in sharp conflict with each other. This is the case with the famous *querelle* on the pre-eminence of long-form poetry (the epic poem) or short-form poetry (elegy, epigram), which we will discuss at more length in relation to Callimachus and Apollonius Rhodius.

An objective detail should be remembered too. Most of the poetry of the Hellenistic Age is from the third or at most the earlier second century, while we have very little of the poetry written from the mid-second and the first century B.C., which had a very important influence on Latin poetry. And what we have was largely written in Alexandria, or at least has links to that city. The only exception, among the poetic genres, is the comedy of Menander, whose theatre was in Athens, as we have seen. This explains why one often speaks of "Alexandrian poetry" practically as a synonym for "Hellenistic poetry." A similar point can be made, *mutatis mutandis*, about the sciences and the work of philologists and grammarians (cf. *The Hellenistic Age* III 1 and VI 1.1).

1.2 The poetic genres

When the refined poetry gave up the link between text and music and lost the close connection between poetic composition and the specific occasion of performance and song (public religious festivals, the symposium, victories in contests, and so on), one of the most significant effects was the abandonment of the complex rhythmic and metrical system that had characterised the lyric output of the Archaic and Classical Ages. The varied and complex metrical structures were far removed from the needs and sensibility of the contemporary culture. The loss in competence by the public and perhaps by the poets too in relation to the earlier lyric metres, which had been matched to the rhythmic modes of performing music and song, caused a profound change in how the various possibilities of Greek metre were deployed, moving towards a simplification, in terms that need to be explained carefully. It should come as no surprise that a considerable part of the profuse efforts that the Alexandrian philologists devoted to the study of past poetic texts, above all lyric and dramatic texts, aimed to reconstruct the metrical and rhythmic structures.

In the poetic output of the period there was a widespread use of traditional metrical forms that had a simple and repetitive structure, which was therefore easy to recognise. The dactylic hexameter continued to be employed mostly in the insuppressible genre of epic (by Apollonius Rhodius and others) and in the derived form of the short mythological poem or *epyllion*, which means "little *epos*" in Greek (by Philitas, Callimachus, Theocritus and others). The *epyllion* was a new genre, a new form of *epos*: its essential elements consist in the fact that the heroes are brought down from their epic grandeur and acquire more "bourgeois" characters; the content is restricted to brief, well-chosen episodes, and all the better if they are unusual and exquisite; the linguistic choices sets up a rivalry with earlier epic, as a competitive imitation played out through deft procedures of reprising and distancing from the prestigious model. The dactylic hexameter was also used, naturally, in the long works in verse on scientific topics, shaped by didactic poetry (Aratus, Nicander: this genre was codified in the Hellenistic Age itself, as has already been noted: cf. *The Archaic Age* II 3.2), and in the new genre of the pastoral or bucolic idyll (Theocritus), but also in the distinctive solution of Callimachus' *Hymns*. As well as the hexameter, the elegiac distich (one hexameter and one pentameter) enjoyed great success too. This is a stanza of epodic type characteristic of elegy and epigram, two lyric genres from the past that survived into the poetic production of the Hellenistic Age (Philitas,

Callimachus, Theocritus and the extensive output of epigrams). With their simplicity and an identical metre, these two poetic forms were distinguished rather by content and tone: elegy is emotional and elevated in style; epigram is confidential, quotidian and immediate.

However, it would be mistaken to think in superficial terms of a mere simplification in Hellenistic metre, one aimed only at eliminating the great variety and complex rhythmic articulations of archaic and classical poetry. It suffices to think of the incredible polymetry of Callimachus' collection of *Iambi* to see that the issue is more nuanced, not to mention the considerable number of Greek metres that take their names from poets of the Hellenistic Period. The experimentalism of Hellenistic-Alexandrian poetry does not bypass the metrical forms. Sadly much of it is lost, but the asclepiadean line certainly owes its name to Asclepiades of Samos (whom we shall discuss shortly in relation to epigram), even though his "lyric" compositions in these metres do not survive, and the sotadean is named after Sotades, a contemporary of Callimachus, from whom a few fragments do at least survive (though we do not know if it is true that he rewrote the *Iliad* in lines of this type). The choliambic verse that the archaic poet Hipponax made famous was used by Herodas, by Phoenix of Colophon and by Callimachus in the *Iambi*, a collection in which many different metres were used, as we have noted: iambic trimeters, trochaic tetrameters catalectic and many others borrowed from archaic lyric.

A phenomenon of major historical importance was the use in stichic form, and hence as recitative, of many metrical sequences that had previously been used within large strophic compositions, sung and accompanied by music. Lines like the phalaecian, the glyconic and the pherecratean are known to us by these names not because they were originally so called. Originally they formed parts of large and complex metrical-rhythmic structures, which followed the lyric-musical modulation of the composition and performance in archaic and classical poetry. The name of the phalaecian is due to the Hellenistic poet Phalaecus, the glyconic to Glycon, the pherecratean to Pherecrates the comic poet, and these figures (whose works are for the most part sadly lost) used them in stichic series, in a declaimed recitative without music. Thus metrical forms that were originally part of a sequence now become autonomous sequences themselves, lines used singly in series. It was an epochal change, linked to the change in kinds of composition and performance, or rather to the fact that certain metrical structures were used with different functions from those for which they had been created and had been used for centuries. The change was decisive also for the way these metrical forms would be adopted in Latin poetry.

2 Elegy and epigram

2.1 Elegy

2.1.1 Narrative elegy: myth and love

The poem in elegiac distichs, a tradition that went back to the Archaic Age, was one of the forms practised most in the Hellenistic Age. Unfortunately very little has been preserved of the vast output in elegiacs during that period, leaving just rare fragments from certain authors. We must therefore adopt considerable caution in interpretation, since it may be inappropriate to extend mechanically to the entire genre characteristics that emerge from what survives.

One of the most significant aspects of this poetry is its narrative character. The poem was centred on telling an episode and describing the background, setting, emotions and mental state. The narrative content was generally drawn from myth, of which the poets demonstrated a careful and cultivated knowledge, often choosing lesser known variants less often treated by their predecessors. The search for the rare and exotic detail is a widespread characteristic in Hellenistic poetry and there is no doubt that this kind of taste is present in the poets, as we will see many times. Admittedly, we cannot but wonder how our present-day evaluation of what was more or less widespread and common in ancient poetry has been influenced by the loss of so much archaic and classical poetry on mythological themes, from cyclic narrative to tragedy, lyrical narrative and elegy itself. In particular, we should not overlook the fact that recent papyrological publications have demonstrated the existence of archaic elegy of a mythological-narrative type, which contained an account of a circumscribed episode from the mythical tradition within a frame provided by a real occasion (Archilochus: cf. *The Archaic Age* III 2.2). As regards themes, the elegiac poets of the Hellenistic Age generally privileged love stories drawn from the mythic repertoire, representing them with effects of pathos, sometimes more subtle, sometimes more intense. As far as we can tell, a special place was held by love stories that were asymmetric and unhappy. Alongside the use of myth, space was also given to the individual emotional experience, which often took on the appearance of an intimate confession inspired by autobiographical events (similarly to what was done in the *Nanno* of Mimnermus). For elegy of subjective-amorous type, a classical precedent is usually seen in the *Lyde* of Antimachus of Colophon (fourth century B.C.), written in distichs, which took its title from the woman beloved by the poet and which recounted unhappy loves from myth, with a consolatory aim (cf. *The Classical Age* VII 1.4).

Another aspect typical of Hellenistic elegy is aetiology (αἰτιολογία), that is, poetry in the form of investigation and revelation of the "cause" (αἴτιον, *aition*) or origin of religious and cultural phenomena and traditions and of names and objects, causes often found in mythological episodes. Already present in the mythographic tradition of archaic and classical Greece, among the Alexandrians the taste for the "cause" (the *aition*) became an aspect of professional research into the past, a "scientific" instrument of antiquarian study, which aimed to explain the "causes" of phenomena and traditions that could still be observed in the present. It is typical of the Hellenistic mentality that the erudite interest in causes/origins became a literary taste, with a conspicuous presence in poetry: out of this, aetiological poetry was born, especially in the form of elegy. The most important and significant instance of aetiological elegy is the collection by Callimachus called simply *Aetia* (i.e. *Causes*). This survives in fragmentary form, but enough of it has been recovered to offer important information on the characteristics of the genre, as we will see in the chapter on Callimachus.

2.1.2 Philitas of Cos

Philitas is the first of the poet-philologists, that is, a Hellenistic intellectual committed to working, at the same time and in an organic way, in both poetic composition and erudite philological research. It is not just a commonplace to record that the two spheres influenced each other in a profound way that allowed these authors to produce artistic creations that were highly learned and sophisticated, together with detailed and documented literary researches. We will meet this convergence of erudite creation and creative erudition several times among the poets of this period, for whom Philitas is a perfect opening figure.

A native of the island of Cos, Philitas (or, in a different spelling, Philetas) lived from 340 to 285 B.C. approximately. He spent part of his life at Alexandria, where he was summoned probably a little before 300 by Ptolemy I Soter to be the teacher of the future Ptolemy II Philadelphus. He returned to his native island, perhaps after around a decade, and on Cos he founded a poetic coterie – it seems that Theocritus took part in it as well as, perhaps, Zenodotus – which promoted the ideal of a cultured, refined and exclusive poetry.

Of Philitas' verse works all that remains are meagre fragments and testimonia transmitted through the indirect tradition. Nonetheless, we can get an idea of his poetics and identify a number of aspects that would be adopted by later Hellenistic poets and also by the Latin poets of the Augustan Period. Latin poets of the first century B.C., especially Propertius and Ovid, ascribed to Philitas a fundamental role in the area of the elegiac genre. It is likely that Latin love elegy owed something, and perhaps a lot, to the influence of Philitas' elegies for a woman called Bittis (or Battis), but unfortunately not even a single line survives that can be securely assigned to them. Brief fragments are preserved of an elegy entitled *Demeter*. The poet was perhaps alluding to the mythical tradition of the visit of Demeter to Cos during her wanderings in search of her daughter Persephone or Chore, which would offer an *aition* of the cult of this goddess on the island. In a little poem in hexameters, or *epyllion* (cf. *The Hellenistic Age* IV 1.2), entitled *Hermes*, the story of Odysseus' stay at the court of Aeolus allowed Philitas to narrate the secret love affair between the hero and the king's daughter Polymele while accentuating the lyricism of the emotional elements of the story in a way unknown in traditional epic. Among his poetic works, the sources record two other collections (though according to some these are just two different titles for the same work), though we do not know whether they were totally or partially in elegiac distichs: the Παίγνια (*Paignia*, literally "Jokes," "Games" or "Light Verse", that is, poetry that is lighthearted in tone or content), and the *Epigrams*.

We have seen in the chapter on philology that Philitas conducted his philological activity predominantly on the Homeric poems, as is attested indirectly but clearly by the polemical work *Against Philitas* written in the second century B.C. by Aristarchus of Samothrace. The erudite study of poetry bore fruit in the composition of a lexicographical work that was quite well known in the ancient world, which collected rare and difficult terms in the Homeric language and technical terminology. This was the work Ἄτακτοι γλῶσσαι (*Ataktoi Glōssai*) or simply Ἄτακτα (*Atakta*, i.e. "difficult words", not in alphabetical order).

2.1.3 Hermesianax of Colophon

One of Philitas' pupils was Hermesianax of Colophon, author of a three-book poem in elegiac distichs entitled *Leontion* (Λεόντιον), from the name of the beloved woman. By recounting the events of his unhappy love, the poet aimed to demonstrate the omnipotence of Eros. Book I told, for example, the unrequited love of the cyclops Polyphemus for the nymph Galatea and described erotic situations in a bucolic setting (we will meet these motifs again in the poetry of Theocritus). A long fragment preserves 98 lines of Book III, which collect in catalogue form the unhappy loves of famous poets and philosophers, from the mythical Orpheus and Musaeus down to the contemporary Philitas. The manner is that of Hesiod's *Catalogue of Women*, which is alluded to by borrowing its presentation scheme and by the special position given to Hesiod among the poets. The characteristics of this singular work include homage to the poetic tradition (in the succession of poets, a kind of acknowledgement of the poet's own artistic and intellectual ancestry), interest in the elegiac theme of unhappy love, a taste for biography and literary history and a recherché style. The work unites in a curious way themes of the "literary history" type and those of love elegy. It is possible that we should attribute to Hermesianax a fragment in elegiac distichs preserved on a papyrus of the second century B.C. (*Suppl. Hell.* 970) that speaks, among other things, of the Calydonian boar-hunt.

2.1.4 Phanocles

In the same poetic line as Hermesianax is Phanocles, of unknown birthplace, who likewise lived in the first half of the second century B.C. In the manner of Hermesianax, Phanocles composed an elegiac collection entitled Ἔρωτες ἢ Καλοί (*Love Affairs, or Beautiful Boys*), structured according to the catalogue scheme and containing the narration of unhappy loves. Unlike Hermesianax, however, Phanocles did not recount the stories of human characters, such as poets and philosophers, but the loves between gods and heroes: Dionysus and Adonis, Tantalus and Ganymedes, and others. As is clear from the title, the myths Phanocles narrated concerned exclusively pederastic love. In one fragment we find Orpheus in love with a boy and torn to pieces by the women of Thrace for having introduced male homosexuality. It seems that every episode included an *aition*. It has been proposed that the same second-century B.C. papyrus discussed in relation to Hermesianax (*Suppl. Hell.* 970) should be assigned rather to Phanocles.

2.1.5 Simmias (or Simias) of Rhodes

A contemporary of Philitas was Simmias of Rhodes, who pursued not only grammatical activity, but also various genres of poetry, including elegy. We have a notice about, and two remaining lines of, a composition of his entitled *The Months*, which narrated myths connected to the festivals of the year, following a scheme later adopted by the Latin poet Ovid in the *Fasti*. He also wrote epigrams and a collection of *Glosses*. We will say more later about his "figured" poems.

2.1.6 Alexander the Aetolian

We have already had reason to discuss Alexander the Aetolian, who was active in the first decades of the third century B.C. as an author of tragedy (he was numbered among the poets of the "Pleiad," cf. *The Hellenistic Age* II 2.2) and as a scholar of tragedy and satyr drama in the first generation of Alexandrian philologists (cf. *The Hellenistic Age* III 2.2); he also wrote epigrams. In the present context he should be mentioned for his elegiac poetry, attested by fragments of the *Apollo*, which recalled unhappy loves prophesied by that god (a little over thirty lines survive), and also fragments of his *Muses*, in which stories of poetic contests provide the opportunity to depict famous poets (less than twenty lines survive). These two works illustrate a need to establish an element of thematic unity, which we will see is a recurring characteristic of the Hellenistic elegy collections and which finds its most distinguished expression in the *Aetia* of Callimachus. We know that Alexander the Aetolian also tried his hand at other genres of poetry, such as *epyllia* and epigrams.

2.1.7 Parthenius of Nicaea

Parthenius lived in the first century B.C. Originally from Nicaea in Asia Minor, he was brought to Rome as a captive in 73. Freed from slave status, he devoted himself to teaching – Vergil was one of his students – and to spreading knowledge and study of Greek poetry, within which he preferred the works and the poetics of Callimachus. Parthenius contributed to the diffusion at Rome of the particular form of elegiac collection structured around the catalogue of unhappy loves. Among his works we may note the *Sufferings in Love* (dedicated to his patron Cornelius Gallus), a collection of thirty-six stories in prose about unhappy love affairs narrated by poets and historians; and a work, perhaps in elegiac distichs, entitled *Metamorphosis* (probably similar to that of Ovid). A few fragments remain from other elegies. He also wrote *epyllia* and *epicedia*. The *epicedion* that he wrote on the death of his wife, in three books with the title *Arete*, was famous. It is also interesting that he translated into Latin some works of the poet Euphorion.

2.2 Epigram

2.2.1 The origins of epigrammatic poetry

The Greek term ἐπίγραμμα (*epigramma*) clearly expresses the origin of this poetic genre: a carved or incised text, an inscription placed on an object (stone, metal or ceramic), the aim of which would generally be to honour or commemorate someone. We have many testimonia to this usage in the Archaic and Classical Ages. The earliest finds bearing inscriptions date to the second half of the eighth century B.C., a period fairly close to the reintroduction of writing into Greece (cf. *Introduction* 3.2, *The Archaic Age* II 1.4.3), for example the famous Nestor's Cup, on which a three-line epigram is inscribed (an iambic trimeter catalectic followed by two dactylic hexameters), which announced the name of the owner and the function of the object. Using a mimetic expressive convention that would be widespread and long-lasting in epigrammatic poetry, the author of the three lines pretends that the words are being spoken by the object itself on which they are written, beginning by saying "I am the cup of Nestor."

Numerous anonymous inscriptions preserve examples of epigrammatic poetry that are funerary or votive in type. The former are found above all on funeral stelae that commemorate the deceased, while the latter are generally dedication inscriptions to divinities, inscribed on monuments or on objects offered to the god in a sanctuary or some other sacred place. The fact that these texts needed to be carved on stone or metal is perhaps the origin of their traditional brevity and incisive expression. They often comprise just one line (a monostich) or couplet (a distich). A consequence of the brevity of the text is the forceful concision of the style, which in a few words informs the reader of the person commemorated or the deity to whom the offering is made, sometimes with a reference to the circumstances of death or the reasons for making the offering and a mention of some other detail thought worthy of note (for example the virtues of the deceased). The most common metre in the Archaic Age is the dactylic hexameter, but already from the sixth century B.C. the elegiac distich had become the usual metre for epigram. Yet examples do also exist of compositions in iambic trimeters or trochaic tetrameters.

Later traditions attribute works of epigrammatic character to poets of the Archaic Age, such as Archilochus, Simonides and even Homer (cf. *The Archaic Age* II 1.10.5). While the case of Homer is clearly a construction made *a posteriori*, we are not able to establish the reliability or authenticity of these attributions to archaic poets, nor the motives that gave rise to them. However, it is likely that epigram made an early entrance, though perhaps a discreet one, into the mainstream of poetry by named authors, in addition to the more widespread, everyday production of anonymous and craftsmanlike epigrams tied to events in life that we have noted.

2.2.2 The epigram in the Classical Age

While the characteristics of the epigram took shape in the Archaic Age – a primarily votive and funerary purpose, brevity, stylistic concision, elegiac distich – during the Classical Age the genre enjoyed a great diffusion and popularity, above all in Attica, and was also influenced by other lyric forms (particularly elegy) and by theatre. The epigrammatic style began to accept stylistic and rhetorical solutions borrowed from other genres, which brought it to a high degree of refinement and led even famous authors to try their skill in the genre. From Euripides an epigram of a single distich is recorded, composed for the Athenian fallen in the Sicilian expedition during the Peloponnesian War, and there is an epigram attributed to Plato (cf. *The Classical Age* XIII 2.1). In this way, probably under the influence of the great lyrics composed in the Archaic Period to honour the fallen of famous battles – we may recall above all the *thrēnoi* and encomia of Simonides for the battles of Thermopylae, Marathon, Cape Artemisium, Salamis and Plataea – the epigram emerged from a specific position and purpose linked to situations of private life, and its standing as a literary genre in the full sense came to be established ever more firmly.

The final step in the literary evolution of the epigram was taken when the term itself to some degree lost its strict etymological sense and began to designate not only texts inscribed on funerary stelae or votive objects, but also in general a brief and summary composition in elegiac distichs that took as topic specific moments and occasions of private life: the epigram ceased to be an inscription and became a text written in an inscriptional style. The original occasion did not disappear entirely, but for the most part it remained as a fictitious pretext and literary convention.

2.2.3 The Hellenistic epigram and the epigrammatic "schools"

We have mentioned the radical difference of Hellenistic poetry from the lyric of Archaic and Classical times. The disappearance of the musical accompaniment and occasions of public performance – fundamental elements of the lyric genres of the Archaic and Late-Archaic Periods – had resulted in the transformation of poetic texts into works intended essentially for declamation or reading in restricted, limited circles, in a manner that is close to that of our own times. While, as we have seen, elegy enjoyed a new heyday with new connotations, we can say that epigrammatic poetry continued to be practised without interruption, enjoying in the Hellenistic Period a renewed and fruitful productivity and becoming autonomous as a true literary genre which attracted poets who practised it as their primary output. Like elegy, epigram responded to the new taste and to the demands of a conception of poetry that favoured short and elegant works, the little gem in a lighthearted tone. Differently from elegy, the epigrammatic genre made it possible to express subjective thoughts and feelings in more immediate and personal tones, using direct references and a more relaxed style. On the other hand, a characteristic trait that epigram shares with elegy is a subjective and autobiographical focus, both being expressions of a more varied range of individual sentiments and attitudes, and epigram clearly accentuates this – though of course with a high level of conventionality in form and content, as a literature founded upon other literature.

The Hellenistic epigram maintained the traditional themes (essentially funerary and votive), but complemented them with other motifs from private life, primarily love and the banquet, which had once been hymned in the form of symposial melic poetry. Other elements that were much practised include the ἔκφρασις (*ekphrasis*), or description of objects or works of art; satire of particular social figures; epitreptic motifs, i.e. moral exhortation; topics and settings of a bucolic type; and, much more rarely, political and civic themes. The occasions for song were usually fictitious, conventional pretexts, a practice that began with the literary epigram and was in accord with the contemporary poetics, which tended to see the work of art as an end in itself rather than as responding to an external purpose of any kind. And so, to give one example, funerary epigrams continued to be written as if they were to be incised in stone, and hence often included an address to the passer-by, even though they were in reality book-poems intended for the page. The original aspects of style – the brevity and incisive expression – remained typical of the genre, but it was an element of its poetic conventionality and certainly not a necessity owed to the space available on an object to be inscribed. The book-based purpose of the texts favoured the production of works in a number of distichs that was slightly higher than what had been traditional. An essential aspect of great importance is that the poetics of the period called for the pursuit of subtle and elaborate refinement in expression, which came into conflict with the traditional pared-down style of epigram. This moved it away from the standards of its early simplicity and permitted and favoured conscious literary games, such as the mixing of stylistic registers, learned and recherché allusion, wordplay, the *pointe* (a barb or joke, often deployed at the end of the poem) and similar elements.

We have thus outlined some general characteristics of Hellenistic epigram. Yet within the large epigrammatic output of the period it is usual to distinguish some approaches or "schools," on the basis of certain choices in style and content made by different authors, which has led to them being indeed quite differentiated. It is a useful grouping for the purposes of explanation and literary history, but it needs to be noted that the definition of "school" is purely a matter of convenience and does not correspond to any real link or association among the poets. And it is necessary to add also that the differences appear clear down to the mid-second century B.C., whereas thereafter they tend to become ever more blurred.

2.2.4 The "Peloponnesian school"

A group of authors working in a Doric setting and language are assigned to the so-called "Peloponnesian school." In this case, the idea of a school is particularly vague and perhaps functions primarily as a counterpart to the "Ionian-Alexandrian" school (see below). The poets of the "Peloponnesian school" favoured simple depictions of landscape and natural scenes and chose a style full of imagery and rich in adjectives.

The female poets Anyte of Tegea (in Arcadia) and Nossis of Epizephyrian Locri (in Calabria) lived in the fourth to third century B.C. Anyte was very famous. Her fellow citizens dedicated a statue to her and she was called "the lady Homer." Around twenty of her epigrams remain, including *epicedia* on the death of animals, descriptions of landscape or little genre scenes. The freshness of the imagery and the delicate notes of the style give her poetry distinctive tones and colour. Nossis refers in an epigram to her aristocratic family and eulogises a victory of her fellow countrymen over the people of the Bruttians. She was famous above all as a poet of love and seems to have taken Sappho as model and inspiration: a special affection for Aphrodite is evident, also in the votive epigrams, and in some portraits feminine beauty is described with grace and sensitivity. Sadly only twelve of her epigrams survive.

Leonidas of Tarentum travelled a great deal. Born in the prestigious Spartan-Peloponnesian colony of Tarentum, he moved from there to Epirus shortly after the Roman conquest (272 B.C.) and travelled throughout Greece and perhaps also in Asia Minor. We have around a hundred epigrams attributed to him (for the most part funerary or dedicatory), in which he speaks of his own deracinated, wandering life and of the poverty that dogged him. We find an interest in people of humble standing, such as herders, hunters, spinners and fishers (who dedicate their working tools as offerings), and a taste for realistic description of objects and craft products. There are also fictitious funerary poems for great poets of the past, such as Homer, Hipponax and Pindar, ecphrastic epigrams upon famous sculptures and a certain taste for macabre scenes and pessimistic tones. It was perhaps an original creation of Leonidas to compose obscene epigrams in honour of Priapus, a divinity of the fields, which gave rise to a genuine subgenre which was quite popular among Latin poets, the *Carmina Priapea*.

We will mention just two other poets, who imitated Leonidas and Anyte very closely. Simmias of Rhodes has already been discussed in relation to elegy: he also wrote epigrams, of which six have survived. Mnasalces of Sicyon in the Argolid flourished around the mid-third century: eighteen epigrams remain.

2.2.5 The "Ionian-Alexandrian school"

A different style and themes were preferred by the poets of the so-called "Ionian-Alexandrian school," who were active in the main cultural centres of the Hellenistic Age (in the Ionian area and at Alexandria). Advocates of a refined and worldly culture, they wrote an urbane poetry with little inclination towards bucolic sentimentalism or lyrical descriptions. The themes of love and of the symposium are central inspirations for the authors of this group. They express their state of mind and the momentary, one-off situation, celebrate the concrete pleasure of a life without too many troubles, the love is physical and material and the pessimistic and pensive tones are absent. The style is usually sober and concise and aims for a very studied and refined simplicity, an elegance able to present itself as fresh and fluent, despite being the result of an exceptional *labor limae* and exquisite technique. It is a poetry of literary and aristocratic circles far removed from humble and popular settings, imbued with a sense of intellectual superiority that gives rise to a refined artistry fully conscious of its own characteristics. The poets working in this current include Alexander the Aetolian (see above), from whom we have two epigrams of uncertain attribution, and others whom we will discuss in more detail later, especially Aratus of Soli and Callimachus of Cyrene. Other than these, the main poets of the group are Asclepiades, Posidippus and Hedylus.

Asclepiades of Samos also worked in lyrical metres (the relevant poems are lost), giving his name to the asclepiadean verses. He lived in the late fourth to mid-third century B.C. and is regarded by the ancient tradition as one of the main adversaries of Callimachus in the matter of poetics. We have thirty-three securely attributed epigrams and fourteen doubtful ones. For the most part these are erotic and address *hetairai* or boys. The theme of love prevails, touching on a great range of varying aspects, with an extraordinary variation in treatments, which runs from a lighthearted attitude to burning passion, from tormented desire to jokes, from delicacy to lasciviousness. In many epigrams the erotic theme is sung against the background of the symposium, accompanied by a taste for drinking and the sentiment of *carpe diem*.

Posidippus of Pella (in Macedonia) and Hedylus of Samos lived in the mid-third century. Posidippus travelled a great deal in the Greek world and Egypt, and was a *proxenos* (ambassador) of the Aetolian Confederacy. It seems that he wrote poems intended for real monuments in various places. Of his work, until a few years ago we knew only thirty epigrams, not all of them securely attributed, in which he at times revealed a more pompous and prolix style than the other poets of the group. Many of them are on erotic topics and recall the manner of Asclepiades, though in a way that feels a little more affected and contrived. A lucky papyrus discovery (*P.Mil.Vogl.* VIII 309) has allowed us to recover another hundred epigrams unknown until now, arranged in a collection that is subdivided by theme (concerning gemstones, auspices, votive, funerary themes, for statues, etc.). Our picture of Posidippus' poetic physiognomy has thus been notably enriched and we can appreciate how he adheres perfectly to the themes and taste of the most refined and polished epigrammatic poetry of the Hellenistic Age.

Hedylus' mother was an elegiac poet called Hedyle and, like Asclepiades, he came from the island of Samos. There he seems to have founded a kind of literary circle, which acknowledged Asclepiades as its master and model for a poetry marked by *joie de vivre* and a taste for the pleasures of *eros* and the banquet. Hedylus, too, imitates Asclepiades, though he does not reach the same standard. Yet, since we have only around ten of his epigrams, our picture of him may be misleading.

Many other epigrammatic poets lived in this period, minor figures who worked primarily in the spirit of Callimachus and Asclepiades. The period from the final years of the fourth to the mid-third century B.C. was thus the first great heyday of the Hellenistic epigram. The strength of the output and the way it caught on so widely meant that the work of this period immediately became a canonical model and point of reference. In the final decades of the third and in the second century, the genre was continued by followers who tended not to be especially original. Two of the more notable figures are Dioscorides and Alcaeus of Messene.

Dioscorides of Alexandria was active in the second half of the third century B.C. We have around forty of his epigrams, mostly from the funerary and erotic genres. Among the love epigrams, his distinctive trait is a more uninhibited realism. In the field of funerary epigram, we find a rich series of epitaphs for poets, from Sappho to contemporaries, which reveals an interest in literary forms that is not common among exponents of this genre. But what is notable above all is his celebration of the Spartan fighters fallen in war, understandable in the period in which many Greeks took the side of Sparta and of the Aetolian Confederacy against the policy of the Achaean Confederacy, which collaborated first with Macedonia and then with Rome. It was a political positioning that derives, once again, from the Greek cities' hopes for freedom and deliverance. A literary reflex of this is "doricism," which is found in celebrations of civil and military ideals linked to the traditional image of the Doric tribe and to Sparta in particular.

In the same context, the Philo-Laconian commitment is shared by Alcaeus of Messene, the most political of the Hellenistic epigrammatic poets. He lived in the second half of the third and the early second century and is an isolated voice in the panorama of Hellenistic epigrammatic poetry, in the aggressive tone (with an iambic flavour) of his poems addressed against Philip V of Macedonia. In one epigram, which according to Plutarch was on everyone's lips, he describes in sarcastic tones the defeat of Philip at Cynoscephalae (197 B.C.), painting the fleeing king as like the swiftest of deer. He trusted the proclamation of Greek freedom by the Roman consul Titus Quinctius Flamininus in 196 and celebrated the event with an encomiastic epigram. Fewer than twenty epigrams survive, including some fictitious epitaphs for poets.

2.2.6 The "Phoenician school"

The cultural career of the so-called "Phoenician school" ran from the second to the first century B.C. Its name derives from the fact that its best known exponents originated in the Phoenician area: Antipater of Sidon, Meleager of Gadara and Philodemus of Gadara. These authors brought to the highest level the tendency towards literary and rhetorical reworkings of funerary, erotic and votive motifs, as can be seen especially in the taste for insistent variation on a single theme and in the repeated, and at times obsessive, use of recherché rhetorical figures. The importance of this group of epigrammatic poets lies above all in having formed the route by which the genre was diffused to Rome (Antipater was the teacher of Lutatius Catulus, the precursor of neoteric poetry; another epigrammatist, Archias of Antioch, was in close contact with Cicero) and in the personal and cultural distinction of, especially, its Gadarene exponents: Philodemus is one of the most interesting figures in the Graeco-Roman cultural landscape of the first century B.C. and made a major contribution to the diffusion of Epicureanism at Rome (cf. *The Hellenistic Age* V 3.4); Meleager, as we will see shortly, was author of an important epigrammatic anthology, which formed the earliest nucleus of the famous *Palatine Anthology*.

Antipater of Sidon lived in the second half of the second century B.C. and moved to Rome, where he was present in poetic and intellectual circles, became the teacher of Lutatius Catulus and was also in contact with Cicero. We know around seventy of his epigrams, which were published some time around 125 B.C. (there is some difficulty in attributing the works, due to confusion with his namesake Antipater of Thessalonica, an epigrammatic poet of the first century B.C. to first century A.D.). Most of them belong to the votive and funerary genres. They are elegant exercises in versification, with infinite variations on the same themes. Imitating all that came before him, he sought by every means to produce pathos, a strong impact and a certain grandeur, deploying all the resources of his linguistic and rhetorical skill.

Meleager of Gadara lived between 130 and 70 B.C. approximately. We get information on his life from autobiographical epigrams: he described himself as a Syrian Phoenician Greek, he was educated in Tyre and at an advanced age he retired to Cosa, where he died. He regarded himself as a spiritual follower of the Cynic philosopher Menippus of Gadara and in his youth he wrote Menippean satires (cf. *The Classical Age* IV 2.2.2). In the epigrams there is however no trace of Cynic philosophy, since, as he states in one of them (XII 101), the wisdom has laid down its weapons before all-powerful Eros. A good description of his poetry is found in his statement that he knew how to unite "sweet tearful Love and the Muses with the merry Graces" (VII 419). That is, he sang of love in its most varied aspects with a rare grace and light touch, with irony and elegance, adding imaginative variants to the re-use of traditional themes. We have around 130 of his epigrams which he himself included in his anthology entitled *Garland*.

Philodemus of Gadara (110–40 B.C. ca.) came to Italy around 70 B.C. and was an established philosopher, playing a fundamental role in the diffusion of Epicureanism at Rome. As a poet (praised by Cicero), he entered the circle of Calpurnius Piso and exerted a major influence on Latin poets such as Horace, Ovid and Propertius. He is an elegant poet, often original, without the artificiality and virtuoso display of Meleager. In his poetry the philosophical stamp can be seen clearly: frugality, modesty and friendship are all Epicurean themes. Love, too, is treated with a certain distance, without passion, and the lovers correspond to the ideal of the pleasant satisfaction of natural needs that should not disturb the mind of the sage.

2.2.7 The tradition of anthologies of Greek epigrams

Aside from the (very many) epigrammatic texts that have survived today inscribed on various objects and the (numerous) ones that are quoted in the indirect tradition, our knowledge of ancient epigrammatic production depends on the tradition of poetic anthologies.

Collections of epigrams by single authors or by various hands must also have been compiled in the earlier Hellenistic Period. We have direct testimony of this in papyrus remnants from the third century B.C. It is also known that in the same period scholars such as the Athenian Philochorus and Polemon of Ilium published collections of earlier inscribed epigrams. Around 80 B.C. Meleager of Gadara made a selection of epigrams composed by forty-seven authors from the sixth century down to his own day and collected them in an anthology entitled Στέφανος (*Stephanos*, Greek for *Crown of Flowers, Garland*). In the proem, which survives (*Anthologia Palatina* IV 1), he assigned to each author the name of a flower or plant. The anthology was organised by thematic sections, each of which was closed with an epigram by Meleager himself, who in this way set himself up in an imagined competition with the preceding authors. The taste for the erudite collection, literary history and rivalry with one's predecessors perfectly matches Hellenistic taste.

Meleager's anthology served as a model for later collections: we will record the main ones here. A continuation of his selection was produced a few decades later in the *Stephanos* of Philippus of Thessalonica, which collected epigrams by authors of the first century B.C. arranged alphabetically, and was imitated by Agathias Scholasticus, a Byzantine historian and poet of the sixth century A.D., whose *Cycle* collected and arranged by topic epigrams by poets of his own time. At the start of the tenth century, the learned Byzantine Constantine Cephalas, drawing on many earlier collections that he was still able to consult (those just mentioned, and others of lesser importance of which some records and some parts survive), put together an impressive anthology of Greek epigrammatic poetry. This was an undertaking that, analogously, matched the taste of its times for creating large-scale learned collections.

All these collections have been lost, but the greater part of their content is preserved through two large later anthologies: the *Palatine Anthology* and the *Planudean Anthology*. The *Palatine Anthology*, which takes its name from its transmission in a manuscript preserved in the library of the Count Palatine at Heidelberg (though half the manuscript is today in the Bibliothèque Nationale in Paris), was compiled in the tenth century by an unknown editor, who used and expanded the collection of Cephalas. It is arranged in fifteen books, each of which contains epigrams that are homogeneous firstly in content, but also in form. For example, the erotic epigrams are in Book V, the votive in Book VI, the funerary in Book VII, the ecphrastic in Book IX, the pederastic in Book XII, and those in other metres than the elegiac distich in Book XIII, forming a total of around 3700 poems and 23,000 lines of verse.

Either the *Palatine Anthology* or a collection derived from that of Cephalas was used, between 1299 and 1301, by the monk Maximus Planudes to create a collection in seven books, which takes its name from him as the *Planudean Anthology*. His autograph copy of it survives today. Although its overall size is somewhat smaller than the *Palatine Anthology*, the *Planudean Anthology* preserves around 390 more epigrams, which the past century have usually (but inappropriately) been published as Book XVI of the *Palatine Anthology*, under the purely conventional title *Appendix Planudea*. It has also become customary to refer to the sixteen books as a whole under the title, which is likewise purely conventional, the *Greek Anthology*.

3 Callimachus: new poetics and philology

3.1 Life

The biography of Callimachus can be reconstructed, with many gaps and uncertainties, thanks to the *Suda* lexicon and some scattered ancient reports. He was probably born at the end of the fourth century B.C. in Cyrene, an ancient Greek colony on the Libyan shore of Africa that had been founded by citizens of Thera. His family was of noble origin and boasted among its ancestors Battus, the founder of the city. Callimachus himself alludes to his own origins in his works: in *Epigram 35* he calls himself "Battiad," i.e. "descendant of Battus" (or "son of Battus," if the *Suda* is right in stating that this was his father's name as well). The *Suda* explains that his family's noble status was accompanied by poverty and so Callimachus had to earn his living by working as an elementary teacher in Alexandria, in the Eleusis quarter of the city. His teaching work and poverty are reflected in some of the poet's verses, but, as always, a degree of caution is needed when attributing a precise force to autobiographical references that we read in poetic texts.

A decisive turn in Callimachus' life and career occurred when he came into contact with the court of Ptolemy II Philadelphus (283–246 B.C.) in Alexandria. Probably he soon took up a position within the Museum founded by the king and stayed on there in the first part of the reign of his successor, Ptolemy III Euergetes (246–221). Despite the large number of Callimachus' works and the variety of his scholarly interests, it appears that he never held the position of ἐπιστάτης (*epistatēs*), the most senior position within the Museum. His name does not appear in the sources (an Oxyrhynchus papyrus and the *Suda* lexicon) that allow us to reconstruct the list of librarians of the great Alexandrian library: after Zenodotus, the position passed to Apollonius Rhodius, and Callimachus was not included in this succession (cf. *The Hellenistic Age* III 2.2). Nonetheless, for the rest of his life he remained in Alexandria, in the environment of the royal court and its cultural institutions.

Callimachus' close relations with the Ptolemaic court are attested by frequent encomiastic references to the monarchs in his works. The poet must have enjoyed particular favour at the court of Ptolemy Euergetes, who, soon after his accession to the throne (in 246/5 B.C.) married Berenice, daughter of Magas, king of Cyrene

(Callimachus' homeland), bringing again Cyrene under Ptolemaic rule. This event must have particularly affected Callimachus, as is shown by the frequent, telling presence of references to Cyrene in his later works and the fact that the queen was the dedicatee of some of the most beautiful and famous poems in the *Aetia*, his most important and elaborate work: the *Victory of Berenice* and *The Lock of Berenice*.

The date of his death, like that of his birth, is unknown, but should in all probability be set around 240 B.C. The latest dated works are those dedicated to Queen Berenice: the *Lock* is not certainly later than 246, while the *Victory* probably refers to a chariot victory at the Nemean Games of 244.

3.2 The works

The entry in the Byzantine *Suda* lexicon that gives us various notices on the life of Callimachus states that he wrote more than 800 *biblia* (βιβλία, that is, "rolls" of papyrus: a single work might easily take up several rolls) and a little later it provides a list of titles, including poetic, dramatic and scholarly works, of which nothing survives (it also seems rather unlikely, given his poetic principles, that Callimachus wrote dramatic works).

3.2.1 The lost works

Some of the works in verse recorded by the *Suda* lexicon (*Arrival of Io*, *Semele*, *Glaucus*) had a mythological theme. There is a polemical intent in the little poem *Ibis*, a wilfully obscure poem full of invective against a person unknown to us, whom the lexicon has no hesitation in identifying as Apollonius Rhodius (we will see below that this identification, despite its long pedigree, is today considered unlikely).

Among the prose works reported by the *Suda* we find a series of writings on topics from literature, language, antiquarian study and historical geography which reveal, among other things, a particular interest in paradoxography, that is, notices of strange and marvellous objects and events. For example we find: *Table of the Glosses and Compositions of Democritus*, *Local Month-Names*, *Foundations of Islands and Cities and Their Changes of Name*, *On the Rivers in Europe*, *On Strange and Marvellous things in Peloponnesus and Italy*, *Collection of Marvels in All the Earth According to Localities*. The authenticity of these learned works is debated, whereas another important work mentioned by the *Suda* and by other ancient sources is certainly by Callimachus: the *Pinakes* or *Tables*, in 120 rolls (the full title is *Tables of All Those Who Were Eminent in Any Kind of Literature and of Their Writings*). As we saw in the chapter on philology (cf. *The Hellenistic Age* III 2.2), this was a catalogue of the patrimony of books assembled at the Library of Alexandria, which was so rich that it can be considered a kind of repository of Greek literature. The authors, arranged alphabetically, were given first a brief biography, followed by the list of works, quoting the *incipit* and noting the length of each work. Probably similar in kind was the work *Table and Register of Dramatic Producers in Chronological Order from the Earliest Times*, most likely based on similar investigations by Aristotle and in a Peripatetic context (*Didascaliae*). In the list in the *Suda* lexicon there are no *hypomnēmata* or monographs in literary criticism, such as the *Against Praxiphanes*, the existence of which is known to us from other sources.

3.2.2 The surviving and fragmentary works

It is striking that the list in the *Suda*, for reasons unknown, completely omits all the poetic works that survive today either complete or in fragmentary form – the *Hymns*, the collection of elegies entitled *Aetia*, the *Iambi*, the little mythological poem *Hecale* and the *Epigrams* – which are today the works that form the profile of Callimachus the poet.

As we will see, especially the collections of the *Hymns* and the *Aetia* reveal in their structure that they are the result of an editorial decision by Callimachus. For the first time, in a way quite similar to what often happens in the modern world, the author has also been the editor of his own texts, the philologist of himself, determining the precise and complex physiognomy of his own works by a carefully studied arrangement within the overall poetic collection. Evidently Callimachus composed his poetic texts over time, whenever the occasion for the poem occurred and following his inspiration. Then, in a second stage, he collected, ordered and arranged the poems in books according to a formal or thematic criterion, no differently from how he himself and the philologists at the Museum worked when editing the classical texts.

The sequence of works intended by Callimachus in his edition seems to be reflected in the collection of *diēgēseis* (διηγήσεις; that is, summaries or resumés in prose), transmitted by a papyrus of the first or second century A.D. preserved in Milan (*P.Med.* 18). The edition opened with the *Aetia* and continued with the poems in iambic metres and the short poem *Hecale*. A definite trace of Callimachus' editorial intervention is the *Epilogue* to the *Aetia* (fr. 112 Pfeiffer): the poet indicates metaphorically that he is about to pass on to the *Iambi*, which are called the "pedestrian Muse," in counterpoint to the "winged" poetry of the *Aetia* themselves. The *Epilogue* hence must have been composed as a conclusion to the *Aetia* and, at the same time, to create a link to the work that followed. It is important to note that the editorial operation thus involved not just a purely mechanical joining, even if a very carefully chosen one, but also interventions to bring the texts into harmony.

Beginning from the edition prepared by the author, these works continued to be read without interruption from the Hellenistic to the Byzantine Age. Their favourable reception is attested by the quantity of the indirect tradition and the amount and wide diffusion, in all periods (from the end of the third century B.C. to at least the end of the seventh century A.D.), of papyrus fragments of editions, commentaries and explanatory summaries (the *diēgēseis* already mentioned), as well as by exegetical work and commentary, which began at a very early stage.

Fragments of a papyrus (preserved in Lille and dated to the late third or early second century B.C.) written in a period quite close to Callimachus' own time provide the start of Book III of the *Aetia* intercalated with explanatory notes, showing that great interest must have been generated by his works, and exegetical study on them must have developed at an early stage.

The *Hymns* and a fair number of *Epigrams* have been preserved in late collections of hymnographic and epigrammatic poetry respectively (which we will discuss more specifically later), having entered these collections after being excerpted from the edition of Callimachus. Yet the majority of Callimachus' poetic work did not make it through the sifting of the Byzantine Era. This serious gap is only partly bridged by the indirect tradition and the substantial finds on papyrus and parchment, which have restored to us in the course of the past century a considerable number of fragments of these works (a number that has been increasing over the past few decades, raising hopes for new acquisitions in the future).

3.3 The *Hymns*

The Byzantine manuscript tradition has preserved a group of six *Hymns* by Callimachus dedicated to divinities and religious festivals. Parts of these are also attested by many fragments on papyrus and parchment that range in date from the first century B.C. to the sixth/seventh century A.D.

As we have seen in relation to the lyric poetry of the Archaic Age, the hymn (ὕμνος) was one of the earliest forms of choral lyric (cf. *The Archaic Age* III 1.2.3; we remember the hymns of Alcman, Pindar, Bacchylides), with the fundamental characteristic of praising a divinity or hero on the occasion of a public religious festival. The surviving *Homeric Hymns*, composed in hexameters, include a notable narrative section on the stories of the god in question and probably formed a sort of prooemium that the rhapsodes would present before they performed passages of epic, so these would be hymns that were not sung but recited. Certain lyric hymns intended for the symposium had a different form and manner of performance, for example those composed by Alcaeus. At an unknown date between the sixth and thirteenth century A.D., a collection was made of hymns by various authors, a kind of selection of Greek hymnographic poetry, which has survived in a few manuscripts. It runs from the *Homeric Hymns* to those of the Neoplatonic philosopher Proclus (fifth century A.D.) and also contains the *Hymns* of Callimachus, which have been preserved in the Byzantine manuscript tradition thanks to this collection.

The order in which the six works are arranged seems to correspond to a precise and coherent logic, so it is probable that it goes back to the editorial arrangement of Callimachus himself and that this was respected in the transmission. The first four hymns (*To Zeus*, *To Apollo*, *To Artemis*, *To Delos*) have traditional characteristics, being composed in an epic-Ionic dialect and with a "cletic" structure and content, that is, as an invocation of a divinity whose attributes are listed and whose merits are illustrated by narrating mythical episodes. These first four hymns revolve around the gods Zeus (*Hymn* 1) and Apollo (*Hymn* 2-4), as well as the human figures associated with them – namely kings and poets – whose reciprocal relationship came to hold special importance in Hellenistic culture.

The collection closes with two hymns (*On the Bath of Pallas* and *To Demeter*) that differ from the previous ones in some shared characteristics, including the decision to use the Doric dialect (rather than the traditional Ionic diction of epic) and their structure, which centres on a detailed narration of a mythical episode. This decision to give room to a mythical tale connected to cult has been seen as a direct influence from contemporary narrative elegy. However, the most significant trait shared by these two hymns is their "mimetic" character, that is, the attempt by the author to imitate and reproduce the real, lively atmosphere of the ritual occasion. This aspect is generally assigned to a late stage of Callimachus work and it is also found, though in less fully developed form, in the *Hymn to Apollo*. In that work, the evocation of the festival of the Carnea celebrated at Cyrene in honour of the god should be linked to the return of Cyrene to Ptolemaic rule in 246/5 B.C.

Following the convention of the poetic and theological tradition, the collection opens with the *Hymn to Zeus*, king of the gods and symbol of regal power. The citation of a half-line from Hesiod (line 79, "from Zeus come kings": cf. *Theogony* 96) begins a reflection on the privileged relationship between Zeus and rightful sovereigns and introduces the praises of Ptolemy Philadelphus (or, according to others, his father Ptolemy Soter). This poem is considered to be the earliest of the group.

The three hymns that follow (*Hymns* 2–4) all centre on the divine figure of Apollo. The importance and centrality given to Apollo in the collection of hymns is explained both by his fundamental function as the god of poetry (which is particularly marked in Callimachean poetics, as we will see) and by his role as guardian deity of Cyrene, Callimachus' homeland. In *Hymn* 2, *To Apollo*, the god is celebrated by recalling his roles, including that of guardian of archers and bards and as the divinity who presides over the foundation of new cities. It is in this context that we find a recollection of the foundation of Cyrene and of the establishment of the festival of the Carnea. The Libyan city of Cyrene was the third most important venue of this festival, after Sparta and Thera (Thera was a colony of Sparta, and Cyrene a colony of Thera). The hymn ends with the polemical motif of the contrast between long-form and short-form poetry, which we will discuss again below. The recollection in *Hymn* 3, *To Artemis*, of the mythical story and attributes of Artemis, sister of Apollo, begins with a contrived device: the poet imagines the goddess as a child seated on the lap of her father Zeus, whom she asks to be allowed to assume the attitudes, divine attributes and shy and savage lifestyle that would then become typical of her. In the rest of the hymn, Artemis is represented with characteristics that are largely the same as those of her brother Apollo. *Hymn* 4, *To Delos*, has as its object of celebration the cult of Apollo practised on this Aegean island since the time when Latona, wandering because she was being pursued by Hera, gave birth there to the twins Apollo and Artemis. From that day forth, the island too stopped wandering around on the sea. Central to the hymn is an encomium of Ptolemy

Philadelphus, whose birth on the island of Cos is prophesied by Apollo from his mother's womb (lines 162–190).

Hymn 5, On the Bath of Pallas (Εἰς λουτρὰ τῆς Παλλάδος), reflects a processional moment in the Argive cult of Athena. The statue of the goddess was brought to the bank of the river Inachus and disrobed, washed, sprinkled with ointment and then dressed again. The mythical episode on which it turns is the bath of Athena that was fatal to Tiresias, at that time still a boy, who was struck blind forever since he had accidentally seen the goddess's nude body. Thereafter, moved to pity by the prayers of the young man's mother, Athena granted him the gift of prophecy (lines 57–133). The text ends with the invitation, addressed to the women participating in the rite, to welcome the goddess. The last hymn in the collection, *Hymn 6*, is dedicated to a particular moment in the cult of Demeter (perhaps at Alexandria, on the model of the Athenian rites at Eleusis), namely the procession that accompanied the return to the temple of the sacred basket of the goddess, filled with the first fruits of the fields. The poem centres on the episode of Erysichthon, who was condemned by the goddess to the punishment of insatiable hunger for having impiously cut down a poplar sacred to her (vv. 24–117). The ending of this hymn, too, is an invitation to the women to greet the goddess's arrival in song.

The *Hymns* of Callimachus no longer had the old function of accompanying the real processional march of the faithful at religious events, but have become detached from the actual ritual moment. Already from the moment of their creation they were literary texts intended for a cultivated reading public, the fruit of the fusion or contamination of elements of the cletic and narrative "Homeric" hymn with the sympotic lyric hymn. They are texts detached from the concrete circumstances of a cultic event that had tied the older hymns into precise characteristics of structure and content, yet they are still inscribed into this ancient and distinguished poetic tradition, whose typical motifs they develop with originality. Callimachus' versatile personal approach, of innovating in relation to the tradition, emerges in their linguistic variety (the Homeric language in the first four hymns, the Doric dialect in the last two) and in their metrical innovations: *Hymns* I–IV and VI are in hexameters, in conformity with the model offered by the *Homeric Hymns*, but they present metrical characteristics unknown to Homer; and *Hymn* V is in elegiac distichs, perhaps in order to emphasise the influence of elegy – another element of mixing of genres – on the decision to place a narrative episode at the centre of the poem.

3.4 The *Aetia*

So far as we can tell, Callimachus' most important work, both in the significance it came to hold within Hellenistic poetic theory and in its enormous influence on contemporary and subsequent authors (down to the Latin poets, above all Catullus and Ovid), is the *Aetia*. This is a collection of elegies (about forty of them have been identified) composed at different times and then brought together and arranged in four books and published by Callimachus himself.

The title (in Greek Αἴτια, literally *Causes*) alludes to the shared character of all these works: they tell the origin of religious festivals, myths, cults, institutions, cities and names, in accord with a taste that was both erudite and poetic and which fits well into the context of the cultivated and refined work of the Alexandrian Museum. An interest in aetiology is an aspect of the antiquarian research of the Alexandrian philologists, with the aim of explaining the "causes" of the formation of traditions and cultural phenomena. Its transposition into poetry found an outlet in many genres, among which aetiological elegy holds a prime position (cf. *The Hellenistic Age* IV 2.1.1).

The *Aetia* are often considered to be the outcome of Callimachus' multifaceted poetic and philological activities, a kind of *summa* of his life's work as scholar and literary figure, the fruit of the final years of the poet's life. This vision, while evocative, needs more precision. The aetiological elegies must have been composed at different times, but Callimachus' old age – perhaps when the poet turned to producing a complete edition of his works – must have been the time when they were arranged editorially as an organic collection with a view to publication, dividing them into four books, inserting the elegies into an overall frame and composing a *Prologue* (in which, at line 6, the poet declares "the decades of my years are not few") and an *Epilogue* (where, as we have seen, we find the formula of the transition to the "pedestrian" poetry of the *Iambi*: fr. 112 Pf.). We will discuss the *Prologue* further below, in the section on Callimachean poetics (cf. below 3.8).

The overall structure of the collection, which can be reconstructed from its many surviving fragments, corresponds to a clear organising logic. The elegies are contained within a "frame" represented by the meeting and dialogue of the poet with the Muses. Callimachus imagines that he meets the goddesses of poetry in a dream, following the model of Hesiod's *Theogony* (a model mentioned explicitly and cleverly imitated in fr. 2 Pf.). He presents to the Muses some questions and receives from them brief responses. The goddesses, as the personification of knowledge, allude specifically to the cultural heritage guarded and studied at Alexandria in the Museum, the "house of the Muses."

An example of how every individual *aition* is inserted into this macrostructure based on the fiction of the dream and the question-and-answer scheme is given by the first elegy, The Graces (frr. 3–7 Pf.). The poet asks why in the cult of the Graces at Paros it is not permitted to use *auloi* or garlands. The explanation is given (so we are told by a preserved scholion) by the Muse Clio: this custom originated at the time when Minos, during a sacrifice to the Graces on the island of Paros, received news of the death of his son Androgeus. The king did not interrupt the sacrifice, but bade the *aulos* players be silent and laid aside the wreath that had garlanded his head, as a sign of mourning. The poet then asks a second question, on the true genealogy of the Graces, and the Muse replies that they are the daughters of Dionysus and the nymph Coronis.

It is not clear if the frame created by the dialogue scheme, set up at the start of Book I and identifiable in fragments of Book II, also formed the structure of the following books. There are hints that point in that direction (frr. 76 and 86 Pf.), but it seems that the two final books were less closely tied to the initial fiction of the encounter with the Muses and the dialogue with them. There are indications that Books III and IV were designed and arranged by Callimachus as a pair that was fairly distinct from the first pair and defined by structural and thematic aspects of their own. The most significant link is established in the clear connection between the elegy that opens Book III and that which closes Book IV, both addressed to Queen Berenice, with the effect of ring composition. These two poems are, respectively, the *Victory of Berenice*, and *The Lock of Berenice*, both already mentioned. They were composed not earlier than 246 B.C., so it must have been placed at this key position within the collection by Callimachus in his old age when he was preparing the definitive edition of his works.

The *Victory* must have been over 150 lines long and our text of it has many gaps. In common with the whole collection of the *Aetia*, it is of course in elegiac distichs, but this fact is a very marked innovation in departing from the traditional form of this type of lyric composition, which was usually intended not for recitation or reading, but for choral song accompanied by instrumental music (a similar case is Callimachus' *epinicion* for Sosibius, fr. 384 Pf.). Transposing an epinician theme into an elegiac form is one of the playful moves of refined erudition and poetic experimentalism in mixing genres that are characteristic of Callimachean and Alexandrian poetics. No one who (like the learned readers of this poetry) knew the *epinicia* of Pindar and Bacchylides would have been indifferent to this. The text celebrates a victory in the chariot race won by the team of Queen Berenice at the Nemean Games (perhaps in 244 B.C.).

The poem has the typical structure of an epinician ode, which includes an initial reference to the occasion and a brief mention of the athletic event concerned, followed by the mythical element, which is in this case the struggle between Heracles and the Nemean lion unleashed by Hera: it is the *aition* of the Nemean Games. The treatment of the myth has some quite interesting aspects. Heracles' labour remains in the background, while great space is given to the hero's encounter with the aged herder Molorcus, who offers him hospitality. Molorcus has been reduced to wretchedness by the repeated incursions of the lion and has to engage in a furious battle with mice who are eating him out of his house and home (the herder is here the counterpoint to Heracles and is modelled on the heroic-comic example of the pseudo-Homeric *Batrachomyomachia*). The hero promises the herder that he will compensate him with herds of animals if he returns victorious from his labour. There is an obvious thematic affinity with the *Hecale*, which we will discuss shortly.

The final *aition* of the collection is again a homage to the Cyrenaean queen. The text has come down to us in a fairly fragmentary state, but we can easily reconstruct the sense of the lost parts thanks to the imitation of this poem by the Latin poet

Catullus (*Poem* 66). When King Ptolemy III left for the war against Syria (246–241 B.C.), in exchange for the safety of her new husband the queen Berenice had vowed to offer to the gods a lock of her hair, which she ordered to be cut off and which was guarded in a temple. When the lock mysteriously disappeared, the court astronomer Conon took the opportunity to celebrate the queen, declaring that the vanished lock of hair had been transformed into a constellation which he had recently discovered and which did not yet have a name (cf. *The Hellenistic Age* VI 1.2). With fine poetic originality, Callimachus imagines the lock itself, taken up into the heavens, addressing the queen and explaining to her what had happened and lamenting its removal from her presence.

For other notable poems in the collection we can reconstruct the content and the distinctive way that Callimachus has reworked it, and so we are able to appreciate the variety of stylistic registers and thematic areas that characterise the *Aetia*. For example, a famous elegy is the one that tells of the love of Acontius and Cydippe in Book III (imitated by the Latin poet Ovid, *Heroides* 21 and 22). Long fragments of it survive (67–75 Pf.), which allow us to pick up the parallels with motifs and expressive forms from different genres, ranging from New Comedy to bucolic poetry to the later novel.

> Acontius is aflame with love for the beautiful Cydippe. At the suggestion of the god Eros, during a festival in honour of Artemis, on Delos, Acontius throws an apple in the girl's direction, on which he has inscribed the phrase "By Artemis, I will marry Acontius." By reading the phrase aloud, according to popular belief Cydippe has bound herself by an oath to the love of Acontius. But the young woman's father has promised her in marriage to another man and Acontius laments his own despair by wandering alone through the countryside far from all human contact and confiding his suffering to the plants of the forest. Three times the father of Cydippe is about to celebrate the wedding of his daughter according to his own intentions, but each time she falls fatally ill. When finally the oracle of Delphi reveals that Cydippe is bound to Acontius by an oath, the girl's father consents to their marriage.

The refined beauty and charm of these poems, which can be reconstructed to some extent yet are for the most part disfigured by a tradition that is cruelly selective and which is for us dependent on the accidents of discovery of the fragments, can only make us regret that the *Aetia* have not been preserved in their entirety.

3.5 The *Iambi*

Some telling clues, including the *Epilogue* to the *Aetia*, already mentioned (fr. 112 Pf.), and the sequence of works in the admittedly fragmentary testimony of the *diēgēseis* on papyrus, confirm that in Callimachus' edition the *Aetia* were followed by the *Iambi*. We do not know if Callimachus himself gave this title to the collection of poems we are discussing here, but it seems unlikely: the *Suda* lexicon mentions some μέλη

(*Songs*), which some believe should perhaps be identified with the collection that we know as the *Iambi*.

The title makes clear that these are, in general, poems inspired by the lively and aggressive style of the archaic poetry of Archilochus and Hipponax. In reality it should be said that Callimachus draws inspiration from the archaic genre as is his wont, by innovating and expanding its characteristic metres, forms and content, knowingly adopting a variety of metres and topics that was unknown to the iambic authors of the Archaic Age and which would have been unthinkable in that context.

This very variety and range of forms is the origin of a quite controversial debate among modern critics. A number of papyrus testimonia (including the papyrus of the *diēgēseis*) attribute to the collection seventeen poems (the same number as the *Epodes* of the Latin poet Horace, who owes so much to Callimachus). Yet some scholars have argued that the final four poems should be excluded, regarding them as too distant from the iambic model in their form and content. Further, *Iamb* 13 seems apt as a final poem, since it contains declarations on poetics, in the same way as *Iamb* 1 does (which would thus create ring composition). Other scholars have maintained, with good arguments, that the collection consisted of all seventeen poems, giving credence to the ancient testimonia and observing that *Iamb* 13, in which Callimachus makes a programmatic announcement of his distance from the traditional norms of the genre in the name of variety (the *diēgēsis* of the poem call this πολυείδεια, i.e. "variety of forms"), fits very well as a poem placed to precede the works that depart further from archaic iambic. This seems all the more likely given that the degree of novelty (in metre, language and content) increases gradually over the course of the collection, a pattern that must be the result of a conscious arrangement.

From the metrical point of view, most of the poems respect the traditional appearance of iambic-trochaic poetry. Poems 1–10, 12 and 13 are in fact in iambic and trochaic metres: choliambs (or iambic trimeters scazon), iambic trimeters, trochaic trimeters catalectic and epodes. But the other four or five poems (14–17 and perhaps 11) are in various lyric metres. The criterion of variation is at work in the choice of language too: while some poems preserve the Ionic dialect of the iambic tradition, others are written in the local Doric dialect of Thera and Cyrene. As we have already noted, finally, the decision to favour variety applies also to the content: alongside compositions characterised by an aggressive tone and addressed to contemporary figures, following the model of the *iambikē idea* of the verse of Archilochus and Hipponax, we find poems that treat topics that had habitually been reserved for elegy or epigram.

Among the poems of more traditional stamp we may note those (1–5) that take as their target contemporary figures, pillorying their vices: this is moral polemic that makes use also of illustrations of a type drawn from fable (that is, by inserting stories whose protagonists are personified animals and plants). *Iamb* 6 is a *propemptikon*, that is, a poem of farewell, to a friend who is about to set off for Elis in order to visit the statue of Olympian Zeus sculpted by Phidias. *Iamb* 12 is addressed to another friend, to celebrate the birth of a girl. *Iambi* 7, 9–11 and (perhaps) 14 and 17 are *aitia* of cults and proverbs; *Iamb* 8 is an epinician, *Iamb* 15 a sympotic song in honour of the Dioscuri and Helen; *Iamb* 16 sings the apotheosis of Queen Arsinoe II, wife of Ptolemy Philadelphus, who died in 268 B.C.; finally, *Iamb* 13 (like the opening poem) contains literary polemic.

> *Iambi* 1 and 13 contain interesting declarations of poetics and statements of metapoetic type. In *Iamb* 1, with great and ironic inventiveness, Callimachus imagines that the poet Hipponax is speaking in the first person and declares that he has arrived from beyond the grave "bearing an iamb that does not sing polemic / with Bupalus" (lines 3–4). This programmatic statement of abandoning the harsh tones and unbridled aggression distinctive of traditional iambic poetry, which is paradoxically put in the mouth of the greatest historical exponent of archaic iambic poetry (with a whole series of expressive elements, starting with the choliambic metre, that allude parodically to Hipponax's own style), is a knowing metaliterary joke staged by Callimachus to express his own very original position. Hipponax continues by calling upon the learned scholars of the Alexandrian Museum to gather in front of the temple of Serapis and inviting them to lay down their quarrels and embrace modesty and mutual harmony. To this end, he relates the famous anecdote of the cup of Bathycles, by way of illustration.
>
> The Arcadian Bathycles, at the point of death, decided to award a precious goblet to the wisest man. The goblet was offered in turn to each of the Seven Sages, beginning with Thales, but each of them declined it, not considering himself the wises. In the end, the cup returned to Thales, who decided to dedicate it to the god Apollo.
>
> Of *Iamb* 13, which we are able to read only in severely lacunose form, we learn from the *diēgēsis* that it was a response by Callimachus to those who rebuked him for the "variety of forms" of his works. Callimachus declared that he adhered to the positions of the tragic poet Ion of Chios (cf. *The Classical Age* V 3.1), which assimilated the poetic art to a *technē* that, once learned, puts the poet in a position to practise various forms: "on the other hand, no one criticises a craftsman if he constructs tools of a different form." The programmatic content is confirmed by the marked use of technical terminology that can be detected in the fragments, which mention literary dialects (fr. 203, 18 Pf.: "in Ionic, in Doric and in mixed language"), types of verse (fr. 203, 31 Pf.: "pentameter, heroic verse," i.e. hexameter; cf. lines 43–45) and poetic genres (fr. 203, 32 and 44 Pf.: tragedies and tragic poets) and refer, at the start and close, to Ephesus and Ionia, the homeland of iambic-trochaic poetry.

3.6 The *Epigrams*

In the epigram collection of the *Palatine Anthology* (which we have discussed in the section on epigram: cf. *The Hellenistic Age* IV 2.2) there are 63 poems under the name of Callimachus, some of which are of contested authenticity, and we have a few other epigrams by Callimachus from other sources. The themes treated are those usual in this genre: funerary (we may note *Epigram* 35, a single distich composed by the poet for his own tomb), votive and erotic (the latter being on homoerotic themes). Especially important are those on literary subjects, some in which the poet voices opinions on the poets of the past, but above all those that treat questions of poetics. A clear allusion to the learned and recherché character of his poetry is the ending of *Epigram* 31 (*Ant. Pal.* XII 102): "Even such is my love: it can pursue what flees from it, but what lies ready it passes by." Famous is *Epigram* 28 (*Ant. Pal.* XII 43): "I hate the cyclic poem, nor do I take pleasure in the road [i.e. in a poetry] which carries many to and fro. I abhor, too, the roaming lover, and I drink not from every well; I loathe all common things (πάντα δημόσια)."

3.7 *Hecale*

Among the poetic genres at which Callimachus tried his hand with impressive results, we should record the epyllion or "little epic," i.e. a short poem in hexameters with mythological content. This was a genre that – as we have seen (cf. *The Hellenistic Age* IV 2.2 and what we said on the poem *Hermes* by Philitas: cf. IV 2.1.2) – connects to the epic tradition but innovates in its form and content and, in particular, by giving room to the more marginal, less well known and less heroic aspects of a myth.

We know that in the twelfth century at Athens a complete copy of the *Hecale* still existed, which was subsequently lost. Today we have only fragments and quotations, from which it is difficult to conjecture the original length of the work or to reconstruct the plot in detail. We are informed about the content, fortunately, by an *Argument* to the work that is preserved via two fragments.

> Theseus had arrived one evening from Athens in the plain of Marathon to confront the terrible bull that was plaguing the area. Overtaken by a storm, he found a welcome in the humble home of an old woman called Hecale. The next day, at dawn, Theseus leaves Hecale's house and, finding the bull, succeeds in overpowering it. The hero returns to the old woman's house to reward her for her hospitality, but finds that she has died suddenly. He decides to offer homage to her by establishing a new Attic deme to which he gives the name "Hecale" and by founding the sanctuary of Zeus Hekaleios.

The humble welcome of Hecale, *aition* of the institution of the cult of Zeus Hekaleios, is discussed also by the Imperial-Period biographer Plutarch (*Lives, Theseus* 14), whose source was the Attidographer Philochorus (fourth to third century B.C.). Perhaps Callimachus too was inspired by the account of Philochorus, but the mythical episode of Hecale was already known at least from the fifth century B.C. onwards, the date of an image on pottery that very probably depicts the old woman in the act of offering a tray to the young Theseus. The age of the tale does not alter the fact that Hecale's story is in essence a marginal episode in the rich saga centred on the figure of Theseus. In Callimachus' little poem, the change in the point of view is clear: the hero is in a sense shifted to second rank while the true protagonist becomes the old lady, who did not spare her poor home and few goods to ease the weariness of the young man and then died before she could enjoy his gratitude. The shift in the point of view of the story, by which the heroic labour and the hero himself lose their central position and attention is turned to the simple and very human heroism of a poor old woman, is the most significant and striking novelty of Callimachus' poem.

Hecale in a certain sense represents epic according to the taste of Callimachus, that is, without its heroic connotations or the characteristic elements of the traditional *epos* (such as great length) and oriented rather towards the tones and subjects of aetiological elegy. Alongside frequent brief echoes of Homer and continual allusions to typical elements of the epic repertoire (e.g. the motif of the hero asked by fellow banqueters to tell his story, with Odysseus at the court of the Phaeacians parallel to Hecale, when invited by Theseus, at her frugal table), we find detailed and realistic descriptions of the country life of which the old woman is part. Emblematic of the fusion of epic and elegiac elements are the lines (fr. 263 Pf., which some regard as the ending of the poem) in which Theseus promises to preserve the eternal memory of Hecale, drawing on a closural motif typical of the *Homeric Hymns* (final invocation of a divinity, with the promise that the poet will sing of her again): "Go, gentle among women, along the road which heartrending pains do not penetrate. Often, Mother, we shall remember your hospitable cottage, for it was a common homestead for all."

3.8 Callimachean poetics

When discussing the works of Callimachus we have seen how many explicit references to his own conception of poetry pervade his poems, often in a prominent position at the start of a collection (as is the case in the *Aetia* and the *Iambi*). A characteristic of the Hellenistic poets is a firm and deep awareness of being artists who make individual choices, which are ascribed more value the more they differ in an original way from those of other poets. By bringing together the various impulses that we have mentioned, it is possible to reconstruct an organic and unitary picture of Callimachus' poetics.

One of the cornerstones of these poetics is an aversion for composing long-form poetry (and thus the traditional epic poem) and a preference for the short poem that is structurally and stylistically "light": "lightness" (λεπτότης), is the term that expresses the essential quality of this poetry. The reason for this choice lies in the fact that long-form poetry demands an improbable degree of continuous inspiration and composition, without which the final work will be full of impurities and imperfections and will not command a consistent standard of form and thought.

This idea is expressed by Callimachus through some forceful and famous literary images, such as that used by Apollo in Callimachus' hymn to that god (*Hymn* 2, 107–113) in response to provocation from Jealousy: "The flow of the Assyrian river is vast, but it draws along much refuse from the land and much garbage on its waters. Not from any sources do bees carry water to Deò (Demeter), but from what comes up pure and undefiled from a holy fountain, a small drop, the choicest of waters."

However, the text that is by far the most significant from this point of view, for its thoroughly allegorical frame and for the impassioned tone of its programmatic declaration, is the *Prologue* to the *Aetia* (fr. 1 Pf.).

At the start of his most important work, Callimachus rails against his opponents, without naming them, but identifying them with the Telchines, ancient figures of divine magician-craftsmen who were jealous of each other and who were located by the mythographic tradition in the islands of the Aegean: "Often the Telchines mutter against me, against my poetry, who, ignorant of the Muse, were not born as her friend, because I did not complete one single continuous song [on the glory of] kings (...) or on heroes in many thousands of lines, but turn around words a little in my mind like a child, although the decades of my years are not few." We learn from the scholia that in the lines that immediately followed, which are badly mauled by lacunae, Callimachus responded to the Telchines' criticisms by citing the example of Mimnermus of Colophon and Philitas of Cos, two poets who tried their hand at both short-form and long-form poetry and achieved better results in the former. Poetry cannot be judged for its length, as is done by Callimachus' detractors Telchines: "Be off, destructive breed of Bascania, and hereafter judge poetry by its art, not by the Persian *schoinos* (i.e. a unit of measurement for long distances)." High-flown song does not suit the poet: "do not expect a loudly thundering song to be born from me: thundering is not my job, but is the work of Zeus." From his first attempts at poetry he had been taught by Apollo himself to nurture a "slender (λεπταλέην) Muse", to "go where big waggons never go," and not to launch the chariot "along a wide road, but along untrodden paths," even if this would mean that his course would be "more narrow." The poet has followed the advice of the god: he prefers the sharp verse of the cicada to the loud braying of asses.

There is a long tradition of critics accepting an ancient notice that is today near-unanimously regarded as false, according to which differing views on poetics led to a fierce personal hostility between Callimachus and his (presumed) student Apollonius Rhodius. Some ancient scholarly sources (the *Suda* lexicon, scholia) do indeed identify Apollonius either as one of the Telchines of the *Aetia* prologue or as other anonymous figures against whom Callimachus railed in his poems. Yet this identification has no secure basis at all and very likely arose from an ancient biographical reconstruction based on inferences from the texts themselves, without any documentary support. We will discuss this again in relation to Apollonius Rhodius (cf. below 5.2). In fact, it is more likely that the direct opponents of Callimachus were students of the school of Aristotle (the Praxiphanes against whose theses Callimachus wrote a monograph was from a Peripatetic background), which, in the footsteps of its founder, continued to assign a fundamental role to epic poetry and tragedy. It is not mere chance that, at the start of the *Aetia* (fr. 2 Pf., *The Dream*), Callimachus polemically chose as his model Hesiod, the first creator of a poetry of truth-telling, that is, one inspired by the truth of the content, in an implicit opposition to Homer. On the harsh polemics in which Callimachus was involved, we should recall how in *Iamb* 1 he sarcastically censured the atmosphere of vicious rivalry that flourished within the Museum of Alexandria, while inviting his colleagues to turn to modesty and harmony.

A prerequisite of the short-form, refined poetry favoured by Callimachus is also his aristocratic exclusivity. In *Epigram* 28, cited above, he expressly declares that he does not like poetry which, to meet the facile taste of the masses, draws on the epic repertoire and appeals to easily impressed tastes: he rejects the road travelled by many in all directions, the inconstant lover and the things that belong to everyone.

The elitist aspect is deeply implicated also in the learned and erudite character of this poetry, which appeals to knowledge that only a few possess.

We saw, when discussing *Iambi* 1 and 13, how Callimachus insists also on the freedom to practise different forms of poetry, to treat as he pleases the traditional forms and contents and to combine them in an original and innovative variety, following his own personal creativity. This is a conception of poetry that sees the poetic product as the result of an art (in Greek τέχνη) that has its own rules and characteristics, which an artist in command of them can deploy as he pleases and according to his ability. In the prologue to the *Aetia*, the Telchines are invited to judge poetry "by (the canons) of art (τέχνη)" that has been deployed and displayed by the author.

> Very important for Callimachus' poetics is the element derived from aetiological types of poetry, such as those that constitute the entire collection of the *Aetia*. However, as we have noted, the taste for aetiology is not in fact restricted to elegy alone, but is a trait of his poetics in general. Aetiological works appear in the *Iambi* and interest in an *aition* emerges also in the *Hymns* and *Hecale*. We have stressed how this taste for the causes and origins of cults, traditions and customs has affinities with the antiquarian interest that motivated Callimachus and the philologists of the Alexandrian Museum to pursue erudite research. It is thus a component of poetics that is inseparable from philological activity.

On the other hand, Callimachus was well aware also of the risks run by a poetry based too strongly on scholarly competence, if the latter is applied obsessively. An elegiac distich on Acontius and Cydippe (*Aetia* III, fr. 75, 8–9 Pf.) clearly shows that poet-philologists such as Callimachus were aware of this problem: "Truly much knowledge is a difficult evil for whoever is not master of his tongue: this man is really a child with a knife." The lines form an ironic self-deprecating joke, since the poet pretends to interrupt himself at the last moment, just before he accidentally reveals some details of the Eleusinian mysteries, which would be against the strict law of the cult. But it should also be read as a declaration of poetics, in which Callimachus denounces the way that a propensity for curiosity and erudite stories may expand to the point that it overwhelms the sense of (poetic) decorum and (religious) permissibility.

3.9 Language and style

Callimachus' poetic language fundamentally follows in the footsteps of the Homeric tradition, but does so with copious and eye-catching elements of innovation. His dactylic hexameter introduces new rules and more strictness than the Homeric one. Into the traditional linguistic mixture used in the hexameter and the distich, Callimachus, with his taste for experimentation and fondness for combining forms, adds forms of the *koinē* and, in the iambs, dialect elements. We have seen how he innovates by using the Doric dialect in *Hymns* V and VI, *On the Bath of Pallas* and *To Demeter*. And we have observed in the discussion of the individual works how the style is generally shaped to pursue a refined and recherché expression and to play with allusive references to elements from different contexts and to the models of the past.

3.10 The reception of the works

Callimachus had many emulators already in the Hellenistic Period and his work enjoyed enormous success in Latin culture. His works were widely diffused, especially in the most sophisticated literary circles of Republican and Augustan Rome, and they influenced many authors, beginning from Ennius, whose prooemium to the *Annales* picked up the motif of the dream that is present in the prooemium to the *Aetia*. Among the works that had the greatest influence on Latin poetry we should note the elegies, for which Callimachus, along with Philitas, was considered a model; the *Iambi*, which contributed to the formation of the Roman genre of satire; and the epyllion, which was emulated by neoteric poets such as Helvius Cinna, Licinius Calvus, Catullus and the author of the *Ciris* attributed to Vergil. More generally, Callimachean poetics had an enormous resonance not only in Greek culture, but also in the Roman literary world, which adopted the taste for short, light poetry and the thoroughly Alexandrian sense of stylistic refinement and vigilant care in composition.

4 Didactic poetry

4.1 Following in the footsteps of the hexameter tradition

We have seen how in the course of the Archaic and Classical Ages the great poetic mainstream of the hexameter tradition came into being. Identified primarily with Homeric epic narrative, it then hosted other, related genres: the theogonic and didactic *epos* of Hesiod, the grand cosmological expositions of philosophers such as Parmenides and Empedocles, the philosophy of Xenophanes or the wisdom literature of Solon and Theognis. Beginning from fantastic tales of war and adventure, drawn from myth and adopted as the paradigmatic model for a world of aristocratic values, therefore, the content of hexameter poetry, even when it kept intact its value for education and orientation in society, had in part shifted towards exhortation to ethical behaviour and philosophical explanation of the structure of the universe. This range of topics did not convince Aristotle, who in the *Poetics* (1, 1447b 13–23) refused to accept the term "epic poet" for those who used the hexameter to expound topics that concerned not the imitation of nature, but nature itself: "Homer and Empedocles have nothing in common except their metre."

During the Hellenistic Age, alongside the hexameter epos on mythological topics (such as the *Argonautica* of Apollonius Rhodius), a certain success was enjoyed also by the more strictly didactic strain of hexameter poetry. The significant progress of science and its constant diffusion, inspired by the investigations carried out within the Peripatetic school and the Alexandrian Museum, can be considered some of the motives for specialisation on technical and scientific content in hexameter poetry in this period. A shared point of reference and literary model for both Aratus and Nicander, the two principal Hellenistic didactic poets, is Hesiod, above all the *Works and Days* with its technical repertoire of farming practices that are recalled in connection with the ethical theme of justice.

When we discussed Hesiod, we made clear how in the Archaic and Classical Ages the problem of a "didactic" genre within hexameter poetry never arose, since poetry in general was regarded as a source of knowledge and education (cf. *The Archaic Age* II 3.2). It is in the passage cited above from Aristotle's *Poetics* that we find the first clear indication of a distinction at a theoretical level between a narrative hexameter poetry and one with "technical" content intended for instruction. A definitive codification occurred only in the Alexandrian Era, within the debate on the definition of literary genres. By that time the self-awareness of the genre seems to be fully established in the works of poets who are explicitly "didactic," whose literary and artistic goal is specifically to set a given discipline into verse. Didactic poetry was then traced back to Hesiod, who was seen as the inventor of the genre and was taken as a model. In the didactic poetry of the Hellenistic Age, the main intention lay in the choice of theme: setting into verse a given discipline, dedicating one's own poetic effort to the exposition of disciplinary knowledge with complex theoretical implications (astronomy in the case of Aratus and aspects of medicine in the case of Nicander), in which the heritage of traditional knowledge was set alongside the results of current scientific observation.

A problem that has not been entirely resolved is the question of what level of scientific competence these poets actually possessed. From reading their works it would seem that their knowledge of the disciplines that they treat was purely amateur. They drew on specialist scientific sources, making the effort to embellish topics that were in themselves unpoetic, using all the ornaments of hexameter diction. Consequently the choice of a technical and scientific topic must have been for these authors subordinate to a purely literary goal, within a poetic conception that was typically Hellenistic, privileging the choice of rare and unusual themes that would allow the poet to demonstrate his virtuoso ability to the full. Once again, we need to avoid the mistake of thinking that the genre of didactic poetry was really responding to the need for a manual to teach the foundations of a discipline to whoever wanted to learn it.

On the other hand, we should not overlook another aspect, that is, that works such as that of Aratus – and this is an attested use – did aim for popularisation, that is, they formed a reference-text for basic and elementary information on astronomy, which needed to be accompanied by commentaries that would pursue in more depth the technical aspects of the topics treated. Further, we have a concrete example of a manual in verse intended for school use: the *Periēgēsis* attributed to Pausanias of Damascus (second half of second century B.C.), long mistakenly thought to be a work of

Scymnus of Chios and hence known as the *Periēgēsis* of Pseudo-Scymnus. Composed in iambic trimeters for ease of memorisation, it consists of an ethnogeographical compendium with elements of mythography, without any literary ambition.

4.2 Aratus of Soli: astronomy in verse

A slender manuscript tradition has preserved the didactic poem of Aratus entitled *Phaenomena*, together with scholia and notices about the author's life.

Aratus was born in Cilicia, at Soli, around 315 B.C. and after completing his early studies in Asia Minor he moved to Athens, where he attended the teaching of Zeno, the founder of Stoic philosophy. From the age of forty he spent his life in the turbulent but wealthy courts of the Diadochi: around 276 he settled at Pella, capital of Macedonia, at the court of Antigonus Gonatas, to whom he dedicated a *Hymn to Pan*; from there he moved to Syria, to the court of Antiochus, before returning to Macedonia. He died around 240 B.C.

Like many other intellectuals of the period, Aratus combined artistic with philological work. We have reports that he produced an edition of the *Odyssey* and we know that he composed numerous poetic works, including *epicedia* (i.e. funerary poems), epigrams (two are preserved in the *Palatine Anthology*) and brief occasional poems, which the sources call by the title *Catalepton* (Κατὰ λεπτόν: "brief and refined compositions"). But the literary sphere in which he was primarily distinguished was hexameter poetry on scientific themes, with the goal of popularisation. We know that he wrote *Iatrica* (Ἰατρικά), a work on a medical topic that is now lost, but we do still have the poem called *Phaenomena* (Φαινόμενα), on the topic of astronomy.

The poem consists of 1154 hexameters and opens with a hymn to Zeus (lines 1–18), which recalls Hesiod as model and reveals clearly the Stoic vision of the cosmos as inhabited and governed by the providential presence of the divine. The hymn ends with the poet's request to the god and the Muses that they help him in the composition of the work. From the point of view of content, the poem falls clearly into two distinct parts. The first part (lines 19–732) describes the constellations and tells the stories of the mythical figures from which they received their names. This structural arrangement allows Aratus to pursue numerous digressions on mythological topics, of which the longest (inspired by the Stoic concept of justice) concerns the sojourn among humans of Δίκη (Justice), who then abandons the Earth due to the steady corruption of the human race (a variation on the Hesiodic theme of the five human races). The second part of the poem (lines 733–1154) was known already in the time of Cicero by the title *Prognostica* (Προγνωστικά) and it contains ideas about meteorology, to enable identification of the signs that permit forecasts of atmospheric phenomena.

Aratus drew his scientific material for the *Phaenomena* from some specialist works: for the description of the map of the heavens he made use of treatments of astronomy by Eudoxus of Cnidus (fourth century B.C.: cf. *The Classical Age* XIII 2.6.2);

for the elements of meteorology he probably drew on material of Peripatetic origin, perhaps from a work on this topic by Theophrastus (we have a later version of this work under the title Περὶ σημείων or *On Weather Signs*). Various individual passages of the *Phaenomena*, in which Aratus misunderstands or completely distorts the explanations contained in his sources, show that he did not in reality possess deep scientific competence.

The poem makes extensive use of epic diction and of the distinctive features of didactic poetry. As is the norm in learned Hellenistic poetry, to understand the text fully it is necessary to recognise and correctly interpret the references to models: to Hesiod, but also the philosophical poems of Parmenides and Empedocles, from which the author of the *Phaenomena* knew the intractable difficulty of fitting the metre and diction of epic verse to an unusual subject-matter.

Aratus' poem found a notable resonance in the Hellenistic world and, as we have already noted, it was also used as a text for school instruction. But its fame is linked above all to the enormous popularity it enjoyed among the Romans, to the extent that it can boast a long series of Latin translations (we may note here those by Cicero and by Varro Atacinus, of which fragments survive) and the reprise of some parts of it in the *Georgics* of Vergil (Book I).

4.3 Nicander of Colophon

There are serious difficulties in identifying precisely the works written by Nicander, a native of Colophon who was active around the mid-second century B.C. The problems are caused by confusion with a namesake, another poet from Colophon who lived around a century earlier. Different ancient sources muddy the attributions when ascribing biographical details and works to one or the other. Considering the shared name and a shared link to the cult of Apollo, we may suppose that the two had some family relation: the earlier Nicander is recorded in an inscription found at Delphi, while the later one occupied a hereditary position as priest at the sanctuary of Apollo of Claros, near to Colophon.

The later Nicander was the son of a certain Damaeus and dedicated a poem to King Attalus III of Pergamum (138–133 B.C.). His oeuvre included various works in verse, including the *Eteroioumena* (Ἑτεροιούμενα; "Things Transformed"), which told myths of transformation in five books, a thematic criterion that would later be adopted by the Latin poet Ovid in the *Metamorphoses*. This poem is lost but a record of its content has reached us through a mythographical work in prose by Antoninus Liberalis in the second century A.D. The latter used Nicander's poem, but we do not know exactly how and to what extent he depended on it, and so the use of this source is rather problematic.

On the other hand, we do have preserved two short hexameter poems on the topic of pharmacology, which display an obvious affinity to each other in structure and content. The *Theriaca* (Θηριακά, a title that can be translated into English as *Remedies against Poisonous Animals*) opens with a short prologue of seven lines containing the dedication to a certain Hermesianax and then the poem narrates the origin of animal venoms from the blood of the Titans, before proceeding to present in general terms the most poisonous animals and the most effective antidotes (lines 8–144). Next, reptiles are described (lines 145–492) and the medicines needed to halt the effects of their bites (lines 493–714). Then follows the description of other poisonous animals, including spiders and scorpions (lines 715–836). The final part of the work contains a list of remedies (lines 837–956), followed by two lines (957–958) in which the author again addresses Hermesianax and mentions his own name as a closing seal (σφραγίς) to the work.

The *Alexipharmaca* (Ἀλεξιφάρμακα, i.e. *Antidotes against Poisons*) opens with the dedication to a certain Protagoras (lines 1–11). Then the author surveys numerous poisons, arranged according to the natural order (poisons of animal, vegetable and mineral origin); the description of the symptoms and effects produced by each of them is accompanied by the prescription of the appropriate remedy (lines 12–628). In this case, too, the work ends with two lines (629–630) that contain an address to the dedicatee and the author's seal.

The especially intractable material, with its need to introduce a large series of technical terms and provide necessary explanation, has left its mark by conferring a certain heaviness to the style of the two surviving poems. Despite the author's efforts to make such a technical subject appealing and effective as literature, it is inevitable that there is a certain repetitiveness due to the lists and repertories that structure the work, using expressive formula typical of medical language (such as the prescriptive imperative of medical recipes).

A number of other works in verse, of which a few fragments remain, are cited under the name of Nicander, but the problems of attribution have not been settled. Perhaps to be attributed to the Nicander of the second century B.C. is a work *Ornithogonia* (Ὀρνιθογονία), which collects mythical stories of transformations into birds. Other works concern technical and scientific topics, from agriculture to medicine: the *Georgica* (Γεωργικά) on horticulture, the *Melissourgica* (Μελισσουργικά) on the world of bees (their possible influence on Vergil's *Georgics* is debated) and the *Prognostica* (Προγνωστικά) inspired by the medical work of that name by Hippocrates.

5 Hellenistic epic and Apollonius Rhodius

5.1 Epic in the Hellenistic Age

5.1.1 Evolution of the genre

In presenting didactic poetry, we noted that the most traditional hexameter poetry of all, the epic genre, continued to flourish also during the Hellenistic Age. To take a step back, we may recall that from the Archaic to the Classical Age the establishment of first lyric and then theatre had pushed epic into second place, to an extent that caused the genre, though it was still practised abundantly, to lose vigour and liveliness in production and, especially, in innovation (cf. *The Classical Age* VII 1). One may talk of innovative impulses in mythological epic in the case of Antimachus of Colophon, who lived in the fifth to fourth century B.C.: some characteristics of his poetry anticipate, to some degree, developments in poetics that were realised fully in the Hellenistic Age (cf. *The Classical Age* VII 1.4). When Callimachus expressed his dislike for long-form poetry, he meant to refer above all to epic on the Homeric model, which poets contemporary to him practised following the familiar norms of the past, in order to meet the demands of an audience inclined to traditionalism. We should avoid the mistaken view that learned poetry of the Alexandrian-Callimachean type was the dominant fashion among the broader public. Beyond the restricted and select audience of the Alexandrian cultural elites, to whom the exclusive and refined output of the learned poets was addressed, there was a wider audience that took part in a whole series of collective occasions such as poetic contests and religious festivals, in the course of which itinerant poets, in the manner of the older rhapsodes, continued the custom of epic recitations. As we noted in our introduction to the Hellenistic Age, in this period there was a growing gap between a sophisticated high culture and a popular culture that was advancing along different paths (generally more conservative ones).

The learned Callimachus, therefore, directed his disapproval at this kind of unoriginal epic production, but not against the no less learned and sophisticated Apollonius Rhodius, as the widespread ancient tradition of a polemical rivalry between the two would have it (as we have mentioned in relation to Callimachus and to which we will return shortly). Apollonius' poem, the *Argonautica*, does not exhibit the features that Callimachus railed against, but seeks and fully achieves the very ideal of originality and literary elaboration that is one of the cornerstones of Alexandrian poetics.

5.1.2 The lost epic output

The *Argonautica* of Apollonius is the only Hellenistic epic poem to survive today. If we bear in mind that, as we have just mentioned, it held a highly distinctive position and represented a novelty within the genre, we can also see how the loss of the remaining output makes it much harder, and in part impossible, to evaluate its characteristics fully. It is at any rate generally believed (also on the basis of Callimachean polemic) that much of the remaining epic output was composed of works of little originality, which repeated the old system of epic forms and heroic values, in order to follow the taste of a general public disinclined to indulge artistic novelties.

For many authors all that remains is their name and the titles of their works, but there are some notices that, taken as a whole, give an idea of what has just been said above. The mythological themes were the ones that held the greatest appeal. Among the sources for the content of Apollonius Rhodius' poem, the ancient commentators mention the works of two Hellenistic epic poets, Cleon of Curium (on Cyprus) and Theolytus of Methymna. The latter also composed a poem on a Bacchic topic, as did Neoptolemus of Parium, author of, among other things, a lost *Poetics* that was one of the sources for Horace's *Ars poetica*. Poems on the *Theban Cycle* were composed by Antagoras of Rhodes and Menelaus of Aegae in Macedonia. On the saga of Heracles there were epic poems by Phaedimus of Bisanthe in Thrace, Diotimus of Adramyttium in Asia Minor and Rhianus of Bene on Crete.

Rhianus was a versatile figure. He was active in the second half of the third century B.C. as a poet, an erudite and a philologist (whose philological work was mentioned above, cf. *The Hellenistic Age* III 2.2). He wrote a mythological poem *Heraclea* about Heracles and some poems on ethnographic topics on the history of the Greek peoples, namely *Thessalica*, *Achaica*, *Eliaca* and *Messeniaca*, to which two papyrus fragments have been hypothetically assigned.

Like those of Rhianus, poetic works on themes from history and ethnography were produced by Demosthenes of Bithynia and Polycrates of Mende. Other authors, Simonides of Magnesia and Musaeus of Ephesus, composed poems that aimed for encomiastic praise of figures of royal rank: the former celebrated Antiochus I Soter (281–261 B.C.), son of the *diadochos* Seleucus I, founder of the dynasty of the Seleucids; the latter wrote for the dynasty of the Attalids reigning in Pergamum.

5.2 Apollonius Rhodius

5.2.1 Life

On the life of Apollonius we have some records in the *Suda* lexicon and in two short biographies that precede the text of the poem in some manuscripts. The meagerness of the surviving information is exacerbated by the frequent discrepancies within it, to the point that very little can be reconstructed with certainty.

He was born in the late fourth or early third century B.C. in Ptolemaic Egypt. The ancient sources disagree on his place of birth: Naucratis (a city on the Nile around 80 km south-east of Alexandria) or, more likely, in Alexandria itself. The surname "Rhodius" or "of Rhodes" has nothing to do with his native land, but derives rather from time spent on the island of Rhodes: he spent a period of voluntary exile on that island after the failure of the first circulation of his poem and the citizens of Rhodes granted him citizenship. The ancient anecdotal tradition claims that in his youth Apollonius was a pupil of Callimachus in Alexandria who later engaged in polemics against his teacher over their deep differences in poetic theory. As we noted already in the chapter on Callimachus, this tradition, which has enjoyed wide and long-lasting acceptance, has been strongly contested and may be an invention made up in the ancient world. What is certain is that Apollonius worked at Alexandria and devoted himself to varied scholarly studies and researches at the Museum there, earning the prestigious distinction of succeeding Zenodotus as director of the Library. He will have held this position for more than twenty years, from around 260 B.C. (when Zenodotus died) to Ptolemy III's accession to the throne in 246. As the director (ἐπιστάτης) of the library, in a custom that had previously been practised and would later become established, Apollonius also held the role of tutor to the son of King Ptolemy II, the future Ptolemy III Euergetes.

Other details, of doubtful reliability, are provided by the mentioned two biographies preserved in the manuscripts. They claim that Apollonius suffered a serious public embarrassment on the occasion of an ἐπίδειξις, a public recitation of his poem, or rather parts of it (from the scholia we can see that it concerned only Book I). He therefore chose to go into voluntary exile on the island of Rhodes, where he set about revising the work entirely. He then made a return to Alexandria, where it was the success of the second edition of the *Argonautica* that earned him the nomination as head of the Library. Today it is seen as likely that the poem was produced over a long enough period that Apollonius could have made public some parts of it at a young age. A first edition of part of it, or προέκδοσις, is mentioned in the scholia to Book I, which cite textual variants that differ between the first and second editions. Therefore we should not reject the reports of a first public recitation and a long gestation of the poem prior to the definitive version.

The stay on Rhodes, too, is an event that should not be considered an invention, yet the sequence presented by the ancient biography poses too many difficulties, above all because it is very hard to imagine that the initial failure, exile, return, success and directorship of the Library could all have happened before 260 B.C., when the poet was at most fifty years old. Further, one biography ends with the honours conferred on Apollonius at Rhodes. What is more likely, perhaps, is that the voluntary exile to Rhodes was not connected at all to the eventful composition of the *Argonautica* and belongs rather to the final years of the poet's life. A notice in the *Suda* lexicon says that Ptolemy III summoned Eratosthenes, a pupil of Apollonius, to Alexandria. It is usually held that this presumably occurred when the king ascended the throne in 246 B.C. and that it was then that he conferred on Eratosthenes the position of librarian. In that case, it would be understandable that Apollonius, probably disappointed by his former student, would have withdrawn to Rhodes. The date of his death is unknown.

5.2.2 The works

The only work by Apollonius that has been preserved entire is the *Argonautica* (Ἀργοναυτικά), a hexameter poem on a mythological topic, on which the author's fame depended already in the ancient world. We also have some meagre fragments of minor works, which can be classified into two distinct groups: poetic works and philological works in prose, a combination that, as we have seen, was characteristic of the Hellenistic Age and of Alexandrian culture in particular.

The former group includes the Κτίσεις or *Foundations*, in hexameters, which must have been inspired, in a spirit at once antiquarian and artistic, by the ancient historiographical genre of this name; it narrated the foundations of Alexandria, Naucratis, Caunus, Cnidus and Rhodes. The little poem *Canobus* (Κάνωβος), in choliambics, takes its name from the mythical helmsman of the ship of Menelaus (or, according to another version, of the god Osiris), who died in the Nile delta (where there is an island bearing his name) from the bite of a serpent and who was honoured by being transformed into a star (*katasterismos*, a literary motif that we have met in Callimachus' *The Lock of Berenice*). This work must have been inspired by the taste for aetiology and will have narrated the origin of Alexandrian cults. We also have records of epigrams by Apollonius, but the only surviving one attributed to him is probably spurious and takes as its theme the poetic rivalry with Callimachus.

Among the works of philology (on which cf. also *The Hellenistic Age* III 2.2) the sources cite some monographs on single authors of the Archaic and Classical Ages, such as Archilochus, Hesiod and Antimachus. His main philological work was on the text of Homer, the results of which deeply influenced his own poetic creation and certainly were set out, at least partly, in his work *Against Zenodotus*.

5.2.3 The *Argonautica*

The *Argonautica* are preserved via an abundant transmission that includes dozens of papyri of the Graeco-Roman Period and more than 50 manuscripts from the Middle Ages and Renaissance, supplemented by a rich indirect tradition.

The poem tells the mythical story of the conquest of the golden fleece by Jason and his companions, who set sail in the ship Argo and are hence called the Argonauts. The work is subdivided into four books, making a total of around six thousand lines, and it has a fairly linear structure. The first two books tell of the Argonauts' long voyage by sea from Pagasae in Thessaly to Colchis on the Black Sea. The topic of Book III is the eventful stay in Colchis, where the love story between Jason and Medea unfolds, and Book IV tells of the capture of the golden fleece and the adventures faced by the heroes on their way back to Thessaly.

> *Book I.* The work opens with an invocation to Apollo, followed by a rapid summary of the situation before the action begins: Pelias, king of Iolcus after usurping the throne of his brother, has commanded his nephew Jason to go on an impossible mission, namely to bring back the golden fleece, in return for which the crown will be restored to him. The many heroes who participate

in the adventure are presented, in a catalogue that takes as its model the Catalogue of Ships in the *Iliad*, but which is distinguished from it by the psychological and biographical depth in which the characters are presented. After Jason has bade farewell to those dear to him – particularly dramatic tones mark his leavetaking from his mother Alcimede – the heroes gather in assembly for the final preparations. Heracles is chosen as the leader of the expedition, but he declines it in favour of Jason. The ship Argo is launched and rites are celebrated to propitiate and win the favour of Apollo. During the sacrificial banquet, the belligerent Idas displays an insolent arrogance that provokes a reaction from the other heroes, but peace is restored by the bewitching song of Orpheus, who accompanies himself on the lyre as he sings a cosmogony with a Hesiodic flavour. At dawn the heroes embark and raise anchor. The rest of the book tells the first part of the voyage to Colchis. The first stage of the journey is to the island of Lemnos, where the women have killed all the men; by divine will, the arrival of the Argonauts will prevent the extinction of the Lemnians (Jason has a relationship with the queen Hypsipyle which prefigures that with Medea). After a year, reminded by Heracles of their mission, the heroes take to the sea again and reach Cyzicus. In alliance with the local population of Doliones they defeat the Giants but then, after setting sail and being driven back by the winds, they again encounter the Doliones. The two groups fail to recognise each other and, when conflict arises, the Argonauts slaughter their former allies. During a stop in Mysia, Heracles wanders away from the ship to look for his squire Hylas, who has disappeared (he has been abducted by a nymph at whose spring the young man had wanted to draw water). When the Argo sets sail, Heracles and Polyphemus, who had in vain run to the aid of Hylas, remain ashore. On board, a discussion arises and Telamon insinuates that Jason was jealous of Heracles and so had intentionally provoked his loss. However, the sea-god Glaucus explains to the Argonauts that the loss of the two heroes is part of a divine plan.

Book II. This book tells the second part of the voyage, up to the arrival at Colchis. In the country of the Bebrycians the Argonauts encounter the king Amycus who challenges to a boxing match whoever reaches his land. Pollux takes up the challenge and prevails over the brutal opponent thanks to his skill and the Argonauts exterminate the population. The heroes then encounter Phineus, the seer condemned by Zeus to blindness and a life of hardships for having revealed part of divine science to mankind. The Argonauts free him from the harassment of the Harpies, who continuously steal his food, and he predicts the itinerary that they will follow and the dangers they will face, until Aphrodite will resolve everything. The ship sets sail again and escapes various hazards including the clashing in the midst of the waves of the Symplegades cliffs at the entrance to the Black Sea. In the country of the Mariandyni they are welcomed by the king Lycus, who gives them as guide his son Dascylus. The seer Idmon, who had predicted his own death, is killed by a boar, and the helmsman Tiphys falls victim to a disease. Avoiding the country of the Amazons, the Argonauts encounter various peoples with bizarre customs: Chalybes, Tibarenians and Mossynoecians. On the island of Ares they find and help shipwrecked sailors: these are the sons of Phrixus, who had set off from Colchis for Orchomenus to recover the goods of their grandfather Athamas, and they accompany them as far as the mouth of the river Phasis, in the land of the Colchians.

Book III. This book, which takes as its subject the opposition between the Argonauts and Aeetes, king of Aia in Colchis, is dominated by the love story of Jason and Medea, the daughter of the king, set in motion by the will of Hera and Athena and the initiative of Aphrodite. After the assembly of the heroes has decided to attempt an amicable agreement with Aeetes, Jason and some companions reach the palace. Here his first encounter with Medea takes place; the god Eros, son of Aphrodite, pierces Medea's heart and enflames her love. The hero Argus presents to the king the request for the Fleece. At first the king, who fears a plot, reacts with rage. Then, when Jason persists, he consents to a pact that Jason must overcome a terrible triple test: to plough a field with bulls that breath fire, sow in it dragon's teeth and fight the giants that will rise from the sown field. Argus advises Jason to ask Medea's help. She, in the meantime, is undergoing her own psychological drama and spends anxious hours seized by the desire of love and the anxious doubt about whether to help the strangers and so come into conflict with her father. After overcoming the temptation of suicide, she resolves to prepare a magic potion that will tame the bulls of Aeetes. She goes to the temple of Hecate to meet Jason. He asks her help and she agrees, receiving in exchange the promise of fleeing with him to Greece and of marriage. The following day the test takes place, in which Jason succeeds, aided by the magic arts of Medea.

Book IV. Shaken by fear of her father, Medea gives the Argonauts the opportunity to seize the golden fleece by using a magic potion to put to sleep the dragon that guards it. The ship Argo sets sail, pursued by the Colchians, and enters the river Ister (the Danube). When Apsyrtus, the brother of Medea, who is leading the pursuit, catches up and corners them, the Argonauts are on the point of making a deal and handing over Medea, but Jason kills Apsyrtus who, in dying, stains his sister with his blood. The need to purify themselves from this contamination prompts the heroes to take a long diversion through the Adriatic. Travelling along the rivers Eridanus and Rhone, they emerge into the Tyrrhenian Sea and arrive at the isle of Elba, from where they proceed to the abode of Circe, who completes the purificatory rites. The voyage continues, encountering hazards, following the route previously taken by Odysseus. They too overcome Scylla, Planktai and Charybdis and flee from the Sirens, who are overcome by the song of Orpheus. After approaching Sicily near the pastures of the cows of the Sun, the ship lands at Drepane, city of the Phaeacians. Here the Argonauts find other Colchians, who want to return Medea to her homeland. The king Alcinous decides that he will judge the matter and, in order to prevent the departure of Medea, her wedding to Jason takes place. The ship sets off again on its voyage, but near Greece it is forced by a storm onto the coast of Libya. Instructed by the local nymphs, the heroes carry the ship across the desert to Lake Tritonis, from where they are able to return to the sea. After other misadventures near Crete, the ship halts at Aegina and finally reaches the gulf of Pagasae in Thessaly where the voyage began.

The story of Jason was quite popular and well known, being known already to Homer, who in the *Iliad* and *Odyssey* dramatised the adventures of the next generation of heroes after the Argonauts. Among Apollonius' more immediate sources, the scholia to the *Argonautica* indicate poems of that name by Theolytus of Methymna and Cleon of Curium (see above), as well as the part of Antimachus' *Lyde* that told of Medea's unhappy love for Jason. Apollonius departs from the traditional tale in some significant ways. It is hard to say whether he found them already in one of his sources, but it is certain that he gave them his own distinctive treatment. Among these we may note, in the backstory prior to the voyage, that in Apollonius' version Jason returns to Iolcus not in order to advance his dynastic claims but to seek reconciliation with Pelias, while the latter wants to be rid of his nephew because the oracle has foretold that he will die by the hand of one who appears before him with one bare foot, and Jason, arriving at Iolcus, has lost one of his sandals. Other modifications of the common version of the myth concern details that clearly aim to soften the image of Medea as diabolically violent and bloodthirsty. The most important change is certainly the metamorphosis of this character, which is presented by Apollonius by changes to the account of the horrible deaths of Medea's brother and of King Pelias in ways that reduce her responsibility. Apsyrtus, who was trying to capture his sister, is killed by Jason, though admittedly in a trap devised together with Medea, while the death of the usurper Pelias does not occur within the poem itself, but is merely announced as a punishment by Hera for neglecting her cult.

5.2.4 Epic model and Hellenistic poetics

The poetry of the *Argonautica* was long considered to be an unsuccessful imitation of Homeric *epos*, the result of an attempted emulation in an era when cultural values, poetic taste and the function and ways of enjoying literature had undergone profound changes. This judgement has been superseded thanks to a better understanding of the text, which, by simultaneously citing its epic model while also distancing itself from it, aims to define a new conception of the genre. The reuse of elements that are constitutive of epic does not mean passive repetition of its traditional characteristics, but is the precondition for a literary product that, by skilful artistic work of variation and differentiation, of allusion to the traditional norm and divergence from it, expresses the new sensibility of its contemporary world.

There are numerous episodes and details in the *Argonautica* that, through a skilful play with intertextuality, use this technique of variation to cite the text of the Homeric poems. The poet makes his own literary competence productive in creating a work in which allusion to the model (explicit or veiled), by varying expressive or thematic elements, continuously generates a depth of meaning. Detailed analysis of Apollonius' poetic diction constantly reveal a relation with archaic Greek epic through allusion and variation, imitation and distance, confrontation and emulation. These aspects are present in the very warp and weft of the poem's expressive fabric and they demand an interpretation that is at all times attentive and accomplished, capable of catching the infinite number of ways and means that the poet's erudite art calls upon in order to "dialogue" with his model, allowing him to treat it as an admired rival. Often the interaction between the poet and his model is complicated by the fact that Apollonius also mixes into the relationship elements drawn from Homeric exegesis. His reuse of, or rather his relationship with, the model is often mediated by an exegetical penumbra that forms part of his "Alexandrian" professionalism as an erudite grammarian. The first consequence of this way of making literature is that ignorance of the model (including its exegetical framework, to some degree) will prevent comprehension of the poetic text.

One of the most obvious citations is the catalogue of heroes at the start of Book I of the *Argonautica*, which has been shaped with an eye to the Catalogue of Ships in the *Iliad*. Analogously, the episode involving Jason's relationship with Hypsipyle on the island of Lemnos, which delays by a year the progress of the voyage in search of the golden fleece, is constructed on the model of the love of Odysseus and Calypso, the nymph who detained him for seven years on the island of Ogygia. In the story of the assembly of the women of Lemnos, on the other hand, what is at work is a kind of "reversal" of a situation typical of Iliadic epic, the assembly of warriors. Some interesting examples of this dynamic relation to the Homeric model are found in a comparison of Book IV with the *Odyssey*. The return journey of Jason and his companions in part repeats the itinerary followed by Odysseus in his voyage towards Ithaca, reusing the famous episodes of Scylla and Charybdis, the Sirens, the cows of the Sun and Circe. The narrative proceeds in the shadow of Homer, in the sense that it presupposes familiarity with the model in order to recognise the citations of it in the text and content. But at a structural and thematic level, there is a substantial difference between the return of Odysseus and that of Jason, since the former involves a voyage from Troy to Ithaca that progressively moves forward, and in which the heroic character of the protagonist is made clear. The voyage of Jason, to the contrary, follows a circular course that leads it back to its point of departure, implying that the adventure is an inconclusive wandering that made no progress, and it is telling that the most frequent sentiment of Jason and his companions is uncomfortable lack of confidence in the face of the difficulties and misadventures that persistently arise. The relation to the model, as we have said, does not aim to be a sterile repetition or imitation, but rather an original revisiting of it, endowed with new meanings. Thus the exordium of Book IV, which contains the request to the Muse to sing the sufferings of Medea, briefly alludes to the *incipit* of the *Iliad* and *Odyssey*, which are fused in a suggestive synthesis – with the significant difference that in this case the declared object of the song is not the trials of war or a hero's adventures, but the sufferings of a woman's love. The final line of the book and of the poem takes on a significant implication that underlines the literary and philological self-awareness of Apollonius' artistic creation: it clearly picks up *Odyssey* 23.296, which was regarded by the Alexandrian philologists as the line that marked the true end of the Homeric poem.

The *Argonautica* is thus not simply yet another poem composed in the wake of Homer (works of this kind were circulating in Apollonius' day too, as we have seen), but is the result of a complex cultural operation by a learned poet, who intended to re-found the genre of epic. Apollonius achieved this literary goal essentially by innovating in the narrative technique, by drawing on modes of narration borrowed from other genres.

One of the genres with the strongest presence for Apollonius in the composition of the *Argonautica* is dramatic poetry. It has been observed that the general structure of the poem (four books ranging from a minimum of 1285 to a maximum of 1781 lines each) picks up that of the tragic tetralogy. The influence of tragedy can be seen also at the level of content and in the organisation of the material. In the first place, the narration proceeds in large part through episodes that are linked but autonomous. As well as the motifs relating to heroes, warriors and adventures, which are typical of traditional epic, we find to a large degree the theme of love, treated in Book III at length and in psychological depth. And the story proceeds through dialogues, monologues, preparation of action and interior development of the characters, which all closely recall dramatic technique.

The depiction of the emotional development of Medea, whose passion for Jason is the true motor of events, has been seen as influenced by the image of this heroine created by Euripides in the tragedy *Medea*. The Medea of Euripides and that of Apollonius have the same energetic initiative, which compensates for the essential passivity of Jason, and both authors draw on the technique of not presenting the action itself, but rather the development of the protagonist's interior drama of hesitation and resolution, which is expressed in charged and dramatic monologues.

Another reflection of the dramatic representation of the epic story is the demystification of the traditional hero. The typical figure of the hero as monolithic in his bravery and physical vigour is personified in the poem by Heracles. The companions acclaim him as leader of the expedition and the choice of Jason is just a subsequent act of homage. It is Heracles who is the spokesman for their collective conscience while the adventure is languishing during the prolonged stay on the island of Lemnos and, significantly, the heroic Heracles departs the scene already before the ship reaches Colchis. The counterpoint to the semi-divine Heracles is Jason, a sort of anti-hero or "bourgeois" hero. It is interesting that Apollonius represents the companions of Jason as troubled by losing Heracles (to the point that Telamon insinuates that Jason had had an active role in the loss). This is confirmation of the difference from the heroic model that is expressed by the two figures. Oppressed in his fragile humanity by the tragic encounter with his own fate, Jason is the opposite of the traditional hero: his recurring and accustomed attitude is in fact dejection in the face of the tests he must face and which he overcomes not by his own personal virtues but by the providential help of other characters. Among these Medea stands out: in relation to her Jason plays an essentially passive role. It is thanks to the love of Medea, not the courage of Jason, that the Argonauts take possession of the golden fleece. And the conclusion of the entire story, as we have seen, is the completing of a circle that leads back to the point of departure.

In place of the essentially linear and uniform narration of traditional epic, Apollonius substitutes a greater freedom in organising the time of the narration: it tends to coincide less and less with the time of the story, in relation to which the author at times accelerates the narrative, by selecting from the material, abbreviating and cutting typical scenes and watering down the repetition and formulaic character proper to epic, but at times the author slows down the narrative, above all by introducing digressions and giving great space to the psychological component of the characters.

Another innovative aspect of Apollonius' epic compared to traditional epic is the simultaneous presence of the mythic past and the historical present. This is ensured by the aetiological interest in the origin of names, usages, cults and foundations of cities, as is present above all in the parts of the poem that recount the wanderings of the Argonauts (Books I–II and IV). The author's cultural sensibility and scholarly competence become functional aspects in a precise poetic conception that tends to historicise myth, using it to provide an explanation of historical data relevant to the present. As well as this narration of myth as a foundational element of the historical present (or *aition*: an element of Alexandrian poetics that we have recalled a number of times), we may add the wish to explain the mythical story in its entirety, jettisoning the traditional practice of narrating just one segment of a saga, which was itself set within the material of legendary cycles. This "narrative self-sufficiency" is achieved by Apollonius by using the technique of analepsis, that is, by recalling the mythical background. Epic narration thus becomes a site in which the unity of myth and history is achieved, in a continuum that runs from the most remote and obscure eras to the present.

An instance of this unity through poetry is the explicit presence of the author within the narration, a sort of *medium* who ensures the link between reality and the material that is subject of the literary narration. Breaking the rigid traditional convention of anonymity and objectivity in epic narration, Apollonius frequently intervenes in the first person to comment on his own tale with metaliterary observations, such as when he reminds himself not to deviate too far from the course of the main narrative. This is an aspect of narrative technique that expresses well the self-awareness and compositional mastery of the Hellenistic poets: we have seen how Callimachus, in the elegy on Acontius and Cydippe, breaches the literary convention by chastising himself for the excess of following the story where he pleases (*Aetia* III fr. 75, 8–9 Pf.).

Seen from this point of view, the distance between the aesthetic conception of Callimachus and that of Apollonius is sharply reduced and perhaps vanishes altogether, except for the decision to apply it to different genres, and hence to different literary problems. The ancient legend of the two poets' rivalry seems to have emerged, on the one hand, from the earliest of the many distortions of Apollonius' work, and on the other hand (as already noted) in all likelihood from a biographical study based merely on off-hand deductions from the texts and a fondness for reconstructing supposed rivalries and polemics between authors supposedly mirrored in the texts (the case of Pindar and Bacchylides comes to mind too). Beyond this, the real difference between the two consists at most in the fact that Callimachus resolved the question of the outmoded character of epic poetry by declining to practise it, whereas Apollonius, to the contrary, proposed to revitalise epic from within, by deciding to test himself on the most prestigious and toughest of the traditional genres, advancing and renewing the structures and expressive modes that had always belonged to it.

Admittedly Callimachus declares several times that he has little sympathy for long-form poetry, which he sees as lacking the continuous inspiration it requires, and he shows that he does not share the Aristotelian judgement that primacy in poetry goes to epic and tragedy. These are points that, to the contrary, apply fully to the poetry of Apollonius, who creates a new epic crossed with tragedy. However, there is a basic aesthetic affinity between Callimachus and Apollonius that is defined by the idea of a poetry that is elaborately refined, addressed to a sophisticated public able to catch the subtle and highly literary skein of allusions and deviations from the model, sometimes imperceptible to all but an expert ear, but always charged with meaning. Like the poetry of Callimachus, the *Argonautica* is an aristocratically exclusive work: one that plays the literary game of mixing different forms of expression (epic and tragedy) according to the Alexandrian precept of πολυείδεια ("variety of forms"); and one in which the use of antiquarian and geoethnographic competence, the erudite selection of the mythical variants and reconstruction of the connection between the mythical past and the present, thanks to the interest in aetiology, are foundational aspects of literary creation. These starting assumptions underlying all Apollonius' work make him the author not of an anachronistic imitation, but of a true revisiting of *epos* in the light of the most up-to-date poetics of the Hellenistic Age.

5.2.5 Language and style
The language of the *Argonautica* is of course that of Homeric diction, which, notwithstanding the possibility of some deviation, remains the basis of expression in the *epos*. We have already spoken above of the intertextual relations to the model, including at the level of linguistic expression. However, the innovative intentions operate at the level of language and style too, leading the author to update the morphology and vocabulary and to use a more complex syntax than that of Homer. In accord with the poetic norm of variation, as happens at the level of typical scenes, Apollonius reinterprets epic formulary by taking every opportunity to break with the typical repetitiousness that was linked, as we know, to the oral origins of archaic Greek epic.

5.2.6 Later reception
In the same way as with Callimachus, the poetic works of Apollonius Rhodius had a vast resonance in the Latin world, where there were some important "translations" or reworkings of the *Argonautica*. Famous among these are those of Varro Atacinus (first century B.C.) and Valerius Flaccus (first century A.D.). But the poem influenced Latin poetry more generally, becoming important above all for the formation of a poetics of epic in the Augustan Period. It is hard to measure the debt of Vergil to Apollonius, which can be seen in the story of Aeneas and Dido narrated in Book IV of the *Aeneid*, which is in large part modelled on that of Jason and Medea.

6 Theocritus and bucolic poetry

6.1 Bucolic-pastoral poetry and Hellenistic poetry

In the landscape of the literary production of the Hellenistic Age, bucolic or pastoral poetry occupies an important space. The genre, traditionally ascribed to the initiative of its "inventor" Theocritus of Syracuse, appears for us moderns too to be closely linked to this Syracusan poet, who, however, did not create it from scratch but picked up impulses and motifs that were already present in previous literature. In the archaic and classical tradition we can trace a seam of naturalistic and pastoral poetry, in various aspects including the setting and way of life, the oldest expression of which is in the Homeric poems themselves. There we find elements drawn from real rural life in the description of the shield of Achilles in Book XVIII of the *Iliad,* as also in the Polyphemus episode narrated in Book IX of the *Odyssey.* Further aspects and contexts from the world of the countryside and the life of herders were abundantly present in satyr drama. However, the most significant aspect, it seems, is that this poetic current had a wide diffusion above all at the level of popular culture, in the context of Sicilian rustic traditions. From here Theocritus must have drawn inspiration in order to "found" a new literary genre that was refined and stylised to a high degree, carrying out a very conscious and studied transformation of forms and contents as regards their modes, level and audience.

The medieval manuscripts that have transmitted the works of Theocritus preface them with a short treatise on bucolic poetry attributed to the grammarian Theon, who lived in the Augustan Period (cf. *The Hellenistic Age* III 2.4). Reconstructing the origin of the genre, the author of the little treatise presents three different versions, with the common element being a direct relation between pastoral poetry and popular and rural cult forms of the goddess Artemis in Laconia or Sicily. A cultic and religious connotation is in reality completely absent from Theocritean bucolic poetry and is perhaps to be explained as the product of ancient erudite studies following the pattern of the cultic origin of dramatic poetry proposed by Aristotle in the *Poetics.*

Represented by Theocritus and in the following century by Moschus and Bion, "sophisticated" bucolic poetry of the Hellenistic Period reached quite elevated levels of formal refinement and literary stylisation, moving decisively away from what must have been the level of the popular production of previous and contemporary times. The themes linked to the rustic world were adopted into the mainstream of the Hellenistic conception of poetics, with its starting assumptions that are more typical of a learned and exclusive poetry and the idea of the artistic product as an end in itself ("art for art's sake").

6.2 Theocritus of Syracuse

6.2.1 Biographical notices

The sources for our limited knowledge of Theocritus' biography consist of a *Life* preserved in the medieval manuscripts, information contained in the *hypotheseis* and in scholia to his poetry and some other scattered testimonia. A few details can be extracted from the works themselves: unfortunately these are not many but, as well as the uncertainty inevitable in biographical inferences drawn from poetic works, in this case we also need to consider the timeless character of bucolic poetry and the setting in a mythical past of the short epic narrative poems.

A first uncertainty is the poet's precise chronology. Since in some works he refers to persons and events that can be dated around the years 280–270 B.C., his date of birth should probably be placed around 300 B.C.

Theocritus' native land was Syracuse (as we learn also from some references in *Idyll* 28, *The Distaff*). Close connections to Sicily are also attested by *Idyll* 11 (*The Cyclops and Galatea*), where Polyphemus is in line 7 called ὁ Κύκλωψ ὁ παρ' ἁμίν, "Our countryman, the Cyclops," and 16 (*The Graces or Hieron*), in which the poet addresses encomiastic words to the Syracusan tyrant Hieron II, who took power in 275 B.C. But other hints indicate that he must have spent long periods away from Sicily.

The knowledge of the island of Cos that emerges from *Idyll* 7 (*The Harvest Festival*) leads us to assume that he spent time there. The mention in that idyll of Philitas, the poet and philologist with close connections to the Egyptian court of the Ptolemies and whose poetic excellence Theocritus acknowledges (line 40), seems to confirm that he spent part of his life on the island and that he perhaps belonged to the famous school of Philitas. A further trace of Theocritus' familiarity with this geographical area comes from other poems, which reveal botanical knowledge more characteristic of the eastern Mediterranean environment than of that of Sicily.

From the setting of *Idyll* 15 (*The Women from Syracuse*) we can deduce that Theocritus made a journey to Alexandria. The existence of significant connections to the Ptolemaic court is well attested by the composition of an encomium (*Idyll* 17) to Ptolemy II Philadelphus (283–246 B.C.) and by the eulogising tones used towards the king here and there in Theocritus' work. The encomium is dated to 273/2 B.C. and so cannot be much later than that for Hieron of Syracuse, from whom Theocritus evidently failed to win protection. Some suppose that at Alexandria Theocritus knew Callimachus and came into contact with the cultural world of the Museum. We cannot be certain of this, which at a biographical level is purely hypothetical (although it seems hard to imagine that when visiting Alexandria Theocritus would not have made the acquaintance of these circles), but from precise references contained in the surviving work it is apparent that Theocritus knew at least the poetry of Callimachus and Apollonius Rhodius. Unlike them, however, it is practically certain that he did not hold any official position within the Ptolemaic cultural institutions.

6.2.2 The works

As we will see, the works of Theocritus have survived, via the medieval manuscripts, within a heterogeneous corpus that includes poems attributed to him that are in reality spurious, and also works by other poets, such as Bion, Moschus, Simmias and anonymous poems. Some papyrus fragments attest interventions by Hellenistic grammarians, a sign that the work of Theocritus was edited and studied in the ancient world, even before the grammarian Artemidorus of Tarsus published the collection of the bucolic poets in the first century B.C. (cf. *The Hellenistic Age* IV 6.3).

Among the thirty-one poems of the strictly Theocritean corpus, thirty are transmitted by the medieval manuscripts, while we possess the first part of one other (*Poem* 31) thanks to a papyrus. The authenticity of some poems is debated or rejected, namely *Poems* 8, 9, 19–21, 23, 25 and 27. The most famous poems in the corpus are those linked to the theme of love in a pastoral or rural setting, in which goatherds and other herders compete in poetic competitions, often with a background of love, within the rustic context of a stylised countryside. These are the bucolic idylls, in Doric dialect, a genre of which Theocritus was and is considered to be the "inventor": these are poems 1, 3–7, 10 and 11 of the corpus. The term "idyll" (εἰδύλλιον) in antiquity designated all the Theocritean poems, that is, not just those on bucolic topics, as is the preferred usage today. The significance of the term, which is a diminutive of εἶδος, is not clear. Perhaps it indicated generically a "small composition" and was adopted by the Alexandrians to designate short poems on various topics. It was probably the particular importance of the bucolic poems within the Theocritean corpus that resulted in the term eventually coming to designate these poems only, for which reason today the term "idyll" is used specifically for this genre of poem.

Aside from the bucolic idylls, therefore, Theocritus' output is quite varied and picks up important poetic genres typical of the Hellenistic Age: the epyllion (cf. *The Hellenistic Age* IV 1.2), in Ionic-Homeric dialect (poems 13, 22, 24, 26), and the mime (cf. *The Classical Age* V 4.1.2) in Doric-Syracusan dialect (2, 14, 15). Other poems pick up various forms of traditional lyric: sympotic and homoerotic poems, which in content and form reprise the Aeolic tradition and Anacreon (12, 29, 30), encomia (16, 17), an epithalamium (18) and a dedicatory epigram (28). In general all these works, in their recollection of lyric genres of the ancient archaic and classical tradition, are characterised by the mixture of different genres and forms, a procedure that corresponds to a specific decision on poetics (as has been noted a number of times already) which matches the general Hellenistic conception of poetry and which to different degrees characterises most of Theocritus' work. Of *Poem* 31, as we have said, we have only around thirty lines thanks to a papyrus. Finally, the manuscripts of Theocritus and the *Palatine Anthology* have also transmitted twenty-four epigrams under this poet's name.

6.2.3 The bucolic idylls

The manuscript tradition unanimously transmits as the first poem of the Theocritean corpus the idyll called *Thyrsis* or *Song*. This exhibits some of the recurring characteristics of the bucolic genre, such as dialogue and poetic song among herders and tones of melancholic nostalgia, and seems to take on an exemplary and programmatic standing. The idealised representation of nature and its inhabitants is a consistent trait of the genre, in which the herders and the people of the countryside are primarily singers and poets. A herder asks Thyrsis to perform a song, offering as gift, among other things, an inlaid wooden bowl. The theme chosen by Thyrsis concerns Daphnis, a mythical figure of the pastoral world – a herdsman of great beauty who was brought up by the nymphs of the woods – whose death is narrated in an obscure and allusive way. The song therefore takes on the tones of funerary lament and describes herders, animals and gods who hurry to the man's deathbed.

Idyll 3 (*The Goatherd*) is the subtly ironic representation of a pastoral serenade by a lovestruck goatherd outside a cave where the herdswoman Amaryllis lives, following the urban fashion of the *paraklausithyron* (the "serenade outside a closed door"). *Idyll* 4 (*The Herdsmen*) is the direct dialogue (i.e., not set out by a narrator's voice) between the goatherd Battus and the cowherd Corydon. The two converse on various topics, drawing a stylised picture characteristic of the rustic world and its people.

The Goatherd's Performance (and) Shepherd's Performance is the title of *Idyll* 5, which is regarded as one of the most important of Theocritus' works, since it stages in the form of a direct dramatic dialogue a bucolic contest, i.e., a verbal competition between herders to win a prize.

> The dialogue is between the goatherd Comatas and the shepherd Lacon: after a tightly-woven exchange with mutual insults, the two challenge each other in pastoral song before the wood-cutter Morson, whose judgement will fall on Comatas.

The structure of the poem seems to reflect the real habits of this type of rural competition, in its strongly aggressive tone based on the power of quick repartee. The definition of this type of competition as "amoebaean song" derives from the Greek adjective ἀμοιβαῖος, which means "exchanging" or "reciprocal" and refers to bantering exchanges. As is clear from this poem, victory goes to whichever of the two contenders has given the best "return" to the opponent, by responding well enough to his insinuations and insults.

The agonistic motif returns, but in peaceable tones, in *Idyll* 6, entitled *The Bucolic Singers*.

> The herders Daphnis and Damoetas confront each other in song, recalling the unrequited love of the cyclops Polyphemus for the nymph Galatea. The nymph embarks on a lover's quarrel, making a fool of the cyclops who is madly in love with her. Damoetas, who impersonates Polyphemus in the fiction, responds to the questions of Daphnis.

Within the collection, and in general in Theocritus' work, particular importance is held by *Idyll* 7, *The Harvest Festival* (*The Thalysia*), in which literary critics have detected a veiled but authoritative declaration about poetics. A bucolic contest set in the rural countryside of the island of Cos (where, as we have said above, Theocritus must have spent time and perhaps was part of the group around Philitas) provides the occasion for a kind of consecration of the poet himself as inventor of the bucolic genre.

> The author, in fact, stages himself in the guise of the herdsman Simichidas, who recounts in epic tones an episode that occurred during his voyage to Cos on the occasion of the Thalysia harvest

festival in honour of Demeter. With two of his friends he encounters the goatherd Lycidas, who is regarded by all as a great poet. After an exchange of banter, Simichidas proposes a bucolic contest. The two compete in turn in pastoral song and at the end Lycidas definitively grants to Simichidas the baton that he had offered as a sign of hospitality, in recognition of his poetic skill. The idyll closes with the description of a luxuriant natural scene where perfumes and colours run riot.

In the dialogue between Lycidas and Simichidas some literary questions are touched on that were very much current in the third century B.C., such as the dispute on long-form poetry (of which we have spoken repeatedly in relation to Callimachus) – Lycidas condemns the traditional epic poem. Further, the gift of the baton to Simichidas has been seen as a symbol of Theocritus' investiture as a bucolic poet by a semidivine figure, which is how Lycidas is presented. The model for this episode seems to be the gift of the poet's sceptre to Hesiod by the Muses (prooemium of the *Theogony*), matching the preference for Hesiod that we have encountered many times among the Hellenistic poets.

Idyll 10 (*The Laborers*) leaves the strictly bucolic model and presents the dialogue and alternating song of two rural labourers, Milon and Bucaeus. The hardship of labour and the emotion of love are the topics of their song, which draws on popular traditions. *Idyll* 11 (*The Cyclops and Galatea*) returns to the theme of the unhappy love of Polyphemus (who is here presented, following a less common tradition, as a young herdsman) for the nymph Galatea. The story is inserted into the frame of a letter sent by Nicias, a doctor of Miletus who is a friend of the poet.

6.2.4 The other "idylls"

In the Theocritean corpus we find another series of poems, for which we shall retain the traditional generic term "idylls," which are clearly built on the traditions of mime, epyllion and other poetic forms, sometimes with obvious mixing of genres.

Mimes go back to the work of Sophron (cfr. *The Classical Age* V 4.1.2) and their greatest Hellenistic exponent is Herodas (cf. below 8). It should be said that the elements of this poetic genre (above all the realism of the situations described and of the form of expression) recur in much of Theocritus' work, yet some of his poems are more obviously structured according to the canons proper to mime. Poems 2, 14 and 15 are termed urban mimes, that is, they have an urban setting (whereas *Idyll* 4, which we have mentioned above, could also be considered a rural mime).

Idyll 2 (*The Sorceresses*) is set on Cos and has as its protagonist Simaetha.

The woman is in love with a man who does not return her love and she is seized by contradictory feelings, of passion and revenge. During the night, while she is preparing a magic potion assisted by a slave called Thestylis, Simaetha recalls her own love story leading up to her present unhappiness. In the finale, the nocturnal quiet seems to soften the woman's troubled state of mind.

In *Idyll* 14 (*Aeschinas and Thyonichus*) Aeschinas is in dialogue with his friend Thyonichus, explaining to him the reasons for his disappointment in love; since Cynisca, the woman he loves, does not return his feelings, he intends to enlist as a mercenary.

The most famous mime of Theocritus is *Idyll* 15 (*The Women from Syracuse*, or *The Women at the Festival of Adonis*).

> The protagonists of the mime are Gorgo and Praxinoa, two women from Syracuse who live at Alexandria, the elegant capital of the Ptolemies. The impressions of the two provincials as they come into contact with the varied and astonishing reality of the metropolis is the lens through which Theocritus presents a vivid image of the Graeco-Egyptian city. The annual festivities in honour of Adonis are underway, which Queen Arsinoe wishes to be particularly magnificent. A series of small scenes and little episodes, linked by the conversation of the two women, leads us from a domestic, family setting onto the streets of Alexandria, lively and colourful for the festival, and from there to the palace of the Ptolemies, the epicentre and climax of the festivities.

Some of the poems are epyllia, that is, short poems on a mythological subject (of the type of Callimachus' *Hecale*).

In *Idyll* 13 (*Hylas*) the motif of the letter to the friend Nicias returns, providing the frame for the narration of Heracles' love for the youth Hylas, who was abducted by the nymphs when he was drawing water from a spring. The text shows obvious parallels with the account of Apollonius Rhodius (*Argonautica* Book I), which is an earlier work. The mixture of literary forms different and distant from each other, such as the religious hymn, epic narrative and dramatic dialogue, characterises *Idyll* 22 (*The Dioscuri*), which likewise picks up motifs present already in the *Argonautica* of Apollonius Rhodius. The figure of Heracles returns in *Idyll* 24 (*Baby Heracles*), which narrates the famous episode of the infant hero killing the snakes sent by Hera. *Idyll* 26 (*The Bacchae*), which is of debated authenticity, takes as subject the killing of Pentheus, guilty of opposing the introduction of the cult of Dionysus, by his mother Agave; the final part of the poem follows the pattern of a hymn.

The adoption of literary genres from the older and more authoritative tradition can be seen more strongly in some of the poems, which evoke other forms. The erotic-symposiastic tradition is the inspiration for *Idyll* 12 (*The Beloved Boy*), in hexameters and Ionic dialect. *Idylls* 16 and 17 are linked by their shared encomiastic content: the former (*The Graces or Hieron*) is addressed to the tyrant Hieron of Syracuse; the second (*Encomium of Ptolemy*) is dedicated to Philadelphus. *Idyll* 18 (*Wedding Song for Helen*) builds on the very ancient tradition of wedding poetry, combining it with epic narrative about this heroine, the wife of Menelaus. In *Idyll* 28 (*The Distaff*) we have an example of a dedicatory epigram in Aeolic language and metre: the poem accompanies the gift of a golden distaff given by the poet to the wife of his friend Nicias. Aeolic lyric on homoerotic themes is picked up in *Idylls* 29 and 30, entitled *Love Poem to a Boy* (Παιδικά), which derive from sympotic poetry of the Alcaean type.

6.2.5 The *Epigrams*

Thanks to the manuscript tradition of the corpus and to that of the *Palatine Anthology*, we know twenty-five epigrams attributed to Theocritus that are probably authentic. They pick up themes and forms from the epigrammatic tradition and can be divided into funerary, dedicatory and ecphrastic poems. Among the last group a series of lyrics is preserved that is centred on the description of statues of famous poets, such as Archilochus and Hipponax. It should be emphasised that these customary themes are accompanied, above all in *Epigrams* 1–6, by the bucolic motifs dear to this poet.

6.2.6 Theocritean poetics

Theocritus' concept of poetics fits fully into the Hellenistic-Alexandrian literary vision that we have tried to elucidate in the previous chapters. The preference for short-form poetry, with limited content and elaborate, sophisticated form, is an element shared by this poet with various other contemporary figures, above all Callimachus. What is perhaps the most interesting expression of Theocritus' advanced artistic research is the mixing of different genres, which we have seen in the survey of the works. This is an artistic choice that responds to a poetic taste that was widespread in Alexandrian poetry, but which in the texts of Theocritus is taken to unique levels of experimental boldness and sophistication.

However, Theocritus' original contribution comes from his choice of a pastoral setting, with its creation of a language of imagery and style that would be a success in Rome (the *Bucolics* of Vergil) and have an immense resonance much later, in some important literary moments of the medieval and modern Ages (Boccaccio, Sannazaro, Tasso). The peculiarity of Theocritus' choice consists in taking a humble social world as a space to express a refined and elite poetic sensibility. The representation of the rustic world of herders is done with a forceful degree of realism, a significant contribution to which is made by knowledge of specific aspects of pastoral society as well as of the plants and animals raised and frequent use of language that tends to reproduce colloquial expression. In the same way, there is a realistic foundation to the re-use – which is to a certain extent an element of erudition – of the very ancient popular usage of holding bucolic contests.

Yet it is clear that this representation appears in Theocritean poetry in a form far removed from true realism in the modern sense of a reflection of concrete reality. The bucolic world is completely idealised. The traits and contents adopted from the real setting of the natural world and the work in the fields serve to construct a poetic world that is completely transfigured as literature, subordinated to the artistic goal of asserting poetic values that are highly sophisticated and the fruit of intellectual reflection. The statements of poetics themselves that are scattered throughout the works and the polished use of the crossing of genres are manifestations of Theocritus' exceptionally high level of artistic self-awareness.

6.2.7 Language and style

In Theocritus' poetry it is the Doric dialect that is most prevalent or, to put it better, a strong Doric colouring combined, in the frequent use of hexameter and distich, with an essentially Ionic-Homeric linguistic base. Since the use of Doric was foreign to the hexameter of the Homeric epic tradition, this linguistic fact is important in itself. The quantity of Doricisms varies, but it remains the case that the strongest impression given by the metre and language is of an artificial language created by a very studied and sophisticated literary blending. Also contributing to this is the generous use of colloquialism and popular forms of language, intermixed with the other elements mentioned above. By far the most common metre (with few exceptions) is the hexameter, used not only for genres traditionally composed in other metres, even lyric poetry, but also in ways that would be absolutely unthinkable in the epic tradition: colloquial addresses and amoebaean dialogue are the most striking examples.

6.3 The bucolic corpus: Moschus, Bion and the "figured" poems

We have already referred to the fact that the medieval manuscript tradition has preserved a collection or corpus of bucolic poetry consisting of works attributed to Theocritus, Moschus, Bion, Simmias and anonymous poems. Some hints lead us to believe that the creator of this collection was the first-century B.C. grammarian Artemidorus, who aimed to bring together in this way a set of work that was homogeneous in character, but for which he did not have a complete edition. Less secure is the idea that Theon, son of Artemidorus, produced an edition of the work of Theocritus alone that was known at Rome (we may recall that knowledge of Theocritus' work was fundamental for the poet Vergil). Theocritus, therefore, unlike Callimachus, was not the editor of his own work and it is for this reason too that the poems transmitted under his name are not all in fact authentic. The corpus that has preserved his poems, as we have said, contains (as well as texts by other authors) also some bucolic texts attributed to him that are spurious. The two most important authors of the bucolic corpus inspired by Theocritus' manner of poetry are Moschus and Bion.

Moschus, originally from Syracuse, lived in the second century B.C. and, according to ancient tradition (the *Suda* lexicon), was a pupil of the great Alexandrian philologist Aristarchus of Samothrace. In the surviving works we can clearly see the influence of Theocritus, both at the generic level of composition and in the language and style. His most important surviving work is an epyllion of 166 hexameters entitled *Europa*, on the story of the young woman abducted by Zeus in the form of a bull. We then have a long epigram in hexameters, *Eros the Runaway*: Aphrodite makes an announcement in which she reports the flight of this god and provides a kind of identikit that describes the fugitive's features. An epigram in elegiac distichs is preserved in the *Palatine Anthology*. Other works that are of some interest should be regarded as inauthentic: the little poem *Megara*, in which the mother of Heracles, Alcmene, and his wife, Megara, lament the death of the Heraclids and foresee the death of Heracles. Also spurious is the *Lament for Bion*, which exhibits clear reminiscences of the *Thyrsis* of Theocritus and probably should be assigned to a pupil of Bion.

Bion of Smyrna too probably lived in the second century B.C. and, like Moschus, took as his model Theocritean bucolic poetry. He was the author of a *Lament for Adonis*, on the unhappy fate of the mythical lover of Aphrodite. Dominant in this work are the pursuit of pathos, the expressive charm of musical effects and a taste for minute description. These can be seen in the account of the death of Adonis, with the choral lament and the grief of the goddess.

The bucolic corpus includes six works called "figured" poems, since the lines of verse that constitute them have a length and arrangement on the written page that reproduces the silhouette of the objects about which they are written. It is possible that they were intended to be carved or written on real objects, but this is by no means a necessary assumption. The experimental and playful character of these poems, which are true literary divertissements, is the origin of the name given them already in antiquity: τεχνοπαίγνια (*technopaignia*, i.e "games of art"). The earliest of the surviving "figured" poems are *The Axe*, *The Wings* and *The Egg*, attributed to Simmias of Rhodes, whom we have already mentioned above (cf. above 2.1.5). Another, *The Panpipe* (Σῦριγξ), is attributed by the tradition to Theocritus, but modern scholars take a different view. The final two poems are both entitled *The Altar*: one in Ionic dialect is attributed to a certain Besantinus and one in Doric dialect is assigned to a certain Dosiadas.

7 Ancient genres and new poetics

7.1 Selection and preservation

Our knowledge of the poetry of the Hellenistic Age comes primarily from the preserved works of authors of great artistic and intellectual stature such as Callimachus, Apollonius Rhodius and Theocritus. This is the result of the sifting done by the passage of time and by the selection made already by the ancients themselves. But it is also the case that the real cultural depth of these figures has meant that attention tends to focus on them. Yet we should not deny that the production of poetry was a widespread and fertile cultural phenomenon in this period and that sadly much of it is irrecoverably lost. We may recall again that the majority of surviving Hellenistic poetry is from the third or at most the first part of the second century B.C. and was written in Alexandria or, if not, has links to Alexandria, while we have very little of the poetry written from the mid-second through to the first century B.C. (which had a very important influence on Latin poetry). Epigram is the only genre for which extensive documentation has survived from the second century and so continues for us without a break until the Late Antique Period. We also know little about authors and poetic movements outside Alexandria, and so our information suffers from geographical limitations as well as chronological ones.

Yet still within this picture, alongside the three major figures, a number of other poets have been noted and considered already in the previous chapters, from Philitas to the major epigrammatists, from Aratus to Nicander, to Moschus and Bion and various other less important figures. Now we should recall some further important poets, who, for various reasons, have played a prominent role in the history of Greek literature but who cannot be relegated to the undifferentiated limbo of the category "minor poets."

7.2 Lycophron of Chalcis

The name of Lycophron is linked equally to the history of poetry and to that of philology of the Hellenistic Age. As we have already noted (cf. *The Hellenistic Age* III 2.2), in the early phases of Alexandrian philological activity (when Zenodotus was librarian), Lycophron was given the task of studying the texts of the authors of Attic comedy (whereas Alexander Aetolus was concerned with tragedy). Unfortunately, we know very little about his philological work, since practically nothing has survived. In his poetic output, Lycophron was a productive and appreciated author of tragedies. We still have one original work from him, entitled *Alexandra*, in iambic trimeters and inspired by the forms and contents of major tragic poetry.

The authorship of the work has been doubted, since it seems to contain a reference to the battle of Cynoscephalae in 197 B.C., an event that can be securely placed after the death of Lycophron, whose date of birth should be set around 330 B.C. However, the chronological discrepancies within the work can easily be explained as the result of interpolations by later authors. Lycophron's homeland was Chalcis, on the island of Euboea. At Eretria, another city on that island, he received his training from the philosopher Menedemus (the founder of the so-called school of Eretria, which was heir to the school of Elis of the Socratic philosopher Phaedo). A turning point in the poet's life occurred when, around 285 B.C. he moved to Alexandria, where he worked at the Library. We do not know the date of his death.

Lycophron's researches and scholarly interests flowed into a treatise *On Comedy*, which seems to have contained, in particular, detailed analyses of glosses typical of comic poets. On the literary side of his output, in antiquity he seems to have found great fame as an author of tragedies, winning a place among the poets of the "Pleiad" (cf. *The Hellenistic Age* II 2.2). Late sources attribute dozens of theatrical works to him, of which all that survives is a single brief fragment (from *The Sons of Pelops*).

Alexandra consists of a long, unbroken monologue of tragic type (that is, a *rhēsis*) in 1474 iambic trimeters. On the day that the young Paris leaves for Sparta, from where he will return after abducting Helen, a servant reports to the Trojan king Priam the prophecies that he has heard from the king's daughter Alexandra, another name of the prophetess Cassandra. The narrative voice of the servant forms the frame, at the start and close of the work, for the young woman's words.

> The messenger speech reproduces word for word the prophecies of Alexandra-Cassandra, which foretell the Trojan War, the city's fall and the subsequent sufferings of the Greeks on their home-ward journeys, a counterpoint to the troubles suffered by the Trojans (in a compensatory logic found already in the *Trojan Women* of Euripides). The adventures of Odysseus, within the account of the *nostoi*, holds a central position in the overall organisation of the work (lines 648–819). Then follows the account of the destiny of the Trojans after the Fall of Troy, linked to the foundation and later greatness of Rome. The returns of the Greeks and the Trojan diaspora prompt the description of the first colonisation of the western Mediterranean, based essentially on the historical account of Timaeus of Tauromenium (cf. *The Hellenistic Age* VIII 1.4.3). Then there is the recollection of the earliest conflict between Europe and Asia, beginning from mythical origins (the abduction of Io), following a traditional scheme already attested by the start of *The Histories* of Herodotus. The prophecies close with the lament of Alexandra at the incredulity of her fellow citizens. Then the servant brings the monologue to an end and only at this point do we learn of the circumstances in which he had heard what he has just reported: Priam had set him to guard his daughter, who is being held in prison (lines 1467–1471).

Continuous interest in *Alexandra* in the ancient world is attested by the existence of scholia and of a commentary produced in the twelfth century by the Byzantine scholar Johannes Tzetzes. He considered the work to be a dramatic monody, evidently seeing in it a combination of expressive means drawn from lyric and those of a theatrical character. There is no doubt that, following a poetic approach perfectly at home in Alexandrian literature (Callimachus and Theocritus come to mind), Lycophron has undertaken a crossing of different genres: tragedy, lyric and *epos*.

The style of Lycophron, which is proverbially obscure and oracular in type, privileges the connotative aspects of metaphorical language through a generous use of hidden allusions and ambiguous reference, arcane and erudite imagery, cryptic and enigmatic expression. The effect of obscurity is accentuated by the use of rare and exotic words and *hapax legomena*, a mixing of dialects and the use of archaisms. The result is a text charged with meanings and bristling with interpretive difficulties.

7.3 Euphorion of Chalcis

Euphorion of Chalcis lived in the mid-third century and was enthusiastically committed to the poetics of Callimachus, whom he chose as his own model. His birth can be placed around 275–270 B.C. He completed philosophical and grammatical studies at Athens, he spent time in Thrace and towards 220 he was summoned by Antiochus III (223–187 B.C.) to direct the library of the city of Antioch. It seems that he was never at Alexandria. He died and was buried either in Antioch itself, or in Apamea on the Orontes.

We know many titles of his works, though we cannot always detect their nature, and for some of them we have a small number of fragments. The *Suda* lexicon provides us with the titles of three poetic works in hexameters: *Hesiod*, *Mopsopia*, *Chiliades*. The second of these may have been about stories and legends of Attica, given that Mopsopia is another name for Attica (probably from the name of Mopsopus, a mythical Attic king and hero). The *Chiliades*, in five books, contained a collection of oracles that came true after a thousand years. We do not know if the title *Curses or The Cup-Thief* – we have a fragment of it thanks to a parchment find – refers to an independent work or to a section of the *Chiliades*: the poet mentions mythological examples of cursing someone who has robbed him. It seems that invectives were also contained in *Thrax* which was probably an epyllion. There are also two surviving epigrams.

From the fragments, and also on the basis of ancient judgements, Euphorion appears to have been a typical representative of Hellenistic poetry, or, better, of Alexandrian poetry, since, despite his apparent lack of direct connections to Alexandria, his inspiration seems in its poetics and style to be very close to Callimachus, indeed he appears to have been one of his strictest followers.

7.4 Sotades

A contemporary of Callimachus and Theocritus, Sotades had close connections to Ptolemy II Philadelphus, writing a poem on the occasion of his marriage to his sister Arsinoe. Legend has it that the king was offended, since the poet described in obscene terms, and as an impious act, the union between the two royal siblings. For this, Ptolemy decreed that Sotades be thrown into the sea shut up in a lead chest.

It is attested by fr. 1 that the work did indeed contain scurrilous and obscene jokes about the wedding pair. In the same poem (assuming that fr. 16 too was part of it) Sotades underlined the incestuous nature of the union, comparing it to the noble mythical parallel of the wedding between Zeus and his sister Hera. The verbal aggression, both joking and obscene, directed at the newly married couple is in some respects part of the customary ceremony from the archaic tradition. What is certain, however, is that in this period, while poets such as Callimachus and Theocritus addressed the king in refined encomia, the tone chosen by Sotades must have sounded like an insolent, as well as courageous, criticism.

His fame in antiquity depended on two different literary aspects. The first is the production of poetic texts with licentious content, for which Sotades was included among the poets called "cinaedologues" (with reference to the licentiousness of the *cinaedi*). The poet's primary role in this thematic sphere is revealed by the ancient testimonia about poems "in the manner of Sotades" or "Sotadeans," some of which survive, and about some poets who imitated him, who were called "Sotadici." The second aspect is the frequent use of a type of verse, the ionic tetrameter *a maiore*, which takes its name from him as the sotadean verse. It is said that he rewrote the *Iliad* in lines of this type.

7.5 Iambographi: Phoenix and Cercidas

Iambic poetry enjoyed great success during the Archaic Age and its aggressive and polemical tone then provided meat for ancient comedy. As an author of iambics in the Hellenistic Age we have already encountered Callimachus, and in the next chapter we will discuss Herodas in relation to the particular form of the *mimiambus*. Here we will recall two other poets who were distinguished in this ancient genre: Phoenix and Cercidas.

Phoenix of Colophon was born towards the end of the fourth century B.C. and was author of a collection of songs in at least two books. The surviving fragments are in choliambic lines and are characterised by themes and motifs that are common in the genre, such as a popular tone and moralising themes. His model, so far as we can tell, is Hipponax. Athenaeus has preserved two quite extensive texts: a funerary epigram on the Assyrian king Ninus (24 lines) and a poetic imitation (21 lines, entitled *Korōnistai*, i.e. *Beggars*) from the *Korōnisma*, a popular song of itinerant beggars. Further, a florilegium on papyrus conserves a poem in 23 lines, partially damaged, addressed to those who live amid abundance without knowing that true riches lie in wisdom.

Cercidas of Megalopolis in Arcadia lived between 290 and 220 B.C. He held political, diplomatic and military positions in the Arcadian League, which was led by his city against Sparta, and he pursued legislative activity (we may recall, among other things, a provision he proposed that would oblige the youth of the city to memorise the Catalogue of Ships from the *Iliad*). He was a follower of the Cynic philosophy, which has left clear traces in his poems, the *Meliambi*, i.e. "sung iambics." In the surviving fragments, motifs typical of Cynic diatribe are predominant, such as criticising vicious habits and devotion to pleasure and urging a return to the autarky of living according to nature. Cercidas was also the author of choliambics (in the manner of Hipponax). From the archaic iambic tradition he also adopted the traits of inventing fantastic and expressive verbal compounds and mixing linguistic forms (using Attic and epic forms alongside the Doric base).

7.6 Melinno

Under the name of the poetess Melinno all that remains is a hymn to Rome in sapphic stanzas, preserved by Strabo (who describes her as "Lesbian," evidently due to the metre, but the language displays only sporadic elements of Aeolic dialect). A scholarly knowledge of the Greek literary tradition, from Homer to the lyricists to the theatre, is combined in this text with the exaltation of Rome and its power (a motif that will be reprised with vigour by the Latin poets of the Augustan Period). The dating is debated: for the most part this poetess is placed in the Roman Republican Period, in the second to first century B.C.; other date her later, to the first to second century A.D.

8 Mime and Herodas

8.1 Mime: a dramatic genre of popular origin

In ancient Greek the term μῖμος (*mimos*) designated both the actor who publicly performed short realistic and parodic imitations of attitudes and situations from everyday life, and also the genre of these representations itself. It is an artistic form that can be connected to burlesque and buffonesque theatre, which was certainly of popular origin and diffusion, structured in short, fast scenes in which the dominant role was played by gesture, vocal articulation, facial and physical mimicry and dance movements.

The genre seems to have had its origin in the western Greek world, probably in Sicily, and it absorbed aspects of popular and burlesque theatrical practice from Italic culture. We may note its affinity with *phallophoria* (ritual ceremonies in which a model of a phallus was carried in procession), with the phlyax (the tragicomic form to which Rhinthon gave literary standing in the fourth century B.C.) and with Megarian farce (cf. *The Hellenistic Age* II 2.4 and *The Classical Age* III 1.4). Companies of travelling players used to improvise spectacles in public squares and private houses. The object of the representations were often human "types" that lent themselves to caricature, characteristic figures drawn from the world of professions, such as the vainglorious and boastful soldier or the charlatan who tries to hawk his latest idea. The actors' recitation was done in large part by improvising, on the basis of a generic plot that functioned as a basis for improvisation. The popular character of the genre is revealed also in the fact that, normally and in contrast to comic and tragic theatre, the actors of mime recited their lines with uncovered faces and without specific types of footwear. For this reason, the mime actor was called *planipes*, "barefoot," by the Latins. The performance might be sung to musical accompaniment or just recited, and it might require several actors or just one solo mime.

The earliest author of literary mimes seems to have been Sophron (cf. *The Classical Age* V 4.1.2), who lived at Syracuse in the second half of the fifth century B.C. The lively dialogues in rhythmic prose and Doric language that he composed were enjoyed by Plato, who contributed to their diffusion at Athens and perhaps drew inspiration from them for the ironic characterisation in some of his philosophical dialogues. The wide diffusion of Sophron's work favoured a revival of the genre during the Hellenistic Age. At that time the output became specialised into dialogue mimes, close to the model of Sophron, and lyrical mimes, that is, sung to the accompaniment of the cithara or *aulos* (the term μιμαυλός, *mimaulos*, probably refers to an "*auletes for mimes*"), in which situations typical of traditional lyric poetry, above all love, were represented in parodic tones and humorous exaggeration. It also seems that in the Hellenistic Age mime enjoyed a new heyday at the popular level, with new performances of a realistic character offered by companies of actors. The ancient sources mention different forms of mime, such as *hilarōdia* (i.e. "cheerful song"), which stuck to moderate tones in its recitation, and the *magōdia* (i.e. "song of the *magos*" i.e. enchanter, charlatan), which was open to more comic aspects and a taste for the obscene.

Mime in the manner of Sophron was thus revived in the works of Hellenistic poets, but in a cultural and literary context of greater sophistication. We have already spoken of the mimes among Theocritus' works; in the present chapter we will discuss the mimes of Herodas.

8.2 The *Mimiambi* of Herodas

Of Herodas (the name is transmitted also in the form Herondas) we know very little and that little is in large part deduced from his preserved works, with the problems we have repeatedly mentioned. The theories about his origins alternate between a city in a Doric context (perhaps Syracuse) and the island of Cos, on the basis of the mention of that island in some of the mimes and of the discovery in inscriptions on Cos of personal names used by Herodas for his characters. The era in which he lived is the third century B.C. and the cultural setting to which he belonged is that of the cultured and lively Alexandria of the Ptolemies.

We knew very little of Herodas' works – just a few fragments from the indirect tradition – until the publication in 1891 of a papyrus roll of the first century A.D. (*P. British Museum* 135) containing eight mimes and the start of a ninth in choliambic or scazontic verse, which gave rise to the ancient name "mimiambi." The papyrus is badly damaged in the final part, so the texts of the eighth and ninth mimes are severely lacunose.

The decision to use choliambs should be considered a precise poetic positioning: along with the traditional mimetic-dramatic character and *verismo* of the genre of mime, Herodas intended to add also the liveliness and quick-witted realism of iambic poetry in the manner of Hipponax, who was generally regarded as the inventor of the choliamb. The *Mimiambi* consist of scenes from daily life, featuring characters of different social positions and with strong characterisation. The language, too, is marked by realism, reproducing slang forms from popular speech.

Mimiambus 1, *A Matchmaker or Procuress*, takes its name from the protagonist Gyllis, who tries in vain to persuade Metriche, whose husband is away in Egypt, to give in to the desires of a lover:

to tempt the woman, Gyllis boasts of the qualities of the suitor, who is described as rich and as a man of impressive physique.

In *Mimiambus* 2, *A Brothel-Keeper*, the manager of a brothel delivers a speech to the judges of Cos, accusing the merchant Thales and calling for him to be condemned to a heavy fine because he entered the brothel by force and tried to abduct one of the girls, by the name of Myrtale. *A Schoolmaster* is the title of *Mimiambus* 3: Metrotime entrusts to the teacher Lampriscus her son Cottalus, who is running wild, so that he may subject him to a harsh punishment. The master takes the woman at her word and starts to whip Cottalus, until the boy, freed, runs away with a sneer.

Mimiambus 4, entitled *Women Dedicating and Sacrificing to Asclepius*, has as its protagonists two women, Cynno and Coccale, who arrive at the sanctuary of Asclepius on the island of Cos to thank the god for a cure. On the visit, the women are impressed by the beauty of the sanctuary, which provides an opportunity to describe the works of art contained in it. The mime ends with the announcement to the women that the sacrifice that they had requested has been propitious.

The title of *Mimiambus* 5, *A Jealous Person*, alludes to Bitinna, who has been cheated on by her lover, who is also her slave, and now she intends to subject him to a severe punishment. She has him bound but, before the punishment has taken place, the pleas of the slavewoman Cydilla make her relent from her decision.

In *Mimiambus* 6, *Women in a Friendly or Private Situation*, Metro has seen in the house of her friend Nossis a tempting leather phallus that belongs to Coritto, and so she goes to see the latter to ask for the name of the leatherworker who made it. By doing this, Metro gets into trouble: Coritto had lent the phallus to Eubule, who had then lent it to Nossis unbeknown to its owner. Coritto is furious, but in the end she calms down and fulfils Metro's request.

Mimiambus 7 has the title *A Cobbler* and is set in the workshop of Cerdon. His client Metro has brought two friends to buy shoes and the leatherworker tries to persuade them to make a purchase, praising the merits of his products and showering the potential clients with flattery. The two women make purchases and Metro receives in return from Cerdon the promise of a pair of shoes as a gift.

Mimiambus 8, *A Dream*, differs sharply from the previous ones in the allegorical character of its content, the interpretation of which is particularly difficult. A character narrates to a slavewoman that he has had a dream: a goat that he was bringing through a wood had eaten some leaves of oak within a sacred precinct, provoking a violent reaction from some herders engaged in a rite in honour of Dionysus. The herders killed the goat and made a wineskin out of its hide. They then set a challenge to see who could jump on the wineskin without falling. No one succeeded except the narrator himself, but he receives not the promised prize but just rebukes from an old man. Of the attempts at interpretation, the most likely solution is that the allegory in the mimiambus has a polemical literary meaning: the contest with the herders symbolises the competition of Herodas with his rival poets, who are represented as incapable of producing the "lame" Muse of the choliamb in the manner of Hipponax.

The final mimiambus contained in the papyrus, no. 9, is too lacunose and damaged to be able to reconstruct the content.

The most prominent aspect of these poems is the mimetic ability displayed by their author in the representation of little everyday scenes in quite different contexts and registers: the judicial setting of *Mimiambus* 2, rendered with a careful use of the technical procedural language and with reference to precise moments in the legal process; the familiar and confidential tones of women's conversation, reproduced in the dialogue of the two visitors to the temple of Asclepius, in *Mimiambus* 4; the humorous licentiousness of the two friends in *Mimiambus* 6; and the colourful garrulity of Metrotime in *Mimiambus* 3 or of the leatherworker who is the protagonist of *Mimiambus* 7.

As well as these purely literary aspects of the realistic slices of everyday life contained in the *Mimiambi*, these poems also have a documentary importance for cultural history, aiding the reconstruction of settings and social contexts that are otherwise unknown. One eloquent example is the fact that *A Schoolmaster*, aside from the exaggerations due to the genre of mime, is a powerful and expressive testimony to the didactic method and specific practice of the elementary instruction employed in the author's times, including the use of harsh corporal punishment.

Herodas' shrewd artistic vision and his taste for the reuse and variation of literary models emerge very clearly in the mimiambus *Women Dedicating and Sacrificing to Asclepius*. The motif of devotees who go on pilgrimage to the temple is one of the most frequent themes in the sphere of realistic mime, from *The Women Viewing the Isthmian Festival* of Sophron to *The Women from Syracuse* of Theocritus; but the theme was known also in comedy, if Epicharmus composed a play called *Pilgrims*. The fully literary character of this mimiamb of Herodas is confirmed by the use of the digressive technique of describing the monuments and art works (*ekphrasis*), a typical and widely used element throughout Alexandrian poetry.

A decisive confirmation that Herodas should be ranked among the learned poets trained in the Alexandrian approach is offered by *Mimiambus* 8. In the summary above we noted the most likely interpretation, which sees this allegorical poem, with its motif of the dream, a theme that since Hesiod had played the role of introducing an author's reflections on his own artistic activity, as a polemical and articulated declaration of poetics. The statement of his own originality and artistic primacy (in having combined the *Hipponactean* iambic with the dialogue of mime) invites comparison with the proud declarations of a poet of the stature of Callimachus (to whom the Latin author Pliny the Younger likened Herodas) and establishes that the author of the *Mimiambi* fully belongs to the erudite setting of contemporary debate on poetics.

It is not clear in what form these poems were published, but their high level of literary craftsmanship leaves no doubt about the cultural level of the audience to which they were addressed and rules out the notion of a popular audience. Their recherché and precious formal character leads one to suspect a performance style that had a low degree of spectacularity, for example being read aloud within restricted circles, which would make it possible to appreciate the artistic fabric of the text. Another possibility is that the mimes were declaimed by a solo actor, who would take care to give a different rendering to each character in the performance. A further hypothesis is, to the contrary, that the mimiambs were recited by a troupe of actors in a true theatrical presentation. In support of this last interpretation, there are some factors shared with theatrical works: the dialogue structure of the mimes, which sometimes involve several characters; the observation of unities of time, place and action; the use of dramaturgical expedients, such as the technique of the "aside" in

Mimiambus 1 or references to objects and persons present "on the stage" put in the mouth of the characters; and the absence of any descriptive interventions by the author.

The linguistic texture of the mimes of Herodas is Ionic with Attic forms. Similarly to the iambic poetry of Hipponax, which beneath apparent expressive immediacy conceals a studied awareness of language and stylistic registers, the *Mimiambi* too show a studied use of vocabulary alluding subtly to terms and expressions from the literary tradition. Alongside elegant and refined forms from high literature, these texts accept stylistic features and expressive forms borrowed from the popular language, such as the use of metaphor, proverbial sayings and neologisms, reused in an erudite linguistic tapestry.

V The Hellenistic Philosophies

1 The primacy of ethics and the problem of happiness

1.1 General characteristics

The profound political and cultural changes experienced by the Greek *poleis*, above all the end of their age-old independence, could not but have a series of striking consequences for philosophical reflection and how it related to the citizens' life and activities. The shift of the centre of gravity from the heart of the city to the great capitals of the Hellenistic kingdoms, with the consequent weakening of the spirit of active and committed participation in government by all the citizens, directly affected the role and function of the philosopher too. A philosopher no longer felt – and indeed no longer was – able to exert direct influence on decisions concerning the community and events in the *polis*. A distancing from civic reality was inevitable: the philosopher and the citizen-politician were no longer the same individual. The collective addressed by the philosopher was no longer the population of the city, but a circle of followers who individually, within their own private sphere, wanted to receive instruction on wise conduct and a reassuring existential model.

The new interlocutor, or rather the new target, of the philosophers was now the personal conscience of individuals who had their own needs and problems, which were to be addressed and solved with a private form of wisdom. Despite clear differences, which were often characterised by lively polemics, the Hellenistic philosophies had some traits in common. A first essential point is the primacy of ethics, which were geared towards reflection that was practical in character, with the goal of pointing out models of living that could grant serenity and happiness in human life. Yet it is important to note that the Hellenistic philosophies were organised into genuine "systems" composed of precise subjects: physics, which studied the fundamental characteristics of the world (and so provided the foundations for the other parts); logic, encompassing theory of knowledge; and ethics, the themes of which stood in an organic relation to the other parts of the system. The primary importance of ethics cannot be understood outwith the overall framework in which it was set, as we will see.

Philosophical reflection generally seems at this time to have been responding to a pressing demand for ethical values that might provide criteria for behaviour and an existential framework for individuals, since their collective and personal identity had lost its traditional setting and their political frame of reference was undergoing further continuous changes in perspective, from the various Hellenistic kingdoms to the arrival of the Roman conquerors. A sense of insecurity took hold in people's minds. A demand for reassuring values that could shelter them from a certain precariousness perceived in their changing circumstances was therefore linked to a demand for

https://doi.org/10.1515/9783110426328-025

proposed and suggested ways of living that would make it possible to achieve a private ideal of unshakeable happiness and peaceful existence.

Ethics, the discipline able to provide the tranquillity and imperturbability of the sage, thus came to hold primacy within philosophical reflection. All this explains the substantial rejection by thinkers of the Hellenistic Age of the dualism that had been the foundation of Plato's vision of the world. Picking up and developing an orientation that was already present in Socratic thought and above all in the Socratic schools, the Hellenistic philosophers decisively rejected the metaphysical support on which Plato and Aristotle had based their ethics. The Hellenistics, instead, focused all their "ontological" research on the sensible physical world and on identifying principles that are immanent in the reality of the world, in the conviction that it is possible for man to pursue a happy life in this world.

1.2 The philosophical schools in the Hellenistic world

The landscape of philosophy in the Hellenistic world includes the development of old and prestigious schools as well as the birth of new schools of thought. At Athens the Academy of Plato and the Peripatos of Aristotle continued to exist, with very different results and differing success. The Socratic schools, which had germinated out of the fertile thought of Socrates, also continued to develop. In the final years of the fourth century B.C. some important and original philosophical currents then arose, which were in turn structured into schools under the leadership of a founder and then his successors (or scholarchs) chosen from among the most loyal and capable disciples. These currents are Scepticism, Epicureanism and Stoicism. Both in continuity and in breach with the preceding philosophical tradition, Greek thought of the Hellenistic Age succeeded in formulating concepts and realising new ethical models of real importance that had an enormous influence on Roman civilisation and then on the culture of the medieval and modern eras.

We have already traced the development of the Peripatos after Aristotle (cf. *The Classical Age* XIII 3.8). After Theophrastus (and so around 287 B.C.) the next scholarch was Straton of Lampsacus, who held the position until his death around 270. All his works are lost and only fragments survive. Straton (with the by-name ὁ φυσικός, "the scholar of nature") abandoned the metaphysical aspects of Aristotelian doctrine and proceeded along the predominantly "scientific" path of Theophrastus, marking a further stage on the way to the independence of the various sciences from philosophy, which would develop in full in the Hellenistic Age and in particular at Alexandria. He was dedicated above all to the study of nature, holding that it could be explained on the basis of the elements, taking into consideration the Aristotelian doctrine of bodies and of movement (the great astronomer Aristarchus of Samos was one of his pupils). Probably in the final years of the fourth century he was summoned to Alexandria by Ptolemy I as one of the tutors of the future Ptolemy II and he stayed there for some time, before returning to Athens in 287 to become scholarch. A few years later another pupil of Theophrastus moved to Alexandria, namely Demetrius of Phaleron, who remained there until his death (cf. *The Classical Age* XIII 3.8.2; *The Hellenistic Age* I 2 and III 2.1). The impulse toward natural science, erudition, historical and literary research developed above all in Alexandria and its cultural institutions, where it was a key source of fruitful work – the scientific disciplines yielded their best and most abundant fruits outside the traditional and institutional setting of the Aristotelian school (cf. further below, *The Hellenistic Age* VI 1.1). The school itself, under the scholarchs after Straton (figures of little importance: Lyco, Ariston of Ceos, Critolaus, Diodorus of Tyre), continued to teach the thought of the master but without any originality. A new impulse towards Aristotelianism came from the publication of Aristotle's esoteric writings at Rome by Andronicus of Rhodes (second half of the first century B.C.: cf. *The Classical Age* XIII 3.3 and 3.5). The rekindled interest gave rise to a rich exegetical activity, which culminated in the second and third centuries A.D. with the great commentary of Alexander of Aphrodisias and continued for many centuries, producing the impressive output of Aristotelian commentaries in Late Antiquity and the Byzantine Age.

Also discussed above was the early phase of the Academy after Plato, the period known as the "Old Academy" (cf. *The Classical Age* XIII 2.6). The works of Xenocrates of Chalcedon (scholarch after Speusippus, 339–314 B.C.) are lost and little can be reconstructed from the fragments. He stressed some religious aspects of the late Plato regarding the conception of the cosmos. In the field of ethics he maintained that virtue alone is not sufficient for happiness, approaching a problem that would be of great interest to the Hellenistic philosophies. It seems that he was the first to introduce the longlasting tripartite division of philosophy into logic, physics and ethics. He was followed as scholarch by Polemon (314–270) and Crates of Athens (270–268). In the spirit of the times, both of them emphasised ethical problems, neglecting the theoretical aspect of Platonic thought. After Crates, the next scholarch was Arcesilaus of Pitane, with whom the Academy took a decisive sceptical turn: we will discuss this shortly, when treating scepticism.

We have already provided sufficient treatment of the Socratic schools, which took us down to the third century and so fully into the Hellenistic Age (cf. *The Classical Age* IV 2.2). We will here note only that, among the developments of Socratic philosophy applied to the practical life, what stands out in the Hellenistic Age is the provocative testimony and pungent social polemic of the Cynics. In the Hellenistic philosophical landscape, Cynicism is an important component: a movement rather than a school, inspired by the model of Diogenes and his immediate followers (cf. *The Classical Age* IV 2.2.2) and followed also by poets such as Cercidas of Megalopolis (cf. *The Hellenistic Age* IV 7.5). The link to Socrates was stressed already by the ancients, who also saw in Cynicism a precursor of Stoicism. In fact a succession was traced (in Greek the term is *diadochē*: the authors of *Diadochai*, *Successions*, set out to identify and establish the teacher-student successions in the various schools): Socrates – Antisthenes – Diogenes the Cynic – Crates of Thebes – Zeno.

The new schools of thought were Scepticism, Epicureanism and Stoicism. Scepticism picked up a faint but constant thread that already ran through sectors of the philosophy of the Classical Age, namely the idea of the fallibility and imperfection of human knowledge. Epicureanism takes its name from the founder, Epicurus of Samos, who around 306 B.C. opened his school at Athens. The central problem of all his reflection was the search for a way of leading one's life that would guarantee individual happiness. The same issue held primary importance in Stoicism, the philosophical current that originated in the school founded by Zeno of Citium, likewise at Athens, around 300 B.C. As we will see, the answers given by the Stoic philosophers were some distance from those of the Epicureans. The latter identified happiness with the satisfaction of elementary needs (and so wisely indulging nature), but the Stoics identified, rather, the *logos* as the universal principle immanent in the cosmos, a rational law to which the sage conformed, finding in this the happiness of virtue.

2 Scepticism

2.1 *Skepsis* in Greek thought

The term *skepsis*, "investigation," "research" and then "doubt," in a philosophical context indicates a type of research inspired by methodic doubt which never reaches secure conclusions or certain advances, and sometimes even comes to deny the very possibility of knowledge. A similar pessimistic concept of the possibility of knowledge is found here and there in the thought of the philosophers of the Classical Age, above all in the thought of the Sophists and Socrates. A "sceptical" issue can be seen at the origin of both the Sophists' relativism about subjective truths and also the continuous demystification of acquired convictions practised in the thought of Socrates, which rarely arrives at the "truth," the existence of which, however, was taken as given. There is a pessimistic current of thought about the possibilities of human knowledge, which was pushed aside by the epistemological confidence of Platonism and Aristotelianism. Scepticism reacted against this optimism about the human attainability of certain and absolute knowledge.

2.2 Pyrrhon and Scepticism

Pyrrhon of Elis (in the western Peloponnese) lived from roughly 360 to 270 B.C. and is recorded by the ancients as the initiator of Scepticism. In his native city he was able to attend the teaching of his fellow countryman Phaedon, the disciple of Socrates, and it seems that he also heard lectures by Socratics of the Megarian school (cf. *The*

Classical Age IV 2.2.4). In his personal and cultural formation a quite significant role was played by the journey he undertook to the East following the expedition of Alexander the Great. Also participating in that journey was the Democritean philosopher Anaxarchus of Abdera, from whom Pyrrhon learned the doctrine of Democritus, above all as regards ethical aspects linked to the imperturbability of the sage. On that occasion, then, he came into contact with various forms of eastern wisdom, in particular with the asceticism of the gymnosophists (i.e., the Brahmans, the Indian priestly caste with whom the Greeks came into contact in the time of Alexander the Great), who trained themselves to a life without emotions or disturbances and to indifference to bodily suffering.

Once he had returned home, Pyrrhon began his philosophical teaching. In homage to the idea that a lived philosophy is superior to speculative activity, which had marked the lives also of Socrates and Diogenes, he left behind no writings on his thought at all, entrusting it solely to oral conversation. To attempt to reconstruct his doctrines it is therefore necessary to rely on testimonies scattered through various later sources, such as the section on him in Book IX of the *Lives of the Philosophers* by Diogenes Laertius and a collection of citations in other authors, including some Latin ones. We can also use the fragments of lost works by his student Timon of Phlius (whom we shall discuss shortly), though he already represented a form of thought different from that of his teacher. By any reckoning, the use of these materials is subject to many doubts and uncertainties. In reconstructing genuinely Pyrrhonian thought, we gain very little help from the three books of *Outlines of Pyrrhonism* by Sextus Empiricus, a philosopher and medic of the second to third century A.D., which bring together a tradition that knew practically nothing of Pyrrhon's own ideas anymore.

In Pyrrhon's thought, ontological problems are addressed in unequivocally pessimistic terms, but precisely this ontological pessimism opens up the prospect of a happy human life. An important testimony, which goes back to Timon (see below), reports that Pyrrhon maintained that all things are equally indifferent and that one cannot express a judgement on them; therefore, neither our sensations nor our opinions tell us what is true or false, so we should be without opinions, uncommitted and indifferent. Since it is impossible for humans to rely on the objectivity of the real such that certain and justified judgements could be expressed, consequently nothing is true in an absolute way and it is not possible to distinguish anything from anything else. Reality appears to the human eye as indifferent or indistinct and, since it is impossible to state anything about it, it is also useless to do so. This idea of the vacuity of any statement about the real is expressed by Pyrrhon with the term ἀφασία (*aphasia*, "inability to talk"). This radical pessimism in ontology and gnoseology extends its consequences also in the ethical sphere: man is not in a position to determine moral principles that correspond to absolute truths and cannot pronounce judgements on what is just or unjust, true or false, good or bad. Since everything is indifferent, in his lived ethics the sage conforms to this characteristic of reality: things lose their value and significance, and man is thus withdrawn from passions and from needs that are not elementary and gains the tranquil indifference to external occurrences, *ataraxia*, that is the rule of life that achieves happiness.

As we have said, Pyrrhon's disciple and interpreter of his philosophy was Timon of Phlius in the Argolid (ca. 320–230 B.C.), a multifaceted figure – a travelling thinker, poet and dramatist. He expounded and popularised his teacher's theories in various works in prose and verse, of which all that remains are fragments and testimonia. He wrote the Ἰνδαλμοί (*Indalmoi*, i.e. *Images* or *Appearances*) in elegiac distichs, which gave a portrait of his teacher sketched through a meeting at a temple of Amphiaraus, and the *Silloi*, poetic satires in hexameters composed on the model of the work of that name by Xenophanes of Colophon. In this last work there was a dispute between philosophers and a descent into Hades in the company of his model Xenophanes, in which the author violently mocks the philosophers (including some contemporary ones, such as Epicurus and Zeno) immersed in interminable and insoluble disputes in search of absolute truths, which are counterpointed by the quiet and serenity in which Pyrrhon is found.

2.3 Scepticism and the Academy

In the overall picture of the currents of scepticism, Pyrrhon remains an isolated thinker. The sceptical phase of the Academy is entirely distinct and independent from him and his teaching. Academic Scepticism developed rather from a scepticising interpretation of the Socrates of the Platonic dialogues and within the landscape of the anti-theoretical tendencies of the Socratic schools.

The successor to Crates as scholarch, Arcesilaus of Pitane (on the Aeolic coast of Asia Minor, at the mouth of the River Caicus), who lived from ca. 315 to 240 B.C., found in Socrates the sceptical method that he applied to his teaching. He adopted the Platonic distinction between knowledge and opinion, assigning a negative value to the latter, but decisively called into doubt the possibility of the former. In sum, he affirmed the precariousness of them both, to the point that he practically denied that knowledge is possible and identified as the most correct approach the suspension of judgement about anything, in Greek ἐποχή (*epochē*). Arcesilaus directed a polemic against the Stoics on the possibility of acquiring certain knowledge, even by an intuitive route (the reply was that Arcesilaus was contradicting himself, since he affirms that one cannot know anything certain, yet affirms that this proposition is certainly true). But the scepticism of Arcesilaus seems less radical than that of Pyrrhon, since he admits the existence of a rational capacity, which can be acquired on the basis of natural instinct.

The firm convictions of the Stoics in gnoseology were opposed polemically also by Carneades (ca. 219–130 B.C.), who gave a probabilistic direction to Scepticism. All representations are deceptive, but he admits that man can express certain judgements and can try to approach the truth via approximations guided by the criterion of verisimilitude. In 155 B.C. he took part in the Athenian diplomatic mission to Rome to defend the Greek philosophers, who had been subject to hostility from the Roman government. In the manner of the ancient Sophists, he made a vivid impression on his audience with a display of dialectic in which he demonstrated the equal validity of opposing theses on the topic of justice.

A sceptical orientation and anti-Stoic polemic also characterise the thought of Philon of Larissa, who was head of the Academy from roughly 110 B.C. He moved to Rome in 88 B.C. and was the teacher of Cicero. More moderate tones were adopted by his pupil Antiochus of Ascalon (second to first century B.C.). The latter's pronounced eclecticism was open also to points of contact with Platonic thought and Stoicism (interpreted as a kind of disguised Platonism) and he admitted Stoic elements into his own doctrine, gaining some success among the many people who aspired to a moderate and conciliatory form of thought.

3 Epicureanism

3.1 Optimism without hope

The philosophy of Epicurus, insofar as we are able to reconstruct it from his preserved or fragmentary writings and from indirect testimonia, is one of the most original and fascinating forms of thought conceived by Hellenistic civilisation. The most intriguing aspect lies in its combination of views that appear to be mutually opposed. On the one hand, there is the harshness and disenchantment of its vision of reality, which leaves neither man nor nature any escape from the fate of death and corruption and which acknowledges that human existence has a propensity towards pain and evil. On the other hand, there is the idea that this awareness of the human condition is a necessary preliminary step towards recognising the perfect route to personal happiness. This happiness takes the negative form of the absence of pain and disturbance and the positive form of the prospect of a quiet and serene existence in which it will be possible to enjoy true pleasures. The fascinating "contradiction" in the thought of Epicurus would seduce a sensitive poet such as the Latin author Lucretius (in whose poetry, however, the awareness of pain that pervades nature seems to overwhelm confidence in individual happiness) and many other Roman thinkers.

3.2 Life and works of Epicurus

The founder of Epicureanism was born at Samos in 341 B.C. His father Neocles was an Athenian citizen who had settled on that island as a colonist and therefore Epicurus too enjoyed all the rights of Athenian citizenship. According to Strabo, he completed his *ephēbia* together with Menander, his exact contemporary. His first contacts with philosophy brought him close to Platonic thought and to the atomism of Democritus. Very soon he worked out the first philosophical developments of his own and began to teach at Lampsacus (in the Troad) and at Mytilene. Perhaps in 307 (the date is not entirely secure) he settled definitively at Athens, where he remained until his death in 270. In 306 at Athens he opened his school, which was generally known as the Garden (in Greek κῆπος, *kēpos*), since it was located in a building surrounded by a garden, where Epicurus also lived and led a communal life with his followers. Very soon, for those who sympathised with Epicurus' thought the Garden became the symbol of a genuine refuge from the troubles and evils of life and of a place where one could cultivate the prospect of individual happiness.

Ancient tradition attributes to Epicurus a fairly large number of works, around 300; proportionally, very little survives. The philosopher and historian of philosophy Diogenes Laertius (third century A.D.) has preserved for us three letters from Epicurus, which form a sort of compendium of his thought: the *Letter to Herodotus* addresses physics, the *Letter to Menoeceus* takes ethics as its topic, and the *Letter to Pythocles* concerns the celestial phenomena. Also preserved is a collection of forty *Principal Doctrines* (Κύριαι δόξαι), which contain instructions for moral conduct in the brief form of maxims; further, a manuscript in the Vatican Library preserves a collection of other moral sayings (*Gnomologium Vaticanum*). To these major remains of his thought should be added firstly a number of fragments of *On Nature*, a work of thirty-seven books, which have been restored from carbonised papyri (so far as it is possible to read them) from the Epicurean library found in the excavation of Herculaneum, and many other fragments that can be recovered from the indirect tradition.

An important document of Epicurus' thought and its reception is a grand inscription that a follower of Epicureanism called Diogenes of Oenoanda (in Lycia) had carved on stone and set up in a portico in his city in the second century A.D. The text contains a brief exposition of Epicurean physics and ethics, together with passages from letters that do not otherwise survive. Finally, for the reconstruction of Epicurus' doctrines, the testimony of various other authors is fundamental. Among these the first place must without doubt go to the poem *De rerum natura* of Lucretius, who was avowedly inspired by Epicurean thought.

3.3 The doctrines

We have spoken of the centrality that came to be held by the problem of ethics in Hellenistic philosophies, focused on the search for individual happiness. Epicureanism perfectly represents this outlook. Epicurus on the one hand rejected Plato's metaphysical realities and ultramondane beliefs represented by the world of the Ideas and the doctrine of the immortality of the soul; for Epicurus, too great a role was played in these beliefs by human hopes and fears. On the other hand, he also rejected the narrow conception of earthly happiness foreseen by Aristotle, who identified its source in the knowledge gained by the philosopher. Epicurus instead sought a happiness that truly belongs to human life in its self-sufficient finiteness, which frees human existence from illusory hopes and false fears and which would be accessible to all people through their very humanity itself. For these reasons, Epicurus conceived philosophy as a genuine practical help for humans in their aspiration to happiness. For that reason, a particular place is given to the problem of the fear of death and of the gods and to reflection on human needs.

In order to be able to discuss this moral reflection, it is necessary to begin from Epicurus' conception of physics, which in a certain sense constitutes the premise of his ethics. Epicurean physics is modelled on Democritean atomism: all reality is material and is constituted by minuscule indivisible particles of matter, the atoms, the aggregation and disaggregation of which produces the generation and corruption of things. Within this deterministically mechanical conception, Epicurus introduced a new element: in the regular flow of indistinct atoms a swerve occurs (παρέγκλισις, *parenklisis*, translated as *clinamen* by Lucretius), which determines their various, accidental combination into various forms. This explains the differentiation and multiplicity of the cosmos and the possibility of free will that is typically human. This way of reconciling determinism with the idea of human freedom is one of the fundamental elements of Epicurus' physics and is necessary in order to understand his ethics.

Epicurean reflection on knowledge derives from this atomistic materialism. Along the same lines as Democritus, Epicurus holds that objects give off effluvia or simulacra of atoms which produce sensation when they strike our sense organs. Thus the material character of sensory experience is itself the guarantee of its truthfulness. It follows from this for Epicurus that knowledge from the senses is more reliable than opinion obtained by judgement. The human capacity to conceive abstract and universal thoughts is owed to the fact that the continuous experience of sensations permits the mind to foresee and anticipate phenomena even in their absence. Abstract reflection is thus a process of anticipation or prolepsis of phenomena that can be grasped in and for themselves only through the senses.

As we have said, Epicurean ethics essentially takes the form of a search for happiness, identified by Epicurus in pleasure (ἡδονή). The individual can pursue true happiness only by eliminating fears and illusory hopes and by reflecting on the quality of his own fundamental needs. This vision of philosophy as an instrument of liberation from the anxieties of existence inspired Epicurus to coin an effective metaphor: philosophy is a "pharmakon," a medicine that remedies the evils that afflict humans. This "medical" character of philosophy, which heals the illnesses congenital to human nature, conveys the predominantly ethical associations of Epicurean thought, with its aim of providing a guide through the confusions of the individual life. Four fundamental propositions of Epicurean doctrine form the so-called *tetrapharmakon*, a kind of catechism for the care of the soul and the achievement of happiness: pain can easily be borne; death is nothing to humans; there is no need to fear the gods; pleasure can easily be achieved.

Epicurus also included in his materialistic conception the idea of the soul and of the gods. The human soul is corporeal and is composed of lightweight, fine atoms which disaggregate on the death of the individual. The soul is hence mortal. In a famous passage of the *Letter to Menoeceus* (125) he demonstrates the irrationality of the fear of death for anyone who has been persuaded of the mortality of the soul: "Therefore, the most terrible of evils, death, is nothing to us: since when we are here, death is not, and when death is here, then we are not. Death therefore does not exist either for the living or for the dead, since for the former it does not exist, while for the latter, they no longer exist." The fear of punishments that could come from the gods is, for Epicurus, likewise without foundation. If the gods have not eliminated evil, then they are either wicked, if they do not want to do so, or else powerless, if they are not able to do so, but that cannot be the case. The presence of evil in the world demonstrates that the gods are distant and indifferent to human life: they live beatifically in the celestial regions that separate the different worlds that exist (the *intermundia*, in Lucretius' term) and do not care at all about what occurs on earth.

Once he has liberated humans from the psychological chains that have imprisoned him in a state of fear and illusion, Epicurus turns to the material limits of existence, which deprive the individual of the opportunity of gaining true pleasure and hence happiness: these are the needs, whose satisfaction can be the source of happiness or unhappiness. He distinguishes three types of need: the natural and necessary ones, such as the need to eat; those that are natural but not necessary, such as the need to eat in a refined and sophisticated way; and those that are neither natural nor necessary, such as the pursuit of power or wealth. Epicurus recommends that one maintain a different attitude in relation to the different types of need: the first kind are to be pursued, the second are admissible, the last kind must be absolutely avoided. Thus the hedonistic doctrine professed by Epicurus (which in later centuries was often interpreted as a permissive yielding to the base pleasures of instinct) in reality takes the form of liberation from superfluous needs and the balanced satisfaction of the primary needs.

We can see clearly at this point how, in the Epicurean conception, happiness is guaranteed by the return of humans to a state of harmony with nature, which inspires in them the desire for pleasure, demanding at the same time that it be satisfied in a way that is balanced and without excess. This obligation to return to natural reality is combined with the substantial rejection of everything that constitutes a construction of human society that gives rise to suffering and trouble for the individual. To be able to pursue happiness it is necessary to arrive at a state of detachment from the world and from the superfluous needs, a state of imperturbability (in Greek ἀταρασσία, *atarassia*) that preserves the sage from the very possibility of suffering evil or pain. It is a private and individual conception of happiness, which requires detachment from the changeability and tumultuousness of society as a whole. It takes the form, in fact, of a sort of distancing from the world: λάθε βιώσας, "live unnoticed," one of the most famous of Epicurus' precepts, fully expresses this obligation to set oneself apart from collective life; from this arises the sage's firm rejection of any form of active political commitment. The only form of "society" that is accorded a positive role in the path to happiness is interpersonal friendship, the community of the group of disciples and followers, with whom one can devote oneself to the collective practice of philosophy (συμφιλοσοφεῖν).

3.4 The school after Epicurus

At the death of Epicurus, his doctrines were adopted by the members of the school who were closest to him. Among them, Metrodorus of Lampsacus (ca. 331–ca. 278 B.C.) was the most important, as one of the "founders" of the school after Epicurus, but he predeceased his teacher. Therefore, Hermarchus was Epicurus' successor, followed by Colotes of Lampsacus (ca. 310–ca. 260 B.C.) and Demetrius Lacon (second to first century B.C.). For all these figures, important fragments have been restored by the Herculaneum papyri. Diogenes of Oenoanda has already been mentioned above. However, no figures emerged from the school who could compete with the philosophical stature and personal charisma of Epicurus.

One figure of real importance was Philodemus of Gadara, a philosopher and poet (cf. *The Hellenistic Age* IV 2.2.6) who lived in the first century B.C. (110–40 ca.). Significant parts of his many important philosophical works have emerged from the papyri in the Herculaneum library. He contributed strongly to the popularisation of Epicureanism at Rome, where its most important fruit was the poem of Lucretius already mentioned.

Epicureanism did not outlive the ancient world. The cohesiveness and firm dogmatism of Epicurean thought in fact hindered it from adapting to changing times and circumstances. Its disappearance should in part be connected to the competitive conflict with the doctrines of strongly religious stamp that were spreading from the end of the Hellenistic Age and the early Imperial Period (above all the mystery religions and Christianity). These proposed an otherworldly happiness that better satisfied the deep and widespread demand for spirituality.

4 Stoicism

4.1 A rational response to the problem of happiness

From the point of view of diffusion and duration over time, Stoicism can be considered the most important of the philosophies born during the Hellenistic Age and one of the most important ones from the ancient world as a whole. Its firm focus on a moral and also religious orientation meant it could respond particularly well to the demand for spirituality that runs through the Hellenistic Period and ensured that it later met with wide acceptance also in Roman culture of the late Republic and Imperial Period. The historical evolution of the movement in fact covers quite a long span of time, from the third century B.C. until at least the second century A.D., with a marked influence also on medieval and modern thought.

As well as the ethical and spiritual aspects of Stoicism, another reason for its success was its – so to speak – 'intermediate' character between Platonic idealism, whose complex metaphysical framework was rejected by Stoicism, and the materialistic hedonism of Epicurus, which was accused of elevating the mere satisfaction of animal instincts to the purpose of human life. Individual happiness in this world, identified by the Epicureans in the pleasure demanded by natural instinct, was for the Stoics rather the realisation of the virtuous life, indicated by the rational component, or *logos*, that is present in every human.

The movement took its name from the Stoa Poecile (Στοὰ ποικίλη), the famous "Painted Portico" at Athens adorned with paintings by Polygnotus. Here the founder of the school, Zeno, carried out his philosophical teaching. Since he was not an Athenian, he could not own private property (as was the case with Epicurus, the Academy and the Lyceum) and he was therefore obliged to teach in a public location. On the basis of the evolution of thought within the movement, three phases are distinguished in the Stoic school: the Early Stoa, which covers the third century B.C. and is represented by Zeno, Cleanthes and Chrysippus; the Middle Stoa, which covers the second and first centuries B.C., represented by Panaetius and Posidonius; and the Late Stoa, which developed in the Imperial Period (first to second century A.D.) with the figures of Seneca, Epictetus and the emperor Marcus Aurelius.

4.2 Zeno and the Early Stoa

Born around 333/2 B.C. at Citium, a city founded by the Phoenicians on Cyprus, Zeno came to Athens for commercial reasons around 311 while he was still young, according to the sources. Obliged to stay in the city for a lengthy period due to the wreck of his merchant ship, he came into contact with the Platonic Academy and with Socratic thinkers, including the Cynic Crates. Around 300 Zeno founded his philosophical school at Athens, delivering lectures in the Stoa Poecile; from then on, he and his followers were known as "the philosophers of the Portico", namely the Stoa. This circumstance characterised the Stoic school as being something different from the type of institution organised like the Academy or the Garden: it presented itself as a location where a group of philosophers and friends met freely to talk about philosophy. Zeno died in 263 or 262 of suicide, according to tradition, in order to escape the frailties of old Age, which were preventing him from remaining true to his own principles.

At the founder's death, Cleanthes of Assos (in Mysia) became head of the school and remained so for thirty years until his death in 232 B.C. He stressed the religious associations of Zeno's doctrines. Cleanthes did not have a sharp or creative personality as a philosopher and so the Stoa passed through a period of crisis. It seems that Cleanthes too chose suicide, at quite an advanced age, letting himself die of hunger. A new impulse arrived when the leadership of the Stoa was taken over by Chrysippus of Soli, in Cilicia (around 280–205 B.C.), who took the initiative of giving systematic order to the doctrines that had been worked out within the school. Diogenes Laertius attributes to him the composition of around 700 written works, of which a small part has survived in fragments, but not one complete work. Our knowledge and image of the earliest phase of Stoicism essentially derives from the clear and unified picture drawn up by Chrysippus in his grand theoretical systematisation, which long constituted the tradition of "official" doctrines of Stoicism. In reality it is not easy to distinguish within the system worked out by Chrysippus what should in fact be attributed to Zeno and what was a later development of Stoic thought.

4.3 The doctrines of early Stoicism

There are innumerable sources on Stoic thought, thanks to the diffusion and enormously wide acceptance enjoyed by this philosophy across the centuries. However, only fragments remain of the works of Zeno, Cleanthes and Chrysippus, aside from Cleanthes' *Hymn to Zeus*, which is the only completely preserved text from the Early Stoa. The reconstruction of the thought of both the founder and of the other two figures is therefore particularly problematic, since it is often difficult to attribute specific doctrines to Zeno or to one or the other of his two successors. There is better documentation, and hence we are better informed, in the case of Chrysippus.

Stoicism too (like Epicureanism) gave primary importance to ethical reflection and its central problem, the search for happiness. This interest was accompanied and matched by a special sensitivity to the existential state of the individual. Something that emerges particularly in Stoic thought is the need to situate the ethical problem within a coherent and organic system of thought, as can be seen in, among other things, the tripartite organisation of the matter of philosophy into three areas: physics, logic (with a distinction between theory of knowledge and dialectic) and ethics.

The Stoics, like the Epicureans, had a materialist conception of the world, but they denied the existence of atoms: they rejected the idea of an ultimate indivisibility of matter, regarding matter as infinitely divisible. For the Stoics reality is made up solely of material bodies, which have two aspects: an active one, by which they act, and passive one, by which they "suffer." They also believed that the cosmic order was the result of a universal principle that was immanent and rational and endowed with providential will, which oversees the various phenomena of nature, directing them towards a precise end. This principle is the *logos*, which is occasionally qualified also as *physis* (φύσις, "nature"), *pneuma* (πνεῦμα, "breath", "air") or *pyr* (πῦρ, "fire") and is sometimes given a divine connotation. Things are launched on their process of generation and corruption by the *logoi spermatikoi* (λόγοι σπερματικοί, i.e. the "seminal reasons") innate in them. These are fundamental structures that organise being and becoming according to constant forms. This causes things to follow a preordained path, which is watched over by the *pronoia* (πρόνοια) or providence of the universal *logos*. The Stoics therefore believed in the existence of a preordained destiny, but understood this in a way that is quite far removed from any threatening or tragic aspect, seeing it instead as a notion that is entirely rational and founded in the *pronoia* of the immanent *logos*. The organic consistency ensured by the *logos* of the cosmic system, viewed as an organism in which every part fulfils its function, results from the ensemble of reciprocal correspondences, or *sympatheiai* (συμπάθειαι), which set the different parts of the universe into relation with each other. From this organic vision of the world arises the idea that every entity and every event has a precise role and is endowed with its own value. In the natural scale, i.e. the hierarchy of the various entities, the human being stands at the top: it is the most mature being, since in it is manifested to the greatest degree the universal λόγος. The latter is linked to the soul, which is material and fulfils different functions; however, all these functions obey a dominant principle, which guides them according to rational criteria.

The moment of cognition is conceived as a material experience (another point of contact with Epicureanism) carried out by the sense organs, on which corporeal entities leave an imprint, a sort of "stamp" (τύπωσις) that produces impressions; these can then be conveyed to the mind by speculative means through the phenomenon of prolepsis. What differentiates the Stoics, in this case, is their confidence in the positive and decisive role of judgement formulated by human reason in regard to impressions that are not immediately clear. There are impressions that impose themselves evidently and others that do not have this force: the soul-*logos* expresses a judgement, granting or denying its own assent. In the sphere of dialectics (that is, as regards the organisation of reasoning and discourse), one of the Stoics' most important advances was the distinction between the object, the word that designates it and the meanings that the latter can take on. The meaning is the only non-material element and it is firmly distinguished from the word (which can take on different meanings). In the doctrine on judgement, the Aristotelian theory of the syllogism was revised and modified in an empirical-sensory direction, in the light of the Stoic conception of knowledge, linking the premises to statements about real data about facts.

For the Stoics, too, interest in theoretical speculation, while regarded as fundamental, was surpassed by an interest in practical living, though knowledge provided the foundations and guide for ethics. We have already noted how Stoicism, by locating human happiness in the recovery of harmony with nature, identifies "nature" with the rational, providential principle that determines its ordered harmony. The Stoics did not accept the Epicurean vision that identified happiness with the pleasure given by satisfying the fundamental needs, nor the vision of the human as an instinctive being. For the Stoics man is a rational being, and so the happiness of the sage consists in conforming oneself to the law of the *logos*, that is, to the virtue (ἀρετή) of behaviour that is good, just, temperate, in accord with the world inhabited by the *logos* and hence detached from the instincts and irrational passions; the latter are manifested in unregulated behaviours and are entangled in unworthy material desires. The Stoic sage's detachment from the world is identified with the absence of disturbances, with apathy (ἀπάθεια, *apatheia*), that is, the absence of the irrational passions that lead one away from the serenity of the natural order. For this reason, Stoic moral teaching takes the form of a call to an austere way of life, foreign to any temptation or concession towards behaviours that are not virtuous.

As we can see, this is the opposite pole from the Epicurean conception of happiness as the balanced satisfaction of the need to experience pleasure. For the Stoic, happiness is inherent in the righteous life in itself, even when it brings troubles and sufferings. To follow the universal *logos* means to live in accord with the world and with other humans, finding the profound meaning of human life in the conscious realisation of justice. This conscious conformity with the natural law is so strong and so firmly rooted in the sage that, in material circumstances that render it impossible, suicide becomes admissible; this was the choice made by Zeno and his disciple Cleanthes, according to tradition, as by other famous Stoics, such as the Roman Seneca.

The notion that the realisation of the natural law brings harmony among men gives rise to other quite significant aspects of Stoic thought. One of these is the perception that the philosopher's political and social commitment is a duty inherent to his function or mission of summoning consciences to the virtuous life. This is a position that, on purely speculative bases, also runs through Platonic thought, in an opposite direction to the Epicurean precept "live unnoticed". A second aspect is the substantially egalitarian and cosmopolitan vision of human society, which is joined in fraternity by sharing in the single divine *logos*.

4.4 The Middle Stoa

In the second and first century B.C. Stoicism presented a phase of thought that was distinct from the earlier form and which is personified in the figures of Panaetius and Posidonius. Panaetius of Rhodes (ca. 185–110 B.C.) worked out a mitigated form of the rigid moral principles endorsed by the school and opened up its traditional teachings to aspects from different philosophies, above all Platonism and Aristotelianism, developing a philosophical system of an eclectic type. He was convinced that the greatest Greek philosophers belonged to a single great speculative tradition, with goals that were substantially unitary.

Posidonius of Apamea, on the River Orontes (Syria), was born around 135 B.C. and was a pupil of Panaetius at Athens when he was around eighteen years old. Around 100 B.C. he spent a month in Cadiz; the experience of observing the ocean is the foundation of the work *On the Ocean*, in which he linked the tides to the movements of the sun and moon and explained the birth of small islands and arms of the sea by the rising and falling of the sea floor. He made many journeys for research purposes and finally settled at Rhodes, where he opened his school and had among his pupils many young members of the most prestigious Roman families, including Cicero (77 B.C.) and Pompey (66 and 62 B.C.). In 87/6 he went to Rome as ambassador of the Rhodians. He died around 51 B.C., perhaps during a period spent at Rome. He shared with Panaetius the eclectic approach, declining to see the truth as being contained exclusively within the Stoic dogmas, and so he opened up Stoicism to the contributions of the other schools, in particular to Platonic and Aristotelian influences. He accentuated the religious component in Stoic thought, meeting the pressing demand for spirituality that was widespread in his times. He accorded an important role to the divine and to the value of astrology and divination and took an interest in eschatological problems relating to the end of worldly realities.

VI The Sciences

1 Mathematics, astronomy, mechanics

1.1 The centrality of Alexandrian scientific culture

The mathematical sciences, the natural sciences and medicine form a chapter of great importance for the Hellenistic Age and would merit a much larger and deeper treatment than is possible in a manual of literary history. The extraordinary development that the sciences underwent in this period is in large part tied to the conditions established in Alexandria thanks to the cultural policy of the Ptolemies and in particular the institution of the Museum (cf. *The Hellenistic Age* I 1). Of course, one should not generalise this absolutely, as if for the sciences there was only Alexandria and nothing beyond it, since we know that other centres were also active in these fields. However, there is no doubt that in the Hellenistic Age Alexandria stands out in an exceptional way in this area too.

A considerable spur for scientific knowledge was given by the developments in the Peripatos after Aristotle, which had followed the predominantly scientific path marked out by Theophrastus. The presence in Alexandria in this period of two Peripatetics of the stature of Demetrius of Phaleron and Straton of Lampsacus (called ὁ φυσικός, "the scholar of nature," teacher of the astronomer Aristarchus of Samos) is a significant link (cf. *The Classical Age* XIII 3.8.2 and *The Hellenistic Age* III 2.1). The impulse towards research on nature, erudition, history and literature was transplanted to Alexandria in particular and the scientific disciplines yielded their best and richest fruits outside the traditional, institutional Aristotelian school. Many scientists of the Hellenistic Period (and also of the first centuries of the Empire) had some level of close and prolonged contact with the Museum, even if we cannot prove that they worked there – in truth there are no explicit testimonia for the mathematicians and astronomers, aside from Theon of Alexandria (philosopher and mathematician of the fourth century A.D.), who is said to have been a member of the Museum. Yet the city and institution guaranteed conditions and research opportunities that were wholly exceptional, given the independence and freedom that the scholars enjoyed (without being distracted by the practicalities of life) and the resources available to them. According to an old historiographic model, in the Hellenistic Age Alexandria was the centre of the new sciences (including philology and grammar), whereas Athens continued as the traditional seat of philosophical studies at its old and new schools (the Academy and Peripatos, Epicureanism and Stoicism). There is some truth in this view, but it is too rigid to do justice to the much more complex and nuanced reality, if for no other reason than that it is mistaken to think of an Alexandria that was purely "scientific," in which no form of philosophy was practised.

https://doi.org/10.1515/9783110426328-026

The problem should be stated in terms of an evolution and transformation of the intellectual scene. Up to the Classical Age, in fact, the scientific studies of which we are speaking (including the science of language and grammar) belonged fully to the philosophical mainstream. A fundamental aspect of science in the Hellenistic Age is the ever greater specialisation of the various sectors of knowledge and, consequently, a distancing of science from the traditional philosophical sphere. The various sciences' path to independence from philosophy began in the developments at the Peripatos noted above; in the Hellenistic Age and in particular at Alexandria this process reached its full conclusion. The emancipation essentially concerned the problem of the foundations of the various disciplines. This process was followed, for example, by grammar as a science of language, independent of philosophy, and the same applies to the scientific disciplines: they sought and found their principles within themselves, applying procedures that philosophical thought had created and refined, but independently of the philosophical systems themselves. This conception can be illustrated perfectly by the example of Euclid, who constructed geometry out of elements furnished by geometry itself, using rules and procedures of thought furnished by philosophy.

Typical of Hellenistic science is its predominantly theoretical character, which privileged pure research over applied research, and epistemological aspects and formal methods over practical realisations. There is no doubt that this was the prevalent tendency, but once again one should not over-generalise. The development of mechanics (as we shall see shortly) certainly did not entirely exclude practical realisations. Medicine was strongly committed to a knowledge of the human body and its functions that was more theoretical than functional, i.e. without concrete therapeutic applications (and this brought a great increase in knowledge thanks to the fact that at Alexandria it was possible to practise dissection of cadavers, forbidden elsewhere), but it is also true that this tendency provoked a reaction from the "empirical" school, which set the emphasis on therapeutic practice, and that in this period dissections of cadavers were carried out with the goal of knowledge about human anatomy.

After the ventures of Alexander the Great the opening up of the eastern world to the Greek spirit of observation and investigation had major consequences for the development of the sciences. The opportunity to gain immense knowledge of new areas and new populations prompted important developments in geographical and ethnographical science, cultivated by outstanding figures such as the Platonist Eudoxus of Cnidus (author of a geographical text describing the Earth) and Dicaearchus of Messana (who pursued his geographical and geological interests by undertaking research journeys and who wrote a work cited as the *Tour of the World*). A curious figure is Pytheas of Massalia, active in the second half of the fourth century B.C., author of a work *On the Ocean* of which only fragments remain but which was sharply criticised by Dicaearchus. Pytheas claimed to have travelled from the coast of the Iberian peninsula along the north-west and northern European coast and on to the far north. His journey invited incredulity but his work found great success and it is often cited. Among the historians of Alexander the admiral Nearchus left lively accounts of his voyages of exploration. We will discuss these topics in relation to historiography, but we may record here at least the extraordinary figure of Eratosthenes of Cyrene, grammarian, philologist, scientist and poet, who applied a mathematical method to cartography (he drew the first map based on a network of meridians and parallels) and to the measurement of the circumference of the Earth, in which his calculation was out by only 300 km (cf. *The Hellenistic Age* III 2.2 and VIII 1.4.4).

1.2 Astronomy

Eudoxus of Cnidus. In connection with the developments at the Academy after Plato (cf. *The Classical Age* XIII 2.6.1) we have already spoken of Eudoxus of Cnidus, an astronomer and mathematician who lived in the first half of the fourth century B.C. In the field of astronomy, Eudoxus formulated the mathematical model of the celestial spheres, which was then perfected and adopted also by Aristotle, who interpreted it as a physical reality. It was a geocentric system which was in fact far from successful in explaining all the observable anomalies in the motions of the celestial bodies. The great astronomer Aristarchus of Samos (ca. 310–ca. 230 B.C.), a pupil of the Peripatetic Straton of Lampsacus, attempted to overcome the difficulties by proposing the revolutionary idea that the Sun was at the centre of the universe and that the Earth was one of the planets that circled it. Of his writings we have only a short work *On the Sizes and Distances of the Sun and Moon*, but we have nothing on his heliocentric theory, though it is cited in an unambiguous testimony by Archimedes: "Aristarchus believed that the fixed stars and the Sun remain motionless, that the earth revolves in the circumference of a circle about the sun, which lies in the middle of the orbit." The theory did not meet with success, probably because its lack of elaboration meant that it produced predictions of celestial phenomena that were less precise than the geocentric system of the celestial spheres; it was adopted only by Seleucus of Seleucia (second century B.C.) and then abandoned. As is well known, resistance due to preconceptions and religious superstitions meant that the heliocentric theory would be reconsidered by the scientific community only in the time of Copernicus.

    Hipparchus of Nicaea. Already Apollonius of Perge (cf. next section) and Hipparchus of Nicaea (who worked on Rhodes and whose dated astronomical observations fall in the period 147–127 B.C.) returned to the geocentric system, which had been shown to have a greater capacity for predicting celestial phenomena. Aristarchus' approach persisted, however, in conceiving astronomical studies not as a physical explanation of the cosmos but as a mathematical one, an instrument to calculate the apparent motion of the celestial bodies and predict the phenomena.

From Hipparchus, one of the greatest ancient astronomers, sadly only one minor work survives: *Commentary on the Phaenomena of Eudoxus and Aratus*. We know that he reached results of great importance above all as regards the position of the stars (he catalogued around 850 of them) and the discovery of the precession of the equinoxes. For this reason his researches and his astronomical observations form a constant point of reference in the *Almagest* of Claudius Ptolemaeus.

Conon of Samos. We should also mention Conon of Samos, an astronomer and mathematician active in the first half of the third century B.C. He corresponded with Archimedes, who regarded him highly and was upset by his early death. He is famous because, thanks to his observations of the celestial phenomena, probably around 245 he discovered a new constellation, which he chose to see as the transformation into stars ("catasterism") of the lock of hair that Queen Berenice II of Cyrene had dedicated to propitiate the victory of King Ptolemy III Euergetes (246–221) against Seleucus II (the cue for the famous poem *The Lock of Berenice* by Callimachus, imitated by Catullus). A notice records that he undertook observations of eclipses of the Sun, but this is uncertain. We know from Apollonius of Perge that, as a mathematician, Conon studied conic sections (cf. next section).

1.3 Mathematics and mechanics

Euclid. The most famous mathematician of the ancient world, Euclid, lived in the fourth to third century B.C. The ancient sources say that he was active at Alexandria in the reign of Ptolemy I, who died in 283 (but not everyone is convinced of the reliability of these notices). Of his works the following survive: *The Elements*, *The Data* (in which the foundations were laid for the so-called "method of analysis and synthesis"), works of applied mathematics such as *The Optics* and *Catoptrics* (which studies the phenomena of reflection), a treatise of astronomical content and one on musical theory. His most mathematically advanced treatises are all lost. The most important work is the *Elements*, in thirteen books, which constitutes the birth of geometry as it has been taught until modern times. In truth, this immensely famoush manual does not contain substantial innovations, yet it does not limit itself to collecting theorems that were already known. For the first time it ordered what was known into a unitary whole and so geometry was elevated to the rank of an independent, abstract, rigorous science. The systematic framework, which is Euclid's most important contribution, is provided primarily by the foundations that underly geometry. He begins from the definitions of the terms of geometrical discourse (point, line, figure, surface, angle and so on); he then moves on to the fundamental rules, formed by the famous five postulates; then follow the axioms, self-evident concepts that do not need demonstration, but which make possible the demonstrations of theorems and the solution of problems, by which the geometric corpus is developed.

Archimedes. Undoubtedly one of the greatest mathematicians and scientists of antiquity was Archimedes of Syracuse (ca. 287–212 B.C.), who corresponded with Conon and Eratosthenes (cf. previous section). He lived mostly in his native city, where he formed friendships with the tyrant Hieron II (who died in 215) and his successor Gelon. He died during the capture of Syracuse by the Romans under Claudius Marcellus in 212. In the field of mathematics Archimedes worked in line with the positions systematised by Euclid, using and perfecting the deductive method: he studied the solution of geometrical problems such as calculating the area of the circle and the length of the circumference. In the field of mechanical technology, Archimedes is famous for the construction of war machines used in the unsuccessful defence of Syracuse against the Romans and of an irrigation pump that exploited the principle of the perpetual screw. On the theoretical level, he formulated the fundamental principles of statics (in particular the laws of leverage) and of hydrostatics (the famous principle of Archimedes on the floating of bodies in liquids). His importance in matters of method should be underlined: the novelty lies in deploying procedures derived from mechanical technology to solve problems of pure science in geometry and mathematics. Archimedes discovered a series of theorems by translating them into physical terms and solving them by employing physical concepts (such as the principles of the lever), in order to demonstrate them a posteriori in a rigorously mathematical setting. In the demonstration he provided, therefore, no account at all was given of the route by which he had arrived at his findings, due to the persistence of the idea that mechanics stand at a lower level than pure science. Mechanics in fact achieved an extraordinary development in the Hellenistic Age and, as the figure of Archimedes himself illustrates, this often occurred in close connection with mathematics. Mechanics was used primarily to build war machines, hydraulic machines or machinery for construction, but also to create devices designed to be astonishing and spectacular at festivals or ceremonies.

Thanks to the respect and wide reception that Archimedes enjoyed down the centuries, there are reasons to believe that his works have reached us almost complete in medieval or Renaissance manuscripts. Some of them are transmitted incomplete or as compilations and a very little is now known only in Arabic or Latin translation, but the works known to us only by their titles are few in number and, it seems, not of primary importance. Our knowledge of the manuscript tradition of Archimedes and of his surviving works in Greek has increased thanks to the discovery of what is usually cited as "The Archimedes Palimpsest." This is a Byzantine manuscript (*Hierosol.* 355) consisting of folios that originally belonged to at least six codices dating to the tenth century, which were then over-written in the first half of the thirteenth century to produce a prayer book. The palimpsest was known in the early twentieth century and already at that time (in 1907) it was used to edit the works of Archimedes. The manuscript subsequently disappeared, only to re-emerge many years later when in 1998 it was acquired at auction by an American billionnaire. It has since been thoroughly studied in great depth. Deciphered with the most advanced technological instruments, the lower writing has revealed various works of Archimedes, a commentary on the *Categories* of Aristotle and parts of two orations of Hyperides (cf. *The Classical Age* XIII 3.5.1 and XII 4.3). As regards Archimedes, the tenth-century folios present seven works, affected by lacunae of various extent. For three of the works (*On Floating Bodies, Stomachion, Method*) the palimpsest is the only witness in Greek, for *Stomachion* and *Method* it is the only witness at all. To get an idea of the extent and importance of the works of Archimedes, we here give a list of the surviving treatises, with a brief note on the content of each.

1. *On the Sphere and Cylinder* (Ἀρχιμήδους περὶ σφαίρας καὶ κυλίνδρου, *De sphaera et cylindro*): on calculating the area of the lateral surface of the cylinder, cone and conic frustum; the volume of conic rhombuses; the volume of the sphere and the area of its surface; the surface-area of segments of a sphere and the volume of sectors (Book I); the volume of segments of the sphere and problems related to them (Book II).

2. *On the Measurement of a Circle* (Ἀρχιμήδους κύκλου μέτρησις, *Mensura circuli*: transmitted in compendium form): on calculating the area of the circle and length of the circumference; an estimate of the ratio of the circumference of a circle to its diameter.

3. *On Conoids and Spheroids* (Ἀρχιμήδους περὶ κωνοειδέων καὶ σφαιροειδέων, *De conoidibus et sphaeroidibus*): the properties and volumes of segments of helixoids, paraboloids and hyperboloids of revolution.

4. *On Spirals* (Ἀρχιμήδους περὶ ἑλίκων, *De lineis spiralibus*): the properties of the spiral, applied to calculating the length of the circumference.

5. *On Plane Equilibriums* (Ἀρχιμήδους ἐπιπέδων ἰσορροπιῶν ἢ κέντρα βαρῶν ἐπιπέδων α′ β′, *De planorum aequilibriis*): laws of equilibrium; centres of gravity of parallelograms, triangles, trapezes (Book I), segments and truncated segments of the parabola (Book II).

6. *Sand-reckoner* (Ἀρχιμήδους ψαμμίτης, *Arenarius*): estimate of the number of grains of sand in the universe.

7. *Quadrature of a Parabola* (Ἀρχιμήδους τετραγωνισμὸς παραβολῆς, *Quadratura parabolae*): on calculating the area of a segment of a parabola, first by a mechanical method, then by a geometrical demonstration. In reality the title cannot have been *Quadrature of a Parabola*, which we find in the manuscripts, since the term *parabolē* (παραβολή) for the parabola was introduced later; the work is cited instead as *On the Section of a Right Cone* (Περὶ τῆς ὀρθογωνίου κώνου τομῆς), the name used by Archimedes for the parabola.

8. *On Floating Bodies* (Ἀρχιμήδους ὀχουμένων α′ β′, *De insidentibus aquae* or *De corporibus fluitantibus*): elementary hydrostatic laws; conditions for floating of segments of the sphere (Book I) and of paraboloids (Book II).

9. *Stomachion* (Ἀρχιμήδους στομάχιον, *Stomachion*: we do not know the exact meaning of the word): geometry of planar tiling (we can read only the start of the work).

10. *Method* (Ἀρχιμήδους περὶ τῶν μηχανικῶν θεωρημάτων πρὸς Ἐρατοσθένην ἔφο-δος, *Methodus*): on calculating the area of a segment of a parabola; the volume and centre of gravity of the sphere, spheroids and their segments, the segment of paraboloids, the segment of hyperboloids, calculating the volume of a cylindrical cut and a vault.

Apart from the *Method*, the language used by Archimedes has the Doric colouring characteristic of the Greek spoken and written in Sicily. It is very likely that the works were collected and preserved in the Library in Alexandria, where at the start of the sixth century A.D. some treatises were given commentaries by the Neoplatonic philosopher Eutocius. It was perhaps in this period that a revision was made of the text of *On the Sphere and Cylinder* and of *On the Measurement of a Circle*, which removed the Doric colouring from both works and reduced the second one to the stingy compendium that survives.

Ctesibius of Alexandria. Ctesibius, active in the first half of the third century, was the son of a barber in Alexandria and was picked up by Ptolemy II Philadelphus (283–246 B.C.) on account of his abilities as an inventor. His work is lost, but later authors (Philon and Heron) provide notices about his researches and inventions. He studied the action of air under pressure, built war-machines (a catapult), a pump and a waterclock, among other things. He had no theoretical tendencies, but it is probable that he meant a great deal to his successors. Philon of Byzantium, who lived in the third to second century, followed in his footsteps. From a compendium of his that collected technologies, entitled Μηχανικὴ σύνταξις (*A Treatise of Mechanics*), perhaps in four books or in nine, the fourth book alone survives in Greek, on war machines; in Arabic or Latin translation we also have the fifth book, on pneumatics, i.e. the discipline concerned with the construction of instruments activated by pressurised air and by fluids, and parts of Books VII and VIII, again on military instruments defensive and offensive; the sixth book, on the construction of self-moving objects (automata), is lost, but was discussed by Heron (on whom see below).

Apollonius of Perge. Euclid's great work of systematisation did not address conic sections, and this topic was taken up by Apollonius of Perge in Pamphylia, who lived from the second half of the third to the early second century B.C., whom we have already noted in relation to astronomy and who too was in contact with Alexandria. Almost the whole of a work called *Conics* is preserved, in eight books (Books I–IV are preserved in Greek, Books V–VII in Arabic translation, Book VIII is lost), a topic for which he had a predecessor in Conon (see previous section), whom he mentions at the start of Book IV. Apollonius studies the properties of the curves arising when a cone is cut by a plane: circumference, hyperbola, parabola, ellipse. Some regard this work as the masterpiece of ancient mathematics; the mathematical analysis of the curves in this work remained the basis of later studies through to the Modern Age.

Heron of Alexandria. The date of Heron of Alexandria, known as ὁ μηχανικός ("the inventor"), is problematic, even given the fact that he must certainly have been later than Philon of Byzantium and Archimedes (whom he cites) and earlier than the mathematician Pappus (third to fourth century A.D.), who cites him; some scholars place him in the first century A.D. Tradition links to his name many works on various themes. In the field of mathematics he provided rigorous geometrical foundations for the procedures of measuring and decomposing geometrical objects, both planes and solids; he also wrote a commentary on *The Elements* of Euclid. In mechanics, it seems that Heron in his writings compiled a kind of repertoire of all that had been discovered and invented in the course of the Hellenistic Era: *Pneumatica*, on devices moved by air pressure and water; *Mechanics*, in three books; *Dioptra* and *Catoptrica*, on optical instruments for measuring distance, mirrors and similar instruments; and *Belopoeica*, on the construction of war catapults. Heron is also famous for a work on the construction of self-moving machines or automata (Περὶ αὐτοματοποιητικῆς), which were used on various occasions, above all in temples, to create astonishment and wonder. It is difficult to say whether any given machine or instrument that he describes was invented by him. It may be unwise to attribute to him a genuinely mechanical workship at the Museum or the construction of a large number of different kinds of device. Many of his works are preserved, in part in Greek and in part in Arabic translation; some of the works published in modern times in his *Opera omnia* are in reality Late Antique or Byzantine compilations.

2 Medicine

2.1 Medicine at Alexandria: "dogmatists" and "empiricists"

Alexandria under the Ptolemies appears to have been the most lively and important centre for the study of medicine in this period. The Alexandrian Library was a centre for collecting numerous texts on medicine too, the majority of which went back to the fifth or fourth century B.C. It is likely that some of them were already attributed to Hippocrates, but some must have been anonymous. Many treatises on medical topics were then collected, arranged and studied. The first securely attested and systematic work of exegesis on these texts was done by the so-called Empirical school (on which see below), which was begun in the third century at Alexandria by Philinus of Cos and was committed to studying a group of works that were regarded as genuine compositions of Hippocrates. It seems that the first nucleus of the *Corpus Hippocraticum* was formed in Alexandria in the third to second centuries. Thereafter the whole collection was expanded until, in the first centuries of the Imperial Period, it reached something like the size of the surviving collection today.

In the Hellenistic Period advances in medicine were linked above all to studies of anatomy, due to the practice of dissection, including vivisection, of animals and people (using cadavers and people condemned to death). Galen (second century A.D.) informs us that, aside from rare exceptions, this was done almost exclusively in Alexandria. Unfortunately the medical texts of the Hellenistic Period are lost and our information depends completely on the indirect tradition, i.e. on the notices provided by medical authors of the Imperial Period. Two important figures represent a turning point in anatomical discoveries: Herophilus and Erasistratus.

Herophilus of Chalcedon worked in the first half of the third century. He was a pupil of the doctor Praxagoras of Cos and concentrated on anatomical studies. He discovered the connection between the brain and the nerves (which he distinguished into sensors and motors), studied the structure and functions of the brain and formulated an encephalocentric theory. He introduced much anatomical terminology that subsequently remained in use (in some cases up to modern times). Erasistratus of Ceos too lived around the first half of the third century, but it is not certain if he worked in Alexandria. He too concerned himself with the nervous system and the brain, some parts of which he described accurately. Of particular importance is his analysis of the vascular system: he discovered the cardiac valves and attributed to movements of the heart the contraction and relaxation of the veins and arteries, which were first distinguished by his master Praxagoras. Yet he did not manage to discover the essential function of the heart, since he believed that only the veins carried blood whereas the arteries circulated a vital breath (in the cadavers he had found the arteries drained).

Around the mid-third century a pupil of Herophilus, Philinus of Cos (whose *akmē* is placed a little after the mid-point of the century), deviated from the positions of his teacher and inaugurated at Alexandria the so-called Empirical school. Philinus and his followers defined themselves as "empiricists" on the basis of the following considerations: if medicine was founded on an entirely anatomical and physical basis, it would deny the uniqueness of the individual patient and so lead to the assumption of a perfect analogy that may be false; the belief that a living organism can be understood perfectly by dissecting a cadaver may give rise to incorrect analogical inferences. For the Empiricists, knowledge of the human body and its functioning seemed theoretical and detached from the proper goal of medicine, which is the therapeutic practice of healing the sick. Deductions and extrapolations run the risk of compromising the efficacy of medicine, which ought to be based on a single case in its specificity and to consider the individual reactions to the illness and to the therapy. The Empirical school was thus reacting against the approach of the two principal medical authorities of the period, Herophilus and Erasistratus, who had built an impressive theoretical framework for the discipline.

The Empiricist doctors devoted themselves to the study of certain works regarded as genuinely by Hippocrates, though already the school of Herophilus had shown interest in some Hippocratic texts, above all in their linguistic and lexical aspects. Bacchius, a member of the Herophilean school, in fact wrote the first lexicon to Hippocrates (*Lexeis*, a title that recalls the work of Aristophanes of Byzantium, from whom Bacchius seems to have adopted it), based on a group of around twenty texts included among those that today form the *Corpus Hippocraticum*. Bacchius' lexico-graphical interest was accompanied by an interest in editorial matters, since he was also the first editor known to us of a Hippocratic text, *Epidemics III*. The Empiricist commentaries that followed built on Bacchius' work, and their characteristics, so far as we can reconstruct them (above all those of Zeuxis, second century B.C., and of Heraclides of Tarentum, first century B.C.), reveal close affinities with the commentaries on literary texts produced in Alexandria (cf. *The Hellenistic Age* III 1.1), since they deal with the similar problem of establishing the text, and make use of glossaries or comparisons with other ancient texts, often poetic ones. Yet the authors of the Empiricist commentaries were professional doctors, interested primarily in the medical training of their pupils. The Empiricists rejected theorisation of any kind that would distance them from direct experience; they denied that anatomical knowledge was useful for therapy and maintained that medicine is built up over time through the accumulation of single therapeutic experiences, which have led to the recognition of certain drugs' utility or of the particular features of certain illnesses. "Experience" for them is a concept that is based on the observations of the individual doctor, but which also presupposes the long history of the discipline, the cumulative observations of the doctors of the past.

The study of the Hippocratic texts thus began out of a scientific need for professional training within the discipline, but the means that made it possible to profit from experience were those offered by Alexandrian grammatical and philological training: the Hippocratic texts were transmitted to the Library in a situation similar to that of the Homeric poems, in copies of different provenances and low reliability, and were written in a language that was already far from that in which the works of the Alexandrian doctors were composed. Editions and commentary were therefore tasks closely tied to the work of the Empiricist doctors, just as was the case in the work of the philologists concerned with poetic texts. At the same time, the Empiricists were the first to construct an image of Hippocrates as their precursor and so their practice of commenting upon Hippocrates was a task that also had ideological value.

It is on the basis of these views that the "empiricist" doctors defined themselves as such, identifying differences of method from the others who were the target of their criticisms. Only later were the latter defined as a group as "dogmatists"; this label did not correspond to a school or precise group and it encompassed figures very different from each other (the most authoritative were Herophilus and Erasistratus). Therefore the identification of two tendencies or even schools of Alexandrian medicine, one "dogmatist" and one "empiricist," was for the ancient authors a convenient historiographical categorisation, but one that does not correspond to a concrete historical reality.

2.2 The Methodist school

The teaching of Asclepiades of Prusa in Bithynia (second to first century B.C.) about the pores (πόροι) and corpuscles (ὄγκοι), based on the atomist theory as defined by Epicurus, gained wide acceptance among the medical authorities and formed the basis for the teaching of the so-called Methodist school, which, according to the ancient sources, was founded around the mid-first century B.C. by a student of Asclepiades, Themison of Laodicea in Syria. Themison seems to have laid the first (theoretical?) foundations of the "method" and to have expounded his ideas in a large number of written works, unfortunately lost, of which we know only the titles (e.g. Περὶ περιοδικῶν πυρετῶν, *On Recurrent Fevers*; Περὶ ὀξέων παθῶν, *On Acute Diseases*; Περὶ χρονίων παθῶν, *On Chronic Diseases* etc.) and various fragments. While some ancient sources present Themison as the founder of the school, the author of the pseudo-Galenic work Εἰσαγωγὴ ἢ Ἰατρός (*Introductio sive medicus*) considers that its "perfectioner" (τελειωτής) was Thessalus of Tralles in Lydia (whose *floruit* is placed around the mid-first century A.D.). This opinion is generally accepted by scholars for other reasons too, since it is reflected in the ancient texts on this topic and above all by the fact that Thessalus himself is presented by Galen as completely unconnected from all the Methodists who preceded him (but also from all the other medical authorities altogether). On the other hand, the theory of the "commonalities" (*koinotētes*), as it is known to us from Galen, is the one defined by Thessalus, and for that reason Galen always talks of the "commonalities of Thessalus" (Θεσσαλοῦ κοινότητες). The term indicates general and evident characteristics, which are common to all illnesses. Thessalus and his followers questioned the significance of the theoretical branches of medicine (anatomy, physology, theories of pulsations, theory of fevers etc.) and tried to simplify to the greatest degree possible the methods of diagnosis and therapy. In accord with the doctrine of the "commonalities," he distinguished only two pathological conditions, that is two *koinotētes*. The first is called *stegnōsis* (στέγνωσις), "state of tension" or "constipation": *stegnōsis* was the result of intense contractions of the muscles of the body, a consequence of which is the diminution or total stoppage of bodily secretions. The second "commonality," called *rhysis* (ῥῦσις), "state of relaxation" or "flow," on the other hand was provoked by an excessive relaxation of the muscles, with the opposite results to those of the previous condition. These two basic *koinotētes* were supplemented later by a third "mixed" one, the *memigmenon* (τὸ μεμιγμένον), defined as the alternation of *stegnōsis* and *rhysis* in the patient, or their simultaneous presence. It is plausible that among the Methodists a therapeutic approach to illnesses existed that corresponded to the mechanistic analysis of the causes that gave rise to them. Thessalus composed various medical writings, but also theoretical works; the latter included (based on what Galen says) above all the one *On Commonalities* (Περὶ κοινοτήτων) and the one *On Comparisons* (Συγκριτικά), in which he set out to promote and defend his theories. The Methodist school (Μεθοδικὴ αἵρεσις) won many followers, perhaps more than any other school, and numerous names of Methodists are recorded in ancient catalogues of doctors, including Antipater, Mnaseas, Dionysius, Menemachus, Olympicus, Apollonides, Soranus and Julianus. Of these the most celebrated was Soranus of Ephesus (first to second century A.D.), known principally for his famous treatise *On Gynaecology* (Περὶ γυναικείων).

2.3 The Pneumatist school

The Pneumatist school was founded in the mid-first century B.C. by the doctor Athenaeus of Attaleia in Pamphylia. Athenaeus followed the teaching of the Stoic Posidonius at Rome (cf. *The Hellenistic Age* V 4.4) and was influenced principally by the theory of the *pneuma*. As is well known, the Stoics accorded great importance to the *pneuma*, which they considered to be the cohesive principle of the All (Σύμπαν), and Chrysippus, especially, had equated it to divinity. Athenaeus attempted to give medical expression to this theory and to explain, based on *pneuma*, the physiological functions of the human organism (that which is κατὰ φύσιν, "in accordance with nature") as well as the causes of illnesses (that which is παρὰ φύσιν, "contrary to nature"). In his theory the *pneuma* that is breathed in, after undergoing some transformation in the body, becomes subtler (λεπτότερον) and hot (θερμόν): the "vital *pneuma*" (ζωτικὸν πνεῦμα), locating itself in the left cavity of the heart, and from there it is diffused throughout the body. The air breathed in constitutes the primary material of the continuous renewal of the *pneuma* itself. When, in the best conditions, the *pneuma* moves through the body and without hindrance reaches all the organs and parts, then the person is healthy, whereas every confusion in its distribution provokes the appearance of different illnesses. Precisely on account of this regulatory role that they gave to the *pneuma*, Athenaeus and his followers were called Pneumatists. Yet it should be noted that both Athenaeus and the Pneumatists who came after him incorporated into their medical system also the fundamental Hippocratic theories (theory of humours, of critical days, etc.). Unfortunately the written work of the founder of the Pneumatist school is completely unknown to us, except for the title of a treatise (περὶ βοηθημάτων, *On Remedies*) and some fragments. A direct student of Athenaeus was the doctor Theodorus, while a little later (first half of the first century A.D.) Magnus was author of the treatise Περὶ τῶν ἐφευρημένων μετὰ τοὺς Θεμίσωνος χρόνους (*On Discoveries after the Time of Themison*). At work towards the mid-first century A.D. was Aretaeus of Cappadocia, who was concerned with various medical questions and in particular with pathology and therapeutics; his eight books of treatises on these topics are the only surviving (almost intact) works of the Pneumatist medical school. Perhaps contemporary to Aretaeus was Agathinus Lacedaemonius, who professed not only tolerance towards the theories of other medical schools, but also their inclusion within the medical system of his own school, though naturally with the absolute condition that such theories not conflict with the principles of the Pneumatists. By this approach he elaborated a new tendency within the Pneumatist school, called "Eclectic" (ἐκλεκτική). As would become evident later, this activity of the school of Agathinus would determine the development of the school, since all the later Pneumatist medics known to us were "Eclectics" (ἐκλεκτικοί). The direct pupil of Agathinus, Herodotus, should obviously be considered an Eclectic. He worked at Rome and was probably the teacher of Sextus Empiricus (see *The Roman Imperial Period* VII 1.3.1), and the same is true of Leonidas of Alexandria, known principally for his interest in surgery. Among the most famous Pneumatists/Eclectics was Archigenes of Apamea in Syria, who worked at Rome in the Trajanic Period and wrote works on almost every sector of medical science. Contemporaries of his were Philippus and Heliodorus, while the last known Pneumatist should probably be seen as Antyllus (first half of the second century A.D.), who wrote an excellent description of the surgical treatment of arterial aneurism. If indeed Ablabes "physician and Pneumatist" (ἰατρός καὶ πνευματικός; ca. 400 A.D.) should be considered a doctor of the Pneumatist school, then we should date the survival of the school at least to the fourth to fifth century A.D.

VII Oratory and Rhetoric

1 The triumph of *technē*

1.1 A scarcely documented output

Given the near-total loss of the output of the rhetors of the Hellenistic Age, it forms one of the obscure chapters of ancient literature. Of all that was written in the three centuries between Aristotle and Dionysius of Halicarnassus (first century B.C.), either in the production of manuals to teach the *technē* or in oratorical practice, very little has been saved. One of the reasons for this lies in the preferences of the authors of the subsequent Imperial Period, who favoured and wanted to emulate the Attic orators of the fifth and fourth centuries B.C., passing over Hellenistic rhetoric, which was thus hit by a kind of *damnatio memoriae*. The schools of the Imperial Period, modelled on classicism, rejected the oratory that had developed above all in Asia Minor in the three centuries after the death of Alexander, and preferred to return to the authors of the Classical Period.

Dionysius of Halicarnassus, for example, saw in this period the beginning of oratorical decadence. Later, Flavius Philostratus, in his *Lives of the Sophists*, omitted any treatment of the Hellenistic Age and passed directly from Aeschines to Nicetes of Smyrna, an author of the Neronian Period, who "found the science of oratory reduced to great straits" (1, 19). Thus the picture that we can reconstruct of post-Aristotelian oratory and rhetoric prior to the Augustan Era is strongly shaped by the negative judgements of the ancient authors and consequently by the indirect sources, which are at times miserly in the information they provide and often highly critical, to the point that they just "skip over" the Hellenistic Period. Of importance too are the notices, names and opinions transmitted by Latin authors such as Cicero in his rhetorical works and Quintilian in the *Institutio oratoria*.

Although our knowledge is hence extremely lacunose, nonetheless at least two aspects emerge clearly. One is the liveliness of the specialist debate on poetics and style, which, although it emerged from a school setting, ultimately exerted a broad influence on Graeco-Roman culture. The other aspect is Athens' loss of hegemony in this sector, to the advantage of the numerous centres of eloquence that flourished throughout the Hellenistic world, particularly on the island of Rhodes and the cities of Asia Minor, while – at least as far as we know – rhetoric and oratory were relatively little cultivated at Alexandria. Thus, in the partial view enforced by the selection of the preserved material, the Hellenistic Age appears as the era of Alexandrian philological and grammatical erudition and poetry, whereas rhetoric and oratory remain marginal and forgotten.

https://doi.org/10.1515/9783110426328-027

1.2 The interest in technique

The loss of the Greek cities' political liberty contributed to a depletion in deliberative oratory, which did not entirely disappear but was drastically scaled back. One can easily grasp how the changed political and social conditions, with power in the hands of a monarch and his court at the capital of a kingdom, would have offered little room to develop oratory that aimed to determine the decisions of a deliberative assembly.

In consequence, the attention of rhetors shifted focus from the effective deployment of the *logos* in the life of the assembled people and the public decisions of the *polis*, and preferred instead to pursue technique and formal virtuosity that were better suited to captivate and impress any audience whatsoever. This prevailing interest in technical aspects was not in itself a novelty: we have seen that during the Classical Age a conception of oratory as *technē* was developed, i.e. as an activity which required for its exercise a whole series of instruments and expedients, and that this conception produced a literature of "manuals" (i.e. the *technai*) that aimed to teach the foundations and tools of the trade. During the Hellenistic Age, however, the disappearance of the real occasions of political debate led to a particular concentration on technical aspects, which ultimately came to be studied and valued for their intrinsic value and not for the sake of their function in prompting a decision. Through this the study of *inventio* and in particular of the *staseis* (which we will discuss shortly) became established, and the key to oratorical success came to be seen in formal play, virtuosity and the use of existing models.

An aspect of this turn of rhetoric in a technical direction is the central importance that came to be held by the *meletē* (μελέτη), "exercise" (corresponding to the Latin *declamatio*). This was a fictitious declamation, the practice of composing a deliberative or forensic speech on invented themes, detached from any real occasion and composed for purely literary purposes, making virtuosic use of the whole gamut of means of verbal persuasion. In this case too, this is not an original innovation. Fictitious speeches had been composed as exercises already in the Classical Period and we have seen how important these were in the activity of the Sophists. The novelty consists rather in the extension of the use of fictitious declamations, which in a short time became the most usual form of oratorical composition. These were no longer an exercise with a view to a real debate, but rather a form of bravura performance to be used for public displays in which one could show off one's talent and win the favour of the audience present at the "spectacle." This kind of declamation was practised quite widely during the Hellenistic Age, but its products have not been preserved and we can now get an idea of what it was like only by an indirect route: the Greek sources are much later (from the fourth century A.D. onwards); the best source is the work of Seneca the Rhetor, a Latin author who lived in the early Imperial Period, who recorded more than thirty Greek declaimers of the Late Republican and Augustan Periods, almost all from Asia. However, it should be added that it was a practice so deeply rooted in taste and culture that it also had a decisive influence on other literary genres such as historiography and novel, which for that reason help to reveal its characteristics.

2 The schools of rhetoric

2.1 Hegesias of Magnesia and Asianism

One of the principal exponents of the rhetoric of Asia Minor was Hegesias, originally from Magnesia on the Sipylus in Lydia, an enormously successful rhetor who lived in the late fourth to early third century B.C. His output included a historical work, the *History of Alexander* (on which see below), as well as forensic and epideictic speeches; all that remains of these are a few fragments. His style, as it emerges both from the surviving fragments and from the references in ancient testimonia, appears redundant due to an abundance of often brash rhetorical figures and a profusion of metaphors, antitheses and parallelisms. The pronounced taste for sound-effects and the use of bold imagery was immensely popular with his contemporaries and Hegesias set the fashion for years. The proponents of Atticism, on the other hand, who (as we shall see shortly) hoped for a return to the simplicity of the classics, sharply dismissed him. For example, Dionysius of Halicarnassus (*De compositione verborum* 18) maintained that Hegesias had not left a single page "that has been felicitously composed."

The Atticist rhetors regarded Hegesias as the initiator and main exponent of Asianism, one of the most important rhetorical tendencies of the Hellenistic Age, which originated at the turn of the fourth to third century B.C. above all in areas of Asia Minor (from which the term "Asian" for this rhetoric derives) and it had a powerful influence on Roman oratory of the Republican and Imperial Periods. Unlike the ancient witnesses, modern scholars do not identify a single figure as founder of this oratorical tendency and prefer to stress the continuity of the style and its characteristics with the earlier Sophistic of Gorgias, Hippias and Alcidamas. Asianism, in fact, took to the extreme the use of expedients meant to impress, which aimed to rely on *pathos* and taking emotional hold of the audience, managing to astonish and captivate it. The expedients included the overwhelming use of rhetorical figures, in particular aural ones; the pursuit, often obsessive, of studied rhythmical sequences in speech; and a general tendency towards poetic prose. Although all these elements are in fact found in the style of Hegesias, Asianism should not be identified with a single school of rhetoric but rather with many of them. It was an orientation in taste, a tendency in style, and not a true school in a strict sense. The decisive aspect for these stylistic choices was in fact the oratorical direction taken by the individual teachers, who did not necessarily come from Asia Minor or pursue their activity in that area of the Hellenised world. The term "Asianism" was anyway formulated by the opponents of this tendency, with the aim of disparaging it: as a polemical generalisation, those teachers who were committed to a florid, emotional and redundant style were called "Asians."

The teaching of the Asianist rhetors was based above all on the exercise of declamation and commanded a large number of pupils from all over Greece and from Rome. Thereafter, with the rapid shifting of the political centre of gravity in the Mediterranean from the east to Rome, the most successful Asianist rhetors found in Rome the crowning success of their career, when their public displays won the enthusiastic support of the Roman public.

2.2 Atticism

The origin of "Atticism" poses significant problems. First of all we should specify that by this term we refer to a stylistic doctrine that takes as its unchallengeable models, to be studied and imitated, the Attic orators of the Classical Period. However, the abstract "Atticism" is a modern term: the ancient sources simply indicate the Attic orators as the models to be studied and imitated, setting them in opposition to the negative example of the more recent "Asianist" rhetoric, which is defined by Dionysius of Halicarnassus (1, 10–26) as insufferable in its theatrical exhibitionism and without culture, a courtesan who has usurped honours and duties above her station. The earliest attestation of this orientation is found in Cicero's rhetorical works *Brutus* and *Orator*, written in 46 B.C. (but not the *De Oratore*, which is from 55 B.C.), where it is presented as a counterpoint to Asianism. In the Augustan Period, then, the sources note as Atticists the Latins Julius Caesar, Licinius Calvus and Brutus and the Greeks Dionysius of Halicarnassus and Caecilius of Caleacte. It is very likely that the origin of Atticism itself should be located in the widespread desire for a defence and rebirth of classical culture, or "classicism," which is found broadly and comprehensively above all from the Augustan Period.

These authors set themselves in opposition to the "bad taste" of the Asianist style, which was bombastic and aimed at provoking *pathos* in the audience; the harsh criticisms addressed to Hegesias show that the polemic against the Asianists even reached tones of violent rivalry. The Atticists preferred the more sober, clear and linear style of the models of the fifth and fourth century B.C. The speeches of Lysias seemed to meet these formal characteristics better than others. From this perspective Atticism represents the culminating moment of a phenomenon by which older authors were rediscovered and appreciated, and so gained the status of "classics" according to a definition that has remained firmly in place up to the present day. On the other hand, the characteristics of this phenomenon seem less strange when we reflect on the fact that an admiring attitude towards models from the past is a fairly widespread aspect of Greek culture. In particular, the adoption of authors of the fifth century B.C. as models is found already in rhetors of the fourth century such as Isocrates, and we have already spoken at length of the great interest that the authors of those centuries held for the scholarly and poetic cultures of the early Hellenistic Age.

The difficulty in separating Atticism from the general classicising tendency that began in the Augustan Age also prevents us from establishing precisely the origin of this stylistic and oratorical taste. Thus, while some scholars trace the earliest roots of Atticism back to the second century B.C., others prefer to shift it to the first century, creating a link between Atticists in style and analogists in grammatical theory on the one hand, and Asianists and anomalists on the other. In general today the preference is to set Atticism within the widespread desire for a defence and rebirth of classical culture, in opposition to the less purist and rigorous concept of Asianism. It is undeniable that such a defence occurred above all from the Augustan Age and early Imperial Period onwards. Hence, while Asianism characterises the stylistic and rhetorical choices of the Hellenistic Age, it is towards the end of the period that we record the reaction that led to the rejection of the Asianist taste in favour of a return to the style of the "classics" of the fifth and fourth century.

2.3 The Schools of Rhodes

Alongside the schools of various cities of Asia Minor, Rhodes became one of the principal centres of rhetorical training, above all from the late second century B.C., although the island's cultural life had certainly flourished in earlier times (among those who taught there were the orator Aeschines, the Peripatetics Eudemus and Praxiphanes and Posidonius; Dionysius Thrax had had a school of grammar there). For the Rhodian schools of rhetoric too we have only indirect notices, due to the loss of the works of even such a first-rank exponent of rhetoric as Apollonius Molon. Cicero (*Brutus* 51) and Quintilian (*Institutio oratoria* XII 10, 18) tell us that the Rhodian rhetors practised a type of eloquence that was inspired both by the Attic authors of the past and by the Asianist tendency, though without sharing all the stylistic excesses of the latter. According to Dionysius of Halicarnassus (*Dinarchus* 8), they took as their stylistic model the speeches of Hyperides. One thing remains a constant in all the sources, however: Rhodes was for decades a cultural centre of primary importance in the Mediterranean area, a point of contact between different rhetorical and philosophical tendencies. The old rivalry between rhetoric and philosophy was represented in the typical form of the opposition between the schools: the authoritative rhetor Apollonius Molon wrote *Against the Philosophers*, while the philosopher Posidonius aimed an attack *Against Hermagoras* (the rhetor, on whom more below). But these were no longer the times of Isocrates and Plato, nor of the Platonic condemnation of rhetoric. At this time rhetoric and philosophy should rather be understood as two curricula within higher education, but they were not exclusive and it was certainly possible to acquire a good standard of instruction in both.

2.4 Hermagoras of Temnos

One of the rhetors with the greatest influence on contemporary and subsequent rhetoric was Hermagoras of Temnos in Asia Minor, who was active in the second century B.C. We know nothing of his life, but we know that his *Technē* was an enormous success. According to the testimony of Quintilian (*Institutio oratoria* III 1, 16), he marked a decisive change in eloquence, inaugurating an approach that was principally concentrated on *inventio*. His work, which is lost, was not organised according to the parts of the speech, but rather according to the tasks of the orator: finding the arguments, arranging them, expounding them, memorising them, and reciting them to the public. Hermagoras introduced the system of the *staseis* (στάσεις, the *status* in Latin), that is, of the positions that the rhetor needed to adopt on the question under discussion. For this system we have only a much later exposition (in the work of the rhetor Hermogenes, second to third century A.D.), but it was in wide use in teaching and continuously underwent systematisations and updatings. Hermagoras proposed four possibilities: to decide if the offence had been committed; what the offence was; how it was to be judged; and whether it was necessary to raise questions of legitimacy or competence. Corresponding to these possibilities were the four *staseis* of the orator: *stochasmos* (στοχασμός, *coniectura*), *horos* (ὅρος, *finitio*), *poiotēs* (ποιότης, *qualitas*) and finally *metalēpsis* (μετάληψις, *translatio*).

Our information about Hermagoras' rhetorical doctrine derive from much later Greek sources or from Latin sources, since the Romans adopted his method and made wide use of it. Quintilian records that the doctrine was followed by Athenaeus, Apollonius Molon, Areus, Caecilius and Theon.

VIII Historiography

1 Problems and tendencies in Hellenistic historiography

1.1 Loss of texts and problems of reconstruction

In the Hellenistic Age historiography bore rich and important fruit, recording and interpreting the events of a historical period that saw the whole lifespan of the Hellenistic kingdoms and the establishment of Rome as the dominant power in the Mediterranean. Unfortunately the very varied historiographical output that lies between the exploits of Alexander and the Roman conquest of Egypt has in large part been lost. All that survives whole is some books of Polybius, fifteen books of Diodorus' work and the first two *Books of the Maccabees* of the *Old Testament*. We must conclude sadly that from this important and complicated historical period, which saw the transition from the empire of Alexander to the Hellenistic kingdoms and finally the Roman conquest of the whole Mediterranean, we do not even have a continuous historical narrative: the surviving part of Diodorus comes down only to the year 301, while Polybius begins in summary form in 264 but in detail only from 220 B.C.

All the rest is known to us only in a quite fragmentary way, often through the use made of it and the judgements passed on it by later historians (including Latin ones), especially those of the Imperial Era, for whom the Hellenistic historians were often a primary source. In general there are few true fragments preserved: the documentation is for the most part formed by indirect testimonia, of different degrees of reliability. These are mainly identified where a later historian is said to have used one of his predecessors as a source. In cases like this – an emblematic case is that of Timaeus, the source of Diodorus – it is a crucially important and extremely difficult task to delimit what precisely belongs to the source and what to the person who used it; the results are often highly hypothetical. Situations such as this pose major problems in reconstructing lost texts and strongly influence the picture that we can form of the characteristics of Hellenistic historiography in its various currents. They also influence the judgements we pass on Hellenistic historiography.

1.2 The panorama of Hellenistic historiography

Despite the serious loss of many works, the panorama of historiography in the Hellenistic Age appears extremely varied and lively. To give some lines for orientation, we have tried to group the authors in certain ways, while separating Polybius due to his special importance. The exposition here is organised on a fundamentally chronological basis. The character and absolutely exceptional significance of the figure

https://doi.org/10.1515/9783110426328-028

and ventures of Alexander the Great gave rise to a whole genre of historiography, that of the Alexander Historians, with all their shared characteristics; these are the subject of the next section. In the sections that come next we have then brought together different forms of historiography that were produced, broadly speaking, in the era of the Diadochi, but which are also very different from each other: these run from the so-called dramatic historiography to the local historiography produced in various settings in the Hellenistic kingdoms, from Timaeus to a group of scholars and polymaths who also wrote historical works. Two chapters are then devoted, respectively, to Polybius and to a group of historians later than him.

At the start of the Hellenistic Age, Alexander and the fortunes of the kingdoms that arose out of the dismemberment of his empire stood at the centre of historiographical interest. From the third century B.C. onwards, beginning with Hieronymus of Cardia and Timaeus, Rome emerged as the hegemonic power in the Mediterranean and steadily captured the attention of historians as its expansion overwhelmed the Hellenistic kingdoms. In the history of world empires, the Roman Empire becomes the successor to the Macedonian Empire. One reason why the figure of Polybius stands out is because with him Rome is definitively placed at the centre of history and historiography. After him, Posidonius reflected in critical tones on the exercise of power and rule by the Romans. In the second and first centuries B.C. a debate on Rome's empire, its legitimacy and its historical causes developed, with learned antiquarian research playing a role in this. A theme such as the origin of Rome in Aeneas and the Trojans took on a value as propaganda that would perhaps not have been guessed at first.

When Thucydides prefaced his account of the Peloponnesian War with the *Pentekontaetia*, in which he ran through the roughly fifty years that separate the Persian Wars from the conflict between Athens and Sparta, he was picking up at the point where Herodotus stopped, revealing the idea that historical exposition ought to proceed continuously. From then on, the work of most Greek historians quite clearly displayed a desire to continue the narrative from where it had been left by a predecessor, who was evidently chosen as an authoritative point of reference. Both the *Hellenica* of Xenophon and the *Hellenica* of Theopompus were presented as direct continuations of Thucydides, but the so-called *Hellenica of Oxyrhynchus* too seem to have been written with this aim. In a certain sense an ideal "historical cycle" was created, though the connections do not appear as clearly to us in the subsequent period, which included the rise of Macedonia and then of Alexander the Great and the fortunes of the Diadochi. This is the period addressed first by the *Philippica* of Theopompus and then by the Alexander Historians and those who recounted the events of the Hellenistic kingdoms. Later Polybius in his *Histories* stated explicitly that he is picking up at the point where Timaeus broke off his account, i.e. in 264, the year when the frontal confrontation between Rome and Carthage began. Posidonius then continued with his *Histories after Polybius* and *Histories on Pompey*. One can easily see that, compared to this, it was a very different decision to compose a "universal history," as was done for example by Ephorus and Anaximenes and, in the first century, by Diodorus Siculus.

1.3 The Alexander Historians

1.3.1 The birth of a genre

The enormous importance and resonance of the achievements of Alexander the Great in the relatively short span of a dozen years, from his accession to the throne in 336 B.C. to his premature death in 323, and the exceptional character of his personality gave rise to a genuine historiographical genre, which consists of the works of the Alexander Historians.

Beginning from the travel accounts of the men who accompanied Alexander in senior military positions (such as Aristobulus, Nearchus, Ptolemy, Callisthenes, Medius and Onesicritus), of which some meagre fragments survive, a literature developed that combined an essentially historiographical intent with aspects of biography, encomium and adventure story, and a taste for narrative and description that gave these texts a decidedly literary flavour, at the expense of faithful historical reconstruction. Alexander's court dignitaries and generals had direct access to knowledge of Macedonian history and, from that point of view, their testimony should have been regarded as reliable and precious. In reality the history of Alexander was very soon packed with legends and extraordinary episodes, put into circulation by the very people who had participated in his expeditions, of a kind designed to cast an aura of encomiastic exaltation, with little respect for the truth about the facts. One should add that the writings on Alexander's achievements generally reflected the ideological orientations of the official propaganda, which encouraged a reading of the expedition to the East as a war brought by the West to avenge age-old wrongs, as the ultimate outcome of the ancient confrontation between Greece and Persia or, to the contrary, as an unexpected opportunity for different peoples to meet and fraternise under shared Graeco-Macedonian rule.

These more-or-less contemporary works on the figure of Alexander are almost wholly lost. The earliest preserved account of the expedition is that of the historian Diodorus, who lived in the Augustan Period. Quite important testimonies are transmitted by Plutarch (first to second century A.D.) in his *Life of Alexander* and by the historian Arrian (first to second century A.D.) in his *Anabasis of Alexander*. Arrian, who understood his task as being to follow the most trustworthy sources, declares that he was basing his account on Ptolemy and Aristobulus, while in the *Indica* he draws on the Alexander Historians to reconstruct the return journey by sea from India to Susa. To these Greek sources we must add the Latin authors Quintus Curtius Rufus (first century A.D.) and Justin (second century A.D.). The so-called *Alexander Romance* of Pseudo-Callisthenes dates to a period after the second century A.D.: in it the literary aspect of narrative novel has definitively overwhelmed the historiographical aspect (on which see below).

One of the characteristics of the historiography centred on Alexander is the encomiastic outlook of the historical reconstruction. It is believed that this approach began with Callisthenes, the conqueror's official historian. Since it was well known that many of the king's actions did not conform to the prescriptions of traditional ethics (drinking, taking a second wife, the killing of Cleitus and Parmenion), he was not praised as a perfect human being or as a model to be followed, but rather as a superman who was above normal human standards. Not everyone wanted to engage in the adulation of Alexander. For example, we have fragments of a hostile pamphlet written by Ephippus of Olynthus (a contemporary historian about whom we know very little, see below). Yet the encomiastic current was in the majority by a wide margin and very soon became ingrained in the cultural tradition. Down the centuries, many conquerors invited a comparison with Alexander, and so in the schools of philosophy and of rhetoric he was long a figure who was used as an exemplary model for moral lessons.

Another peculiar aspect of this historiography is its fantastic elements. Strabo (II 1, 9), an author of the Augustan Period, accused the historian Onesicritus, one of the officials who accompanied Alexander, of inventing things on a grand scale, making Alexander travel into a world inhabited by improbable events and beings and preferring the marvellous to the truth. Given the characteristics of the figure of Alexander and the course of his life, the conditions were ripe for the inclusion of an element of novel, an interest in the extraordinary and fantastic and a stylistic search for effect and the chance to rouse emotions. On the other hand, the adventurous aspect, linked to the journeys to unknown and distant lands, was translated into a rebirth of interest in and study of ethnography. This favoured a return to historiography of the Herodotean type, shaped by geographical and ethnographic themes, with a taste for usages and customs of remote and hitherto unknown peoples. This element is present both in the Alexander Historians and in the works of local history that we shall discuss shortly.

So far as it is possible to reconstruct, the Alexander Historians seem to have had some important aspects in common: an affinity in their concept of politics; a shared literary tradition and a certain familiarity with prior Greek literature; a core set of scientific knowledge; and often some interest in philosophy. Further, they wrote for a Greek readership whose ideas and prejudices they knew well.

1.3.2 Authors and works contemporary to Alexander

The Royal Ephemerides. We begin with the *Royal Ephemerides*, cited explicitly by Arrian and Plutarch. These are a daily diary (this is the meaning of the Greek word *ephēmeris*) which described the final days of Alexander's illness in Babylon. Doubt has been cast on their supposed derivation from a journal by a court official, held by the chief secretary Eumenes of Cardia, which was used by Ptolemy as his principal source for the history of Alexander, and the authenticity of the document has been contested by modern scholars. The most important contribution they make, if they are authentic, is in the account of Alexander's death, which Plutarch claims to be following to the letter. They supported the position that the king died of a natural cause, due to his excessive drinking, against the theory that he was poisoned.

Callisthenes. The role of official historian of the expedition was probably assigned to Callisthenes of Olynthus (under whose name the so-called *Alexander Romance* circulated, though it was written later than the second century A.D.). A relative and pupil of Aristotle, he cooperated with him in scientific research (Aristotle asked him to acquire Eastern writings about astronomical observations) and in erudite studies (an inscription at Delphi pays homage to Aristotle and Callisthenes for their work on the victors at the Pythian Games). It was Aristotle who introduced him to the Macedonian court. Callisthenes joined the following of Alexander and composed his account of the expedition to the East simultaneously with the advance of the army. However, in the course of the expedition he fell into disgrace in the king's eyes. First he refused to engage in *proskynesis*, i.e. prostration before the king, an expression of the divine conception of monarchy adopted by Alexander following the customs of oriental kings. Then he was accused of having taken part in a conspiracy (the so-called "Page's Conspiracy") and was arrested and executed before the expedition returned to Babylon. Due to Callisthenes' premature death, his account of the expedition was obviously left incomplete. He also wrote some *Hellenica*, which narrated Greek history from 387/6 (the King's Peace) to the accession of Philip to the throne of Macedonia in 359, largely filling the historical gap left by the two works of Theopompus, the *Hellenica* (which ended at 394 B.C.) and the *Philippica* (which began with Philip's accession to the throne). At the point where the latter ended, Callisthenes picked up again with his history of Alexander. These choices suggest that Callisthenes was following the Isocratean school and the rhetorical historiography that it championed, although the ancient sources do not record him as a student of Isocrates. The sources mention other works by Callisthenes: a *Periplus*, which probably offered accounts and mythological explanations of geographical names, and a collection of *Apophthegmata* or famous sayings. Polybius criticised in detail Callisthenes' lack of precision and his style. This negative judgement contributed to the loss of his works (a few quotations survive).

Onesicritus. Onesicritus of Astypalaea was born before 375 B.C. and was a pupil of the Cynic philosopher Diogenes. He joined the following of Alexander in the final part of the expedition, in the Indian region; during the return voyage from the River Indus to the Persian Gulf he was the chief helmsman of the royal flagship, subordinate to the admiral Nearchus. His personal connections to the king are attested also by the fact that in 326 B.C. Alexander invited him, as an exponent of the Cynic school, to a meeting with some Indian wise men. Two works of his are recorded about the king: Πῶς Ἀλέξανδρος ἤχθη (it is not certain if the title means *How Alex-*

ander Was Educated) and an encomium of the king. A large part of his historical work was devoted to the events of the Indian phase of the expedition and it included a narrative of the return voyage. On this latter point he was criticised by Nearchus, who wrote an account on the same topic. Onesicritus indulged in telling fantastic episodes (such as a meeting between Alexander and the Amazons), which earned him the criticism of Strabo (who called him a "helmsman not just of Alexander but of the improbable") and the curiosity of later authors, who were attracted by his taste for the marvellous and strange. Already in the ancient world (Diogenes Laertius) a certain affinity between Onesicritus and Xenophon was noted, beginning in their respective biographies: both abandoned the study of philosophy for military adventure; played a prominent part in a dangerous return journey; admired their fallen commanders and glorified them in their writings; and enlivened their narrative by discussing the local customs and the fauna and flora of the countries they saw. The similarity between the two authors seems also to have held good at the level of style, but of Onesicritus' writings not a single fragment survives in his own words and so no comparison is possible.

Ptolemy. Our essential source for knowledge of the work of Ptolemy, son of Lagus, is Arrian, who held him in high regard for various reasons: he had accompanied the expedition of Alexander; he had written after the king's death, when there was no longer any motive for adulation; and Ptolemy himself was a king, so one could expect him not to lie. In some historical episodes in which Ptolemy seems to have been involved, it is likely that Arrian has drawn on Ptolemy's own account: the clarity with which Arrian describes the military operations carried out by Ptolemy himself supports this theory and allows us to appreciate his competence as a military historian. While our knowledge of his work is scant, we know his biography with some precision. A Macedonian by origin, Ptolemy was one of the most trusted commanders in Alexander's army. After the long struggles that followed the king's death, he assumed royal power over Egypt with the title "Soter" (i.e. "Saviour"), inaugurating the dynasty of the Ptolemies or Lagids. According to the general opinion, Ptolemy wrote his work on Alexander in the final stage of his life, perhaps just a year or two before his own death in 283 B.C. The reasons that prompted him to give an account of his experience with Alexander (aside from the ambition of setting out his credentials as Alexander's heir in imperial status, in competition with the other Diadochi) are likely to have included the desire to correct existing versions and dispel the mythical and romantic haze that was thickening around the figure of Alexander. From the testimony of Arrian, it is certain that Ptolemy was talented and experienced in military command and had a close personal connection to Alexander and a direct, first-hand knowledge of the king's thinking and of official documents. All these are motives that may have led him to provide his own authoritative testimony to the events, giving more space to the military operations in which he participated.

Nearchus. Nearchus was born around 360 B.C., of Cretan origin, and was a childhood friend of Alexander. Following the severe quarrels that broke out in 337 between Alexander and his father Philip, king of Macedonia, Nearchus was expelled from the kingdom. He returned on the death of Philip and took part in various military missions, in 334 becoming governor of Lycia and Pamphylia, a position that demanded experience of naval command, to prevent any operations by the Persian navy. He was named commander of the Hydaspes fleet and, after sailing down the rivers Hydaspes, Acesines and Indus, in 326 he was made admiral of the fleet that had to find a route from India to Babylon and explore the countries on the coast to be encountered during the voyage. His account of this difficult undertaking was the Περίπλους τῆς Ἰνδικῆς (*Circumnavigation of India*). On the death of Alexander, Nearchus took part in the struggles for the division of the king's immense domains, siding with Antigonus Monophthalmos and then with Demetrius Poliorcetes. Our knowledge of his work derives from the summary of it given by Arrian in his *Indica*, where we also find extracts of interest for ethnography and natural history (a description of India and of the voyage from the Hydaspes to Babylon). He was responsible for the official report of the expedition. No one has ever accused him of distorting the facts and Arrian treats him with great respect, taking for granted that he is reliable. Since his work is lost, we cannot know what literary form it took (it was certainly not just a transcription of the official report), nor its length or original title. It is possible to detect some literary influences: there are elements that the narrative of the *nostos* of Alexander shares with the account of the *nostos* par excellence of the Greek literary tradition, the *Odyssey*; in his rapid descriptions of places, Nearchus reveals the influence of the ancient genre of the *periplus*, which enjoyed a lively return to popularity.

Aristobulus. We do not know Aristobulus' country of origin. Although he never appears in military expeditions, he received positions from Alexander that suggest that he had skills of a technical nature, as engineer or architect. His work and that of Ptolemy are the principal sources of Arrian's *Anabasis*, who states that he trusts their reliability because they both accompanied the king on the expedition and because they wrote after his death, when there was no longer any motive to say anything but the truth. Aristobulus began from Alexander's accession to the throne and also narrated the first campaigns. In the account of the episodes concerning the king's behaviour (drinking, executions) he sought to play down the negative sides and to justify the excesses, endeavouring to provide a consistent characterisation of the king. While it would not be possible to talk in his case of real adulation of Alexander, episodes were included that aimed to present the king in an ideal and virtuous light. For example, Aristobulus is the source of the anecdote according to which Alexander preferred to throw to the ground a helmet full of water that he had been offered, in order not to quench his thirst before his soldiers, tormented by thirst, were able to do so. Aristobulus' descriptions of the tomb of Cyrus at Pasargadae and that of Sardanapalus at Anchiale are admired by modern archaeologists for their precision. This accuracy seems to reflect the author's technical skills and recurs in his citing of precise figures for distances, time, money and so on. It seems that Aristobulus avoided or at least played down the mythical and marvellous elements present in other narratives about Alexander. For example, he rejected the episode of the encounter between Alexander and the Amazons (like Chares and Ptolemy), though he did not deny the existence of the Amazons, whom he simply leaves in their traditional territory near Colchis. He did not try to eliminate the miraculous element entirely but, when he speaks of it, his is often the least sensational version. Despite the fact that it was used extensively by Arrian, we know nothing precise about the literary characteristics, style, composition or length of his work.

Marsyas. Marsyas of Pella, born around 356 and died after 294, probably accompanied Alexander for some stage of the expedition into Asia. We know nothing other than that he participated in the battle of Salamis in the spring of 306 B.C. We do not know when he died precisely. According to the *Suda lexicon*, Marsyas composed a history of Macedonia (*Macedonica*) in ten books, from the earliest kings to Alexander's march into Syria after the Egyptian campaign; he also wrote an *Education of Alexander* and twelve books of *Attica* are also attributed to him.

Chares. Among the Alexander Historians who claimed to have written on the basis of their own direct experience, some aimed principally at their target audience's interest in gossip and scandal. Their work made a strong contribution to the genesis of the romanticised tradition about the figure of Alexander. We may recall here Chares of Mytilene, Alexander's εἰσαγγελεύς (chamberlain or master of audiences). His work, perhaps with the title *Histories of Alexander*, had at least ten books and probably consisted primarily of anecdotes. Examples include the long account of the five days of wedding ceremonies at Susa, cited by Athenaeus among the passages that were intended to show Alexander's luxurious habits, and the account of Callisthenes' refusal to prostrate himself before the king, which may have been witnessed by Chares himself.

Ephippus. Ephippus of Olynthus must have been born before the year 348 B.C., when his city was destroyed, and he held military responsibilities as an official in the Macedonian army. The work *On the death (or funeral) of Alexander and Hephaestion* (in 323 and 324 respectively) should probably be attributed to him. As far as we know, he is the source of five fragments transmitted by Athenaeus concerning details of dishes, drinks and behaviours at the court of the Macedonian commander that were little suited to the Hellenic style. The fragments reveal a strongly hostile attitude towards Alexander and one inclined to accept all the stories that showed him in a bad light. We do not know what role personal reasons may have played in this, such as the destruction of his native city Olynthus and the execution of his fellow countryman Callisthenes.

Cleitarchus. The surviving fragments of the work of Cleitarchus, (Τὰ) περὶ Ἀλεξάνδρου (*On Alexander*), in more than twelve books, are few and of little significance. Despite its popularity in the late Roman Republic and the first centuries of the Empire (it was used by Diodorus, Curtius Rufus, Plutarch and Arrian, though the last of these never names him), ancient judgements on his work were harsh. Cicero, Quintilian and Strabo regarded Cleitarchus as an orator rather than a historian. Greek rhetors did not find his style attractive, regarding it as tasteless in its vocabulary choices (Demetrius, *On Style*) and pompous (the treatise *On the Sublime*). Unlike the authors considered so far, nothing suggests that Cleitarchus personally participated in the expedition of Alexander; since his father Dinon wrote *Persica*, his knowledge of the East does not imply that he had actually visited it. Some fragments reveal a tendency to manipulate the reconstruction of facts to obtain an effective story. For example, he told an episode in which Alexander was dragged to safety by Ptolemy (and perhaps made this the origin of the title "Soter") in the battle at the city of the Malli, although Ptolemy himself said that he was not present at this battle (this adulation of Ptolemy, among other things, is in accord with the notice that claims Cleitarchus was an Alexandrian). His use of the miraculous confers a romantic tone on his work: he does not reject the history of the fantastic encounter of Alexander with the Amazons, and describes it in a colourful and dramatic way; he also elaborates on the motif of Alexander as following in the footsteps of Dionysus in his journey to India. Cleitarchus is definitely a historian who does not master the details, narrating events in which he himself did not participate. He works by drawing on other authors, reporting their testimony or else altering it without a qualm. A work such as his was easily able to win more interest than the honest but unappealing works of Aristobulus or Ptolemy. His literary tendencies and his style make him an author of Alexandrian taste and a precursor of Asianism.

1.3.3 Authors later than Alexander

The later tradition around the figure of Alexander includes not only historical works but also contributions from the schools of philosophy and rhetoric. Among other things, a corpus of themes developed that was a widely shared inheritance to be used by the rhetorical schools in their exercises. Among the historians surveyed above, Onesicritus belonged to the Cynic school and was a student of Diogenes; Callisthenes and Cleitarchus gave their work a marked rhetorical stamp.

Anaximenes. We have already mentioned Anaximenes of Lampsacus, a rhetor and historian who lived approximately from 380 to 320 B.C. and knew Philip and Alexander personally. His fame as a rhetor was notable and the *Rhetorica ad Alexandrum* has been attributed to him, a work transmitted in the Aristotelian corpus (cf. *The Classical Age* X 1.4). He pursued a dispute against Theopompus, whom he tried to discredit by putting into circulation a harsh invective against Athens, Sparta and Thebes called the *Trikaranos*, composed in the style and under the name of Theopompus. He must have had a great talent for imitation. The learned scholar Didymus maintained that *Oration* XI of Demosthenes should be attributed to Anaximenes. Dionysius of Halicarnassus said that Anaximenes did not achieve full success in any of the fields that he attempted and that his style was weak and unconvincing. In fact it is odd that so little has survived of the work of an author who was so famous in the ancient world. As a historian, Anaximenes was an exponent of so-called rhetorical historiography. He wrote a work of universal history, the *Hellenica*, in twelve books, which ran from the origin of time to the battle of Mantinea (362 B.C.), then he continued with two monographs entitled *History of Philip* and *History of Alexander*. From the few fragments, what emerges is a strongly adulatory attitude towards Alexander the Great. Anaximenes had been one of the king's teachers and accompanied him on the expedition into Asia, specifically in his capacity as a historian. Although he is named in the canon of the ten principal historians, it seems that he did not have much influence.

Hegesias. Hegesias of Magnesia on the Sipylus, who lived in the first half of the third century, has likewise been mentioned above for his work as a rhetor. The ancients considered him to be one of the pioneers of the Asianist style. He was a prolific writer. Among the titles of his works we may recall the *Encomium of Rhodes*, *The Philo-Athenians*, *Aspasia* and *Alcibiades* (the nature of these works is not clear). He also wrote forensic or political speeches. We know nothing of his history of Alexander, but Dionysius of Halicarnassus cites a long section of it that is rich in epic echoes, for the purpose of deploring its taste and style.

Potamon. Potamon of Mytilene, who lived in the first centuries B.C. and A.D., spent his final years at Rome as a teacher of rhetoric. The *Suda* lexicon records among his works *On Alexander the Macedonian*, *Chronicle of the Samians*, *Encomia of Brutus and Caesar* and *On the Perfect Orator*.

The "antiquarian historians." The term "antiquarian historians" refers to some authors whose work appears to be characterised by combining rhetorical and antiquarian history with long-standing genres such as the *periplus* (in this perhaps partly influenced by Callisthenes). Among these writers we may record: Menaechmus of Sicyon, to be placed perhaps at the end of the fourth century B.C., author of an erudite work on the Pythian victors, a history of Sicyon, a treatise on music and perhaps a work on bronze sculpture. Anticleides of Athens (third century B.C.), the first Athenian to write on Alexander, to whom a work on the antiquities of Delos and one on a mythological topic entitled *Nostoi* are attributed. Aristus of Salamis, cited by Arrian as an author of histories of Alexander, who lived perhaps around 150 B.C. Finally, a papyrus from Oxyrhynchus (*P.Oxy.* XV 1798) of the second century A.D. seems to preserve fragments of a history of Alexander of some length and provides some interesting details that are not otherwise known.

The Alexander Romance. It remains to consider the so-called *Alexander Romance*, normally called the work of "Pseudo-Callisthenes" since in the manuscripts it is transmitted under the name of the first of the Alexander Historians. It is an account of the achievements of Alexander in which the literary aspect of narrative novel has definitively overwhelmed the historiographical aspect. It is nearly certain that it originated in the Alexandrian Period, but in the Imperial Period different versions came into being and circulated. In the form that we know it, the work was composed at a date after the second century A.D. and has survived in different recensions, derived from an epistolary novel (formed by fake letters supposedly sent to and from Alexander) with the addition of fantastic and encomiastic episodes drawn from the historiography on Alexander.

1.4 Forms of historiography in the age of the Diadochi

1.4.1 Histories of the Diadochi: Hieronymus of Cardia, Duris, Philarchus

If we bear in mind the ideal of the "historical cycle," in which the authors of historiography proceed steadily through the narration of events by continuing the work of their predecessors, after the Alexander Historians it is natural to find a group of authors who treated the following period, i.e. the age of the Diadochi of the first generation and their successors.

Hieronymus. Hieronymus lived between 360 and 265 B.C., was born at Cardia on the Hellespont and was a friend and close collaborator of the Diadochus Eumenes of Cardia, a champion of the unity of the empire bequeathed by Alexander the Great. At the death of Eumenes (316 B.C.) Hieronymus moved into the service of his rival Antigonus Monophthalmos. When the latter too died at the battle of Ipsus (301 B.C.), Hieronymus remained loyal to the Antigonids and became a follower of Demetrius Poliorcetes. He wrote a history of the period after Alexander (*The Events After Alexander* is one of the transmitted titles of the work, along with *History of the Diadochi*, among others), beginning at 323 and continuing to the death of Pyrrhus (272 B.C.). The narrative thus encompassed around fifty years and was probably preceded by an excursus on the early history of Macedonia, to provide the historical background to the events of 323. He was the first Greek historian to treat Rome, the origins of which he recounted. Despite the judgement of Pausanias, from whom it seems that Hieronymus was characterised by a strongly courtly attitude towards the kings who were his patrons, his history was considered authoritative, to the extent that for those fifty years it was the main source of Diodorus, Arrian and Plutarch. Dionysius of Halicarnassus states that his style was dry and unadorned.

Duris. Duris, whose family was originally from Samos but had been forced into exile, was born in Sicily after the mid-fourth century B.C. After returning to Samos around 300 B.C. he became its tyrant and held on to power for around twenty years. We do not know at what stage of life he was a pupil of the Peripatetic Theophrastus. He died around 270 B.C. A prolific and versatile author, Duris wrote works on various topics, of which only fragments remain: works of literary criticism (an interest in the interpretation of literary works was frequent among the Peripatetics), such as the *Homeric Problems*, *On Tragedy*, *On Euripides and Sophocles*; a Περὶ νόμων (*On Melodies*) and a Περὶ ἀγώνων (*On Competitions*), both perhaps on musical topics; works of history of art, such as the treatises *On Painting* and *On Toreutics*. In the field of historiography, Duris was the author of a local chronicle of Samos (Σαμίων ὧροι, *Annals of Samos*), a contribution to a rich tradition of histories of the island, which included a large number of episodic and anecdotal stories and a patriotism that elevated Samos above other cities, even at the expense of historical reality (the invention of the twenty-four letters of the alphabet was attributed to the Samians and it was maintained that Panyassis and Herodotus were from Samos). On the contemporary figure of the tyrant Agathocles of Syracuse (died 289 B.C.), an exceptional personality of great wickedness and boldness, he wrote the work *History of Agathocles*. This figure was the ideal subject for Duris' concept of historiography, in which a prominent role was played by *peripeteiai*, the alternation of successes and defeats, scenes with a tragic flavour and emotive events. A fondness for the genre of biography, typical of Peripatetic circles, cannot have been foreign to this work. Duris' main historical work was the *Macedonica*, which recounted the fortunes of the Macedonian monarchy from the death of Amyntas III (father of Philip and grandfather of Alexander) in 370, probably down to the battle of Corupedium (281 B.C.), and so encompassing the entire phase of the struggles of the Diadochi, with the formation and consolidation of the Hellenistic kingdoms that emerged from the splintering of Alexander's conquests. It is wise to bear in mind that the few surviving fragments, which were mostly selected by a polemical tradition, may produce a disproportionate emphasis on certain aspects over other ones. Certainly there is a clear contradiction between Duris' theoretical assumptions, which praised a faithful and meticulous search for the truth, and their realisation which, for the sake of making the story pleasant and attractive, gives much room to invented details. At any rate, beyond the consideration that he often chose to use good sources, in his favour is the fact that he was a witness to the period he was recounting, and at Samos, which was a window onto both Europe and Asia.

Philarchus. We have very meagre biographical notices about Philarchus, who is traditionally said to have shared historiographical characteristics with Duris. His country of origin is uncertain (Athens, Naucratis or Sicyon), as is his date. According to the testimony of Polybius, he lived in the mid-third century. Recorded are various monographs on historical and mythological topics, as well as his Ἱστορίαι (*Historiai*) in 28 books, which began with the invasion of the Peloponnese by Pyrrhus and ended with the death of Ptolemy III Euergetes, the accession to the throne by his son Ptolemy IV Philopator (who put to death the queen-mother Berenice) and the death of the Spartan Cleomenes (220/19). In this work the author revealed a particular interest in the history of the Peloponnese and of Ptolemaic Egypt. In the manner of Duris, Philarchus was fond of anecdote and the episodic event, with a predilection for dramatic content. We find in his fragments a tendency towards moral instruction through edifying stories, which was probably also influenced by contemporary philosophical conceptions (Stoicism and Cynicism). Again in line with Duris and with a historiography of Herodotean type, Philarchus exhibits curiosity about ethnography and a taste for the miraculous. All these traits attest a dominant influence from Theopompus and Duris, with the latter in particular being the inspiration of Philarchus' preference for the tragic tale and for moving and sensational episodes, in a continuous search for facts that could rouse emotion. These choices, along with the frequent description of women's psychology, led Polybius to call the Philarchean manner γυναικῶδες ("feminine").

Duris and Philarchus are regarded as exponents of the so-called dramatic or tragic historiography. A fragment of the first book of Duris' *Macedonica* conveys significant elements of his literary and historiographic concept. He criticises the historians Ephorus and Theopompus for their lack of μίμησις (i.e. the ability to imitate nature) and of ἡδονὴ ἐν τῷ φράσαι (i.e. a pleasing, graceful style). That is, he rebuked the historiographic school modelled on Isocratean rhetoric for its lack of the artistic imitation of life that produces enjoyment and pleasure. To this is added Polybius' harsh criticism of Philarchus, whom he accused of representing the facts in a dramatic fashion in order to resonate in the imagination of the readers and so to provoke their emotional involvement. This polemic offers us good information about the characteristics of the historiography that Polybius rejected, even though we know well that he was transposing a primarily political disagreement onto a methodological level (on which, however, he had a good point). At any rate, the combination of these elements has led scholars to identify a real historiographic tradition, which is defined as "dramatic" or "tragic history." It is traced to the Peripatetic school, maintaining that Duris (a pupil of Theophrastus) had tried to overcome the Aristotelian view that regarded poetry as superior to historiography (as we read in the *Poetics*: cf. *The Classical Age* XIII 3.5.3) by cancelling the distinction between the two genres and so making historiography a mimetic activity like poetry. This interpretation has today been abandoned and what is emphasised is rather that readers' tastes moved the authors to try to capture their attention by expedients that would pique their interest and entertain them: this, then, was the reason for the lively and captivating scenes represented; the rich pathos in descriptions, with the goal of provoking strong emotions with tragic and sensational episodes; and the battle narratives, which yielded dramatic effects and grand narrative scenes. There was a search for whatever was strange and unusual, and great importance was accorded to the analysis of character and the description of the figures' feelings, as also to anecdotes and love stories. All efforts were aimed at a vivid and pleasing narrative, preoccupied with attracting the readers by entertainment, rather than making them think and reflect on the great problems of politics and human life. However, there are no elements that support the idea that this constituted a real tradition, i.e. a tendency that could be isolated from the general picture of Hellenistic historiography. It is rather the case that we should think of these as choices made by certain authors, with every likelihood that they were influenced by the rhetoric of the period and were trying to meet the demands of tastes that were widespread.

1.4.2 Local history

The exploits of Alexander and the literature that they made possible included an adventurous aspect, linked to journeys to distant and unknown lands, which also translated into a rebirth of interest in and study of ethnography. On the other hand, the Hellenistic kingdoms promoted the knowledge and appreciation of the history and cultural traditions of their territories. It is probable that the writing of local history in various settings was requested or at least favoured by the reigning dynasties. This phenomenon is significant also in the fact that it intensified the cultural exchanges between the Greek world and the civilisations of Asia, opening up of an unusually broad political and cultural horizon.

A disciple of Pyrrhon, the founder of Scepticism, Hecataeus of Abdera visited Egyptian Thebes under Ptolemy I (305–283 B.C.). As well as a work on the Hyperboreans, he wrote the *Aegyptiaca*, which was the principal source of the description of Egypt that we read in Diodorus (I 10–98: the only complete report on Egypt that survives, aside from that of Herodotus). Diodorus shows us that the work was arranged into Egyptian cosmology and theology, geography, Egyptian kings, usages and customs. In Hecataeus' work Egypt was strongly idealised, as a country that was exemplary in its customs and political institutions, the cradle and source of all civilisations, including that of Greece.

Manetho, an Egyptian from Sebennytos (a city in the Nile delta) and a priest at Heliopolis under the first two Ptolemies (Ptolemy I: 305–283 B.C.; Ptolemy II: 283–246 B.C.), played an important role in the introduction of the cult of Serapis. He is a significant example of a non-Greek using the Greek language. His work *Aegyptiaca* was suggested to him by Ptolemy II, to whom it was dedicated. Its aim was to familiarise the Greeks with Egyptian civilisation and religion, probably as a counterpoint to the idealised and romanticised image that they had been given in the work of the same name by Hecataeus of Abdera, which had been published shortly before. The work, in three books, treated the mythical era and Egyptian history across thirty dynasties, drawing on Egyptian documentary material provided by annalistic works, king lists and learned chronicles.

The author of a *Babylonian History* (or *Chaldaica*) in three books, Beros(s)us was priest of Bel-Marduk, the supreme god of the Babylonian pantheon, and was born (as he himself said) at the time of Alexander the Great. He too was thus a non-Greek using the Greek language. The work was dedicated to Antiochus I Soter (281–261 B.C.) and so was in line with the official politics of the Seleucid court. It began with an account of the origins of the world and ended with the death of Alexander the Great. The sources used by Beros(s)us were provided by local documents and traditions: comparison with Babylonian and Assyrian cuneiform texts shows that his account is generally reliable. His work conveyed to the Greeks important astronomical knowledge, although it seems that the report that he founded a school of astrology is baseless.

An ethnographic work on India was composed by Megasthenes, a diplomat and historian, whom Alexander himself had appointed to a satrapy, which he governed until at least 316. He undertook diplomatic missions to India in the years 302–291 and composed his *Indica* based on his personal experience.

1.4.3 Sicilian historiography: Timaeus of Tauromenium

Timaeus was born around 350 B.C. at Tauromenium, a city of which his father Andromachus was the founder (in 358) and tyrant. For reasons unknown to us, Timaeus was banished from Sicily by the tyrant Agathocles of Syracuse (some time between 316 and 312) and he spent his exile at Athens. He himself says (fr. 34) that he remained there at least fifty years, though he may already have been in the city when his banishment was pronounced. At Athens, not being able to take an active part in politics, he devoted himself to studies with the Isocratean Philiscus of Miletus and to the composition of historiographical works. At an advanced age it became possible for him to return to Syracuse. He died aged almost a hundred around 260 B.C.

Timaeus drew the criticisms of Polybius as a "desk-based" historian who wrote about topics of which he had no direct experience (as had also been said of Ephorus). The characterisation of Timaeus as a scholar devoted primarily to book-based research is confirmed by our information about the works he composed.

The *Olympionikai* seem to have been a preliminary task for his principal historical work. It was not merely a revision of the similar work done by Hippias and Aristotle, but rather a new and very accurate synchronised record of the Olympic victors with other eponyms (ephors and kings of Sparta, archons of Athens, priestesses of Hera at Argos), which introduced the chronological system based on Olympiads, accepted for example by Eratosthenes (cf. *The Hellenistic Age* III 2.2) and used by Polybius and Diodorus and which survived into the Late Antique Period.

The *Sikelikai historiai*, divided by the author himself into 38 books, ran from the mythical origins of Sicily to the death of Agathocles of Syracuse (289/8 B.C.). Timaeus maintained that there had been a continuous Greek presence in the West from the Mycenaean Age, with early foundations of *poleis*. This is a very different view from that of Antiochus of Syracuse (second half of fifth century B.C.), but it may have had a predecessor in Philistus (late fifth to first half of fourth century). The large number of preserved fragments, the wide use made of it by Diodorus for Sicilian history up to Agathocles (despite the problems of reconstruction that we have spoken of above: cf. above 1.1) and the polemical judgements on it expressed by Polybius allow us to gain a good idea of Timaeus' work.

Books I–V, also called προκατασκευή (*prokataskeuē*, "preparation"), contained a geography of the West and North and narrated mythical events, foundations of colonies and genealogies; links and synchronisms were established between Greek and western myths, thus laying the foundations for the creation of the myth of Rome's origin from Aeneas. Then followed the his-

tory of Sicily prior to Agathocles (Books VI–XXXIII). The last five books (XXXIV–XXXVIII) took
as their subject the events linked to the figures of Agathocles and Pyrrhus, down to the beginning of the First Punic War (264 B.C.); they were perhaps added to the previous books at a later
stage.

Unlike a Greek author such as Hieronymus of Cardia, who limited himself to narrating the origins of Rome, Timaeus followed the events down to 264, the year in which the first war against Carthage began. The event that will have drawn his attention to the history of Rome was probably the defeat suffered by Pyrrhus in 272 B.C. Southern Italy and Carthage were also taken into consideration and some excursuses gave an account of the situation in Greece.

Notable in Timaeus is the simultaneous presence of some of the different approaches that can be identified in Hellenistic historiography. The ultimate aim that he attributes to his historical research is the truth (and even Polybius, despite his harsh criticism, acknowledges his chronological and documentary accuracy). However, this ideal goal is flouted in practice by the intrusion of a series of personal and subjective tendencies: patriotism, which does not stop even at clear distortion of the facts; deep hatred for tyrants, which leads him to present the figure of Agathocles of Syracuse in a grotesque manner (the distorted description of the tyrant and the surrender to pathos in the description of his victims are marks of a taste that did not disdain the search for effect and the use of rhetoric) and to express negative judgements on Hieron I and the two Dionysii; hatred of Carthage; the decision to completely invent speeches, which thus become purely theoretical exercises; a strongly critical attitude towards previous historians (above all Philistus); and a conception of history that leads him to see continuous divine interventions in historical events. Polybius explains many of Timaeus' shortcomings by attributing them to his book-based erudition and lack of real political and military experience. As with Ephorus, for Timaeus too the work of writing history consisted essentially in the sifting of literary sources.

It is very difficult to get an idea of Timaeus' style, since for the most part we have only testimonia that do not reproduce his exact words. Dionysius of Halicarnassus did not spare him in the classicising condemnation of Hellenistic prose in general. Yet Cicero, who considered him a representative of Asianist prose (cf. *The Hellenistic Age* VII 2.1), called him "rich in ideas and vivid" and regarded his phrasing as "harmonious and elegant." The fact that Timaeus' work formed a point of reference is shown both by the large number of Greek and Roman authors who drew on him, and also by the polemics that he provoked from later historians such as Istrus, Polemon and Polybius. Contrasting judgements have been expressed on Timaeus also by modern historians, who have sometimes ascribed to him a rhetorical and propagandistic concept of history, in which the truth of the facts can be sacrificed to the demands of persuasion, sometimes a rhetorical taste that sought effects in order to move the emotions, yet at other times great scientific fastidiousness. It seems that in reality one may say that the different components coexisted in his work and this simultaneous presence of them needs to be taken into account when relying on the tradition derived from him.

1.4.4 Historians and polymaths

In this section we collect a small group of authors who devoted themselves to different literary and scholarly genres, including historiography or chronography, a genre closely linked to history since it concerns the chronological framework and dating criteria of events.

The fame of Eratosthenes (third century B.C.), as we have seen, is linked above all to philological and scientific studies, which he was able to develop by drawing on the vast patrimony of books in the Library of Alexandria, of which he was director after Apollonius Rhodius. He composed a *Chronographia* in at least twelve books, from the Fall of Troy (dated to 1184/3) to the death of Alexander the Great, in which a fundamental role was played by fixing the chronology of historical events. An example of it is given by the Christian author Clement of Alexandria, who summarised the structure of the work as follows (*Stromata* I 138, 1–3): "Eratosthenes wrote up the chronological timings in this way (τοὺς χρόνους ὧδε ἀναγράφει): from the Fall of Troy to the return of the Heraclids, eighty years; from this event to the colonisation of Ionia, sixty years; the following events down to the government of Lycurgus, one hundred and fifty-nine years; down to the first year of the first Olympiad, one hundred and eight years..." A separate work was devoted to the victors in the Olympic Games (*Olympionikai*); their sequence, with the first Olympiad fixed in the year 776 (the first known victor, Coroebus of Elis, won on that date), was the basis of his chronological system, a choice that was followed by many subsequent historians. For the previous period he used the list of the Spartan kings.

Agathocles of Cyzicus (a city on the Propontis) lived in the second half of the third and the first decade of the second century B.C. He spent part of his life in Alexandria, where he was a student of Zenodotus. There are indications that he also lived and worked in other cities (he may have been at Seleucia and have had connections with Pergamum). A historian, scholar and renowned grammarian, he treated local history (cf. above 1.4.2) in a work Περὶ Κυζίκου (*On Cyzicus*). Agathocles maintained the theory that Aeneas came to Italy after the Fall of Troy (cf. previous section), a point needed to attest the Trojan origin of the Romans, which was a powerful propaganda tool. On this theory, which later became the official version of the origins of Rome, a genuine historical debate arose: as well as Agathocles, it was supported also by Hegesianax of Alexandria in the Troad (a historian, poet and grammarian of the second century B.C.), whereas it was rejected by the scholar and antiquarian Demetrius of Scepsis in the Troad, the author of a commentary on the *Catalogue of the Trojans* in the *Iliad* (second century B.C.).

Agatharchides of Cnidus spent much of his life at Alexandria in the first half of the second century B.C., first as a schoolteacher and then as secretary to Heraclides Lembus, an influential courtier. Since he had free access to the royal archive, it is likely that he was a member of the Alexandrian Museum. Cited as his works are a *History of Asia* in ten books, perhaps down to the period of the Diadochi; a *History of Europe* in 49 books, which included a detailed treatment of Greek and Macedonian history of the third century; and the ethnographic work *On the Red Sea* in five books, with which Agatharchides wished to provide a contribution to the geography and ethnography of the southern part of the world, which had been left out of the descriptions of previous authors. This last work also met a specific interest on the part of the Ptolemies in the commerce and natural history of this region. The sources used must have been the *Royal Hypomnēmata* (the official reports of expeditions, published by the Ptolemaic court) and some eyewitness testimonia, especially those of merchants. Agatharchides also made use – often critical – of previous historians.

Apollodorus of Athens (whom we discussed in the chapter on philology, cf. *The Hellenistic Age* III 2.4) displayed a variety of interests comparable to those of Eratosthenes. He was born around 180 B.C. at Athens, where he studied with Diogenes of Babylon and then moved to Alexandria where he was a pupil of Aristarchus. He left the Egyptian city probably around 145/4 B.C. and settled at Pergamum before returning to Athens, where he died between 120 and 110. The *Chronica*, composed in iambic trimeters to ease memorisation, were dedicated to Attalus II, king of Pergamum (and so were completed after 144). They probably ran from the Fall of Troy (1184/3) to 144 B.C. They recorded not just political and military events, but also notices concerning philosophy, literature and art. The years were identified on the basis of the Attic archons. An appendix, added as a fourth book, extended the work to 120 or 110. Said to be based on Apollodorus is the *Periēgēsis* once falsely attributed to Scymnus of Chios (and hence known as Pseudo-Scymnus) but now ascribed to Pausanias of Damascus (second half of second century B.C.). However, this work of 980 lines falls far below the elegance of Apollodorus' verse, which are often particularly deft and successful in inserting proper names into the metre.

2 Polybius

2.1 A Greek at Rome

Polybius was born at Megalopolis in Arcadia in 205 B.C. (or between 202 and 200, according to others). His father Lycortas was a statesman and leader of the Achaean Confederacy, which brought a large part of the Peloponnese (Achaea, Arcadia, the Argolid and other regions) into confederation, often in conflict with Sparta and Messenia. Polybius received a thorough education, as is shown by, among other things, the points of literary criticism present in his main work: for example, he once addresses a problem of Homeric exegesis (Book XXXIV) and elsewhere he cites expressions from Pindar and Hesiod. An influence from the Peripatos in his formation has been noted. He then began a military and political career, thanks to which he came into contact with the most important figures of the time. He admired Lydiadas, the tyrant of Megalopolis, Cleomenes III, king of Sparta, and the Arcadian Philopoemen, the *stratēgos* of the Achaean Confederacy who pursued a shrewd policy that aimed to safeguard the Greek cities' autonomy despite a fundamental alliance with Rome. Polybius had a significant career, soon becoming one of the most important figures in the Achaean Confederacy, and he took part in numerous military and diplomatic missions. One of these missions, in 190/89 B.C., provided the opportunity to establish an alliance with Rome: a contingent from the Confederacy was next to the Romans in the battle against the Galatians. On another occasion he was part of an embassy to Ptolemaic Alexandria together with his father. In 169 he held the military office of hipparch (cavalry commander), the second most important position in the Confederacy.

In 168 B.C., when the Roman victory at Pydna put an end to the Macedonian hegemony in Greece, the pro-Roman party was predominant in all the *poleis* of the Greek lands. Polybius and other representatives of the Achaean Confederacy who followed the line of Philopoemen had maintained a cautious and luke-warm attitude towards the Romans. Callicrates, a member of the Achaean Confederacy, denounced Polybius to the Roman authorities, accusing him and others of having flouted the commitments made to Rome and of having instead assisted the Macedonians. As a result of this accusation, Polybius was included among the thousand hostages who followed the victor, the consul Lucius Aemilius Paullus, in his triumph at Rome.

At Rome Polybius enjoyed the friendship of Scipio Aemilianus and entered the political and cultural circle of the Scipiones, the powerful and prestigious family that numbered among its members the principal military commanders and officials of the Roman army and which in those years was becoming the key agent of the spread of Greek culture at Rome and the promoter of Philhellene cultural tendencies. The friendship of the Scipiones allowed Polybius to remain at Rome, whereas the majority of the hostages were dispersed to various cities of Etruria. Free from political duties and spurred by new intellectual stimuli, in this period Polybius probably collected material for his writings and reflected on the political experience that had put him in contact with the new hegemonic power by placing him at its very heart, namely the city of Rome. Polybius' military competence cemented his relations with his principal protector. In the role of military counsellor, in 151 he accompanied Scipio Aemilianus on a journey to the Iberian peninsula and the next year followed him to North Africa and southern Gaul, then returning to Italy by the route travelled by Hannibal in the Second Punic War.

Towards 150, thanks to pressure from influential compatriots from the Peloponnese and the personal intervention of Scipio Aemilianus, Polybius recovered his status of free person and left Italy. In the years immediately thereafter he was present at the military events that played the greatest role in establishing Rome's domination of the Mediterranean, namely the destruction of Carthage (Third Punic War: 149–146) and Corinth (146). He may have taken part in the final phase of the siege of Numantia in 134/3, alongside Scipio Aemilianus.

When he returned with the latter to Rome, Polybius attempted to offer a final service to his Greek homeland by softening the anger of the Roman victors and seeking to convince the Greeks to accept the reality of Rome's military superiority. The Romans had set up a commission charged with establishing a new settlement for Greece, but after the commission itself had left Greece Polybius was entrusted with the practical realisation of the new order that had been established. In carrying out this role, he gained the admiration of many cities, which set up statues in his honour.

He died in his homeland at the age of 82 from a fall from his horse. The date of his death is fixed by the date accepted for his birth, and so the possible span runs from 123 to 118.

2.2 The minor works

As well as the *Histories*, which is Polybius' principal work and the only one of which a significant part has been preserved, we should record some minor works that are now lost. They treated subjects which must have in some way flowed into the major historical work. The *Life of Philopoemen* in three books was an encomium of the great Achaean politician poisoned by the Messenians in 183 B.C. The *Tactica* were a sort of manual of military tactics. The work *On the Inhabitability of the Equatorial Zone* was on a geographical topic. With the historical monograph *The Numantine War* Polybius effectively continued the narrative of the *Histories*, which had ended at 144 B.C., down to 133, a date that marked, among other things, the end of the great political and social cohesion at Rome (which occurred following the politics of Tiberius Gracchus) that had strongly impressed Polybius.

2.3 The *Histories*

The composition of the *Histories* must have been drawn out over at least twenty years and they were published after the author's death. The importance of the work lies, even more than in its value as a historiographical testimony of the first rank, in the fact that for the first time a Greek author took as the point of view and guiding thread of his historiography not the internal events of Greece but the steady and unstoppable consolidation of Rome's military and political world power.

Following a practice well established in Greek historiographical culture, Polybius's *Histories* connected with the narrative of Timaeus of Tauromenium, which had stopped at 264, the year in which the confrontation between Rome and Carthage began. Polybius states explicitly that he is picking up at the point where Timaeus stopped his account. His aim was to provide a general contemporary history that was open to the events in Greece, Asia, Italy and Libya, while still remaining focused on Rome as the fundamental point of view. His attention was focused essentially on political and military actions. This was thus a pragmatic historiography, which took as its model the work of Thucydides. Of the forty books of the final version, only Books I–V remain complete, while for the others we have extracts or brief passages.

Most of the *Histories* must have been published only after the author's death, but Polybius had probably already made some books public, perhaps the first four or five. There is a theory that there was an edition of Books I–XXIX that went back to the years 160–130 B.C.: Polybius would then have intervened in his text again with additions and expansions and would have composed the rest of the work after 129. The expansion of the original plan has indeed had the result that some anachronisms remain, such as many passages that presuppose the existence of Carthage, the composition of which must evidently go back to a period prior to the destruction of the city in 146 B.C.

Books I–V are preserved in 22 manuscripts of the medieval and Renaissance Period. From Book VI to XVIII, on the other hand, we have extracts of varying length transmitted by around fifty manuscripts. Other passages from the work, namely extracts from Books I–XXIX, are preserved in the so-called *Excerpta Constantiniana*, an anthology of historical works that was compiled on the order of the Byzantine emperor Constantine VII Porphyrogenitus around the mid-tenth century A.D. Citations contained in lexica and compilations of the Byzantine Period preserve other short passages. Our knowledge of a large part of the work has hence been subject to criteria of epitomisation and anthologisation by scholars and students of the Late Antique or Byzantine Period, who were often moved by didactic aims. This is why what is preserved from Polybius' work includes many biographical and moral portraits of great historical figures and digressions on geographical or military topics.

The proemium. Polybius presents as the subject of his work the roughly fifty years in which the whole world passed under the rule of a single power, Rome. After a summary of historical facts that occurred in the period roughly from 264 to 220 B.C., the true historical reconstruction begins with the run-up to and events of the Second Punic War (218–202 B.C.). For this reason, it is believed that at first Polybius had planned to stop the work at 168 B.C., the date of the battle of Pydna, which marked the end of the centuries-old hegemony of Macedonia and its fall into the hands of Rome (he in fact states with precision in I 1: "in less than fifty-three years"). In reality, during the composition of the work, the material must have grown, leading the author to make an expansion that extended the chronological limit to 144 B.C., two years after the destruction of Carthage and the capture of Corinth (Books XXX–XL). Finally, the monograph on the Numantine War, mentioned above, can be considered another expansion, down to the year 133.

Books I–V. As already noted, these are the only books that have survived entire. Polybius himself calls Books I–II a *prokataskeuē*, i.e. a kind of "preparation" or "introduction," like Book I of Thucydides' history, whose influence is apparent. They contain an exposition of the methodological principles and a statement of the subject of the work, followed by a summary reconstruction of the events concerning Italy and Greece in the years 264–220 B.C., i.e. from the start of the First Punic War in 264 to the years immediately before the Hannibalic War, which began in 218. The subject of Books III–V is the events that occurred in Italy and Greece until the Battle of Cannae (216 B.C.), in which Rome suffered one of the most resounding and dramatic defeats in its history at the hands of Hannibal. Here follows a summary of the content of these five books:

Book I. After some chapters that justify the decision to present the Roman point of view (the greatness of Roman domination) and provide some necessary methodological preliminaries (pragmatic and universal history), we find an excursus on the Roman expansion in Italy until the brink of the First Punic War. A certain amount of room is given to the hostilities with Carthage in Sicily, where Rome took the opportunity to intervene by claiming internal problems in the city of Messana as its pretext. At this point there is a short summary of the period that will be addressed in the first two books: the author states that he has decided to narrate the First Punic War, since the two historians who had addressed it, Philinus of Acragas and Fabius Pictor, lacked objectivity (the one was too pro-Carthaginian, the other too pro-Roman) and had left a narrative that was not truthful. The account continues with the Roman intervention in Sicily, the capture of Acragas and the naval victory of Gaius Duilius at Mylae against Carthage (260), which marks the start of open conflict between the two powers and of the Roman occupation of Sicily. There follows the account of the Roman landing in Africa and their military engagements, up to the decisive victory over the Carthaginian fleet at the Egadi Islands and the surrender of Carthage. The final chapters of the book are on various rebellions of peoples subject to Carthage that occurred after the defeat.

Book II. This book contains a summary report of the historical events in the twenty years after the First Punic War, which ended in 241. The account of the Carthaginian military operations in Spain is interwoven with that on the Roman expedition to Illyria and the conflicts to which the Romans subjected the Gaulish population in order to control the plains of the Po, or Cisalpine Gaul. The author gives quite a detailed description of the plains of the Po, with a digression that gives precise geographical, economic and ethnographic details. There follows a history of the Gaulish invasions into Italy and Cisalpine Gaul down to 221 B.C. The second part of the book (chapters 37–70) is on the history of the Achaean Confederacy, which prompts the author to make specific criticisms of the presentation of these events as expounded by Philarchus (for his misuse of effects of pathos, his failure to recognise the real causes of events, his political factiousness and various mistakes).

Book III. This has as its subject the Second Punic War or Hannibalic War (218–202 B.C.). We thus arrive at the heart of Polybius' historical reconstruction: this "second beginning" of the work is emphasised by some general considerations, developed in the first chapters, concerning the author's goals and the plan of the research conducted. Then the problem of the causes of the war are addressed, dwelling on the distinction between causes, pretexts and beginnings, with examples. He then moves on to the account of the conflict, with Hannibal's capture of Saguntum in Spain in 219 B.C. (an excursus discusses the ancient treaties between Rome and Carthage, providing their text and commenting on it), which constituted the *casus belli*. After a Roman embassy to Carthage with requests that amount to an ultimatum, war is declared; we have the march of the Carthaginians to Italy and the other events as far as the battle of Lake Trasimene (217). The book ends with the account of operations in Italy and of the terrible Roman defeat at Cannae (216).

Book IV. This book is set entirely in Greece and is devoted to the so-called Social War (220–217), in which the Achaeo-Macedonian coalition, the Achaean Confederacy, took sides against the Aetolian Confederacy in various theatres of operations: the Peloponnese, Rhodes and Byzantium, Epirus, Achaea, Aetolia, Elis and so on. There are also sizeable digressions, such as a geographical one on Byzantium and the Pontus Euxinus or those on the influence of music in Arcadia and the wealth of Elis.

Book V. The first 30 chapters of Book V contain the remainder of the Social War. The central part of the book is constituted by the account of the war fought by Ptolemy IV and Antiochus III for possession of Coele Syria (219–217 B.C.). After a digression on the earthquake at Rhodes and on Greek solidarity with the stricken city, we have the narration of the final phases of the Social War, which was ended by the Peace of Naupactus. The book closes with a picture of the situation in Greece and the East, an account of other peripheral military events and the announcement of the transition to the theme of the institutions of Rome.

Books VI–XL. As we have seen, the books of the *Histories* after Book V have not survived whole. We have only extracts and fragments of them that have reached us indirectly. The surviving parts are more extensive for Books VI–XVIII and more meagre for the subsequent ones.

Book VI was of key importance in the organisation of the work. It examined the institutional order of Rome, with an analytical description of how the state was structured, accompanied by general reflections on political philosophy (which we will discuss further below). So far as we can reconstruct it, Polybius presented in the first chapters (3–10) the classification of the different forms of state, linked to each other by a cyclical progress demonstrated by the examples of Rome and Lycurgus. A sketch of the early history of Rome preceded the description of the city's political (11–18) and military institutions (19–42). The picture thus drawn is compared to other regimes, especially that of Carthage (43–56).

In the remainder of the work, Books VII–XL, the narrative proceeded on an annalistic basis, except in a few cases where the author preferred not to break up events that were closely interconnected, in which case the unit of the year is exceeded. The temporal structure is based on the succession of Olympiads, but made more precise by reference to the natural cycle of the seasons, Roman consulates, the *strategiai* of the Aetolian, Achaean and Boeotian Confederacies and Rhodian prytanies. The geopolitical setting remains that set out in the first part, i.e. the events in West and East. Each book contains the events of one Olympiad or half-Olympiad, i.e. a period of four or two years respectively; however, certain particularly eventful years take up a whole book. Among the most striking characteristics of Books VII–XL, which (we repeat this once again) have come down to us in the form of epitomes or anthologies, if not entirely as fragments, we again note deeper reflections on historical method. Book VIII contains, among other things, a specific criticism of the monographic form employed in the historiographical sphere and a long polemical digression against Theopompus. An attack on the monograph form returns in Book XXIX, where it is said that authors of monographs are led to inflate their own material. Book IX opens with a restatement of the superiority of pragmatic historiography, which aims to be useful to politicians, over traditional accounts of genealogies and foundations, the purpose of which is principally enjoyment. In Book XII Polybius aims harsh criticisms at Timaeus (we will return to this), reproaching him for an incorrect methodological approach and specific errors. Other passages (evidently selected in the work of epitomisation) have preserved for us Polybius' account of crucial moments in Greek and Roman history, such as the appearance on the scene of two outstanding men, Scipio at Rome and Philopoemen in

Greece (in Book X, concerning the years 210/9–209/8) or the closing events of the Second Punic War down to the decisive battle of Zama (203/2 B.C., at the start of Book XV).

2.4 Polybius' sources

For past events to which he was not a witness, Polybius used the historical reconstructions of previous authors, about some of whom he had critical reservations in general or in detail. In particular, the sources for the history of Hannibal were necessarily writings by his predecessors, either from the Carthaginian side or the Roman one. His own contemporary times involved events to which he was witness or had experienced himself; the close link to some of the most authoritative members of the Roman aristocracy must have given him a chance to gain a rich yield of first-hand information; he also used contemporary historians such as C. Acilius, A. Postumius Albinus and Cato. Polybius also consulted archival sources, for example for the well documented reconstruction of the treaties between Rome and Carthage. Further, one cannot underestimate the role that must have been played by oral reports that he was able to collect, bearing in mind also the many journeys he undertook to learn about the theatres of war that he was preparing to describe. The need to have direct knowledge of the physical context of events is one of his precepts.

Book-knowledge and direct experience (including through the military activity he conducted in the Achaean Confederacy) are the origin of Polybius' interest in and accuracy about the aspects linked to topography and geography. Much room, and hence much importance, is given to excursuses about geography (for example on Italy, II 14–17; on Arcadia, IV 20 ff.; on the Black Sea region, IV 38–44) and topography (Leontini, VII 6; Acragas, IX 27; Alexandria, XXXIV 12; New Carthage, X 9–11). This interest is explained by the author himself as being due to the need for direct observation of events or at least of their scene. The whole of Book XXXIV was dedicated to the discussion of geographical questions: he rejected the description by Pytheas of Massalia and the mathematical and astronomical measurements of the Earth carried out by Eratosthenes.

2.5 Polybius' conception of history and historiography

We have seen how on many occasions in his work Polybius turned to discussion on historiographical method and expressed positions that indicate a personal theory of history. The ideas that he set out must have been the fruit of deep reflection made at different times, before and during the composition of his work, which gradually flowed into it as he clarified his thoughts. For this reason, in the *Histories* we do not find a systematic theoretical treatment of history, but rather a group of scattered reflections at different points in the work. Nonetheless we can identify some principles, which reveal a substantial consistency in his thinking.

In the excursus in Book VI on the Roman constitution and the forms of government, two theories can be identified, for which we know of various precedents in Greek political and philosophical thought: that there is a periodic change in constitutions, in which one type degenerates into another; and the idea of the mixed constitution, which guarantees an equilibrium between different powers through a balanced combination of monarchical, aristocratic and democratic elements. Polybius saw the constitution of Rome as the realisation of the mixed form of government and he saw this factor as the reason for the success and longevity of Roman power. In what remains of Book VI, however, we can detect later additions, which play down this positive assessment of the Roman constitution, introducing pessimistic thoughts about the city's future development. These less enthusiastic notes should probably be traced to Polybius' direct experience of the crisis that the Republic entered during the social conflicts linked to the Gracchan reforms.

Polybius' analysis is not entirely original and reworks Plato and above all Books II–III of Aristotle's *Politics*, which the historian follows both in the classification of different types of constitutional form or *politeia*, and also in the description of the ways in which they degenerate from one into the other (though this idea can be found already in Herodotus). Aside from Plato, all the authors cited by Polybius on this topic belong to the Peripatetic tradition. The idea of the mixed constitution and its excellence goes back at least to Thucydides (VIII 97, 1–2) and it too is found in Plato.

Polybius' original contribution to the theoretical picture described above probably consists in the idea (perhaps derived from a late Pythagorean concept) of the ἀνακύκλωσις (*anakyklōsis*), or cyclical return of the same forms of constitution, a consequence of the successive transition from one to the other. This vision – that there is a repetitive character to the natural dialectic between regimes – enjoyed much success in Renaissance political theory. The constitution of Rome, too, despite its excellence, was in the end embroiled in the general idea of cyclical transformation. Polybius' analysis thus holds an inevitable prediction of the decay of the Roman constitution, which would not be able to escape the ineluctable law of *anakyklōsis*. In this sense, a suggestively symbolic value was assumed by the episode in Book XXXVIII in which Scipio, facing the dramatic spectacle of Carthage burning, foresaw the end of Rome.

There are numerous passages that indicate the goal of historiography as the exposition of truth (I 14, 6; II 56; XII 26b, 4; XVI 14 ff.). This statement of the need to reconstruct truthfully, which might seem obvious and a matter of course for a modern reader, is in reality an element that distinguishes Polybius' thought from some forms of historiography of the period. We have seen in the previous chapter how a mimetic type of historiography became established, which, devoted entirely to the pursuit of the story's dramatic effect, for that purpose often ended up by falsifying reality (Duris and Philarchus). Beginning from different assumptions, the historiography of Timaeus too, with the characteristics that we have noted, produced distortions of the historical truth (for example, Polybius criticises Timaeus for inventing speeches from scratch: XII 25a).

One of the first consequences of this scruple about truthfulness is the great importance given to finding the causes in which historical facts originate and which determine their course. Thucydides had distinguished between accidental causes, αἰτίαι (aitiai), and the true reason, ἀληθεστάτη πρόφασις (alēthestatē prophasis), of the events, but without applying this terminology rigidly and sometimes using the term προφάσεις (prophaseis) to indicate the accidental causes. In the footsteps of other authors, Polybius rigorously adopts Thucydides' terminology from the "methodological" chapter (Thucydides I 23) and accuses the other historians of not having properly understood or correctly used the threefold distinction between prophasis, aitia and ἀρχὴ τοῦ πολέμου (i.e. the casus belli: this last concept recurs in Thucydides I 118, 2). Linked to the problem of historical causes is the analysis of the causal relation between the development of a state and its constitutional arrangement. From this idea derives the thesis that the expansion of Rome was due to the excellence of the mixed constitution. Within the problem of causes, much attention is paid also to the motives and objectives that inspired the actions of political leaders. By this route the biographical element enters historiography.

Much space is given to the incidence of tychē (τύχη: "chance") in determining events. In Polybius' work different conceptions of tychē are interwoven, with it at times seen as a kind of providential ruler of the world, at times as an entity "jealous" of human prosperity (in the manner of the traditional Olympian gods), at times as an irrational force that limits, sometimes dramatically, the space for a rational understanding of the historical process. The importance given by Polybius to the role of tychē is a sign of the essentially agnostic sentiment that underlies his thought. To this almost hypostasizing religious vision of chance, he sets up as a counterpoint the idea that official religion is in fact an invention by the ruling power in order to govern the masses better and to condition their outlook.

In the fundamental aspects of his thought, Polybius picks up motifs and lines of thinking from Thucydides, who turns out to be his model of thought and of historical and political analysis. The idea that the aim of historiography ought to be truth gives rise also to a rigidly utilitarian concept of it. Knowledge and understanding of history are useful in the present moment for people and, in particular, for politicians. The historian's goal is therefore to collect and point out the important experiences concealed in the events. This vision often leads Polybius to adopt a very marked didactic attitude and to intervene with observations and comments in the course of his narration of the facts, rather than being content to let them speak for themselves. Providing specific knowledge to other politicians is the goal, ruling out any intention to provide pleasure or enjoyment as goals in themselves. Historiography thus returns to choosing as its exclusive theme a major contemporary problem, a major event of the present day, which makes possible a direct and precise knowledge of the decisive factors in history. This utilitarian end implies also a pragmatic conception, in which the historian's attention is essentially turned toward political and military events, to the actions of peoples, cities and royal dynasties, unlike the enjoyable genealogical histories of the mythical era and of traditional themes such as colonisations, foundations of cities and family relations among dynasties (introduction to Book IX). The historian must carry out a detailed study of the sources; acquire precise knowledge of geography and topography; and have direct political and military experience (XII 25 ff.). Polybius considers very important this last requirement, which is not met by "desk-bound" historians such as Ephorus, Theopompus and particularly Timaeus. In Book XII Polybius collects some errors by Timaeus about Africa, Sardinia, Italy and Sicily, also discussing the criticisms that Timaeus had made of other authors and castigating his method. It cannot be denied that many of these criticisms have little or no foundation. It is a fact that Polybius aimed to discredit Timaeus, who was the most important Greek historian to have concerned himself with the West and Rome, and he wanted to make very clear his own superiority as a literary figure and as a man moulded by political and military experience.

Polybius aimed to write a history that would have universal range and significance, i.e. one that gave an account of events concerning the whole known world, following the form adopted by Ephorus (the only historian whom Polybius credits as his predecessor in the field of universal history). And he knew very well that his theme met this requirement, since the Roman hegemony represented as never before the achievement of unity across the entire known world. He understood very well that the Roman point of view offered him a unitary vision of universal history and allowed him, in his capacity as historian, to overcome the varied complexity of the facts in order to see and show their deep causal chains. We know that in the time of Dionysius of Halicarnassus there was debate on the value of different ways of organising narratives and Dionysius castigated Thucydides on the ground that his annalistic procedure had fragmented the episodes. The annalistic scheme subdivided by seasons was even more inadequate for a history that encompassed events of the entire inhabited world. For this reason, Ephorus had chosen a narration κατὰ γένος (i.e. "thematically organised"), whereas Polybius evidently remained tied to the Thucydidean model.

Various passages (I 3, 3 ff.; III 32; VII 7; VIII 4; XXIX 12) examine the relation between universal history and monographic writing and, as we have seen, the latter is harshly criticised. In fact, the *prokataskeuē* of Books I–II goes through the events in grand scenes. A truly universal vision of the historical panorama is adopted by Polybius for the facts after 220, beginning from Book III. The universal unity of the events after this date is ensured by the ascent of Rome, which imposes itself as a unifying factor. In other words, the rise of Rome to hegemonic power over the whole

Mediterranean world makes a treatment of individual episodes in independent monographs inadequate and unsatisfying.

We have seen a number of times how Polybius in the *Histories* aims strong criticisms at his predecessors, to a degree that is not paralleled in what we know of ancient historiographic literature. As well as polemic against Philarchus, the most brash example is offered by the repeated rancorous attacks on Timaeus. Despite all these polemics, Polybius himself is in fact doing no more than retrace the path already pioneered by Thucydides and continued by other, later historians. Thucydides had identified the epochal importance of one event (the Peloponnesian War; in the case of Polybius, the imperialistic expansion of Rome) which serves as a unifying pole to which the other events are firmly connected. Thucydides' insight was followed up by the authors of *Hellenica*, who organised the narrative of Greek history around the current hegemonic power in each period. After Athens, it was the turn of Sparta, Thebes and Macedonia. The *Philippica* of Theopompus, so harshly attacked by Polybius, far from being a monograph on one sector of events as accused, in fact identify Philip of Macedon as the fulcrum of the general historical situation of the time. Polybius' barbs are fully justified, however, when he criticises contemporary historiography, from which he is sharply distinguished by achieving a rigorous return to the methodological model of Thucydides.

To what extent was Polybius' strong insistence on historiographical truth reflected in his actual practice? In reality his serious urge towards objectivity and impartiality ran up against some specific, and perhaps inevitable, limits of the author. In first place is Polybius' patriotism, which led him to give his homeland an excessively large space within the universal framework of the *Histories*. Further, Polybius was by no means a stranger to political passion. For example, when he harshly casts criticisms at Philarchus, he certainly is not just doing so, as he would like us to believe, for reasons of method, but on account of differences in opinion on events involving the Achaean Confederacy. We can see that many attacks on previous historians are the result of a superficial or misleading reading of their accounts, or they are better explained in political differences. Despite sincere efforts towards impartiality, in the narrative of the encounter with the Carthaginians Polybius' pro-Roman sympathies are clear, as can easily be explained by his close personal relations with the Scipiones and his general admiration for Roman power. The tendency to pro-Roman partisanship is found for example in the narrative of the background to the First Punic War. He criticises the exposition of the historian Philinus of Acragas on the ground that it is too pro-Punic and that of Fabius Pictor for being too pro-Roman, but ultimately follows the latter. At the level of method, too, Polybius sometimes commits errors similar to those that he castigates in others, revealing a certain incoherence. For example, while he in theory demands the direct reproduction of speeches or at least of their content, in fact he himself ends up making his historical figures say whatever the situation demands, in the manner of Thucydides.

2.6 Language and style

The language used by Polybius is the Hellenistic *koinē*, close to the language of the chancelleries, with which it in fact has some affinity. It is Attic in its grammar, but less Attic in lexicon and syntax, which are those of the *koinē*. As well as these aspects, there are also effects from a pronounced Graeco-Roman bilingualism. At the level of style, his historical account is weighed down by prolix methodological reflections, jumps forward or back in the flow of the narrative, a certain solemn pomposity and didactic tone in his expression. Often he gives the impression of not being particularly careful and of not ranking rhetorical embellishments highly, even though there is no lack of rhetorical figures, poetic vocabulary and quotations from poets in his work; he also makes efforts to avoid hiatus. The intolerant judgement that the Atticists passed on Polybius' style (Dionysius of Halicarnassus, *De compositione verborum* 4, 30) was generally the case in relation to the prose of the Hellenistic Age.

3 Historiography after Polybius

3.1 Posidonius of Apamea

The figure of Posidonius (135–51 B.C.), together with that of his teacher Panaetius, is associated primarily with his role as an exponent of the Stoic school in the phase known as the "Middle Stoa" (cf. *The Hellenistic Age* V 4.4). His extensive output, the product of a very wide culture and great intellectual gifts, covered all fields of knowledge. No complete works have survived, but we have many titles and a generous series of fragments. In the present chapter we will limit ourselves to discussing his works on historical topics.

Born at Apamea on the River Orontes (Syria) around 135 B.C., Posidonius was a pupil of the Stoic Panaetius at Athens at around eighteen years of age. He made some journeys for study purposes and finally settled at Rhodes, where he opened his own school, which was sought out by major Roman figures such as Pompey and Cicero. In 87/6 he went to Rome as ambassador of the Rhodians, where he met Marius, by now elderly and in a bad way. Posidonius died around 51 B.C., perhaps during another stay in Rome.

The *Histories after Polybius* continued Polybius' work, covering the period 144–86, i.e. down to the year of Marius' death. The work was used by Diodorus in his Books XXXII–XXXVII, by Strabo and by Athenaeus, so modern scholars try to reconstruct its content from the hints that can be detected in these authors. This was followed by the *Histories on Pompey*, which must have come down as far as 59 B.C. It seems that these two works combined geographical and ethnographical interests (which are expressed in the attention given to barbarian peoples and the problems of slavery) with the rigour of historiographical method inspired by Thucydides. In these works, Posidonius included the knowledge he had gained in the course of voyages that took him to the land of the Ligurians, in southern Gaul, to Spain, North Africa, Sicily, Italy and the Adriatic region. Cicero (as we know from a letter to Atticus, dated to June 60) would have liked Posidonius to write a historical work on his consulate of 63 B.C. (of the kind that he had dedicated to Pompey) and for this reason he sent him a *hypomnēma* about the events that occurred during it. But Posidonius refused, saying that his reading of the *hypomnēma* had made him even less inclined to consider a work on this subject.

Posidonius believed that humanity was undergoing a progressive decadence, which was particularly detectable in the eastern world; he set up as counterpoint to the Roman world's simplicity, justice and religiosity, characteristics that for him justified Rome's rule. In the Roman world too, however, after the destruction of the Carthaginian enemy in 146 B.C., its moral fibre had been sapped and troubling cracks had appeared. Posidonius, with decided oligarchic tendencies, expressed a highly critical judgement of the values of Roman society after the destruction of Carthage, which according to him was headed on the road to grave decline. He did not question the legitimacy of the conquests or rule of Rome, admittedly: his critique was aimed rather at the ways and forms in which the Romans exercised power. The problems of poor governance were manifest above all in the administration of the provinces, something that anyone who was not born at Rome or did not live there could learn at first hand. The moral and political decline of the ruling class and consequently of the structure of the state was clearly perceived. He located the causes in the lust for power and riches, arrogance and excessive luxury. Yet the idea that the symptoms of decline might be due to moral reasons both public and private did not prevent him from thoroughly analysing the profound changes brought about by the enormous expansion of Rome's rule, including social changes at various levels and changes in culture and mentality. In the past there was a tendency to overestimate the role of Posidonius, but it is undeniable that his influence on the historical concepts of Sallust and Tacitus were of great importance.

3.2 Diodorus Siculus

Our information on Diodorus' life is derived in essence from the little that he himself says about it, in particular in the general introduction to his work. He was born perhaps around 90 B.C. at Agyrion, in inland Sicily not far from Enna, and lived to around 30 B.C. (his work makes no mention of the victory of Augustus at Actium in 31 B.C.). He himself tells us that the writing of his historical work occupied him for thirty years and that in doing so he travelled a lot in Europe and Asia and spent time at Rome. We do not know his family background but from various hints it seems that he had a liberal education that gave him a knowledge of rhetoric, the poets and philosophical literature, despite the fact that he does not seem much inclined toward speculative thought. His religiosity is revealed in his appeals to respect the gods and his records of the punishments that befell the impious. However, he also seems to be open to the rational explanations of religion known as "Euhemerism."

This term derives from the name of Euhemerus of Messana, who lived in the fourth and third century B.C. and advocated a rational interpretation of religion. He wrote a work entitled *Sacred Scripture*, in which he recounted a voyage that he had made into the East, where on an island he had found an inscription that told of the actions of the ancient kings of that place, whose names were Uranus, Cronus and Zeus, who had been divinised and worshipped as gods on account of their achievements and good deeds. The idea seems to have been inspired by the wish to legitimise the divinisation of the Hellenistic kings, but it gave rise to an "ideological" orientation that utilised this mechanism in order to give a rationalist explanation of religious beliefs.

Diodorus seems to be practically untouched by the debate that developed over the legitimacy of Roman power, the way it was exercised and the elements of decadence that beset Roman society. His work, the *Library of History*, is a grand compilation with the aim of setting out in an organised way the whole history of the world from its origins to the conquest of Britannia by Caesar (54 B.C.). The author himself lays out the main lines of his work when he presents (I 4, 6) the organisation of the material in its 40 books. Entirely preserved are Books I–V and XI–XX; of the others we have fragments and a series of extracts (the latter produced by order of the Byzantine emperor Constantine VII Porphyrogenitus, as we saw also in the case of Polybius). The following, in summary, is the content of the work:

Books I–VI were on the origin of the world and the mythical events prior to the Trojan War for which it is not possible to construct a precise chronological framework. The first three books narrate the traditions of "barbarian" peoples (Egyptians, Assyrians and Medes, Indians, Scythians, Amazons, Hyperboreans, Arabs, inhabitants of the Islands of the Blest, Ethiopians, Ichthyophagi; then a series of myths on Uranus, Cybele, Cronus, Dionysus, Ammon and their ventures in the East); then Books IV–VI set out myths concerning Greek peoples (Book VI is lost: it seems that influence from the rationalism of Euhemerus was important in it).

Books VII–XVII set out the events that occurred from the Trojan War to the death of Alexander of Macedon, according to the chronology of Eratosthenes and of Apollodorus of Athens. Book VIII perhaps began with the first Olympiad (776 B.C.), from which point the narration became annalistic, switching between events in Greece, Sicily and Rome. Books XI–XV relate Greek history from the expedition of Xerxes (480 B.C.) to the rise of Philip II of Macedon (360 B.C.); Philip is the subject of Book XVI, while Book XVII is on Alexander the Great. In this section Roman history remains rather overshadowed.

Books XVIII–XL had as subject the history of the Hellenistic Age, down to the Gallic Wars of Caesar. Much importance is given to the histories of the Diadochi and to Sicilian events (above all to the reign of Agathocles). Only with Book XXII, where the history of Pyrrhus is narrated, did Rome take on importance, becoming the centre of the narrative in the following books, which are on the First (XXIII–XXIV) and Second (XXVI–XXVII) Punic War. The final part of the work is on Caesar, down to the conquest of Britannia (54 B.C.).

After a process of collecting material that one may imagine was long and complex, the writing of the work seems to have taken place following the chronological sequence of the periods treated. Each book has a prologue and conclusion, making its unity clear to the reader, even where the length is considerable. The prefaces and conclusions underline the division into books with clear indications, recalling what went before and announcing what will follow, often accompanied by some general reflection. The exposition has an annalistic structure and Diodorus is well aware that this often disrupts the narration of events that were spread out over multiple years. Much attention is given to chronology (excepting the mythical period): beginning from the Fall of Troy, Diodorus avowedly follows the chronology of Apollodorus of Athens, but we do not know if he adopted an annalistic style of exposition already from the fall of Troy to the first Olympiad. The succession of Olympiads forms the basic chronological scheme, into which were inserted the dates provided by the lists of eponymous magistrates at Athens and Rome. Diodorus' chronology, while not without uncertainties and errors, is fundamental for us for some periods, such as the history of Philip, the Diadochi and the Sicilian tyrants. At times, faced with the prospect of an account that is too fragmented, Diodorus prefers to present a continuous account, such as for the deeds of Dionysius the Elder (Book XIV). At other times, for facts that did not find a place in the main narrative but which he does not want to pass over, Diodorus gives a brief summary at the end of a chapter or collects them without any logical connection in a supplementary chapter. Often events that took place over a long span of time are grouped together in a single year, or they appear as events that are repeated in several years, all in a rather arbitrary way, which poses serious problems for present-day historians using Diodorus' information as a source.

In the preface he declares the goals of his research: he intended to compose a universal history from the origins to his own times, in such a way that the readers can draw great moral and political profit from it, by enriching themselves with the experience of previous generations, so that they can avoid their errors and act righteously. This is a restatement of the ancient motif of the utilitarian purpose of historical knowledge. Diodorus holds that no prior historian had written a true universal history: some had overlooked the barbarian peoples, others had given credit to mythical traditions that are too hard to grasp in their entirety, others are flawed in their chronology, others never finished their work. In addition, all these attempts were already old and the previous two centuries of history had not yet been systematised into a global account. Diodorus declares that he wishes to remedy these faults and gaps. The historiographical principles stated in the work are essentially based on the search for and respect for the truth. The model adopted by Diodorus is the work of Ephorus (cf. *The Classical Age* XI 2.5), expanded by the addition of mythical history.

Narrating the mythical traditions is a difficult undertaking for a historian, such that many had declined to deal with this part of the past. Diodorus, to the contrary, says that he has taken great care over mythical history, since demigods and heroes had accomplished many exceptional deeds. He has drawn information from the mythographers, his predecessors, and believes that myth has a historical foundation and so it is important to know about it. His attitude to the material varies from radical criticism, which moves him to declare a myth to be purely fable, to a careful treatment that distinguishes between different versions, seeking a reconciliation by means of a rationalism that is at times naïve. Despite his knowledge of Euhemerism, Diodorus is revealed rather as an adherent of conceptions that see the gods as great cosmic forces. An important place in his concept of history is also held by *tychē*, seen as the cause of the type of event qualified as παράδοξον ("unexpected"), one that confounds human predictions.

The project of a universal history implies unceasing researches in the works of his predecessors and a compilatory procedure. By reason of this in-depth work on the sources, the various sections of the *Library* preserve traces of the authors from which they derive, even down to the language. This does not mean that the author declined to examine critically the material that he collected, as becomes clear from the very choice of authors used and from his personal reflections. Nineteenth-century critics were primarily concerned to identify the sources used by Diodorus, proposing a series of theories, often unfounded, with the main shared assumption that the *Library of History* was compilatory in character and that the historian took a passive attitude towards his sources. This then led to the idea that a single source was used for long stretches of the work (Ephorus for Greek events; Timaeus for Sicilian ones; Hieronymus of Cardia for the history of the Diadochi) and to the idea, more recently, that there was a principal source supplemented by one or two secondary sources, with interventions that could be attributed to Diodorus himself. Consequently, after a long period of disparaging the work of Diodorus, accusing him of having little originality and of being deferential towards his historiographic sources, today there is a tendency to reconsider his personal gifts and the usefulness of the *Library*, if only for the large quantity of reports and traditions that it has preserved for us that would otherwise have been irrevocably lost.

Diodorus seems not to have slavishly followed the authors that he used, nor to have distorted then in a dishonest way. When it is possible to compare him with the older source (which unfortunately does not happen often), Diodorus' transcription appears to be faithful and does not misrepresent the original, which is often followed quite closely. The narrative passages, however, are composed more freely and Diodorus uses his own language, which is often less colourful than his source. There is no lack of evidence of a critical spirit. For example, he chastises Herodotus for an excessive taste for stories that are extraordinary and diverting. Recent analyses have shown that in the book on Egypt, in which some have wished to see the exclusive influence of Hecataeus of Abdera, an effort has been made towards a synthesis through the comparison of several sources. The way that modern scholars have conjecturally extended the influence of authors such as Ephorus, Timaeus or Theopompus across the whole of large parts of Diodorus' work is often arbitrary and the very variety of the theories advanced should advise caution (also as regards the problem of the reconstruction of lost authors, such as the three just mentioned). At the least, one should acknowledge in Diodorus some specific merits, such as the fairly frequent mention of the sources used (which is what makes it possible to recognise them), the use of important and reliable authors for the different sections (including Latin sources) and, as we have just noted, the preservation of a historiographical legacy that would otherwise have been doomed to disappear.

In language and style Diodorus displays a regularity and simplicity that should be considered a mark of the personal way in which he used his sources, seeking to amalgamate their accounts into a uniform narrative that is easy to understand. The style does not indulge in rhetorical embellishments and makes no use of speeches put into the mouths of the historical figures.

3.3 Nicolaus of Damascus

To reconstruct the biography of Nicolaus of Damascus, we have not only the testimonia of various ancient sources, but also the remains of his *On My Own Life and Education*, a lost autobiographical work of which some fragments survive. Born in 64 B.C. at Damascus to a rich and powerful family, he was able to receive an excellent Greek education. He was an adherent of the Peripatetic philosophy and wrote various commentaries on the Aristotelian system, none of which survive. He held all the highest political offices in his homeland, establishing close ties to King Herod. In the 30s B.C. he was named tutor to the sons of Antony and Cleopatra and later he became tutor also to the sons of Herod. In the years after the battle of Actium (31 B.C.) Nicolaus probably got to know Augustus and held various diplomatic positions that put him in contact with the Roman authorities. On Herod's death (4 B.C.) he accompanied the king's son to Rome to support his claim to succeed his father. It seems that at that time he settled permanently in Rome, where he devoted himself to studies and the writing of his works. We do not know the date of his death.

Nicolaus was a polymath and also a philosopher of the Aristotelian school. His lost works included tragedies and comedies, a compilation on an ethnographic topic and a compendium of Aristotle's philosophy, of which a Syriac translation survives. His most important work is the *Historiai*, a universal history in 144 books, which perhaps ran down to the year 4 B.C. Sadly only fragments and extracts survive, in this case too, as with Polybius and Diodorus, transmitted thanks to the historical collection ordered by the Byzantine emperor Constantine Porphyrogenitus. So far as we can tell, Nicolaus' universal history must have been in general of the same type as that of Diodorus. It is certain that it had the distinctive feature of being written by a direct witness of the Middle Eastern region, who was able to speak knowledgeably of the causes of events in those areas. It is interesting that he used direct dialogue to make his historical account more vivid.

The *Life of Augustus* in thirteen books is likewise known to us only in fragmentary form. It was a biography and encomium (we may recall other examples of this such as *Evagoras* by Isocrates, *Agesilaus* by Xenophon and the *Life of Philopoemen* by Polybius), based at least in part on the *Autobiography* of Augustus himself. The account survives in the part that narrates the period from Augustus' childhood to October 44 B.C. Much space is given to the conspiracy against Caesar and the events leading up to it. There is a plausible theory that the first book ended with the death of Caesar and the second opened with the problem of his testament and the adoption of Octavian.

3.4 Castor of Rhodes

Castor, who lived in the first century B.C., was the author of a *Chronicle* in six books that came down as far as 61/0 B.C., the year in which Pompey completed the reorganisation of Asia subject to Rome. The work was based on the king lists of Sicyon, Argos and Attica (beginning from Cecrops) and on the Athenian archons, as well as on the list of kings of Alba and of the kings and consuls of Rome (beginning from Aeneas). Unlike Apollodorus, Castor also introduced mythical history and took account of the history of the West and of Rome. His *Chronicle* was much used in the ancient world: Varro, Plutarch, Julius Africanus and Eusebius all drew on it.

3.5 Anti-Roman historiography

We have seen above (cf. 1.2) that the problem of the origins of Rome became important in the second century B.C., as the role of Rome gradually grew and became consolidated as an international power of vast reach. This topic was a tool of propaganda and there was no lack of polemical voices on the Greek side, who denied the Trojan origins of the Romans and underlined their original barbarism. The problem was whether or not to legitimise the rule of Rome and its hegemony over an immense territory (cf. also Posidonius). The debate took place in the first century, when the war of more than a decade by Rome against Mithridates, king of Pontus, seemed to take on the significance of a Greek attempt to recover some degree of freedom from the rulers. An anti-Roman public discourse began, appearing in historical works favourable to Mithridates.

It was a fact that not everyone who was Greek in culture was integrated into the Roman empire or ready to take on the role of legitimating the new rulers in the eyes of the Greek world. There was no lack of critical voices, though their works are mostly lost. The decisive response came in the Augustan Age, with the Roman history of

Dionysius of Halicarnassus, who endorsed Rome's legitimacy in dominating the world, for the sake of culture. An interesting case is that of Timagenes of Alexandria, a rhetor and historian, who came to Rome in 55 B.C. as a prisoner of war. Thereafter he lived and worked at Rome, it seems primarily as a rhetor, given that he is cited as an eminent rhetor together with Caecilius of Caleacte. He won the favour of Augustus, but then fell into disgrace and was welcomed into the house of Asinius Pollio. Of his works we have a collection of fragments, most of which perhaps belonged to a work called *On Kings*. One fragment speaks ill of Pompey, which reveals to us that the work included contemporary history. It is likely that his work had an anti-Roman orientation, though we know too little of it to be sure of his positions.

IX Judaeo-Hellenistic Literature

1 The Jews of Alexandria and the *Septuagint*

1.1 The *Bible*, the fundamental text of Jewish culture

The name "*Bible* of the Seventy" or "Septuagint" (from the Latin for "seventy," and often cited simply by the Roman numeral LXX) refers to the oldest and most widely circulated Greek version of the Hebrew *Bible*, which was produced in the third century B.C. in the cultural ferment of Alexandria, where there was a lively and numerous Jewish community. The name in fact encompasses also the books known as "deuterocanonical", i.e. composed directly in Greek at a more recent date, which are rejected by the Jewish canon but accepted in the Christian one.

This weighty collection of books of various genres and contents (texts that are historical or mythological in character, collections of laws, books of wisdom, preachings of prophets, hymns and prayers) not only collects the entire literary production of the Jewish people, but also forms the very core of their historical and cultural identity, in that religious identity assumed a totalising value for the Jews, which had the capacity to involve deeply every aspect of life.

1.2 The *Septuagint* in the ancient sources. The *Letter of Aristeas*

The translation of a text like this obviously presents very distinct problems. It is clear that, if one credits the idea that the words contained in these books are of divine inspiration, it follows that the text must be translated with absolute fidelity. That the translators were conscious of this concern is shown by the very manner in which the work of translation took place, as is described in a precious ancient text that has survived and in other testimonia.

The *Letter of Aristeas to Philocrates* (or *Book of Aristeas*) is a text set in the third century B.C. but probably written in the second century B.C. by a learned Jew of Alexandria who presents himself as an eye-witness to the events and who gives an account of the translation in positive terms, with the clear intention of defending its textual, theological and religious reliability, i.e. its value as a faithful witness to the divine revelation, despite the change in language from Hebrew to Greek. The author speaks of real teamwork by 72 translators (six for each of the twelve tribes of Israel: the name "*Bible* of the Seventy" or "Septuagint" is thus a rough indication of the authors of the translation), who were gathered at Alexandria by the king (apparently Ptolemy II Philadelphus, 283–246 B.C.) on the initiative of the Peripatetic Demetrius of Phaleron, with the goal of having a Greek version of the law of Moses, in order to add it to the collection of laws preserved in the Library of Alexandria. Ac-

https://doi.org/10.1515/9783110426328-029

cording to the account in the *Letter*, the translators produced the Greek text in collegial collaboration in the exceptionally short time of 72 days. Thereafter, public readings from the translation were given in Alexandria and it won the agreement and
official approval of the people and the highest authorities. An anathema was also
solemnly pronounced against anyone who dared to change even a single word of it.

Philo of Alexandria (first century A.D.: cf. *Roman Imperial Period* VI 1.1) and
some Christian authors present a different version of events, which attests even
more strongly the concern with fidelity to the original Hebrew words, as well as the
incontestable authority that the *Septuagint* had already acquired. On this account,
the 72 did not work together as colleagues, but instead translated independently of
each other and at the end their translations had all turned out to be identical: this
was irrefutable proof that the Greek translation, just like the original text, had been
divinely inspired.

The translation of the *Septuagint* therefore became the official version of the sacred text, beginning from the Jewish community of Alexandria and on to Christian
authors, and it was accorded the same authority as the original. It is easy to imagine
what its importance will have been for the Greek-speaking Jewish communities,
such as that at Alexandria, and for the diffusion of the *Bible* across the vast area of
the Hellenised world. The translation, therefore, may have been above all a response to a practical need for religious liturgy and instruction, in a context in which
the literary language was predominantly Greek. But if the authority assumed by this
translation made it a text of fundamental importance among the Jewish people,
even more important are the consequences arising from the subsequent adoption of
this text by the Christians, through which the *Bible* came to play a part in the culture
of the Graeco-Roman world.

1.3 Alexandria and Judaeo-Hellenistic culture

As we have seen, the sources, including the *Letter of Aristeas*, agree in seeing the
basis of the translation in an impulse external to the Jewish community, namely the
wish of Ptolemy and the Alexandrian scholars to complete the book holdings of the
famous Library. In reality, it is the opinion of scholars today that one should think
rather of a first impulse coming from the Alexandrian Jewish community for the
practical reasons mentioned above. Also, it is likely that existing translations of
individual books passed into the Greek *Bible*. The report about the role played in the
events by the king and of the scholarly circles of the Hellenistic capital is perhaps an
invention or amplification of a real event, with the aim of legitimising the translation itself and the Jewish culture that had promoted it.

The *Letter of Aristeas*, with a long description of a banquet held at court during
which the king exchanged information and discussion with the Jewish scholars,
clearly has the aim of providing a legitimation of this cultural venture; it is a sugges-

tive, idealised representation of the particular reality of Alexandria in the third century. As the capital of Hellenic culture and seat of an important Jewish community, the city was a privileged site of encounter (and so also of conflict) between these two different cultures. The details of the text's approval by the king and its preservation in the Library, which are narrated in the *Letter*, also have the aim of guaranteeing that the Alexandrian translation would hold a very special value.

Even if it is correct to hypothesise that the initiative for the translation of the *Bible* came from within the Jewish community (which would reduce the level of external interest in this text, which the sources attribute to figures outside Jewish culture), the operation nonetheless remains of exceptional importance. It is in fact the first translation into Greek of a major text in an oriental language, a cultural undertaking without precedent and a unique occasion of encounter and communication between different cultures.

The language of the translation is rich in Semitisms and syntactic constructions that are unusual in contemporary literary Greek. Above all this second aspect is due in certain cases to the needs of fidelity to the original, to the point that at times the translation risks becoming almost incomprehensible. However, some elements of the "language of the LXX" (as it is known) are in fact attested also by papyrus fragments containing documents or private letters found in Greek-speaking Egypt. They must therefore be part of the language in everyday use, which seems to have had an influence on this particular form of the *koinē*.

It is not possible to say much with certainty about the translation's fidelity to the Hebrew original, in the form in which it survives. For it is an open problem that in more recent times it received additions of a novelty that is rather troubling. In the Greek text of the *Septuagint* there is a large series of additions, omissions or modifications of various kinds that affects practically all the books of the *Bible* and which are usually described as a text that has been modified from the original – in sum, an "erroneous" text. In 1947–1957 at Qumrân, in the Dead Sea region, some ancient text scrolls were found in a cave, which can be dated to the centuries from the second B.C. to the first A.D., containing thousands of written texts, which have not yet been published in their entirety. Among these there are various books of the *Old Testament*, which we can hence now read in manuscript versions that are considerably older (by around a millennium) than the one that has been transmitted, which dates to the tenth to eleventh centuries A.D. The documentation that has been made public has already allowed us to confirm that variants present in the text of the *Septuagint* in fact match those of the scrolls from Qumrân, which should mean that the translation was made from an original that differed in part from the Hebrew version preserved in the medieval manuscripts, and which was much older.

1.4 Other Greek translations of the *Bible*

We have information about other, later translations of the sacred book of the Jews or its parts. However, all that remains is brief fragments, above all thanks to the work of Origen (second to third century A.D.), whose work entitled *Hexapla* set alongside each other in six parallel columns the Hebrew text, its transliteration into the Greek alphabet and four different translations, including the *Septuagint*. Of the oldest translation, ascribed to a certain Theodotion, we know almost nothing. An extremely literary translation of the entire Hebrew *Bible* was completed by the Jew Aquila at the time of the Emperor Hadrian, in a Palestinian context. Thereafter, around A.D. 165, Symmachus produced a translation that was widely praised for its literary value; unfortunately nothing has survived by direct transmission.

2 Jewish literature in Greek

2.1 Aristobulus and biblical exegesis

As well as the *Bible* translation of the *Septuagint* and the *Letter of Aristeas to Philocrates* already discussed, another figure from Alexandrian Jewish circles was Aristobulus, from whom a few fragments of biblical exegesis have survived via the works of Christian authors, such as Clement of Alexandria (second to third century A.D.) and Eusebius of Caesarea (third to fourth century A.D.), whom we will discuss in the section on the Imperial Period. This Aristobulus, interpreter of Scripture, lived under Ptolemy VI Philometor (181–145 B.C.), a king to whom he dedicated a work that seems to have contained a general interpretation of the *Pentateuch*, i.e. the first five books of the *Bible*. As far as we are aware, Aristobulus is the only Jewish author before Philo of Alexandria to have applied the method of allegorical exegesis to the explanation of the biblical text. In this way the text of the *Pentateuch* moved from its more restricted value as a history of the Jewish people and became the source for a religious (or, better, ethical) doctrine of wider validity. In the fragments we find that Aristobulus insisted repeatedly that the doctrines of Greek thinkers (such as Pythagoras, Plato and Socrates) were derived from Jewish wisdom. He is thus fully part of the ambience of Alexandrian Judaism, in which Greek and Jewish culture met.

2.2 The *Exagōgē* of Ezekiel

The *Exagōgē* is a tragedy in around 270 lines, attributed by the tradition to an author by the name of Ezekiel, who is usually placed in the second half of the second century B.C. The theme is that of the people of Israel's bondage in Egypt, down to the crossing of the Red Sea. The protagonist is of course Moses. Through the work of

Eusebius, we have a collection of fragments, which are enough to reveal inspiration from Greek classical theatre, in which the biblical content is clothed. The language is borrowed mainly from Attic tragedy, with influences from the *koinē*. It uses the conventional iambic trimeter, though with some liberties compared to the classic tragedians.

2.3 *Joseph and Aseneth*: the novel

We do not know the author of this novel, which tells the fortunes of the *Bible* character Joseph and of the daughter of an Egyptian priest. The girl, named Aseneth, falls in love with Joseph and converts to the Jewish religion in order to marry him. The language is the Greek of the *koinē* (with some Semitisms) and the theme is in accord with the Greek novel (cf. *Roman Imperial Period* IX 1): a love that encounters obstacles on the way to its achievement.

The Roman Imperial Period

I The Period

1 The Roman Imperial Period

The traditional periodisation distinguishes Greek literature of the Hellenistic Age from that of the Roman Imperial Period, taking the Augustan Age as the pivot between the two eras. To our historical and cultural sensibilities this chronological turning-point seems very significant, because then Rome changed from a republic to an empire and because it is the transition from the era before Christ (B.C.) to the era after Christ (A.D.). In the actual development of literature, of course, this chronological division is, as always, just conventional but, in this sense, it is useful in describing the process by which literary forms evolved.

Commonly the definition of the Imperial Period or the Roman Period of Greek literature encompasses roughly the first five or six centuries A.D. The literature of the sixth century, i.e. of the age of Justinian, can be seen either as the final phase of ancient literary civilisation or as the first manifestation of Byzantine (medieval Greek) literature. A further distinction, which is useful and is adopted ever more widely today, is to speak in the case of literature too of a "Late Antique Period," an idea that varies from a very expansive model, encompassing the centuries from the second or third to the eighth A.D., to a more restricted one that limits the period to the fourth to sixth centuries. In general it seems useful to take the era of Constantine (306–337) as the starting-point of the Late Antique Period, since that was when ancient civilisation took on the characteristic fusion of Roman, Greek and Christian elements that would be distinctive of the following centuries. With the necessary flexibility (and without denying that it is artificial, though convenient, to apply to literature time-periods fixed by the death of emperors), we may keep in mind the following periodisation: by Greek-language literature of the Early Imperial Period we mean from the Augustan Age to the third century (let us say until the reign of Diocletian: 284–305), reserving the term Late Antique Period for the fourth to sixth centuries.

Although concepts of climax (or top) and decadence are steadily giving way to less naïve historiographical criteria that restore the more profound sense of the idea of historical development, there is no doubt that for Greek literature the Augustan Period marked a new rise. Then in the course of the second century literature in Greek underwent a remarkable expansion and flourishing, which has led some to talk of a "rebirth." This period is identified principally with the decades of the rule of Hadrian (117–138) and the Antonines (138–180), decades that were felt to be "enlightened" by intellectuals and artists and those valued by the Greek and Roman upper classes. A change took place in the cultural landscape of the empire, by which in the course of the second century, probably with a combination of social and political motives, a general weakening of culture in the Latin language resulted

https://doi.org/10.1515/9783110426328-030

in the predominance of literary production in Greek, which then continued in the following century. While a large number of writers (as we shall see) staked out fundamental advances in Greek literature in the course of the second and third centuries, in the same period Latin pagan literature appears to have been in a phase of crisis: Apuleius, Fronto and Aulus Gellius are the most notable names of the second century, while in the third it is the already growing Christian literature that offers the major figures, namely Tertullian and Cyprian.

Aside from these distinctions for the sake of orientation, which cannot always be applied with ease and which, above all, are certainly not absolute, it remains a general fact that Greek literature exhibits a considerable flourishing throughout the whole chronological span from the Augustan Age to around the mid-third century, a period that turns out to be a crux in many respects. It is where one naturally locates the complex problems connected to the progressive establishment of Christianity and so of the birth and growth of a Christian literature, in both Greek and Latin. But together with this it should be remembered and emphasised that, as regards the various mechanisms of preserving and transmitting classical culture, this period marks the second most significant and consequential stage (second after the effects of Alexandrian philology) in the selection of authors and texts, the activity of exegesis and edition and the production of copies.

The development of literature in Greek in the Imperial Period reveals a clear prevalence of prose over poetry. It is in the prose genres, in fact, that we find a notable richness of prominent personalities, movements and important works. In the sphere of historiography, in the literature (typical of the period, as we shall see) that lies between oratory, rhetoric and philosophy (though a philosophy that did not create new systems), in literary criticism, in the varied scene of scholarly production (grammar, philology, lexicography), Greek literary civilisation of the Imperial Period yielded results of profound and striking interest and developed its own original historical function.

2 The fortunes of Greece in the Imperial Period

The starting date of the Imperial Period is traditionally set in 31 B.C., the year of the battle of Actium. In the vicinity of this location on the eastern coast of Greece the warships of Octavian defeated the fleet led by Antony and Cleopatra, who retreated to Egypt and chose to take their own lives. In this way Octavian became the sole and uncontested heir to the unfinished absolutist project of Julius Caesar. The following year Egypt too, as last of the Hellenistic kingdoms, entered the Roman sphere.

In the years immediately thereafter, Octavian accumulated in his own person a series of offices and powerful roles expressed in the titles that he adopted: the military position of *imperator* (commander in chief of the army), the religious one of *pontifex maximus* and the civic and honorific position of *princeps* (first citizen). Four years after Actium, when Octavian was accorded the epithet *Augustus*, his *de facto* political, military and religious supremacy was given a formal endorsement. His ostensible reverence towards the Senate was from then onward just a shrewd expedient and façade, useful in legitimising his actions. In a painless transition, after around five centuries the Roman Republic had returned to absolute monarchy, despite the persistence of the old Republican institutions as apparently still vital and intact: the Senate, the *cursus honorum* and consulate, the popular assemblies and the army.

In 27 B.C. Augustus restructured the administration of the Roman territories. Greece (officially called the province of Achaea) was included among the senatorial provinces, i.e. among the areas of the empire that were already pacified and did not require the intervention of the army for their control. The role of Greece thus took a secondary position in the political events of the empire, but the same cannot be said of the Greeks themselves. Not only did they continue to meet the Roman social elites' demand for cultural *paideia* and to respond to the ruling class's need for education, but they integrated into imperial society and ultimately accepted the historical inevitability of the dominating power. However, this point should not be generalised or treated as absolute: there was no lack of resistance, hostility and open dislike towards Rome in various times and places, as we shall see in the next section.

From this perspective, the Roman nationalism of the first emperors (Augustus, 27 B.C.–A.D. 14, and Tiberius, A.D. 14–37) encountered a particular form of Hellenism, fed by antiquarian longing for the past physiognomy of the *polis*. Some Greek cities thus embarked on an almost museum-like fate through the nostalgic resurrection of obsolete political, cultural and religious forms. At Sparta the institutions of the Classical and Archaic Ages were revived along with the archaic constitution of Lycurgus, while the Amphictionic Council of Delphi gained a new and vigorous impulse. Yet a very different idea was gaining ground already in the Augustan Age – that Rome was the true heir to the splendours of the Greek cities and that in this sense it was pursuing their cultural path.

After the extravagances of Caligula (37–41) and the lukewarm Hellenism of Claudius (41–54), the highpoint of Philhellenic attitudes among the first emperors was reached with Nero (54–68), who in 67 intended to pay homage to the ancient grandeur of Greece by abolishing its status as province and proclaiming its freedom (this is what earned him the byname *Zeus eleutherios*). The accession to the throne of Vespasian (69–79), founder of the Flavian dynasty (Titus, 79–81; Domitian, 81–96), marked a return to Roman nationalism and a scaling back of the role and image of Greece, which from 74 (the year when the philosophers were banished from Rome and Italy) was again reduced to a province and made subject to tribute.

The first century of our era ended with the experience of the despotism of Domitian. His successor, the elderly senator Nerva, remained in office for just two years (96–98), but he inaugurated a practice that was destined to guarantee the empire a period of stability for at least a century. Beginning from Nerva, the emperors undertook to designate their successor by adoption, choosing him not just on the basis of blood relation but above all taking into account the real political abilities of the men around them. We therefore speak of the "adoptive emperors" (Nerva, Trajan, Hadrian, Antoninus Pius, Marcus Aurelius, Commodus, whose reigns run from 96 to 193) and of an "orderly" phase of political, military and economic management of the empire.

The second century represented a new era of Hellenism opened by the renewed interest of Trajan (98–117) in the eastern provinces of the empire. His successor Hadrian (117–138) and the Antonines (Antoninus Pius, 138–161; Marcus Aurelius, 161–180 and his co-emperors Lucius Verus and Commodus, who then became successor to Marcus Aurelius until 192) gave the impulse for a cultural policy of reclaiming Hellenic civilisation, with the aim of refounding it in an original and vital way. One of the typical phenomena of the period, linked to the project of renewing Hellenic culture and promoted by the emperors themselves, was the practice of euergetism: people with great resources and great munificence could win lustre and honours by constructing grandiose and monumental public buildings in the Greek cities. Following this came a rebirth of many urban centres in Greece and the Hellenistic world, which came to play an important role in the culture of the era.

It is at the very end of the second century that one notes the first signs of a gradual eclipse of ancient Greek culture. From this point of view, there is a symbolic significance to the invasion of Greece by the barbarian people of the Costoboci (ca. 170) in the reign of Marcus Aurelius. In the latter half of the following century – which was characterised by the substantial decay of literature and by an ever more accentuated militarisation of the empire – the phenomenon of barbarian invasions began to take on a troubling scale on the north-eastern borders, threatening the very survival of Hellenistic and Graeco-Roman civilisation.

The final phase of the empire created room for a new cultural phase beginning from the reign of Constantine (A.D. 306–337), which opened what we have defined as the "Late Antique Period," with the transfer of the capital to the ancient Byzantium, now rechristened Constantinople. The spread of Christianity led to the emergence of new literary currents and poured fresh streams into the Graeco-Roman cultural tradition, which was now sustained by the values and goals of the officially recognised religion, to the point that one may talk of the "Christian empire." Even the extreme attempt to restore paganism and the ancient polytheistic beliefs, supported by the emperor Julian the Apostate (A.D. 361–363) and matching the aspirations of the most elevated and traditionalist echelons of Roman society, was no more than a final coda by intellectuals unwilling to accept the process of fusion and integration underway between Romano-Hellenistic and Christian culture.

The establishment of a separation into a western and an eastern empire would result, on the one hand, in the formation of a caesura between the two spheres also in culture, but on the other hand it guaranteed in the eastern part the readoption and preservation of the traditional inheritance of Greek-language civilisation. Through this channel, in the intense activity of innumerable episodes of selection and transmission of ancient texts, in what was essentially an attitude of emulation and conservation of the works of the past, the inheritance of Greek civilisation was passed on to the Byzantine empire. The periodisation that we have indicated stops at the reign of Justinian (527–565), with whom we set the end of the Late Antique Period of Greek literature. In the course of their thousand-year history the Byzantines would become guardians of that tradition, finally passing on their witness in turn to Italian humanism.

3 The bilingual empire: integration and resistance

Among the different aspects that give the Imperial Period its distinctive form, one should not overlook the fact of language. Through the Hellenistic kingdoms, Greek had had an immensely wide diffusion through the whole eastern region in the common literary form called the κοινὴ διάλεκτος (*koinē dialektos*, "common language") and it continued to hold this role as international language also in the Graeco-Roman world of the Imperial Period. The Roman ruling class normally knew Greek, whereas there were not many Greek-speakers who were able to use Latin well (especially in the eastern provinces).

Further, after Augustus there was a process of rapprochement between the provinces and Italy, resulting in ever greater homogeneity between centre and periphery. The eastern Greek or Hellenised regions, countries with very ancient and refined cultures, generally did not understand their relation to the Roman conqueror in terms of a necessary assimilation or cultural adaptation to it (unlike what happened in many Romanised areas in the West), but rather turned the relation on its head, into one of exerting a powerful and profound cultural influence on the conqueror.

The first three centuries of the Imperial Period were characterised by the ever deeper roots struck by Greek culture within the overall borders of the Roman Empire. Rome's confirmed hegemonic position ensured that the world of Greek-language culture found in it an ever greater pole of attraction for literary figures, artists and philosophers. Undoubtedly Latin literature had been enriched by Greek models right from its origins, and continued to be, but in the Imperial Period the process by which the culture in fact became bilingual was completed decisively. Greek historians, rhetors, scholars, scientists and philosophers wrote in Greek for a both Greek and Roman public. An ever more Hellenised Rome and an ever more Romanised Greece – this is just a formula to say that the coexistence was by then not just a reality but also an effective and active basis of culture. In a Graeco-Roman world, the Roman Empire itself was in reality the cradle and guarantor of Greek cultural vitality and literary production.

While in the course of the Hellenistic Age there had been room for anti-Roman debate and historiography, in the Augustan Era the Greek historian Dionysius of Halicarnassus definitively established an idea of Rome as the prestigious guarantor of the reclamation and conservation of Hellenism's deepest traditional values. The path to integration had been opened up for everyone, and in the following centuries there was no shortage of cultured figures who pursued this path in the intellectual, political and social life of the empire. For an intellectual such as Dio of Prusa, for example, hostility towards the despotism of Domitian (shared also by the Roman senatorial class) was just one blip in a long line of excellent relations created by appreciation and harmony both with Vespasian and Titus and then with Trajan, who was celebrated as a model of the wise and enlightened emperor. The *Encomium to Rome* by Aelius Aristides (second century), which paints Rome as a classical Greek *polis*, illustrates well the highest point of concord between Greek intellectuals and the Roman Empire and it exerted a notable influence on political and historiographical thought of the second and third centuries, or at the very least it was strongly in accord with it.

However, one should not yield to the seductive image of invariably idyllic harmony between the different components. The history that produced the different forms of syncretism between pagan and Judaeo-Christian culture was fairly complex and nuanced and underwent not only absorptions and reconciliations into new amalgams, but also troubles and rifts. And one should recall expressions of disquiet and instability in the Greek intellectual world under the hegemony of Rome. The flourishing and development of religious and mystery movements, the rise in mystical tendencies and occult superstitions (often mixed up together with philosophical doctrines), the wandering through the cities of soi-disant ascetics and wonder-workers, the practice of magic and divination – these are various instances of the resort to the irrational, which attest the bubbling that was not far, and not only, under the surface of an era full of suffering and troubles.

Finally, there were genuine factors of dissent, which found expression in critical voices and positions not integrated into the nascent Graeco-Roman culture, or simply standing aloof from it. For example, Plutarch in his *Lives* set Greek and Roman on an equal plane to each other, yet believed that young Greeks of noble families should restrict themselves to the autonomous politics of their cities, evidently without participating directly in the central political life of the empire. Lucian, in his ironic picture of the world around him, certainly does not seem entirely reconciled to it and at times seems to adopt the image of a Greek intellectual by no means burning with pro-Roman sympathies. Anti-Roman resistance could thicken around the temples of the eastern zones, places in which the political and social elites had the ability to organise the consensus, and for this reason the Romans attempted to subject them to conditions. A particular but important case is that of the Jewish world, never entirely quiet or pacified in the alternative between collaboration and opposition, even for intellectuals who wrote in Greek (for example Flavius Josephus). Real dislike for Rome is found in the varied collection of *Sybilline Oracles*, and an under-current of anti-Roman expectations at times finds expression in apocalyptic litera-ture. Tendencies running counter to Rome, which are absent from the literature of the higher echelons, found space in the Christian apologetic of the second century (a literature that was closer to the popular classes) and in the protest preaching of the so-called popular Cynics, who are depicted as crude and vulgar figures who spent time in humble settings and gave voice to malcontents and attempts at revolt.

Another characteristic of the period is the diffusion of what we may call the lit-erature of entertainment, with the aim of pure enjoyment by the public. This too can be seen as a symptom of a desire for escapism, which perhaps betrays a certain feeling of disharmony with reality. Apart from the success of the novel, there was also a rich output of romanticised and adventurous history, collections of fantastic letters, works of political disengagement, of reading for pleasure or escapism. This work is predominantly in prose; yet there are also examples in poetry and above all in forms of spectacle aimed at pure entertainment. This genre of literature came to take on the role that had in previous periods been played by a large swathe of the historiographical output, which had been aimed primarily at enjoyable amusement.

4 Classicism, Atticism and the Second Sophistic

Characteristic of Greek culture of the Imperial Period is a set of literary phenomena, primarily in the rhetorical, linguistic and stylistic sphere, that could be generally and generically termed classicism. At least on the stylistic and formal level, the cultural renewal of the Augustan Era had as its most fundamental feature the phe-nomenon of Atticism. This was the view by writers that they should take as model for their style and linguistic choices the Attic authors of the fifth and fourth century B.C., who were vigorously prescribed as models for study and imitation by anyone committed to the art of writing. This choice thus essentially became a problem of models, above all in the later developments of this current and in the numerous differentiations in individual tastes and positions. Dionysius of Halicarnassus and Caecilius of Caleacte in the Augustan Period are the two principal figures noted as initiators or promoters of the Atticist approach in letters. Such forms of classicism had a natural continuation in a broad and varied movement that developed from the late first century, flourishing vigorously in the second and until the first decades of the third, for which it is conventional to adopt the term (used already in the ancient world) of the "Second Sophistic."

This whole complex of phenomena is centred in various ways on the desire to return to the authoritative and sanctioned literary models of the Classical Age and to the ideals that they represented. It seems on the cultural level to be a clear form of demand by the Greeks for their own original traditions and their own cultural identi-ty, and one that had a significant political force. Cultural prestige and political or social position were often closely interlinked, as becomes clear if one considers the figures who were most outstanding among the rhetors and sophists, philosophers and historians. It must have seemed to the Greeks that the ancient ideal of the sage guiding society had found some kind of realisation. This tendency was for the most part incarnated by the higher classes of the eastern Greek provinces. Well integrated into the imperial structure at every level and often operating at the centre of power, they saw in the Roman empire, and entrusted to it, the role of supporter and the historical function of guarantor of a world in which they could cultivate and develop their own culture, finally bringing it to the hoped-for new renaissance. Thus it is not at all paradoxical, indeed perfectly comprehensible, that this highest level of integration, among men of culture who were originally and traditionally Greek, was matched by the highest level of defence of their own proud and autonomous identity.

Operating at a similar level is the appeal to the past as a fount and foundation of security, as is evident in the development of the various philosophical schools, which continued the traditional doctrines and literary genres in which they had been expressed. There was a proliferation of re-readings and reinterpretations of the thought of the great philosophers of the Archaic, Classical and Hellenistic Ages and there developed a luxuriant doxographic and exegetical literature. Philosophy and rhetoric thus proceeded in harmony, thanks, among other things, to the common choice of the past as the perennial model and indispensable source of knowledge. Still moving in the footsteps of tradition, the old debate between the two disciplines continued, but without the harsh and quarrelsome tones of other periods, and perhaps one may say that the relation had become one of integrative cooperation. The figure of the sophist was often that of a rhetor-philosopher or a philosopher-rhetor. Holding the balance, or rather the halfway point, between oratory and philosophy are figures such as Dio of Prusa and Lucian, as well as Plutarch and Aelius Aristides (the distinction between literary genres is thus often only a matter of convenience, and the one that will be presented in what follows is also a matter of convenience), who in different ways, often with irritation, criticisms and objections, or else with complete identification, nonetheless developed their activity in the mainstream of the life of the empire. In every case, the key and dominating element in every intellectual activity involving words remained the omnipotent rhetoric, the true stamp of the spirit of the time.

Linked to these aspects is the strong development of the activity of interpreting and commenting on ancient authors, with the aim of providing the basic models of culture with a philological and exegetical apparatus that was indispensable if they were to be enjoyed in the most knowledgeable, deepest and richest way. The foundations of this activity had been laid in the Alexandrian Era, but in the Imperial Period it unleashed its greatest energy for collecting material, and so exerted a decisive influence on the transmission of the material to future centuries.

5 The literary genres in the Imperial Period

As we have said, the Imperial Period exhibits a clear prevalence of prose over poetry. The poetic genres maintained their vitality, but rarely offer great original creations. In the sphere of poetry, the genre that yields the most significant results is without doubt the epigram. After the great phase of Hellenistic epigram, the themes and style of the models were reprised and varied in a rich output, always made up of brief compositions, for the most part in elegiac distichs, which ran in a first phase from the Augustan Period to the second century A.D., then entering a decline and regaining vigour some centuries later in the age of Justinian. Alongside epigram, hymnography is the only traditional lyric genre still represented in what survives of Greek poetry of the Imperial Period. From Mesomedes of Crete, a citharoedus and lyric poet of the second century, we have in total thirteen poems in various metres, including religious hymns to pagan divinities and descriptions. Epic-didactic poetry, which went back to the most noble origins of Greek literature and had yielded splendid fruit in the Hellenistic Age, continued to be cultivated also in the Imperial Period, until an important blossoming in the Late Antique Period. Entering into the tradition of hexameter poetry were some works of uncertain chronology on Orphic topics (two short poems and a number of hymns) and collections of oracular poetry (*Sybilline Oracles* and *Chaldaean Oracles*). We may note finally the fables in iambic metre of Babrius and the theatrical genre of mime, which existed alongside the now well-established custom of restaging tragic works of the Classical Age (above all by Euripides).

Among the prose genres, rhetoric, understood as an institutionalised, formalised and normative discipline with schools and currents of taste engaged in an active literary criticism, without doubt constituted the intellectual activity that in this period exerted a kind of dominance, by itself informing the entire human creative sphere concerned with words. Historiography echoed the assumptions of rhetoric, moving, from the conceptual point of view, within the Romano-centric vision inaugurated during the Hellenistic Era above all by Polybius. The centrality of Rome is expressed both in pro-Roman tendencies, which from Dionysius of Halicarnassus onwards saw Rome as a Greek *polis* able to reunite different cultures within the universal horizon of the empire, but also in the anti-Roman tendencies inspired by dissidence of various kind and origin. The novel is perhaps the greatest novelty to be noted in the panorama of Greek literature of the Imperial Period. Although the earliest surviving testimonia attest that the genre existed from the second century B.C., the novels that have survived complete through the Byzantine manuscript tradition belong to the Imperial Period, and it seems that we should date to this era the greatest success and diffusion of these entertaining narratives (which continued in the Byzantine Period, both in prose and verse).

Among the most important Hellenistic manifestations of the Jewish cultural ambience expressed in Greek, we have noted for the Hellenistic Age the translation of the *Old Testament* known as the *Septuagint*, achieved in the setting of the strong Jewish community of Alexandria. The diaspora of the People of Israel outside the territories of Palestine produced the birth of various Jewish communities in different settings with an already well-established Greek culture (the most conspicuous of these Graeco-Jewish communities was in Alexandria), where a cultural identity that was never obscured was married to the deep absorption of Hellenism. From the second half of the first century A.D., the texts of the *New Testament* launched an ever richer and larger Christian literature, which produced an original constellation of literary forms and genres. Compared to the terrible loss of Hellenistic philosophical literature, the richness of what has been preserved from the Imperial Period is striking, though it continued to plough the furrow of doctrines born in the past, without producing a truly new current of thought. Alongside the output of speculative work and commentary, tied above all to the Academic and Peripatetic schools, we may note the output of two important philosophical-religious movements seamed with mysticism: Neopythagoreanism and Neoplatonism.

It is not always easy to identify a strictly "scientific" literature as distinct from philosophical literature. Disciplines such as geography, astronomy, mathematics and medicine underwent important development in the Imperial Period, which brought forth a copious literature dedicated expressly to it. Finally, a chapter that should not be neglected in Greek culture of the Imperial Period (one again in close continuity with the Hellenistic Age) is constituted by the whole area that can be connected to the concept of erudite literature, as mentioned above: philology, grammar, lexicography, antiquarian and doxographical collections and repertoires of material of every kind.

Tab. 2: Chronological Table of the Principal Historical Events (the first dates are B.C.).

31 (2 September)	Battle of Actium
30	Death of Antonius and Cleopatra; Egypt becomes a Roman province
27	Creation of the province of Achaea
27 B.C.–A.D. 14	Augustus is *imperator*
14–37	Tiberius
37–41	Caligula
41–54	Claudius
54–68	Nero
67	Nero abolishes the province of Achaea
68–69	Galba
69	Otho, Vitellius
	Year of the Four Emperors
69–79	Vespasian

74	Vespasian banishes the philosophers from Rome and Italy; restores the province of Achaea
79–81	Titus
81–96	Domitian
96–98	Nerva
98–117	Trajan
117–138	Hadrian
138–161	Antoninus Pius
161–180	Marcus Aurelius
161–169	Lucius Verus co-emperor
170 ca.	The tribe of the Costoboci invades Greece
178–180	Commodus co-emperor
180–192	Commodus
193	Pertinax
193	Didius Julianus
193–211	Septimius Severus
198–211	Caracalla co-emperor
211–217	Caracalla
209–212	Geta co-emperor
212	Edict of Caracalla (*Constitutio Antoniniana*)
217–218	Macrinus
218–222	Elagabal
222–235	Severus Alexander
235–238	Maximinus Thrax
238–284	Period of "military anarchy" (about 20 emperors)
253	Barbarian incursions (Goths, Burgundians and others) on the coasts of Asia Minor
256–262	Barbarian invasions by land in Asia Minor
267	Invasion of Greece by the Heruli
284–305	Diocletian and the tetrarchy
305–313	Tetrarchy
313–337	Constantine sole emperor
313	Edict of Milan (also known as edict of Constantine)
361–363	Julian the Apostate
379–395	Theodosius emperor
380	Edict of Thessalonica
391	Destruction of the Serapeum of Alexandria
393	Last Olympic Games
395	Death of the emperor Theodosius and division of the empire into a western and an eastern part

410	The Goths under Alaric sack Rome
476	Deposition of Romulus Augustulus and end of the western Roman empire
527–565	Justinian emperor of the East
529	Justinian decrees the closure of the philosophical schools of Athens

II Rhetoric and Literary Criticism

1 Rhetorical tendencies in the Rome of Augustus

1.1 The establishment of Greek rhetoric at Rome

If we had to name an intellectual activity in this period that exerted a kind of domination, shaping by itself practically the whole human creative sphere involving words, it would be rhetoric, understood as a discipline that was institutionalised, formalised and normative, with different schools and currents of taste.

The flow of intellectuals and teachers of rhetoric from Greece to Rome became ever more numerous from the late Republican Era onwards, and under Augustus a very striking level of exchange was occurring between Italy and the Hellenised East. Dionysius of Halicarnassus, for example, lived and worked in Rome for more than twenty years. Prompted in part by the Roman ruling class's insistent demand for cultural instruction, the official recognition of teachers of rhetoric occurred under the Flavian dynasty. In A.D. 74 Vespasian issued an edict in which he decreed a tax exemption for those teaching rhetoric and grammar in any city of the empire. After that, he set up in the capital a professorial chair of Greek eloquence and one of Latin eloquence at state expense. In these years a lively literary debate is attested, facilitated by the frequent cultural exchanges and by the establishment of a culture that was, so to speak, fluid and malleable, favourable to encounters and mixtures.

In this debate an important role was played by some elements of a different nature. To cite two quite different ones, we should remember the improvement in communication routes and the road network that was promoted by Augustus and the diffusion of the epistolography with rhetorical and critical content. These are two factors that made easier the cultural exchange between rhetors and intellectuals in various cities of the empire. No less weight should be given to the intensification of literacy and the book market, which diffused ideas, fashions and tendencies. The opportunity to access texts was facilitated also by the growth of private libraries (from the late Republican Era on, private houses were often planned with spaces for libraries), as well as the public ones (the first of them all being the ancient and prestigious Library of Alexandria, but there were also others, such as those at Pergamum and Antioch). According to tradition, the first public library at Rome was set up at the wish of Asinius Pollio in 39 B.C. It was followed by other initiatives, the main one being that of Augustus, who promoted the establishment of a Greek library and a Latin library.

In our introduction to the Imperial Period we mentioned one of the main aspects of rhetoric of the Augustan and later periods, which embraced the world of letters in its entirety: Atticism, i.e. the outlook that led writers to choose the Attic authors of the fifth and fourth centuries B.C. as their model for style and linguistic choices.

https://doi.org/10.1515/9783110426328-031

This phenomenon is part of a more general classicising taste, the origins of which we have already discussed in the part on the Hellenistic Age (cf. *The Hellenistic Age* VII 2.2). It is important to clarify that Atticism cannot be identified with a system or school of rhetoric. It was essentially a phenomenon of taste and it took the form of the problem of choosing models, above all in its later developments and in the numerous differentiations of individual tastes and positions. In the Augustan Age, as we shall see shortly, the rhetorical debate involved figures of the first rank such as Dionysius of Halicarnassus, Caecilius of Caleacte and the anonymous author of the treatise *On the Sublime*.

1.2 Apollodorus of Pergamum and Theodorus of Gadara

It was long believed possible to interpret a large part of the rhetoric of the first century B.C. and the first century A.D. on the basis of the controversy between Apollodorus of Pergamum and Theodorus of Gadara, teachers of rhetoric at Rome, and between their respective schools, the "Apollodorans" and the "Theodorans." Despite the loss of the works by these two rhetors and their schools, we are able to reconstruct their doctrines at least in some part, thanks to a certain number of later testimonia.

Apollodorus of Pergamum lived between 104 and 22 B.C., taught rhetoric at Rome, wrote an *Art of Rhetoric* (Τέχνη) and was the teacher of the young Octavian. The approach taken in his rhetorical doctrine was strongly rationalistic and was based on a rigid idea of the means and goals of eloquence. He therefore carefully classified all the parts and kinds of speech, with the goal of creating a very detailed system of rules, which were to furnish the student constantly with the arguments, expedients and stylistic possibilities needed to produce a successful oration.

A different approach was proposed in the rhetoric championed by Theodorus of Gadara, who lived between 70 and 6 B.C. He was the teacher of Tiberius at Rhodes and wrote a historical work *On Coele Syria*, the treatises *On History* and *On the State*, an *Art of Rhetoric* and a linguistic manual *On the Similarity of Languages and on Demonstration*. Following an approach closer to Stoicism, Theodorus maintained that eloquence had to reserve for itself a certain freedom of expression and inspiration. He too, naturally, conceived the learning of eloquence as the mastery of a *technē*, yet he did not hold that it should dictate rules and norms set out in a rigid and meticulous way, but that a degree of space should also be allowed for the emotional charge of the *logos*.

In studies of the history of rhetoric, the controversy between the two schools was "dramatised" by the repeated generalisations of scholars, until they saw it (groundlessly) as an ideological conflict that opposed free and natural inspiration (Theodorus) to a rigid, scientific but dry normative system (Apollodorus), even seeing it as opposing anomaly to analogy as expressions of, respectively, freedom and normativity. All this was a gross misunderstanding by historians and critics, and one that unfortunately is still sometimes repeated. In reality there was a more limited divergence, on some precise points of the rhetorical system and the structural scheme of the speech, in which Apollodorus granted less freedom than Theodorus. It was thus a strictly technical contrast within the school of rhetoric, which in all likelihood did not deviate at all, in any of these teachers or pupils, from the context of an Atticist classicism that was already well on the way to becoming established.

2 Dionysius of Halicarnassus

2.1 A key figure

The most important representative of the rhetorical culture of this period is Dionysius of Halicarnassus, active at Rome between 30 and 7 B.C., and also a historian of great importance. He is the ancient author from whom we have the greatest number of preserved works of rhetorical criticism. These form a series of essays based on a sharp and rigorous stylistic criticism that was firmly anti-Asianist (for Asianist rhetoric cf. *The Hellenistic Age* VII 2.1), since he was one of the most fervent proponents of the Atticist taste and tendency. More recent research, freed from the prejudices of some nineteenth-century philologists who saw in Dionysius above all an insignificant *Graeculus*, has re-evaluated his exceptional role as intellectual bridge between Greek and Latin culture, in the important crucible of innovation that was Rome of the Augustan Period.

We know little of his life. It seems that he was born around 60 B.C. in the same city on the coast of Asia Minor that had also given birth to Herodotus, and that at around the age of thirty he had moved to Rome, where he supported himself by working as a professor of rhetoric and formed links with the main families of the city. He belonged to the circle of the jurist Quintus Aelius Tubero and was a friend of the rhetor Caecilius of Caleacte. We hear nothing more of him after 7 B.C., around which time his work on the history of Rome was published.

2.2 The works

Dionysius was the author of a Ῥωμαικὴ ἀρχαιολογία, *Roman Antiquities*, which narrated the history of the city from its legendary origins to the First Punic War. In this way Dionysius linked up from behind to the work of Polybius, who had begun with the events of 264 B.C., although Dionysius' historiography is very far removed from the character and pragmatic intentions of Polybius' work. Of the twenty books in which it was composed, the first ten and part of the eleventh have survived, as well as two late epitomes. It is a historiographical work in which the rhetorical and ideological component seems to take priority and shape the treatment. More than the truthfulness and reliability of the sources, more than the task of documentary research, Dionysius was interested in writing a history according to the models of language, style and cultural outlook of Athens of the fifth and fourth century B.C. To this end, annalistic sources are deployed in an uncritical way as regards how they correspond to the facts. Nonetheless, Dionysius' Atticism is not rigorous and extreme. In his prose many expressions and lexical elements of the Hellenistic *koinē* appear, which sharply undermines the ideal of Attic purity. The work is of value predominantly for the fact that it bridges gaps in periods, especially in the Archaic Age, that are poorly attested by ancient authors and, perhaps above all, for its admiring attitude towards Roman history and institutions, with the ideological perspective of supporting and boosting the Roman Empire in the eyes of the Greeks, essentially on the basis of a claim that the Romans were originally Greek. But we will discuss this work at more length in the section on historiography (cf. *The Roman Imperial Period* III 1.2).

In this chapter we are concerned in detail with the various rhetorical works that have survived, which contain simultaneously both theoretical aspects and stylistic analysis. Dionysius regarded himself as a rhetor and literary critic (this is of course a modern term, but it conveys the idea well enough) and the intensity of his interest in studying authors' style clearly shines through his writings (even though the material treated may make them seem rather dry). His analysis gives a lot of space to the quotation of passages from the authors he discusses. For this reason, Dionysius is also a very important source of many lost authors, fragments of which he transmits in large numbers, some of considerable length.

The work *On Literary Composition* (Περὶ συνθέσεως ὀνομάτων, *De compositione verborum*) takes part in the complex debate on style that was fairly lively in his time and also included the anonymous treatise *On the Sublime* and the work *On Style* by a certain Demetrius, which we will discuss shortly. Dionysius' treatise is concerned with one of the key topics of ancient rhetoric, namely the art of σύνθεσις ὀνομάτων (*synthesis onomatōn*) or of the arrangement of words in a phrase. Dionysius comments on and analyses in detail long passages of the best authors, which he proposes for imitation by his pupils, with the aim of illustrating which style is suited to each subject. The criteria considered concern essentially rhythm and euphony, as well as lexical propriety. First of all he defines the nature, effects and methods of *synthesis*, then its goals and the means of achieving it. At this point he identifies three types of *synthesis* or *armonia* (ἁρμονία), that is to say, the aural and euphonic qualities that characterise the different forms of expression: the austere or severe form (αὐστηρά), represented by authors such as Antimachus and Empedocles in epic, Aeschylus in tragedy, Antiphon in oratory, Pindar in lyric and Thucydides in historiography (he dwells on the last two of these with a special analysis); the refined and elegant form (γλαφυρά), typical of Sappho (whose *Ode to Aphrodite* he records in full), Isocrates and Euripides; and the mixed or moderate form (εὔκρατος), present in Homer, Stesichorus, Alcaeus, Sophocles, Herodotus, Demosthenes and Plato. The closing chapters dwell on the relations between prose and poetry and on the possibility of assimilation between the two, i.e. a poetic prose and a poetry similar to prose. In this final part, too, various fragments of lost poetry are recorded.

The three-book treatise *On Imitation*, of which we possess only fragments, addressed one of the key topics of rhetoric of the Imperial Period, namely the theory of *mimesis* or imitation. The basic idea is that one cannot dispense with the close familiarity and imitation of the classic authors, in particular the Greek ones, with the principal authors being passed in review in Book II (both poets and prose authors). Here again we have the central problem of the choice of models. Among the authors favoured by Dionysius are Demosthenes, for his capacity of matching style to circumstance and for the intensity of his versatile and emotionally rich periodic style. It was precisely in the late Republican and Augustan Period that Demosthenes was established as the orator par excellence, both in the Latin world, with Cicero, and the Greek one, with Dionysius and the anonymous author *On the Sublime*.

The survey of works, although summary, reveals the intensity of the discussions and the liveliness of the public debates about ancient authors, the analysis of their style and the question of which models to choose. Dionysius also wrote *The Ancient Orators* in two books, of which the first survives, including treatments of Lysias, Isocrates and Isaeus. Of the second book, the parts on Hyperides and Aeschines are lost, while the section *On the Style of Demosthenes is preserved*. Matching the positive judgement that emerges from the treatise *On Imitation*, Demosthenes is here presented as an orator who knew how to choose the best from each style and from all the authors, developing an individual style that was able to meet any need and personifying the eclectic ideal that Dionysius proposes to his ideal pupil.

Another two monographs by Dionysius on stylistic criticism are also preserved: one on Thucydides and one on Dinarchus, which is mutilated at the end. Lost are some works in which the author, still on the basis of stylistic criteria, treated questions of authenticity and attribution (concerning Lysias, Isocrates and Demosthenes). Finally, three works take epistolary form: two are addressed to his friend Ammaeus and one to a certain Gnaeus Pompeius Geminus, probably a Greek who did not live at Rome. The first *Letter to Ammaeus* aims to deny any relation between the eloquence of Demosthenes and Aristotelian rhetoric; in the second *Letter* some peculiarities of Thucydides' style are examined. In the *Letter to Gnaeus Pompeius* Dionysius reprises some criticisms of the style of Plato that he had made in the essay on Demosthenes and on which he had received objections.

3 The rhetorical and stylistic debate

3.1 Caecilius of Caleacte

On this rhetor, younger than Dionysius of Halicarnassus and a convinced promoter of Atticism at Rome, we have only very meagre notices. According to the *Suda* lexicon he was of slave origin and Jewish faith; his true name had been Archagathus. Plutarch, in his biography of Demosthenes, criticised him for being too anticonformist, perhaps on account of his innovative tendency in establishing models and criteria of stylistic composition. His work is completely lost, aside from a few fragments. He wrote a treatise *Against the Phrygians*, in opposition to the Asianist orators, whom he polemically called "Phrygians," and one entitled *On What Differentiates the Attic Style from the Asian Style*. It seems that Caecilius is responsible for the first formulation of the canon of the ten Attic orators.

A large part of Caecilius' celebrity is derived from the polemic launched against his theories in the treatise *On the Sublime*, which attributes to him a similar work on the same subject, which is the target of the polemic, and a commentary on Lysias.

3.2 The treatise *On the Sublime*

The treatise Περὶ ὕψους (*On the Sublime*, i.e. concerning the problem of stylistic sublimity or of the most elevated style) is one of the best known works of rhetoric and stylistic criticism from the ancient world. It has come down to us in lacunose form and lacking its final part. In the surviving part, it addresses varied topics of rhetoric with a critical and stylistic edge and sensitivity that has no parallels in Greek and Latin rhetorical treatises. The fame of *On the Sublime* among modern authors has been exceptional, to the point that it has obscured other rhetorical treatises from the ancient world that are no less interesting, though admittedly more dry and schematic. Also favouring the anonymous author is the fact that he displays an ability to express himself with great succinctness and beauty and has been able to turn rhetorical criticism into a work of art of a high standard.

As we mentioned, the treatise was composed as a polemic against a work by Caecilius of Caleacte on the same theme, which is mentioned at the start of the work: "Caecilius' little treatise on the Sublime (...) appeared to us to fall below the level of the subject" (par. 1). In other words, the author believes that Caecilius has not succeeded in bringing out the essential points of the topic or in providing an adequate explanation of them. What the sublime consists in and the means by which it may be obtained are the central topic of *On the Sublime*. According to the author, the ability to achieve the sublime resides in innate natural gifts, such as high sentiments and the capacity for extraordinary sensitivity, but it is not possible to develop or realise its potential to the highest level without a suitable training.

The sublime consists "in a consummate excellence and distinction of language," an element that has allowed poets and prose authors to reach the summit of their art: "For the effect of genius is not to persuade the audience but rather to transport them out of themselves." The sublime is thus compared to a lightning bolt that reduces to cinders whatever it touches and which focuses the entire power of the orator (ch. 1, 3–4). Then a list is given of the five sources of the sublime: to aim for elevated thoughts; having an attitude that is passionate, vigorous and full of enthusiasm; commanding solid competence in creating rhetorical figures of thought and of speech; expressing oneself in a noble way; and placing the words according to a dignified and solemn register (ch. 8). The treatise, with its numerous quotations from past authors analysed with finesse, provides examples of the rhetorical expedients and above all the figures that help to raise the tone of a statement (for example metaphors, hyperbaton, periphrases and similes); further, it warns against those elements that can reduce and lower an elevated style, for example the use of a broken or agitated rhythm, of members of the period that are too quick or composed predominantly of short syllables, since they seem "bolted together, as it were, at frequent intervals with rough and uneven joins" (ch. 41). The models of *On the Sublime* are Homer, Pindar, Sophocles, Demosthenes and Plato (the last of whom had been criticised by Caecilius). The author's judgement on Homer is famous in his comparison of the two Homeric poems, according to which the *Iliad* was the work of Homer's maturity, as befits its consistently sublime tension, the passion for military ardour, the theme of war and the tendency towards action, whereas the *Odyssey* was the work of the poet's old age, when the taste for storytelling, description and the characters' personalities is preferred: "in the *Odyssey* one may liken Homer to the setting sun; the grandeur remains without the intensity" (ch. 9, 13). The final preserved chapter (ch. 44) speaks of the causes of the decadence of oratory in the author's own times: an anonymous philosopher who is his interlocutor maintains that the cause is political, namely the vanishing of democratic liberty, the only sustenance for great political oratory; the author himself, to the contrary, speaks of a moral cause, which he identifies in an excessive love of money and pleasure that pushes every other value into second place.

The problem of the identity of the author has always been central to critical debate on the text. It is in fact difficult to set the treatise in a precise critical or rhetorical tendency, except for the open polemic with Caecilius. The manuscript tradition attributes the treatise to a Dionysius Longinus, an author who has not been identified with any person otherwise known (this attribution is the source of the conventional name "Pseudo-Longinus" by which the treatise is sometimes cited). In the past there was a tendency to identify this Longinus with Cassius Longinus, a rhetor of the third century, minister of Zenobia, queen of the city of Palmyra. However, this theory has been abandoned for some time: the cultural climate that emerges from the treatise, the importance assigned to pathos and to the emotion that words can arouse, as well as the observations on the grandeur of thought that elevates the spoken word, as well as other elements, cannot be dated to such a late period. The attribution offered by the manuscript tradition has been explained as arising from someone who did not know the author of the treatise and decided to attribute it conjecturally to two of the most eminent critics and rhetors of the ancient world, Dionysius of Halicarnassus and Cassius Longinus. This person would thus have written the alternative "Dionysius or Longinus," as is found at the end of the contents summary of the Paris manuscript that transmits the work, where folio 1^v reads

Διονυσίου ἢ Λογγίνου περὶ ὕψους ("*On the Sublime* by Dionysius or Longinus"), whereas in the same codex at the start of the treatise (folio 178ᵛ) the title is Διονυσίου Λογγίνου περὶ ὕψους ("*On the Sublime* by Dionysius Longinus"). The next step would thus have been the loss of the disjunctive "or" and so the emergence of a non-existent "Dionysius Longinus." However, there are also scholars who believe that this was the correct name of the author: a rhetor called Dionysius Longinus of whom we have lost all other trace, as has indeed happened to various others. Other proposals that have been advanced identify the author with the rhetors Hermagoras or Theon. Today the problem of authorship in the strict sense appears less dramatic, since scholars prefer to focus on the dating and on placing the work into a precise cultural context, which seems much more important than the mere attribution of a name. The most recent scholarship holds that the author was a Greek who was certainly active at Rome, with a preference for placing him in the cultural climate of the Augustan Age or a little later, in the first half of the first century A.D., which sets him in the context of the rhetorical and stylistic debate that we have been examining here and the discussion of models of style in the context of Atticism.

3.3 Demetrius

An interesting stylistic treatise entitled Περὶ ἑρμηνείας, *On Style*, known also by the Latin title *De elocutione*, has survived with attribution to a Demetrius, who was confused in the ancient world with Demetrius of Phaleron, though the work has nothing to do with him (cf. *The Classical Age* XIII 3.8.2).

   The content of the work has no parallels with the Aristotelian work of the same name. It is devoted entirely to problems of style and establishes a system (distinctive to this work) that considers four styles or χαρακτῆρες (*charaktēres*): the simple or plain (ἰσχνός), the elevated or solemn (μεγαλοπρεπής), the vehement or terrifying (δεινός) and the elegant or refined (γλαφυρός), which are illustrated in detail with numerous quotations from classical authors, among whom the most prominent are Homer, Xenophon and Demosthenes. We know nothing of Demetrius nor of the period in which his treatise was written, with scholars ranging between the Hellenistic Age (in a Peripatetic context) and the first to second century A.D. The language and style of the work, which contains numerous post-classical forms, seems to give more support to the latter theory.

4 The spread of rhetoric in the Imperial Period

From the Augustan Period onwards, rhetoric had been establishing itself as the dominant discipline both in education and in culture, while the teachers of eloquence saw their role recognised both by the authorities and by the public, which often arrived *en masse* to attend the declamations. The schools of rhetoric were the principal centres of culture and cultural debate and remained so through to the Late Antique Period. As is evident from the *Institutio oratoria* of Quintilian, interest centred on the didactic and pedagogical problem, on the ethical goal of the rhetor's intervention in society, and on his relation to power. All this was thanks to an unprecedented diffusion of rhetorical teaching into all the regions of the Roman Empire and also to a notable circulation of books and letters of literary critical content.

Rhetoric had long before definitively ceased to intervene directly in political life and see it as its principal goal, and had instead become the general, shared basis of the cultivated person's education. Rhetorical and philological studies in this period are marked by a strongly technical cast: an interest in complex problems is dominant, such as those concerning figures (σχήματα) and tropes (τρόποι). Authors such as Hermogenes reached an extraordinary level of abstraction and systematic rationalisation of the discipline (an element that found success also among the Neoplatonic philosophers). Together with its technical character, which definitively fixed the terminology and norms of the system, in rhetoric both in Greek and in Latin a tendency to erudition became established in both education and research: the preservation and imitation of models from the past are aspects that became ever more strongly rooted and wholly indispensable.

In school-teaching what dominated was a rhetorical practice that was based essentially on two tools: the preparatory exercises (προγυμνάσματα), whose fundamental elements were narration (διήγημα), comparison (σύγκρισις), and description (ἔκφρασις); and the fictitious declamations (μελέται), through which the skills acquired were demonstrated by putting into practice the results of the exercises. However, it cannot be denied that in this period, too, the majority of the output has been lost and the surviving works are often lacunose or reworked by later authors. For example, two significant rhetorical manuals have come down to us in the form of a summary: this is the case with the treatise *On Figures* by Alexander, son of Numenius, who lived around the mid-second century A.D., and the so-called *Anonymus Seguerianus*, a text of the third century on the parts of the speech, taking its name from its first modern editor (Séguier de St. Brisson, who published it in 1840).

Among the better attested works, we note the collection of *progymnasmata*, the earliest of which goes back to Aelius Theon, a rhetor from Alexandria who lived in the first century A.D. His preparatory exercises, which gave students the means to compose various types of oratorical passage, were arranged by level of difficulty. Later they were superseded by the *Progymnasmata* of Aphthonius of Antioch (fourth to fifth century), whose work was widely used in the Byzantine Period, and by that of the sophist Nicholas of Myra (fifth century).

An author who has been notably re-evaluated by recent scholarship is Menander Rhetor, from Laodicea (on the river Lycus in Asia Minor), who lived in the late third and early fourth century. He wrote commentaries, all of which are lost, on Hermogenes of Tarsus (see next section), on the *Progymnasmata* of Minucianus of

Athens (a rhetor of the second century, also author of a rhetorical *technē*: nothing of his work survives), on Demosthenes and on Aelius Aristides. Two surviving treatises are attributed to Menander, both of them concerning the composition of epideictic speeches. In the first one we read the rules for composing eulogies of gods, cities and regions, in the second those for composing speeches for public and private occasions of various kinds.

Once again the panorama that opens before us is very incomplete due to the loss of the majority of the original works. We can hardly form an idea of the liveliness and richness of the ideas about rhetoric in this period, which the indirect tradition attests for us but which have inevitably been flattened and homogenised in the repertoires compiled for schools that have survived.

5 Hermogenes of Tarsus

The fate of the rhetorical production of the Imperial Period was in part escaped by Hermogenes, whose work, for its originality and strongly rationalist foundation, appealed to the Neoplatonic philosophers and profoundly influenced later rhetors. From this rhetor, born at Tarsus in Cilicia, who lived roughly between 160 and 240, we in fact still have five treatises: *On the Staseis* (i.e. the *status*, the essential points and qualifications of a speech) and *On the Ideas*, both of which are certainly authentic; and also *Progymnasmata*, *On Invention* and *On the Method of Eloquence*, whose authorship is debated. Taken as a whole, these works constitute a sort of rhetorical *technē*, which provided a complete training course for an orator, from the preparatory exercises to the stylistic categories called "ideas" in the sense of "forms" of style.

Hermogenes' method marks a break from previous authors. He considers rhetoric to be a science, an ἐπιστήμη (*epistēmē*), of which he is undertaking the rigorous rational systematisation. Its fundamental parts, *inventio* and *elocutio*, are therefore analysed by beginning from abstract principles of universal validity. The texts, i.e. the written or oral utterances that fall under our experience and analysis, are none other than the concrete realisation of abstract categories, realisation that takes place through the combination of possible stylistic choices. These categories are called "ideas," i.e. abstract forms that constitute a sort of stylistic potentiality. There are seven of them: clarity (σαφήνεια), beauty (κάλλος), grandeur (μέγεθος), vigour (γοργότης), character (ἦθος), truth (ἀλήθεια) and the effectiveness of eloquence (δεινότης). The last of these is perfect, because it results from the combination of the others. If these are defined with maximum precision, each one can be pursued by the orator by applying in successive stages the rules of combination prescribed by the *technē*.

The novelty of Hermogenes consists in his rejection of literary criticism based on the method of critical comparison and stylistic analysis of texts of the authors, as practised for example by Dionysius of Halicarnassus or Demetrius in *On Style* (and which goes back to Aristotle's *Rhetoric*). Hermogenes instead proposes an abstract study of the stylistic forms in their essence. In his works, therefore, we do not find any type of illustration based on quotations from authors. With him a real change in outlook occurs, by which rhetorical doctrine becomes a rarefied science and arrives at total abstraction, detached from the use of concrete examples that would be provided by contact with texts. Instead he offers a set of essential norms, intended to be exhaustive and able to be applied always and everywhere, like an art of combining elements from a pre-established grid. Yet, despite the substantially theoretical approach, even in Hermogenes the idea of the "model" retains its full force: the paradigmatic author is Homer, followed by Plato and Demosthenes.

The influence of Hermogenes on later rhetoric was exceptional, if one bears in mind that his ideas were widely adopted by Aphthonius in the fourth century and cited and commented upon without interruption into the Byzantine Era. The *Suda* lexicon calls Hermogenes' work "the manual that everyone has in their hands."

III Historiography

1 Historiography in the Augustan and Imperial Periods

1.1 A Romanocentric historiography

1.1.1 The legacy of Hellenistic historiography

The central focus of much Greek historiography of the later Hellenistic Age, at varying levels of explicitness and elaboration, had been the expansion of Rome's rule and its consolidation as hegemonic power in the Mediterranean area, which was already seen as the unifying aspect on which the historical development hinged. The main themes treated by historiography in Greek, both in pro-Roman writings and in covertly or avowedly anti-Roman ones, had been varied: the political and ethical problems connected to Rome and its rule over the known world, with the changes this had brought about in civic structure throughout the world and in the conquered territories (contacts with new peoples in East and West, changes in political and economic structures, habits of thought and cultural reference-points), the legitimacy of power and of the Roman claim to command the world and how to understand and justify this imposing phenomenon (the right of the strongest or the right of the best? and in this case: who were the best, and why?). It is obvious that in the Imperial Period historians' horizons became ever more firmly and naturally Romanocentric.

Broadly speaking, in the final century of the Hellenistic Age themes treated included the moral decadence and corruption of the political class, greed for power and riches and the exploitation of the provinces by misgovernment and oppression that caused anti-Roman revolts, at times open, at times more covert. These were topics that prompted reflection on the ways in which Rome exercised its rule, but also offered valid grounds to feed anti-Roman public debate and historiography (such as the pro-Mithridates and pro-Parthian historiography), in which political motives were not absent, including in the attitudes of the more humble classes and the mass of the people (cf. *The Hellenistic Age* X 3.5). One instance of this centrifugal tendency is the voice of the Jewish historian Flavius Josephus, who lived in the first century A.D. and took part as an officer in the Jewish revolt against Roman rule that culminated in the destruction of the Temple at Jerusalem and the Jewish diaspora (A.D. 70). Through his own experience of political and military engagement, he worked out an advanced concept of the empire as being based on violence against the subjugated (who therefore had no other option but to maintain moderate positions in relation to the conqueror) and in his *Jewish War* he argued polemically against pro-Roman historiography (we will treat Flavius Josephus in the section on Judaeo-Hellenistic literature: cf. *The Roman Imperial Period* VI 1.2).

Already in the time of Augustus, as we will see shortly (but cf. also above), the anti-Roman tendencies provoked a reaction from Dionysius of Halicarnassus, author

https://doi.org/10.1515/9783110426328-032

of the *Roman Antiquities*. In his interpretation, the thesis that the Romans were originally Greek made it possible to regard the history of Rome as an integral part of the history of Greece. It was thus possible to understand the empire, which had been brought by Augustus to the highest degree of ecumenical power, as a new cultural unity centred on the values of the classical Greek world. They were guaranteed by the rule of Rome in harmony with the educated upper classes of the Greek eastern provinces, which were an organic part of its political and social structure.

1.1.2 The establishment of a universal culture

This positive, universalistic vision of the empire (conquered by force of arms but thereafter characterised by government exercised by persuasion and built upon reconciliation, peace and social stability) was founded already on the first achievements of Augustus. Shared in its essential aspects by Nicolaus of Damascus and Philo of Alexandria, for example, from then on this vision was steadily consolidated by many Greek intellectuals (there are explicit testimonies to it in the speeches *On Kingship* by Dio of Prusa and in the *Encomium to Rome* by Aelius Aristides) and would become ever more firmly established as the basis of Greek pagan historiography in the second and third centuries, which as a general rule reflects the outlooks of the upper classes, already conscious of belonging to a single imperial ruling class. This Greek historiography about Rome is of great importance also in light of the fact that Latin historiography after Tacitus (who died probably around 117) did not produce significant works, aside from imperial biographies, until Ammianus Marcellinus, a Syrian of Greek language and culture who wrote in Latin in the fourth century, connecting with the end of Tacitus' *Historiae*.

On these ideological foundations it was possible for history to be conceived and written in much the same way as politics was lived: the most important historians of the period mostly came from the eastern, culturally Greek provinces, almost always had political experience themselves and so had concrete knowledge of the current problems in the life of the empire. The predominant historiographical model hence follows the pragmatic tradition of Thucydides and Polybius, a model firmly linked to contemporary reality and to the actions that were or could be exercised upon it. This idea of historiography does not necessarily require that it recount facts contemporary to the historian. It was also possible to draw experiences from the past that were relevant to the present and to current problems, and any historiographical theme could be animated by a moral and civil sense, by a direct or indirect political commitment.

1.2 Dionysius of Halicarnassus

1.2.1 Rhetor and historian
When we sketched the profile of Dionysius of Halicarnassus as rhetor and literary scholar, we noted that in the years of the Augustan principate he was active at Rome, where he supported himself by working as a professor of rhetoric. We do not know if the historian Livy was among those who he met in Rome, but it is certain that Dionysius was able to use at least the first books of Livy's immense work, which was published gradually from 25 B.C. onwards and whose first fifteen books treated the same period as Dionysius' work.

1.2.2 The historiographical work
Dionysius' *Roman Antiquities*, Ῥωμαϊκὴ ἀρχαιολογία, probably published in 7 B.C., treated in twenty books the history of Rome from its origins to the start of the First Punic War (264 B.C.). It thus completed, from behind, the narrative of Polybius, setting out the history of Rome from the start to the point at which Polybius' work began. Books I–X survive whole, Book XI with lacunae and there are fragments and extracts from the others. Book I is devoted to the historical problem of the origins of Rome, which was quite contested during the Augustan Period and was inevitably loaded with important ideological and symbolic meanings, Books II–IV tell the history of the regal period, while the later books concern the Republican Era, down to the First Punic War.

Book I addresses the topic of the prehistory and foundation of Rome. It includes a lengthy discussion of the traditions and legends of Italian ethnography, based on the examination of very varied sources, especially annals, but also with reflections on language, topography and archaeology. This draws a picture (in which the model of Roman antiquarianism of the first century B.C. can be detected, above all that of Varro) in which the history of the individual peoples of prehistoric Italy leads to the image of Rome as having been born out of a fusion of peoples who were Greek or of Greek origin and had gradually come to the land of Italy (this migration theory, well known to Greek history and ethnography, explained the composite character of the Roman population).

Writing at a time when there was great interest in the Etruscans, Dionysius shows that he is properly informed about them. Although he is using an annalistic source that is aligned against them, he reveals sympathy for the Etruscans (as was already the case in Posidonius: cf. *The Hellenistic Age* X 3.1). Further, he rejects the widespread theory, accepted by Varro, that the Etruscans were Pelasgians and hence Greeks; similarly he rejects the theory of Herodotus that they were of Lydian origin. Instead he maintains that they were autochthonous to Italy, a view that tends to create a clear distinction between Etruscans on one side and Greek-Romans on the other.

For the periods after the origins, less space is given to this type of innovative research and it leads only to supplements, adjustments and corrections to the picture that had hitherto been offered by the historical tradition, which could no longer be overturned. Dionysius is conscious of having no real predecessors in Greek in treating Italian ethnography and the history of archaic Rome. He rejects both purely constitutional histories and simple annalistic lists of facts. Nonetheless, the Roman annals were in fact the only model to which he could refer and the only pool of information on which he could draw in a serious way. His scrupulous but generally uncritical use of the sources allows us to recover part of the Roman annalistic tradition, beginning from the second-century authors writing in Greek, whose outlooks he seems to have preserved by following their organisation.

Characteristic of his work are the comparisons made between Roman and Greek institutions, which were already found in the works of Cato and Varro but which are here expanded thanks to Dionysius' taste for institutional and religious problems: with this topic too he wants to demonstrate the Greekness of the Romans and their superiority. The basis of the work is in fact the proposal to demonstrate that the Romans were originally Greeks. By this means Dionysius was able to overcome the opposition between the Greek and the Roman world, which had provoked hostility and entrenched positions in historiography too. He thus places himself in the centripetal tendency of Greek historiography, which sought to trace back to Greece the peoples with whom Greeks came into contact. The earliest Roman historiography too, responding to specific political and diplomatic intentions, had sought to set the origins of Rome in close relation to the Greek world (Fabius Pictor, Cato, Varro). Dionysius' interpretation of Roman history is, among other things, a recognition of greatness of Rome while reconciling this with the pre-eminence of Greek civilisation.

Dionysius belongs to a strand of rhetorical historiography and has clear sympathies for dramatic historiography, with Theopompus as its model (cf. *The Classical Age* XI 2.6). At times he engages in polemic with the criticisms made against Theopompus by Polybius. Dionysius' rhetorical and literary works, which were produced at the same time as he was working on the Roman history, are, so to speak, the methodological laboratory in which he refined his study of models, worked out his stylistic and rhetorical theories and theories of compositional technique and reconsidered the means and goals of historical narrative. In particular the speeches, of which there are many in the work, echo the imitation of Thucydides, Demosthenes and Isocrates. They are generally reworkings of the speeches that Dionysius found in his sources, as can be seen from many of the questions they address, which are connected to Roman history of the second and first century B.C.

1.3 Greek historians of the Imperial Period

1.3.1 Appian of Alexandria

What we know of Appian derives from his own work and from the letters of Fronto, the Latin rhetor (ca. A.D. 100–170) who was his contemporary and whose partially extant correspondence also contains a letter from Appian to Fronto. Born at latest in A.D. 96 at Alexandria, he died around 165. At Alexandria he moved up through the stages of a brilliant political career until his skill in forensic eloquence led him to Rome, where he pleaded cases in the presence of the emperors and was made *procurator Augusti* thanks to the intercession of Fronto.

The *Roman History* was Appian's principal work. In the preface to it, the author speaks of his *Autobiography*, which is unfortunately lost and was unknown already to the Byzantine patriarch Photius, in whose *Library* we find a precious epitome of the *History*. The work consisted of twenty-four books, thirteen of which survive only as fragments or in the epitome of Photius. What is preserved is, as well as the prologue, Books VI, VII, the first part of VIII, the second part of IX, the first part of XI, XII and XIII–XVII (the civil wars). In this work, which began from the origins of Rome and went down as far as Trajan, Appian wanted to compare the valour of the Romans with that of other nations and he divides the narrative by the provinces acquired from time to time by the empire. The result of this is a sort of collection of histories, the sequence of which is dictated by the chronological succession of the first hostile contacts by the Romans with each nation, within which is set the history of the civil wars, with the narrative ordered by the protagonists. The final book aims to demonstrate the current military and economic power of the Romans. Here and there, some interesting autobiographical references are brought to light.

> In the preface, after briefly describing the borders reached by the empire and the peoples over which it ruled and a very quick overall sketch of Roman history, the author refers to the imperial polity, praising it as unequalled in extent and duration and comparing the glory of Rome with the experiences of Greek and Asian, Macedonian and Egyptian hegemony. Luck and wisdom, united into an unbeatable ardour, had allowed the Romans to achieve their current greatness.
>
> Book I tells the events of the regal period. The narrative begins with Aeneas who, after long wanderings, lands at Laurentum, marries Lavinia and founds the city of Lavinium; on the death of his father-in-law Faunus, Aeneas succeeds him in the kingdom and names his subjects Latins. Three years later he is killed by the Rutuli and is succeeded by Ascanius, who dies four years later after founding Alba and is succeeded by Silvius. The genealogy from Silvius to Numitor and Amulius leads down to the birth of Romulus and Remus to Rhea Silvia (they are thus descendants of Aeneas through their mother and of unknown family on their father's side). Next follows the period of the seven kings of Rome, with the hostilities between the Romans and Sabines. Book II, which bears the title *The Italian Book*, surveys famous episodes and figures of archaic Rome, including the war with the Volsci, Coriolanus, Publicola, Valeria, the Fabii, Appius Claudius, Camillus and Marcus Manlius. Book III, *The Samnite Book*, takes as its subject the wars fought by Rome against the Samnites, with the related conflict with Tarentum and King Pyrrhus. Book IV, *The Celtic Book*, tells of the Gauls' sack of Rome and other campaigns against Rome,

until reaching the Gallic campaigns of Caesar. Book V, *The Sicilian and Island Book*, concerns the Roman occupation of Sicily.

With Book VI, devoted to Roman ventures into Spain, Rome's horizons widen to encompass the European continent and the fateful and decisive confrontation with Carthaginian power. Book VII is on the figure of Hannibal and Book VIII on the conquest of Carthage and Numidia. The Roman ventures into Macedonia and Illyria take up Book IX, those in Greece and Asia Book X, those in Syria Book XI; Book XII discusses relations with King Mithridates.

Books XIII to XVII have as their subject the civil wars fought at Rome between the late second and first century B.C. It is our only continuous account of the era from the Gracchi to the battle of Actium. Appian's attention is on the effects provoked by the civil wars in the provinces, on the acceleration of the process of annexation of Egypt and on the slippage, connected to that, of the constitutional form towards a monarchical system.

Books XVIII–XXI are on Egypt. Book XXII includes the events of the first century of the empire. The final Books XXIII and XXIV are on Dacia and Arabia respectively, as well as showing the current military and economic power of the Romans.

Appian depends on earlier sources, but it should be recognised that he has the knowledge to draw on valid sources for the history of the provinces and to use this material shrewdly. For the parts concerning the Late Republican Age he reveals awareness of how economic, political and social forces interact. His work is also the first overall evaluation of Rome from the point of view of the provinces. The architecture of his historical account, based on the progressive annexation of the regional areas reduced to Roman provinces, recalls the model of Herodotus, whose influence, alongside that of Thucydides and Xenophon, is highlighted also in Appian's language and style.

However, his style does not imitate any particular historian, nor is it marked by an intransigent Atticism. While he avoids hiatus (which was felt to be aurally harsh) and uses a classicising phrasing, the use of participles and prepositions recalls the *koinē*. Influence from Latin is detectable in the formation of compounds, the meaning of certain terms and the syntax, as well as, obviously, in admitting transliterated Latin terms.

1.3.2 Arrian of Nicomedia

Lucius Flavius Arrianus was born at Nicomedia, capital of Bithynia, into a local aristocratic family. Since he held the consulate in A.D. 130, his date of birth must be placed between A.D. 85 and 90. His entirely Greek background led him to perceive Roman culture as something foreign, but his name implies that his family, which must have belonged to the social elite of Nicomedia, had received the Roman citizenship in the Flavian Era. From an early age he attended the lectures of Epictetus, with whom he stayed in Nicopolis for some time, developing interests of a philosophical character. He held priesthoods and civic offices and also held military positions of some importance in the Roman army in the Danube area. He visited Athens, where he was initiated into the Eleusinian mysteries; it seems that he was part of the circle of Gaius Avidius Nigrinus, Roman legate in Achaea. During the reign of Trajan he formed family ties with the future emperor Hadrian, either through their shared friendship with Epictetus or perhaps during his stay at Athens. With Hadrian's accession to the throne, the doors of the Senate were opened to him despite that fact that he was damaged by Nigrinus' fall from grace, proving that his ties to the *princeps* were already very strong. Various documentary traces have led to the theory that he held prestigious positions within the emperor's entourage. He was *consul suffectus* in A.D. 129 or 130; after the consulate he obtained the consular governorship of Cappadocia, which he held for at least six years, until 137, distinguishing himself in military ventures of some prominence. His proconsulate ended before the death of Hadrian (A.D. 138) and we know no more about his public career. He retired to Athens, where he received honorary citizenship and was eponymous *archōn* in 145/6. He perhaps lived until the reign of Marcus Aurelius, who ascended the throne in 161.

Arrian began to write in his youth and he gained a certain fame above all in philosophical studies, for having published his notes from the lectures of Epictetus as well as composing some works of his own. The teaching of Epictetus prompted the writing of two short works on philosophical topics: the compendium of ethics called the *Enchiridion* ("manual," translated into Latin by Angelo Poliziano and into Italian by Giacomo Leopardi) and the *Discourses*. The latter were in eight or twelve books (four of them survive): Arrian asserts that he has limited himself to recording the teacher's lessons, without literary elaboration, and that he decided to publish because his youthful notes had already been put into circulation in some way. Of Arrian's lost philosophical works what has survived are fragments of essays on meteorology entitled *On Celestial Things* and *On Comets*, which show that he did not limit himself to questions of ethics but also discussed problems of natural philosophy.

The figure of Arrian is for us associated above all with his historiographical work, in particular his works on Alexander the Great: the *Anabasis of Alexander* and the *Indica*. The two works contain cross-references and the author probably planned them together. In particular, the treatments of the geography of India in the two works are clearly complementary, since we find in them different material from the same sources distributed between the two works.

The main one of these works has been known since the Byzantine Era as the *Anabasis of Alexander*, a title that may not go back to the author, but could have been modelled on the *Anabasis* of Xenophon, who set the pattern also for the subdivision into seven books. The work is based essentially on the accounts of Ptolemy and Aristobulus, chosen as custodians of the genuine tradition about Alexander out of the many available sources (cf. *The Hellenistic Age* VIII 1.3). The *Anabasis* is intended as a literary monument to the achievements of the Macedonian king. Arrian declares that he is certain that his work will meet with success and will set an end to the falsehoods that are told about the great commander. It may be presumed that the work ought to be dated to the final years of the reign of Trajan, when Arrian was around thirty and was already a mature and successful writer. In fact, the work's qualities made it an admired model of historiography already in antiquity.

The historians of the Imperial Period had the habit of postponing notices about themselves until after the first chapters of their work. In chapter 12 of Book I of the *Anabasis*, Arrian states that he has no need to give his name: what is important is his work, which will be the celebration of Alexander just as Homer's work is the celebration of Achilles. He feels fully capable of such a work, worthy of the first rank in Greek letters, just as Alexander was in arms.

A sort of supplement to the *Anabasis* is offered by the *Indica* (Ἰνδικὴ ξυγγραφή), which in the manuscript tradition forms in practice the continuation (placed as an eighth book) of the *Anabasis*. It is written in Ionic dialect, in homage to the archaic tradition of historical ethnography. The first detailed description of India that we posses is that of Herodotus, but the region must have been described by Scylax of Caryanda and naturally it had a place in the Periēgēsis of Hecataeus of Miletus. Thereafter, Ctesias of Cnidus had composed a *Description of the Earth* and a monograph entitled *Indica*. From Ctesias until the expedition of Alexander, there seem to have been no new contributions to Greek knowledge of India. In the Hellenistic Age *Indica* were composed by Megasthenes, who between 302 and 297 B.C. took part in numerous embassies to the Indian king Chandragupta on behalf of the king Seleucus Nicator. In the Hellenistic Era a geographical tradition also began (Agatharchides, Eratosthenes) in which the Indian region was not absent. The Hellenistic tradition on India finally reached the writers of the Roman and Imperial Periods from Strabo to Pomponius Mela to Pliny the Elder. From the late first century A.D. is the *Periplus of the Red Sea*, which is very rich in precise indications for the traveller. The geographical data were then systematised in the *Geography* of Claudius Ptolemaeus (second century A.D.; see below IV 4).

Arrian's work treated the return voyage of Alexander's royal fleet from the mouth of the Indus to the Persian Gulf. The account is preceded by a description of India (chapters 1–17), which is a second-hand report (Arrian does not appear to have ever visited these regions) and is based on a critical use of previous sources (Ctesias, Onesicritus, Nearchus, Megasthenes, Eratosthenes). For the account of the journey (ch. 18–43) the author follows the logbook of Nearchus, as is reflected in the monotonous style and formulae, which are repetitive and so give the account a reliable tone. The choice of the Ionic dialect is linked to the ancient character of the literary genre of the *periplus* and travel account, which was traditionally Ionic, but Arrian's language is a mannered Ionic that seems not to have any correspondence with linguistic reality nor to follow precise or rigid norms.

Recorded among Arrian's lost works are two biographies (*Timoleon* and *Dion*), a *History of the Diadochi* in ten books and two ethnographic works entitled *Bithyniaca* and *Parthica*. As well as the works connected with the figure of Alexander the Great, also preserved are a *Periplus of the Black Sea*, the work *The Order of Battle Against the Alans* and an *Essay on Tactics*. Dated to 136/7, the latter work expounds some principles of Greek and Macedonian tactics and provides a vivid description of the training methods of the Roman auxiliary cavalry. The author praises the alacrity with which the Romans assimilated the tactics of others and the innovations introduced by Hadrian after the conflicts with the Armenians and Parthians. The work ends with a panegyric of Hadrian (ch. 44).

We have already mentioned the use of the Ionic dialect in the *History of India*. More generally, the most characteristic trait of Arrian's style is his conscious and proud imitation of Xenophon, whose very name Arrian liked to bestow on himself: the later tradition records that he was known as the "new Xenophon." Proof of his favoured connection with this Athenian historian emerges from the works themselves: Xenophon's account of the journey of the Ten Thousand is a constant source of inspiration for the narration of the exploits of Alexander. Further, imitation of Xenophon is clear and explicit in the *Periplus of the Black Sea* and in the *Cynegeticus*, while Xenophon's *Agesilaus* may have inspired the lost biographies of Timoleon and Dion.

1.3.3 Cassius Dio

The large amount of information that we possess about Cassius Dio's life comes from his own historical work (Books 71–80). He too (like Arrian) was born in Bithynia, at Nicaea, around A.D. 155 (or in 163/4), into an affluent family of high social class. His father Cassius Apronianus was a senator and governor of Cilicia and of Dalmatia. Any family relation with the great rhetor Dio of Prusa, which some have attributed to him, is very uncertain, however. He must have gained the favour of Hadrian and the other emperors of the second century, in a period of economic and cultural prosperity, in which the Greek and eastern world aroused great interest. We know nothing of Cassius Dio's education, except that he must have also pursued the study of law, since he states that he had worked as an advocate under Pertinax. He made a long series of journeys and in 180, the year of Marcus Aurelius' death, he was at Rome. It is not certain whether he was already a senator by that year or if his career began only in the reign of Commodus, who held power from 180.

With the era of Commodus things changed suddenly for the worse, but Cassius Dio managed to maintain his position as senator. Pertinax honoured him in various ways and made him *praetor*. He made it through the very brief reign of Didius Julianus unscathed (28 March–2 June, A.D. 193), although he had some fear of him since he had attacked him in court cases. Under Septimius Severus (193–211) the initial hopes for an improvement in the political climate were followed by disappointment, when the emperor's autocratic tendencies and character became clear. It appears that at that time he had been sidelined and his career had suffered a kind of "freeze" between 195/6 and 217, but some scholars place Cassius Dio's first consulate in the reign of Septimius Severus itself. The misdeeds of Caracalla, too, were given an appropriate treatment in the *History* of Cassius Dio, whose relations with this emperor were largely cool.

In 217 he was at Rome, where he heard the proclamation of Macrinus' elevation to the throne. He passed a judgement on this emperor that was not entirely negative and received from him the position of *curator* of Pergamum and of Smyrna, where he spent the winter of 218–219 and from where he returned to his native city of Nicaea to recover from a sudden illness. He then held office in Africa (223) as legate or proconsul. He was linked by both friendship and collaboration with the mild and cultivated emperor Severus Alexander (222–235). On returning from Africa he was sent as *legatus Augusti pro praetore* to Dalmatia (224–225) and to Pannonia Superior (226–228), where he lost the sympathy of the troops due to the rigid discipline he imposed on them. In 229 he had the privilege of holding the consulate alongside the emperor. After this he left Rome and retired definitively to Nicaea, the city of his birth, where he dedicated himself to the composition of his historical work. He died around 230.

Dio's weighty *Roman History* consisted of eighty books and covers the chronological span from the landing of Aeneas in Italy to A.D. 229. Surviving out of these, though with some lacunae, are Books XXXVI–LX, on the events from 68 B.C. to A.D. 47, and fragments of other books. Additionally, the contents of the work are known through some compendia of the Byzantine Period. A compendium of Books XXXVI–LXXX was made in the eleventh century by the Byzantine historian Johannes Xiphilinus. Based in part on this compendium by Xiphilinus is another compendium by Johannes Zonaras (twelfth century), concerning Books I–XXI (events down to 146 B.C.) and XLIV–LXXX, which Zonaras inserted into his *Universal History*. Finally, substantial passages of the work have been preserved in the *Excerpta Constantiniana*, compiled in the tenth century by order of the Byzantine emperor Constantine VII Porphyrogenitus.

> The chronological criterion adopted by Dio is annalistic in type, based as far as possible on the succession of the consuls, even in the Imperial Period. The narrative is subdivided into decades like those of the Roman historian Livy. Books I–II told of the settlement of the Trojans in Latium and the regal period of Roman history. With Book III the history of the Republican Period began. The second decade started with the First Punic War (Book XI) and the following decade with the Third Punic War (Book XXI). The wars fought by Rome against Mithiridates were the subject of Book XXXI. In Book XLI the account of the civil war between Caesar and Pompey begins. The remaining part of the work (Books LI–LXXX) was dedicated to the history of the empire, the start of which is placed in the year 31 B.C. (battle of Actium). Book LII contains a famous debate between Octavian, Agrippa and Maecenas on the appropriateness of Octavian leaving power and allowing a return to the Republic. Books LIII–LVI treat the principate of Augustus, while the following ones, down to Book LXXX, covered the period between Tiberius and the Severans.

Cassius Dio states that he had composed a collection of prodigies that foretold the coming of the emperor Severus Alexander. Further, he says (LXXII 23, 2) that he had decided to write about historical matters because he had been urged to do so by a divinity in a dream. His narrative of the first years of the reign of Severus Alexander earned the favour of the latter and the public to such a degree that he decided to begin a work that would tell the entire history of Rome. We are informed that he spent ten years collecting the material and twelve years composing the work. The part subsequent to the death of Septimius Severus, which was contained in the final books, was a further expansion of the original plan.

Dio made large use of Roman historiographical sources, drawing from a wide variety of authors. Since many of the sources that he used are now lost, even the compilatory parts of his work are of great interest for us. For example, in compiling the first books he used the Roman annalists of the second generation (Valerius Antias, Claudius Quadrigarius) and it is likely that he had also read Livy and Dionysius of Halicarnassus. For the Punic Wars his sources were Polybius, used with a certain freedom, and Livy, especially for Rome's internal politics. For the Gallic Wars the main source was Caesar's account, while for the wars between Caesar and Pompey he made use especially of Livy. For the empire from Augustus to Marcus Aurelius a number of sources have been identified, perhaps including Tacitus, who in general was read rarely or not at all in antiquity.

Dio's use of sources was not mechanical, but rather aimed to pursue an artistic, political and moral objective. Further, while for the period prior to Marcus Aurelius the documentation was based on a large number of historiographical works, for the following period Dio's personal political experience plays a fundamental role, as does the opportunity for direct consultation of official documents of various kinds. He employs great scrupulousness in establishing the truth, and the essential honesty of his account is certainly one of the merits of Cassius Dio's work. On the other hand, in one passage (LXXII 18) he explicitly states that he does not want to dwell on the details in the narrative, since they would not be consonant with the solemn dignity of history.

The historian's political thought finds expression at various points of the work, particularly in the many speeches, of varying length, that offer a field for the author's rhetorical display. What emerges from them is a lively and acute sense of the state, from which arises the pre-eminence of the common interest above that of the individual. On the level of institutional structures, Cassius Dio's preference is for monarchical government, though it should be accompanied by collaboration with a Senate composed of the best citizens, including those from the provinces. Fundamental importance is assigned to the observance of discipline by all members of the civic and political body.

Cassius Dio's commitment to Atticism is not enough to raise him to the heights of stylistic excellence: in the passages in which he imitates Thucydides, he remains rather below his model. A variety of styles is the dominant impression, probably due also to changing between sources. The narrative parts are monotonous (in some cases weighed down by obscure explanations of laws or Roman customs or by intricate political situations), but this is countered by the elaborate rhetorical means deployed in the speeches.

1.3.4 Herodian

Now that we no longer accept his identification with Tiberius Claudius Herodianus, the *legatus proconsulis* in Sicily, our information about the historian Herodian is reduced to the meagre notices that he provides about himself in his historical work. His place and date of birth are unknown. He was certainly not of Italian origin (some hints in his work lead us to suppose an Anatolian origin), and he was perhaps born around 180. From his own words we learn that he lived at Rome for some time; that he was a public official, though probably without reaching the higher ranks; and that the chronological span of his life coincides roughly with that of the period which he narrated, from the late second to the first half of the third century A.D.

The *History of the Empire after Marcus* (Τῆς μετὰ Μάρκου βασιλείας ἱστορίας βιβλία ὀκτώ) relates in eight books the events from the death of Marcus Aurelius (in A.D. 180) to the accession of Gordian III (in 238). The severe judgements passed on the latter emperor tend to rule out a publication of the work during his reign, making a date towards the mid-third century more likely, in the author's old age.

The historical narrative begins with an account of the death of Marcus Aurelius, who is praised for the liberality of his empire and mourned by all. Herodian declares at once that he will use the figure of this emperor as the standard by which to evaluate his successors. Among these, the most praised is Pertinax: the rule of the liberal emperors (Pertinax, Macrinus, Severus Alexander) is equated to that of the aristocracy, while those who sought the agreement and support of the Praetorians (Commodus, Didius Julianus) or the legionaries (Caracalla, Maximinus Thrax) are said to be cruel tyrants. As well as this attempt to classify the emperors, the historical account is subordinated to specific political ideas that guide the narrative: what emerges is a fairly negative assessment and scorn for the military, which would not tolerate wise administration of power, and a sympathy for the well-to-do classes and the Senate. The opinions of these classes are often identified with those of the entire people. Despite the fact that this ideological position heavily shapes the account, Herodian does still attempt to be objective.

Unlike other historians of the Imperial Period, in the case of Herodian the problem of his sources is relatively minor, since he is addressing contemporary topics so his use of written sources must have been intermittent and occasional. However, there must have been some relation between his work and the contemporary historical work of Dio, who was a little older than Herodian.

Herodian's style has prompted strongly negative judgements from modern scholars, since it combines the worst arsenal of rhetoric with language that is poor, sloppy and pedantic and drenched in repetitions, unnecessary and pleonastic explanations and mechanically applied commonplaces. The work is also suspected of having falsified the narrative for the purpose of rhetorical embellishment, though it is likely that this is true only of details. Nonetheless beneath this blanket of carelessness Herodian conceals hints of the classical historiographical tradition that he seeks to imitate, as is demonstrated emblematically by the opening pages of his work, with their clear echoes of Thucydides.

1.3.5 Dexippus

The Athenian Publius Herennius Dexippus, who lived in the third century A.D., belonged to the prestigious family of the Kerykes, of the deme of Hermos. He held various public offices (among other things, he was eponymous *archōn*) and in 267 he repelled an invasion of Herulians. As his work the Byzantine patriarch Photius recorded: a *Chronicle* in twelve books, which covered the historical period from the origins to 269/70 and which was continued by Eunapius of Sardis (see below); a *history of the Diadochi* in four books, which was a shorter version of Arrian's history; and a work entitled *Scythica* (Σκυθικά), which recounted the war against the Germanic invaders. The preserved fragments reveal the marked influence of Thucydides.

1.3.6 Military treatises: Polyaenus

Although it is fairly far removed from the systematic approach and specialist expertise exhibited by the Πολιορκητικά (*Poliorkētika*) of Aeneas Tacticus (fourth century B.C.: cf. *The Classical Age* XI 2.8), the Στρατηγήματα (*Stratēgēmata*) of Polyaenus belong to the genre of military treatise.

We know that the author was from Macedonia, lived in the second century during the reigns of the Antonines and in 162 dedicated his work to Marcus Aurelius and Lucius Verus, on the eve of the Roman campaign against the Parthians. The *Stratēgēmata* in fact aimed to be the cultivated literary rhetor's contribution to the military operation: in eight books he collects the descriptions of 900 military expedients and episodes of warfare, compiled with antiquarian and book-based expertise from authors and historians of different periods, from Herodotus to Plutarch. While in the first three books the anecdotes are arranged chronologically, the other five adopt a thematic arrangement by category.

2 Historiography in the Late Antique Period

2.1 Historiography and Christianity

With the establishment of Christianity as official religion of the empire, endorsed by the Edict of Constantine in 313, the whole of Roman society and the balance of power itself encountered striking changes of enormous consequence. The state set up the Church as its interlocutor, beginning the history of a complex and delicate balance that would mark the fortunes of Europe for many centuries: during the fourth century, the Church took on a role of great importance in imperial politics, with the aim of using ecclesiastical organisation to restore the unity and preserve the empire's dominions.

In the section on ancient Christian literature (*The Roman Imperial Period* XIII) we will see that the fourth century was also an era in which a powerful and productive rivalry flourished between pagan culture, sustained by the rich and noble traditions of the past, and the nascent Christian literary culture, with its task of constructing its own "classics" and comparing them to the output of paganism. In this context of Christian attempts to produce a greater cultural breadth, a new and distinctive current was born within the genre of historiography, namely ecclesiastical history. In the following centuries, other historians, faced with the general consolidation of Christian culture, took different paths. This is the case with Zosimus, the pagan historian of the fall of the Western Empire under the assault of the barbarian invasions, and of Procopius of Caesarea, whose interest was in sketching the figure and exploits of the emperor Justinian.

2.2 Eusebius of Caesarea and ecclesiastical historiography

The initiator of ecclesiastical historiography is generally seen to be Eusebius of Caesarea, who was the first to feel it necessary to give the Church its own historical narrative, as a clear sign of its new identity and a vehicle for the Christian point of view in the interpretation of human history.

Born in Palestine around 260, Eusebius escaped the last terrible anti-Christian persecution, unleashed by Diocletian. Around 314 he became bishop of Caesarea and was a moderate supporter of the heretic Arius, but at the Council of Nicaea he was exonerated from the charge of heresy and subscribed to the orthodox creed. After the death of Constantine he wrote an encomiastic biography of the emperor (though its authenticity has been contested). Among other things, he composed a *Chronicle*, which has survived only in epitomised versions which are based in their turn on an edition of Eusebius' work that had been supplemented and reworked by others. Nonetheless, it is a very important source, given the quantity of historical and chronological data that it preserves. He died around 339/40.

Eusebius was the author of both apologetic and exegetical texts (cf. *The Roman Imperial Period* XIII 2.3), but his most innovative and original work is certainly the *Ecclesiastical History*, in ten books in its definitive version, which tells the story of the Church from its origins to A.D. 324 (the defeat of Licinius and reunification of the empire under Constantine). With its lists of bishops and collections of documents, quotations and disparate notices, it is certainly not a work for pleasant reading nor even an organic historical treatment: more than anything else it is a rich collection of material, even in its disorder. However, its importance for us is notable, since it offers a real goldmine of notices and testimonia about people, events, liturgical practices and heretical movements. The model of classical historiography is here fundamentally modified by the fact that what is placed at the centre is not the fortunes of the emperors, but rather those of the Church and the Roman state of which it was part. This point of view has been seen as a new expression of the tradition of Greek historiography that had proceeded according to the series of hegemonic powers, in a universalist external framework in the manner of Diodorus. At times the narrative splinters into individual biographical narratives, which owe a lot to the philosophical and scholarly biographies of the Hellenistic Age.

After this, other authors such as Philostorgius, Socrates, Sozomen, Theodoret of Cyrrhus (fourth to fifth century) and Evagrius Scholasticus (sixth century) devoted themselves to the history of the Church, understanding their histories as a reworking and continuation of Eusebius. In particular, the *Ecclesiastical History* of Theodoret (ca. 393–466; cf. *The Roman Imperial Period* XIII 2.6.3) aimed to complete that of Eusebius, using the earlier works by Socrates and Sozomen. Theodoret's history treated the period between 323 and 428, primarily taking an interest in the Arian controversy, about which it records very important testimonia from the Antiochene party and a rich documentation.

2.3 Zosimus

Aside from some meagre notices transmitted by the Byzantine patriarch Photius (*Library* 98, 84b 4 ff.), the little that we know of Zosimus is what he tells us himself. Since we have no other information on his country of origin or the precise period in which he lived, we have to draw on his work itself to deduce that he lived in the latter part of the fifth and early sixth century. In particular, the fact that he describes the Roman Empire as depopulated, destroyed and occupied by barbarians, suggests that we should place his historical work after the end of the fifth century, that is, after the advance of the peoples who brought about the end of the Western Empire. The only manuscript to transmit the work informs us that he was a count (*comes*) and had been an advocate of the imperial treasury (*advocatus fisci*). We can further deduce that he was a convinced pagan and hated Christianity, that he possessed a certain literary culture and spent at least part of his life at Constantinople, revealing quite an accurate knowledge of its topography. It is possible that he was a pupil of the rhetor-philosopher Procopius of Gaza, as is revealed by influences from Neoplatonic doctrine present in his work.

In the manuscript that transmits it, the historical work is preceded by the title Ἱστορία νέα, which should be understood in the sense of *History of the Contemporary Age*. The work is unfinished and the final sections reveal clear signs of a rushed and unrevised publication. From a notice by Photius and from the epitome that entered the *Excerpta* of Constantine Porphyrogenitus we can infer that it was originally six books in length. The strongly anti-Christian outlook of the work must have resulted in a publication that was to some degree clandestine and restricted to a small and limited circle, the dispersal of which must also have been responsible for the oblite-ration of notices about the author.

After a brief preamble, the narrative begins with the reign of Augustus, gradually becoming more detailed through the Imperial Period as it comes nearer to the au-thor's own times. The rather abrupt conclusion concerns the events of the summer of 410, a little before the sack of Rome by Alaric's Visigoths. Depending on which source he from time to time uses, the length and detail of Zosimus' account vary sharply. This aspect, together with failings in the style and elaboration of the narrative, espe-cially in the final book, are clear marks of a rushed, non-definitive publication.

> Book I opens with a preamble (ch. 1–5) containing some reflections by the author and a quick survey of Greek history, with just a mention of the Roman Republican Period and strong criticism of the monarchical regime established by Augustus. With chapter 6 the history of the Imperial Period begins, which except in a few cases is reduced to little more than a dry enumeration of emperors. The narrative becomes much more detailed for the history of the events of the second half of the third century, probably corresponding to a change of source. The end of Book I and the start of Book II are lost, due to a lacuna in the manuscript of the work. Book II sets out the final events of the pagan empire: the abdication of Diocletian and Maximian means the depar-ture of the last two emperors committed to paganism and the end of the era in which the ancient religion was respected and practised. Constantine and Licinius established the celebrations of Christianity, provoking, in Zosimus' view, the decadence of the empire, which had not upheld its vows to the gods. Then follows the history of Constantine and his sons. Book III is largely dedicated to Julian, the emperor who achieved the pagan restoration and who was hence espe-cially dear to Zosimus, while in Book IV, which covers the period A.D. 364–395, what is especially interesting is the negative portrait of the emperor Theodosius. Zosimus is the only historian to provide a continuous account of these events from a pagan point of view. Book V covers only fifteen years, separately addressing the narrative of events concerning the eastern part of the empire and those concerning the western part. Book VI, finally, which is very short and full of confusions and contradictions, concerns the events in the West between the end of 409 and the summer of 410, but without narrating the capture of Rome in 410.

Identifying the sources used by Zosimus is a particularly complex task, but at least one secure point can be fixed thanks to the testimony of Photius: according to the Byzantinte patriarch, Zosimus based his work primarily on the historical account of Eunapius, which covered the period from 270 to 404 (cf. *The Roman Imperial Period* III 2.5 and XI 6). Other identified sources include Olympiodorus of Thebes (cf. *The Roman Imperial Period* III 2.5). Another finding of researchers is that Zosimus was not at all independent in relation to his sources: he does not seem capable of combining different sources and seeks out a different source only when the first one comes to an end. On the other hand, his history should be considered independent of the available historiographical models and a work of originality in its overall design and in his re-cording of the recent decline of the empire.

Zosimus indicates Polybius as his model, both in basic outlook and in form, and he aspires to play the same role as Polybius in recounting the decadence of the em-pire. In one passage (I 57, 1) he explicitly states: "while Polybius set out how the

Romans founded their empire in a brief period of time, I am about to narrate how they swiftly destroyed it through their foolish presumption." In Zosimus' historiographical interpretation, the factors determining the fall of the empire include the establishment of Christianity, carried out by Constantine, and the collapse of the ancient religious traditions. In the generalised diffusion of Christian ideology, the voice of Zosimus remains almost isolated and offers us the possibility of comparing the pagan point of view on emblematic figures such as Constantine and Theodosius with the Christian view attested by Ammianus Marcellinus and Eusebius of Caesarea.

Photius praises the concision, sobriety, purity and pleasing character of Zosimus' language, contrasting it to the ornate style of Eunapius, one of his sources. The work in fact lacks rhetorical ornament (we may note, among other things, the absence of direct speeches), but often he also slips into monotony and tedium. On the other hand, there is no lack of evidence of the author's literary culture. Some lexical choices and expressions seem to allude to Herodotus, Thucydides, Euripides, Xenophon and Demosthenes.

2.4 Procopius of Caesarea

While Eusebius is the initiator of ecclesiastical historiography and the historian of Constantine, and Zosimus is the pagan historian of the fall of the Western Empire under the assault of the barbarian invasions, the figure of Procopius of Caesarea combines a return to pragmatic historiography in the tradition of Thucydides and Polybius, focused on political and military events, with an interest in the person and exploits of the emperor Justinian. This latter aspect makes his work especially important, since he is not only our main source, but often our only one, for the long period of the reign of Justinian.

2.4.1 Biographical notices

Procopius was born between A.D. 490 and 507 at Caesarea in Palestine, a cosmopolitan city with rich cultural traditions, from a family that probably belonged to the wealthy Christian upper classes. In 527 he became adviser to the general Belisarius, who at that time was *dux* in Mesopotamia, and Procopius was present as an eye-witness at the majority of the events of which he was later the historian. He was with the Roman troops in the East until 531, then returned with Belisarius to Constantinople. He left with him in 533 on the campaign against the Vandals in Africa, in which he entered Carthage with the victorious Byzantine troops. He was at Carthage in 536 during the great revolt, then joined Belisarius in Italy and undertook various duties in his service. In 540 he entered Ravenna with the Byzantine troops, after which he probably left Italy and returned to Constantinople (he may have been recalled after the emperor's change in attitude towards Belisarius). In 542 he was at Constantinople, where the plague was raging. As far as we can tell, he did not return to Italy with Belisarius in 544, but the detail of his narrative of events in 546/7 suggests that in that period he was indeed in Italy. After this date, we know nothing certain about his movements.

2.4.2 The works

Three works by Procopius are preserved. The major work is the historical one, *The History of the Wars*, which narrates the wars fought by the generals of Justinian for the defence and expansion of the imperial territories, with a marked focus on achieving the project of reunifying the Roman Empire by reconquering the West. The other works are *De aedificiis (Buildings)* and the *Secret History* or *Anecdota* (Ἀνέκδοτα), the topic of which is the events behind the scenes in the life of the court, which the author pitilessly bared.

The composition of the *The History of the Wars* must for the most part have fallen in the 540s and must have depended on notes and diaries kept in the preceding period. The *Wars* are therefore a history linked to the first part of the reign of Justinian, the history of an era of successes. The eclipse of Belisarius after his recall in 548 had a major effect on Procopius' attitude: in the final part of the work the general's role is viewed with ever greater disenchantment. This atmosphere of disillusion that pervades the final part also allows us to adopt a date of roughly 550 for the *Secret History*, in which the author states that he wanted to give the true explanation of the *Wars*, collecting there all the things that he was unable to say in the public work. The work was supposed to remain secret and its publication would certainly have been quite dangerous.

The Wars. This, the most strictly historical work, in eight books, tells the course of the Bellum Persicum (Books I–II, A.D. 530–532 and 540–549), the *Bellum Vandalicum* (Books III–IV, African campaign until 535) and the *Bellum Gothicum* (Books V–VII, Italian campaign A.D. 535–550). A second proem at the start of Book VIII attests the later composition of this final part of the work, which provides an update of the events that took place in all three zones addressed by the preceding books (the East, Africa and Italy) and continues to the defeat of the Goths in 553. The sources of the historical narration are essentially Procopius' own direct experience and oral reports, which would be easily acquired when treating contemporary facts. Written sources come into play only when the work departs from the main narrative into historical and ethnographical digressions.

> *Bellum Persicum.* This narrates the war against the Persians. The theatre of operations is well known to Procopius from his youth and through his direct experience of it with Belisarius. The narrative is preceded by a summary of Persian history from the early fifth century. Book I proceeds from the battles of Dara and Callinicum to the Nika revolt, which broke out at Constantinople in 532, and which Belisarius helped to suppress, entering the hippodrome with troops loyal to the emperor and massacring the rebels there, and on to Belisarius' posting to Africa (535). Belisarius was not yet the famous hero, the greatest Byzantine general, but in this period he

already enjoyed Procopius' support and admiration. Book II, which treats the events connected to Belisarius' second mission to the East, is largely devoted to the incursions of Khosrow in Mesopotamia and Syria. Attention then returns to Constantinople on the occasion of the plague of 542.

Bellum Vandalicum. This treats a campaign that, according to Procopius, had been chosen by Justinian against the general opinion. The venture was at first marked by Belisarius' greatest and most brilliant victories, culminating in the triumph celebrated at Constantinople in 534 and the consulate in the following year, as is emphatically underlined by the historian, but thereafter it was necessary to confront the hard struggle against the Berbers, the mutiny of the Byzantine army and a whole series of events that were negative to some degree, which was ended by the definitive defeat of the Berbers. In the pages of the *Bellum Gothicum* Procopius would present harsh criticisms of the conduct of the African campaign: he makes a series of reproaches against Justinian, including of not having made any effort to ensure the loyalty of the new subjects.

Bellum Gothicum. Here Belisarius, still consul, conquers Sicily and enters Syracuse as triumphator. He besieges Naples and enters Rome as victor. The city is then besieged for a year (537/8) by the Goths, but in the end they are forced to retreat. Procopius was again with Belisarius in 539, when the Franks entered Italy and moved against the Byzantines, and in 540, at the siege of Ravenna (on that occasion some Goths offered Belisarius the throne, but he refused and entered Ravenna in the name of Justinian). Procopius then returned to Constantinople together with the general when the latter was recalled. Procopius probably did not return to Italy again. From the vivid narrative of Belisarius' first Italian campaign the text passes to the much more subdued and disappointed account of the second campaign, when the great Belisarius did not achieve any results. The account becomes ever more openly critical of the general, reaching a highpoint of dissent in Book VII. With Book VIII, written in 554, Procopius' crisis of disillusionment has passed through its worst moments, but he is very far from the optimism that buoyed the start of the work.

Overall, *The History of the Wars* maintains an attitude towards Justinian that is cool and distant, as becomes ever more accentuated as the work proceeds. Its hero, at least in the initial part, is Belisarius. In relation to the general, too, a progressive disillusionment is clearly perceptible, reaching its highpoint around 550, the time of the publication of Books I–VII and the composition of the *Secret History*. At times Procopius passes a favourable judgement on barbarian leaders such as Theodoric, whom he eulogises near the start of Book I, or Teia, whose heroic death at the battle of Mons Lactarius in 553 he recounts with great sympathy. This favourable judgement of the Goths is the counterpoint to an ever more critical attitude towards Justinian, whom he reproaches for his negligence in the conduct of the final part of the war in Italy.

The Secret History. The *Anecdota*, rediscovered only in the seventeenth century, form an alternative history of the same period recounted in *The History of the Wars*. The author's aim is to declare the true causes of several events about which he had been obliged to be cautious in his historical work (though only the first section of the *Secret History* matches this intention, whereas the rest is a critique of Justinian's imperial policies). For this reason, Procopius has been accused of having adopted an insincere or else naïve attitude at the time of composition of *The History of the Wars*.

It has even been doubted whether the work is authentic, due to the apparently irreconcilable contrast to the rest of Procopius' work. From internal elements it seems that the work was probably written around 550, when Procopius' disappointment in Belisarius and in Justinian's policy were at their highpoint. It is not a private text, in the sense that it has been constructed in a literary way and is introduced by an elaborate preface modelled on those of Diodorus and Polybius, but it was in all probability intended as a clandestine publication.

> The initial chapters (1–5) are about Belisarius and his wife Antonina. There follows an account of the origins and youth of Justinian and his wife Theodora (6–10) and the description of the emperor's greed and misgovernment (11–14); chapters 15–17 centre on the figure of Theodora, her crimes and depravities, while the final part (18–30) presents Justinian as the murderer and oppressor of his subjects. In the portrait of the protagonists Procopius paints a black picture and is inspired by obvious hostility and malice. Antonina, wife of Belisarius, is said to be the descendant of charioteers, dissolute, mother of many children before she married the general, unfaithful even after marriage and the friend and accomplice of the empress Theodora in her misdeeds. Belisarius is presented as dominated by his wife, fearful and cowardly, to the point that his tactical choices are determined by jealousy; he is very rich but also very greedy. The empress Theodora had from her youth abandoned herself to base and unnatural sexual practices, on which Procopius dwells with crude realism, and revealed a similar shamelessness in her performances as a circus actress, by which she seduced Justinian. The quite widespread image of a Theodora who was an exemplary model of femininity is overturned by Procopius, who attributes to her the most grim intentions and most dissolute vices. All aspects of Justinian's politics are attacked pitilessly: the rulers throw the life of the state into confusion, do not shy from lies and crimes in order to appropriate others' possessions, invariably choose the most corrupt administrators and intervene heavy-handedly in religious questions, often as a pretext to get their hands on the possessions of anyone forced to abjure. The sleepless industriousness of Justinian (which in *De Aedificiis* is a proof of his *pietas*) is here a sign of demonic force aiming to do wrong without interruption or else to control his subjects. The representation of the emperor as demoniac or even as the prince of demons is intended to underline the exceptional character of his wicked excesses, which exceed the very bounds of human nature.

The De aedificiis. The work entitled *De aedificiis*, in six books, was composed after the war against the Goths and before May 558, the time of the first collapse of the cupola of Hagia Sophia, which Procopius does not mention. The principal theme of the work is the development of monumental building promoted by Justinian's policy of constructing churches, fortifications and aqueducts. However, the list of buildings is far from complete and the selection of material at times seems arbitrary. Through the description of the grandiose building works achieved by the emperor, who is given an obsequious and openly eulogising treatment, Procopius constructs a genuine panegyric of the ruler.

> The material is divided among the six books according to a geographical principle: in Book I the subject of discussion is Constantinople, in Book II Asia, in Book III Armenia, in Book IV the Balkan peninsula, in Book V the rest of Asia, in Book VI Africa. Guided by some hints (including the absence of any mention of Italy and the lack of accuracy of some parts) it has been held that the

work is incomplete, or at least had not been revised. Another proof of its unfinished character may be the lack of uniformity in the stylistic level, though the author claims in the preface to be fully committed to an elevated style. It is likely that he had access to official documentation, but much of what he writes has an anecdotal character and presents a mixture of credible notices with others that appear unreliable.

2.4.3 Aspects of Procopius' historiography

The quality of Procopius' narration is quite variable. Without doubt he was able to boast of his direct knowledge of a large number of sites and facts that he discusses in his works, though often, also in cases of this type, one finds distortions of the reality for political or personal motives. It is rare for him to declare the source of his information. Hence all his works need to be evaluated critically, also in cases where the information he provides seems to derive from official sources or accounts that his position would have made easily accessible to him.

Scattered through *The History of Wars* there are long geographical digressions. We encounter a series of historical and ethnographic excursus on the origins or history of certain peoples, for example on the Vandals and the Franks. The aim of these digressions is to introduce the narration of historical events in a way that is appropriate for literature. This obvious purpose influences both the manner in which the excursus are organised and also the notices themselves that they contain, requiring a certain caution in using them. The direct speeches, too, although they sometimes genuinely shed light on the dynamics of the events or help to characterise a person, in general appear to be purely rhetorical compositions that indulge in a heavy-handed moralism and so demand to be read with sharp critical awareness.

The History of Wars is a traditional military history, in which the events are organised according to an annalistic rhythm of Thucydidean type, by winters and summers. Matching this model is the fact that the work is based essentially on autopsy and on contemporary facts. The narration of military events leaves little room for internal politics or life at Constantinople, an aspect that we find also in the continuation of Procopius' work by the Byzantine historian Agathias. The subdivision of the narrative on the basis of theatres of operation forces Procopius to refer several times to the same fact and does not promote clarity about chronological connections between different events.

The account of the plague at Constantinople is clearly inspired by imitation of the famous account by Thucydides of the plague at Athens, but there are also strong differences between the two narratives. Procopius uses the Thucydidean distinction between *prophasis* (πρόφασις, *the true reason*) and aitia (αἰτία, *the accidental causes*) but does not highlight any plausible human cause and does not trust scientific analyses, in line with the Christian polemic against scientific and pseudo-scientific thought. Consequently, all that remains is for him to explain the plague as an effect of divine will, obscure to mortals. In the episode of the Nika revolt, too, which is present in all three of Procopius' works, he does not give any real analysis of the causes, essentially escaping into a generic profession of faith in the mystery of divine providence. Despite the fact that religion was a fundamental element of the political life of the time, the traditional conventions of the genre of historiography often hinder the author from considering together the theme of politics and the theme of religion.

The relationship between Procopius and Justinian and his judgement on the emperor's expansionist policy appear in *The History of Wars* to be filtered through the historian's close personal relations with the general Belisarius. Procopius' critical attitude and discontent, which emerge over the years, are always directed against very precise persons and actions and do not even minimally touch on the substance of the imperial system or the project of reunification and reconquest. In the *De aedificiis* Justinian is the object of a panegyrical treatment insofar as he is considered as the incarnation of the imperial dignity. On the other hand, sometimes the criticisms made by Procopius against imperial decisions demonstrate the modesty of his gifts in historical and political analysis, through his inability to grasp connections and relations between different phenomena and decisions. For example, the eulogy of Justinian's military policy is accompanied by violent criticism of fiscal policy, which is an indispensable condition for the former.

The element of greatest disharmony in Procopius' ideological panorama is without doubt the *Secret History*, with its harsh hostility and invective tones against Belisarius and the emperor, extended also to their spouses, which seem incompatible with the favourable attitude and respectful criticism expressed in the other works. However, it should not be denied that the form and content of Procopius' three works must have been influenced to a not insignificant degree also by the different literary genres from which they took their cue: historiography in *The History of Wars*, panegyric in *De aedificiis*, invective in the *Anecdota*. Bearing this factor in mind, it can be said that, beyond the major differences that separate them, the three works can still be traced to the same cultural background. They have in common also certain peculiarities of language and of periodic rhythm, which comes to constitute a unifying stylistic element, which is perhaps a more significant criterion than the objective differences.

To attempt an assessment of Procopius' historiographical work: we may say that, despite its limitations, it has a validity of its own and exhibits great vitality. The vagueness of the military terminology, the lack of precision in geographical questions, the tendency to anecdote, the disposition towards tendentiousness and the exclusion from the account of certain aspects, such as religion, that had great weight in the history of the sixth century – all these are some of the undeniable failings of which the author can be accused. Nonetheless, they should not lead us to deny that *The History of Wars* constitute a work of great breadth and grandiose conception, which aspires to provide a history of the wars of Justinian in the style of Thucydides. The greatness of the events seemed worthy of the undertaking and Procopius, thanks to his social position and circumstances, was the best qualified author to treat them.

2.5 Other historians of the Late Antique Period

Here we will collect together and briefly treat some other figures who belong to the rich panorama of Late Antique historiography.

The Athenian Praxagoras lived in the Age of Constantine, and devoted a historical monograph to the emperor. Photius has preserved a summary of his work.

Eunapius of Sardis lived between 345 and 420, was educated in part in his home city and in part at Athens, but then returned and settled in Sardis as a teacher of rhetoric. An exponent of the Neoplatonic current of philosophy and known for the composition of the *Lives of the Philosophers and Sophists* (cf. *The Roman Imperial Period* XI 6), he is recorded as a historian for his work of universal history in fourteen books, the *Hypomnēmata historica*, in which he continued the narrative of Dexippus, covering the chronological span from A.D. 270 to 404. So far as we can tell from the fragments and extracts and from the indirect tradition, as a convinced opponent of the Christians, Eunapius exalted the figure of the emperor Julian the Apostate and tried to add new lustre to pagan culture.

Together with Eunapius, we mentioned as a source of Zosimus the Egyptian Olympiodorus of Thebes, who lived in the fourth and fifth century. He wrote a historical work in twenty-two books, on the emperor Theodosius II, of which Photius has preserved an extract. It concerned the Western Empire in the period 407–425 and was rich in notices and anecdotes on the barbarians, based on his own personal experience (in 412 Olympiodorus had been ambassador to the Huns).

Olympiodorus' knowledge of barbarian cultures and historical interests were shared with the Thracian Priscus of Panion, who in 449 took part in the embassy sent by Theodosius II to the Hun king Attila. He was author of a *Byzantine History*, in eight books, concerning the period 433–471. Fragments of it have survived via the work *De legationibus* of the Byzantine emperor Constantine Porphyrogenitus.

Malchus of Philadelphia in Syria, who lived in the fifth and sixth century, wrote a history in seven books that began from the reign of Constantine. The preserved fragments concern the years 474–480, which seem to have continued the account of Priscus.

IV Geographical and Periegetic Literature

1 Authors and literary forms

The celebrated tradition of Greek geography, understood as a scientific and philosophical discipline often in a close and natural connection with historiography,
found expression during the Roman Era in extensive treatises that profited from the
rich legacy of knowledge already acquired. In the past, for an author such as Herodotus, so attentive to geographic, ethnographic and cultural aspects, history and
geography were mixed together and no particular place was assigned in a work to
one or the other. In the historical work of Ephorus, on the other hand, two books
were specifically dedicated to the geography of Europe and Asia (IV–V) and this
decision was explicitly theorised by Polybius, according to whom geography is a
part of history and the historian should find a suitable place for it in the narrative.

A clear change can be identified in the work of Artemidorus of Ephesus (late
second century B.C.), who wrote Ἰωνικὰ ὑπομνήματα (*Ionika hypomnēmata*, i.e.
"Dissertations on Ionia") and eleven books of Γεωγραφούμενα (*Geōgraphoumena*,
i.e. "Geographical descriptions"), in which he described the known world in the
manner of the ancient Mediterranean periplus, perhaps for the first time since Hecataeus on a scale that constituted a geographical equivalent to universal history. In
this process, the distinction between works of geography and works of history took
on new force, which may have precedents in the ancient tradition of logography. As
we shall see shortly, in the Roman Era this distinction was adopted by Strabo. Of
Artemidorus' works only fragments in the indirect tradition remain. Recently a large
papyrus from a private collection, published in 2008, has restored materials that
may go back to the *Geōgraphoumena*, which would increase quite considerably our
knowledge of Artemidorus' work, but the authenticity of the witness and its content
is the subject of the most heated debate, leaving open various possibilities: a modern falsification, an authentic piece of Artemidorus or a fragment of a writing in
some way derived from his work.

A symbol of the compilatory and systematic conception of knowledge is Claudius Ptolemaeus, who lived in the second century A.D., a multifaceted scientific figure
who was competent in the most varied disciplines and whose works took the character of overall systematisations of the knowledge acquired in various fields. Among
other things, we glimpse here *in nuce* the selection of basic disciplines of scholastic
education, which were concretised as the "quadrivium," i.e. the scientific programme of medieval education: geometry, arithmetic, astronomy and music.

Dating to the Augustan Period are the seventeen books of the *Geography* of
Strabo, which have survived almost entire. The work is of universal scope, presenting a general description of the known world (Europa, Asia and Africa). The ancient
literary genre of the *periēgēsis*, i.e. the description of things seen while travelling,

https://doi.org/10.1515/9783110426328-033

intended as a guide for visitors, merchants and soldiers, also continued in the Hellenistic and Imperial Periods and was often cultivated by writers of history too.

The *periēgēsis* in verse is represented above all by Dionysius Periegetes (we shall mention him again when discussing didactic poetry). In prose, the most important work of *periēgēsis* is undoubtedly the *Description of Greece* in ten books by Pausanias, who lived in the atmosphere of admiration and reclaiming of the ancient past that characterised the central decades of the second century. In bringing together all the regions of central and southern Greece in a single description, the author took the opportunity to offer a large number of precious antiquarian notices, which are often of decisive importance in the fields of art history and archaeology.

2 Strabo

2.1 Biographical notices

The main source about the life of Strabo is his *Geography*, the only one of his works to survive. He was born at Amaseia in Pontus around 64 B.C. into a distinguished and politically important family (his maternal grandfather had been a friend and officer of Mithridates Euergetes, king of Pontus). Although in the Augustan Period Pontus was a Roman province and the family did not have any current political relevance, nonetheless his family must have maintained a patrimony sufficient to allow Strabo to devote himself freely to studies and journeys. At first he studied grammar at Nysa with Aristodemus, who was already tutor to the sons of Pompey; his education then continued thanks to contact with prominent cultural figures of the time, such as the grammarian Tyrannio, the Peripatetic philosophers Xenarchus of Seleucia and Boethus of Sidon (with whom he said he had studied Peripatetic thought). He knew well Posidonius of Apamea, who had a major influence on him, perhaps particularly in the combination of historical and geographical interests. There are elements of an eclectic education, but within this (as we can infer from some passages of his work) Strabo cultivated particular sympathy for Stoic philosophy.

He visited Rome for the first time in 44 B.C., but later stayed there on other occasions and was in contact with the influential politician Publius Servilius Isauricus. In 25–24 B.C. he was in the following of Cornelius Gallus in Egypt; he returned there again in 20 and lived for some years in Alexandria. He lived to see the beginning of the principate of Tiberius (who ascended the throne in A.D. 14) and died after A.D. 23 at an advanced age.

2.2 The lost historical work

In all probability we should put down to chance (and not to intentional choice) the fact that the tradition has preserved Strabo's *Geography* but not his *Historica hypomnēmata*. Of the few surviving fragments of the latter, three are transmitted by Strabo himself, in passages of the geographical work where he speaks of the method and content of his own historical work.

Written before the *Geography*, probably between 29 and 25 B.C., it consisted of 47 books and continued the narrative of Polybius. It is likely that Strabo used as his sources the same works that he mentions in his *Geography*. Among these Posidonius stands out, who likewise continued the work of Polybius. We know nothing about the chronological organisation, but it is likely that Strabo used the Polybian model of Olympic years. A fragment attests that in the historical work space was given also to biographical interests (it is not by chance that some fragments have been preserved in the biographies of Plutarch). This perhaps had the aim of idealising certain figures and providing prompts for moral instruction, and so went beyond the military and political pattern of the Thucydidean type, resulting in a greater variation in narrative forms. On the historiographical criterion adopted by Strabo, from the fragments we can glean a refusal, inspired by Polybius, to accumulate facts of little importance, with a consequent downgrading of precision in details. Further, in one passage of the *Geography* he defends the use of testimony from others, given the impossibility of achieving "autopsy," as restoring dignity to the faculty of hearing relative to the faculty of sight.

Worthy of some reflection is the fact that Strabo's work picked up directly from the *History* of Polybius and not that of Posidonius, who had already continued Polybius. A desire to compete with Posidonius seems clear. Strabo probably did more than just add to the historical data already set out by Posidonius and attempted to rewrite the events according to interpretive lines of some originality. The advancing decadence of Roman society, as Posidonius had seen it, was no longer persuasive in the era of peace and prosperity of the Augustan years. The historical and political problems that had tormented Polybius and Posidonius, along with any resistance or mental reservation against Roman rule, had vanished by the time of Strabo, who had the opportunity to reread the past in a way that justified the present state of prosperity. Strabo's historiographical vision of Rome is illuminated by Book VI of his *Geography*, where the description of the geographical foundations of Italy's supremacy is followed by a historical sketch that is absolutely favourable to Rome. Strabo characterises Rome's hegemony as a necessity, and sees in it an indispensable educational role and the role of political guide, all viewed in the optimistic perspective of a civilising mission that fell to the victors.

The question has often been raised of Strabo's attitude towards the Augustan ideology, in the belief that it is possible to identify traces of an evolution from initially critical positions to a substantial and convinced adherence. From the remains of Strabo's work, what emerges is admiration for the greatness of the empire and for the role of the emperor as guarantor of well-being and security. He seems sincerely attracted to the principate of Augustus and incapable of seeing its limits and defects. Strabo remains a man of Greek culture and mentality, who is carrying out the fundamental historical role of passing on to the Roman world the immense patrimony of civilisation that had been accumulated by his own world and which is itself guaranteed by this evolution. In this basic attitude, his agreement with Dionysius of Halicarnassus cannot be overlooked.

2.3 The *Geography*

The work was probably written at the end of the reign of Augustus and the first years of the reign of Tiberius. In the monumental introduction (Books I–II), the author attempts to make explicit the foundations of a composite literary genre, which concerns history, as well as the mathematical and astronomical sciences and physics. Beyond the author's statements, however, it remains an open question what the specific goal and addressees of the work were. Yet we can still grasp the pragmatic character of a work of this type: Strabo lets us glimpse his tendency towards Stoic thought, which championed a knowledge that was not just theoretical but oriented towards action and concrete commitments, in an ethical tension aimed towards the good of humanity. With the *Geography* he aimed to be useful to the society of his time and to those who administered it, accepting with good grace the reality of Rome's imperial dominion over Greece and the world.

Strabo does not limit himself to the geographical localisation of the sites, but produces research that, on the one hand, goes beyond modern geographical interests, and on the other cannot be directly translated onto maps, since it is anything but systematic and accurate in locating sites. These aspects of structure and content, together with a form that is not particularly appealing, has yielded it limited success and a lack of appreciation since his own times, to the point that, for example, he is cited neither by Pliny the Elder in the *Naturalis historia*, nor by Claudius Ptolemaeus. Strabo had to wait until the nineteenth century for reassessment and appreciation.

The *Geography* consists of seventeen books, which have survived almost entire. The first two contain the introduction; the actual description of the known world begins from Book III, proceeding clockwise along the northern coast of the Mediterranean, from the Iberian peninsula to Asia, and finishes with the southern coast of the Mediterranean (Libya).

> In the introduction (Books I–II) some general problems of geography are treated: the goals and characteristics of geographical research, with a critical assessment of the works of his predecessors (the series of which he begins with Homer, whom he discusses at length) and of the

genres they used, dwelling also on the historians (Ephorus, Polybius) and the "physicists" (Posidonius, Hipparchus) who had devoted parts of their work to geographical problems and descriptions. Geography, a discipline that demands great breadth of knowledge, including specialist knowledge, is linked to the sphere of activity of the philosopher and is seen as indispensable for the needs of political and military life. The specialist requirements should not allow geography to end up beyond the reach of anyone who is concerned by its problems.

Book III is devoted to the Iberian peninsula. Strabo reveals an interest in the ancient customs of the Iberian peoples, in relation to the evolution they have undergone with Romanisation, the events of which are given a great deal of space. The author acknowledges the value of the Augustan peace, which allows peaceful development and cultural growth while abandoning barbarian practices. In Book IV Gaul is described, the parts of which are assimilated to geometrical forms. In this case too, a great interest emerges in the events of Romanisation and the consequent acculturation of the barbarian peoples, which is manifested in their adaptation to urban structures. Italy is the topic of two books: Book V describes the plains of the Po, Liguria, Tyrrhenia, Elba, Corsica, Sardinia, Umbria, the Sabine country, Latium and Rome, Picenum and the interior of the peninsula, Campania, Samnium and the territory of those Piceni who had moved to the Gulf of Poseidonia; Book VI describes Lucania, Bruttium, Sicily, Iapygia and the coast between Bari and Picenum and contains a conclusion on the peculiar characteristics of Italy, which permitted the Romans to achieve such great power (natural defences, ports that, though few in number, were of excellent quality, variety in climate due to the extent of the peninsula in latitude and altitude, rich resources in water, minerals and forests). The section on Italy and on Roman supremacy concludes with a historical excursus on Rome's conquests. Book VII takes as its subject northern and eastern Europe, delimited by the River Rhine, the arc of the Alps, the Adriatic Sea, the regions north of Greece and by Macedonia and Thrace up to the Straits, the Black Sea and the River Tanais, the conventional frontier between Europe and Asia. This is an immense area, and one that is quite varied from a physical point of view, but which offered a landscape of human geography that was yet more complex. Following the procedure typical of geographical descriptions in antiquity, Strabo proceeds from West to East. After treating the countries of the Germans, Cimbri and the still unexplored lands of the far North, the treatment of central Europe follows the natural axis of the Danube. The end of the book is lacunose and fragmentary. The description of Greece and the Aegean islands is covered in Books VIII–X. After a general introduction, which discusses the previous geographical tradition on Greece from Homer onward and announces the intention to take the sea and coast as a guiding thread through the description itself (as Ephorus had done), Strabo divides Greece into five peninsulas, beginning from the Peloponnese. The final part of Book X contains the description of Crete, the Cyclades and Sporades.

Books XI–XVI describe the continent of Asia, subdivided as follows: northern and western Asia, except the Anatolian peninsula: the coasts of the Maeotis and Euxine as far as Colchis, Iberia, Albania, the Caucasus, the western coast of the Caspian Sea, Hyrcania, the Däae, Massagetae and Sacae (the last three belonging to the group of Scythians), Parthia, Aria, Margiana, Bactriana, Sogdiana, the Taurus, Media, Armenia); Asia Minor; India and Persia; Assyria, Syria and Arabia. The last book, finally, treats the regions of the continent of Africa: Egypt, Ethiopia, Libya.

Strabo is conscious of the profitable interrelation between geography and historiography: problems posed by the one can be illuminated by the tools of the other, in such a way as to yield an explanation and comprehension of complex phenomena. In particular, he highlights how military campaigns have allowed geography to make great advances, through the discovery of new countries and a better knowledge of the peoples of the world. For example, when in the *Geography* he describes the region of Pontus, he is conscious of making accessible to the public recently acquired information that had been collected thanks to Roman military ventures in that area. Similarly, Strabo gives a lot of room to notices of an ethnographic and historical character, drawing them above all from Posidonius, whose researches certainly owed a lot to the recent wars fought by Rome, and from the tradition of the *periplus* for the description of the sea coasts and riverbanks. In the same way, in Polybius and the historians of Alexander and of the *Diadochi* Strabo was able to find knowledge that derived from the presence in the Macedonian army of central European troops and from oral sources, official memoranda and military reports.

Despite the many cues for narrative that are present in the work, Strabo's style remains rather dry and monotonous: his goal is a simple exposition of data and facts, without troubling to pursue appealing details or rhetorical embellishments.

3 Pausanias

3.1 Biographical details

We do not know either the native land nor the precise dates of Pausanias. Yet it is clear that he wrote during the period from Hadrian (117–138) to Marcus Aurelius (161–180) and that his work fits fully into the atmosphere of reassessing Greek culture in the central second century. From various passages in the work we learn that he was at least partly contemporary to Hadrian; on the other hand he mentions the invasion of Greece by the barbarian Costoboci, which occurred between 166 and 180, and the celebration of the triumph of Marcus Aurelius over the Quadi, Marcomanni and Sarmatians, which took place in 176. In conclusion, we will not go far wrong if we set his lifetime roughly between A.D. 100/110 and 180.

In his work *Description* (*periēgēsis*) *of Greece*, Pausanias reveals very great familiarity with Asia Minor, to the point that it has been conjectured that his native land, or at least the place where he lived, should be sought in that area. A significant clue supporting this is the fact that he devotes a long digression to the Ionians of Asia in Book VII of his work, within the description of Achaea, where the Ionians were traditionally said to have originated. A further element that leads in the direction of placing Pausanias' origin in western Asia Minor is provided by the evident affinities with the historiographical method of Herodotus (who was from Halicarnassus) that are present in the *Description of Greece*.

Pausanias himself tells us of his numerous voyages, which gave him the opportunity to collect information and gain experience and which bring him close to the figure of Herodotus. He travelled to Syria and Palestine, Egypt as far as Thebes and the oasis of Ammon, and he visited Rome and its environs, as well as Capua and Pozzuoli (less likely, however, are voyages to Sicily and the Straits of Messina). In Greece, as well as the central and southern part that is the subject of his work, he visited Thessaly, Macedonia and probably Epirus. Of the timing, reasons and manner of his travels we know nothing, but it is enough to know that they existed, in order to place Pausanias alongside the figures of the sophists of the second century, who were itinerant within the vast borders of the pacified empire.

3.2 The *Description of Greece*

The geographical work entitled *Description of Greece* consists of a description of the central and southern region of the peninsula, pursued along a precise itinerary from Attica to the Peloponnese (travelling clockwise) and from Boeotia to Naupactus (the regions of the coast looking out towards the Peloponnese, from East to West). The geographical description is supplemented by a myriad of notices concerning history, anecdotes, mythography, artworks and antiquarian aspects of various kinds. Through this, the work takes on for the modern scholar the significance of a precious reservoir of information about the ancient world, which ranges from topography to history of art, from epigraphy to myth. The variety of facts transmitted in the *Description* make it quite precious for scholars of the ancient world, in particular those concerned with artistic and archaeological aspects of Greek culture. It is an indispensable point of reference, for example, for scholars of Greek architecture and sculpture. In this respect it is notable how scrupulous Pausanias is in describing sculpted works, with a specific interest in their material, from which, among other things, he derives information for chronological reflections. To take another example, notable importance is accorded to epigraphic documentation collected by Pausanias, which is today in large part lost in its material form but is still accessible through the *Description* for scholars of ancient inscriptions.

  In the manuscript transmission the *Periēgēsis* is divided into ten books: I Attica and the Megarid; II Corinth and the Argolid; III Laconia; IV Messenia; V–VI Elis; VII Achaea; VIII Arcadia; IX Boeotia; X Phocis with Delphi and Ozolian Locris to Naupactus. Some statements by the author cast light on a stratified compositional approach, carried out in successive phases. For example, in Book VII there is an allusion to the *ōdeion* (a hall for musical performances) built at Athens by Herodes Atticus, which is not mentioned in the book on Attica, which must therefore have been written prior to the construction of the building. In sum, it seems that the composition of the work should be placed between 155/160 and 180 and that there were two main phases of composition, though the extent of each is debated. Doubts have also been raised about the completeness of the work: in some passages the author seems to promise a treatment of other Greek regions, and a late author (Stephanus of Byzantium, see below) has preserved a quotation from Pausanias that mentions a city of Euboea, Tamyna, that does not in fact appear in the text of the surviving work.

We have mentioned the numerous journeys undertaken by Pausanias to the East, West and Greece. We should regard as fruits of these journeys the digressions included in the work concerning regions distant from Greece (on the Dead Sea, the Colossus of Memnon, the Temple of Diana at Capua, the works of Trajan at Rome). These passages make clear their character as additions, through the fact that they could easily be removed without any loss to the context.

The practice of first-hand travel to the regions that are the subject of geographical and antiquarian inquiry can clearly be traced back to the model of Herodotus, who identified autopsy and the collection of local (often oral) sources as the surest criterion in historical research. It is not by chance that in the *Description of Greece* the testimony of Herodotus is reported almost always as being trustworthy and only occasionally supplemented or corrected. As regards Herodotus, however, in Pausanias we can observe a significant reversal of perspective in the changed historical circumstances. Herodotus described peoples foreign to a Greek public at the moment when it was at the highpoint of its political, economic and cultural development. Pausanias, on the contrary, is a Greek originally from a peripheral area who, a little nostalgically, assigns to his work – in this era of renewed philhellenism – the function of refreshing the ancient grandeur of the motherland in the eyes and memories of the dominant powers at Rome.

The reference to Herodotus and to journeys leads us to touch on a quite important aspect of the documentary method adopted by Pausanias. As well as the experience gained by direct viewing of sites and monuments, in the collection of material for the work he also contributed an intense engagement with written sources. As we have said, alongside the elements that are purely descriptive, much space in the work is also given to historical and antiquarian, mythographic and anecdotal aspects, for which Pausanias could easily draw on previous historiographical works. While Herodotus plays a primary role, we see little drawn from historians such as Thucydides and Xenophon, although they are used for the *Pentekontaetia* and the Peloponnesian War. For the following years we find affinities with historiography on the Isocratean pattern, and for Hellenistic history Pausanias cites Hieronymus of Cardia and the autobiographical memoirs of King Pyrrhus. It is less easy to determine the role played by Polybius and Plutarch. One of the peculiarities of Pausanias is his wide use of local historians, who were guardians of regional curiosities and civic traditions, on whom he relied in order to enrich his work with rare or little known notices.

His interest in documentation that is varied, precious and locally sourced leads Pausanias also to draw on literary sources, preferably archaic ones. Among the authors most cited are Homer and Pindar, sometimes mentioned to settle differences between other sources. Not a few quotations are drawn from other works in epic genres that are today lost. Other authors mentioned are Asius of Samos, Cinaethon of Lacedaemon, Hesiod, Aristeas, Panyassis, Apollonius Rhodius and Euphori-on. The *Description of Greece* is a precious source also of poetic verses from archaic lyric and elegiac. Pausanias shows less fondness for Attic theatre, in which his sym-pathy, for ideological reasons too, goes to Aeschylus.

It was once hypothesised that the genesis of Pausanias' work was essentially book-based. But this judgement has been radically altered by more recent studies, according to which he skilfully combined a vast number of notices of many different kinds drawn from sources for which he used his own direct experience of "autopsy" thanks to his numerous journeys. To maintain (as has been done) that Pausanias had described not the Greece of his own times, but that of three centuries before, is to overlook his distinctive attitude, which is idealistic and classicising as it turns towards the past and is less attracted by the monuments of the late Hellenistic and contemporary ages.

3.3 The *Description of Greece* and the Greek historiographical tradition

In the past not enough attention was paid to the fact that, in homage to the tradi-tional pursuit of originality, the main goal pursued by Pausanias and his work was that of supplementing and correcting the historical and geographical works by those who had preceded him, avoiding repetition of their contents. In many passag-es he states that he will pass over a topic or a description because it has already been treated by others. In some cases of this type he proposes corrections or adds some marginal details. Elsewhere Pausanias says that among so many possible topics he has preferred to choose those that lend themselves to an overall narrative. In sum we can conclude that, while availing of a large quantity of original and un-published historical and antiquarian material, Pausanias has chosen not to rewrite a history of Greece (and so to inscribe himself in the historiographical tradition of *Hellenica*) and has preferred to take a new path: to draw up a geographical itinerary of the Greek regions and *poleis*, selectively inserting into this framework supple-ments and corrections to what was already known from previous historical narra-tives.

These criteria fit parts of the work such as a section of Book I which, although taking its cue from the description of monuments preserved at Athens, in reality provides a history of the early Hellenistic Period. Similarly, a large part of Book IV supplements Herodotus' account of the Messenian Wars. Likewise, the detailed description of Sparta, carried out with a sort of inventory of the city's monuments (64 temples, 21 *herōa*, 3 altars, 18 tombs, the market, the marble theatre, 8 porticos, etc.) seems to have its justification in the desire to refute Thucydides' judgement on the modest aspect of the monumental city.

The project of intervening on questions already treated by others only when cor-rections and original contributions are to be made is often achieved by drawing on oral traditions, in polemical opposition to written sources that had by then become canonical and codified. Significant from this point of view is the abundant presence in the work of verbs and expressions that refer to the sphere of speech. Pausanias' attitude towards these traditions is not inspired by naïve credulity: in a way not unlike that of Herodotus, according to whom the historian should report what is said but is not obliged to believe it, he often distances himself from the testimony reported or adopts a neutral attitude towards it.

Of a similar kind is Pausanias acceptance of historiographical traditions that are minor, lesser known or less often repeated and the use of documentary sources such as inscriptions. For numerous original inscriptions Pausanias reports the text, either by drawing it from an intermediate source or by inspecting it in person, and archaeological discoveries continue to provide confirmations of the authenticity of these inscriptions.

The same approach of selecting and supplementing moved Pausanias in the description of works of art, to which he applies his own criterion of "reading": in well known monuments he proceeds by allusion and brief references (one example may stand for them all: the Parthenon), but in contrast he likes to dwell and linger on the lesser known and rare monuments, with a genuinely antiquarian taste. Further, he reserves particular attention for works of the archaic and classical Periods, and shows great interest in old buildings, even those that are dilapidated and ruined. Yet there is also no lack of interest in a similar selection of Hellenistic buildings or those from the better periods of the Roman domination, such as the Augustan, Trajanic and Hadrianic Periods, evidently in homage to the author's own political preferences.

3.4 Reception

The *Description of Greece* was quite little used in antiquity. The reason for this limited success should be sought in all likelihood in the very character of the work, which was wholly aimed at a classicising renewal of the past glories of Greece and was hence tied to the tastes and interests of the cultivated classes of the second century. Its circulation was thus bound to fail after the Antonine Era, through the fading of the ideological and cultural conditions in which it had been produced. Interest in Pausanias came to the fore again in the Byzantine Age, in the recurring phases of "renaissance" and classicising returns to the Greek past, beginning from Stephanus of Byzantium (who lived in the sixth century and was author of a geo- and ethnographic encyclopedia).

4 Claudius Ptolemaeus

4.1 An encyclopaedic scientist

Despite the fact that Strabo had introduced a decisive turn in a historical and ethno-graphic direction in geographic exposition, an older tradition reckoned geography among the scientific disciplines and this was the strand that was picked up in the second century A.D. by the versatile and industrious figure of Claudius Ptolemaeus. He worked in various spheres of science, concerning himself not only with geogra-phy, but also astronomy, astrology, mathematics, geometry, harmony and optics: we will discuss him again in the chapter on scientific literature (cf. below VII 2). In the sphere of geography Ptolemaeus distinguished himself by the composition of large works concerning whole fields, which collected and elaborated the materials and advances of previous research. By picking up the old approach of Eratosthenes (cf. *The Hellenistic Age* III 2.2), he sought to order and interpret geographical knowledge in a mathematical mode.

4.2 Biographical notices and principal works

Ptolemaeus was born around A.D. 100 in Ptolemais in Upper Egypt and he spent part of his life at Alexandria, where he contributed to the rebirth of the Museum. There he was occupied for several years collecting material for the composition of his principal work, the manual of astronomy in thirteen books entitled Μαθηματικὴ σύνταξις ("systematic mathematical treatise") and then known as Μεγίστη σύνταξις ("the greatest systematic treatise") or (from the Arabic translation of the title) *Alma-gest*. The work is emblematic of Ptolemaeus' systematic mentality, which aimed to reduce the observation and description of the heavenly bodies to a mathematical calculation of an organic whole.

As well as other works of astronomy and the disciplines mentioned above, Ptol-emaeus composed his *Geography* in eight books – the full title is *Geographical Guide* (Γεωγραφικὴ ὑφήγησις) – with the aim of providing an instrument for the construc-tion of maps, that defined the astronomical position of around 8000 locations on Earth, indicating their latitude and longitude. Despite the inaccuracies (due to his adoption of the calculation of the Earth's circumference by Posidonius, which was less precise than that of Eratosthenes, and to the use of imprecise traveller's ac-counts as the sources for the distances), this work enjoyed great resonance until the Middle Ages, gaining much success for the rigour and breadth of the topics treated.

V Plutarch of Chaeronea

1 Plutarch and Graeco-Latin culture

In the complex cultural landscape of the Imperial Period the figure of Plutarch stands out as an authoritative witness to his times. Endowed with vast cultural breadth and multiple interests, he embraced in himself the awareness and weight of responsibility that characterised his generation: the awareness of being the heir to the immense legacy of the past Greek civilisation and the responsibility of turning himself into a forceful interpreter and continuator of it.

Plutarch incarnated this role as upholder of Hellenic culture perfectly and fulfilled it in complete harmony with the historical climate of Graeco-Roman society in the first to second century A.D. In his attempt to recover and revalue Greek *paideia*, in a context of advanced political and administrative Romanisation, some of the motivations at work were connected to the peculiar relationship between Greece and the imperial power of Rome. He inscribed himself into the implicit but already age-old and evident dialectic of integration and competition between the two "nations" and cultures, which played out on the two different levels of political domination, on one side, and primacy in artistic, literary and intellectual civilisation in general, on the other. The political supremacy of Rome was already, for Plutarch too, an undisputed and incontrovertible matter of fact, yet it was still the potentials of the Greek heritage that seemed to be rich enough to function as guide in revitalising and energetically inspiring the present era.

Plutarch is every bit a man of his time, as he draws on forms of thinking and organising knowledge that were becoming established in the first centuries of the empire: a tendency towards synthesis and eclecticism in philosophical matters; the accentuation of normative aspects and rhetorical components in the field of literature; in general a deep sense of continuity and of an endless debt owed to the past ages, the results and goals of which were indispensable points of reference for contemporary man. This insistent retrospective gaze was thus not nostalgia, intellectualism or antiquarian pedantry, but a firm and convinced trust in the continuity and vivid actuality of Hellenic civilisation.

2 Life

Plutarch's homeland was Chaeronea in Boeotia, where he was born on a date that we cannot pin down with absolute certainty, but which should be placed around A.D. 45. The figures of his father Autobulus, grandfather Lamprias, great-grandfather Nearchus, brothers Lamprias and Timon and his wife Timoxena recur in his works, in which the sense of family is very marked. He had three sons and one daughter. The latter died at the age of two while he was away from home. In that

https://doi.org/10.1515/9783110426328-034

circumstance he sent to his wife a heartfelt, and still extant, *Consolation*. He certainly received careful training in rhetoric, an obligatory and indispensable component of education at the time. The school curriculum would next have included philosophy. As his teacher in this sphere he cites the Platonic philosopher Ammonius, whose lectures he attended at Athens. Here he entered the Academy and devoted himself to assimilating the thought of Plato with passion and depth.

During his adult life he held civic offices at Chaeronea (as eponymous *archōn*, superintendent of public buildings and head of the construction police), in accordance with Platonic-Stoic ethics, which urged political engagement and obedience to civic duties. His political activities must have included a large component of diplomatic contacts and missions to the Roman authorities. His diplomatic activity also gave him the opportunity to undertake a series of journeys: to Greece, Egypt and probably Asia Minor; he stayed at Rome on a number of occasions from the Flavian Period onward and visited the cities of northern Italy. At Rome he gave lectures and won the admiration of leading figures in the emperor's entourage, some of whom appear as dedicatees of his works. Through the intervention of his influential friend Lucius Mestrius Florus, Plutarch also acquired the Roman citizenship.

As his fame grew, Plutarch accumulated prestigious positions and public awards. From A.D. 95 he was priest of Delphi; it seems that he received from Trajan the honour of *ornamenta consularia* and from Hadrian missions on embassies between Rome and Greece; later he was *epimelētēs* of the Delphic Amphictiony. At Chaeronea, where he spent the last part of his life, pupils both Greek and Roman sought out his instruction; many of them have left quite vivid traces in his works, in which they figure as protagonists or dedicatees. He died around A.D. 125 at an advanced age.

3 The Plutarchan corpus

We possess an ancient catalogue of Plutarch's works, preserved in the *Suda* lexicon, which attributes it to one of Plutarch's sons by the name of Lamprias. Yet it does not appear that Plutarch had any son of this name (though one of his brothers was called Lamprias) and the question of the author of the catalogue is a thorny problem. The catalogue proper is preceded by a letter which "Lamprias" sent to an anonymous addressee along with the list of his father's works. Some modern scholars believe that the list reproduces a catalogue, datable to the third or fourth century, of the writings of Plutarch preserved in some library; according to others the letter is a forgery of the thirteenth to fourteenth century.

The catalogue includes the titles of 227 works in a total of 278 books, out of which today there survive 83 works in 87 books (and fragments of around another 15 works). Yet the list does not include 18 other surviving works nor a further 15 for which we have notices in the indirect tradition (i.e. the catalogue is incomplete).

Therefore a great deal has been lost out of an immense output, but there is also a great deal that has survived. The extant works fill a whole library shelf; they include some works that we can identify as inauthentic or doubtful, but they are known overall by the obvious name the *Corpus Plutarcheum*. Within this, two large categories of writings are traditionally recognised: the collection of biographies entitled *Parallel Lives* (Βίοι παράλληλοι, often simply *Lives*) and the shorter works of moralistic content under the collective name of *Moralia* (Ἠθικά).

The *Lives* are generally regarded as a work of Plutarch's maturity. As for the *Moralia*, one possible chronology sets in his juvenile period the rhetorical works written with dazzling tones and effects, while to the author's maturity would be assigned the works that show more substance in their content and greater attention to philosophy and to ethical and religious duties, along with a more robust formal originality. All this is of course conjectural and susceptible to subjective evaluations.

4 The *Lives*

The ancient tradition has preserved almost complete the collection of biographies entitled *Parallel Lives*, which for the most part set alongside each other the lives of a Greek and a Roman figure that present some affinity or common feature.

A total of 50 biographies survive, which can be grouped as follows: 22 pairs (but in one case four lives are set in comparison: *Agis and Cleomenes* on the one hand and *Tiberius and Gaius Gracchus* on the other) and four single biographies: *Aratus*, *Artaxerxes* (the Persian king, i.e. a non-Greek), *Galba* and *Otho*. The chronological span of the *Lives* ranges from the mythical past (*Theseus* and *Romulus*) to contemporary history: an important section of the collection was in fact formed by the lives of the Roman emperors up to the Flavians, but all that survives from this part are the *Lives*, just mentioned, of *Galba* and *Otho*. Many biographical pairs, finally, are accompanied by a closing *synkrisis*, i.e. a close comparison of the two figures. The *Lives* were probably all written after A.D. 96.

The biographies are transmitted in manuscripts that can be traced back to two recensions, or ancient editorial arrangements: one in two volumes, and one in three. In the two-volume recension, which is probably the earlier one, the *Lives* were arranged according to the chronology of the Greek figures, from *Theseus–Romulus* to *Philopoemen–Flamininus*. In the tripartite recension, attested by the majority of manuscripts, the *Lives* were arranged according to the ethnic of the Greek figure, from Athenians to Spartans, with the figures in chronological order within each subdivision. Its three volumes ran as follows: from *Theseus–Romulus* to *Demosthenes–Cicero*; from *Phocion–Cato the Younger* to *Alexander–Caesar*; and from *Demetrius–Antony* to *Agesilaus–Pompey*. According to a modern hypothesis, the collection opened with the lost pair *Epaminondas–Scipio*, preceded by a general preface and by the dedication.

We provide here a list of all the *Parallel Lives*, following the order attested in the tripartite manuscript transmission: *Theseus–Romulus, Solon–Publicola, Themisto-cles–Camillus, Aristides–Marcus Cato, Cimon–Lucullus, Pericles–Fabius Maximus, Nicias–Crassus, Alcibiades–Caius Marcius Coriolanus, Demosthenes–Cicero, Pho-cion–Cato the Younger, Dion–Brutus, Paulus Aemilius–Timoleon, Sertorius–Eumenes, Philopoemen–Flamininus, Pelopidas–Marcellus, Alexander–Caesar, Demetrius–Antony, Pyrrhus–Caius Marius, Aratus, Artaxerxes, Agis and Cleomenes–Tiberius and Gaius Gracchus, Lycurgus–Numa, Lysander–Sulla, Agesilaus–Pompey, Galba* and *Otho*.

The biographical pair *Theseus–Romulus* is one of the few that concern "histori-cal" persons whose figures are lost in the mythical tradition. Plutarch is conscious of the fact that they belong to a period for which it is not possible to achieve proba-ble or certain knowledge, but he maintains that what is still necessary is "purifying Fable, making her submit to reason and take on the semblance of History" (*Theseus* 1, 5). In these two *Lives* the erudite character of the work is accentuated, with quota-tions from all kinds of authors and statements attributed to various traditions not further specified. The biographical reconstruction in this case therefore takes the form of a learned report or summary of the various opinions and traditions around the two figures, who were weighed down with centuries of historical and erudite reconstructions and poetic and literary elaboration. The author is inclined towards the rationalistic versions, to the point that he omits some famous details of myth; where there is a contradiction between sources, he sometimes dwells on specific odd variants. There are also aetiological sections on toponyms, rites and festivals, for which Plutarch undoubtedly drew on the Attidographers and the Athenian local historians and, for Rome, on antiquarians such as Varro and Juba.

The biographies of *Demetrius* and *Antony* belong to Plutarch's full maturity, be-ing datable to A.D. 116 to 117. Prominent in this biographical pair is the role assigned to the mutability of fortune, which determines the existential arc of the two figures. The figure of Demetrius Poliorcetes is complex and nuanced, but essentially to be condemned. He is introduced, after notices about his family, by a physical and psy-chological portrait whose qualities and defects are set up in counterpoint. Yet his initial positive qualities are gradually, and then rapidly, corrupted by his defects, in a deterioration that was promoted by the adulation of the Athenians, which fed his *hubris*. After some attempts to get back on track, Plutarch's Demetrius ends by re-nouncing his previous ambitions and abandoning himself to drink, gambling and pleasure. Similarly, Antony achieves the highest levels of power thanks to his gifts, but his youth is branded immoral by Plutarch. Octavian, shrewd and calculating, and Cleopatra, beautiful and flattering, bring his failings to the fore and become insuperable obstacles. The role assigned to Cleopatra is emblematic of Plutarch's conception of women: love for the Egyptian queen destroys all the good that remained in Antony (from chapter 25 of the *Life of Antony* the figure of Cleopatra takes on great prominence, to the point that this is almost a double biography).

Plutarch must have set about composing the *Lives* with the double aim, which was dear to him, of reminding the Romans of the glorious past of the Greek world and inviting the Greeks to adopt a conciliatory attitude towards Rome. Plutarch was in this way inviting the intellectual and political elites of the empire to discover the grandeur and dignity of Hellenic civilisation, a goal fully achieved a few decades later with the advent of Hadrian and the Antonines. As well as this aim there was another one, equally important: to place his contemporaries in the presence of great figures of the past, from whose high qualities or vices they could draw significant and useful moral lessons. One can detect how Plutarch liked to draw his figures in chiaroscuro brushstrokes, refraining from constructing images that are absolutely virtuous or vicious and instead trying to mingle qualities and failings. For this reason even a negative pair such as *Demetrius* and *Antony* takes on an edifying role, to the extent that, as Plutarch explains in the preface, the negative example can point us by contrast towards the righteous life.

4.1 Plutarch's *Lives* and the relation between biography and historiography

In the famous introduction to the *Life of Alexander*, Plutarch clearly sets out his programme as a writer of biographies and not of historiography, founded on his intention not to repeat what had already been narrated by the historians, but rather to attend to the particular and everyday aspects that often reveal a person's character better than is done by political and military events of major significance (ch. 1): οὔτε γὰρ ἱστορίας γράφομεν, ἀλλὰ βίους, "I am not writing history but biography." Plutarch continues by observing that "in the most illustrious deeds there is not always a manifestation of virtue or vice, nay, a slight thing like a phrase or a jest often makes a greater revelation of character than battles where thousands fall, or the greatest armaments, or sieges of cities."

It cannot be ruled out that this proemium may have been placed at the beginning of the *Life of Alexander* to justify the author's failure to present exhaustive information when faced with the very rich historiographical tradition in this case. On the other hand, its content undoubtedly has a general conceptual and programmatic significance that can be extended to the entire collection, as is demonstrated by the presence of the same concepts at the beginning of the *Life of Nicias*. Here (ch. 1) Plutarch criticises authors such as Timaeus who were so bold as to narrate the events concerning this Athenian general by entering into competition with the inimitable account of Thucydides. Plutarch, to the contrary, has limited himself to running through in a succinct way the events already expounded by others, while concentrating his research on lesser known aspects and episodes and so "not gathering meaningless historical data, but recording data which promote the understanding of character and personality" of the figure.

Thus by using the genre of biography Plutarch maintains the ability to intervene with supplements and corrections to the prestigious tradition of classical historiographical models, declining to engage in a risky and over-ambitious competition with them. In a similar way, some decades later Pausanias would use another "secondary" or "alternative" genre, the *periēgēsis*, as an original route that allowed him to intervene through supplements and corrections to the historiographical narrations of the past (cf. above IV 3).

Notable inspiration for the genre of biography had come in the Hellenistic Age both from Peripatetic circles (attracted by the problem of ethics and so by the description of the *ēthos* of eminent figures) and from the world of Alexandrian erudition (which aimed rather at the collection of materials and documents: cf. *The Hellenistic Age* III 1.6). However, these forms of biography essentially dealt with literary and philosophical figures; it is not clear whether there was an output of *Lives* of political figures before those written by the Latin author Cornelius Nepos, who lived in the first century B.C. and who can hence to a certain degree be seen as the model for Plutarch. If one wishes to trace the genesis of political biography, one should remember that the monographs *Agesilaus* by Xenophon and the *Life of Philopoemen* by Polybius do not fit this genre, but belong rather to the genre of prose encomium. On the other hand, one should not overlook the fact that substantial biographical elements concerning political figures are present within works earlier than the Imperial Period and Nepos. One possible example is the (lost) digression that Theopompus devoted to the Athenian demagogues: if that consisted of narratives of biographical type, then it should be considered the earliest attestation of political "biography," but it is important to keep distinct what can be regarded and labelled as "biographical interest" from what constitutes a genuine biography as an autonomous genre.

It is likely that the genre of biography had constituted a familiar source of information only or predominantly for figures from literature and philosophy, whereas those who sought information about political figures would essentially turn to historical works. We know that this was Plutarch's mode of working and that he then corrected and supplemented the information that he found among the historians with information drawn from his own researches (of varying depth) in erudite and antiquarian writings. This is the reason why his *Lives* are for us the source of numerous fragments of lost works of various genres, above all from the Hellenistic Era.

4.2 Peripatetic influences on Plutarch's *Lives*

Various elements of biography within the Peripatetic school exerted an influence on Plutarch. Among these, one that emerges clearly is the need to identify a person's *ēthos* by characterising his way of thinking and acting. This is the case, for example, of the Athenian general Nicias, whose representation by Plutarch turns entirely on his superstitious character, or of Alcibiades, who is seen as a scheming, ambitious flatterer.

Aristotle asserted the importance, for the formation of an individual's *ēthos*, not just of *physis*, but of *proairesis*, i.e. the free and voluntary faculty of decision and choice. This conception assumes great thematic importance in Plutarch's biographies. Even figures who are fundamentally negative are not to be condemned right from the start, as a matter of nature: the negative developments of their existence depended on the choices, conscious and voluntary to some degree, that aligned them towards evil through a prevalence of vices and corruption. Another recurring theme drawn from the typology of the Peripatetic *bios* is the *metabolē* (μεταβολή), i.e. the change that sometimes occurs in a person's character, subverting expectations.

Some would also ascribe the very distinction between history and biography to the theorisations dear to Aristotelian circles, a distinction that occurs in quite similar terms also in Cornelius Nepos (*Life of Pelopidas* 1, 1). Finally, the collections of famous sayings and witticisms, or *apophthegmata,* have also been ascribed to the enthusiasm for forming collections, which derived from Peripatetic approaches.

5 *Moralia*

The generic name *Moralia* or better, in Greek, Ἐθικά (*Ethica*), a title drawn from the edition produced by the Byzantine scholar Maximus Planudes, designates a collection of around 80 works, only part of which are in reality on moral topics. The literary form of these essays is also varied. In the more substantial works, Plutarch often uses dialogue and so inscribes himself, at least formally, into the prestigious Platonic tradition. These include *dihegematic dialogues*, i.e. those reported by one of the participants, *dramatic dialogues*, i.e. characterised by direct speech, and *mixed dialogues*, in which the conversation is retold within a direct dialogue. There are also monographs in treatise form (historical-critical and antiquarian), declamations of the type used in school and rhetorical education and diatribes in the tradition of popular philosophy, on ethical themes and addressed to a non-specialist, popular audience.

Solely in order to give a clear organisation to the exposition, we may distinguish within the whole of the *Moralia* three groups of writings: philosophical and pedagogical works (both popularising and specialist); ethical and political ones; and others on miscellaneous topics (including scientific, literary critical, and erudite or antiquarian themes).

5.1 Philosophical and pedagogical writings

Among the writings on ethical topics with a popularising character, we may record first of all a pair of treatises that focus on the symptomatology of human characters and behaviours, as *How to Tell a Flatterer from a Friend* (*De adulatore et amico*) and *Concerning Talkativeness* (*De garrulitate*). Specific moral questions, addressed by contrasting typical characters and attitudes, are the topic of essays such as *Whether Vice Be Sufficient to Cause Unhappiness* (*An vitiositas ad infelicitatem sufficiat*), *On Envy and Hate* (*De invidia et odio*), *Desire and Grief – Psychical or Bodily Phenomena?* (*De libidine et aegritudine*, authorship of which has been contested) and *Virtue and Vice* (*De virtute et vitio*). Some works are decidedly paraenetic, i.e. they offer moral advice: *On Moral Virtue* (*De virtute morali*), *On the Control of Anger* (*De cohibenda ira*), *How a Man May Become Aware of His Progress in Virtue* (*De profectis in virtute*) and *On Tranquility of Mind* (*De tranquillitate animi*). In the work *How to Profit by One's Enemies* (*De capienda ex inimicis utilitate*) it is stated that one should not treat a vanquished enemy with spite, lest one incur his revenge sooner or later. The treatises *On Brotherly Love* (*De fraterno amore*) and *On Affection for Offspring* (*De amore prolis*) are testimonies to the intensity of Plutarch's feelings in relation to the family, which we find addressed also in a more intimate sphere in the works *Advice to Bride and Groom* (*Praecepta coniugalia*), *Consolation to His Wife* (*Consolatio ad uxorem*, addressed to his wife on the occasion of the loss of their little daughter Timoxena) *and The Dialogue on Love* (*Amatorius*). In the last of these writings it is stated that physical attraction between spouses, while important, is a less lasting aspect than the strong bonds forged by shared affections and by reciprocal support.

Different tones and contents are found in a series of more specialised works, which address precise philosophical questions raised by the traditional Greek schools of thought. These works constitute for us a precious mine of information on the individual schools, as well as on the eclectic orientation of Plutarch's thought, which is essentially Platonic-Stoic in character. Three treatises are devoted to anti-Stoic polemic: *On Stoic Self-Contradiction* (*De Stoicorum repugnantiis*), *The Stoics Talk More Paradoxically Than the Poets* (*Stoicos absurdiora poetis dicere*) and *Against the Stoics on Common Conceptions* (*De communibus notitiis contra Stoicos*). Plutarch agrees with Stoicism on the duty of constant effort in favour of other people and the thesis that a divine providence regulates the world, but on the other hand he does not admit the conception of a mortal soul subject to the alternation of cosmic cycles, nor the belief in divinity as immanent. There are also three surviving writings with anti-Epicurean content: *That Epicurus Actually Makes a Pleasant Life Impossible* (*Non posse suaviter vivi secundum Epicurum*), *Reply to Colotes in Defence of the Other Philosophers* (*Adversum Colotem*) and *Is "Live Unknown" a Wise Precept?* (*De latenter vivendo*). Out of Epicurus' thought Plutarch would retain almost nothing and he attacks it from all angles. Platonic topics are addressed in the treatises *On the Generation of the Soul in the Timaeus* (*De animae procreatione in Timaeo*) and *Platonic Questions* (*Platonicae quaestiones*). Not authentic, but of great importance for our knowledge of ancient thought, is the *On the Views held by Philosophers* (*De placitis philosophorum*).

We can also assign to the philosophical theme the writings on theological and religious subjects, a sphere to which we can see that Plutarch, who long held the prestigious office of priest of Apollo at Delphi, was very sensitive. Some of these treatises confront single questions. *The E at Delphi* (*De E apud Delphos*) offers a round up of possible interpretations of the letter epsilon that could be read at the entrance to the temple of Apollo at Delphi. In *The Oracles at Delphi No Longer Given in Verse* (*De Pythiae oraculis*) the topic of the decline in the metrical form of oracular responses by the Pythia introduces the problem of the decline of oracles themselves, which is also the theme of *The Obsolescence of Oracles* (*De defectu oraculorum*): the speakers in that dialogue propose various explanations of the phenomenon, including the momentary disappearance of the demons, intermediaries between the divine and human spheres, the depopulation of Greece and the increase in human perversity. The work *Isis and Osiris* (*De Iside et Osiride*), as well as attesting to the spread of Egyptian religion within the empire, offers a wealth of information on it: it presents a syncretistic reading of cult practices, priestly careers and mythology, in the light of rationality and allegorical interpretation, with the aim of escaping the snares of superstition, which is considered worse than atheism. *On the Sign of Socrates* (*De genio Socratis*) addresses the traditional problem of the *daimonion* of Socrates. Fideistic tones characterise the *On the Delays of the Divine Vengeance* (*De sera numinis vindicta*), a valuable dihegematic dialogue on the ineluctable execution of divine justice, in which Plutarch himself takes the stage in the role of fictitious narrator.

Particularly interesting, and with a certain success also among modern readers, are some works on pedagogical topics, which are useful both for the reconstruction of this sphere of ancient thought and for understanding the principles of Hellenic *paideia* professed by Plutarch. The treatises *How the Young Man Should Study Poetry* (*De audiendis poetis*), *On Listening to Lectures* (*De audiendo*) and *The Education of Children* (*De liberis educandis*) address particular questions of method and content in the education of the young, a motif that is present also in many other writings of Plutarch. A text that is perhaps more important, *De liberis educandis*, is subject to serious doubts about its authenticity, though the work seems to have a close connection to the practice of school-teaching and to Plutarch's own teaching approach. Its rediscovery in the West had a major influence on humanist pedagogical theory.

5.2 Ethical and political writings

We can collect in this group some writings on political and moral topics, two aspects that are in fact often inextricably mixed together in Plutarch's thought.

One of the more important political works is the *Precepts of Statecraft* (Πολιτικὰ παραγγέλματα or *Praecepta gerendae rei publicae*), in which Plutarch reveals a pragmatic attitude towards the now unavoidable Roman domination of Greece, while well aware of the limits that it imposes on local politics. Consequently, he indicates that the first task of the wise politician is to maintain peace and security by avoiding the risk that rivalries and conflicts, an endemic evil in the Greek world, might force an intervention by the rulers. The application of this proposal implies that political man should possess moral virtues such as self-control and rectitude. Some treatises on political topics have a didactic and paraenetic tone, such as: *Whether an Old Man Should Engage in Public Affairs* (*An seni sit gerenda res publica*), *That a Philosopher Ought to Converse Especially with Men in Power* (*Maxime cum principibus philosopho esse disserendum*), *To an Uneducated Ruler* (*Ad principem ineruditum*) and *On Monarchy, Democracy, and Oligarchy* (*De tribus rei publicae generibus*; perhaps from Plutarch's school).

5.3 Treatises on miscellaneous themes

Plutarch reveals polymathic gifts and a vast breadth of culture in a long series of other writings on miscellaneous topics, ranging from rhetoric to literary criticism, from natural sciences to historical and antiquarian learning. In this he in a sense becomes the heir to the Aristotelian conception of knowledge, a systematic and encyclopaedic idea that does not set limits or walls between the different spheres of knowledge.

One series of texts of rhetorical character reveals by their very form that they were composed in a youthful phase, when Plutarch had not yet matured into his attitude of moderate reserve in relation to rhetoric, which would later become clear. Some are so far from the balance typical of Plutarch that some critics even exclude that they could have been intended for publication. We may note the writings that address themes typical of epideictic declamation, such as the discussion of the role of *Tychē* in human affairs: *Chance* (*De fortuna*), *On the Fortune of the Romans* (*De fortuna Romanorum*), *On the Fortune or the Virtue of Alexander* (*De Alexandri fortuna aut virtute I–II*) and *Were the Athenians More Famous in War or in Wisdom?* (*De gloria Atheniensium*).

Exegetical essays were devoted to the works of Hesiod (we have parts of a *Commentary*, which was extensively used by later commentators), Aratus and Nicander. The "catalogue of Lamprias" also cites a commentary on Euripides, of which nothing survives. Some writings were true monographs on authors of the past. The best known out of this group is perhaps the *On the Malice of Herodotus* (*De Herodoti malignitate*), a sort of polemical *pamphlet* against the historian, who is held to be guilty of factiousness in judging the attitude of Thebes during the Persian Wars. We may also recall the *Comparison between Aristophanes and Menander* (*Aristophanis et Menandri comparatio*), which survives in an abbreviated form, from which emerges a judgement in favour of the more recent comedian. Interesting but spurious are the *Lives of the Ten Orators* (*Decem oratorum vitae*), which presents a series of biographies of the most important Greek orators, the work *On the Life and Poetry of Homer*, which is rich in material from Alexandrian philology, and the treatise *On Music*, which is one of our primary sources on this subject.

Among the writings on scientific topics, the themes that emerge are physiology, biology and zoology, though these also feature the principles of ethics. The *Advice about Keeping Well* (*De tuenda sanitate praecepta*) maintains the importance of a balance between good physical condition and serenity of mind. In *On the Eating of the Flesh* (*De esu carnium*) Plutarch asserts the necessity of avoiding unbridled consumption and of respecting the ancient habits, codified by Pythagoras and Empedocles, that denied man's right to the lives of animals, prefiguring the possibility of metempsychosis, and exhorted them not to eat meat. Halfway between an essay on nature and rhetorical writing of the epideictic type lies *Whether Land or Sea Animals Are Cleverer* (*De sollertia animalium*), in which Plutarch aims to demonstrate the capacity for reflection and understanding in animals on land and sea. The thesis is picked up again in *Beasts Are Rational* (*Bruta animalia ratione uti*), in which Gryllus, one of the companions of Odysseus transformed into a pig, states that animal existence has some aspects that are better than human existence. In *Concerning the Face Which Appears in the Orb of the Moon* (*De facie in orbe lunae*) Lamprias, brother of Plutarch, reports a learned dialogue on the marks on the surface of the moon and on the possibility that the moon holds forms of life.

A characteristic series of writings has the typical traits of the literature of scholarly compilations, in which the central thematic motif is a pretext for accumulating around it a large amount of disparate information drawn from various places. Antiquarian interest is foundational to collections of data and anecdotes such as *The Roman Questions* (*Quaestiones Romanae*) and *The Greek Questions* (*Quaestiones Graecae*). The frame of a symposium provides the background to *The Dinner of the Seven Wise Men* (*Convivium Septem Sapientium*), in which we find a fusion of gnomic and symposiastic literature, and to the *Table-Talk* (*Quaestiones convivales*), in nine books, which is a work of maturity in which very varied themes are treated within the traditional frame of the banquet. Other writings collect the sayings of famous figures (*apophthegmata*), matching a taste and curiosity that accord with the idea (expressed in the *Life of Alexander*) that often a triviality, a phrase or a joke can reveal someone's character better than famous political and military undertakings. Among these we note the *Sayings of Kings and Commanders* (*Regum et imperatorum apophthegmata*), dedicated to Trajan; the *Sayings of Spartans* (*Apophthegmata Laconica*); and the *Sayings of Spartan Women* (*Apophthegmata Lacaenarum*).

Modern scholars have often debated the origin, purpose and also the real authorship of these miscellaneous collections. Older theories regarded them as later forgeries, as created out of material drawn from Plutarch's works, or as works that Plutarch himself put together by reusing the documetnation used in the *Lives*, but these ideas now seem to have been superseded. Scholars today tend to see in the miscellaneous works a varied legacy of preliminary documentation, which formed the principal instrument of Plutarch's "workshop" and which was probably produced by adding to pre-existing selections with the fruits of his own deep and extensive reading. It is possible that the publication of these works, which were created, so to speak, for private use, was posthumous and goes back to the initiative of Plutarch's admirers, who aimed to publish his entire written legacy.

5.4 The primacy of ethics

We have observed how the name Ἠθικά (*Ethica*), in Latin *Moralia*, is a term that strictly speaking is not appropriate to the entire collection of writings known under this title. Yet we should recognise that there is hardly any piece of writing by Plutarch in which an ethical element cannot be identified. This is a clear mark of the author's great interest in moral reflection, i.e. reflection that aims to define the norms to which individual behaviour or *ēthos* conform.

It is necessary to underline once again the importance that *ēthos* (in the literal sense of "character," "behavioural propensity") assumes in the *Parallel Lives* too. Just as the *Moralia* include abundant historical exempla and anecdotes, which are offered as paradigms of vices and virtues, so also in the *Lives* the ethical interest informs and guides the historical and biographical narrative. This interaction between history and morality is perhaps one of the most significant traits of Plutarch's intellectual personality and it emerges clearly as a unifying factor in the dense exchange of materials, quotations, data and anecdotes between the two groups of works, i.e. *Lives* and *Moralia*.

Plutarch's marked interest in moral philosophy should not come as a surprise. We have seen how, from the Hellenistic Age, the problem of ethics had held a central position in philosophical reflection in the principal schools of thought, from the Academy to the Peripatos, from Stoicism to Epicureanism. Plato, in relation to whom Plutarch reveals a kind of intellectual devotion, had outlined the important function of the philosopher in society as a guide of collective action; the Stoics, picking up this aspect of Plato's vision, regarded it as an inescapable imperative that the sage engage ethically and politically in person. Beyond the substantial eclecticism of his thought and the criticisms made also of Stoicism, Plutarch is clearly inspired by these Platonic and Stoic premises. He chooses to interpret them in a mystical and religious key in his own reflection and activity as a productive writer, granting the ethical demand a primary position and foundational role in thought and life.

6 Language and style

One of the characteristics of Plutarch's personality is his very fine sensibility as a writer of vast literary culture and refined stylistic gifts. His chosen language is an Atticism that is not extreme, but softened by the presence of the *koinē*, attentive to the goal of guaranteeing clear and precise diction. Above all in the *Moralia*, however, there are also passages of great conceptual density, with a matching syntactical complexity. Plutarch's preferred stylistic register, too, is the middle, plain level, which aimed to achieve clear and appropriate expression and to provide pleasure in reading by a skilful balance in the use of rhetorical devices. His rigorous tendency to avoid hiatus is commonly taken as a criterion to determine whether a work is authentic.

7 Reception

Plutarch's work enjoyed swift and immense success already from the period straight after his death. Testimony to this is the presence in the corpus of numerous apocryphal works, evidently introduced in order to ensure they would gain circulation and attention. The conceptual outlook of the *Moralia* guaranteed appreciation by the pagan Neoplatonics, but also by the Christian authors of the fourth century, who saw in them certain points of agreement with Christian morality. The *Lives* on the other hand met with particular favour above all in the Modern Era, beginning from their rediscovery in the West in the Renaissance, and they exerted an important influence on European culture in the following centuries (Shakespeare, Alfieri, Foscolo, Leopardi).

VI Jewish and Christian Literature

1 Jewish literature in the Greek language

1.1 Philo of Alexandria

1.1.1 Philo and the Alexandrian setting
The versatile and complex figure of Philo is a fruit of the eclecticism typical of the philosophical culture of his age and of his Alexandrian setting, where there was a very large Greek-speaking Jewish community, to which Philo belonged (as we mentioned already when discussing the *Septuagint* translation of the *Bible*, cf. *The Hellenistic Age* IX 1.3).

The little that we know of his life is drawn from his works. The only secure notice about him is that he represented the Jewish community of Alexandria on an embassy to Rome in A.D. 39/40 to argue the case of the Jews of his city before the Emperor Caligula, who in 38 had been subjected to a full persecution by the Prefect of Egypt, Aulus Avillius Flaccus. Philo's date of birth is unknown, with hypotheses ranging from 30 to 10 B.C. His death should be placed in the reign of Claudius (A.D. 41–54), perhaps around 45.

From Philo's works there remain a total of 35 treatises, which for convenience can be grouped on the basis of their subjects, whereas it is in general difficult to suggest a chronological order for their composition. One group is composed of writings of a strictly philosophical character, such as: *On the Eternity of the World*; *On Providence* (fragmentary); *Every Good Man Is Free*; *Alexander, On the Fact that Animals Possess Reason* (which survives in an Armenian version). Another group is formed by an allegorical commentary on parts of the *Pentateuch*: we may note the *Allegory of the Laws, On the Confusion of Tongues, On the Migration of Abraham*; the work entitled *Questions and Answers* has survived in fragments, except for four books *On Genesis* and two *On Exodus*, which we know from an Armenian translation. Other works, in which allegory has less importance, constitute an explanatory reflection on biblical history and the Mosaic Laws: *On the Account of the World's Creation Given by Moses, On Abraham, On Joseph, On the Decalogue* and others. Finally, there are some apologetic writings in defence of Judaism, among which we may note *On the Embassy to Gaius, Flaccus, Hypothetica* (*Apology for the Jews*) and *Moses*, which is written in an anecdotal spirit that accords with the canons of Hellenistic biography.

The eclecticism of the learned Philo, who seems to have had an assured command of a large number of works by Greek philosophers, is dominated by the polarity between the Hellenic philosophical culture, on one side, and Jewish culture and faith on the other. He is confident in the possibility of using concepts and methods

https://doi.org/10.1515/9783110426328-035

from Greek philosophical thought to elaborate Jewish thought, creating an original synthesis with deep roots in classical culture but leading to developments outside it.

The character of these works, which often hinge on paraphrase and explication of passages of Scripture, in general makes Philo's style rather stilted and monotonous. However, it should be stressed that his way of writing nonetheless reveals sound preparation and attention through its careful form, even though for the most part the result is not very appealing.

1.1.2 Philo and the *Bible*: allegorical interpretation

Of fundamental importance for the Jewish Philo is exegesis of the biblical text, for which he exploits, with methodological awareness, the resources of allegorical interpretation that were copiously provided by the Greek tradition. In substance, alongside the exegetical tools already typical of Jewish culture he sets the weapons of allegoresis employed on texts of classical authors. From this perspective he is adopting the intuition of Aristobulus (cf. *The Hellenistic Age* VIII 1.3.2), by successfully and systematically applying this interpretive instrument, consolidated in the study of pagan authors, to the foundational text of Jewish culture. Through Philo's work the allegorical method reached the Christian exegetes of the sacred text, among whom, as we shall see, a special place is held by Origenes (second to third century).

Beginning from the assumption that every word of Scripture is the bearer of a divine message, Philo concentrates on the *Pentateuch* in his exegesis, but holds that the so-called historical books of the *Old Testament* (from *Joshua* to *Maccabees*) too must go beyond their mere value as historical narrative and description to become bearers of a higher moral and theological instruction that embraces and surpasses traditional philosophical speculation. This is the goal of allegory, which becomes a means of understanding this extraordinary source of communication with God at a deeper level. It also moves beyond whatever materialistic and anthropomorphic elements may exist in the images of divinity and the story that are presented by the sacred text, in order to bring the biblical content to more satisfying theological conceptions, also in the light of the principles of traditional philosophical speculation. For example, for Philo, the invitation to Abraham to leave his own country is an invitation to man to free himself from worldly goods; likewise the exhortation to separate himself from his family is read as an exhortation to the human mind to distance itself from the body. It is evident that elements of classical philosophy are here being included but re-read in a different light, with original results that would have important consequences in the reflections of later thinkers, both Christian and otherwise.

1.1.3 Philo's thought

The thought of Philo seems to elude every attempt at synthesis and on many points scholars have expressed diametrically opposed opinions. In part this is due to the variations connected to the formula of his own very original eclecticism, which exploits terms and concepts from classical philosophy, bending them to express contents that, despite analogies, are sometimes totally foreign to traditional Greek thought. Another aspect that should be borne in mind is the role of Scripture. As is traditional to Jewish culture, Philo's own reflections were founded and elaborated on the basis of the sacred text, and due to this very feature his work, developing in the form of commentary and interpretation rather than as an organic synthesis, frequently presents a disjointed picture in which different elements are prominent at different times. Clearly present at the basis of his thought are Platonic conceptions, but also Stoic, Pythagorean and Aristotelian ones. Yet even the terms and concepts that apparently stay in closer contact to traditional philosophy take on new values and original meanings within Philo's vision, the result of his own personal elaboration.

Philo's God is absolutely transcendent and stands outside the intelligible world, which is His creation. The definition of Being is the only positive definition that can be given of this God whom, beyond the intelligible world, man cannot otherwise define. One thinks here of the expression in *Genesis*: "I am He Who is." God is not a demiurge of the sensible world, but properly a creator who brings the world from non-being into existence. One of the points that has caused scholars the most difficulty is the fundamental concept of *Logos*, which in this absolute divine transcendence explains the creation of the world and permits the maintenance of a link between God and the created world. In the treatise *On the Account of the World's Creation* it is stated that the intelligible world is none other than the *Logos* of God in the act of forming the world. This *Logos* may therefore seem to be the divine *Nous*, but at times it is even defined as an autonomous entity produced by God (for example, it is called "first-born Son") and in other passages this transcendent model, on which the world was formed, seems also to have an aspect that is immanent to the world of which it is the guide and principle of preservation, the chain that keeps it united. It is through the *Logos* that a link is created between God and the created world, and this determines a providential vision of the events of history. By a voluntary gift from God himself, man has received a spark of divine origin, which permits him to look upon divinity. This is a gift that is configured as grace which cannot be earned by man by his own actions, but it is lost by anyone who does not live according to virtue.

Philo's immaterial *Logos* leads to a resolution of Plato's irreconcilable dualism between the Ideas and sensible reality. Conceptually it is sharply distinct from the material *logos* of the Stoics, with which, however, it seems to have affinities of a different kind, such as the conception that it is the link that unites in a coherent way all that is created. According to Philo, however, human reason, although guided by

divine revelation, does not have the capacity to acquire full knowledge of the essence of God, which is achievable only by means of ecstatic contemplation, something that is bestowed exclusively by God himself.

1.2 Flavius Josephus

1.2.1 A witness of the first rank

The figure of Flavius Josephus is notable also for his close involvement in the tensions and events that convulsed the Jewish world in the first century A.D. (we have
already mentioned this in relation to historiography: cf. *The Roman Imperial Period*
III 1.1). As an exponent and protagonist of nationalistic Judaism and convinced
opponent of Roman domination in Palestine, he then found himself forced by events
to recognise Rome's military superiority and to become a proponent of necessary
coexistence with the rulers on the part of his subjugated and dispersed people.

The tension between Romans and the Jewish world had begun in the period
when Pompey had captured Jerusalem and profaned the Temple (63 B.C.) and was
continued through the ever more intrusive Roman interference in Palestine. Alongside the High Priest, Caesar had set up Antipater as a procurator (ἐπίτροπος), whose
son Herod defeated the leader of the anti-Roman resistance Ezekias and had him
killed. The deterioration of relations had led to the birth of the Zealot movement
(one of the factions that would then go on to characterise political life in Jerusalem),
which produced the revolt of A.D. 6 led by Judas son of Ezekias, as a result of which
Judaea ended up being a simple protectorate and became a territory under direct
control of Rome. Some years later, in A.D. 66, the provocative attitude of the governor Gessius Florus unleashed a new revolt, led by Menahem, son of Judas and
grandson of Ezekias. The Roman garrison was massacred and the troops stationed
in Syria, which had invaded the region in order to punish the rebels, were severely
defeated. The conflict continued to unfold until it was definitively ended by the
destruction of Jerusalem by Titus and the diaspora of the Jews (A.D. 70).

1.2.2 Life

Flavius Josephus was born at Jerusalem in A.D. 37 or 38. He belonged to one of the
most prominent families of the city: his father had been part of the priestly nobility,
his mother (according to what he claims in a context where he is defending himself,
which hence is not beyond suspicion) was descended from the royal family of the
Hasmoneans. He received an education appropriate to his social rank: on the subject of Greek education he himself admits that he had not achieved a flawless accent, but he had no equals among his fellow countryment in his Jewish training,
which included the study of the biblical *Laws*. Josephus had passed through the
apprenticeship of young Jews: he spent the fifteenth year of his life learning and

practising the rules of life of the Jewish sects (Pharisees, Sadducees and above all the Essenes), he then spent three years of penance and ascesis in the desert and on his return he chose the sect of the Pharisees (usually the great priestly families were adherents of the Sadducees).

In 64, after an adventurous journey in the course of which he suffered a shipwreck in open sea, he arrived at Rome to plead the cause of some priests that the procurator Marcus Antonius Felix had referred to the imperial tribunal on flimsy charges, probably because he considered them to be leading proponents of anti-Roman resistance. At Pozzuoli Josephus made the acquaintance of an actor of Jewish origin who was admired by Nero (and Poppaea), which smoothed his path to victory in the trial and led Poppaea to send him on his way with rich gifts. It has been noted that in the lengthy account that he presents of these facts there is a singular omission, certainly by choice: there is no mention of the Great Fire of Rome in 64.

As we have already noted, when the Zealot Revolt lead to conflict between Jews and Romans in 66, Josephus was involved in the first rank, holding an important military position in Galilee, where he found himself confronted by serious episodes of insubordination. Sticking to the political approach of the Pharisees, Josephus adopted a cautious position in relation to the praise of those who wanted war without adequately weighing the dangers to which it would expose the country. The Sanhedrin of Jerusalem felt forced to prosecute the conflict, but the extremist anti-Roman line was taken above all by movements active in Galilee. The difficulties encountered by Josephus in maintaining discipline in the ranks in this region is explained by the fact that the Galileans cannot have appreciated a commander-in-chief sent from Jerusalem who was relatively unconvinced of the ideals of the revolt and of the possibility of victory against Rome. To this were added the serious and objective gaps in Josephus' military training, which he can be seen to be unaware of in his works.

After attempting the vain defence of some cities, in the face of the advancing legions led by Vespasian and his son Titus, Josephus surrendered to the Romans, in accord with his conviction of the necessity of a treaty with Rome. Vespasian's ascent to the throne in July A.D. 69 led to Josephus' liberation; he then became a collaborator of Titus, the destroyer of Jerusalem. His changed attitude towards the Roman rulers had emerged already after his surrender: he joined the imperial army in the occupation of Galilee (67), Peraea, Idumaea and Judaea (68) and in the campaign led by Titus that led to the conquest and destruction of Jerusalem (70).

The continued setbacks encountered by the Jews confirmed for him the idea that the injustice that reigned in his native land had moved God to abandon his people and to become allied to the Romans. And so the true enemies of the fatherland were those who in their folly had wanted at any cost the war that had ended in the destruction of Jerusalem, and not he who had worked for his people by trying to appeal to Titus' clemency.

Josephus received land in Judaea from Vespasian and Titus, was the latter's guest in his residences in Rome and received an annual pension. After the death of Titus, he enjoyed the protection of Domitian (81–96). At Rome, where he had retired and where every so often he was subject to accusations and slanders arising from his ambiguous positions, he completed the composition of *The Jewish War*, the *Jewish Antiquities* and other works. He died in the early years of the second century.

1.2.3 Chronology and general character of the works

Josephus' first audience consisted of the Jews of the Mesopotamian diaspora, whom he addressed in order to dissuade them from any anti-Roman inclinations. It was for this reason that at an early stage he wrote *The Jewish War* in Aramaic. Thereafter he addressed a more heterogeneous public including the Romans themselves and translated his work into Greek (the probable title is Περὶ τοῦ Ἰουδαϊκοῦ Πολέμου, "On account of the Jewish War") with the help of some assistants, whose role and influence is debated. It is likely that this change in audience led to a series of modifications, such as the detailed description of the zones in which the conflict took place, which would have been superfluous for readers in the Jewish diaspora but useful to a wider Greek-speaking readership. Josephus' writings in a certain sense became the official history of the glorious exploits that marked the accession of Vespasian and Titus: the latter in particular warmly supported Josephus' work, gave it his own *imprimatur* and saw to its circulation. The publication of the Greek translation took place between 75 and 79.

The Ἰουδαϊκὴ Ἀρχαιολογία, normally translated into English as *Jewish Antiquities*, was published in 93 94 with the support of an influential friend named Epaphroditus, who should perhaps be identified with the famous freedman of Nero of that name. Josephus narrated the history of his people from its origins to the start of the war in 66.

Three other works by Josephus are dedicated to Epaphroditus, which all share an apologetic intention. At some date later than 100 we should place *The Life of Josephus*, composed as a polemic with the Jewish historian Iustus of Tiberias, whose history of the Jewish War had tried to cast Josephus in a bad light in front of the Romans. The work *Against Apion* is devoted to the defence of Judaism from slanders made against it by the Greek world.

The *Fourth Book of Maccabees*, transmitted among the biblical texts, is attributed to Josephus by the late antique historian Eusebius of Caesarea (cf. *The Roman Imperial Period* III 2.2), but this attribution cannot be accepted.

1.2.4 The historical works

Josephus' main historical work, *The Jewish War* in seven books, is very clear in his essential support for the Roman cause and for Greek culture, which had been introduced and spread by the Romans. In this work his pro-Roman tendency and Jewish nationalism meet in an original synthesis, expressed emblematically by the theory that freedom should be preserved by force and courage so long as one succeeds in maintaining it, but when it is lost it is better to bow one's head and submit. Consequently, the figures of the anti-Roman resistance are branded as brigands, just as the Romans regarded those who rebelled against their rule, and even as traitors. Nonetheless, while the title of the work takes its reference from a Roman point of view (*War Against the Jews*) and while the interest of his imperial protectors was focused in this work, the author visibly maintains the point of view of someone who is telling the story of a war of the Jews against the Romans.

> The actual narrative of events is preceded by a lengthy and detailed introduction, which identifies a long series of background events before the war, beginning from the conflict between Antiochus Epiphanes and the Maccabees. Much space is given in the first part of the work to the emblematic figure of Herod I the Great, around whom the author focuses the nostalgic evocation of his country's greatness; for the public and private events of the king's life he used the *Historiai* of Nicolaus of Damascus, Herod's friend, ambassador and counsellor (cf. *The Hellenistic Age* X 3.3). In second rank is a series of figures from this period who were equally important. The following period is treated in more succinct and rapid form, with some striking overstatement of the role of Jerusalem in relation to Roman politics.
>
> Within Book II begins the account of the war, in which the author reworks his memories and notes. Among his sources he probably also used the *hypomnēmata* of Vespasian and Titus. While Vespasian is praised in encomiastic tones and with some distortion of the historical truth, even greater is the praise of Titus and his clemency. The powerful and praised Roman army had to adopt a waiting tactic (which Vespasian, according to Josephus, regarded as the most suitable and safe) and went to great trouble in gaining the upper hand over the tiny enemy. This strategic power and calm was opposed by the force, inspired by faith, of those who fought to defend Jerusalem. Aside from the distortions that we have mentioned on ideological and encomiastic patterns, comparison with other surviving historical sources on this period (Tacitus, Suetonius, Cassius Dio) and with archaeological data shows that Josephus' account is fairly reliable.

The 20 books of the *Jewish Antiquities* (Ἰουδαϊκὴ Ἀρχαιολογία), composed directly in Greek and published around A.D. 93–94, were intended to complete the story of the historical events preceding the period narrated in the *Jewish War*. They contain a Jewish ancient history shaped by the biblical tradition, with the addition of free embellishment and inventions (Books I–XI), followed by a historical account up to the time of Nero, based on various sources, including again Nicolaus of Damascus (Books XII–XX). The model is Dionysius of Halicarnassus, who is alluded to both by the title of the work and by the number of books.

In this work there are two references to Jesus and to the existence of the Christians, the larger of which, the so-called *Testimonium Flavianum* (*Jewish Antiquities* 18, 63–64), has been the subject of extensive polemics among scholars. At present the dominant hypothesis is that the passage began from an authentic reference, which would thus be one of the earliest non-Christian testimonies about Jesus, but that the passage of Josephus has been expanded at a later date by Christian interpolators who added an explicit mention of the resurrection and of the fact that Jesus was to be identified with "the Christ," expressions that are unlikely to derive from the Jewish author Josephus.

1.2.5 Reception of the historical works

After the fall of the Flavian dynasty, interest waned in the works of Flavius Josephus and the facts narrated in them. However, they gained new wind in the Christian world, which saw the *War* as the account of an epochal moment in the history of the Holy Land, and the *Antiquities* as the true history of the Jewish people. The extensive reception of the *War* is attested by the translations, reworkings and epitomes produced during Late Antiquity and the Middle Ages. We note a late antique version of Book VI, which even came to form part of the canon of the Syriac Church as the *Fifth Book of Maccabees*, and the Latin translation or reworking in five books produced by the so-called Hegesippus (fourth to fifth century), which had the goal of converting Jews. In the tenth century a Hebrew paraphrase was produced, from which derive, through subsequent reworkings, the Arab translation of the eleventh century, the Ethiopian translation and two Armenian versions.

1.2.6 Language and style

Following the tendency of his time, Flavius Josephus was committed to an Atticising taste. Consequently his style is inspired by models of classical Greek historiography and makes ample use of the resources of rhetoric. A certain stylistic roughness is found in *The Jewish War*, probably due to the fact that it is the translation of an original version in Aramaic.

2 The first centuries of Christian literature: the *New Testament*

2.1 Christianity and literature

Despite the serious conflicts and incomprehension that grew up quite quickly between the Christian and Jewish communities from the dawn of the present era, historically the Christian religion was deeply and naturally grafted onto the Jewish religion, as is shown above all by their shared foundation in the sacred texts of the *Old Testament*. Jews and Christians saw and see them as the fruit of divine revelation, to the point that in their case, as in the similar one of Islam based on the Qur'an, we speak of the "Religions of the Book." As we will see, the Christian *Bible* accepted into its canon, in addition to the sacred books acknowledged by the Jews as inspired by Yahweh, also some texts that the Jews considered to be edifying but which they did not include among those that were divinely inspired, as well as a number of writings concerning the figure of Jesus that form the *New Testament*.

2.2 The writings of the *New Testament*

The teaching of Jesus was purely oral, but very soon his message began to be diffused and transmitted also through a series of written works. The 27 texts of differing character that bear the earliest surviving written testimonies concerning the figure and actions of Jesus were collected under the name of the *New Testament*. The Latin word *testamentum* translates the Greek διαθήκη, in the sense of "pact, alliance, covenant," with reference to the pact established between God and men through the incarnation and sacrifice of the Christ. The expression "New Testament" (Καινὴ διαθήκη) thus establishes a relation with the previous pact made with the Chosen People of the Israelites, namely the *Old Testament* (Παλαιὰ διαθήκη).

Considered to be direct and truthful testimony to the events of the apostolic period, the writings of the *New Testament* quite quickly assumed a distinctive role in the development of the communities of the new religion. Since they were regarded as divinely inspired, they were set alongside the sacred texts of the Jewish religion and made the foundation of Christian doctrine. A true canon, or an official list of the books considered to be sacred and bearers of the revealed message, would not be formed until rather late. In general the Christian communities accepted from the start the writings of the *Old Testament* as Scripture, but did not feel the need to form a specific and precise canon of the *New Testament* until around the second half of the second century. For the previous period, we have indications that across a vast geographical area at least the four *Gospels* and the *Letters* of Saint Paul (except the so-called *Letter to the Hebrews*) were considered to be inspired texts, since they were authoritative vehicles of the apostolic tradition. However, with the increasing number of works composed in imitation of the writings of the apostolic period, and above all with the rise of the first contested theological controversies, the need to order the works and establish a canon became all the more pressing. The earliest list of sacred texts known to us is in a palimpsest of the eighth century found by the scholar Ludovico Antonio Muratori (1672–1750), who published it in his *Antiquitates Italicae Medii Aevi*. The text, known as the *Canon Muratori*, seems to be the late Latin translation of a Greek original from the end of the second century. Compared to the current catholic canon, the Muratori canon does not include the *Letter to the Hebrews* or a large part of the catholic epistles, whereas it contains a second *Apocalypse*, that of Peter; it also mentions the *Shepherd* of Hermas among the works worth reading though they do not form part of the canon (cf. *The Roman Imperial Period* XIII 1.2.7).

The present canon was established only at the start of the fourth century, though some uncertainties persisted. Excluded from it were a certain number of writings about the actions of Jesus that had proliferated but which the Church did not accept among the canonical writings, and which have since been known by the name of the *New Testament Apocrypha*. These include some gospels, some epistles and other texts such as the *Apocalypse of Peter* and the *Shepherd* of Hermas that we have just mentioned. The 27 texts included in the canon are for the most part arranged in the manuscripts in the following order:

- five works of narrative character, namely the four *Gospels* (Εὐαγγέλια): *According to Matthew, According to Mark, According to Luke, According to John*; and the *Acts of the Apostles* (Πράξεις ἀποστόλων);
- a group of 21 epistles sent to Christian communities, namely: 13 *Letters* attributed to Paul; the *Letter to the Hebrews* (which has from the earliest testimonia been recognised as being of Pauline inspiration but which clearly, also for linguistic reasons, cannot be attributed to Paul); the so-called 7 "catholic" letters (the term, in use from the third century, derives from the Greek καθολικός, *katholikos*, "universal" or "general"): one is attributed to James, two to Peter, three to John and one to Jude;
- the *Revelation* or *Apocalypse* (Ἀποκάλυψις) of John.

The extraordinary cultural importance of the *New Testament* naturally lies above all in the fact that it is the bearer of a strong and penetrating revolutionary message. Alongside this is the fact that the texts that compose it present stylistic characteristics that are in many ways different from those of the classical Greek texts that had been considered model works. In their engagement with pagan thought and literary models, the authors of the *New Testament* writings produced another phenomenon of historical significance, namely the birth of a new culture and a new literature with its own distinctive characteristics.

2.3 The *Letters* of Paul of Tarsus

The oldest *New Testament* texts are almost certainly the letters of Paul. The canon consists of 13 Pauline epistles, grouped on the basis of their addressees and their length, from longest to shortest; these are followed by the *Letter to the Hebrews*, which is placed last, despite its length, since already in antiquity it was considered not to be authentically the work of Paul, but merely belonging to his circle (for which reason it was long excluded from the canon in some oriental churches). When the *Canon Muratori* cites these epistles, it places first those to the Corinthians, a possible indication that the original collection was formed at Corinth. Yet it is clear that the letters immediately found success and were circulated by the addressees also to other communities.

The life of Paul can be reconstructed in large part thanks to the epistles (in particular the *Letter to the Galatians*) and to the testimony of the *Acts of the Apostles*. Some public figures cited in the epistles also allow us to propose a relatively precise dating of the main events of his life. Paul was a Jew born in Tarsus in Cilicia. As he himself said, he was taught at Jerusalem according to the rules of strict rabbinical observance and in a first phase he was an opponent of Christianity. After his conversion, which occurred miraculously on the road to Damascus following a vision of Christ (perhaps in the year 30 or 34), and followed by some years of silence, Paul dedicated himself actively to the spread of the Christian gospel in particular among the pagans, undertaking three major missionary voyages (the dates proposed for them are 45–48, 50–52 and 53–57), with intervening visits to Jerusalem. On the second of these journeys he was in Greece and came to Athens, where the *Acts of the Apostles* (17, 22–31) recount how he addressed a speech to the Athenians on the Areopagus, which was not a great success but is seen as the first encounter between the Greek world and the Christians. Thereafter, he was arrested in the Holy City, spent two years in prison in Caesarea and was then transferred to Rome since, through his place of birth, he was a Roman citizen and so enjoyed the right of appeal to the emperor. He reached Rome in 61, where he was kept in prison but not forced to halt his preaching for that reason. The account in *Acts* breaks off at this point and our information about the following period of Paul's life has to be based on less reliable testimonies. Paul seems then to have been freed and to have undertaken another missionary voyage, but, arrested again, he was beheaded in Rome in the year 67.

Paul is undoubtedly a figure of primary importance. His epistles demonstrate an extraordinary speculative depth and a capacity for doctrinal elaboration, which had fundamental consequences for the subsequent development of the Christian religion. To him is owed above all the definitive opening up of Christianity to non-Jews, or gentiles (a term calqued on the Greek *ethnikoi* in Paul's text), moving beyond the conception of a Jewish Christianity, which had risked limiting the new religion within the circumscribed sphere of Judaism. His ideas of opening up the religion were sometimes opposed, but the very widespread usage by Christian writers of calling him "the Apostle" as an antonomasia (or "the Apostle to the Gentiles") gives an idea of the importance attributed to him, despite the fact that by his own admission Paul had never known Jesus.

A first group of canonical epistles includes, in chronological order: two *Letters to the Thessalonians*, the second of which is of debated authenticity; a *Letter to the Galatians*; and two *Letters to the Corinthians*. These are the fruit of Paul's wish to remain in contact with the communities in which he had managed to preach or which he himself had founded, and to which he clearly felt connected by a strong personal bond. While the epistles also contain important considerations of a general character, they often arise out of particular practical necessities: to resolve disputes within the communities, to respond to requests and provide clarifications on theological topics as well as to indicate basic norms of morals and behaviour.

The topics are in many cases set out in some disorder. After the introductory formulae, Paul addresses the individual problems in question, sometimes returning a number of times to themes closer to his heart, then passing from the particular to the general, introducing reflections and recommendations of a broader scope. This diffuse character can be explained in various ways. In some cases material in different epistles may have been combined into one; more generally, we should bear in mind that these are not theological tractates, but rather writings that arose from precise and concrete situations, and so some references that are obscure to us must have been clear to the addressees of the message, since they referred to the particular real cases.

Next in chronological series is the *Letter to the Romans* (datable to 57–58), composed by Paul in order to make contact with the local community in view of an imminent visit. This is the text in which the greatest attention has been given to matters of doctrine. Paul here presents an articulated picture of his own theological vision, underlining on the one hand the continuity between the *Old Testament* and the new doctrine that was its fulfilment, and on the other hand – and this is the fundamental core of Paul's thought – that the coming of Christ brings about the surpassing of the *Old Testament* vision, permitting man's justification by means of faith in Jesus and not by observance of the Jewish Law.

Another group of letters goes back to the period in prison in Rome. The very short *Letter to Philemon* is a simple, familiar note in which Paul requests that the rich Philemon of Colossi receive kindly, as befits his Christian faith, the slave Onesimus who had returned to him after escaping. We then have the *Letter to the Philippians*, the *Letter to the Colossians* and the *Letter to the Ephesians*. This last letter, which is almost certainly not authentic although it conforms to Paul's thought, is presented as a sort of encyclical to the Churches of Asia Minor. There we find fully developed the image of the Church as Body of Christ, in which those who have been saved by his redemption take part without any distinction, in particular without distinction between those who come from the Chosen People and those who converted from paganism, the gentiles.

There are then the three short letters called "pastoral," i.e. addressed not directly to communities, but rather to individual "pastors" (literally "shepherds") of souls: the two *Letters to Timothy* and one *Letter to Titus*. Their authenticity is now generally rejected, on the basis of some stylistic characteristics and certain details in the structure of the Church that seem to belong to a later period.

In reality, these are not the only letters about which doubts have been raised over their authenticity. Quite serious questions concern in particular, as already mentioned, the second *Letter to the Thessalonians*, due to its striking discrepancies from the first one; the arguments against the *Letter to the Colossians* seem less significant. Parts of the *Second Letter to the Corinthians* and of the *Letter to the Romans* (ch. 16) may have been added to the original text, perhaps by drawing on other letters now lost.

The style of the letters reveals the character of the author. Paul expresses himself with firmness and enthusiasm, relying on an original manner of writing that is full of vehemence. This becomes clear above all in the first group of epistles, which were composed to resolve specific queries posed by the Christian communities. Sometimes we find there anacolutha, broken phrases and expressions that are elliptical to the point of obscurity, yet at the same time effective through their immediacy, due to the ardour with which Paul expounds and defends his own point of view.

The Letter to the Hebrews. The *Letter to the Hebrews* has the appearance of an elaborate doctrinal exposition: excepting the final greetings, it has the characteristics of a theological discourse more than of an epistle. It is today universally considered not to be by Paul. The thought and style of the author do have affinities with those of Paul, yet depart from them in a significant way. References to the Temple of Jerusalem lead us to suppose it was written before 70, but some think the date is later. However, it is certainly prior to 96, the year in which it is cited by Clement of Rome (cf. *The Roman Imperial Period* XIII 1.2.1). The letter addresses the topic of the superiority of the Christian religion over the Jewish one, of which it is the fulfilment. The argument used by the author is the superiority of Christ over the angels and Moses, of the priesthood of Christ over that of the High Priest, of the celestial sanctuary over that of the Temple, and of the sacrifice of Christ over animal sacrifices. In the second part there follows an exposition of sacred history.

2.4 The narrative texts: the *Gospels* and the *Acts of the Apostles*

Before treating the epistles that do not form part of the Pauline corpus and are of later date, we should discuss the narrative writings: the four *Gospels* and the *Acts of the Apostles*.

The title Εὐαγγέλιον literally means "good news" (*god spel* in Old English translation, from which the modern word "gospel" derives) and appears at the start of the *Gospel According to Mark*: Ἀρχὴ τοῦ εὐαγγελίου Ἰησοῦ Χριστοῦ υἱοῦ τοῦ Θεοῦ ("The beginning of the 'good news' of Jesus Christ, the Son of God"). The "good news" of Christ is the salvation of humanity achieved by the coming of the Son of God on earth, his death and resurrection. This also explains the narrative character of these writings: they are texts aimed not only at transmitting a particular doctrine, but above all at telling of the achievement of divine incarnation in the history of humanity, via the historical event of the life and ministry of Jesus of Nazareth.

Yet this does not mean that the *Gospels* aim to be a strict chronicle of the events of the life of Jesus, i.e. works that meet precise criteria for historiographical research and reconstruction. Even where the same materials are used or even the same episodes narrated, in each *Gospel* the material is organised in a different form, in such a way as to match the overall design devised by the author, without the intent to reconstruct the real, exact sequence of events. Every one of these writings therefore presupposes some theological reflection by the authors, who evidently accorded greater significance to the organisation of the material concerning the preaching of Christ than to the reconstruction of the actual sequence of individual episodes. The different perspective in which the individual evangelists present the same events also justifies the fact that multiple *Gospels* were accepted into the canon. It should also be noted that the authors alternate narrative sections and speeches, creating what is now considered to be a genuinely new literary genre.

The first three *Gospels* (those of Matthew, Mark and Luke) are called the synoptic *Gospels*, since their content is largely in agreement, to the point that their text can be presented in parallel in three columns, i.e. in a synopsis. In the course of the centuries numerous theories have been advanced to explain these similarities, which it would be simplistic to explain as due merely to the fact that the three works concern the same topic or are based on similar oral testimonies. Already Saint Augustine in the fourth century assumed that the *Gospel of Matthew*, at that time considered to be the earliest, had been abridged by Mark, and then later reworked, along with that of Mark, by Luke, i.e. Augustine hypothesised a use of the earlier texts by the evangelists who wrote later. This thesis had a long history and from the second half of the eighteenth century solutions were proposed based on different chronological sequences. In the same period the hypothesis arose of a lost shared source of the three synoptic *Gospels*, known as the *protevangelion*, which would have been written in Aramaic. A different theory again, called the "theory of the *diēgēseis*," presupposes that in a first phase some short, distinct narratives (in Greek *diēgēseis*) had been composed, which were subsequently combined and reworked by the evangelists into the form of the current texts. Finally, others have considered that oral tradition could have stabilised at an early stage and was later fixed in written form by the evangelists.

Of particular importance is the "theory of the two sources," which combines and develops the previous theories: Matthew and Luke would have used the text of Mark, which is regarded as the earliest, with the addition of a second source that is now lost (called "Q" by scholars, from the German *Quelle*, "source"), which would have consisted of a collection of *logia* (speeches and sayings) of Jesus. This general theory, of which different variants have been proposed, is today widely considered to be the most convincing, above all as a result of in-depth studies on the form and structure of the synoptic *Gospels*, which have aimed to highlight traces indicating the use of pre-existing material.

Despite the strong similarities in content and structure, the fundamental fact remains that in each of the synoptic *Gospels* the material is presented in a different form. The study of these differences, or of the editorial work done by each author, allows us to elucidate the particular aims of each evangelist and the interests of the communities to whom each text was addressed or in which it was formed.

2.4.1 The *Gospel of Matthew*

The first in the canonical order is the *Gospel according to Matthew*. This is the one that makes the most effort to stress the link between the teaching of Jesus and the *Old Testament*. A very large number of *Old Testament* quotations are introduced to this end. The author is thus clearly a Christian of Jewish origin addressing a Judaeo-

Christian community, for which continuity of the teaching of Jesus with the *Old Testament* must have had a fundamental importance. A confirmation of the origin of the author lies in the fact that he does not find it necessary to explain Jewish customs or Aramaic terms. The date of this and the other *Gospels* is quite difficult to determine. The theories range from a date before A.D. 70 (destruction of the Temple of Jerusalem) and 90. The text does not give the name of the author, which tradition identifies with the publican Matthew whose conversion is narrated in 19, 9. However, this identification is hardly verifiable and does not fit well with the widely accepted theory that the author made use of the *Gospel of Mark*: the identification would imply the unacceptable scenario that an eyewitness (Matthew) used the narrative of a disciple (Mark) who had not personally known Jesus. An ancient testimony speaks of the existence of a *Gospel of Matthew* in Aramaic, for which reason it has been thought that the Greek text that survives today is a translation of the Aramaic original. At present it is believed that there were indeed some writings in Aramaic that lie behind the text of Matthew and which were used as sources. However, the formal characteristics of the Greek text make it hard to suppose that it is a work of simple translation and lead us rather to think of it as a profound reworking of this original material.

The *Gospel of Matthew* has a more elaborate structure than the other synoptic *Gospels*. The episodes are carefully grouped by thematic nuclei that hinge on speeches and statements of Christ. The syntax is based on symmetrical structures and parallelisms, in which a Semitic influence seems to be noticeable.

2.4.2 The *Gospel of Mark*

The second *Gospel* is attributed by tradition to a certain Mark who is said not to have been one of the apostles but rather a witness to the preaching of Peter. In fact, it is hard to suppose that this text could have been used by Matthew and Luke, as seems to have happened, if its testimony had not enjoyed a certain authority due to the fact of being based on the preaching of an apostle. If Mark is then to be identified with the "John called Mark" spoken of in the *Acts of the Apostles*, his work would be linked to the ministry of Paul, with whom there do in fact seem to be affinities in thought. In 14, 51–52, in the middle of the account of the Passion, there is a reference to a mysterious young man who followed Jesus just after he had been arrested and who managed to escape capture, leaving in the soldiers' hands the linen cloth that he had been wearing. This detail, which is entirely redundant in the overall sense of the story, has led some to believe, even already in antiquity, that behind this youth is concealed the evangelist himself, who would thus have been smuggled into the narrative. In that case, we would need to suppose that the author of the *Gospel* had personally known at least some of the events narrated.

For this *Gospel*, which seems to be the earliest, various dates have been proposed. Those who see in it references to the Neronian persecution suppose a date around 63; others see possible allusions to the destruction of the Temple in 70 and for that reason prefer a date after that year. Recently, on the basis of a papyrus fragment found in a cave at Qumrân in the region of the Dead Sea (on the Dead Sea Scrolls cf. *The Hellenistic Age* IX 1.3), a date before 50 has even been proposed; but nothing prevents us from supposing that in reality the papyrus, which anyway preserves a section of text limited to a few letters, restores a fragment belonging to a tradition earlier than Mark and used by him (the attribution of text to *The Gospel of Mark* is not certain anyway). The abundant use of expressions inspired by Aramaic, the tendency to parataxis and the importance given to Judaea lead us to suppose an author of Judaean origin. However, the fact that the Aramaic expressions and references to local customs are always accompanied by explanations confirms that the text was written for a community of gentiles, i.e. converts to Christianity of non-Jewish origin. The presence in the language of the text of Latinisms (for example σπεκουλάτωρ, i.e. *speculator*, in 6, 27) suggests that it was addressed to a Latin-speaking community. Indeed, in accord with its possible links to Paul, some have hypothesised that it was intended for the Christian community in Rome itself.

Compared to the other *Gospels*, that of Mark is shorter and has a simpler, barer narrative. However, beneath the apparent simplicity we can recognise a clear compositional design that organises the episodes according to a geographical criterion, presenting the preaching of Jesus as a journey that, through various stages, concludes at Jerusalem. The narrative opens with the preaching of John the Baptist, without references to the infancy of Jesus, and from the start the author's interest is directed towards demonstrating that Jesus is the Messiah and is Son of God. In some of the manuscripts the narrative ends abruptly with the flight of the women from the tomb of Jesus, which had remained empty after the resurrection, but in another part of the tradition the text is completed by a brief recounting of the appearances of the risen Christ (of which there are three different versions of different length), which is generally considered to be a later addition, though it was known already to Justin and Irenaeus of Lyons.

2.4.3 The *Gospel of Luke* and *Acts of the Apostles*

The *Gospel of Luke* presents some traits that are more canonical and, so to speak, classical. In a contrast to the other *Gospels*, the author prefaces the text with a prologue in the first person, in which he dedicates the work to a certain Theophilus and names the sources he has used, which were earlier writings and the accounts of eyewitnesses, in particular the Apostles.

In this case too, the author's name is transmitted only by tradition. The attempt to identify this Luke with a doctor of that name cited in the letters of Paul is today generally rejected, despite the fact that the evangelist's thought reveals links to that of Paul. In some sections of the *Acts of the Apostles* (which are attributed, as we shall see, to the same Luke and likewise dedicated to Theophilus) the first person plural is used in accounts of the missionary voyages of Paul. This could mean that the author was a companion of Paul, but it could also be due simply to the word-for-word adoption of sections of a travel diary written by a companion of Paul, who need not be identified with the author of the *Gospel*.

Luke, if that is indeed the author's name, is an educated person who uses a language that is much more classicising than the other synoptic authors, although he does not avoid some Semitisms, above all in the sections in which the words of Jesus are reported. The prologue reveals the classical culture and stylistic care of the author. What emerges above all is a desire for clarity and order, attested by the introductions to individual parts of the text and by the phrases commenting at the end of some sections. There is little interest in a strictly Judaising tradition, whereas much attention is given to expressions that stress the refusal by some Jews to acknowledge Jesus as Messiah and the consequent opening up of Christianity to gentiles. His work was hence clearly conceived for a community of Christians of pagan origin.

The same Luke who was author of the third *Gospel* also composed the *Acts of the Apostles* (Πράξεις ἀποστόλων), these too dedicated to Theophilus. In fact, as is made explicit in the prologue, from the point of view of content *Acts* is the natural continuation of the account in the *Gospel*. The topic is the formation and organisation of the first communities after the death and resurrection of Jesus, following the descent of the Holy Spirit at Pentecost and the spreading of the "good news" from Jerusalem to Rome by means of the preaching of Peter and Paul. The point of view of the account is thus aimed not just at providing a complete picture of the Church from its origins. Rather, it aims to present the action of the Spirit in the formation of the early communities and the spreading of the word to Rome, without giving a precise picture of the actions of the individual apostles, as one might have assumed from the title. The choice of Peter and Paul has the further aim, by reconciling the positions of these two authoritative figures, of representing how the opposition was overcome between those who saw Christianity more as a continuation of Judaism and its universal character.

2.4.4 The *Gospel of John*

The *Gospel* attributed to John, or "the Fourth *Gospel*," presents a different structure from that of the synoptic *Gospels*. First of all, the ministry of Jesus is spread over three years, rather than a single year as in the synoptic *Gospels*. Then, some episodes are narrated that are absent from the synoptics, while others are omitted that are of special importance in the latter (such as the institution of the Eucharist at the Last Supper, which nonetheless seems to be taken for granted in some imagery used in the text). The fundamental difference lies in the complex theological elaboration with which the material is presented by the author, who is revealed as familiar with the subtelties of rabbinic speculation and of some concepts of pagan philosophy. These characteristics have earned the text the title of "the theological Gospel."

As we can see from the use in some passages of the first person plural, the author presents himself as an eyewitness to the events, but the text of the *Gospel* does not suggest an identification with the apostle John. The mention on several occasions of a disciple described as the disciple "whom Jesus loved," without specifying his name, has led some to suppose that we should see in him the author himself, but the interpretation of this figure is still debated. The final chapter, which in fact has the air of an addition, seems to have been composed at a later stage by another author. In this last chapter it is stated that word has spread that the anonymous beloved disciple would never die; this claim is then said to be incorrect, a sign that at the time when this chapter was written he must have been dead.

John's Gospel is considered to be the latest, but its speculative character makes it even more difficult to suggest a date in this case. The traditional identification of the author with the apostle John would require an early date, but at the start of the nineteenth century it was thought that the theological elaboration of the text was the result of more extended reflection and dated to the mid-second century. On the basis of the differing datings, the interpretations of the work, too, vary to some extent: it remains an entirely open question what relation it may have had with Gnostic currents (on Gnosticism cf. *The Roman Imperial Period* XIII 1.5.2) or with the spirituality of some Jewish sects. Yet a papyrus fragment dated to 110–130 seems to bolster the thesis of an earlier date, which is now generally fixed around the year 100. Some sections seem to attest a knowledge of the synoptic *Gospels* and it has been noted that sometimes it seems almost to be assumed that readers have a knowledge of the information contained in them. Others prefer to suppose that the author of the *Fourth Gospel* simply used the same material employed by the authors of the synoptic *Gospels* but not those *Gospels* themselves. From some incongruent elements in the structure it has been supposed that the text has come down to us in a version that is not definitive. A theory has also been proposed that, based on the characteristics of the work, assumes the use by the evangelist of three sources: a collection of miracles, a collection of revelation speeches and a narrative of the events concerning the Passion. However, the problem of its composition remains quite controversial.

The work opens with the celebrated hymn to the divine *Logos* that shineth in darkness (some suppose that here a pre-existing hymn has been reworked), which introduces the core of John's message: the incarnation of the divine Word, distinct from the Father, but indissolubly linked to him and in perfect harmony with him. This *Logos*, pre-existent prior to the creation and endowed with all the prerogatives of the Father, is identified with the incarnated Christ and his work is perpetuated by the subsequent action of the Spirit. John's eschatology is consequently an eschatology that has been realised, i.e. without looking to the second coming of Christ at the end of days.

2.5 The *Letters* of John

Within the *New Testament* we find other writings transmitted under the name of John, namely three of the catholic epistles and the *Apocalypse*.

The second and third epistles contain little more than brief exhortations and greetings, but the first is characterised by a long exhortation in which the epistolary character is less obvious. Whoever wrote them presents himself simply as "the elder": he does not make his own name explicit, but despite this the three epistles seem to belong to the same author and to reflect the situation of the same community of addressees. Some scholars are inclined to accept that the author of these letters is also the author of the *Fourth Gospel*, or at least to consider them the work of an author very close to him in theological point of view. However, opinions on this differ.

The letters are addressed to a community in deep crisis due to "false prophets" who claim to be able to know and see God and to be free from sin even while rejecting the reality of the incarnation. The author does not engage in polemic with these figures, but directly addresses the faithful at risk of submitting to their influence, with a firm and impassioned exhortation, reminding them, above all in the first letter, of the criteria on the basis of which communion between the faithful and God–Love is realised.

2.6 The *Apocalypse*

It would be hard, however, to maintain that the author of the *Fourth Gospel* is identical to that of the *Revelation or Apocalypse* (Ἀποκάλυψις). The latter presents himself by the name of John and claims to be a prophet, but he never states that he was one of the twelve apostles. The language that he uses, packed with Semitisms, is sharply different from that of the author of the *Fourth Gospel* and the differences are such that they cannot simply be ascribed to the different literary genres of the two works. While some of the imagery used in this text seems to have a connection to expressions present in the *Fourth Gospel*, the content of the two texts seems to diverge on many points. References to the persecution of the Christians has led to a preference for a date a little after the Neronian persecution (65–70), or towards the end of the reign of Domitian (91–96), but it has also been proposed that the current text includes sections from different periods.

The genre of apocalypse (a term that means "unveiling" or "revelation," from which the alternative English title *Revelation* derives) was a genuine genre of Jewish literature. The apocalyptic writings illustrated revelations received by the author through visions, which were often full of complex symbols and allegories (the higher reality that was revealed, in order to be expressible, required in itself a language of this kind), in general with an eschatological background. The vision is more than a simple contemplation of celestial realities and is directed towards the realisation in history of the divine plan, for which the visions were a preparation.

The interpretation of John's *Apocalypse* is faced with the difficult problem of the precise meaning of the complex symbols present in it. Some of the images, which are transparent enough even for modern readers, allow us to identify clearly, for example, the violent anti-Roman polemic that pervades the text. However, many aspects of the content remain obscure.

> John, on the island of Patmos, has a vision in which he is invited to write "to the seven churches which are in Asia," acknowledging the merits of each, but also firmly reproaching the communities whose ardour was ebbing. There follows a vision of the heavenly throne surrounded by complex imagery of prophetic inspiration. "He that sat on the throne" has in his hand a scroll sealed by seven seals. The breaking of the seals by the Lamb opens the way to a further complex series of symbols: at the breaking of the first six seals, four horses each of a different colour advance with their riders bearing calamities; there follows the vision of two distinct multitudes of the elect preserved from these scourges. At the breaking of the seventh seal "there was silence in heaven about the space of half an hour." At this point seven trumpets are assigned to seven angels: at the sound of the first six we have visions of calamities that strike the Earth. There follow two visions that turn on an angel and a sealed little book and on two "witnesses." At the sounding of the seventh trumpet the heavenly temple is opened. At this point we find a vision of a woman giving birth attacked by a dragon, then of a beast with ten horns and seven heads that comes from the sea and of a beast with two horns that comes from the land, which seduce the inhabitants of the Earth. This vision is counterpointed by that of the Lamb and of those who are with it. Then there is the vision of seven angels and seven cups bearing seven scourges. Here is introduced the vision of the "great whore," called "Babylon the Great," and her defeat is announced. We then have the description of two distinct battles between the divine and the infernal powers, divided by the reign of a thousand years of Christ and those who were faithful to him. The work closes, after the final victory and the judgement on the nations, with the vision of the New Jerusalem, which descends from heaven resplendent, "having the glory of God."

The visions clearly indicate various phases of sacred history, with the struggle of the divine powers against the demoniac powers. The fulcrum of this history is the figure of the Lamb, the symbol of Christ as sacrificial victim. However, we are still far from achieving a unanimously accepted deciphering of all the images in detail. In general, further, it is debated to what extent such visions are a presentation of the battle that will occur at the end of time and to what extent, to the contrary, they refer to an eschatology that has already been realised, as a figuration in prophetic language of the salvation already achieved by the death and resurrection of Christ. The assumption of one or the other of these two perspectives alters any reading of the work considerably.

2.7 The *Letters* of James, Peter and Jude

To complete the writings of the New Testament canon, still to be considered are the letters of James, Peter and Jude.

The *Letter* of James, which entered the canon only at a very late stage, is a work by a strongly Judaising Christian. It presents a series of moral norms in line with the traditional teaching of the *Old Testament* and is the only surviving text in the canon to attest an interpretation of Christianity opposed to that of Paul. The epistle is directed to the "twelve tribes that are in the diaspora" (a fairly vague expression) and in the initial greeting the author says that he is called James. The ancients identified him with the apostle James the Great, but there are no indications that would prove this identification. The notable insistence on the necessity of works to make faith effective leads one to assume it is a polemic against an extremist position of Pauline thought. From this a general dating later than the epistles of Paul has been deduced, but we cannot say much more than that.

The first *Letter* of Peter, on the other hand, enjoyed an early success, but it is quite difficult to find proof of the attribution and the learned author seems to have little in common with the image of the fisherman Peter that is transmitted by the *Gospels*. The epistle is generically addressed to the faithful of five churches of Asia Minor, which are said to be "in the diaspora" (but the expression could have a figurative sense). The author states that he is in Babylon, which is probably an allusion to Rome, the New Babylon. The epistle alternates between fervid exhortations of a moral character and doctrinal sections, with particular attention to the problem of suffering, which even the faithful must undergo in this life.

The *Letter* of Jude is a short text full of obscure allusions. The author presents himself as Jude the brother of James (not to be confused with the apostle Judas who betrayed Jesus), who is mentioned in the *Gospels of Mark* and *of Matthew*. He wanted to warn his addressees against mysterious "false doctors," in whom some wish to see the representatives of a Gnostic movement (cf. *The Roman Imperial Period* XIII 1.5.2), declaring that a judgement condemning them has already been issued. The author, who is clearly of Jewish-Christian origin, picks up the tones and expressions of Jewish apocalyptic. There are references to some *Old Testament* texts, which after A.D. 90 were officially excluded from the Jewish canon as apocrypha; this suggests for this text a date earlier than that.

The *Letter* of Jude is picked up and reworked in the *Second Letter* of Peter, in which, however, the quotations from the apocryphal books of the *Old Testament* do not appear. For this text a quite late date has been proposed, after 90 and perhaps even close to 150. Interesting in this epistle is the reference to the delay of the *parousia* (παρουσία, "advent"): the Christians of the first generations had in fact been awaiting the imminent Second Coming of Christ and the end of days. The aim of the letter is to reassure the disconcerted faithful about the delay of these expected events.

VII Philosophical and Scientific Literature

1 Philosophical literature

1.1 General characteristics of philosophical thought

1.1.1 Under the sign of continuity

In our treatment of the philosophical output of the Hellenistic Age, we noted how relatively little of it has survived. In a surprising contrast to this grave loss, a comparatively rich amount has been preserved of the philosophy of the Imperial Period. As regards speculation and the elaboration of thought, on the other hand, this period lacks real originality and continues to plough the furrow of the doctrines that arose in the classical and Hellenistic Ages, without producing genuinely new currents of thought. The two great schools that maintained the legacy of Plato and Aristotle, the Academy and the Peripatos, continued their life. In parallel, important developments occurred also in the other schools of thought that arose in the classical and Hellenistic Ages, such as Cynicism, Scepticism, Stoicism and Epicureanism. Among these, it is Stoicism that found the greatest acceptance, at least in the first two centuries of the empire, outshining the other schools and enjoying a huge diffusion that was almost undifferentiated across all social classes. It was a Stoic education that was received by the philosopher-emperor Marcus Aurelius, who took a concrete step to promote the preservation of the ancient philosophical heritage in A.D. 176 by establishing four separate professorial chairs intended for the study and teaching of the Platonic, Aristotelian, Stoic and Epicurean doctrines respectively.

In some cases, under the influence of eastern religiosity and eclectic and syncretistic tendencies, speculative philosophy pushed the assumptions of older, now renewed doctrines to reach conclusions that had the character of philosophical religion and even mysticism. This is the case above all with Neopythagoreanism and Neoplatonism. The latter, in particular, constituted the true novelty of philosophical thought of the Imperial Period and reached the highpoint of its development in the third century. After starting out in open contrast to Christian doctrine, in its later developments from the fifth century onward Neoplatonism ultimately came to be profoundly influenced by Christianity and to influence it in turn.

A general tendency should be underlined in philosophy in the context of the Graeco-Roman world of this period, which continued an orientation that has already been highlighted for the Hellenistic Age. Leaving aside the specific doctrinal model, in every school or tendency a primacy of ethical goals emerged in a marked way and the practice of philosophy took on the appearance of a guide and therapy for the soul, which was presented as capable of directing and improving human conduct in the face of life's challenges. What took prime position was hence an exhortatory or

https://doi.org/10.1515/9783110426328-036

consolatory character of thought and of philosophical reflection (it is not by chance that, among other things, the genre of *consolationes* was developed).

Continuity with the thought of previous centuries was achieved both in the form of speculative procedures and in the rediscovery of the authentic content of doctrines of the older founders and schools. This approach often led to the splintering of doctrines into separate currents or the development of syncretistic forms. From this point of view the figure of Philo of Alexandria is emblematic, a Jewish theologian and philosopher (whom we discussed in the chapter on Jewish-Christian literature; cf. *The Roman Imperial Period* VI 1.1.3), who made an important and productive effort to reconcile Greek and Jewish thought in an organic syncretism, opening the way for the later phases of fusion between classical paganism and Christianity. Philosophical literature gradually developed other outputs typical of the period, such as doxographical collections and the imposing commentaries on the works of the founders. In the course of the Imperial Period this landscape of exegetical and reconstructive production expanded, being enlivened and stimulated by a perceived rivalry between the various schools and not without expressions of a superficial philosophical dilettantism, the fruit above all of unfounded intellectual pretentions (we may read a parody of this in the *Hermotimus* of Lucian; cf. *The Roman Imperial Period* VIII 2.3.1).

1.1.2 Philosophy, rhetoric and literature

A serious lack of true philosophical originality was thus counterpointed by a more widespread presence in society of the culture and language of philosophy. Many aspects of intellectual life came to be pervaded by philosophical themes, above all in the vast sphere of rhetoric. Philosophy became less professional and emerged from its restricted circles, addressing itself to a broader public in new literary forms. Philosophy and rhetoric often went hand in hand, in the person of the philosopher-rhetors who delivered public lectures and exhibitions and diffused their teaching in various ways (cf. *The Roman Imperial Period* II 1 and VIII 1.1.2).

Characteristic figures of the centuries of the empire were those who worked between philosophy and oratory, in the sense that their works could be understood as contributions to either of these spheres. This is the case with intellectuals and writers (whom we shall discuss or have discussed in various chapters) such as Plutarch, Dio of Prusa, Favorinus, Aelius Aristides and Lucian as well as Synesius and the emperor Julian (cf. *The Roman Imperial Period* XI 7 and 5). Plutarch was moved by a foundational Platonism, but one that was able to accept other influences from the philosophical tradition, though it led him into polemics above all with the theological conceptions of Stoicism and Epicureanism. In Dio the elements of Cynic-Stoic diatribe (in which Socrates too played a role, alongside the main model, Diogenes) were used above all in the function of public discourse. Lucian appears essentially as an eclectic who, in the rationalistic and satirical image that he presents of his times, directs sarcasm also against the petulance and pettiness of contemporary philosophers. Another follower of Platonism, though not without eclectic elements, is Maximus of Tyre (late second century), he too a rhetor and sophist, from whom we have around forty orations.

1.2 The Academy and the Peripatos

1.2.1 The Academy: Middle Platonism

The label "Middle Platonism" defines the developments of the Platonic Academy in the period from the first century B.C. (i.e. after Antiochus of Ascalon: cf. *The Hellenistic Age* V 2.3) to the start of the third century A.D. (the period of Plotinus, the greatest exponent of Neoplatonism). The importance of this period of activity by the school lies predominantly in the intense and decisive work commenting upon the Platonic text and interpreting Platonic thought, which was a determining moment in the formation of later Neoplatonic thought. The speculative sphere that attracted most of the work of deeper conceptual elaboration was metaphysics, with particular interest above all in the theological dimension of Platonic investigation, approached in a religious key. The metaphysical and theological cast of this work was a reaction against the rigorous dogmatism of the late Hellenistic Academy and anticipated substantial aspects of Neoplatonism. It was a strong renewal of Plato's dualism, which led to polemics against Epicureanism and Stoicism.

Beyond this, we should acknowledge that we cannot form a well-founded and documented image of Middle Platonism on a strictly philosophical plane. We could fastidiously list the names of at least five or six philosophers in a strict sense, only then to say that their works are lost and we cannot form a valid picture of their thought. The category of eclecticism, for this period of the Academy, has been used in a misleading way, prompted above all by the fact that we lack the works of the philosophers and tend to pass judgments based on authors who are quite distinctive individuals and are each eclectic in their own way.

We have already spoken of the work of Plutarch, but we note here that the *Moralia* include numerous short philosophical works with a Platonic-Stoic approach and hermeneutic character (we cite *On the Generation of the Soul in the Timaeus* and the *Platonic Questions*), while other writings typically have a religious orientation (Plutarch had a special devotion to Apollo of Delphi). From the Latin writer Apuleius, author of the novel *The Metamorphoses*, we have the first two books of the work *On Plato and His Doctrine*, on the life and teaching of the master. We may recall, finally, the Διδασκαλικός or Εἰσαγωγή, i.e. an *Introduction* to Platonic thought, attributed to a certain Alcinous.

1.2.2 The Peripatetic school

The determining event in the history of Aristotelianism in the Imperial Period is naturally the publication of the writings of Aristotle from his own private library by Andronicus of Rhodes in the second half of the first century B.C. The diffusion of the esoteric works renewed interest in the Peripatos and gave a notable spur to studies of the founder's thought (cf. *The Classical Age* XIII 3.5).

The history of Aristotelianism in the Imperial Era is substantially a history of exegetes and commentators, aiming to explain and deepen the master's theories, which continued almost without interruption from the early Empire to the Late Antique Period and, through the extremely important mediation of Arab culture, in which quite important and authoritative translations and commentaries flourished, reached the Byzantine and Latin Middle Ages. Among the Greek commentators of the Imperial Period we may recall at least Alexander of Aphrodisias, who lived in the second to third century, without listing the other names in this rich literature, whose preserved works include many of great significance. However, we note here Simplicius (sixth century), who taught at Athens at least up to A.D. 529, when Justinian closed the city's philosophical schools, and who attempted a reconciliation between some Aristotelian and Neoplatonic doctrines. His Aristotelian commentaries are an important source of information on the Presocratics.

1.3 Other philosophical schools

1.3.1 Scepticism

Even though in the Roman world an adherence to Stoicism, of differing degrees of depth and commitment, was predominant, other traditional philosophical schools that had arisen in the Classical and Hellenistic eras also continued to accept adepts and to undergo developments of varied importance and significance. In reaction against the dogmatism professed in the Platonic Academy by Philon of Larissa and Antiochus of Ascalon, in the second half of the first century B.C. the Sceptic Aenesidemus of Cnossus renewed traditional critiques based on an inquiring and doubting attitude (*skepsis*) and reaffirmed the need for suspension (*epochē*) of judgement in the sphere of knowledge.

An important exponent of Sceptic doctrine was Sextus Empiricus, a philosopher and doctor who lived in the second to third century. His second name is to be explained by his membership of the Empiricist school of medicine, which based its approach on therapeutic practice, in critical opposition to the approach of the Dogmatist medics (cf. *The Hellenistic Age* VI 2.1). Sextus wrote three books of *Outlines of Pyrrhonism* (Πυρρώνειοι ὑποτυπώσεις), so called from the name of the founder of Scepticism, Pyrrhon of Elis. However, the exposition of the Sceptic doctrines is the result of much later reworking and is heir to a tradition that by now no longer knew much about Pyrrhon himself. Sextus was also the author of two polemical writings,

Against the Professors (Πρὸς τοὺς μαθηματικούς) and *Against the Dogmatists* (Πρὸς τοὺς δογματικούς), respectively books I–VI and VII–XI of a single work in eleven books, in which he refuted the scientific claims of the various disciplines and the claims to philosophical validity in the fields of logic, physics and ethics, to arrive at suspension of judgement as the only prudent possibility.

1.3.2 Cynicism
Attention is merited by the developments in Cynicism that are present in the Graeco-Roman philosophical landscape from the first century onwards with fairly different approaches and at different levels. On the one hand, we can see the influence of Cynic-Stoic thought on a cultivated and refined rhetor such as Dio of Prusa; on the other, we can record expressions that are more typically and radically linked to the non-conformist and contrarian thought and practice of the Cynic tradition, such as the preaching by the masses of so-called "popular Cynics." The nature of these figures is rather hazy, hovering between the philosopher and the parasitical charlatan. Portrayed in the sources as rough and vulgar people, they found support among the lower social classes, whose discontents and attempts at revolt they voiced. Sometimes seen as similar to the Christians, the Cynics could, depending on the point of view, take on the appearance of defenders of the poor and oppressed popular classes or of dubious political agitators and plotters. Hostile distrust of philosophical conceptions of this type should be seen as the reason for the episode of banishing philosophers from Rome by the emperor Vespasian in A.D. 74. At the heart of the Cynic phenomenon in the Imperial Period we find the citing of the ancient paradigmatic figures Diogenes and Antisthenes, the acceptance of elements of Stoic thought and the adoption of openly political interests.

1.3.3 Stoicism
During the late Hellenistic Age (second to first century B.C.), thinkers such as Panaetius and Posidonius had reinterpreted the ideas of the original Stoic founders in the light of a less rigorous spirit and a greater attention to religious phenomena, passing on the legacy of the school (in this softened and enriched form) to the world of the Roman social and intellectual elites. In the first two centuries of the empire, Stoic philosophy had a wide resonance at Rome, being accepted at various levels of the social scale. This final ancient phase of Stoicism, which takes the name of the "New Stoa," accentuated the ethical component of the traditional doctrine, to the point that the philosopher increasingly assumes the appearance of a teacher of moral virtue and guide to practical life and his teaching takes the form of therapy or medicine for the soul. The paradigmatic figure of this consciously constructive role of the sage is the Latin philosopher Lucius Annaeus Seneca (ca. A.D. 4–65) who, as tutor and then counsellor of Nero (at least until, in 59, he lost the emperor's favour), had hoped to realise the plan of a political power enlightened by philosophy and the

pursuit of the good. Exponents of this phase of Stoicism who wrote in Greek are Epictetus and the philosopher-emperor Marcus Aurelius.

Epictetus. Born around A.D. 55, Epictetus of Hierapolis, in Phrygia, was at Rome a slave of Epaphroditus, an influential freedman of Nero. His servile status did not prevent him attending the lectures of the Stoic Musonius Rufus. After gaining his freedom, he devoted himself directly to philosophical teaching, until in 89, he was forced to leave Rome when Domitian decreed the expulsion of philosophers. Epictetus then transferred his school to Epirus, to Nicopolis, where his students included the historian Arrian of Nicomedia and where he died around 135. We owe to Arrian (cf. *The Roman Imperial Period* III 1.3.2) the preservation of a large part of Epictetus' thought, collected in two works based on notes taken during the lectures: four books of *Discourses* and the *Manual* (*Encheiridion*), which attest to the familiar, everyday character of this philosopher, who liked to entrust his teaching to conversations that were neither systematic nor written down. His rigorous adherence to the ethics of the Early Stoa (rejecting the compromises considered by the Middle Stoa) did not exclude influences from other schools of thought, primarily the Cynics (to which the Greek title *Diatribai*, translated as *Discourses*, alludes). It seems central to his thought, and characteristic of his status as slave and then freedman, that he reflected on freedom, which was understood as a conscious and serene acceptance of necessary reality and as independent of our will.

Marcus Aurelius. An interesting and original Stoic figure was the emperor Marcus Aurelius Antoninus, born at Rome in 121. After training in rhetorical studies under the guidance of Fronto and Herodes Atticus, he turned to philosophy and embraced Stoicism. Adopted by the emperor Antoninus Pius, whom he succeeded in 161, he was long embroiled in wars on the eastern and northern borders of the empire. He died in 180, in the course of a military campaign near Vindobona (Vienna). In his spare time from political and military life, he composed in Greek a work in twelve books *Meditations* (Τὰ εἰς ἑαυτόν, literally "to himself"), containing brief, incisive reflections in which, however, the abbreviated style is the result of careful rhetorical choice. The Stoicism of Marcus Aurelius is pervaded by a vein of very personal inner trouble, which arises from an awareness of the transience of existence and a perception of the vanity of human action. This position does not cohere with the doctrinal presuppositions of the school (namely the goodness of nature and faith in divine providence) and it anticipates the sense of unease and existential disquiet that would characterise the following century. This singular figure of philosopher-emperor is more generally distinguished by the search for an interior dialogue, translated into the personal, "diary" form of the work, in a period in which philosophy tended rather to be oriented towards opening up outwards.

1.3.4 Epicureanism

The pursuit of Epicureanism, without, it seems, any conceptual developments that moved beyond the original teaching of Epicurus, is only barely attested in the Imperial Period. Yet precious information is offered by a long inscription erected in the second century by an enthusiastic follower of Epicurus, Diogenes of Oenoanda (in Lycia) in his city. The inscription contains extracts from Epicurean doctrine, quotations from select passages and letters. The persistence of interest in the doctrines of the Garden and the existence of followers of this school is also reflected in the establishment of a professorial chair of Epicurean philosophy (alongside others) at the wish of Marcus Aurelius and in the frequent polemical jabs against Epicureanism in the works of Christian authors.

1.3.5 Neopythagoreanism and mystical currents

The term Neopythagoreanism refers to the development of Pythagorean thought in the period from the mid-first century B.C. to the second century A.D. Pythagorean philosophy had won new success in the Hellenistic Age, when works were composed and attributed to Pythagoras, primarily on mathematical and symbolic topics. The best known is entitled *Golden Verses*, is of quite uncertain date and was probably reworked in the Imperial Period. The school underwent a decisive turn in a religious direction, though adopting elements of Platonism, through the work of Eudorus, who was active in Alexandria around the first century B.C. The figure of Pythagoras was reinterpreted as that of an outright wonderworker and the apocryphal writings attributed to him were read as expressing a religious message.

In the first century A.D. a prominent figure was Apollonius of Tyana in Cappadocia, author of a *Life of Pythagoras*. Apollonius' characterisation as a travelling magus or holy man and wonderworker with an ascetic lifestyle and his transposition into the dimension of legend owe a lot to the romanticised biography composed in the early third century by the Neosophist Flavius Philostratus (*Life of Apollonius of Tyana*: cf. *The Roman Imperial Period* VIII 1.2.8). A *Life of Pythagoras* was also written in the second century by Nicomachus of Gerasa in Arabia, while we owe to Numenius of Apamea in Syria, who was active in the second half of the second century, the definitive fusion of Neopythagoreanism with contemporary developments in Platonism. Numenius is often considered to be a kind of link between Middle Platonism and the subsequent Neoplatonic developments. Neopythagoreanism did not find much popularity and the imperial power often showed outright hostility to it, with official acts that took the form of real persecutions.

The tendency to accentuate the theological aspects, which led into practices belonging fully to mystery religion and into mystical approaches, found expression in other currents of thought that enjoyed wide popular diffusion and which were open to the influence of oriental religiosity. We may recall in first place the corpus of the *Hermetic Writings*, a collection of texts attributed to Hermes Trismegistos. Hermeticism was a mystical and ascetic doctrinal tradition in which Egypt came to be seen as the place of origin of ancient knowledge. Likewise halfway between philosophical thought and religion lies Orphism and the oracular literature of Egyptian and Chaldaean inspiration (*Sibylline, Delphic* and *Chaldaean Oracles*: on this whole literary production, cf. *The Roman Imperial Period* XII 3).

1.4 Neoplatonism

1.4.1 The twilight of Greek philosophy
The last philosophical movement to emerge from the roots of Hellenic civilisation and the most flourishing one in Late Antiquity was Neoplatonism, the mature fruit of the theological and religious tendencies of Middle Platonism and of the other manifestations of philosophy and religion of the early Imperial Period. In the course of the third century the Egyptian Greek Plotinus, starting from some intuitions of the Platonist Ammonius Saccas (teacher also of Origen of Alexandria and of the rhetor Cassius Longinus), achieved a synthesis of Platonic, Aristotelian and Stoic speculations, arriving at the construction of a complex and original philosophical system, in which religious elements also played a primary role. At the threshold of Late Antiquity, the prodigious career of Greek thought thus in a certain sense achieved the fulfilment of its experience, summarising and metabolising the immense heritage of contents and instruments for rational investigation, reread in the light of a religious demand that had by then spread deeply in contemporary society.

The style and language of these authors generally have in common a need for precision in expression and terminology that matched the rigour of the philosophical contents. The style becomes formal and elliptical in the dry systematic expositions. In general they wrote substantially according to Atticism, but softened by the *koinē*.

1.4.2 Ammonius Saccas
The founder of the movement is generally said to be Ammonius Saccas, a figure whose historical outline is not well defined and who is little known also as regards his thought. Tradition says that he was a native of Alexandria of humble origin (the surname "Saccas" seems to allude to the modest clothing that he wore) and that he abandoned Christianity for Platonic philosophy. In the manner of Socrates, he professed oral philosophical teaching, leaving no writings at all. The difficult task of reconstructing his thought thus has to work via indirect testimonies, above all the works of his disciple Plotinus, in which however it is almost impossible to distinguish what belongs to the teacher and what, to the contrary, is an original elaboration by the disciple and author. Ammonius Saccas was also the teacher of the Christian philosopher Origen of Alexandria (cf. *The Roman Imperial Period* XIII 1.6.3), of

his namesake Origen "the Pagan" (in whose thought, it seems, an approach on a Middle Platonist pattern persisted) and of the rhetor Cassius Longinus (cf. *The Roman Imperial Period* II 3.2). Ammonius died around 242.

1.4.3 Plotinus and the School of Rome

The teaching of Ammonius had a powerful and inspiring effect on Plotinus, his disciple from 232 onward and the true initiator of Neoplatonic thought. Our information about him derives above all from the biography written by his pupil Porphyry of Tyre, who succeeded him in the leadership of the school that he founded. For this reason, we have a good knowledge of the events of his life.

The biography of Plotinus falls entirely in the third century and gravitates between Egypt and Italy. He was born in the Egyptian city of Lycopolis around 205 and already in adulthood (aged almost 30) he turned to the study of philosophy, attending the lectures that Ammonius delivered at Alexandria. He did this for around a decade. Wishing to learn Persian customs and mentality, in 242 he enrolled in the Roman army and left on military campaign in the East in the following of the emperor Gordian III. He escaped from the disastrous fate of this venture (in which the emperor himself died) and in 244 returned to the West and settled at Rome, where he founded his philosophical school. His lectures were attended by senior members of the Roman senatorial class and by the emperor Gallienus himself, who gave him his protection. Suffering ill health and over 65 years of age, he retired to the villa of a friend at Minturnae in Campania, where he died around 270.

Initially Plotinus preferred oral teaching (following the example of his own teacher). He began to write only at an advanced age, intending his writings for internal circulation within the circle of his pupils (they are thus esoteric writings, which tend to lack formal ornament). We owe to the initiative of his pupil Porphyry the collection and stylistic elaboration of the tractates of the master, which were collected in the work entitled *Enneads*. The title refers to its structure, which consists of six groups each with nine texts, to form a total of 54 tractates. The material is arranged according to precise thematic criteria: *Enneads* I–III have as their topic man and the universe; *Enneads* IV and V concern the Soul and the Intellect; the final *Ennead* addresses the theme of the divine One.

Plotinus' philosophy is a continuous discourse on the metaphysics of Plato, from whom it takes its start in a systematic reworking that ultimately differs greatly from the point of departure. The fundamental Platonic concepts that inspire Neoplatonic reflection are, on the one hand, the opposition between reality and the world of ideas and between the soul and the human body, and on the other hand the ascent that the human soul accomplishes in order to raise itself to the contemplation of pure ideas. In the thought of Plotinus a central role is played by the conviction that God is absolutely unattainable by the human mind and that, hence, it is not possible to state anything positive about him, except that he is One. The universe is configured not as a voluntary creation (which would imply a change in God), but rather as an emanation of the One (in the manner of light that emanates from its source without this causing it to be impoverished), through the intermediate terms of the Intellect (understood as the singularised identity of that which thinks and that which is thought), the World Soul (which supervises at the same time the unity and multiplicity of the corporeal cosmos) and Matter (conceived as the substrate on which Being is impressed and hence, in itself, as a "non-Being"). Through these mediating terms, although distant and differentiated from the One and for that reason itself perishable and imperfect, the whole multiple reality comes to participate to a certain degree in Being. In man and in the whole universe, where there is a trace of the divine order, therefore there is a tendency towards a rejoining with the common principle constituted by God-One, in which all alterity and multiplicity, a sign of impurity and imperfection, is annulled, returning to be a pure and perfect identity.

This metaphysical vision is foundational to the ethical conception, since the material and corporeal world, multiple and differentiated fruit of the emanation of the One, is configured as distant from the highest Good, with which the One is identified, and in a certain way opposed to it, although it encloses in itself a trace of the divine. From this it follows that man can again pursue the good and happiness, from which he comes, by distancing himself from the multiplicity of the corporeal, which is heavy and imperfect, and by tending towards rejoining with the One. This occurs through a gradual path backward, which completes the circle drawn by the process of emanation: from the One to the multiple, from the multiple to the One. The path of ascent is divided by Plotinus into different stages or degrees, the first of which is the abandonment of the passions that make the human soul a slave to egoism, while the final one is the ecstatic vision of the One, which has the character – at its conclusion – of an experience of intuitive type and no longer a logical and rational one. However, we should take care not to assimilate Plotinus' thought too easily to a form of mysticism, underlining the spiritual detachment from reality to the point of a kind of ecstasy. There is undoubtedly in him a powerful religious sentiment, which is continually emphasised, but it proceeds via a rigorous exploitation of reason (*logos*) and the intellect (*nous*). In this last major exponent of Greek rationalism, the most vivid and profound religious needs are joined with the search for rational responses to the questions of philosophy.

The thought of Plotinus reveals his singular relation to Platonic doctrine also in the political sphere. While the purpose of a large part of Plato's research was to define the role of philosophy in society and to configure the mission of the sage in relation to active politics, for Plotinus, to the contrary, the speculative dimension ultimately appears as an alternative to the human collectivity itself. Mistakenly believing that he had the support of the emperor, he cherished the dream of founding a city of philosophers in Campania based on the ideal city outlined in Plato's *Laws* (Platonopolis was to be its name), an ivory tower for himself and his followers, separate and distant from the human community.

1.4.4 Porphyry

The disciple and successor of Plotinus at the head of the Neoplatonic school at Rome, Porphyry was born at Tyre in Syria around 234 and died in the imperial capital around 305. The sources attribute to him around 70 works on different fields and themes, from literature to religion to philosophy, but only 10 survive. Among the lost or fragmentary works we may note philosophical, rhetorical and erudite treatments of various kinds as well as commentaries on Homer (in particular the *Homeric Questions*, of which we have considerable remnants from various sources), Plato, Aristotle, Claudius Ptolemaeus and other authors. Only fragments remain also of the work *Against the Christians* in 15 books, an impassioned defence of pagan civilisation against the unceasing advance of Christianity.

Among the preserved works, those that deserve to be noted are in the first place two biographical writings, the *Life of Pythagoras* and *On the Life of Plotinus*, the second of which appears as a preface to the edition of the *Enneads* that was produced by Porphyry himself. The propagandistic aim of these biographies explains the idealised presentation of the two figures, who are encircled by a halo of quasi-divine religiosity and, in the case of Pythagoras, an aura of miracles and wonder-working.

We should also mention: the *Eisagōgē*, an introduction to Aristotelian logic, translations of which would go on to enjoy a lasting success into the Middle Ages and were copiously studied and commented upon; and a group of writings on themes from moral philosophy, namely *On the Return of the Soul* (also known as *De regressu animae*), *The Impulses of the Soul Towards the Intelligible* and *On Abstinence*, in four books. This last monograph is for us a precious testimony to ancient dietary concepts, since in it Porphyry comes to maintain the necessity of a vegetarian diet, starting from the criticism of blood sacrifices and of a meat-based diet and also drawing on precepts from Pythagorean doctrine.

His commentary on Ptolemaeus' *Harmonics* is an important source for knowledge of treatises of music theory that are otherwise lost. Porphyry brings out the debate on the quantitative or qualitative nature of sound and the reflections on the role of reason and sense perception as cognitive instruments of musical phenomena. Finally, much interest has been provoked by the monograph of Homeric criticism entitled *The Cave of the Nymphs*, which presents a commentary on *Odyssey* XIII 102–112 using the instruments of allegorical interpretation, an ancient exegetical method that continued to find great success, also in Christian circles. The Homeric description of the cave of the Naiad nymphs near the port of Ithaca is paraphrased and explained in metaphysical and cosmological terms, imbued with concepts belonging to Neoplatonic thought.

1.4.5 Iamblichus and theurgy

A decisive turn of Neoplatonism in a mystical and religious direction was brought about by Iamblichus, originally from Chalcis in Syria, who lived approximately from 250 to 325. A pupil of Porphyry, he founded his own school in Syria, perhaps at Apamea, where he conceived an original syncretistic marriage of Neoplatonic thought with Orphism and Neopythagoreanism, drawing also on religious doctrines of Chaldaean and Egyptian origin (a sphere of thought and spirituality attested by Orphic, oracular and Hermetic literature, on which cf. *The Roman Imperial Period* XII 2 and 3).

Iamblichus followed the example of Porphyry by composing philosophical commentaries on works of Plato and Aristotle, which are not preserved. His interest in oracular literature is attested by a work in 28 books, now lost, entitled *Chaldaean Theology*. As had been done already by the Neopythagoreans Apollonius and Nicomachus and his Neoplatonic teacher Porphyry, Iamblichus composed a *Life of Pythagoras*, which has been transmitted as the opening book of a ten-book work on Pythagorean doctrines that is partially preserved (Book II is a general introduction to philosophy known as the *Protrepticus*, Books III and IV treat mathematics and arithmetic). But the work that is most revealing of the figure of Iamblichus is the essay *On the Mysteries of Egypt* (a title established since Marsilio Ficino, often known simply as *De Mysteriis*), whose authenticity is doubted by some. The work offers an anti-rationalist and theurgical reading of Neoplatonic principles, maintaining the possibility of achieving contact with God by recourse to practices of magical and symbolic occultism and evocative occultism (θεουργία, "theurgy") modelled on the *Chaldaean Oracles*.

1.4.6 The School of Athens: the epigoni of Neoplatonism

In the fifth century, while the exponents of the now triumphant Christianity spoke from the prestigious sees of Alexandria and Antioch and while in the political and cultural landscape of the empire an ever more dominant role was taken by Constantinople, Neoplatonic thought found its seat of choice in Athens, the ancient cradle of Hellenic civilisation and philosophical culture, by now reduced to a marginal and peripheral role. Here Plutarch of Athens (who lived until roughly 430) founded a new Neoplatonic school, leadership of which passed in 431/2 to the Alexandrian Syrianus, author of works of philosophical, literary and rhetorical exegesis following the Orphic-Pythagorean line inaugurated by Iamblichus.

A student of Plutarch and Syrianus in the School of Athens was Proclus of Byzantium-Constantinople (410–485 ca.), who became head of the Academy, he too producing many philosophical commentaries; we note here the commentaries on Plato's *Timaeus*, *Parmenides* and *Republic*. He was also the author of various works of literary-critical, scientific and philosophical content, from which we note the monograph *Platonic Theology* and the systematic exposition of Neoplatonic theology entitled *Elements of Theology*. Here Proclus brought to completion Plotinus' conceptual elaboration, introducing the Henads (the term means "unities" and is found already in Plato) as intermediary entities between the One and the process of differentiation of the multiple. The Henads that emerge from the One are the principal gods, from whom descend a further complex hierarchy of beings. Proclus applied to the doctrine of emanation and return to the One a dialectical and circular structure in three phases: "immanence in itself," "procession from itself" and "reversion to itself" of the unique divine Being. Finally, from Proclus we have seven *Hymns* in hexameters, transmitted in the same collection of the Byzantine Era that has also preserved the *Homeric Hymns* and the *Hymns* of Callimachus. In these compositions Proclus sets out to achieve, in the ancient form of a religious hymn addressed to a pagan divinity, a syncretistic synthesis of traditional polytheism and the philosophical-religious spiritualism elaborated by Neoplatonic thought.

1.4.7 The School of Alexandria

In conclusion we may mention the philosophical school of Alexandria, which in reality does not exhibit an organic and formal structure like that of the Athenian school. Alexandria offers, rather, some significant figures among the thinkers and scholars of ancient philosophy.

Among these, the original figure of Hypatia stands out, a philosopher and scientist with many cultural interests who in 415 fell victim to the fanaticism of a group of Christians who murdered her. A disciple of Hypatia was Synesius of Cyrene, who died quite young in 413, a rhetor and philosopher who converted to Christianity (cf. *The Roman Imperial Period* XI 7, XII 2 and XIII 2.7.2). Here we limit ourselves to noting his *Hymns*, with a syncretistic character that reveals a singular and significant accord with the *Hymns* of Proclus.

Other Alexandrian Neoplatonists are Hierocles (fifth century) and Simplicius (sixth century), in whose works we can see a strong influence from Christian thought. This opened the doors to comparison and integration between the developments of late antique Neoplatonism and its old enemy, a prelude to the development of a Christian Platonism. It seems that Hierocles was a pupil of Plutarch of Athens. Photius preserves fragments of two of his works, a *Commentary on the Golden Verses of the Pythagoreans* and an essay *On Providence*. Simplicius, originally from Cilicia, at Alexandria attended the teaching of Ammonius, disciple of Proclus, and at Athens that of Damascius. He left the city in 529, when Justinian's decree closed the Neoplatonic school. A few years later, after returning to Athens, he composed some philosophical commentaries. What survives are those to the *Manual* of Epictetus and to the Aristotelian works *On the Heavens* and *On the Soul*, the *Physics* and the *Categories*.

2 Scientific literature

2.1 Scientific culture in the Imperial Period

In the course of the Imperial Period the scientific disciplines underwent important and fertile growth, matched by a rich literature expressly dedicated to them. During these centuries, the distance between science and developments in philosophical thought steadily reduced, above all in the role that came to be played in the philosophical sphere by the tools of mathematical research. Consequently, it is not always easy to distinguish a strictly "scientific" literature from the philosophical literature: the distinction risks becoming a modern imposition of a division that did not exist.

We have already recalled in relation to geography (cf. *The Roman Imperial Period* IV 4) the versatile and important figure of Claudius Ptolemaeus, who lived in the second century and whose activities in study and research touched on countless spheres of scientific thought, from astronomy and astrology to geography and applied geometry and from optics to music theory. His works take the character of overall systematisations of the knowledge acquired in various fields and were a point of reference for many centuries. He was distinguished and subsequently valued above all for his studies in astronomy, as well as in geography. In the Museum of Alexandria he must have found an atmosphere and instruments well suited to the collection of data useful in composing his major work, the great treatise on astronomy entitled Μαθηματικὴ σύνταξις ("systematic mathematical treatise"), in thirteen books, later known as Μεγίστη or Μεγάλη σύνταξις ("the greatest systematic treatise") or *Almagest* (from the Arabic version of Μεγίστη, *Megistē*). There Ptolemaeus worked out in every detail a complete geometrical model of the movements of the celestial bodies. His main results are compiled in the *Handy Tables*, a treatise composed exclusively in numerical tables.

Other works by Ptolemaeus are: the manual of astrology called *Tetrabiblos* (in four books), a treatise on optics (which survives only in a Latin translation from the Arabic) and one on music theory. As regards geography, Ptolemaeus compiled a *Table of Illustrious Cities*, which was in its turn included both in the *Handy Tables* and in the very large collection of geographical coordinates that forms the core of the eight-book *Geography* (Γεωγραφικὴ ὑφήγησις, i.e. "geographical guide"). Its purpose was to provide elements and data to draw a map of the known world. In the manuscripts the geographical work is accompanied by geographical maps, the origin of which have long been debated by scholars. The treatise *Harmonics* (to which Porphyry wrote a commentary) is a systematic overall treatment of music theory, which picks up and critically compares the traditional doctrines of Pythagoras and Aristoxenus. The basic question is about the prevalence of reason versus sense perception in establishing the validity of musical data.

The mathematician Diophantus, in modern times called "the father of algebra," probably lived and worked at Alexandria in the third century A.D. Of his *Arithmetica*, a collection of problems originally in thirteen books, there remain six books in Greek and another four in Arabic translation. The work is foundational to the study of indeterminate equations and is the first example of the systematic application of a symbolic notation in mathematics. To him an epigram in the *Palatine Anthology* (XIV 126) is attributed, an epitaph for his own tomb that proposes in the form of a riddle an equation from which it is possible to deduce that he lived to the age of 84.

In the same field of mathematical research, the work of Pappus of Alexandria, who lived in a period around A.D. 320, constitutes a precious store of earlier material. In this field too, great energy was devoted to commenting upon and preserving the works of the tradition (especially the *Almagest*), now that, above all in Neoplatonic circles, mathematics often came close to dialectic and theology and moved away to some extent, at least in its goals, from the strictly scientific aspect of the Euclidean model (cf. *The Hellenistic Age* VI 1.3).

2.2 Medicine and Galen

Medicine too flourished to a significant degree, but the works that have reached us today are a tiny part of the literary output of that period. The rich Greek pharmacological tradition is today summed up in the work of Pedanius Dioscorides (first century), originally from Anazarbus in Cilicia. In his work *Materia Medica*, in five books, he collected the precious pharmacological experience he had accumulated as a military doctor in the reigns of Claudius and Nero. Other medics and authors of writings on medicine are: Aretaeus of Cappadocia (first century), from whom a work survives on the causes and therapy of acute and chronic illnesses, which for centuries was admired by doctors for its clarity; Rufus of Ephesus (first to second century), from whom we know a good number of works also via the Arabic tradition; and Soranus of Ephesus (first to second century), from whose many works all that remains is one gynaecological treatise.

Galen. The highpoint of medical studies was reached in the second century with the work of Claudius Galenus of Pergamum, known in English as Galen, who was perhaps the most important and best known doctor in the ancient world after Hippocrates. His multifaceted personality and immense output are of significance also for the history of philosophy and of philology.

Galen was born at Pergamum in A.D. 129 or 130. His father Nikon, an architect and landowner with good economic resources and broadminded opinions, ensured that he received a reasonably good philosophical education (with teachers from the four most important schools: the Platonic, Peripatetic, Stoic and Epicurean schools). A dream is said to have prompted his father to direct him towards medicine. His anatomical apprenticeship therefore began very early, when he was just seventeen, with the medic Satyrus, who was at that time staying in Pergamum in the following of an important Roman statesman.

Around A.D. 150, on the death of his father, Galen moved to Smyrna to attend the lectures of another anatomist, Pelops, a disciple of Numisianus. After this he decided to meet in person with Numisianus, who was at Corinth, but who most probably died in the meantime. Galen therefore went to Alexandria, since it was at that time the major centre of studies of anatomy (cf. *The Hellenistic Age* VI 2.1). He stayed there for some time and then returned to Pergamum, where for some years he very successfully fulfilled the role of doctor to the gladiators. He went to Rome in 161 or 162, at the start of the reign of Marcus Aurelius. Here his patron was a certain Eudemus, who was linked to a circle of eminent figures with Peripatetic tendencies, who, among other things, attended a private anatomy course delivered by Galen himself. The most important of his works of this period is the *Anatomical Procedures*.

In his two Roman Periods, between 162 and 166 and again after 169, he wrote, among other things, *On the Doctrines of Hippocrates and Plato*, in which he outlined his own doctrine by using these two authors as points of reference, and the great anatomical and physiological treatise *On the Function of the Parts of the Human Body*, in which he reworked and updated the tradition of Aristotelian biology. He returned to Pergamum for a certain period and was then at Rome from 169 until his death, which occurred perhaps in 216.

Out of Galen's immense work a large part still survives, although a number of works, especially those of non-medical character, have been lost. His literary output embraced very different fields: philosophy (moral and logical), linguistic and grammatical analysis (*On Names in Medicine*, *Notable Attic Words*, *Hippocratic Glossary*), commentary and exegesis of the writings of Hippocrates, Plato and Aristotle (he wrote commentaries, which partly survive, on Hippocratic works, on Plato's *Timaeus* and Aristotle's *Categories*) and strictly medical fields such as anatomy and physiology, therapy (with pharmacological works) and pathology. He also wrote works of a propaedeutic character such as the *Protrepticus to the Art of Medicine*.

Galen was an intellectual figure of encyclopaedic formation, who reflects the characteristics of the better provincial elites, the most vital part of Roman society in the second century. He had an enormous influence on the subsequent history of medicine, in Late Antiquity and the Middle Ages, but in his own time he may have been known as a philosopher as well as a doctor. He also deserves a place, not necessarily in the second rank, in the history of philology, for his writings on literary critical, linguistic and rhetorical topics and for his commentaries on various authors (in this sector he still needs to be studied and evaluated thoroughly). Galen himself tells us of his own output in a bio-bibliographical work *On My Own Books* (and also in the briefer *On the Order of My Own Books*) and in autobiographical references scattered through his works.

Among these, two new acquisitions deserve to be noted, namely the two short works Περὶ τῶν ἑαυτῷ δοκούντων (*On My Own Opinions*: previously known only in a problematic Latin version, based on an Arabic translation) and Περὶ ἀλυπίας (*On the Avoidance of Grief*: previously completely unknown), which were discovered in 2005 in a manuscript preserved in a monastery at Thessaloniki and published already in 2005 (in the case of the first work) and two years later (in the case of the second).

The treatise *On My Own Opinions* is a sort of intellectual biography (a rare if not unique case in the ancient world). Having reached old age, Galen evidently felt the need to reconsider his own works, in the already cited *On My Own Books* and *On the Order of My Own Books*, and then to pin down his own ideas on some controversial doctrinal points in the work *On My Own Opinions*, which may be his last work. *On the Avoidance of Grief* is a sort of epistolary *consolatio* "in reverse," in which Galen reminds the friend to whom he is writing, who is grieving on his behalf, of the immense damage done by the great fire at Rome in A.D. 192 to Galen's own huge collection of books and to those of the magnificent public libraries on the Palatine. From this we gain not only a vivid and engaged autobiographical testimony to the event and to the author's temperament, but also a large amount of information useful for reconstructing the cultural history of the time, in particular as regards the history of the book and of libraries.

Medicine after Galen. Many doctors after Galen devoted themselves to producing compendia and manuals drawn from the writings of their predecessors, but the majority of their writings have been lost. However, we should recall Oribasius of Pergamum, who lived in the fourth century and was personal doctor to the emperor Julian; his works enjoyed great success in the Middle Ages.

2.3 "Parascientific" literature

2.3.1 The *Corpus Hermeticum*

In the period of the Roman Empire there was some diffusion of so-called "Hermetic literature," attributed to Hermes Trismegistos (whose name, in Greek Τρισμέγιστος, means "thrice greatest"). This divinity, mediating between the divine and human worlds, was assimilated to the Egyptian god Thoth or Teuth, the inventor of writing, a magus and wonderworker, and the revealer of a doctrine that we would today define as parascientific: a comprehensive mixture of alchemy, astrology and philosophy.

In the sphere of Hermetic literature it is conventional to distinguish two thematic groups: the earlier works, which are of occult character and in which much space is given to alchemy and astrology, and the more recent ones, which should perhaps be placed in the first centuries of the Imperial Period and which are theological and philosophical in character. The *Corpus Hermeticum* in a strict sense belongs to this second group and consists of seventeen treatises composed in the second to fourth century and collected during the Byzantine Era, plus a series of fragments that appear in the *Anthologion* of John of Stobi. The strong symbolism and the continuous reference to Egyptian ritual practices make the Hermetic doctrine extremely obscure, though there are clear references to Platonic and Orphic-Pythagorean philosophical religion. For example, one of the truths revealed by Hermes Trismegistos concerns the *Logos*, son of the Supreme God, while much space is given to the dualistic conception of reality, conceived as an opposition between good and bad, light and darkness. The reception of Hermetic literature in the centuries of the later empire (a period that has been called an "age of anxiety") should be explained by its salvific message, which is offered to the initiate capable of freeing himself from the bonds of the body and rejoining with divinity.

2.3.2 Artemidorus and the interpretation of dreams

Attention to dreams and the study of their meanings was a constant in the Greek world, as is attested by a specific literary tradition on this topic, going back to the earliest philosophers (for example the Pythagoreans and Sophists) and to Hippocratic medicine. Others who addressed the topic of dreams include Aristotle, Epicurus and the Stoics, who offered differing interpretations. Among the later exponents of this parascientific tradition, Artemidorus has left the only complete treatise to have survived today.

Artemidorus was born in the second century A.D. at Ephesus, but in his work he says he is from Daldis, native city of his mother, in homage to Apollo Mystes, the "Apollo of the Initiates," who enjoyed a special cult in this city of Lydia. The *Onirocritica*, in five books, is the only work that survives of this author who, according to the *Suda* lexicon, wrote also on divination by means of birds and chiromancy, activities for which he became famous among his contemporaries. Of his life we know very little at all. Following a fashion common at that time, he travelled very widely throughout the empire, gathering on his journeys "eyewitness" material for his collection of dreams and interpretations.

The *Onirocritica*, which presents a classification of dreams into the theorematic and the allegorical, attributed a divine origin to dreams and for that reason Artemidorus considered them an essential moment in the prediction of the future. Theorematic dreams are easily intelligible, because they present a meaning that is wholly clear, and they come true soon. Allegorical dreams demand more effort to interpret and the event foretold by them usually takes place after a long period of time. By privileging the moment of classification, Artemidorus avoids the need to indicate what behaviour should be followed on the basis of the interpretation of the dream. The work is cited by Sigmund Freud in his *Interpretation of Dreams*.

VIII The Second Sophistic and Lucian

1 The Second Sophistic

1.1 Character of the Second Sophistic

1.1.1 The primacy of rhetoric

For the cultural moment that we conventionally call the "Second Sophistic" (already mentioned above, cf. *The Roman Imperial Period* I 4), our main source is the *Lives of the Sophists* by Flavius Philostratus (cf. below 1.2.8). There we find, among other things, the term "Second Sophistic," which was evidently owed to the desire to assert a proud connection to the classical Sophists, with the aim of reviving their glorious past. Philostratus presents us with a very different picture from the one that we can draw for ourselves on the basis of our knowledge (and our opinions, to be truthful). Philostratus' work does not include Lucian and gives rather limited space to Dio of Prusa, Favorinus and Aelius Aristides (who are for us authors of the first rank), while it bestows the role of renewers of the Sophistic upon Nicetes of Smyrna (Neronian Period) and his disciple Scopelianus, and is then dominated by the long biographies of Polemon (88–144 ca.) and Herodes Atticus (second century), figures who were certainly very famous and influential in their time, but who have been almost totally erased by time.

The main, most widespread and significant expression of imperial rhetoric and oratory is seen by Philostratus in the *meletē*, an exercise consisting of fictitious declamations that originated in schools and then became a genuine form of exhibition or show with a major cultural impact, though to our eyes it has a fairly minor and primarily documentary value (cf. *The Hellenistic Age* VII 1.2). Even when we find it appropriate to downgrade the significance of Philostratus' work or to correct the relative importance of its components, we could not consider denying altogether the value of the picture it offers us, despite the different selection of material presented to us by our tradition. It is likely that an accurate historical reconstruction will come by combining these two classes of data and taking different factors into account.

In the introduction to his *Lives of the Sophists*, Philostratus clarifies that the Second Sophistic is both inspired by and contrasted to the earlier one, represented by rhetor-philosophers such as Gorgias: it preserves the specifically rhetorical aspect of the earlier movement, but the new one prefers to treat themes drawn from history, i.e. specific topics from real life. Modern scholars are much more keen to mark a clean break between the First and Second Sophistic, since the interests and topics treated by these two cultural currents seem entirely unalike and their role in society is different too. With the Neosophists the share of the philosophical component is reduced and the share of the political component watered down, while the concept of rhetoric takes on a new significance, more aligned with the formal and

https://doi.org/10.1515/9783110426328-037

cultural tendencies of post-Hellenistic eloquence than with those of the Classical Age.

Philostratus sets the heyday of the Second Sophistic in the second century A.D. with Herodes Atticus, yet it was lively already in the first century A.D. and remained so until the sixth. This is the long period in which the successful rhetor held a prestigious social position and one that was officially recognised by the state authority. Often, as Philostratus himself does not fail to highlight, the sophists had close links to the Roman emperors. This was the case for Dio with Trajan, for Polemon with Hadrian and Antoninus Pius and for Aristides with Marcus Aurelius. Herodes Atticus was the tutor of Marcus Aurelius and Lucius Verus, while Antipater, another Greek rhetor active at Rome in the second and third century, was tutor of Caracalla and Geta. The Antonine emperors, in particular, became protectors of the sophists, which favoured the creation and development of numerous schools of rhetoric. The sophists in their turn became a kind of counsellor and collaborator of the emperors, for which reason it has been concluded that these rhetors were of greater importance in Roman history than in Greek history. There is no doubt that Greek and Roman culture at no other time influenced each other reciprocally in such a fundamental way as in this moment.

1.1.2 Star orators and intellectuals

Although Philostratus does not take the time to explain what he means by "sophist," the rhetors in this intellectual current can be seen to share at least three broad elements: erudition and the preeminence of form; the cosmopolitan tendency of their teaching, and hence continuous relocations across all regions of the empire; and the theatrical character of their displays.

The sophist was for the most part an intellectual star, who shaped opinions and set cultural trends when he expressed himself in public. Fully involved in the political and social life of the empire, he also managed to accumulate vast riches. The key to popularity lay above all in his bravura performance as lecturer, an ability that worked by its impact on the public. It was not enough that the oration be composed according to precise formal criteria (even in the Second Sophistic, for example, the divergence between Atticists and Asianists remained), but it was also necessary to make skilful use of intonations, diction, vocal approach and appropriate gesture.

Possessing a vast and refined cultural background, which ranged from the classical authors to contemporary ones, capable of treating with ease philosophy, literature or social questions, these "itinerant rhetors" produced oratorical performances in both East and West, putting on their shows equally before educated audiences and vast crowds. The audiences attracted were sometimes so numerous that it was not sufficient to bring them to the *akroatērion* ("auditorium" or lecture hall), but it was necessary to use the *bouleutērion*, the *ōdeion* or even the theatre. To a degree otherwise unparalleled, the rhetor and literature became spectacles, inheriting techniques and tricks from the art of theatre. The Neosophists were able to recite an oration that had previously been scripted, for the most part designed to meet the refined tastes of a select audience, but they were also able to improvise on the basis of requests from the audience. This was not always an innate talent: the schools of rhetoric trained improvisation, for example teaching the use of repertoires on various themes, mostly historical and philosophical, the key points of which were committed to memory and reworked as needed. At the basis of this profession, therefore, was the constant exercise of declamation and memorisation. To give an example: Herodes Atticus declaimed in the presence of his pupils every day.

1.2 The "rhetor-philosophers"

1.2.1 Philosophy and eloquence

By the expression "rhetor-philosophers" we conventionally designate in particular Dio of Prusa and Maximus of Tyre, who combined the profession of rhetor with an interest in conceptual approaches drawn from philosophical thought. As we shall see, however, for these authors the philosophical component did not constitute the central element or true substance of their speeches. It was rather a source of inspiration or even a pretext for composing rhetorically elaborate speeches intended to astonish and capture the public's admiration. The predominant aspect is without doubt that of a complacent Atticist eloquence, following the fashion of the times, and of a refined and cultivated use of literary models. This formal interest in rhetoric marks a major difference from the rhetor-philosophers of the Sophist movement of the fifth century B.C. To adopt a simplistic formulation (with the advantages and disadvantages of that genre), we may say that, unlike the case of the Sophists of the Classical Age, for these rhetors philosophy was at the service of eloquence and not vice versa.

1.2.2 Dio of Prusa (or Dio Cocceianus), called Chrysostom

Dio, who from the third century onward was given the epithet of Chrysostom ("golden mouthed") to mark his excellence in oratory, was born between A.D. 40 and 50 at Prusa, in Bithynia, a region of Asia Minor, to a wealthy family. From his youth he devoted himself to legal advocacy. He then moved to Rome, where he became one of the main rhetors at the imperial court. He fell into disgrace under the emperor Domitian, for reasons that are unclear to us (it is thought that he was damaged by his friendship with Flavius Sabinus, a cousin of the emperor who was executed in 82), and was forced to pursue a life in exile outside Italy. Philostratus tells how Dio had set off, taking with him, with a polemical intent, nothing but Plato's *Phaedo* and Demosthenes' oration *De Falsa Legatione*. After his moment of success as a rhetor, this period of Dio's life is presented as having the character of a philosophical phase, pursued according to the rules of poverty of the Cynic-Stoic school and with the aim, so loudly proclaimed in his works in these years, of removing from mortals the desire for luxury and riches. In 97, under Nerva, his exile was rescinded and Dio, now back in Rome, achieved even greater success than before. He had excellent relations with Trajan, who attended his declamations: he gained Roman citizenship and took the name of Cocceianus. He also held sensitive government positions. Our last information on Dio is transmitted by Pliny (*Epist.* X 81–82), who says that he was involved in a trial for embezzlement around 111. He is said to have died a little after this.

With Dio the relation between eloquence and philosophy is close but, as he himself admits, his decision to pursue philosophy was due above all to his novel and unexpected life circumstances. The philosophical component in his speeches appears as a surface patina, above all as a source of motifs and examples that were easily understood and would make an immediate impression on the audience. In his works Atticist eloquence dominates, nourished by a refined and cultivated use of literary models, relegating the philosophical component to a secondary level.

The corpus of his writings consists of 80 texts of heterogeneous character. There are speeches that were delivered in reality, short treatises on moral topics set out in the form of an oration, lectures and a letter on a topic of literary history (Oration 18) sent to an important person, perhaps the emperor Nerva. Not all the works in the corpus are authentically by Dio. It is believed that Orations 37 (*The Corinthian Discourse*) and 64 (*On Fortune* 2) should be ascribed to his disciple Favorinus (on whom see below).

Almost all of Dio's speeches are hard to place chronologically. In all likelihood dating to the period of his exile are the "Diogenic Orations" (Orations 6, 8, 9, 10), so called because they centre on the figure of the Cynic philosopher Diogenes of Sinope and his disdain for worldly goods, especially riches (but even in this case what predominates is a certain simplification and stylisation of Cynic philosophy). Dio returns to the theme of disdain for possessions also in Oration 79, *On Wealth*. Of a more sophistic character is one of his most famous orations, the Olympic Oration (*Man's First Conception of God*, Oration 12), which features the sculptor Phidias expressing his conception of the divine and of art. An oration of literary content is Oration 52 (*An Appraisal of the Tragic Triad*), in which, following a typical sophistic taste, the plays entitled *Philoctetes* by the three great tragedians are compared, in which (with Aristotle) Sophocles is given a middle position between Aeschylus and Euripides.

Writings now lost are: the work of historical geography *Getica*, a source for the *Historia Gothorum* of Jordanes (sixth century), who seems to have confused the Goths with the Getae; the works *Against the Philosophers*, *Reply to Musonius*, *In Defence of Homer*; and sophistic *paignia* such as the *Encomium of the Parrot*, the *Encomium of the Mosquito* and the *Encomium of Hair*, which got a response, around three centuries later, from Synesius with the *Praise of Baldness*.

A famous speech by Dio is *The Euboean Discourse, or The Hunter*. In the incipit the author declares that he is going to tell "a personal experience of mine; not merely something I have heard from others." This concerns the encounter, after a shipwreck, with a hunter and his family who live in a hovel in an isolated area of the Euboean countryside, rejecting the so-called civil life and limiting contacts with the city as far as possible. Dio sings the praises of a poor, natural, autarkic life, according to the Cynic-Stoic ideals that he preached. This idealisation is counterpointed by the frenetic and alienating life of the city, in which ordinary people are forced to live by their wits in a degrading misery. Woven through the whole oration are commonplaces drawn from idyllic and bucolic literature, from Cynic-Stoic diatribe and from philosophy. The bookish references are numerous, such as the literary quotations from Homer, Hesiod and Euripides that close the oration. Above all in the second part, the result is cold and mannered. The less artificial and more intense section concerns the encounter with the hunter, a handsome man with fine, healthy features, and his speech about his chosen lifestyle.

A typical characteristic of Dio's style is brusque transition, within the same oration, between different tones, registers and sometimes topics. Some modern scholars have held that this apparent incoherence may be a result of alteration and reworking of Dio's texts by later editors. This theory has been met with bafflement, since the texts' lack of cohesion and the stylistic heterogeneity of many orations seems to be an intentional characteristic of Dio, who treated a number of topics with often differing approaches and outlooks and took pleasure in this mixture as well as in continual allusions to other authors. Further, ποικιλία (*poikilia*, "variety of style") is a characteristic of the writers of this period (of Lucian and Aelian, among others), who pursue it by choice. In accord with the fashion of the sophists, the play with literary allusions is very well developed both in the philosophical texts and in those that are strictly rhetorical. The models of Attic style preferred by Dio are Plato, Demosthenes and Xenophon.

1.2.3 Maximus of Tyre

Like Dio of Prusa, Maximus of Tyre, who lived in the second century, combined his rhetorical output with a conspicuous philosophical component. He too was a famous lecturer and spent a certain period of time in Rome. He wrote 41 *Dissertations* (Διαλέξεις) according to the motifs and stylistic features of the Neoplatonic thought that was in vogue at the time, adopting an Attic language that is clear and at the same time flashy, full of vivid rhetorical features. Although he was an adherent of Neoplatonism, in his works a strong eclecticism predominates, which leads him to mix different philosophical orientations and models. Maximus mostly privileged popular themes drawn from Cynic-Stoic philosophy, adapting them to his particular vision, according to which divinity is the highest good, to be attained only through the intellect. Interesting in his conception of divinity is the presence of *daimones*, conceived as semidivine beings, intermediate between god and man.

1.2.4 Favorinus of Arles

Born around A.D. 85 at Arles, the ancient Arelate, in Gallia Narbonensis, Favorinus mastered Greek language and culture, probably by studying in Marseilles. He was a pupil of Dio of Prusa at Rome and got to know the principal intellectuals of the period in the course of numerous journeys in Greece and Asia Minor. Plutarch dedicated the work *On the Principle of Cold* (*De primo frigido*) to him. He rapidly won great fame, such that the Corinthians dedicated two honorary columns to him. However, he fell into disgrace with the emperor Hadrian for reasons unknown to us and in 132 he was exiled to Chios. With the ascent to the throne of Antoninus Pius he was able to return to Rome, where he opened a school of rhetoric attended by Aulus Gellius and Herodes Atticus. He seems to have died around 143.

Favorinus wrote a very large number of works on the most varied topics, as was the tendency at the time. His works are mostly lost, except two orations included in the corpus of Dio of Prusa, *On Fortune* 2 and *The Corinthian Discourse*, and the speech *On Exile*, which was rediscovered thanks to a papyrus published for the first time in 1931. There are also some surviving fragments, mostly found in Diogenes Laertius.

> In the oration *On Fortune* 2, Fate is defended against the charge of often provoking ruin among humans. The speech *The Corinthian Discourse* treats the custom of dedicating statues and columns to illustrious figures, an honour that Favorinus himself had received. The oration *On Exile*, which has survived but without the start and end of the text, was composed during the years of enforced absence from Rome. By adopting the tone and recurring themes of the *consolatio*, Favorinus sets out to soften the worries of exile with the moral and intellectual support of philosophy.

The arguments and motifs are those of the Cynic-Stoic school, while the language is the Attic of Plato and Xenophon, the two models preferred by Favorinus. The style is rendered artificial by the presence of many rhetorical figures and the insistent pursuit of rhythmic clausulae.

Among the lost works of Favorinus we may note the *Miscellaneous History*, in 24 books, which, through its erudite and encyclopaedic character, became the inspiration for a number of authors including Aulus Gellius, Athenaeus, Aelian and Diogenes Laertius. Favorinus also addressed philosophy in *The Pyrrhonian Modes*, in 10 books, and the *Memorabilia*, in 5 books, in which he recounted in anecdotal form the biographies of the principal philosophers. Sophistic works of a paradoxical cast are the declamations *On Quartan Fever* and *On Thersites*.

1.2.5 Herodes Atticus

A member of a rich and noble family of Athens, Herodes Atticus lived between A.D. 101 and 177. He was a renowned sophist, at the head of one of the most prestigious schools of eloquence in Athens. He was named consul at Rome and became teacher of rhetoric to the future emperors Marcus Aurelius and Lucius Verus. Thanks to his wealth, he advanced the adornment of Athens with numerous public works, including the *ōdeion* and the Ilissus stadium. His patronage of the arts and his generosity became proverbial in the ancient world.

According to Philostratus, who gives a long profile of him in the *Lives of the Sophists*, Herodes Atticus was a pupil of Favorinus, Polemon and Scopelianus, the principal sophists of the period. Philostratus praises his rhetorical ability and style: Herodes, he said, a devotee of Atticism, had achieved great effects by simplicity of expression and the ability to create harmonious periodic structure, succeeding at the same time in giving vehemence to his attacks. He was assiduously dedicated to his studies, which he did not neglect even during banquets or at night during intervals from sleep. Philostratus knew "very many letters by Herodes, discourses and diaries, handbooks and collections of suitable passages in which the flowers of antique erudition have been collected" (II 565, 9). What survives today is just the oration *On the State*, which some even regard as spurious and a much later work; those who do not contest Herodes' authorship of the oration believe instead that it subsequently became the object of imitation.

1.2.6 Aelius Aristides

With Aelius Aristides we meet one of the second century's most interesting personalities, not only for his extraordinary oratorical ability, acknowledged by many ancient authors, but also for his autobiographical account of the illness that he suffered all his life in the *Sacred Discourses*, an exceptional text and in some respects a disconcerting one.

He was born in A.D. 117 in the Mysian hinterland of Asia Minor to a rich family of landowners. The main rhetors of the period were his teachers: he studied linguistics and literature in Phrygia with the grammarian Alexander of Cotiaeum (who later became the tutor of Marcus Aurelius) and the sophists Aristocles of Pergamum and Polemon of Laodicea. He then moved to Athens, where he was linked to Herodes Atticus. He travelled a lot, despite his precarious health, which was accentuated by a "neurotic" attitude that obliged him to spend two years at the Temple of Asclepius at Pergamum to seek a cure: he became ill towards the end of 143, when he was about to leave for Rome, was stricken by various forms of illness and never truly recovered. The *Sacred Discourses* are the diary of his illness and attest an alternation of phases of health, during which the famous orator was able to devote himself to his beloved activity as rhetor, and exhausting relapses. He too spent time at Rome, in 143/4, but the journey greatly weakened him. Philostratus records that he died, perhaps in his homeland, perhaps in a location in Ionia, at the age of 60 or 70.

Like other Neosophists, Aelius Aristides too wrote an enormous amount. His corpus consists of 55 texts, not all authentically by him, that are very diverse in topic and style: encomia of persons and cities, prose hymns, historical and mythological declamations, polemical writings and pamphlets, which were read, commented upon and taken as models down to the Byzantine Period (along with Thucydides and Demosthenes, Aelius Aristides was in fact one of the three authors indicated by the Atticists as the best models for the *lexis attikē*). Among the epideictic speeches we note the encomia for cities, such as the *Panathenaic Oration*, in which he sings the praises of Athens in the footsteps of Isocrates, and *To Rome*, in which he recognises the merit of the Roman Empire in having established universal peace. Among the declamations (*meletai*) preserved, the most famous are the two *Sicilian Discourses* and *On the Peace with the Lacedaemonians – On the Peace with the Athenians*. There are three so-called "anti-Platonic" discourses: in the oration *In Defence of the Four*, he acquits Miltiades, Cimon, Themistocles and Pericles on the charge made against them by Plato in the *Gorgias* of having made Athens great politically but not morally; in the orations *In Defence of Oratory* and *To Capito* he lauds oratory and its educational and social function, countering the positions voiced by Plato.

The *Sacred Discourses* certainly form one of the most singular texts that the ancient world has left us. It consists of four speeches called "sacred" because they were written under the inspiration and guidance of Asclepius, the healing god in whom Aristides trusted to gain his healing. It is an autobiography, which originally consisted of more than 300,000 lines of text but was later extensively pruned by the author himself, concerning the course of his illness and the advice offered to him by Asclepius, mostly in dreams. In the *Asclepieion* of Pergamum, where Aelius Aristides had gone to be cured, the rite known as "incubation" was indeed practised: those admitted for healing were expected to record their dreams and to follow the indications provided by the divinity during sleep. This type of medical treatment tended to privilege an intimate communion with the god, which also suggested to Aristides topics and occasions for his compositions. The modern reader may perhaps feel puzzled when faced by the obsessive precision with which Aelius Aristides notes the circumstances and reasons why he vomited, was purged, sweated, abstained from bathing or was moved by the god to bathe, for example in the cold waters of a river in midwinter. The four speeches seem like the tortuous and anguished course taken by an individual in search of equilibrium and are a unique document of the religiosity and interior dimension of an intellectual of the second century A.D. The style matches the content: contorted, disjointed, sometimes lush, sometimes dry, characterised by brusque transitions and sudden changes of tone and topic. Yet even with this content, what seems preeminent is attention to the past literary tradition (even in the incipit, for example, Aristides presents two quotations from Homer).

The work of Aelius Aristides that has been preserved illustrates the main tendencies of the literary and cultural movement of the Second Sophistic, but it is distinguished clearly by the marked religious dimension that we have discussed. As was recalled already by Philostratus, Aelius Aristides preferred in-depth preparation to improvisation, "keeping his eye turned to the authors of the past and reinvigorating them with his fertile nature" (II 581, 17–582, 3). He was very scrupulous in his use of rhetorical figures and, in general, in applying the rules of the rhetorical art. In this sense his style appears elaborate and lacking in immediacy, though it in fact varies greatly from work to work. Another characteristic of his writings is his continuous return to the literary tradition, both in frequent references and allusions and in his re-creation of the Attic style of the classics. Aristides even succeeded in reproducing, 500 years later, the rhythmic laws of Demosthenes' prose, i.e. avoiding a sequence of more than two short syllables. This extraordinary ability earned him notable celebrity: the emperor Marcus Aurelius himself was a great admirer.

1.2.7 Aelian

Born at Praeneste in A.D. 170, Aelian, like Favorinus and Lucian, was able to master the Greek language and culture so well that his contemporaries came to call him μελίγλωσσος, i.e. "with honeyed tongue," for the precision, propriety and effectiveness of his style. Philostratus, who tells us about him in the *Lives of the Sophists*, recalls that he mastered Attic like an Athenian from the Attic countryside.

Unlike the majority of sophists, he did not travel around the world but remained settled in Latium, where he died in 235. Little inclined to declamation, he preferred to devote himself to historical, antiquarian and zoological studies. According to the *Suda* lexicon he was a priest, perhaps at Praeneste, in the Temple of Fortuna. He has not been much appreciated by modern critics for his encyclopaedic and anecdotal tendency, but he has left us works of some interest.

His *Historical Miscellany* (*Varia Historia*) in 14 books, which has survived in compendium form (though the first two books are complete), consists of a series of anecdotes, aphorisms, brief tales and notices about famous figures from history and classical culture. Aelian is a mine of information – though often of doubtful reliability (his sources are almost never cited) – including not only on facts, persons and curiosities, but also on the development of the legends and narrative nuclei concerning figures such as Alexander, Alcibiades, the tyrants of Syracuse, Aspasia, Semiramis and others. Aelian, a follower of Stoicism, presents a moralistic approach to the facts, in which he confronts vice and virtue, good and bad.

In the work *Characteristics of Animals*, in 17 books, which survives complete though with later alterations, the author, in an encyclopaedic spirit, collects pseudo-scientific information and curiosities about animals, aiming to demonstrate that they have the same passions, feelings, vices and virtues as humans. Here we can detect the zoological ideas of the Stoics and the often fantastical approach of Hellenistic paradoxography.

Aelian also wrote 20 *Rustic Letters*, which places erotic situations typical of New Comedy into a rural setting, and two works that have been lost: *On Providence* and *On Divine Manifestations*, on a Stoic pattern.

1.2.8 The Philostrati

The ancient world has transmitted various works under the name of Philostratus. The *Suda* lexicon distinguishes three people by this name, all from Lemnos and related to each other, but modern critics have not yet succeeded in establishing with certainty their identity or how precisely the surviving works should be distributed among them. Further, it seems that the short work entitled *Imagines*, recounting 17 pictures, which is a continuation of the 64 *Imagines* of Flavius Philostratus (known as Philostratus II), attests the existence of a fourth Philostratus unknown to the *Suda*.

The one known as Philostratus I, the earliest of the group, is thought to have been a teacher of rhetoric at Athens in the period of the Flavian dynasty and was author of many works in various genres, including at least 40 lost tragedies.

Flavius Philostratus. The best known figure is Flavius Philostratus, or Philostratus II, probably born between A.D. 170 and 180, a sophist active at Athens. He became the tutor of the young Caracalla and Geta and was introduced to the court of the empress Julia Domna, wife of Septimius Severus, and to her coterie of mystical and orientalising writers. In 208 he was part of the *comitatus* that accompanied the emperor to Britannia and in 213 in that of Caracalla in Gaul. On the death of Julia Domna he left Rome and returned to his career as an itinerant sophist. It seems that he died between 244 and 249, in the reign of Philip the Arab.

Among the earliest works of Flavius Philostratus, *The Life of Apollonius of Tyana*, written at the request of Julia Domna, is the novelistic biography of a sort of travelling magus and wonderworker who lived in the first century A.D., famed for his ascetic lifestyle and his wisdom, who became a true legend in the ancient world. Although there are fantastic details, the work remains a valid testimony for reconstructing the philosophical-religious mentality of the period and the magical and mystic beliefs found both among the people and at the imperial court. Also attributed to him is the *Heroicus*, a dialogue that illustrates popular beliefs about heroic myths.

The work for which Flavius Philostratus is most famous is the *Lives of the Sophists*, a sort of biographical history of the Second Sophistic, mentioned already above (cf. par. 1.1). The work contains important information not just on the lives and works of the principal rhetors of the Imperial Period, but also notices about their techniques of composition and declamation and on the schools of rhetoric. Prefaced to the *Lives* is a paragraph in which Philostratus offers a definition of the New Sophistic and identifies Gorgias as the inventor of improvised oratory. He distinguishes between the First Sophistic, with its greatest exponent being Gorgias himself, and the Second Sophistic, which he starts with Aeschines. Philostratus leaves a large gap between Aeschines and Nicetes of Smyrna, who lived around three centuries later, a gap that some scholars have explained as a textual lacuna. However, we cannot rule out that he intentionally chose not to treat authors whom he judged to be of little significance.

Other preserved works by Philostratus are: the *Gymnasticus*, on the ancient sporting traditions of Greece; the *Imagines*, in which, adopting the sophistic technique of *ekphrasis*, he describes 64 paintings in a collection at Naples, for the most part mythological in character; and finally a collection of 73 *Letters*, generally fictitious and on erotic topics.

Philostratus III and IV. To another Philostratus, great-grandson of the previous one and conventionally called Philostratus III, is attributed a letter *To Aspasius of Ravenna*, which treats the epistolary style. Finally Philostratus IV, who lived around the mid-third century, was the author of a small collection of *Imagines*, in 17 pictures, which presents itself as a continuation of the *Imagines* of Flavius Philostratus, i.e. Philostratus II.

2 Lucian of Samosata

2.1 A free spirit

In Lucian we encounter an intellectual in whom the force of reason combined with an irreverent spirit produced works rich in caustic irony towards prejudices and conventional ideas. He is an extraordinary representative of the cosmopolitan culture of the second century, in whom Hellenic civilisation was renewed and reinvigorated through contact with lively elements of eastern culture – a provincial fully involved in the Roman Empire and in the Greek literary and linguistic tradition, to the degree that he became one of its most brilliant and wise exponents.

Although he is generally considered to be a "sophist," his specific, complex activity and output do not make it easy to place him in the framework of the Second Sophistic movement. In particular, his most typical production – the dialogue based on a marriage between comedy and philosophical dialogue, intended to be recited or read – seems much closer to what Philostratus calls *phrontismata* (i.e. works that are thought out and prepared) than to the improvised *meletai* of the Neosophists (though he did also practise these). A distinctive trait of Lucian is his extreme versatility, which allows him to move unproblematically through very different topics. The counterpoint to this is a certain superficiality, or rather absence of depth, that he was able to use to give a light and polished touch to a vast range of themes, but on none of them does he dwell deeply enough to achieve a specific study of it for its own sake or to reach original results. His work as a writer creates a continuous relation, through playful reworkings, to the literature of the past. His writing gains its breadth as a result of his immense knowledge of Greek literature, which is constantly an object of references, allusions and reuses, filtered through his dazzling ability to transform anything into the mix of quick witted irony and piercing intelligence. Only by highlighting and understanding this breadth can his writing be appreciated fully. His work has enjoyed an extraordinary success from the ancient world to the present day; in particular, it was admired and imitated in the Enlightenment, thanks to its penetrating and irreverent rationalism and formal brilliance.

2.2 Life

Secure data on Lucian's life are scarce, since the notices transmitted by the ancient sources are few and there is often debate on whether they are soundly based. From references that we find in his works we can reconstruct that Lucian was born between A.D. 119 and 126 at Samosata, a city on the upper Euphrates that was the capital of Commagene (a region of Syria). Thus he was not a Greek by birth, but a Syrian with a Semitic background. In the work entitled *The Dream, or Lucian's Career,* Lucian recounts how, from the earliest age, he was apprenticed in the art of sculpture with an uncle, but that he soon gave it up, after he broke a marble slab, and chose instead to become a rhetor. His cultural education must have been received among the sophists of Asia Minor and it provided him with a perfect command of Greek language and literature. He was first an advocate and then a successful lecturer. He travelled a great deal, from Asia Minor to Greece and Italy and from Gaul to Egypt, and he also went to Rome, perhaps in 159. He speaks of having an interest in philosophy, which he embraced at around the age of 40. This is the theme of the dialogue *Nigrinus*, dedicated to the philosopher of that name whom he met at Rome. But the very idea of "conversion" is wholly foreign to Lucian's spirit and the dialogue seems rather to cultivate uncharitable feelings towards Rome and the Romans. It seems that the philosophical schools and their doctrines were, rather, one among the very many themes that Lucian treated with the light and somewhat flippant irony that he adopted towards any serious commitments or causes espoused with fervour. Thus in the *Hermotimus, or Concerning the Sects*, composed around 165, rather than sceptically condemning all the philosophical schools, he treats them all with the amused detachment of someone who does not feel, or does not wish to appear, all that involved. In 167 he was present at the Olympic Games, where he was a witness to the suicide of the philosopher Peregrinus, which he represents in often paradoxical tones in the work in epistolary form *The Passing of Peregrinus*. He served as an imperial official in Egypt between 173 and 176. Thereafter he resumed his career as an itinerant lecturer and again went to Athens. Through a reference to the death and divinisation of the emperor Marcus Aurelius, in the work *Alexander the False Prophet*, his death can be dated after 180. The notice reported in the *Suda lexicon*, according to which Lucian had died by being torn to pieces by a pack of wild dogs, is certainly a tendentious legend and it is thought it originated in Christian circles, which were emphatically averse to him.

2.3 The Lucianic corpus

Lucian's surviving output is immense and heterogeneous. The Lucianic corpus consists of around 85 works, some not authentically his, which address a great variety of topics. This is firm testimony to the versatility of his genius, of which we have spoken, and to his abilities as a writer, capable of using different forms to produce arresting variations in his stylistic tones, composing in different keys. The absolute and relative chronology of the works remains entirely problematic, despite frequent attempts to resolve it.

Some rhetorical exercises on typical "school" topics are regarded as sophistic in a strict sense: *The Tyrannicide*, *The Encomium of the Fly*; eight *prolaliai*, i.e. brief preambles, such as the works *Amber or the Swans*, *The Scythian or the Consul*, *Heracles*, *Dionysus*; descriptions of artistic works (*ekphraseis*) such as *The Hall* and *Hippias or The Bath*; epideictic lectures such as *Slander (On not being quick to put faith in it)* or the sparkling *The consonants at Law (Sigma vs. Tau in the Court of the Seven Vowels)*: the joke scenario is an accusation by the letter *sigma* against the letter *tau* before a tribunal of vowels. These texts are often characterised by the search for bizarre and paradoxical arguments, which are pursued, deploying the stylistic features of the Second Sophistic, with great formal refinement and an evident desire to recover, in a modern key, topics and inspirations from classical literature.

In all the rest of Lucian's work, the dialogue form strongly predominates. It is an ancient form which Lucian renews to produce results of great literary value, which we will discuss more fully below. In the corpus there are also two famous narrative works that come close to the genre of novel: *A True Story*, which is certainly by Lucian, and *Lucius or The Ass*, the authenticity of which is debated. Some works are brief treatises, written in epistolary form to a person addressed in the prologue: in *The Ignorant Book-Collector* the satire is against a figure well defined by the title; in the *Apology for the "Salaried Posts in Great Houses"* Lucian defends himself from malicious criticisms made of him when he accepted (in 171) the position of *archistator praefecti Aegypti*; in *On Salaried Posts in Great Houses* he ridicules the renunciation of freedom by Greek intellectuals who live as guests with rich and powerful Romans; and in the famous *How to Write History* Lucian invites us to appreciate the freedom of the historian in a polemic with the panegyrists of Lucius Verus at the time of the second Parthian war (A.D. 161–166). This last work features various sentiments unfavourable to Rome, as we have already noted above in the *Nigrinus*, confirming Lucian's attitude as a "free thinker" who wanted to preserve his own freedom as an intellectual of Greek culture in the Romanised world.

A small group of texts that survive in the manuscripts within the Lucianic corpus are certainly spurious: *The Patriot* (*Philopatris*), *Charidemus*, *Nero*, *Timarion*, around fifty epigrams and some letters. Other works in the corpus have been doubted and contested, but without reaching a firm conclusion that they are inauthentic.

2.3.1 The dialogues

The dialogue is the form used most frequently by Lucian. He himself, with his usual clear self-awareness, defines the novelty of his work in relation to tradition. He in fact states that he has taken the philosophical dialogue, by then reduced to wretched circumstances and out of favour with the public, and has revitalised it by combining it with comedy, thus winning for it "great favour from his hearers, who formerly feared his prickles and avoided taking hold of him as if he were a sea-urchin," as he says in the dialogue *The Double Indictment* (par. 34), composed around the age of 40, and so in his full maturity. This renewal of the traditional and serious philosophical dialogue by introducing a comic, amusing and appealing element, put into Lucian's hands an instrument of great flexibility that allowed him to confront a vast range of themes by pleasant rather than grave means.

Philosophical in content (but treated in Lucian's manner) are dialogues such as: the already mentioned *Hermotimus*, composed around 165, in which he reviews with irony and detachment the various philosophical schools; *Essays in Portaiture*, *Essays in Portaiture Defended*, *Toxaris or Friendship* and *Anacharsis or Athletics*. Some moral dialogues return to the manner of Menippean satire, and sometimes feature Menippus of Gadara himself as a character (cf. *The Classical Age* IV 2.2.2), such as *Icaromenippus or The Sky-Man* and *Menippus or The Descent into Hades*. It is impossible to list all the themes and titles, which run from *Astrology* to *The Goddess Syria* (in which Lucian imitates Herodotus); from the frequent flippant representation of the world of the gods (*The Parliament of the Gods*, *Zeus Catechized*, the group of *Dialogues of the Gods*, on which see below) to the representation of human types, as in *Philosophies for Sale*, *The Parasite* and *Anacharsis or Athletics*; in *Lexiphanes* he criticises linguistic fanaticism with penetrating satire. However, the works that, in the Modern Era, have given Lucian his greatest fame are the four collections that expressly bear the title of *Dialogues* in the manuscript tradition, in which the satirical and, often, paradoxical element gains force from a vivid and graphic style and from the choice of particularly amusing situations.

In the 26 *Dialogues of the Gods* Lucian, moving away from certain bombastic artifices of the Second Sophistic, passes with wit and finesse through the repertoire of classical mythology, from the love affairs of Zeus to the judgement of Paris, from the story of Prometheus to the problem of the paternity of Pan, son of Hermes. The outlook is rationalist and irreverent: in an era of religious syncretism and of a preponderant influence from mystery religions and eastern religions, Lucian succeeds in dissipating even the aura of greatness and idealisation that surrounded the classical myths, bringing out into the open their often shabby motives and intrigues. In the 15 *Dialogues of the Sea-Gods* the background shifts from the heavens to the sea, but remains set in the disputes, spites and affairs of mythological figures such as Poseidon and his son Polyphemus, Triton and the Nereids, the nymphs Doris and Galatea and so on.

A more bitter tone characterises the *Dialogues of the Dead*, in which Lucian offers a glimpse of how the ancient world conceived the reality of the afterlife in thirty situations, marked by real black humour; his polemic is directed against the vanities of earthly life and its empty passions. In the crudeness of some details and the seriousness of certain situations, Lucian is indebted to the moral content of Cynic-Stoic diatribe and to Menippus, already mentioned above, who takes part as a protagonist in some dialogues, as do Pluto, Charon, Hermes, Diogenes and Alexander the Great as protagonists in some of the dialogues. In the 15 *Dialogues of the Courtesans*, Lucian, recalling situations typical of the New Comedy of Menander, sketches a lively social profile of a timeless Athens, in which the private dimension predominates, with characters such as thwarted lovers, dodgy businessmen, young men in love and, above all, pimps and prostitutes. This work too (which is mostly dated to Lucian's first stay at Athens, around 160) imposes a disenchanted and strongly ironic view, in which, for example, the author mocks the fierce competition between courtesans to secure the richest lover, or of the spite and ill will between the younger and older courtesans; with less irony he touches on the theme of girls forced into prostitution by poverty.

2.3.2 *A True Story*

A True Story also enjoys considerable fame. The work, in two books, is intended as a parody of those authors who pass off fantastic topics as real, a polemical intent that is clear already in the title. In the introduction Lucian declares, in opposition to writers such as Ctesias, Herodotus, Iambulus (cf. *The Roman Imperial Period* IX 1.7.8) and even Homer ("forefather of these charlatans"; par. 3), that he has written a story full of falsehood and evasions, to divert the mind of the reader from whatever serious matter occupies it. "I am writing about things I neither saw nor experienced nor heard about from others, which moreover don't exist, and in any case could not exist" (par. 4). The irony is clear even in the choice of expressions, which recall famous declarations of historical truthfulness.

> The fantastic adventures of a group of Greeks begin as they set off, captained by the author, departing for the western Ocean and passing the Pillars of Hercules. From this point on there is a crescendo of amazing inventions, which has no equal in surviving Greek literature. The intrepid travellers end up, in marvellous fashion, on the Moon, take part in a battle between the Sun-ites and the Moon-ites, drop back down to Earth where they are swallowed by a whale, encounter the Corkfeet, who surf on feet of cork, reach the Land of the Blest or the Hereafter. At the end of the second book Lucian promises to continue further, but the new chapters were probably never written.

A True Story is certainly the work in which Lucian's fine intellectualism, his ability to mock human usages and customs, his wish to create a very knowing web of references and allusions to classical and contemporary authors (many of whom are unknown to us) all meet, achieving a result of extraordinary elegance and great wit. Critics believe that this type of brief novel does not date before 180, and so would be one of Lucian's final works.

2.2.3 *Lucius or The Ass*

A particular mention should be made of this other brief novel, Lucian's authorship of which is debated. It tells the adventures of a character called Lucius, who is transformed into an ass instead of into a bird by a mistaken piece of magic. At the end of his troubled adventures, the ass returns to human form by eating rose petals (cf. *The Roman Imperial Period* IX 1.1.3).

The plot is similar to that of the *Metamorphoses* of the Latin author Apuleius, who states that he was inspired by the work of the Greek Lucius of Patras. The question of what the relation is between the text of Lucius of Patras, Pseudo-Lucian and Apuleius is at the centre of a very lively critical debate, which has not yet reached definitive conclusions. The most likely theory seems to be that Lucius of Patras, a sophist contemporary to Lucian (as we are told by the Byzantine Photius) had written a long novel, of which the *Lucius or The Ass* attributed to Lucian is a summary. The arguments for or against Lucian's authorship of the work (or of the summary) are evenly balanced: some scholars see in it evidence of Lucian's typical style, while others highlight late syntactical structures or even blunders that are not in line with Lucian's Atticist purism.

2.4 Style

The corrosive force and extreme clarity of judgement that are characteristics of Lucian's works rely on a supple and vivid instrument: the Attic language. As a partisan of Atticism, Lucian was able to achieve a command of this language, which was geographically and chronologically remote from him, with an extraordinary freshness and aptness. His periodic structures are elegant and agile; the vocabulary, which is precise and open to colloquial forms, can adapt to both abstract content and concrete situations. The copious references to classical authors are never an end in themselves, but strictly a function of the content. We are far removed from certain stylistic artifices and abstractions of the Neosophists, which Lucian himself criticises in dialogues such as *The Sham Sophist or The Solecist* and *A Professor of Public Speaking*. In the former, the target is, precisely, an intellectual *à la page*, convinced that he knows how to use Greek to perfection, but who ends up making grammar errors; the latter ridicules the eloquence of the period as a wholly empty, exterior phenomenon. Lucian counsels reliance on the ancient authors, but with a prudent caution.

The authors most plundered are, across the whole of Lucian's output, Homer, Aristophanes, Menander, Euripides and the classical historians. The result, as has been noted, is never a slavish imitation, but an original creation of typical situations and images, elements that make Lucian not only the champion of satire, but above all a literary figure of the first rank, aware of his own intelligence, able to use it and proud of the Greek cultural heritage.

IX Narrative Literature

1 The Greek novel

1.1 Origins and characteristics of the novel

1.1.1 A "new" genre

The novel in prose is perhaps the most original feature of the landscape of Greek literature in the Imperial Period. The testimonies available today in fact allow us to say that the genre probably existed from the second century B.C. and that in the late Hellenistic Period it underwent considerable growth. The so-called *Ninus Novel* (behind the figure of the protagonist lies a historical person, the ancient king of Assyria: cf. below 1.7.2), a few fragments of which survive on papyrus, is dated around 100 B.C. and is hence the earliest example of which we have direct knowledge. Still probably in the first century B.C. there is *Callirhoe* by Chariton of Aphrodisias (cf. next par.) and the fragments of *Metiochus and Parthenope* and the *Novel of Chione* (cf. below 1.7.4). However, the majority of the novels that have survived entire, via the Byzantine manuscript tradition, belong to the Imperial Period, the era to which it seems we should also date the greatest success and diffusion of this narrative entertainment genre, as is attested by the many papyrus fragments with remains of works that are otherwise lost and for which we do not know the authors. The success of the genre continued also in the Byzantine Period, when various novel-like works were composed in both prose and verse.

1.1.2 The origins of the novel

The origin of the Greek novel has long been debated by scholars, to the point that study of the texts of the novels in their own right has almost seemed to take second place. There is no doubt that the studies on the genre's genesis have yielded a quantity of valid and useful critical observations, which remain a solid scholarly advance, yet today the problem of genesis is addressed with rather less intensity, and even with a certain distancing, and scholars prefer to investigate the various "ingredients" that have in different ways influenced the formation of the narrative genre that we call the "Greek novel" (taking care to resist the temptation to see in it a sort of prototype, not yet perfected, of the modern bourgeois novel).

The theories formulated in the past fixed on an origin in eastern cultures (the majority of the novels have eastern settings) or in the context of mystery religions, or they identified the site of its formation as the rhetorical schools, in the atmosphere of the Second Sophistic. These are all elements that may have played some role and it is still appropriate to consider them, but only together with other elements. Scholars have emphasised the Greek novel's relation to the ancient epic tradition (primarily, of course, the *Odyssey*), which had an influence on the for-

https://doi.org/10.1515/9783110426328-038

mation of the novel's narrative that is undeniable at the level of structures of narration and of subject-matter, and also as a remote model that offered authoritative suggestions. But one certainly cannot overlook the influence of a genre that is formally distant from the novel, such as New Comedy, with its typical plot that wants to see two young lovers happily reunited after being cast out on various adventures by *Tyche*, seeing them as passive heroes at the mercy of misfortunes and misadventures. And finally, when we think of a cultural hinterland for the novel authors, one cannot deny the presence of novelistic material in various literary contexts (one may think here of Menippean satire or the so-called Milesian tales: cf. respectively *The Classical Age* IV 2.2.2 and *The Roman Imperial Period* IX 2.2), nor that of a certain type of historiography intended more for entertainment than for practical purposes, aimed at the amusement of the reader and the enjoyment of the story.

In relation to historiography, one should not overlook the fact that the protagonists of the earliest novels are historical figures. A precedent that may very well have played a role, in this case, is the tradition of romanticised history that bloomed in the Hellenistic Age around the exploits of Alexander the Great. And the earliest of the historians of Alexander, Callisthenes, is the figure who attracted the false attribution of the curious work that goes by the title of *The Alexander Romance* (normally called the work of "Pseudo-Callisthenes"), which has survived in various recensions (and translations) that ultimately go back to an epistolary novel. It is almost certain that its origin is to be placed in the Alexandrian Era, but different versions were produced and circulated in the Imperial Period (cf. *The Hellenistic Age* VIII 1.3).

Today, however, the study of models is no longer pursued in light of a search for the location and genre from which the novel may have emerged through some more or less direct descent, as was done in the last century, but in light of the concept of intertextuality, or the simultaneous presence and operation of other texts and genres within the conception and composition of a work, a relation that is productive of literary references and learned winks by the author to the reader. The novel therefore appears in essence to be the result of an intersection of different elements, fused in the creation of a new genre but, as is always the case, the offspring of one or more traditions.

1.1.3 The themes of the novel

As we have already mentioned, we should distinguish the novels transmitted through the Byzantine manuscripts (i.e. the works of Chariton, Xenophon of Ephesus, Achilles Tatius, Longus and Heliodorus) from those known only partially, by other routes – above all the discovery of papyrus fragments preserved by chance (for example the important *Ninus Novel*, the oldest known, that we have already mentioned). A very great amount has been lost and it is only in the Egyptian area, thanks to the papyri, that we can recover a few scraps.

We have many fragments of unknown authors, all to some degree enigmatic and of differing literary levels, which attest the broad diffusion of the genre across different classes of reader, from the more refined level, informed by literature and rhetoric, to the more popular level with simple tastes. Perhaps due to its aim of entertainment, the novel is a genre that is discussed little or not at all in ancient treatise-writing, and the rhetorical teaching did not bother to give it a name or a definition, nor to make it the object of critical reflection or note its precise physiognomy. This matches the fact that the authors are for the most part otherwise unknown, even in cases where we know their names and origins. It seems clear, then, that for the ancient world this entertainment literature in prose, even in its stronger representatives, was set apart, so to speak, from all that was considered to be more serious and noble. Yet, in what we do know of the genre, we can identify some particular strands.

The novel of love and of adventure. The characteristic and predominant themes are, firstly, *erōs*, incarnated in a love that is permissible but at first thwarted, until it finally wins out, and which remains faithful and therefore tenaciously chaste during the adventures that precede the final reunification; and, secondly, that of the journey, which is long, troubled and full of adventures. The structure-type is roughly as follows. A pair of young lovers are forcibly separated in a double scheme: the separation occurs soon after the wedding in the earlier novels, and in the later ones soon after falling in love, and so before the lovers' physical union. In these latter novels, in fact, the component of sexual fidelity takes on an even more significant value, in an exaltation of the values of fidelity and chastity, especially when facing the temptations and snares of the period of separation. We have already mentioned the predominantly passive character of the protagonists, above all the male ones: they are not the heroes of the action but instead at the mercy of capricious and tyrannical fate (*tychē*), though not a fate so cruel as to prevent the final achievement of their happiness. Onto this motif is grafted a whole range of events that recur to some degree, which provide the body of the narrative and enliven both the central, unifying erotic theme and the basic scheme through a series of *coups de théâtre*, without bothering about realistic representation.

The fantastic novel. Yet love is not the only theme in all the texts known to us. Especially if we take into account those that have not survived entire, we also find the fantastic adventure or travel novel, in which the erotic theme is absent or merely incidental. It seems clear that the selection made by time and tradition, by whatever means and for whatever reasons, has privileged the first type of novel (as described above) while penalising the fantastic novel, sacrificing a greater variety within the genre. This is true not only in relation to content, but also at the level of style and audience.

Connected to the fantastic themes is the brief novel entitled *Lucius or The Ass*, which has survived within the corpus of the works of Lucian, though its authenticity is debated (cf. *The Roman Imperial Period* VIII 2.3.3). It tells of a certain Lucius who, through his inept use of magic potions, transforms himself into an ass instead of a bird and after various setbacks recovers his human form. We know that the same theme, which was then also picked up by Apuleius in his *Metamorphoses or Golden Ass*, was retold in a lost work by a certain Lucius of Patras. This has given rise to a complex and still undecided philological debate, not only on the authorship of *Lucius or The Ass*, but also on the relation of this short work to Lucius of Patras (is it a simple summary, or a shorter reworking with some degree of originality?), on the identity of the latter and on its relation to Apuleius (did he use the work of Lucius of Patras, which would then be the shared source of both Apuleius and Pseudo-Lucian?).

The novels on the Trojan Cycle. We may here mention the novels on the theme of the *Trojan Cycle* of legends, based on the fiction of an "eyewitness account," which is attributed in the tradition to Dictys Cretensis and Dares of Phrygia, long known only in the Latin version. The existence of a Greek original, which had been doubted, is now secure, thanks to papyrus discoveries. They were thus works written in Greek probably in the first century A.D. and later translated into Latin. In *The Diary of the Trojan War* (*Ephemeris belli Troiani*) Dictys Cretensis presents himself as a Greek who had participated in the war and had kept a diary. He is counterpointed by *The History of the Fall of Troy* (*De excidio Troiae historia*) in which Dares Phrygius, a Trojan priest, presents the events of the great war and siege from the point of view of the defeated.

1.2 *Callirhoe* by Chariton of Aphrodisias

1.2.1 A nearly unknown author

The only ancient testimony about Chariton appears at the opening of the novel of which he claims to be author, *Callirhoe* (I 1, 1): "I, Chariton of Aphrodisias, clerk of the lawyer Athenagoras, am going to relate a love story which took place in Syracuse." The ancient sources are otherwise silent and evidence for Chariton disappears until the Humanistic Period, when the text was rediscovered. Only with the recent discovery of passages of the work in some papyri of the second to third century A.D. has it been possible to cast some light on the novel's date, which was once mistakenly placed in the fourth to fifth century A.D. At present, the date given to *Callirhoe* ranges from the first century B.C. to the first century A.D. If, as seems probable, the earlier dating is correct, then this is the earliest novel, and the first novel of love, to have survived complete but for some brief lacunae. A further step in unravelling the complex dating problem may be gleaned from a deeper study of the epigraphic material of the city of Aphrodisias in Asia Minor. At our current state of knowledge, the presence in the city's inscriptions of the names Chariton and Athenagoras has been established: Consequently, we can confirm at least the plausibility of the notice that appears at the opening of the novel.

1.2.2 The plot

Chaereas and Callirhoe, the two most beautiful young people of Syracuse, on their way to the Temple of Aphrodite to participate in a festival of the goddess, meet on the road and fall in love. Although the girl's father, the general Hermocrates, is opposed to the marriage, the people of the city, gathered in the assembly, convince him to grant his daughter's hand in marriage to Chaereas. The couple's wedded bliss is blocked, however, by Callirhoe's former suitors, nobles from the greatest cities of Magna Graecia, who are not inclined to accept rejection.

Making use of Chaereas' naïve and impulsive character, they convince him of Callirhoe's infidelity. Seized by jealousy, Chaereas kicks his wife, leaving her unconscious. It is thought that Callirhoe is dead. In a solemn funeral ceremony, in which the whole city takes part, the girl is shut up in a tomb full of unimaginable riches, which attract the thief Theron and his band of tomb-robbers. Discovering that the young woman is alive, Theron abducts her and leaves for Miletus, where he sells her to a prominent citizen, Dionysius, who had recently been widowed. The meeting between Callirhoe and Dionysius takes place in a temple of Aphrodite and the man, convinced he is seeing Aphrodite in person, falls in love with the girl.

Callirhoe in the meantime discovers that she is expecting a child by Chaereas. To spare the child a future as a slave, she consents to marry Dionysius. Meanwhile at Syracuse Chaereas discovers the truth and, setting off in pursuit of Callirhoe, reaches Miletus, where he is taken prisoner by Mithridates, satrap of Caria. Mithridates is in love with the woman and uses Chaereas to try to detach Callirhoe from Dionysius. The latter, having seized a letter sent by Chaereas to Callirhoe and interpreting it as a trap set by Mithridates, asks for help from Pharnaces, satrap of Lydia and Ionia and enemy of Mithridates. Pharnaces in his turn sends to Artaxerxes II, king of the Persians, who summons them all to Babylon for a court case. Complicating the debate further, Chaereas makes a surprise appearance, reclaiming the woman for himself. During the hearing, Artaxerxes, struck by the beauty of Callirhoe, tries in vain to seduce her. But a sudden rebellion of the Egyptians and the invasion of Syria force the king to leave with his army and with an imposing royal entourage, in which both Callirhoe and Statira, queen of the Persians, take part. Dionysius takes his position alongside the king.

Chaereas joins the Egyptian army and, due to his heroism, he is named admiral of the fleet. He thus succeeds in defeating the Persians by sea, seizing booty and finding Callirhoe. The final victory, however, falls to the Persians, who suppress the Egyptians' revolt. By a trick Chaereas and Callirhoe succeed in fleeing towards Syracuse. Before they leave, Callirhoe entrusts to Statira a message for Dionysius, in which she asks him to raise her son in accord with his noble rank and to send him back to Syracuse once he has reached maturity. In Syracuse, Chaereas and Callirhoe, who had been believed dead, are welcomed in triumph.

1.2.3 The historical background

The events narrated are presented against a real historical background. Callirhoe is the name of the daughter of a real person, Hermocrates, who defeated the Athenian fleet in 413 B.C. Diodorus Siculus informs us that the general had a daughter who was married to Dionysius I, tyrant of Syracuse; and Artaxerxes II too is a historical figure. However, the references in the novel to these real details are not coherent and it is easy to spot many substantial chronological discrepancies. Hence these are elements that have been freely reused and reworked. At no point in the story does the historical component take precedence over a taste for fantasy in narration or over the rapid and at times vertiginous succession of events, which is marked by many *coups de théâtre* and a large cast of characters.

For various reasons we cannot call *Callirhoe* a "historical novel," above all for the vague and imprecise chronological placing of the events, but also for the extreme rarity of descriptions of settings and places and of digressions on habits and customs, despite the fact that the action offers numerous opportunities for this, shifting as it does from Sicily to Asia Minor and from Mesopotamia to Phoenicia. All elements of the narrative are, rather, subordinated to the tension of the plot and the breakneck rhythm in which the adventures unfold before the reader's eyes in all their spectacularity. The impression is that, in making a historical figure the heroine of his story, Chariton was meeting aesthetic and compositional principles that were perhaps already conventional in this literary genre.

1.2.4 The protagonists

Absolutely central is the protagonist Callirhoe, even in comparison to Chaereas, who only in brief sequences manages to steal the scene. The priority of Callirhoe over Chaereas is declared by Chariton himself at the finale of the novel (VIII 8, 16): "So ends the story I have composed about Callirhoe." And even at the start, straight after the presentation of the subject, the author describes Callirhoe first ("her beauty was not so much human as divine, not that of a Nereid or mountain nymph, either, but of Aphrodite herself"; I 1, 2), and then Chaereas ("whose handsomeness surpassed all, resembling the statues and pictures of Achilles and Nireus and Hippolytus and Alcibiades"; I 1, 3). Thereafter whenever the beauty of the two is compared, Callirhoe puts her husband in the shade.

Chariton, however, does not limit himself to making Callirhoe a new Aphrodite or a new Helen, as some critics have maintained, interpreting the novel as a lay reworking of these myths. While the principal characteristic of the heroine, in a stereotype common to all Greek love novels, is beauty, Callirhoe is also endowed with wisdom and manages even in difficult situations to maintain self-control and make the right decision; she is the equal of her antagonists in cunning and trickery, fights to remain faithful to her husband and not to lose the noble status of her family.

Chaereas, to the contrary, is more impulsive and irascible and falls into the traps of his adversaries. When he is seized by despair he weeps and laments and only his friend Polycharmus succeeds in dissuading him from suicide. In the final part, however, there is a redemption for Chaereas: when he manages to capture by a ruse the city of Tyre, impregnable to attack and loyal to the Persians, he becomes the admiral of the Egyptian fleet and succeeds in taking possession of the enemy booty and finding his beloved. However, his attitude to Callirhoe's decision to entrust their son until he reaches maturity to Dionysius of Miletus remains inexplicable.

The centrality of the figure of Callirhoe, together with the positivity of all the female characters of the novel, has led some critics to maintain that the work was intended for a female audience, though this hypothesis has not been confirmed. However, it is interesting that, according to some recent proposals, Chariton may have been the author of two other novels with female protagonists: the *Novel of Chione* and *Metiochus and Parthenope*. Less plausible, on the other hand, is the theory of those who see Chariton as the author also of the *Ninus Novel* (cf. below 1.7).

1.2.5 The spectacular in the narrative

More than the historical dimension, the salient narrative feature of Chariton's novel lies in the search for a fast-paced rhythm characterised by brash *coups de théâtre*, which confer on the story a quite spectacular dimension with a notable visual impact. In the novel there are numerous comparisons and similes that refer explicitly to the sphere of theatre. When Chaereas suddenly appears at the court hearing in Babylon, the author intervenes in the narration with this statement (V 8, 2): "What dramatist ever staged such and extraordinary situation? An observer would have thought himself in a theatre filled with every conceivable emotion. All were there at once – tears, joy, astonishment, pity, disbelief, prayer." More significant is the reference to the theatrical world that characterises the opening of Book VIII, in which the happy ending of the story is presented (VIII 1, 4): "I think that this last book will prove the most enjoyable for my readers, as a *catharsis* to the grim events in the preceding ones."

Some scholars have maintained that the plot of *Callirhoe* has the overall unity of a drama in five episodes, which are to be identified as follows: the wedding of Chaereas and Callirhoe and the troubles of Callirhoe; the adventures of Chaereas; the trial at Babylon; the military triumphs of Chaereas; the "cathartic" finale. On this view, the episodes would be linked together in such a way as to ensure a rise towards the climax at the finale. Further, unlike the other novelists who create suspense by concealing from the reader part of the truth, Chariton uses the very truth of the facts to keep interest alive. There is no doubt that the happy ending of the story, the importance accorded to Tyche in the course of events and the presentation of some characters (including Dionysius, a cultivated, moderate, magnanimous man) relate to comic models rather than tragic ones. In particular, scholars believe that Chariton (and probably the novel of love as a whole) was strongly influenced by New Comedy. A piece of evidence for this is the fact that this novel also includes an interesting quotation from the *Misoumenos* (*The Hated Man*) of Menander. Dionysius regrets acting precipitately by communicating his suspicions to Pharnaces and so risking the loss of his lady at the trial in Babylon, "when he could be in bed, embracing his beloved" (IV 7, 7; cfr. Menander, fr. 9 Sandbach).

1.2.6 The presence of the Homeric model

Another striking factor is the abundance of Homeric quotations that emphasise the salient moments of the story. Homer is cited a full 31 times in the course of the eight chapters of the novel. Among the quotations that recur most frequently is the expression, present already in the first chapter (I 1, 14), "Her knees collapsed and her heart within her" (cf. *Iliad* XXI 114 and *Odyssey* IV 703), which emphasises the moments of greatest emotional tension. In another passage, Callirhoe's beauty is said to be "like unto Artemis or to Aphrodite the golden" (IV 7, 5; cf. *Odyssey* XVII 37 and XIX 54), in a periphrasis that in the Homeric poem refers to Penelope.

Apart from the explicit quotations, there are also many intertextual references in the novel alluding to Homer. For example, the whole section concerning the triumphs of Chaereas echoes the *Iliad* in more or less explicit ways and at the moment when he devises a trick to storm Tyre, Chaereas is likened to the Iliadic hero Diomedes. Further, the scene of the final meeting of Chaereas and Callirhoe recalls the meeting of Odysseus and Penelope.

1.3 *Anthia and Habrocomes* of Xenophon of Ephesus (also known as *The Ephesian Story*)

1.3.1 The author and the work

The *Suda* lexicon preserves our only ancient notices on this author: "Xenophon, an Ephesian, narrator. (He wrote) *The Ephesian Story* (*Ephesiaca*): it is a love novel in 10 books about Habrocomes and Anthia, *On the City of the Ephesians* and other things." On Xenophon, modern critics have debated everything. According to some, the by-name "of Ephesus" refers to the writer's home city, while for others it derives from the topic of his principal work, namely the novel called *The Ephesian Story*. Doubts have been raised also about the truth of the name Xenophon, which, according to some, was adopted by the author of the novel in homage to the historian of that name, either because he was his chosen stylistic model or because he was considered to be the first narrator in the novelistic style.

As regards the dating, the only indications are internal to the work (for example the mention of the career of "eirenarch," an office attested from the Trajanic Period onward) and lead us to suppose that *Anthia and Habrocomes* was composed in the second century A.D. Scholars generally maintain that the text is earlier than the novels of Achilles Tatius and Heliodorus and of course later than Chariton.

Another problem concerns the novel's text itself. The *Suda* lexicon reports a division into ten books, whereas in the version that has survived today the work consists of five books. Given the greater brevity of the text compared to the other surviving love novels, the identifiable lacunae, the internal contradictions and the quality of the story, it has been argued that what survives is not the original text but an epitome, perhaps from the Byzantine Period. According to others, however, it is more likely that the original work consisted of five books and was later expanded into ten. But when was the original produced? On this aspect too we have no certain knowledge.

1.3.2 The plot

The *opening* of the novel seems to be inspired by Euripides' *Hippolytus*: Habrocomes, a boy of sixteen, is full of pride over his exceptional beauty and disdains Eros. The god takes revenge and makes him fall hopelessly in love with a fourteen-year-old girl, Anthia. The two meet at the local festival of the goddess Artemis and at once fall hopelessly in love with each other, even falling sick. The worried parents turn to the oracle of Apollo at Colophon to discover the cause of the sickness. They learn that the two should marry, that they will encounter great misfortunes, but that it will all have a happy ending. Upon returning to Ephesus, the parents consent to the marriage of the two young people. To ward off the oracle's grim prophecies, they (inexplicably) decide to send the young couple far from the city. After a halt at Rhodes, Anthia and Habrocomes' ship is attacked by Phoenician pirates, who bring the pair to Tyre, to their chief Apsyrtus. From this moment on, the two young people are forcibly separated and an interminable series of misfortunes begins for them, ranging from Asia Minor to Egypt, Ethiopia to southern Italy, in a succession of flights from brigands, Indian princes, slave merchants, pimps and soldiers madly in love with one of the two protagonists. The final encounter of the married couple, under the auspices of the oracle of the god Apis, takes place on Rhodes in the Temple of Isis, where Anthia has taken a vow. The couple return to Ephesus, where their love will be lived out in a more peaceful fashion.

1.3.3 A dry narrative

Aside from some books, such as the first, in which the narration is characterised by greater narrative breadth, the novel presents the facts with extreme brevity, removing all descriptions and digressions and limiting the characters' dialogues, monologues and laments. Further, many characters appear in the narrative and then depart the scene without leading to the consequences that they seemed to herald and which the plot requires.

For example, in Book I two Phoenician pirates, Corymbus and Euxinus, fall in love with, respectively, Habrocomes and Anthia, but in Book II they disappear from the narrative without any consequences of their love, which at first sight had appeared impassioned and to presage troubles. In Book IV it is said that Anthia, condemned by the brigands to die in a pit, torn apart by two starving dogs, is saved by the guardian of the pit, a brigand who is in love with her. Several times in the narrative reference is made to the fact that Anthia decides to rear the dogs, which makes it seem likely that in the original story the two animals had a precise role. Yet in the surviving text the dogs too leave the scene without prompting any development of the story.

1.3.4 The religion of *Anthia and Habrocomes*

In the text there are rather heterogeneous elements of religiosity. Great importance is given to oracles. The oracle of Colophon, for example, is the motor of the first part of the plot and nine hexameters are dedicated to it; and, at the end, Anthia is comforted by the oracle of the god Apis, which assures her that Habrocomes is alive and that he will soon be reunited with her. In Book I great prominence is held by two divinities: Eros and Artemis. Echoing the *Hippolytus* of Euripides, Xenophon dwells on Habrocomes' disdain for Eros, whom he considers to be not even a god. Eros, indignant, seeks a trap for the boy and finds it in the festival of Artemis. During the sacred procession to the Artemisium, Habrocomes for the first time sees Anthia, dressed as Artemis the Huntress. Those who see the novel as an allegory of the sacred mysteries of Isis have supposed that that goddess lies concealed behind Artemis, since Isis is the Egyptian goddess to whom Anthia, in the course of the story, will take a vow in order to remain chaste and faithful and who represents the saviour goddess mentioned by the oracle of Apollo. More than in other novels, the pantheon of the *Ephesian Story* presents a mixture of Greek and Egyptian divinities: invoked are not only Artemis-Isis, Apollo and Eros, but also Aphrodite, Hera, Helios, Apis and the river Nile. Of some interest, in relation to the Nile god, is a salvation scene, which recalls some episodes of hagiographical literature. Habrocomes, condemned to death for committing a homicide, is crucified on the bank of the Nile. The youth implores the god Nile not to let him die and the river swells up and sweeps away the cross, dragging the youth to safety. Habrocomes is then condemned to the pyre: again the Nile with his waters douses the flames and saves the hero. A similar "miracle" of salvation is also present in the novel of Heliodorus (see below).

Another trait characteristic of the novel is the considerable presence of Stoic elements. Phrases such as "They have power over my body, but I keep a free soul" (II 4, 4), recurring references to the *Pronoia* (Providence) that governs the world and oversees the troubles of the two heroes, the insistence on virtue as an inalienable interior good, the presence of many positive figures alongside the antagonists – all these are various factors that reveal in the novel a strongly founded moral intent on a Stoic pattern.

This interesting and multiform marriage of religious and philosophical elements gives the impression that the *Ephesian Story*, rather than being a novel of *Pronoia* or a novel of mystery religion, includes in its fabric different suggestions and motifs, which are stratified more or less organically in the version that has survived.

1.4 *Leucippe and Clitophon* by Achilles Tatius

1.4.1 A hit novel
According to the *Suda lexicon*, Achilles Tatius, originally from Alexandria and author of the novel *Leucippe and Clitophon*, at the end of his life converted to Christianity and became a bishop; he had written love stories, essays on the celestial sphere and on etymology and a history of illustrious people. The lexicon also records an interesting stylistic observation: "His style is everywhere the same as that of the love stories." Aside from this, we lack precise references to the period or cultural setting in which Achilles Tatius lived and worked; some scholars consider his Greek

name *Tatios* to be a transcription of the Latin Tatius, while others even see it as transcribed from the Egyptian *Thoth*.

For this novelist too, therefore, the problem of the date was for years at the centre of scholarship, until the discovery of some papyri dating to the second century A.D. permitted us to establish at least a *terminus ante quem*. Further, some historical references contained in the work allow us to set the date of the novel securely in the second century A.D.

It seems, then, that the report about the conversion to the Christian religion and the bishopric (similar to what happens in the case of another novel author, Heliodorus) were a late attempt to rehabilitate an author whose novel presents a strongly erotic component that was a hit in the Christian world. Indeed, *Leucippe and Clitophon* immediately enjoyed wide success that lasted into later centuries. The first quotation from the work occurs already in Eustathius of Antioch (fourth to fifth century) and an epigram in the *Palatine Anthology* (IX 203) also refers to the novel. In the Byzantine Period it was the object of imitation by two novelists: Eustathius (or Eumathius) Macrembolites, in his *Hysmine and Hysminias*, and Constantine Manasses in *Aristander and Callithea*. The work of Achilles Tatius also inspired Torquato Tasso, in the *Aminta*, and other modern authors.

1.4.2 The plot

The author of the novel, in Sidon in Phoenicia, meets the young Clitophon, who tells him his troubled love story. Clitophon, originally from Tyre, was intended by his father to be married to his half-sister. Following the war of the Thracians against Byzantium, a cousin of his, the beautiful Leucippe, moves to Tyre, to the house of Clitophon's father. Clitophon, as soon as he sees the girl, is seized by an irresistible passion. Leucippe does not at once fall in love with Clitophon, but over time she notes and appreciates her cousin's continuous attentions and his attempts at seduction. In order to possess Leucippe, the youth decides to abduct her and flee to Alexandria in Egypt. However, a violent storm causes their ship to be wrecked.

The pair succeed in reaching the Egyptian coast, where Leucippe is captured by the ferocious Nile brigands, the Bucoli (in Greek βουκόλοι, literally "herdsmen"). Clitophon, freed by a garrison of Egyptian soldiers, succeeds in tracking down the young woman at the very moment when, during a sacrifice, the Bucoli seem to be ripping open her belly and dining on her entrails. In reality the girl has been saved by a shared friend of the couple, Menelaus, who succeeds in deceiving the Bucoli with a trick used by theatrical actors, namely to place over Leucippe's body, before the sacrifice, a fake belly full of animal entrails. Having rediscovered Leucippe, Clitophon decides to set off for Alexandria again. Here the young woman is abducted by other brigands who cut off her head.

Clitophon's despair is eased over time by the impassioned suit of a wealthy young widow, Melite, who convinces him to marry her. The two depart for Ephesus, where she lives and where Clitophon has promised to spend the wedding night. In Melite's house he finds Leucippe too (who had evidently escaped from the decapitation somehow), under the false identity of Lacaena, a shaven-headed slave who had been purchased from the pirates. The girl sends a letter to Clitophon in which she reveals her identity to him, reproaches him for his marriage to

Melite and asks, in the name of the fidelity that she alone has maintained, to be freed and sent to Byzantium. Clitophon has in fact not yet consummated his marriage to Melite: only later will she succeed, by furious pleas and cries, in extracting an embrace from the young man. In the meantime Melite's previous husband, the violent Thersander, reappears, intending to avenge himself on the adulterers. He too, however, falls in love with Leucippe. To shock Clitophon, he pretends that Leucippe is dead. The story, after more misfortunes and a trial in which Clitophon is condemned for the killing of Leucippe, ends with the re-establishment of the truth and the chance for Leucippe to demonstrate her virginity. Finally the two young people can be united in marriage and return to Tyre.

1.4.3 A complex and artificial plot

The series of misadventures that the two lovers must confront, the three apparent deaths of the heroine (two of which are genuine horror scenes), the sudden appearance of new characters, who enliven the action and delay the rhythm of the story with flashbacks of their experiences, all ensure that the plot of *Leucippe and Clitophon* does not have the linearity and immediacy of the novel of Chariton nor the narrative simplicity of *Anthia and Habrocomes*. The plot thus becomes almost a pretext for the insertion of long digressions and descriptions in which the author, with erudition and an encyclopaedic taste, flaunts his knowledge in various fields, from figurative art to botany, from zoology to geography.

In the first part of the novel much space is given to digressions and debates on erotic topics, which, in an easygoing and worldly manner, echo the content of some Platonic dialogues, mixed with piquant references to the literature on the *ars amandi*. Drawing on commonplaces (for example from Hesiod) the characters dwell on the inferiority of heterosexual love and the negativity of relations with women, who are dangerous if they are beautiful and intolerable if they are ugly. In the case of this novel one can fairly talk of an "open form" that is able to receive and rework narrative and literary elements of various kinds. The intertextuality of the work is truly multiform: we have echoes of the genres of historiography, novella, epistolography and philosophy, again a taste for the spectacular on a comic and pantomimic pattern and a rhetorical interest in the elaborate descriptions (*ekphraseis*) that were enjoyed so much by the rhetors of the Second Sophistic.

1.4.4 The first-person narrator

A significant point is the use of first-person narration: it is Clitophon himself who retells his own amorous misfortunes to the author of the novel, after meeting him at Sidon in front of a painting that represents the rape of Europa. It is difficult to establish a connection between the subject of the painting and the content of the novel. The *ekphrasis*, which describes the painting in detail with a certain conceitedness, functions as the frame of the novel, a frame that does not close at the end of the final eighth book, as is done in the novel of Chariton in which the author speaks again at the conclusion. The use of the first-person narrator also helps, along with the insertion of anti-heroic characters and the reversal of dramatic episodes into amusing scenes, to ensure the comic and parodic tone of the novel, in which the characters appear to be puppets in the hands of *Tyche*.

Of the two co-protagonists, it is above all Clitophon who lacks depth: the author's comic intentions fasten more gladly on him (in an amusing scene he is cross-dressed as a woman). Leucippe, in contrast, seems better characterised, being aware of her good qualities and proud of them, as does Melite, who is intelligent and impassioned. Moreover, unlike the other novels, the male protagonist does not remain chaste and faithful to his beloved, but is literally carried away by Melite's erotic fury, after months of weary waiting. Due to these elements, some critics consider *Leucippe and Clitophon* to be in reality a parody of the novel of idealised love, supported by its artificial intellectualism and somewhat irreverent taste.

1.5 *Daphnis and Chloe* by Longus

1.5.1 A pastoral novel set on Lesbos

With its notable structural and narrative differences, the novel by Longus entitled *Daphnis and Chloe* deserves a separate treatment.

As is the case also for the other novel authors, the figure of Longus, too, is not certain in detail. The very name Λόγγος (*Loggos,* pronounced *Longos*), which appears in the title of some manuscripts, seems to be uncertain, since the main manuscript that has transmitted the text of the novel records the genitive Λόγου (*logou*) followed by the title of the work, perhaps meaning "[The four books] of the novel (λόγου) *The Pastoral Stories of Daphnis and Chloe*." However, the prevailing view among scholars is that Longus is indeed the name of the author (sometimes with the byname Sophistes, which is a modern addition, dating from the early seventeenth century).

The precision of the descriptions of Lesbos, the island on which the story is set, leads us to suppose that the author was a native of this Aegean island, or that he at least had some particular link to it. This hypothesis seems to be reinforced by the discovery on the island of inscriptions attesting the existence of a family there called *Pompeii Longi*. Other scholars maintain that Longus was a Roman (according to some, of slave status), perhaps originally from Lesbos, with a connection to a Dionysiac cult community.

The date is also uncertain. Through its closeness to the aesthetic and stylistic principles of the Second Sophistic – for example the taste for *ekphrasis*, the refinement of his periodic prose, the simplicity of the locution, the use of figures – it has been thought that Longus should be placed in the late second or early third century A.D. This dating seems to be supported by the reference in the novel to a treasure of three thousand drachmas, a significant sum in the third century, but paltry in the fourth due to inflation.

1.5.2 The plot

The novel opens with a brief prooemium in which the author describes in detail an admired painting on Lesbos, representing a love story. "I sought one who would explain the picture and I composed four books, a votive gift to Love, the Nymphs and Pan." Daphnis and Chloe, two foundlings, are brought up on Lesbos by herders of slave status. Their reciprocal and continuous visits, amid the charms of the rural world, lead the two young people to an irresistible physical attraction, but this does not find satisfaction due to their inexperience in the pleasures of love. They are given their first theoretical education in love by Philitas, a cowherd-poet: the god Eros, who had appeared to him in the garden of his house, has communicated to him that Daphnis and Chloe are under the gods' protection and will find satisfaction through a kiss, embrace and marriage. Daphnis and Chloe know the first two remedies, but are ignorant of physical union.

It is Lycaenium, a charming woman from the city, who will initiate Daphnis into love. Daphnis, however, abstains from making love to Chloe out of fear of the defloration. In the meantime many suitors seek the girl in marriage, but Daphnis, having discovered a small fortune of three thousand drachmas, succeeds in winning her hand. The young people's parents, however, wish to wait until autumn and the arrival in the countryside of the patron Dionysophanes. The latter, seeing the objects that were exposed along with Daphnis when he was abandoned, recognises the young man as his son. Chloe too turns out to be the daughter of a prominent citizen of Mytilene, Megacles. Finally the pair marry, but prefer the rural life to that of the city.

1.5.3 An original formula

The setting of the novel in the pastoral and agricultural reality of the island of Lesbos, the importance assigned to the rhythms of nature and the seasons, the recurrence of the principal motifs of Theocritean and Vergilian bucolic poetry (the song contests, dance, exchanges of gifts, participation of animals and nature in human emotions), not only determine the tone of the novel, which clearly presents a greater lightness and sunniness than novels such as that of Xenophon of Ephesus or Heliodorus, but also differentiate it clearly from them in its motifs and narrative structure.

In *Daphnis and Chloe* the action never leaves the island of Lesbos. In brief, there are no voyages or troubled journeys through strange lands and seas. There are, in short episodes, pirates and antagonists who try to tear the two heroes away from the countryside of Lesbos, but the unity of place is never breached. Another element of difference lies in the absence of the commonplace of the lovers' separation. Daphnis and Chloe are parted only for brief periods, for example during a particularly harsh winter, which forces the herders and countryfolk to stay in their own homes. Yet even on this occasion Daphnis, by using a pretext, manages to see his beloved again. Distinctive also is the mechanism of the couple's falling in love. We are not shown the conventional lightning bolt against the background of the local patron deity's religious festival: in Longus' novel the two young people, living together and sharing the everyday life of their pastoral work, end up falling in love with each other "naturally," each finding their complement in the other.

Another result of this is that the rhythm of the story is slowed, and is punctuated not by a chance succession of adventures and *coups de théâtre*, but by the natural and expected alternation of the seasons. In this sense in the case of *Daphnis and Chloe* scholars have spoken not of a voyage through places, but of a voyage through time, meaning that the maturity of the two young people, reached under the protection and with the complicity of Eros, Pan and the Nymphs, develops with the passing of the seasons, and it is as we reach a new season that a moment of growth occurs for the couple.

Typical of the novel genre, and shaped by a more intense narrative rhythm, is the final double recognition scene. This is a procedure clearly borrowed from New Comedy and here fulfils the function of promoting and crowning the happy accomplishment of the two young people's destiny.

1.5.4 The importance of Eros

In a story without historical details, set outside historical time but inserted into the cycle of nature, the true motor of the action is love, understood as a primeval force. A significant moment is the story of the cowherd-poet Philitas (behind whom the figure of the Alexandrian poet Philitas of Cos seems to be concealed) about the epiphany of Eros, a god who is "young, beautiful and winged" (II 7). According to the Orphic-Pythagorean conception (present also in Plato's *Symposium* and Lucian's *Dialogues of the Gods*), Eros, despite his youthful appearance, is the most ancient god in the cosmos. Some scholars have hence understood *Daphnis and Chloe* not as a novel of simple escapism, but as a religious story intended to reveal to the adept the mystery of Love, the ruling force of natural, human and cosmic life. Alongside this interpretation is set the theory of those who see the novel, through its setting on Lesbos, an important centre of Dionysiac religion, as an allegorical novel dedicated to Dionysus. There are in fact many mentions of Dionysus and Dionysiac festivals, above all in the second part of the novel, when the resolution of the story is about to take place thanks to the important role played by Dionysophanes, true father of Daphnis.

1.5.5 Reception

More than any other ancient novel, *Daphnis and Chloe* has won the admiration of ancient and modern readers, becoming a true bestseller in the humanist and Renaissance Eras. The Byzantines had already recognised the novel as a more than ordinary success, as is attested by the fact that Michael Psellus recommended that youths should begin their reading with topics more serious than the pastoral adventures of Daphnis and Chloe. In the Modern Era the first imitations of the work include the *Arcadia* of Jacopo Sannazaro and, in Spain, the *Arcadia* of Lope de Vega.

Translations, reworkings and revisitings of the novel run through the whole of western culture, from the Italian translation of Annibale Caro (1537) to the ballet *Daphnis et Chloé* to the music of Ravel in the early twentieth century.

1.6 The *Aethiopica* of Heliodorus of Emesa

1.6.1 A different climate

At the end of the *Aethiopica* ("Ethiopian Story") we read: "And so ends the novel of the *Aethiopica* about Theagenes and Charicleia. It was composed by a Phoenician of Emesa, of the race of the Sun, Heliodorus, son of Theodosius" (X 41, 4). We have to wait until the fifth century to get more information about Heliodorus, which is transmitted by Socrates, the Church historian: "In Thessaly this custom [the celibacy of priests] was introduced by Heliodorus, who was bishop of Tricca. Attributed to the same Heliodorus is a love novel, which he wrote in his youth and which is entitled *Aethiopica*" (*Ecclesiastical History* V 22). Socrates' notice is not considered to be reliable, since it seems, as in the case of Achilles Tatius, to conceal a wish to bring into a Christian perspective a pagan author who was so fashionable in the ancient and Byzantine world. Yet it is true that in the novel of Heliodorus, much more than in the work of the other erotic writers, the ideal of purity and chastity, both for men and for women, is given an exceptional moral importance, whereas characters with freer habits are given negative connotations and suffer a sad fate. In other words, in the novel we may note a moralism and a distrust towards the more material and corporeal aspects of life, which presupposes a cultural and religious climate that was in all likelihood later than the second century.

Scholars consider the novel to be not earlier than the third century for reasons internal to the work and also due to the way that Heliodorus defines himself, calling hismself a Phoenician, since we know that Emesa formed part of the Roman province of Syria Phoenicia from A.D. 220.

1.6.2 The plot

Persinna, queen of Ethiopia, gives birth to a daughter with exceptionally pale skin. She therefore decides to conceal the birth of the child from her husband and entrusts the infant to a gymnosophist (for this term, cf. *The Hellenistic Age* V 2.2), Sisimithres, who sends her to Charicles, priest of Apollo. The little Charicleia grows, as a religious server of Artemis, at Delphi, where she meets, during a sacred festival, the very beautiful Thessalian Theagenes. The two are struck by a *coup de foudre*: with the help of Calasiris, an Egyptian priest, Theagenes and Charicleia escape from Delphi to get married. The voyage is extremely troubled: after a shipwreck the pair, along with Calasiris, land in Egypt, where they are taken prisoner by the Bucoli (cf. above on the plot of the novel of Achilles Tatius). Theagenes and Charicleia are separated and after various adventures they find themselves at Memphis, where Arsaces, wife of the Persian satrap who governs Egypt, falls in love with Theagenes and tries to eliminate Charicleia by condemning her to the pyre. However, a stone with magic powers, set in Charicleia's ring, keeps the flames away and saves the young woman. The pair manage to depart from Memphis, but end up in the hands of the Ethiopians, who are at war with the Persians. And so they reach Meroe, capital of the Ethiopian kingdom. Here Theagenes is destined to die in a public sacrifice. At the last moment, Charicleia manages to get herself recognised by her mother Persinna and then by her father Hydaspes and so saves her beloved. Sisimithres decides to ban all human sacrifice and the two young people, who now become priests of Selene and Helios, are allowed to marry.

1.6.3 A flashback construction

The novel does not present a development in chronological sequence, but instead begins *in medias res* with the description of the bank of the Nile where Theagenes and Charicleia, after the wreck of their ship, are found injured and exhausted. From this point the story of the two young people's travels begins, without the reader yet knowing their identity or their past. The background is presented later in a very long flashback, from the second to the fifth book, in a story told by Calasiris to Cnemon, a companion of the protagonists in their misfortunes. With great skill in organising the different events, characters and settings, the story is told not only by the omniscient external narrator (the author), but also by narrators internal to the *fabula* who create variations in style and language. These internal narrators give the diegetic structures of the novel a distinctive complexity, which some scholars have found artificial.

Heliodorus alludes, with a degree of conceitedness, to the structure of the *Odyssey* and Odysseus' retrospective story at the court of the Phaeacians. The principal reference model of the *Aethiopica* is thus Homer, not only at the level of macrostructure, but also in continuous quotations and references to motifs and characters of both the *Iliad* and the *Odyssey*. A work as elaborate and refined as this, however, has multiple literary models. Heliodorus enjoys quoting and alluding to many authors including Hesiod, the tragedians, Aristophanes, Xenophon and Plato. One of the most frequently cited authors is Euripides, whose *Hippolytus*, for example, provides the cue for the "novella" of Cnemon, another lengthy *flashback* in the novel. In the first book, Cnemon tells Theagenes and Charicleia of the attempts at seduction made by his stepmother, the passionate Demaeneta. The latter, rejected contemptuously by the youth, takes revenge on him by falsely accusing him of an attempted assault. Cnemon is condemned, but in the end the truth is established and Demaeneta dies a suicide.

1.6.4 The triumph of virginity

Scholars see Charicleia, above all, with her earnest struggle to preserve her virtue, as the heroine of the *Aethiopica* and consider her to be the key character in the work, being characterised by a spirit of greater initiative than Theagenes. Charicleia in fact has a moral role, in which the capacity for self-control (above all in relation to sexual pleasure), interior balance and temperance become the reference values for Theagenes and the other characters.

The religious elements are of primary importance. It is significant that Charicleia has spent her life among priests (the gymnosophist Sisimithres, the priest of Apollo Charicles, the Egyptian priest Calasiris, until she herself becomes, at the end of the story, priestess of Selene) rather than with her lover. It is interesting that in this case virginity is a value to be guarded, to be protected from the snares encountered on her troubled adventures. The exaltation of this value, not only in women but also in men, is not a part of classical culture, but seems to be the result of a cultural climate and religious setting influenced by Christianity, for which virginity is a virtue and sexual pleasure outside the bonds of marriage came to be forbidden.

1.7 Fragmentary and lost novels

1.7.1 Riches to be discovered

Thanks to the continual discovery of new papyrus fragments, we have a less static and more varied vision of ancient novelistic fiction and countless prejudices on the topic have been overcome. The extraordinary success of the novel among ancient readers is not, in fact, always synonymous with a low-quality narrative product, as people had sometimes tended to believe. The already great richness of forms, motifs and styles in this genre, which includes novels of adventure, fantasy, history, parody and religious mystery, has been further increased by new discoveries. These can sometimes be hard to fit into too rigid attempts at schematisation and catalogisation, and have brought new knowledge and opened up varied outlooks. The fragments of novels that have been found are much more numerous than one might have supposed. Here we will discuss only the longer and more important ones, beginning from the discovery that revolutionised our knowledge on this topic, the publication in 1893 of the so-called *Ninus Novel*.

1.7.2 The *Ninus Novel*

Today we possess four fragments, two more than the two first published at the end of the nineteenth century. Behind the protagonist lies a historical figure, an ancient king of Assyria.

In the first fragment Ninus, a seventeen-year-old Assyrian king, has returned victorious from a military campaign. He addresses Derceia, his aunt and the mother of Semiramis, and boasting of his valour in war and his chastity he asks her for her daughter's hand in marriage. From the fragment we learn that Semiramis is in love with the young man too and Derceia is not against the marriage. In the second fragment we have a military scene: Ninus, together with Greek, Carian and Assyrian troops and 150 elephants, sets out on a march against the Armenians. Reaching enemy territory, he stops for ten days to allow the elephants to rest. The initial part of

Ninus' speech exhorting the troops before battle also appears in the fragment. The third fragment, added to the previous two in 1945, presents a shipwreck and Ninus' despair. The fourth
and last papyrus is too small to allow us to identify the scene.

Thus in the surviving fragments the typical elements of the novel genre appear, namely love and the reversal of fortune (here represented by the military events), to which is added an elegant style (in the speech of Ninus hiatus is avoided and rhythmic clausulae and rhetorical figures are used). Despite the historicity of the characters, their story, as it emerges from the fragments, is conceived in an original way, compared to the versions of Ninus' story that we find in Ctesias, Athenaeus and Plutarch (Plutarch, in *The Dialogue on Love*, or *Eroticus*, turns Semiramis into the concubine of a slave).

The date of the novel is placed in the second or first century B.C. (around 100 B.C.), making it the earliest one of which we have direct knowledge. Its importance is hence exceptional, in that it has made it possible to go beyond mere hypothetical constructions and prove wrong those who set the birth of the genre of the novel in the high Imperial Period in parallel to the heyday of the Second Sophistic.

1.7.3 *Metiochus and Parthenope*

This novel has been restored to us by quite lengthy papyrus fragments, but they are of course lacunose. The motif that inspires it is close to that of *Anthia and Habro-comes* of Xenophon of Ephesus, in its adoption of the motive of contempt for love, moulded on the model of Euripides' *Hippolytus*. Metiochus shows his pride and jeers at the god Eros, who punishes him by causing him to be carried off by passionate love for Parthenope. Historical figures appear in the story, such as Polycrates, tyrant of Samos and father of Parthenope; Anaximenes, the philosopher of Miletus; Hegesipyle, mother of Miltiades and stepmother of Metiochus – the story is thus set in the sixth century B.C.

The work's date is debated. It is generally held that the novel precedes the hey-day of Atticism and was written in the early first century B.C., and thus contempo-rary to the *Ninus Novel*. A theory that would see Chariton as the author of the work has not met with success. According to some, this is not a novel at all, but a dia-logue on an erotic theme.

1.7.4 The *Novel of Chione*

There are three fragments in which the character of Chione appears. According to some she is a princess, according to others a heroine of citizen origin. Due to her beauty, the girl is beset by arrogant suitors, who are obliged to await Chione's deci-sion for thirty days. In the fragments the name Megamedes also appears, who is sometimes interpreted as one of the suitors, sometimes as the man whom Chione loves. It is likely that the novel, in which we can see a thematic allusion to the motif of the Proci in the *Odyssey*, proceeds with the misfortunes of the two lovers, pursued by the suitors. The three fragments have recently been supplemented also by a scrap of papyrus in which Chione appears in conversation with a woman.

The scholarship has not ruled out, for reasons of language, style and situation, that the author of the *Novel of Chione* could be Chariton of Aphrodisias; among other grounds, we know that the fragments of the novel appeared in a codex, now lost, that also contained *Chaereas and Callirhoe*.

1.7.5 Antonius Diogenes and *The Incredible Things Beyond Thule*

We owe to Photius knowledge of the summary of this novel in 24 books, composed at an unspecified time by an author called Antonius Diogenes for his sister Isidora, a "lover of culture," and which is now lost. In the *Library* (166, 111b, 32 ff.) the Byzantine patriarch writes: "It seems that Antonius Diogenes was the earliest author of stories like these, such as Lucian, Lucius, Iamblichus, Achilles Tatius, Heliodorus, Damascius. In fact the source and root of *A True Story* of Lucian and the *Metamorphoses* of Lucius seems to have been in this work (...) As regards the period in which the father of these stories flourished (...) we can only conjecture that he lived not distant from the time of Alexander the Great." Scholars today do not accept Photius' date. The hypothesis that holds most sway places the novel in the first century A.D., but no later than the second century.

Aside from Photius' summary, we also have papyri that transmit some very brief portions of the novel, and a testimony by Porphyry in the *Life of Pythagoras*, from which we learn that Antonius Diogenes had also recounted the life of Pythagoras in his own manner.

> The narrating voice of the novel is that of Deinias, a man who "in search of new experiences" undertakes voyages throughout the world as far as Thule (which should be placed in an idealised Scandinavia), where he meets and falls in love with Dercyllis, a girl who has fled from her native city, Tyre, since she was pursued by a dishonest and perverse Egyptian priest by the name of Paapis. In Photius' summary the journeys had pushed into lands inhabited by unknown and incredible peoples (for example in one city of Iberia the people can see at night but are blind by day), whereas there is hardly any trace of the erotic element, which must nonetheless have played an important role, above all in the character of Paapis. Photius privileges the fantastical scenes, which are often connected to magic, and the extraordinary episodes, above all the voyage to the Moon accomplished by two characters who decide to push north of Thule, beyond the Pole.

The unreal tone and the implausible character of the adventures make this text one of the few fantasy novels of the ancient world. On the other hand, given the presence of many references to Pythagoreanism and the mysteries in the novel, there are also those who have detected a religious intention, based on the motifs of guilt, expiation and redemption.

1.7.6 Iamblichus

The love novel of Iamblichus, *The Babylonian History* in 39 books, is likewise known through the summary of Photius (*Library* 94, 73b 24 ff.). The Byzantine patriarch regarded the author as a writer intermediate between Achilles Tatius, who was judged "trivial and indecent," and Heliodorus, who was "more austere and restrained." According to Photius, Iamblichus was a refined writer, of Babylonian origin but of Greek culture, who lived in the time of Marcus Aurelius (A.D. 161–180) and was an expert in magic. The magical component must have taken on a significant importance in the original text; in Photius' summary it lives on in Chaldaean oracles, incredible apparitions and macabre scenes.

> The protagonists are Sinonis and Rhodanes. Their misfortunes are set in motion by the king of Babylonia, Garmos, who wants to force the beautiful Sinonis to marry him. Rejected, he condemns Rhodanes to be crucified, but he manages to escape with the help of his beloved. The couple's adventures and wanderings, which follow at an insistent pace and bring onto the scene a large cast of characters, including Garmos' two wicked eunuchs, are set predominantly in Mesopotamia. Garmos' persecution ends with his death and Rhodanes' ascent to the throne.

Brief fragments of the novel are found in the *Suda* lexicon and some extracts are found in manuscripts of the fifteenth century.

1.7.7 Lollianus

Lengthy but lacunose papyri have restored to us parts of the *Phoenicica* of Lollianus, an author whose identity is debated, but who lived probably in the second century A.D. and who is connected to the Second Sophistic. It is difficult to reconstruct the plot of the novel. In the fragments there first appears a character who recounts losing his virginity with a girl called Persis. Then he takes part in a scene that is unique in the ancient novel: some brigands, after an orgy, kill a παῖς (either a slave or a child) during a sacrifice and eat its heart. The strong realism of the narration, the protagonists' not entirely moral and chaste behaviour and the content of the novel seem far away from the idealising erotic novels of the authors of this genre whose works have been fully preserved.

1.7.8 Other novels

Iambulus. The work of Iambulus, a Syrian author of the second century B.C., is attested by Diodorus Siculus, who transmits a summary of it (II 55–60). However, it is not clear whether it is a novel in the full sense or rather a chronicle of (fantastic) voyages. The erotic theme is absent, while the description of Iambulus' voyage to an island in the South (perhaps to be understood as Ceylon) takes on absolute importance.

Iambulus, on the death of his father, a merchant, decides to follow in his footsteps. On arriving in Ethiopia, he is captured by bandits who force him, for ritual reasons, into a new voyage by sea. With his companions he disembarks on an archipelago of seven islands, with a mild climate where the fruits grow spontaneously and the people live long and happily, in a sort of communism of goods. The institution of the family does not exist and this, according to Iambulus, prevents the unleashing of rivalries and wars. After staying there for seven years, Iambulus is driven out on account of his immorality and returns to Greece.

The Novel of Sesonchosis. Some papyri from Oxyrhynchus have restored fragments of the *Novel of Sesonchosis*, which seems close to *Ninus* in its historical theme and its period of composition, perhaps the first century B.C. The protagonist is an Egyptian pharaoh of the Twelfth Dynasty, Sesonchosis, who is mentioned under different names by various Greek historians. He loses power and falls in love with the daughter of the new king of Egypt. However, the stylistic level of the novel is less refined than that of *Ninus*.

The Novel of Calligone. The protagonist of the *Novel of Calligone*, of which we have a short papyrus of the second century A.D., is a warrior heroine, a character not otherwise attested in the Greek novel but present in eastern legends. The scene takes place in a military encampment and shows Calligone seized by rage and despair. She wants to kill herself, but is stopped by a certain Eubiotus, who is perhaps her tutor. Calligone declares that she is Greek and, in spirit, as brave as an Amazon.

Herpyllis. A fairly lengthy papyrus of the early second century A.D. describes the conventional situation of a pair of lovers separated by shipwreck during a storm. The protagonists are the young Herpyllis and a boy who is the first-person narrator of the story.

The Diary of the Trojan War (*Ephemeris belli Troiani*). The matter of the *Trojan Cycle* is picked up in a Latin novel of the fourth century A.D., the *Diary of the Trojan War*, in which a certain Lucius Septimius states that he is translating into Latin the war diary of a Greek, Dictys Cretensis, who had participated in the conquest of Troy. Some papyrus discoveries confirm the existence of a Greek original of the novel, perhaps in the first century A.D. (cf. above 1.1.3).

The History of the Fall of Troy (*De excidio Troiae historia*). From the fifth or perhaps sixth century comes the *History of the Fall of Troy*, it too probably a Latin translation of a Greek novel which, from what we read in the Latin version, was composed by Dares of Phrygia, a Trojan priest mentioned in the *Iliad*. In this work the fall of Troy is described from the point of view of the vanquished (cf. above. 1.1.3).

Both these Latin novels enjoyed great success in the Middle Ages, a period in which the Latin West was not able to access the Homeric texts.

The History of Apollonius King of Tyre (*Historia Apollonii regis Tyrii*). The *History of Apollonius King of Tyre* too is likely to be the Latin version, of the sixth century A.D., of an older novel that was probably in Greek (though not all scholars are agreed about its Greek origin). It narrates the tormented story of Apollonius, king of Tyre, who marries the daughter of the king of Cyrene. After the wedding, the two set off on their travels but the woman dies in childbirth. Yet she is only apparently dead and after long adventures and misfortunes Apollonius, in a double recognition scene, rediscovers his wife and child, who has in the meantime become the priestess of Artemis.

2 The novella, the fable, epistolary literature

2.1 The novella

As with the novel, for the novella too the Greeks had no a specific term. They call it by various names, without differentiation: λόγος, ἀπόλογος, αἶνος, μῦθος, διήγημα or διήγησις and πλάσμα without distinguishing between novella, fable, tale or anecdote. The novella was therefore, for a long time, a "non-genre" or, better, a genre that was not seen to have autonomy or specificity.

Yet it is likely that the novella arose before the novel, as is attested by the novella-like inserts present already in authors of the fifth century B.C. In *The Histories* of Herodotus, for example, the whole oriental tale of Candaules, king of Sardis, and his bodyguard Gyges (I 7–14) has a clear novella-like flavour. The distinctive character consists in the realistic setting of the story, which takes place against a background that is popular and often comic. These are characteristics that, joined together, distinguish it from the fable and the novel of love.

An autonomous genre of the novella can be documented with relative certainty only from the second century B.C., the era in which Aristides of Miletus, drawing on oriental repertoires, wrote the *Milesian Tales* (*Milesiaca*). This collection of comic-erotic novellas set in Miletus was particularly enjoyed by the Romans. Cornelius Sisenna, probably the historian (120 ca.–67 B.C.), translated them into Latin and reworked them in a lively style. They passed into mime and the novel, for example into Petronius and Apuleius: famous, in Petronius' *Satyricon*, is the novella of the matron of Ephesus (111–112). The fame of the *Milesian Tales*, a name that very soon came to be assigned to every kind of erotic story, is attested by a notice in Plutarch (*Life of Crassus* 32), according to whom a volume of Aristides' *Milesian Tales* was discovered in the pack of a Roman soldier in Crassus' army.

2.2 The fable

The tradition of fable was already established in archaic and classical Greece thanks to Aesop (cf. *The Archaic Age* VI 2), but rose to new importance in the Imperial Period. The fable, including anthropomorphised animals and with a mainly moral purpose, takes on a standard form inspired by the recurring structure of the traditional texts: the story is preceded by a *promythion*, or preface, and followed by an *epimythion*, or moral, in which the ethical significance of the story is explained.

In the Imperial Period the fable was employed for explanatory and didactic purposes both in school settings and in rhetoric. An interesting collection is that of 40 prose fables transmitted in the *progymnasmata* of the rhetor Aphthonius. Some seem to refer to the *Aesopic Mythiambs* of Babrius, a collection of 143 fables with humans, animals and gods as protagonists, arranged alphabetically and composed in choliambics (the ancient metre of Hipponax). Of Babrius we know almost nothing; the language of his fables, which combines Ionic dialect with the *koinē*, seems to present influences from the language of the *Septuagint*, which opens the possibility that Babrius lived in the East in a period from the first to the third century A.D. The discovery of the *Mythiambs* is relatively recent, having occurred in 1843 in a manuscript in a monastery on Mount Athos.

2.3 Letter collections of the Imperial Period

A genre that won particular success with readers in the first centuries A.D. was epistolography, which is characterised by two elements: the fictitious and strongly literary character of the letters produced and the predominantly erotic themes contained in them. The letter collection containing exchanges of imaginary letters between historical or legendary figures or taken from daily life came to constitute an effective tool for practising composition and was used in the rhetorical schools. Reference is made, in a rather conceited way, to classical and Hellenistic literature and in general to those worldly literary motifs which, coupled with a precious but light style of writing, responded to the entertainment needs of a broad middle-brow audience, perhaps the same audience as for the various forms of the novel and novella.

We may mention here also apocryphal epistolography. Collections of letters, authentic or spurious, that were attributed to famous figures of the past had already been circulating in large numbers in the previous periods. Classic examples are the collections of letters of Socrates and the Socratics, or the group of thirteen letters, some authentic and some spurious, attributed to Plato. Famous also is the case of the *Letters* of Phalaris (tyrant of Acragas in the sixth century B.C.), whose spuriousness was demonstrated by the great English philologist Richard Bentley (1662–1742). In the Imperial Period fictitious letters continued to be produced in the context of rhetorical exercises, as we have mentioned.

Alciphron. The author of the best known letter collection of the Imperial Period is Alciphron, who lived perhaps in the second century A.D. and was imitated by Aristaenetus in the fifth century. We will discuss these collections here, whereas for the letter collections of Aelian and of Flavius Philostratus we refer to the treatments of those authors above (cf. *The Roman Imperial Period* VIII 1.2.7–8). Of Alciphron we know very little. Two eminent Byzantine scholars, Eustathius of Thessalonica and

Johannes Tzetzes, called him an Atticist and rhetor, reports that are too meagre to permit us to reconstruct a biography. He used the Attic language of the fifth century B.C., in a nostalgic reprise of the models of the past that clearly matches Atticist taste. His date is uncertain, nor has it been possible to establish which of Alciphron and Lucian inspired the other; Aristaenetus, who created a fictional letter exchange between the two of them (I, 5, 22), seems to regard them as contemporaries.

> The chosen setting of Alciphron's 123 fictitious letters, namely the Athens of the fourth century B.C., is in itself indicative of the taste of the public of the Imperial Period, which wanted to see itself reflected in a past that was remote but was felt to be close to them. The *Letters of Fishermen, Farmers, Parasites and Courtesans*, in four books, are able to present in all its liveliness the everyday reality of a past world, of which the echo still resounds, formed by "daily news," pieces of gossip, grand love stories, laments and complaints. The first two books present the world of labour at sea and on land in such a way as might please and interest wealthy citizens of the imperial cities, with a strong literary mediation and with a slightly disengaged air. The most savory letters of parasites and courtesans refer to New Comedy, as is revealed explicitly by the letters between Glycera and Menander. Among the other historical figures we find Phryne, the sculptor Praxiteles and Demetrius Poliorcetes.

Aristaenetus. Dating to the fifth century, Aristaenetus composed 50 *Erotic Letters*, in two books, in the manner of Alciphron. However, they lack the conventional letter schema with greeting formulas and reference to the addressee. The "letters" are thus presented rather as passages in prose with erotic content. More than in the case of Alciphron, by making *erōs* the true motor of human existence Aristaenetus makes it the central protagonist of his writings, with debts, of varying degrees of explicitness, to Plato, Hellenistic poetry (above all to elegiac verse), the repertoire of New Comedy and, perhaps, the novel. Among other things, the letter collection of Aristaenetus is a precious source illuminating the different conceptions of love in the ancient world.

X Grammar, Scholarship, Compilation

1 The study of grammar

1.1 The culmination of a tradition

Apollonius Dyscolus and his son Aelius Herodianus, who lived in the second century A.D., are the two most important Greek grammarians of the Imperial Period. Through their work, Greek grammatical teaching received a weighty systematisation, along the lines of the specialised studies initiated in the Hellenistic Age by the great philologists and scholars Aristophanes of Byzantium and Aristarchus of Samothrace, consolidated by Dionysius Thrax and pursued by figures such as Tyrannio and Philoxenus (first century B.C.), Tryphon (Augustan Period), Alexion and Ptolemaeus of Ascalon (first century A.D.). The Imperial Period thus saw the culmination of an impulse towards systematic study of grammatical forms, with its deepest roots in the criterion of analogy, which had been formulated already in the early Hellenistic Age by the philologists of Alexandria and then gradually evolved.

Compared to their prestigious predecessors, the grammarians of this period were less sharply innovative scholars, but were still endowed with enormous technical competence in linguistics and they were also capable of original ideas. What distinguished them from the Alexandrian philologists was above all the changed social role of the grammarian, who was no longer just a specialist scholar of language and literary texts, but was now, rather more than previously, tasked with school teaching activities as the teacher of a discipline that was universally considered to be the first step in a liberal education. Grammar was to provide the first stage of training, as a preliminary study to rhetoric, which had become a pillar of imperial culture (one may think, for example, of the importance of distinguishing the Attic forms, when the taste for Atticism was dominant: this was a skill that could be gained only in a sound grammatical training). In the organisation of teaching in the Middle Ages, based on the seven liberal arts, grammar was in fact the first discipline of the "trivium," which consisted of grammar, rhetoric and dialectic.

1.2 Apollonius Dyscolus

Apollonius Dyscolus was born in Alexandria, where he spent the greater part of his life, aside from a brief stay at Rome. Already in the ancient world questions were raised about the reasons for his byname Dyscolus (from the Greek δύσκολος: "difficult, displeasing"), whether it was due to his character, to his habit of posing difficult questions or to the obscurity of his manner of expression.

https://doi.org/10.1515/9783110426328-039

He wrote various works touching on all the fields of Greek grammar and dialectology, with the intention of providing a systematic theoretical picture of the discipline. For many of these works, only fragments survive, but four are preserved. We have three works on parts of speech: *On Pronouns* (Περὶ ἀντωνυμίας), *On Adverbs* (Περὶ ἐπιρρημάτων), *On Conjunctions* (Περὶ συνδέσμων). His treatise *On Syntax* (Περὶ συντάξεως), in four books, is the only surviving ancient Greek work on this theme, i.e. on the combination and function of the different parts of speech within the phrase, a topic that is not without philosophical aspects, connected to the analysis of language.

The importance of Apollonius' work on syntax should be emphasised, since before and after him grammatical study was for the most part devoted to the treatment of phonetics, morphology and the parts of speech, whereas syntax was addressed only sporadically. For this reason, Apollonius' work subsequently exerted a major influence, also through the works of the Latin grammarian Priscian (fifth to sixth century A.D.), and so reached the Byzantines and through them the Italian humanists.

Recent studies have cast light on how the foundation of Apollonius' thought is the existence of rational correctness in language, based on rules that can be discovered and described and in relation to which it is possible to analyse deviations and discrepancies. Differentiating himself from the prevalent largely empirical approach, which previously had been focused on the observation of the phenomena of speech used by authors (and of the spoken language), Apollonius maintained that language functions on the basis of a rational system of objective and natural rules, the precise determination and application of which indicates the correctness of the meaning of the phrase. While in his study of language the tradition of literary works plays an important role, he nonetheless cites the usage of authors (in particular Homer, from whom he takes the majority of his examples, but without an interest in textual or exegetical problems emerging) as a support and confirmation of the grammatical rules, and not as the source from which they are to be deduced. Previously, this kind of problem (the rational rules of language, the correctness of the meaning of word and phrase) had been the object of analysis essentially just in the sphere of rhetoric and logic. It seems that Apollonius was the first to make a systematic study of syntax (i.e. of the intrinsic relation between the elements of a phrase in relation to its meaning) as a problem of linguistic and grammatical character, and this reveals the basis of his philosophical approach in relation to the problems of language. While a semantic approach like this may suggest Stoic influence, it must nonetheless be emphasised that the Stoics on the one hand analysed the relations between the elements of the phrase in the sphere of logic and, on the other, their semantic studies were essentially devoted to the lexicon. For this reason too the originality of Apollonius' developments emerges, which are thus tied to a figure who is in many ways exceptional.

1.3 Aelius Herodianus

The son of Apollonius Dyscolus, Aelius Herodianus, who was active in Rome in the period of Marcus Aurelius (161–180), was a worthy successor to him, although he was less rigid than his father in observing and applying the rules of analogy. For his studies of language, Herodianus based his work heavily on the tradition of grammatical studies going back to Aristarchus and his school (cf. *The Hellenistic Age* III 2.4).

The preserved materials lead us to recall him above all for his great work done on the general doctrine of accents. Yet we should emphasise that his major work – the *General Prosody* (Καθολικὴ προσῳδία) in 20 books, in which he says he had examined around 60,000 words, as well as problems of accentuation (including those concerning the combination of words within the phrase, as in the case of enclitics), to which he devoted Books 1–19 – also treated aspiration (the breathings), quantities and various morphological problems, such as the division into syllables. This should come as no surprise if we bear in mind that the term *prosōdia* in Greek could indicate everything that determined the sound and pronunciation of a word, and hence accents, quantities, aspiration of vowels, but also separation (ὑποδιαστολή) or union (ὑφέν) of words. The treatment consisted of a systematic exposition, formulating a collection of rigorous rules that indicated the proper accentuation of the different categories of word, identified on the basis of characteristics such as the termination, the number of syllables, the gender and so on (the list is found in the work *On the Nominal Declination*, Περὶ κλίσεως ὀνομάτων). He held that the rules ought to be made either on the basis of the language commonly accepted or on the basis of the criterion and norm of analogy, which "with its art holds together, as in a net, the varied voice of the language of men." As far as we know, Herodianus had at least one predecessor in this field, Heraclides of Miletus (first to second century A.D.), whose *General Prosody* (Καθολικὴ προσῳδία) today survives in around 60 fragments, but the comprehensive system of Herodian's project should clearly distinguish him from any other work of the kind. Two works of this type on the language of the *Iliad* and the *Odyssey* and one on Attic fed into his magnum opus, it seems. From the Homeric part, copious excerpts are preserved in the Homeric scholia, while extracts and epitomes have survived of the remainder, which are found in various manuscripts.

Characteristic of his linguistic thought is the basic idea of relating every specific case to the appropriate general rule and of hence making it governed by this rule. A theorisation of the functioning of this mechanism is found in the Περὶ μονήρους λέξεως, *On Lexical Singularities* (in the sense that they form a rule of their own). In this treatise Herodianus says that the mass of words in a language are subdivided into groups on the basis of some similarity that is shared by the members of the groups (though the similarities are listed there with some discrepancies from those cited in the treatise *On the Nominal Declination*). In the case in which something does not fit, one should not suppose a malfunctioning of the system of rules: it is simply necessary to put the words in the 'right' group. In the case of words that elude every attempt at systematisation, and which hence cannot be collected in any group, it is said that they form a group by themselves, i.e. they themselves constitute a rule. These are the "singular (i.e. anomalous) words" of the title. It should be noted that these are not terms treated as "exceptions" to a rule, but terms that are subject to a rule followed by no others.

Herodianus also wrote on very varied grammatical topics, such as spelling, verbal and nominal inflection, the parts of speech and other topics: we know of around 30 titles of his works. We have a large number of fragments derived from various sources of indirect tradition, but unfortunately the only one of his works to have survived entire is the short treatise *On Lexical Singularities* that we have discussed.

2 The interpretation of texts and lexicography

2.1 Philological exegesis

After a significant flourishing in the Augustan Period (cf. *The Hellenistic Age* III 2.4), in the field of philology and textual exegesis the centuries of the Imperial Period once again saw some figures of importance at work.

Nicanor, a grammarian and philologist of Alexandria (second century A.D.), worked out a well developed system of interpretive signs and is known above all for his writings on the punctuation of the Homeric poems. The results of his studies on the text of the *Iliad* and *Odyssey* flowed into the surviving Homeric scholia tradition. He also worked on the poems of Callimachus and produced a sort of theoretical *summa* of his researches entitled *On Punctuation* (Περὶ στιγμῆς).

Also present in the thematic field of textual interpretation is the figure of the Neoplatonic philosopher Porphyry (234–305 approx.), with works such as the *Homeric Questions*, of which we have extracts mixed in with the Homeric scholia, and the allegorical work on the Cave of the Nymphs in the *Odyssey*, as well as short (lost) treatises on grammatical and rhetorical questions: we have already spoken of him in the chapter on philosophy (cf. *The Roman Imperial Period* VII 1.4.4).

We conclude by recalling the contribution made to the philological and scholarly disciplines by the doctor and philosopher Galen, a scholar with a unique profile. His multifaceted interests led him to produce, as well as an enormous quantity of works on anatomy and medical and scientific topics, also commentaries and works on themes in literary criticism, linguistics, rhetoric and musical harmony. For a detailed account, we refer to the treatment of this author in the chapter on scientific literature of the Imperial Period (cf. *The Roman Imperial Period* VII 2.2).

2.2 Lexicography

In the Imperial Period the work of lexicographical research and collection also continued, in the footsteps of the Alexandrian glossographical tradition, understood as the "science" of difficult and foreign words, which had been inaugurated (at least as far as we know) by the *Atakta* of Philitas of Cos and continued by Zenodotus, Aristophanes and other scholars of the Hellenistic Age (cf. *The Hellenistic Age* III 2.2). The city of Alexandria still long remained the leading cultural centre of this type of study. The continuity with the Alexandrian Age is found also in the fact that the renewal of lexical interests during the centuries of the Empire took place in the sphere of grammar and literary criticism. However, the work of lexicography was also geared towards a purpose of wider impact, namely schoolteaching. The increased distance between the language in general use and the classical literary language, and the demands posed by educational choices in an Atticist spirit, demanded, already at the level of primary education, the recovery of lost lexical knowledge that was needed to read and interpret the ancient authors.

Specialist or thematic lexica. In the Imperial Period there was an enormous development in lexicography, to the point that it may be useful to distinguish the abundant production of general lexica (on which see below) from an equally rich yield of specialist collections, inspired by a specific thematic motive: lexica of dialects, of synonyms, those dedicated to a single author or genre (tragedy, comedy, history), Atticist lexica, onomastic lexica and compilations on particular fields. We shall limit ourselves here to mentioning the most important testimonies.

In the first century A.D. lived the Egyptian Apion, who was a student of Didymus Chalcenterus and succeeded Theon as head of the school of grammar at Alexandria. The *Against Apion* of Flavius Josephus (cf. *The Roman Imperial Period* VI 1.2.3) was a reply to notices hostile to the Jews contained in Apion's historical work, the *Aegyptiaca*. In the sphere of erudite research his importance lies in his composition of a collection of *Homeric Glosses*, which was one of the main sources, along with Aristarchus' exegesis, of his contemporary Apollonius Sophista, the author of a *Homeric Lexicon* that has survived in compendium form.

Onomastic lexicography is attested by an epitome of the *Onomasticon* of Iulius Pollux (second century), he too an Egyptian of Naucratis, a teacher of rhetoric at Athens, who won the favour of the emperor Commodus, and an exponent of the Atticist cultural tendency. The work consists of an ordered collection of words in literary and rhetorical use, from the most varied semantic spheres (religion, law, economy, the sciences, cooking, etc), which are arranged by thematic nuclei (and hence not in alphabetical order) and sometimes followed by brief explanations and quotations from the authors. Particularly useful are the notices about the theatre and masks that are contained in Book IV.

Atticist interests inspired the studies of Phrynichus too, a contemporary and rival of Pollux, whom he reproached for compromising on some linguistic decisions, attesting Phrynichus' position of rigorous purism in expression. He produced a lexicon in 37 books (*Sophistic Preparation*) that is full of examples and quotations from Attic authors, but is today reduced to a meagre epitome, and a *Selection of Attic Verbs and Nouns*, which is preserved.

The lexicographical work of Valerius Harpocration, born at Alexandria and he too probably dating to the second century, is adjacent both to exegetical practice and rhetorical training. His *Lexicon of the Ten Orators* (Λέξεις τῶν δέκα ῥητόρων) recorded and commented upon vocabulary of the Attic orators in the Alexandrian canon (Antiphon, Andocides, Lysias, Isocrates, Isaeus, Aeschines, Lycurgus, Demosthenes, Hyperides and Dinarchus). The original work is lost, but we have two epitomes (of which one is more concise and one is richer). Moreover, it is possible to recover some contents from a Byzantine lexicon whose author used Harpocration (the Συναγωγὴ λέξεων χρησίμων, *Collection of Useful Expressions*, mostly simply referred to as *Synagogē*). What remains of the *Lexicon* is a goldmine of information of various kinds, especially when the term explained concerns the technical spheres of law or Athenian institutions.

Orus of Alexandria too (fifth century) composed an Atticist lexicon, today only partly reconstructible from indirect sources (inter alia, again the *Synagogē* mentioned above), and some treatises on grammatical topics that have not survived. We recall him also in relation to collections of geographical and ethnographical terms, as the author of a collection entitled *How to Express the Names of Peoples*. The work was used, along with others, by Stephanus of Byzantium (sixth century): Stephanus' *Ethnica* was of monumental size, extending to 50 books and, while keeping the geographical theme central, its erudite curiosity encompassed various spheres of what is knowable: history, geography and philological and grammatical erudition. The epitome that has survived is full of interesting antiquarian notices and precious quotations from lost authors.

General lexica. The culmination of general lexicography of the Imperial Period is a work that has reached us in an epitomised and reworked version: the *Lexicon* of Hesychius of Alexandria, who lived in the fifth to sixth century. In a certain sense the last member of the Alexandrian school, Hesychius stands at the end of a rich and for us lost tradition of lexicography, collecting the fruits of his predecessors' labours and providing a sort of summa of Alexandrian lexicography. The starting point of this tradition can be seen in the weighty synthesis in 95 books composed in the first century A.D. by Pamphilus of Alexandria, who aimed to collect in a single encyclopaedic work the whole of the scholarly knowledge gained by the research of the Alexandrian philologists. The lexicon of Pamphilus was epitomised by Julius Vestinus (second century), whose epitome was used a little later, together with various other sources, by Diogenianus of Heraclea (second century). The lexicon of Diogenianus, in its turn, served as the main basis for the work of Hesychius, which has survived incomplete and considerably interpolated. In its current form, with its more than 50,000 lemmata, it is one of the richest goldmines of erudite lexicographical notices to have survived.

2.3 Paroemiography

A particular form of erudite work is represented by the paroemiographical collections, i.e. collections of proverbs arranged alphabetically. The Imperial Period and late antiquity have transmitted some of them, of which one that deserves to be recalled is that produced in the second century by the rhetor Zenobius, which survives in a non-original version. The paroemiographical tradition continued in copious quantity through the centuries of Late Antiquity and various collections have survived, attesting a compilatory activity of considerable scale.

3 Late Antique and Byzantine erudition

One could say that after the second century A.D. the truly creative phase of Greek philology and grammar was already over. However, the Roman Imperial Period and then Late Antiquity were when the decisive stages in the preservation of all this material took place, material that gradually took on forms and characteristics that were preludes to the formation of the great scholiographical collections of the Byzantine Period, and which hence determined what we know of it now. An abundant production began of miscellaneous works of synthesis, in which the stores of exegesis and erudition that had been transmitted were combined, fused and epitomised. Commentaries and scholarly works of various kinds were summarised and abbreviated in various compilations, reduced to doxographical annotations sometimes rich, sometimes meagre. This type of work continued in the Byzantine Period, when very varied interventions were again made, reusing and selecting the transmitted materials. Genres of scholarship were established and diffused, the preserved texts of which are also the works with the richest information for us, i.e. above all scholiography and lexicography (without ignoring paroemiography), which are true reservoirs of the earlier output with its multiple forms (cf. *The Hellenistic Age* III 1 and 2). Scholiographical collections preserved much exegetical material concerning the classical authors, the great (etymological) lexica brought together an enormous yield of notices of all kinds, and compilations of every type selected materials with a view to their endurance and the benefit of preserving them.

Today we have a considerable number of scholiographical collections, above all concerning poets, and of some lexicographical compilations: the so-called *Cyril-Lexicon* (dating perhaps to the fifth century), the lexicon of the patriarch Photius (ninth century) and the *Suda lexicon* (tenth century), the four major *Etymologica* (the *Genuinum, Gudianum, Magnum* and *Simeonianum,* dated from the ninth to the twelfth century), the lexicon of Pseudo-Zonaras (twelfth century) and other minor ones. These are very useful cultural products and are representative of the tendencies in a period that focused assiduously and tenaciously on studying, collecting, summarising and preserving the treasures of learning that constituted the glorious intellectual heritage of many centuries, and so drawing and fixing a cultural identity that aimed to continue as a living tradition.

4 Metrical and musical studies

4.1 Metrical studies and Hephaestion

Notices that can be found in the erudite tradition, as well as the origin of some ancient scholars of metre, lead us to believe that at Alexandria, home of Hellenistic philology, there was also some kind of school of metrical studies. This, at any rate, was where in the second century B.C. a scholar of the calibre of Aristophanes of Byzantium had been the first to devote himself to the colometry of lyric and ancient drama. To the Alexandrian school, and to a theoretical approach similar to it, can be traced the work of Philoxenus (first century B.C.: grammarian and philologist, but also author of *On Metres*, Περὶ μέτρων), Heliodorus (first century A.D.) and Hephaestion, he too a native of Alexandria.

The common theoretical denominator of these metrical writers is the conviction that they can explain the different metrical forms as combinations of some well defined fundamental metres (such as the trochee, iamb, dactyl, anapaest and so on). The theory was set out in a manual of metre composed by Heliodorus, later superseded and replaced by that of Hephaestion, which enjoyed long-lasting fame and authority and was repeatedly the subject of commentaries.

Hephaestion should perhaps be identified with the tutor of Lucius Verus of this name mentioned in the *Historia Augusta*. His *Manual On Metre* (Ἐγχειρίδιον περὶ μέτρων) in its original version consisted of 48 books, which were then reduced (perhaps by the author himself) first to eleven, and then to three and finally to just one book. This last version has survived today and is for us the only extant example of an ancient metrical manual. Hephaestion treated the different types of metre, concerning himself with various problems posed by the metrical composition of poetic works. The manual ends with two precious "appendices," one on the parabasis of comedy and one on the notational signs that are useful for distinguishing the metrical structures of poetic compositions. The importance of the manual lies also in its function as a vehicle of quotations of ancient texts.

It is conventional to describe as a "school" of metre at Pergamum a different theoretical approach to that which was professed by the Alexandrians and which derived the metrical forms from two metrical-rhythmic structures that were regarded as fundamental, namely the hexameter and the trimeter. This approach was followed by the Latin authors Terentius Varro, a scholar of the most wide-ranging interests and vast cultural knowledge (second to first century B.C.), and the poet and scholar Caesius Bassus (first century A.D.).

4.2 Aristides Quintilianus and musical studies

The musicologist Aristides Quintilianus deserves a mention, whose dating is quite uncertain and ranges from the first to the fourth century A.D. In his work *On Music*, in three books, he undertakes to reclaim the musical theory of Aristoxenus of Tarentum (the pupil of Aristotle, whose musical writings have survived in fragmentary form: cf. *The Classical Age* VII 2.1 and XIII 3.8.2). However, he also drew on earlier authors, such as Damon of Oa (fifth century B.C.: cf. *The Classical Age* VII 2.1). Alongside the more technical aspects of rhythm and metre, also treated are concepts concerning music's social function, its individual psychagogic effects and its ethical implications. Pythagorean influence is the source of the interpretation of music in terms of arithmetical ratios (a theme treated by Porphyry in his commentary on the *Harmonics* of Claudius Ptolemaeus: cf. *The Roman Imperial Period* VII 1.4.4).

5 Miscellanies, compilations, anthologies

5.1 Useful and precious compilations

The period including the end of the second and the whole of the third century marks a visible decline in studies and does not see the production of important original works, but the material collected in compilations is often very precious, because it constitutes all that remains of traditions that have been lost, perhaps forever.

Useful, for example, is the work of Aetius, who lived at the turn of the first to second century, who put together a doxographical collection of the opinions of various philosophers in the field of physics. On this topic we return to two works that we have already noted, the *Library* of Pseudo-Apollodorus, datable to the first or early second century (cf. *The Hellenistic Age* III 2.4) and the *Miscellaneous History* (Παντοδαπὴ ἱστορία) of Favorinus of Arles, who lived from around 85 to around 143, which probably inspired subsequent similar works (cf. *The Roman Imperial Period* VIII 1.2.4). From the early third century there are the compilatory works of Aelian (175–235 ca.), of whom we have already spoken too (cf. *The Roman Imperial Period* VIII 1.2.7): the *Historical Miscellany* (Ποικίλη ἱστορία), in 14 books, which has survived in compendium form, except the first two books, which are complete; and the *Characteristics of Animals* (Περὶ ζῴων ἰδιώτητος), in 17 books, which is preserved entire but has been subject to later alterations.

5.2 Athenaeus of Naucratis

Miscellaneous works such as the *The Learned Banqueters* (*Deipnosophistae*) of Athenaeus of Naucratis in Egypt, who lived in the second to third century, belong to the type of work mentioned above. The surviving work extends to 15 books but is a shortened version of the original text, which is likely to have been twice as long; the lacunae of the first three books are in part bridged by an epitome of the Byzantine Period. Athenaeus inserts innumerable notices about literature, philosophy, grammar and antiquarianism into the framework of a learned conversation in the context of a symposium, drawing on an expedient that had already become a literary form and been adopted for example also by Plutarch of Chaeronea (in his *Table-Talk*).

In the first eleven books the author's erudition is concentrated on the theme of food in Greek culture, dissecting its historical and cultural aspects and its material aspects as well as its more typically gastronomic ones. Every detail (the circumstances, procedures, ingredients) provide a prompt for the author to launch his characters into well documented disquisitions on the most varied topics, which are manifested above all in a fastidious and scrupulous care over terminology (for example in Books VI–VIII, on fish) and the ability to cite with ease the classical authors (Plato, Aristotle) as *auctoritates* but without inferiority complexes or excessive veneration. Books XII and XIII address the topic best suited to the symposiastic setting, namely that of pleasure, immediately linked to that of *eros*: in the second of these two books much space is given to an examination of Greek love lyric. Book XIV concerns the usual forms of entertainment at banquets, from buffoon shows to musical performances (interesting here is the digression on instruments) and dance. The final book dwells on the furnishings at symposia, then turns to poetic forms connected to banquets.

As well as being a goldmine of information on a disparate variety of topics (from objects of everyday use to the practices connected to banqueting, from symposiastic lyric to philosophy), the *The Learned Banqueters* is for us an irreplaceable source, thanks to the large quantity of quotations of ancient works, often lost ones. Over a thousand authors and work-titles are cited and more than 10,000 lines, with a massive presence of Middle and New Comedy, which gave a lot of room to everyday situations and language.

5.3 Diogenes Laertius

We know almost nothing about this author, who has left us a work in ten books concerning the lives and works of the Greek philosophers from Thales to Epicurus, known as the *Lives of Eminent Philosophers*. The dating of Diogenes to the first half of the third century is based, among other things, on the fact that he never alludes to Neoplatonic philosophers. The work belongs essentially to the genre of biography, but it links it to other aspects, such as doxography, aspects connected both by their shared erudite nature and by their origin under the influence of Peripatetic researches.

> In the introduction he addresses the problem of the origin of philosophy and declares that he is committed to the custom (of Alexandrian origin) of dividing the philosophers into an Ionic succession and an Italic one, with the resulting breakage of some doctrinal connections. Then follows the treatment of the lives of the philosophers and their doctrines, beginning with the Ionic series (Books I–VII): The Seven Sages (I); Anaximander, Anaximenes, Anaxagoras, Archelaus, Socrates and the Socratic schools (II); Plato (III) and his students (IV); Aristotle and his students, from Theophrastus to Heraclides (V); Antisthenes, Diogenes of Sinope and the Cynic philosophers (VI); the Stoics, from Zeno to Chrysippus (VII), with a lacuna in the final part of the book. The last three books are on the Italic series: Book VIII concerns, among others, Pythagoras and Empedocles; Book IX Heraclitus, Xenophanes, Parmenides, Melissus, Zeno of Elea, Leucippus, Democritus, Protagoras, Diogenes of Apollonia, Anaxarchus, Pyrrhon and Timon; Book X, finally, is entirely devoted to Epicurus, some of whose works it preserves, namely three letters that present a compendium of his thought (*To Herodotus, To Menoeceus, To Pythocles*) and 40 *Principal Doctrines* (Κύριαι δόξαι).

Diogenes uses previous collections of anecdotes and doxography with a compilatory technique that is not banal in its methods, combining alongside each other materials of different origin and quality that seem to him useful in delineating the biographical profiles or forms of thought, in such a way as to construct a sort of "history of Greek philosophy" by profiles of philosophers. The value of the work lies both in its testimony to the interests of the author (whose philosophical alignment is a matter of debate) and of his addressees, and also in the quantity of information that it provides, though this must be taken in an appropriately critical spirit.

5.4 The *Anthologion* of John of Stobi

An emblematic case of the compilatory activity of Late Antiquity is the collection entitled *Anthologion*, in four books, which John of Stobi (often called Stobaeus), who lived in Macedonia, in the fifth century, addressed to his son with didactic intentions. He collected extracts and citations of works by more than 500 Greek authors, predominantly of the Classical and Hellenistic Ages, and he grouped them by topic, treating them in the same way as opinions on various topics: metaphysics and physics (Book I), ethics (II and III), politics and private life (IV). It is thus a work that has, at the same time, the character of an anthology and of doxography. The *Anthologion*, known to us in a form that has emerged from various later interventions and interpolations, has preserved for us in this way a generous hoard of fragments of ancient texts from a large variety of literary genres.

XI Oratory and Rhetoric in Late Antiquity

1 The revival of rhetoric

The third century had marked a phase of decline, but the fourth century was not a period of cultural silence, despite the crisis and social and political difficulties that the Roman empire was passing through. A testimony to this is rhetoric, which, cultivated above all for its educational role, had a renaissance in this century, borne on a wave of reusing and defending the classical authors. The emblem of what is conventionally called the "Late Sophistic" was again the Atticist taste and the imitation of classical models such as Demosthenes, even though these tendencies were realised in different ways from one author to the next (as had anyway been the case also in the previous centuries). Alongside innovative figures such as the emperor Julian, who enlivened the models of a distant past by introducing a new spiritual sensibility, there were also many authors who turned Atticism and its stylistic features into a tool for formal playfulness that was often empty and pursued as an end in itself.

But the real novelty of this sophistic *revival* consisted in the fact that rhetoric became a point of encounter and conflict between paganism and Christianity (which, after Constantine, had risen to become the state religion) and at the same time a connecting link between the classical pagan world of Late Antiquity and the nascent Byzantine civilisation. The centre of rhetorical studies, as of political realities, shifted from Rome to Constantinople, the new capital built by Constantine on the European shore of the Bosphorus, inaugurated on 11 May 330 and called "the New Rome." From then on, rhetors, philosophers and intellectuals poured into it, attracted by its lively cultural developments, and inevitably the contacts brought to the surface the tensions between pagans and Christians. Some rhetors and teachers of rhetoric showed a reaction to the spread of Christianity by defending the moral and intellectual values drawn from the classical tradition. The most troubled and sensitive figures experienced this opposition in terms of an inner tension and sought responses at the religious and philosophical level, for the most part privileging a Neoplatonic direction. An example of this is the work of the emperor Julian, one of the most sensitive and afflicted witnesses to this century. Other authors, such as the rhetors Himerius and Libanius, drew on their reading of the classics with less originality. However, despite the fiery polemic with the Christians, rhetoric was not the site of an intolerant conflict or dialogue of the deaf. The schools of rhetoric generally accepted contacts with the Christian world and by allowing the attendance of students of a different religion they made possible a setting in which classical culture flowed into Christian culture.

https://doi.org/10.1515/9783110426328-040

2 Himerius of Prusa

Himerius of Prusa, son of a rhetor, was born in the early fourth century in Bithynia, at Prusa, which had also been the home city of Dio Chrysostom. He was trained as a rhetor at Athens, where he knew the future emperor Julian. At the latter's invitation he went to Constantinople and in the capital he was a teacher of eloquence. Thereafter he lived and worked above all at Athens, where his students included the Christians Gregory of Nazianzus and Basil of Caesarea. He died at Athens after 384.

From Himerius there remain, in an incomplete form, 24 works including speeches and fictitious declamations, for the most part addressed to imperial functionaries or intended for school use. According to Photius, whose *Library* preserves many quotations from Himerius, he wrote more than 80 speeches. Among the rhetors of this period, Himerius appears to be the one least sensitive to the social and political upheavals of his time and a stern defender of the sophistic tradition. He was a friend of the emperor Julian, to whom, in a speech delivered at Constantinople in 362, he addressed admiring words about his project of renewing the ancient pagan cults, "sweeping away the darkness that prevents us from raising our hands towards the sun" (41, 84–86). In his speeches he privileged content suited to particular occasions and called himself the "friend" of the ancient lyric poets, endeavouring to emulate in his poetic prose the artifices, assonances and musicality of authors such as Sappho, Alcaeus and Anacreon. In fact, the importance of Himerius' work lies also in the fact that he is a mine of quotations and paraphrases of Attic rhetors (Demosthenes, Aeschines) and of various poets.

3 Themistius

Originally from Paphlagonia, Themistius lived between, roughly, 317 and 388. He was at first educated in the school of his father, the sophist Eugenius, and was at an early stage directed towards studies of Platonism and Aristotelianism. He continued his philosophical and rhetorical training at Constantinople, where he then opened an important school. He enjoyed the admiration of the emperors of his time, who trusted him with the role of official court panegyrist, but he was also admired by Christian authors who were attentive to rhetorical culture, such as Gregory of Nazianzus. The emperor Theodosius nominated him *praefectus Urbi* in 383/4 and teacher of his son Arcadius.

Unlike his contemporary Himerius, Themistius' interests and output were linked both to philosophy and to rhetoric, achieving, better than any other rhetor of this period, a marriage between these two disciplines, though in a rather eclectic way. His philosophical leanings led him to reject the title of sophist and to chose a modest lifestyle. His paraphrases of some Aristotelian works (*On the Soul*, *Posterior Analytics*, *Prior Analytics Book I*, *Physics*) enjoyed notable success in the Byzantine

Era and have survived to this day. They were written with an exegetical intention and with the main aim of clarifying the more obscure passages.

While little remains of his philosophical work, from his rhetorical output there survive 34 orations (of which 19 are official speeches), composed on different occasions and topics, as was the fashion of the day. Themistius often voiced support for a state governed by philosophy and regulated by philanthropy, which he considered the leading virtue of an emperor. In the name of this concept, he sought to inspire the emperor Theodosius to a policy of peace towards the barbarians, in particular the Goths (as is attested by Oration 16). His position towards Christianity, too, was particularly moderate: Themistius declares that he favours coexistence between different cults and even maintains the importance of liberty of cult and faith (*Oration to Jovian*).

Themistius' prose is sustained by the reading of the Attic orators, although, as in Himerius, there are also reuses of poetic texts. Although he at times yields to the superficial tastes of his time, we can see in him a certain depth of thought and conviction that is reflected in some pages composed in the "severe style."

4 Libanius of Antioch

Libanius was the most admired rhetor in the fourth century and the Byzantine Period. He was born at Antioch in 314 into a rich family and pursued his studies at Athens. He opened a school at Constantinople in 342 but, following disagreements with his fellow rhetors, he left the city and moved to Nicomedia in Bithynia. In 354 he returned to Antioch, where he pursued the profession of teacher of rhetoric for almost half a century, heaping up fame and honours. Among his students were the Christians Gregory of Nazianzus, John Chrysostom and Basil of Caesarea. He enjoyed the esteem and friendship also of the emperor Julian, with whom he was connected by the defence of the values of paganism against the spread of the Christian religion. The esteem of the emperors translated into public offices: Julian named him quaestor and Theodosius summoned him to hold office as Praetorian Prefect. He died in his native city around 393.

Libanius was an extremely productive rhetor. The fame that he enjoyed in the ancient and medieval world ensured that very many of his works have been preserved. We have 64 orations, a fair number of compositions for use in school and a notable letter collection. Of great interest are the speeches for public and private occasions, in which many contemporary topics arise. Some are addressed to friends: addressed to Julian, for example, is Oration 13, in which he salutes the emperor's accession to the throne, while Oration 17 (*The Lament over Julian*) and 18 (*Funeral Oration over Julian*) were written on the occasion of his death. Dedicated to the emperor Theodosius is Oration 30 (*To the Emperor Theodosius, For the Temples*), in which Libanius attacks in invective tones those who destroy pagan temples and statues while in the grip of religious fanaticism. Also of notable interest is Oration 1, the so-called *Autobiography*, written in the course of around twenty years, from 374 to 393, in which the rhetor traces the story of his life in the terms of an apologia. Among the compositions for use in school, we may note declamations (*meletai*), descriptions (*ekphraseis*), exercises (*progymnasmata*) and *ethopoeiae* (*ēthopoiiai*). In this sphere belong also a *Life of Demosthenes* and the *hypotheseis* (*Arguments*) to the speeches of the great Athenian orator.

Libanius has also left his correspondence of 1603 letters, the largest to have survived from antiquity. The letters are addressed both to Christians and to pagans and treat extremely varied topics. Some are very short, following the fashion of the time, to the point that they can appear enigmatic. In this field, too, Libanius appears to be a sophist in the fullest sense of the word: for him the letter is above all a literary genre and is approached as such, with the greatest formal care and the use of the genre's most typical stylistic features. The imitative reuse of the classics, in fact, is the most striking characteristic of this author, who is for the most part considered to be an essentially superficial figure as rhetor and literary author. Modern scholars charge him with lack of originality, an overblown fondness for tiny, pedantic details to the detriment of the essential point and a formal preciousness that runs over into affectation and superficiality. However, his Atticism, the richness of his vocabulary, his vast knowledge of the classics, in particular of Demosthenes and the Attic orators, all made him famous and admired among his contemporaries and later rhetors.

5 Emperor Julian and the pagan restoration

The son of Julius Constantius, half-brother of Constantine, Julian was born at Constantinople in 331. At the age of six he escaped the massacre of his family, which was probably ordered by his cousin Constantius, thanks to the quick thinking of a Christian priest who hid him in a church. From then on he lived under surveillance and was raised by a eunuch, Mardonius, who directed him towards the study of the classics, a study that he pursued with the help of the best teachers. Julian soon rejected Christianity and from this arises his byname, given to him by the Christians, "the Apostate," i.e. traitor, "he who has committed apostasy" (recanting, defection). He was initiated into the rites of Mithras, Cybele and the Sun, and later to those of Eleusis, and he embraced Neoplatonic philosophy. In 354 at Milan the emperor Constantius proclaimed him Caesar and, perhaps with the aim of getting rid of him, sent him to Gaul. Although he had no military experience, Julian revealed notable abilities as a general and in 357 he defeated the Alamanni at Strasbourg. He won enormous popularity thanks to his military victories and in 361 at Lutetia (present-day Paris) he was proclaimed emperor by the rebellious legions of the West. The following year, on the death of Constantius, he entered Constantinople as the sole master of the empire. The years of his reign were very brief but decisive. He promoted important reforms, such as easing the fiscal burden, reducing the court staff and restoring the classical tradition and the pagan cults against a hitherto triumphant Christianity. Julian did not pursue any real persecution of the Christians, but he barred them from teaching literature and rhetoric in schools. He died in 363 in the course of a campaign against the Parthians, at Ctesiphon, aged just 32.

The ancient sources describe Julian as a nervous man, to the edge of neurosis, animated by an extraordinary faith in the value of the classics and by an exceptional energy. The Christian Gregory of Nazianzus presents a near-caricature of him (Oration 5, 23): Julian had a fanatical character, the gaze of a fool and speech that was often disconnected and characterised by sudden bursts of laughter. A more positive portrait is given by the pagan historian Ammianus Marcellinus (XV 4, 18), who speaks of eyes that were "burning and seductive, which expressed an inner disquiet" and of a personality that was strongly charismatic. We know that he lived frugally and used part of the night to complete his official duties and to devote himself to philosophy and literature. He embraced Neoplatonism and in the art of governance he was inspired by Marcus Aurelius, the philosopher-emperor. He intended to realise the ideal of a state governed by philosophy (in the footsteps of Plato) and chose always to be accompanied by intellectuals and philosophers. He was linked in particular to the rhetors Libanius and Themistius, to whom he addressed an important letter, and to the Neoplatonic philosophers Maximus of Ephesus and Priscus. Modern historians agree in regarding him as the last of the emperors to incarnate the Roman model of a man of both action and thought.

Despite the fact that his life was short and eventful, Julian wrote a lot, but little has survived of his works. Lost are his *Commentaries* on his war in Gaul and the treatise *Against the Galileans*, the disparaging name that he used for the Christians in counterpoint to the Hellenes. In this work, which can be reconstructed from its refutation by Cyril of Alexandria (fifth century), Julian decreed the superiority of the Greeks, among whom he praised the laws of Solon, Lycurgus and other legislators, over the Jews. The latter, following recurring motifs of anti-Christian polemic (it appears that it was modelled on now lost works by Celsus and Porphyry), are considered to be thieves and wrongdoers and generally untrustworthy.

The preserved works are of differing character, including orations, letters and satirical works. Among the more interesting orations, the first three in the corpus are political in character, namely the *Panegyric in Honour of the Emperor Constantius* (Oration 1 of the corpus), the *Panegyric in Honour of the Empress Eusebia* (Oration 2), showing his sincere admiration and respect for her, and the work *The Heroic Deeds of the Emperor Constantius, or On Kingship* (Oration 3). In these speeches Julian, who reveals a clear awareness of the decline of the empire, rejects the tendency, which had begun already under the Severans, to make the emperor a mediator between God and Earth and he prefers to go back to the Platonic conception of the philosopher-king. It is in fact the Platonic virtues of prudence, strength and justice that he makes the foundation of the activities of emperor and state.

The fourth speech in the corpus of Julian's works (*A Consolation to Himself upon the Departure of the Excellent Sallust*) is a *consolatio*, datable around 358/9, which Julian addressed to himself on the departure of his friend Sallust, who is perhaps to be identified as the Prefect of the Orient, Secundus Saturninus Sallustius. The speech *To the Athenian Senate and People* (Oration 5) takes up a position against the actions of Constantius in order to justify Julian's own act of rebellion. In the letter *To Themistius the Philosopher* (6), the dating of which is problematic, Julian discusses with his friend the rhetor the importance of the contemplative life and the gifts that should distinguish the activity of an emperor: while Themistius regarded the emperor as the incarnation of the laws, according to Julian the emperor is subject to the law. Philosophical in content are two orations against the Cynics, *To the Cynic Heracleios* (Oration 7) and *To the Uneducated Cynics* (Oration 9). Two speeches are religious in character and take a hymn-like course, matching Julian's programme of religious restoration: *Hymn to the Mother of the Gods* (Oration 8) and *Hymn to King Helios* (Oration 11). In the first of these, the cult of Cybele is praised in mystical tones and through the use of symbols and allegories; the intention is to achieve religious unification of the empire by celebrating an oriental goddess who had been transplanted to Rome since time immemorial. In the *Hymn to King Helios,* Julian retraces the path he has followed as a devotee, in the context of praise of the solar religion, which had already been embraced by some emperors in the past; a large part of the oration is given over to the description of the solar system, with the distinction between the intelligible, intelligent and visible worlds (with debts to the philosopher Iamblichus).

The *Symposium or The Caesars* (Oration 10), from the year 361, has the features of a Menippean satire. Julian imagines a celestial banquet in which the Roman emperors take part, from Caesar to Constantine: in a sort of competition, Marcus Aurelius emerges as the winner, while the loser is Constantine, who is guilty of being Christian. The work that has brought Julian the greatest fame is the *Misopogon, or Beard-Hater* (Oration 12), written in 363, shortly before he left to fight the Parthians. It is an untypical work that is hard to place in a precise literary genre. The polemical intention of the work is directed against the inhabitants of Antioch, who were spreading libels against the emperor, accusing him of, among other things, wearing a beard in imitation of pagan philosophers. Julian, as was his style, did not respond with repression, but with this satire. In it he pretends to accuse himself but with finesse turns the accusation against the Antiochenes and their habits. From Julian there also remains a collection of around 80 *Letters*, both official and private, which constitutes an important testimony to the character and personality of this ruler.

Verdicts on Julian's works and style are not unanimous. There are some who reproach him for an excessively academic manner of expression, which is sometimes marred by a form that is not all that polished and chiselled, due to the speed with which he composed so many works in a very few years. But others emphasise the effectiveness of a style which, while formally Atticist, is able to be charged with particular intensity precisely because of the jumps and discontinuities and the *inconcinnitas* of the periods and so to become a mirror of a strained and sensitive mind.

6 Eunapius of Sardis

We have already discussed Eunapius (who lived between 345 and 420) in the chapter on historiography in the Late Antique Period, noting his *Hypomnēmata historika* (cf. *The Roman Imperial Period* III 2.5). We note here the work entitled *Lives of the Philosophers and Sophists*, produced on the model of the work of that name written by Flavius Philostratus (cf. *The Roman Imperial Period* VIII 1.2.8). In it Eunapius includes philosophers (such as Plotinus) and rhetors who were his contemporaries, such as Himerius and Libanius but not Themistius. As seems to have happened in the historical work, in the *Lives* too Eunapius reveals great admiration above all for the aims of pagan renewal by the emperor Julian, to whom he devotes an entire book.

7 Synesius of Cyrene

Synesius, who was a Christian and the bishop of Ptolemais, is regarded as the last great rhetor of the fourth century, whose career extended also into the first decade of the following century. All of his work is in fact characterised by a significant and specific rhetorical cast and by the ongoing presence of classical and Neoplatonic ideals.

Born at Cyrene in Libya around 370, Synesius studied at Alexandria at the school of the philosopher and scientist Hypatia (cf. *The Roman Imperial Period* VII 1.4.7); at her school he had the opportunity to acquire and deepen his knowledge of Neoplatonism. Subsequently he was at Athens and Constantinople, where he went on an embassy to request fiscal benefits for his own region. He remained at Constantinople for three years, from 399 to 402, and was in contact with the imperial court. He converted to Christianity, probably at Constantinople. In 410 he was named bishop of Ptolemais and he fulfilled this office in a spirit of self-sacrifice until 413, which is probably the year of his death.

The corpus of Synesius' works that survives today includes treatises, orations, correspondence and hymns. The orations and treatises were for the most part composed prior to his episcopate. Scholars place in his youth the sophistical exercise *The Praise of Baldness*, in which Synesius, at a distance of three centuries, brilliantly refutes the lost *paignion* (παίγνιον) *Encomium of Hair* by Dio of Prusa (cf. *The Roman Imperial Period* VIII 1.2.2). Dating to his time in Constantinople is the speech *On Kingship* (*De Regno*), which was delivered in the presence of the emperor Arcadius in 399 and is one of Synesius' most important works. In it he principally treats the duties and actions of the ideal sovereign, according to the traditional stereotypes, but other subjects of interest also appear, such as distrust of barbarians, above all the Germanic ones who were infiltrating into the magistracies and Roman army to an ever greater degree. Synesius even proposes a national army, composed exclusively of Romans, by eliminating the "barbarian party." In the work *Egyptian Tales, or On Providence* he again addresses, this time in an allegorical manner, the conflict between Roman politicians and magistrates and those of barbarian origin. Another of the more important works is *Dio*, written around 405, presenting Synesius' cultural ideal, which consists of a harmonious marriage between philosophy, rhetoric and the sciences. Dio of Prusa is considered to be the model for this, in opposition both to the philosophers, who are too obscure and incapable of communicating their thought, and also to the anchorites and monks, who are rough and wholly uncultured. Synesius exalts Hellenic civilisation as the salvation from the decadence of his contemporaries. In his work *On Dreams* he discusses the prophetic value of dream visions.

His 156 *Letters* were composed between 393 and the year of his death. They form a precious source on the author's life, in particular on the period of his episcopate. There are also numerous notices on events and personages of the period, as well as debates on contemporary events. The 9 *Hymns*, which did not have a liturgical function, attest the author's deep religiosity, which did not reject the message of the Neoplatonists even after he had crossed over into Christianity. Alongside reminiscences of classical authors, echoes of *Scripture* also appear in the *Hymns*.

Synesius is considered to be a symbol of the religious and cultural syncretism that characterised the centuries of the Roman empire's decline. In his work the memories of classicism and paganism are still tenacious and continuous, while Neoplatonism remains the philosophical foundation on which Synesius bases his thought. After his conversion he accepted the position of bishop without repudiating his wife, who was also a Christian, and without rejecting his prior philosophical training. Due to this distinctive position he was excluded from the number of the Church Fathers, but found favour among the Byzantines. Photius, in his *Library*, admires him for the elevation of his style and the importance of the content. Similarly positive judgements were made later by Michael Psellus (eleventh century) and the humanists, who elevated him to a model of Greek thought.

8 The School of Gaza

Gaza, the city in Palestine, became between the fourth and the seventh century the seat of an important rhetorical school that lasted until the Arab conquest in 635. Its members revealed a sound classical and philosophical training, for the most part Neoplatonic, to the point that it attracted students even from Athens. Gaza thus appears as one of the locations where the cultural syncretism characteristic of this period took shape.

Among the principal rhetors of the school, the one who stands out is Procopius of Gaza, who lived between 465 and 528 and was the author of a *Panegyric of the Emperor Anastasius I*, in which the emperor is compared to Alexander the Great and other famous men of old, and of *Commentaries on the Old Testament*, perhaps his most important work, which was widely diffused in the Byzantine world. Various rhetorical works have been lost, including a *Homeric Paraphrase*, about which Photius informs us.

At work in the same years was the rhetor Aeneas, who wrote 25 *Letters* and the dialogue *Theophrastus, or Of the Immortality of the Soul and of the Resurrection of Bodies*, in which he maintained the Christian doctrine on immortality in opposition to the Platonic one. A friend of Aeneas was the rhetor Zacharias Scholasticus, author of a dialogue *Ammonius*, in which he launches a polemic against the Neoplatonic philosopher of that name, a disciple of Proclus. Choricius of Gaza (sixth century) is the last important member of this school. He has left us an interesting treatise on the theatre known by the Latin title *Apologia mimorum* (*Defence of Actors*), in which he describes the theatrical practices of the Late Antique Period in their most everyday aspects and the organisation of the stage. He also wrote orations and school exercises.

XII Poetry in the Imperial Period

1 Epigram

1.1 A flourishing genre

Throughout the Imperial Period there was a general decline in poetry to the advantage of an exuberant and varied output in prose. It was only with difficulty that poetry found new forms and new motives for inspiration and it often ended up reworking traditional schemes. A case apart is epigrammatic poetry, which was practised without interruption through to the Byzantines. On the one hand the exponents of this genre always kept their eye turned toward the golden age of epigram, the Hellenistic Period, and toward Latin authors, but on the other hand the continued vitality of epigram should be traced to the suppleness of its form and contents, which allowed it to adapt to new tastes on the part of its readers.

In this sense, the forms and thematic ranges of traditional epigram continued and were rejuvenated, with its topics of funerary, political, erotic, dedicatory, convivial, ecphrastic and scoptic verse. Despite continuous and ostentatious allusions to Alexandrian epigram (and also to the epigram of the Archaic and Classical Ages), the principal poets did attempt some innovations in language (neologisms are not infrequent) and metre and, departing from conventional situations, they also succeeded in transposing into verse slices of real life, in very varied styles. This is the case, for example, with the poetry of Palladas, in which harsh autobiographical elements are interwoven, or the languid eroticism of Paulus Silentiarius and Agathias. The dialect used is predominantly Ionic, though in some authors a mannered Doric is present. The metre is the elegiac distich, sometimes replaced, above all in the late poets, by the dactylic hexameter and iambic trimeter.

1.2 The epigrammatic poets of the Imperial Period

Among the principal poets of the Augustan Age we note Crinagoras of Mytilene, author of around 50 epigrams that stand out for their "minimalist" attention to everyday life, which is contemplated in its most minute aspects. The language and style, too, are often simple and linear. His contemporary Antipater of Thessalonica (not to be confused with the Hellenistic poet Antipater of Sidon) wrote around a hundred epigrams on various topics, characterised by notable formal refinement and by the continual desire to compete with the models of the past. In some poems historical figures appear, such as Calpurnius Piso Frugi, a friend of Antipater, and Gaius Caesar, nephew of the emperor Augustus. Also of the Augustan Age is Marcus Argentarius, from whom 37 epigrams survive on various topics, predominantly erot-

https://doi.org/10.1515/9783110426328-041

ic, which echo above all the models of Callimachus and Meleager. Philippus of Thessalonica, who lived in the reign of Caligula and was the author of the *Garland* (cf. *The Hellenistic Age* IV 2.2.7), wrote around 60 epigrams of various kinds, shaped by a moralistic vision of life. More interesting is his language, in which various *hapax legomena* appear. The poetry of Lucillius, who was active under Nero and the author of 125 epigrams, is considered to be more powerful artistically. His scoptic poems use jabs of burning sarcasm to depict persons and types of his era; some scholars consider him to be a precursor of Martial. A contemporary of Lucillius is Leonidas of Alexandria, author of three books of epigrams, the *Charites* (Χάριτες); many of Leonidas' poems have the characteristic of being composed of just a single distich.

Among the poets of the following generation Straton of Sardis stands out, a second-century author of erotic epigrams primarily on homosexual love. His poetry varies greatly in its registers, though predominantly ephebic love is portrayed in its more physical and sensual aspects; sometimes he also uses obscenity, with heavy-handed jokes and double-entendres. Of the same period is Rufinus, from whom around 40 erotic epigrams survive, written in a register of languid and at times lascivious sensuality.

After a couple of centuries of relative silence, in the Late Antique Period the epigram enjoyed another flourishing phase. Among the more interesting and expressive authors we note Palladas of Alexandria, who lived in the fourth to fifth century, under the emperor Arcadius, and was author of around 150 epigrams preserved in the *Palatine Anthology*. He is considered a forerunner of the renaissance of epigram in the age of Justinian. A schoolteacher, Palladas seems to have lived a life of hardship and bitterness, as many of his poems attest. He is one of the epigrammatists in whom the autobiographical element (whether it be real or conventional) is at its strongest, rendered dramatic by a constant sense of frustration in the face of life. Some epigrams, scoptic in character, are addressed to his insufferable wife and women in general and they hence take their inspiration from traditional misogynistic themes. There are also fierce criticisms linked to his profession as schoolteacher, which never allows him to escape from his resented poverty (*Ant. Pal.* XI 378, 1–2: "I cannot put up with a wife and with Grammar, Grammar that is penniless and a wife who is injurious"). There are few erotic or convivial epigrams. Palladas uses expressive resources very skilfully and draws aptly on models. As well as the elegiac distich, he uses the hexameter and the iambic trimeter. He enjoyed some fame from a very early stage.

The final creative phase of ancient epigram belongs to the years of Justinian's empire and presents poets of notable importance. Although they are Christian authors, the topics are those of the tradition: convivial, epideictic, sepulchral and above all erotic, these last perhaps the most intense, in which love takes on tones that are vaguely intimistic and languid, but without altogether abandoning the assemblage of commonplaces and conventions that the genre had accumulated over time. Among the epigrammatists of the Justinianic Age who have left us their works, the two most important are Paulus Silentiarius and Agathias, but we may note also Julian the Egyptian, Macedonius of Thessalonica and Eratosthenes Scholasticus.

Paulus Silentiarius. Paulus Silentiarius (the byname meaning either "usher" or "master of ceremonies at the palace") lived at the court of Byzantium and was a friend of Agathias. He wrote two *Descriptions* in hexameters: the *Ekphrasis of the Church of Hagia Sophia*, which he dedicated to the emperor Justinian and to the patriarch Eutychius, and the *Ekphrasis of the Ambo of Hagia Sophia*. From his output around 80 epigrams of great formal refinement survive in the *Palatine Anthology*. They are for the most part erotic epigrams, with a strong sense of sensuality and abandonment to passion (*Ant. Pal.* V 219, 4: "furtive liaisons are more honeyed than open ones"). The epigrammatic poetry of Paulus Silentiarius is marked by the musicality of the verse and the elegance of his use of past authors, for example Philodemus, Leonidas of Tarentum, Horace and Ovid, which the author brings to life again in new situations. For example in *Ant. Pal.* V 258 Paulus treats with ardour a traditional commonplace theme, the love for a mature woman, seeing it in a perspective of burning sensuality and passion: "your winter is warmer than another's summer."

Agathias. Agathias Scholasticus lived between 530/2 and 579/82 and composed a lost poem entitled *Daphniaca*, a *History* in five books on contemporary events, which is preserved, and a collection entitled the *Cycle*, in which he collected his own epigrams and those of authors of his time, which was incorporated into the *Palatine Anthology*. This collection was arranged in seven sections by topic and not, as had previously been done, in alphabetical order. Of some importance is the prooemium in which Agathias elucidates his editorial criteria. We have around a hundred of his epigrams on various topics, which are elegant in form and arch in their allusions to models. Following the traditional commonplaces of the genre, Agathias often dwells on the precarity of life, which is seen as a brief passage towards death, which it is wrong to fear excessively.

2 Hymnography

2.1 The forms of the hymn

The genre of hymnography, too, continued to be cultivated in the Imperial and Late Antique Periods but, unlike in the past, the genre came to include texts that had long been rejected by the dominant culture, such as magical texts. Of great importance for our knowledge of the spirituality of the period are the *Orphic Hymns*, which, alongside poems such as the *Orphic Argonautica* and the *Lithica*, attest the importance of the cult of Orpheus in these centuries, and the *Magical Hymns*. Other authors such as Mesomedes, Proclus and Synesius stayed close to the motifs and themes of traditional hymnography.

Of Mesomedes of Crete, a freedman of the emperor Hadrian, we have some poems dedicated to various divinities and some profane hymns in anapaestic or trochaic metres, written in the language of the *koinē*. From the Neoplatonic philosopher Proclus we have seven hymns in hexameters, and nine authentic hymns remain from Synesius of Cyrene (cf. *The Roman Imperial Period* VII 1.4.6 and XI 7) written in an artificial literary Doric dialect. Both these authors aim to use the forms of the hymnodic genre to achieve a philosophical-religious syncretism between traditional polytheistic beliefs and the religious and spiritualistic demands of Neoplatonism.

2.2 The *Orphic Hymns*

While the cult of Orpheus is very ancient and had some diffusion in Greece from at least the sixth century B.C., the religious and literary tradition of the *Hymns* that can be linked to Orphism is no less ancient, as is attested for example by Aristophanes, Euripides and Plato. However, most of the testimonia to this form of spirituality are much later. Aside from the Orphic tablets discovered in southern Italy and dating to the fourth to third century B.C., we possess a collection of *Orphic Hymns* that was compiled probably around the second century A.D. (though perhaps with earlier roots). These should be connected to the renaissance of Neopythagoreansim, which gave an impulse to various religious forms characterised by an Orphic-Pythagorean spirituality.

The origin of this hymnographic corpus is uncertain. There are 88 hymns, structured according to the traditional scheme with the invocation of a god, exposition of his prerogatives in a series of epithets and finally the request for help. The metre used is the hexameter and the style is full of epithets and, in general, of terms that are rare or remote from everyday use. The gods most often invoked are those connected to Dionysiac cult, but foreign gods also appear, such as Sabazius, from Phrygia, and Hipta, from Libya.

For the sake of completeness we mention here some other texts belonging to Orphic literature that have already been noted: the poem entitled the *Orphic Argonautica*, of around 1300 hexameters, in which Orpheus narrates the story of the Argonauts; the *Lithica* (*On Stones*), a short poem of around 700 lines in which Orpheus sets out the specific properties of stones; and the cosmogonic poem, of which we have some fragments thanks above all to the remains of the commentary to one such poem preserved in the famous Derveni Papyrus (cf. *The Archaic Age* IV 1.2).

2.3 The *Magical Hymns*

Although the remote literary origins of the hymns on magical topics are certainly earlier than the Imperial Period, the corpus that we possess goes back to a period between the third and fifth century A.D. A literary tradition linked to magic is attested at least from the Hellenistic Period, as is shown for example by the short poem *The Sorceresses* by Theocritus. However, both the Greek and then the Roman authorities, as well as the "official" culture in general, long refused to accept this tradition, even though, above all in the first centuries A.D., scenes of magic and theurgy are an ever more frequent presence in literary works, from novels to poetry. The origin of the *Magical Hymns* is predominantly Egyptian and it is hence not mere chance that these texts have reached us above all thanks to discoveries of Egyptian papyri bearing magical texts and formularies. The structure of each hymn is the canonical one (as with the *Orphic Hymns*), with invocation of the divinity and request for help, using recurring formulas and epithets with symbolic force. The divinities invoked are for the most part Hermes, Hecate and Helios, as well as the Egyptian gods. There is no recurring metrical structure; the language is full of terms special to magic and foreign terms, while onomatopoeic plays on single words or on the litany hold a marked symbolic force.

3 Oracular literature

Among the collections of oracles that have been transmitted from the ancient world, the *Delphic Oracles* present the traditional responses of the priests of the sanctuary at Delphi, one of the most ancient and venerable in the Greek world, to questions from private citizens or public authorities, and sometimes from entire communities or cities. The consultations concerned both private affairs and problems in public life, such as the foundation of a colony or the appointment of a magistrate. Often the oracle of Delphi prescribed "purifications" to remove some contamination scourging the collective. The responses were for the most part made in hexameters and in language that mirrored the language of Homer. It is not rare for them to be presented in the obscure form of riddles or enigmas. Authors such as Plutarch, who was fairly close to the cult of Apollo of Delphi, criticised their excessive ambiguity. No ancient collection of Delphic oracles has been transmitted: the one that we read now has been put together by modern scholars on the basis of literary sources (such as Herodotus) that report the oracles and (to a much lesser extent) epigraphic sources.

The *Sibylline Oracles* (not to be confused with the *Sibylline Books*) acquired this name because they were attributed to the ancient Sibyls, priestesses charged with making known the oracles of Apollo. The first book of the collection opens with a catalogue of the ten Sibyls. The texts present characteristics that differ from those of the *Delphic Oracles*, since they do not consist of responses, either real or supposed, to a consultation, but of predictions about the destiny of humanity. In many cases they consist of prophecies in apocalyptic tones, which foresee events such as epidemics, earthquakes, famines and volcanic eruptions. Put together probably in a Jewish context, with the aim of promoting Jewish culture via a pagan spokesperson, interventions have also been made in them in a Christian context (cf. *The Roman Imperial Period* XIII 1.2.8). The corpus, originally consisting of 14 books (12 survive), has been composed by juxtaposing two distinct collections, with a total of more than 4000 hexameters of modest workmanship, in an imitation, at a low level, of Homeric style. The first collection seems to go back to the sixth century A.D. and is attributed to the anonymous author of the preface. The second was probably compiled after the Arab conquest of Egypt (seventh century) and consists of Book IX to the end. They unite oracles originating in the pagan world but presented in a form that has been deeply reworked and interpolated on the basis of Jewish and Christian motifs. The topics range from the creation of God and of Adam and Eve to the history of Rome, the key moments of which are interpreted in eschatological terms. The series of arguments, often lacking in coherent or organic connections, presents various repetitions and contradictions.

The *Chaldaean Oracles*, likewise in hexameters, are known to us through around 200 rather brief fragments preserved by pagan and Christian authors for the most part linked to late Platonism. The tradition attributes them to a certain Julian, but we do not know if this is the Julian called "the Chaldaean" or his son, called "the Theurge," who lived during the reign of Marcus Aurelius. It cannot be ruled out that the son reused for his edition oracles that had already been collected by his father. The title refers to the wisdom of the Chaldaeans, a people of ancient Mesopotamia who were expert in cosmology and theology. The contents are obscure and not easy to decipher, a difficulty aggravated by the oracles' symbolic and enigmatic form. The byname "Theurge" attributed to their presumed author refers to the practice of theurgy, which was widespread in Late Antiquity, aimed at evocation of the gods and the possibility of acting upon reality by means of them. The *Chaldaean Oracles* present different characteristics from the two previous types: they are neither responses nor prophecies, but treat astrology, theology and philosophy, taking inspiration from Neoplatonic and Neopythagorean motifs. It is difficult to organise the complex doctrine of these oracles into a precise system, though modern authors have found in them many analogies to the work of Numenius (cf. *The Roman Imperial Period* VII 1.3.5). Some fragments celebrate the Father, creator of the Ideas and of the Second Intellect. Great importance is given to Hecate, who is perhaps to be understood as the World Soul, and the doctrine of demons and angels. The *Chaldaean Oracles* had a wide influence on intellectuals and writers of a Platonic orientation, such as Porphyry, Iamblichus, Arnobius of Sicca, Synesius of Cyrene, Proclus and the Byzantine Michael Psellus, who wrote an *Exegesis of the Chaldaean Oracles* (Ἐξήγησις τῶν χαλδαικῶν ῥητῶν).

4 Epic and didactic poetry

4.1 Diffusion of the genre of epic

Alongside epigram, the other two poetic forms that were cultivated with success in the Imperial Period up to the Byzantine Era are epic and didactic poetry. For the sake of a convenient exposition, we shall classify the former as narrative epic of Homeric, romance and historical-encomiastic types, leaving for a separate treatment Nonnus of Panopolis. It should be stated that all the hexameter poetry, despite the innovations and developments of each author, largely continued to follow in the expressive path of the language of Homer, which remained the basis of the poetic language in these genres. Late epic poetry did not develop suddenly in the fourth and fifth century, as had sometimes mistakenly been believed, but rather it flourished without interruption from the first centuries of the Imperial Period onwards and enjoyed a practically uninterrupted tradition. Although very many works of the authors prior to Nonnus of Panopolis and Musaeus, who are perhaps the two most significant representatives of late epic, have not been transmitted or have reached us in an extremely fragmentary form, from the most recent studies we know that in these centuries the epic tradition was deeply rooted in Egypt, thanks above all to poets who wandered from region to region, getting paid to practise their art.

4.2 Narrative epic in the Homeric tradition

We cannot always ascribe originality and talent to the authors of this period, but in the case of Nestor of Laranda, who lived in the first half of the third century, we have an attempted exercise that was at the least bizarre. In his *Lipogrammatic Iliad* (Ἰλιὰς λιπογράμματος, "Iliad Lacking One Letter"), he rewrote the Homeric poem while eliminating from each book the corresponding letter: in Book I the letter *alpha*, in the Book II *beta* and so on.

  Quintus Smyrnaeus. Of a different calibre is the work of Quintus Smyrnaeus (i.e. "of Smyrna" in Asia Minor), an author of whom we know very little. Even his homeland is uncertain, since the adjective Σμυρναῖος ("of Smyrna"), which the author applies to himself (XII 310), refers to the fact that he was inspired by the Muses while he tended his flocks at Smyrna. The era in which he lived is also uncertain: the scholarship ranges between the third and fourth century. He composed *The Events After Homer* (Τὰ μεθ' Ὅμηρον), known by the Latin title *Posthomerica*, in 14 books, in which he narrates the events following the end of the *Iliad*, creating a narrative link to the *Odyssey*.

> The work follows a compositional scheme of 5 + 4 + 5. The first five books, with unified content, present a sort of *Achilleid*, with the narration of the killing by Achilles of Penthesilea,

queen of the Amazons, and of Memnon, king of the Ethiopians, up to Achilles' own death and the contest for possession of his weapons. The next four books are devoted to the conflicts and duels between Greeks and Trojans. The last five books narrate the ruse of the Trojan Horse, the last night of Troy (an episode for which one can observe analogies with Book II of Vergil's *Aeneid*), the return journeys of the Greeks to their homeland and the exploits of Aeneas.

Often accused of transposing into excessively fulsome and "baroque" verse heterogeneous material drawn from mythographic manuals, Quintus Smyrnaeus does not enjoy a great reputation as a poet. Nonetheless, some have seen in the poem gifts of clarity and expressive effectiveness, despite its undoubted prolixity and a certain taste for the macabre which is typically late antique. The poem's models are above all Homer, then Hesiod, the poets of the *Cycle*, Apollonius Rhodius and Lycophron, who are completely revisited and often superimposed by drawing on well worn expedients of the art of allusion that recall those of the learned Alexandrian poetry of the Hellenistic Age. With Homer Quintus maintains a relation of imitation with variations on the model, an operation in which he deploys a technique that is often refined, formed of complex and layered expressive strategies.

Triphiodorus. Contrasting judgements have been made also of the work of Triphiodorus (the name means "gift of Triphis," an Egyptian god), born at Panopolis in Egypt. We do not know when he lived. Some scholars place him, for reasons of style, in the fifth century, but the recent discovery of a papyrus seems to attest an earlier date, perhaps in the third century. His only surviving work is an epyllion in 691 hexameters, *The Taking of Ilios* (Ἰλίου ἅλωσις), which, like the work of Quintus Smyrnaeus, imaginatively completes the material narrated in the *Iliad*. The work, in which much space is given to descriptions, following the rhetorical model of *ekphrasis*, and the pursuit of dramatic narrative effects, fully matches Late Antique taste. Works by Triphiodorus that do not survive are the *Marathoniaca*, the *Lipogrammatic Odyssey*, on the model of the *Iliad* of Nestor of Laranda, and other works cited by the *Suda* lexicon.

Colluthus. Among the last representatives of the epic-mythological tradition we may record Colluthus, originally from Lycopolis in Egypt, who was active in the late fifth and early sixth century. The *Suda* informs us that he wrote the *Calydonian Tales* (*Calydoniaca*), on the myth of Meleager, and the *Persian Tales* (*Persica*), in honor of the emperor Anastasius, a work that has been lost. What remains is an epyllion in 394 hexameters entitled the *The Rape of Helen* (Ἁρπαγὴ τῆς Ἑλένης), the topic of which, the abduction of Helen by Paris and the Greeks' declaration of war on the Trojans that followed it, was contained in the cyclical poem Cypria and in all likelihood had been adapted already in the Alexandrian Age.

4.3 Nonnus of Panopolis

The greatest representative of the renewal of narrative epic on mytholgoical themes in the Late Antique Period and its principal innovator was Nonnus of Panopolis. We know almost nothing about him. We know only that he was a native of Panopolis, a city of Upper Egypt, and that he was living at Alexandria when he composed his poem on Dionysus. The name Nonnus means "pure" or "holy" in Egyptian and was quite common in the Imperial period, above all in eastern and Christian circles. It is likely that Nonnus' career should be placed in the second half of the fifth century, though some set it in the fourth and some in the sixth century

Nonnus wrote two works that are very different from each other: the epic-mythological poem *The Dionysiaca* (Τὰ Διονυσιακά), which earned him great fame in the ancient world, and *The Paraphrase of the Gospel of John* (Μεταβολὴ τοῦ κατὰ Ἰωάννην ἁγίου εὐαγγελίου), a rewriting of the fourth *Gospel* in epic hexameters. The coexistence of the two works raises numerous questions: did Nonnus write first the *Paraphrase*, which is not a simple paraphrase but a rewriting of the *Gospel* text in an elaborate style, and then in his maturity *The Dionysiaca*? Was he always a Christian even though he, like other ancient authors, admired the values of classicism and its mythology in an almost visceral way? Or, as some scholars think, was the *Paraphrase* written in a later period of his life, after a (presumed) conversion to Christianity? At our current state of knowledge, we do not have conclusive answers to these questions: the ancient notices are too sparse. Scholars are inclined to consider Nonnus a true representative of the cultural and religious syncretism that distinguished Late Antique culture and particularly that of the cosmopolitan ambience of Alexandria.

> *The Dionysiaca*, the more important work, recounts the adventures of Dionysus in 48 books, divided in two groups of 24, each introduced by a prelude and an invocation of the Muse. It is an imposing work, which has no equal in scale in the ancient world with its more than 20,000 lines (the *Iliad* and *Odyssey* together amount to a little more than 27,000 lines). The narrative does not begin straight after the birth of the god, but takes its start from a sort of "Dionysiac archaeology," i.e. from the wedding of Cadmus and Harmonia, the rape of Europa and the story of Semele, mother of the god. The central events are Dionysus' ascent to Olympus, his love affairs and, above all, his journey to a fabled India, a journey that is interpreted in a symbolic key, on the basis of the Hellenistic motif connected to the figure of Alexander the Great, the "new Dionysus" and conqueror of the East. The final part of the poem recounts the god's victorious return, his fight against Pentheus and the Giants and his wedding to Aura.

The choice of the myth of Dionysus is justified in the first part of the poem. Zeus had invited this god to earth to comfort humanity with the gift of the vine, just as in the past he had sent Demeter with the gift of grain. The pairing of the two divinities is traditional and has a parallel, for example, in the *Bacchae* of Euripides. The symbolic and soteriological values in the poem are numerous but not always easy to decipher. Further, the loss of many works on Dionysiac topics that were composed in the

Hellenistic and Imperial Period, and which served as models for Nonnus, prevents us from clarifying the meaning of many passages, although it seems, on the basis of the work as a whole, that there is an initiatory motif in the god who dies and is reborn and triumphs over his adversaries after trials and troubles.

Nonnus is an author of fervid fantasies, as is manifested above all in the scenes of orgies and mysteries, which are full of pathos and expressive intensity. The clarity of his narration is diminished by his excessive use of rhetoric and erudition, as well as the dizzying succession of very many secondary scenes, in homage to the tried and true technique of a "story within a story." Further, as Nonnus himself declares in the work's first prooemium, the narrative criterion closest to his heart is ποικιλία (*poikilia*), variety in composition. The principal model of *The Dionysiaca* is Homer, but Nonnus' verse has very little of the Homeric about it: the style, imagery and narration are the result of exultant imagination and compositional exuberance, the language is "baroque" and erudite. The scenes in distant lands have features of fable and the East is seen as a mysterious and unbridled world. Of notable sensuality are the love episodes, for example those that have as protagonists Ariadne and Aura.

Nonnus was also an innovator in his dactylic hexameter, which is full of assonances and musicality and characterised by must stricter rules than either the archaic hexameter or the Callimachean one. Nonnus avoids proparoxytone words at line end (something that reveals an attention to word accent as well as to the quantity of syllables). He does not admit two spondees in succession, unless separated by incision, and he follows particular schemes for the incisions. In this period the pronunciation of Greek was anyway already far from that of the Classical Age and was gradually losing the perception of the quantitative differences and evolving towards Byzantine and Modern Greek. The metrical novelties of Nonnus soon found many imitators.

4.4 The romance epic of Musaeus

The principal epyllion on the topic of love in this period is owed to Musaeus, another author of whom we know almost nothing. The only indication we possess is the epithet γραμματικός (*grammatikos*), i.e. grammarian or teacher of letters and rhetoric, which follows the name Musaeus in the titles of the manuscripts. According to some scholars, Musaeus should be identified with a friend of Procopius of Gaza (cf. *The Roman Imperial Period* XI 8) of this name, to whom Procopius addressed two letters. Other elements for the dating can be inferred from the fact that Musaeus was an imitator of *The Dionysiaca* of Nonnus of Panopolis in the structure of the hexameter, while it seems that he was echoed by Colluthus in *The Rape of Helen*. This implies that Musaeus lived in the second half of the fifth century.

To him we owe an epyllion or short poem in 343 hexameters, *Hero and Leander*, which adopts a legend already known and widely treated by Alexandrian poets and present also in Ovid's *Heroides*.

> During a religious celebration, Leander, a young man of Abydos, falls in love with the very beautiful Hero, a priestess of Aphrodite who lives at Sestos, on the opposite shore of the Hellespont. Leander succeeds in approaching the girl and in declaring his passion for her. In order to meet his beloved, every night Leander swims across the straits that separate the two cities, guided by the light of a lamp lit by Hero at the top of the tower where she lives in seclusion, at the command of her parents. The strait, which is around seven stades across (a little more than a kilometer), is crossed by powerful currents. Not even the arrival of winter can make the two cease their meetings, but in a stormy night the wind douses the flame and the boy is carried off by the waves. The following morning Hero, seeing the body of her beloved on the shore, kills herself by throwing herself from the tower.

The adventure is linked to a very ancient folktale motif and presents numerous features that are typical of the Greek novel: the love story concerns two young people of extraordinary beauty, the passion between Hero and Leander arises in the course of a sacred ceremony, their love is blocked according to the typical scheme of the love novel. But Musaeus sets into these motifs and into the structure of the Alexandrian epyllion elements of great emotional and sentimental intensity. A scene full of sweetness and, overall, of amorous delight is the one in which Hero and Leander speak to each other for the first time and the young man, after declaring his love, intuits from the expression of the girl that she too is in love. While some parts operate at a slower narrative rhythm, there is a more sustained and dramatic pace in the final scene, in which Hero will not renounce Leander even in winter, provoking the death of them both. These are episodes in which Musaeus' skill in mastering the feelings of his protagonists (we may note that no other figures appear in the short poem) manages to move beyond conventional schemes, which are, however, also present in the fabric of the work. The physical and sensual rendering of the nocturnal meetings between Hero and Leander, too, escapes the mannerism of some Greek novelists and is characterised by a certain freshness, which is quite rare in authors of the Imperial and Late Antique Period. Yet Musaeus was still working closely from his models, which are the Alexandrian epyllion, erotic elegy and, among the novelists, Chariton and Achilles Tatius (cf. *The Roman Imperial Period* IX 1.2 and 4). Naturally, in the metre and lexicon his greatest debt is to Homer. The work enjoyed notable success as soon as it was rediscovered in the Humanistic Period and was favoured especially by the romantics.

4.5 Historical and encomiastic epic

Throughout the Imperial Period, alongside the mythological and romance epics, historical *epos* flourished, which for the most part took on celebratory and encomiastic features, since the emperors were the principal patrons and addressees. Among the major representatives of this genre we note Oppian of Apamea, active in the third century, who celebrated the war of Septimius Severus against the Parthians and who was also the author of didactic works (cf. next section). Callistus, *protector domesticus* of the emperor Julian, wrote in honour of the latter a work on his campaign in the East. Among the authors of the Late Antique Period we note Arrianus, who lived probably in the fourth to fifth century, to whom the *Suda* lexicon attributes an *Alexandrias* on the victories of Alexander the Great, and Christodorus of Coptus, in Egypt, who composed a poem on the exploits of the emperor Anastasius I (491–518) against the Persians.

Christodorus was also an exponent of two other literary genres that were particularly popular in this period: the *ekphrasis* and the *ktisis*. The genre of *ekphraseis* (*descriptiones*) consisted of detailed descriptions of objects of craftsmanship, works of art, jewels, arms and armour and other objects, inserted into a poem (the archetype of the genre is the famous description of the shield of Achilles in Book XVIII of the *Iliad*). Beginning already in the mature Hellenistic Era, *ekphrasis* became an autonomous literary genre, also under the influence of rhetoric. Christodorus has left us a short poem in 408 hexameters in the rhetorical and erudite style, preserved in the *Palatine Anthology*: the *Description of the Statues in the gymnasium of Zeuxippus* (an imposing bathing complex in Constantinople). Other exponents of the genre of *ekphrasis* were Paulus Silentiarius and John of Gaza. The *ktiseis* are epyllia on the foundation of cities; among those who tried their hand at them, as well as Christodorus of Coptus, a certain Claudianus, who seems to be different from the Latin poet of that name who is author of the *Rape of Proserpina*.

4.6 Didactic epic

The authors of didactic poems of the Imperial Period addressed very varied topics, often confronting themes from medicine, geography or natural science. These works had a certain success in the Latin world and then in the Byzantine one, although they lack a truly scientific approach to the material, since their aim was rather to rival the models of the past at the level of rhetorical and compositional skill.

To Marcellus of Side, in Pamphylia, who lived in the second century, is owed the hexameter didactic poem *On Medical Matters* (Ἰατρικά), now lost. What does survive, however, is the hexameter poem *Tour of the Known World* by Dionysius Periegetes, originally from Alexandria and he too of the second century: the work, inspired by the genre of the *periēgēsis* in prose, was translated into Latin by Avienus and Priscian and was admired by the Byzantines. Oppian of Anazarbus, in Cilicia, was active in the second to third century and is the author of the hexameter treatise *Halieutica*, or *Fishing* in five books, in which he describes the variety of fish and their habits; the work is dedicated to an Antonine, who is perhaps the emperor Marcus Aurelius. Oppian of Apamea, who was the author also of a historical-encomiastic poem (cf. previous section), wrote a work of didactic character dedicated to Caracalla, *Cynegetica*, or *The Chase* in four books, by which he intended to rival Xenophon and Arrian.

XIII Christian Literature in Greek

1 Christian literature before Constantine

1.1 Under the sign of continuity and difference

With the spread and organisation of the Christian religion, from the mid-first to the second century A.D., a Christian literature also came into being. It is usual to distinguish two phases of this literary history, corresponding to the two quite different phases undergone by Christianity between its origins and the Late Antique Period. In the early centuries, until the Edict of Constantine in 313, Christian writers saw their task as the strenuous defence of doctrine and of their own social role, or indeed of their own lives, but after this date a triumphant Christianity gave rise to a "canonical" literature that was able to address the different spheres of knowledge in total safety, or even with the comfort of open political protection.

As well as considerable elements of continuity, the Christian literary experience presents original aspects that justify distinguishing it from the previous and contemporary literature of pagan inspiration. Further, the literary experiences of Christian authors appear very varied and also differ among themselves, in parallel to the changes in historical and social conditions, which produced an evolution in genres and forms. It is nonetheless possible to indicate summarily some general elements that characterise this literature. Above all, in the first centuries it had strictly practical purposes: the works, be they apologias, commentaries, homelies, polemics or historical writings, were responding to specific and concrete demands in the Christian community. This does not mean that there was no literary interest, no taste for writing or for pure speculation, but such interests were subordinated to the practical goals that moved the author. In the first centuries, therefore, the Christian sphere lacked a literature for pleasure, or one in which the ludic element held a pre-eminent role. The Christian author was a literary militant whose religious duty entirely pervades the work. As we shall see, the themes treated were new and, in many cases, the literary forms were new too, prompted by the needs of the religion and adapting to new demands (new occasions, contexts and addressees).

The positions taken towards classical culture and literature are very varied. They range from an unconditional rejection that extends even to that literature's expressive resources, which were seen as a vain seduction, to a cautious appreciation of it, with an eye to exploiting its expressive forms and tools of thought in a Christian context. Yet the writers were inevitably imbued with traditional culture and literature, even when they made a point of condemning them without reserve due to their paganism, and in reality they remained deeply influenced by them.

New models appeared alongside the classical ones, in particular the *Scriptures*. The Holy Book, which ought to inspire a Christian's every action, took on a very

https://doi.org/10.1515/9783110426328-042

particular role as paradigm that has no counterpart in classical literature. Not only was it an object of study and point of reference for every judgement or opinion on any topic at all, but it was also a model and source of inspiration for every piece of writing. The allusions to and quotations from classical texts were paralleled or replaced by those from *Scriptures*. As in Jewish culture and religion, for Christianity too the written text of the divine revelation took on a central position. For this reason it is easy to understand how not only the content but also the form and expressions of the Holy Book moulded the works of Christian authors deeply.

The influence of *Scriptures* also operated in another direction. In the pre-Christian ancient world the need to comment upon a text had never taken on the importance and significance that commentary on sacred texts came to hold for Christians (only the case of Homer is comparable). This introduced great novelties also from the formal point of view, since a new technical vocabulary came into being. On the one hand new words, sometimes modelled on Hebrew, were introduced to express the concepts of the new religion, on the other hand existing words took on new meanings or were specialised in technical senses. The translations of *Scriptures*, further, did not limit themselves to introducing to the target language stylistic traits of the source language but, through their commitment to an original that was considered to be inspired, they also transmitted syntactical elements that in many cases contributed to deeply modifying the target language, and these came to be used also outside the strictly religious sphere.

Often the texts of the Christian authors have been studied solely for their historical and theological interest or they have been seen as witnesses to a form of decline in the ancient cultural tradition. Many of them do not in fact manage to reach the heights of the greatest writers of the pagan tradition and in some the lack of interest in the stylistic and formal factor is programmatic, since traditional rhetoric was seen as an outcome of pagan culture and a possible tool of deceit, capable of maintaining both what is true and what is false. Further, the need to convey the *Gospel* message also to the more simple and uneducated members of the faithful demanded a profound rethinking of linguistic tools. However, this rethinking was in many cases not resolved by a simple rejection, but by the search for a new literary language capable of conveying the Christian message effectively to a vast audience, and there is no shortage of authors who deserve admiration also from the strictly literary point of view, nor is it acceptable to make generic negative judgements, especially when formulated on the basis of evaluative standards founded on a classicising taste. This literature marks a moment of undoubted novelty, without which it would be impossible to understand and explain the subsequent developments in language and literary production. It is essential, above all, that Christian literature be studied and interpreted as a specific phenomenon, with its own characteristics and its own historical and cultural context.

1.2 The Apostolic Fathers

1.2.1 Clement of Rome

A first group of authors is generally grouped under the name of Apostolic Fathers, since they belong to a period in which it was possible to have direct access to the testimony of the Apostles.

Beyond the *New Testament* writings, the first testimonies that have survived today are for the most part in epistolary form, which was already well represented in the *New Testament* from the letters of Paul onward. The earliest is the *Letter to the Corinthians* by Clement, fourth bishop of Rome, which can be dated to around the year 96. It was written in Greek, which long remained the official language of the Christian communities even in the Latin world. The style is simple but reveals the author's good education, since he shows attention to correctness in language and elegance in phrasing.

Clement, who expresses himself in the plural in name of the entire Christian community of Rome, attempts with this letter to quell some disagreements that had arisen in the heart of the community of Corinth, addressing a strong appeal to the sense of unity and fraternity within the community and an exhortation to humility and obedience. As occurs also in the letters of Paul, without losing sight of the specific, contingent aims, the address is broadened to the point that it becomes an exhortation of general value, accompanied by the indication of a model of Christian life that is modelled on examples drawn from *Scriptures*. We can glimpse traces of the influence of Stoic thought in the statements concerning the harmony that governs the world. The letter also has a special historical interest, both for its notices about the martyrdom of Peter and Paul and the persecution of Nero, and since it attests the position of particular authority, in certain aspects, that the episcopal see of Rome was coming to assume.

1.2.2 Ignatius of Antioch

A little later are the letters of Ignatius, bishop of Antioch (in Syria), who in 110, in the reign of Trajan, was condemned to be torn apart by wild beasts and brought to Rome to suffer this martyrdom. During the long journey transferring him there, he wrote seven letters to various communities of Asia Minor and to that of Rome. Of these letters, three different versions have come down to us, of which one has been expanded by an interpolator probably in the fourth century and another, in Syriac, contains only some of the letters. From Smyrna Ignatius wrote to the communities in Asia Minor of Ephesus, Magnesia and Tralles, to thank them for the delegation they had sent to meet him, and to that of Rome to dissuade them from appealing for the revocation of his sentence. From Troas he sent letters to the churches of Smyrna and Philadelphia and to Polycarp, bishop of Smyrna, asking them to send delegations to

Antioch to express happiness about the end of the persecution, of which he had been informed.

From these writings there emerges a strong sense of the hierarchical organisation of the Church, which already seems surprisingly well developed. There are also frequent appeals to unity. In line with the traditions of Paul and John, Ignatius fights against docetism (the doctrine that attributes to Christ a humanity that is only apparent), maintaining the both human and divine nature of Christ.

The language and style of Ignatius are very different from the orderly and elegant writing of Clement: there are irregularities, Latinisms, neologisms, colloquialisms and a rhythm that is fragmented and full of non-sequiturs, revealing a distinctive expressive efficacy. In this author's love for bold imagery, the commentators have tended to see signs of a typically eastern taste.

1.2.3 Polycarp of Smyrna

From Polycarp, bishop of Smyrna and addressee of one of the letters of Ignatius, we have two letters sent to the community of the Philippians, transmitted in the manuscripts combined as a single letter. We know that around 154 he came to Rome to discuss the divergences between the Roman church and the churches of Asia. At a date ranging between 156 and 177 he suffered martyrdom on the pyre at Smyrna.

The first letter is a brief greeting that accompanied the copy of an exchange of letters which the Philippians had requested from him. From it we gain information, among other things, about how these letter collections circulated and how the epistles of Paul were diffused. In the second letter, Polycarp reassures the community, which had been troubled by the heresy of Marcion (cf. below 1.5.2), exhorting them to Christian virtue and to prayer, in simple tones but with a certain disorder in his presentation of the content and with the support of very numerous quotations from the *Old* and *New Testament*.

1.2.4 Pseudo-Barnabas

We also possess a letter attributed to Barnabas, the companion of Paul in his ministry, but it was regarded as spurious already in the ancient world. In fact the epistolary form is purely a literary conceit and the thought that is expressed there makes it difficult to maintain the attribution of the text to the companion of Paul. Some allusions to historical events have led to a proposed dating that ranges from 96 to 138. The first part of the text is a polemic against the Jews, arguing (as Paul had done) for the allegorical interpretation of the *Old Testament*, but taking this tendency to the extreme, to the point of completely denying that there was any literal force to the sacred text. The second part develops the moral allegory of the two paths, the path of light and the path of darkness. The style is in general maladroit and not very effective. From its polemical content arguing against the literal value of the Mosaic law and from the notable difficulties that it reveals in dealing effectively with the material treated, scholars believe that the author could be a Jewish convert to Christianity, perhaps from the area of Alexandria.

1.2.5 The *Didachē*

The allegorical theme of the two paths is treated also in the first part of the so-called *Didachē* (Διδαχή), the complete title of which is, in English, *The Lord's Teaching to the Heathen by the Twelve Apostles*. This work by an unknown author, the dating of which ranges between the early and mid-second century (though the surviving text may be based on an earlier Jewish work) aims to provide a series of instructions to catechumens and gives us precious notices about a quite early stage of ecclesiastical organisation. After providing some instructions of general character by treating the theme of the two paths, the author addresses baptism, fasting, prayer and the eucharist. The final part speaks about the behaviour to be maintained towards missionaries, about criteria for choosing bishops and deacons and about Sunday worship. The text closes with a reference to the imminent coming of the Lord.

The style is very simple and clear, as we would expect of a text of this kind without any literary ambitions. Particularly interesting, also from a stylistic point of view, are the liturgical prayers included in the text.

1.2.6 Papias of Hierapolis

From Papias, bishop of Hierapolis, we have a few fragments of a work, originally in five books, entitled *Expositions of the Sayings of the Lord*, composed around 130, in which he exploits early oral traditions that he considers to go back to the circle of the Apostles. Some fragments are of particular importance, since they provide ancient reports about the composition of the *Gospels*. We owe to Papias the first testimonies to the millenarian doctrine, i.e. concerning the thousand-year duration of the kingdom of the Messiah on earth. This belief, Jewish in origin, thereafter enjoyed some success and took on very different forms. For example, it appears in a spiritual interpretation also in the *Apocalypse of John*, perhaps in polemic against the literal interpretation of a thousand-year reign.

1.2.7 The *Shepherd* of Hermas

Hard to place is a text known as the *Shepherd* of Hermas, which had a notable diffusion and was included by some among the canonical books (we may note its mention in the *Canon Muratori*, cf. *The Roman Imperial Period* VI 2.2). Hermas gives his own name in the work, where he calls himself a Roman freedman. A reference to Clement, bishop of Rome, may set the author and the work at the end of the first century, but the *Canon Muratori* identifies him as a brother of the bishop Pius, which would shift the date to the mid-second century. We cannot rule out that the work was composed in multiple stages or that it combines materials of disparate origin.

In the work, the structure of which is not homogeneous, an introductory section is followed by five visions, in a tone that is surprisingly close to that of a popular novel. The first four visions are centred on the figure of a matron, who symbolises the Church and invites the author and his family to penitence. In the fifth vision the angel of penitence appears under the aspect of a shepherd (from which the work gains its title) and instructs the author by introducing ten "precepts" and twelve "allegories." The precepts present the virtues and the vices against which the penitent must guard. The same concepts are then reprised, with complex imagery, in the allegories.

Despite the difficulties in interpreting the text, we can see as central to the whole work the theme of penitence, of particular importance to the Christian communities of the first centuries, when it was not always clear how to behave towards those who, after baptism, had relapsed into sin. The language is full of Hebraisms and Latinisms and the style is popular, but quite effective in its naïve narrative taste.

1.2.8 Early Christian poetry

In the mid-second century we also have the first testimonies to a Christian poetry, in the *Odes of Solomon*. These are 42 works that have been transmitted only in Syriac but which in all probability were originally composed in Greek and then translated. The form is deeply influenced by Hebrew poetry which, in the absence of metrical and rhythmic schemes like those of Greek and Latin poetry, work by intensifying the individual concepts with expressive devices in which an essential role is played by the use of repetitions, accumulated synonyms, citations or varied echoes, which create a system of parallelisms and ring structures. There is a strong influence from the *Old Testament*.

Also partly traceable to the early Christian tradition is the collection of the *Sibylline Oracles*, of which we spoke in the chapter on oracular literature (cf. *The Roman Imperial Period* XII 3). These texts, which are a true cento of Homeric verses, were probably composed in a Jewish setting with the aim of diffusing and legitimising Jewish culture by using pagan forms and attributing the message to a pagan figure. These were then in part reworked and increased in number in a Christian setting.

1.2.9 The origins of homiletic writing

In the second century we also have the first examples of the genre of homily. The term "homily," which has, among other meanings, that of "conversation," in liturgy indicates the "preaching" with which the priest addresses the faithful, usually by commenting on the liturgical readings of the day. The genre takes on very different forms depending on the content, aims and audience being addressed. It is based on traditional compositions such as diatribe or, in the case of homilies in praise of a saint, panegyric, but the solutions it finds take notably original forms.

A homily of quite simple tone, full of quotations from *Scriptures* and containing exhortations of a moral character, has been transmitted under the mistaken title of *Second Letter of Clement*. It was probably delivered in Corinth in the second half of the second century. Papyrus discoveries have also restored to us a homily by Melito of Sardis, whose main work was an apologia, now sadly lost (see below). In the homily the institution of Passover narrated in *Exodus* is read as an image of the redemption achieved by Christ. The author is revealed to be a sophisticated rhetor fond of elaborate rhetorical figures and of a style that is at times almost lyrical.

1.3 Christians and pagans: the apologetic writers

1.3.1 The time of persecutions

The spread of the Christian religion in the Roman empire and in the city of Rome itself led to harsh conflict between the political authorities and the communities of followers of the new religion, beginning from the notorious persecution of Nero that began in 64. In a first phase in all likelihood the Christians were considered to be simply a sect within Judaism. With the passage of time, however, the ideas of the new religion, which would totally overturn the canons of culture and traditional life, began to be considered dangerous to society and hence as something to be combatted with persecutions. These were of differing scale in both time and space and we should not think of them as a systematic or continuous action across the entire territory of the empire; it was only the final series of persecutions, promoted by Diocletian, that were systematic and comprehensive in extent. As well as suspicion from the educated and powerful classes, there was also hostility from the masses, who were habitually little inclined to accept novelties and prompt to accept slanderous reports about the new and mysterious sect. From the apologias we discover that the Christians were charged with accusations of a kind that today seem ridiculous: cannibalism, due to a misunderstanding of the rite of the eucharist, which was interpreted as a vicious sacrifice in which the adepts ate human flesh; incestuous relations, due to the preaching about mutual love between "brothers and sisters"; and atheism, due to the refusal to worship the traditional gods and eat the meats burnt as offerings to them. The grand attempt to revitalise traditional pagan culture that was undertaken in the second century by the movement of the Second Sophistic encountered an obstacle in the new religion, which certainly could not be accepted favourably by the educated classes.

Out of these manifestations of incomprehension, a need arose for works of defence, or "apologia," against the pagan accusers and detractors, with the aim of winning acceptance for the new religion by publicly clarifying its character. However, one should not deny that in many cases these writings were at the same time an impassioned defence and an attempt to spread the creed of the *Gospels* by making it better known and explaining its content.

1.3.2 The authors and works

Aristides. If we leave aside an apologia sent by a certain Quadratus (otherwise unknown) to the emperor Hadrian, of which all that remains is a brief fragment, the first apologetic text of which we have sizable testimonies is that sent in the second century by Aristides, an Athenian philosopher, to the emperors Hadrian and Antoninus Pius. From it we have two papyrus fragments, a Syriac version, an Armenian fragment and a version, in part reworked, incorporated into a hagiographical novel of the eighth century. The author sets out to demonstrate the truth of the Christian religion compared to other religions. Picking up motifs in the criticism of traditional beliefs that were already a feature of ancient philosophy, he ultimately argues that reason itself leads one to choose Christianity. With an emotional lyricism he describes the life of the Christians, who have the commandments of Jesus "impressed on their heart."

Justin. The same approach is taken by Justin, a philosopher originally from Sichem (Flavia Neapolis, today Nablus) in Samaria. After following various philosophical schools, he converted to Christianity and went to Rome, where he opened his own school with the aim of deepening Christian thought. He died a martyr between 163 and 167, as we are told in the *Acts of Justin and of his Companions* (see below).

From Justin are preserved two *Apologias*. The first was addressed around 153 to Antoninus Pius, Marcus Aurelius and Lucius Verus; the second is a brief appendix to the first, written a short time later, after the sudden condemnation of three Christians by the Roman prefect Urbicus. The texts contain a firm demonstration of the judicial illegitimacy of persecutions based on *nomen*, i.e. on the mere fact of being Christians. The author treats the characteristics of the religion and the behaviour of its adepts, but he does not limit himself to a general treatment, also addressing specific problems, convinced that the main enemy of the Christian religion is ignorance about it. According to Justin the rigid morality of the Christians helped make them not an element of social disturbance, but loyal citizens, provided that the emperor would renounce his claims to divinity.

The new religion is presented in philosophical terms that can be appreciated by a reader trained in ancient philosophy. Justin is not only talking to the pagans in terms familiar to them, but also reveals a notable openness towards pre-Christian culture, acknowledging that the major pagan philosophers had intuited fragments of the truth, which were then revealed by Christ. We should not see in Justin an attempt at syncretism between Christianity and elements of ancient philosophy: he is firmly convinced that the revelation definitively supersedes prior philosophical thought, but at the same time he avoids making a global condemnation of ancient culture, introducing the concept of the common end (truth) and of a certain continuity between pagan philosophy and Christian religion. An appealing aspect of his writings is his intelligent openness to understanding non-Christian culture, despite the firmness of his own profession of faith.

On a quite similar level is another work by Justin, datable a few years later and entitled *Dialogue with the Jew Trypho*. Here he addresses the delicate problem of the relation of Christianity to Judaism. This work, which has survived with lacunae in its central part, reports a long dialogue between the author and an authoritative Jewish scholar, in which Justin tries to demonstrate the truth of the new religion, in particular by discussing the interpretation of the *Old Testament*. This is certainly a literary fiction, though one may suppose that it could be based on a debate that really took place. The polemic is pursued by Justin firmly, but with intelligent respect for his adversary.

Justin does not seem skilful in organising his material. His arguments follow each other in a way that seems arbitrary and interrupted by numerous digressions. The tone is firm and enthusiastic and he includes not only numerous quotations from *Scriptures* but also quotations and echoes of classical literature.

Tatian. A radically opposite position is taken in the thought of the Syrian Tatian, although he was a disciple of Justin during a long stay at Rome. His *Oration to the Greeks* is a violent invective in which he makes use of the most sophisticated weapons of dialectic and deploys the methods of philosophical speculation in order to set out Christian thought, with the aim of condemning without reserve every aspect of pagan culture. The *pars destruens*, devoted to the criticism of paganism, takes up almost the whole of the work. Tatian parted from the Church after the death of Justin, and founded a rigorist sect in the East and composed the *Diatessaron*, a *Gospel* formed by reworking the testimony of the four canonical *Gospels*, which had a notable diffusion, as is demonstrated by the many translations of it that have survived: the original is lost.

Athenagoras. From 177 there is a *Legatio for the Christians* sent by a certain Athenagoras, of whom we know nothing, to Marcus Aurelius and Commodus. In a peaceable and conciliatory tone and a style that is balanced and inspired by Atticist tastes, with an exposition that is orderly – not a common feature of these writings – the accusations of atheism, anthropophagy and incest made against the Christians are refuted.

Theophilus of Antioch. Theophilus, bishop of Antioch, wrote three books *To Autolycus*, a person unknown to us, whom he addresses describing him as a friend. The work was composed after 180 (the third book contains a chronology of the world from the Creation to 180) and gives autonomous treatments in response to specific questions put to him by Autolycus. Various arguments are presented in it, in no order: a defence of the Christians against the most common accusations; a presentation of the Christian god with an allegorical interpretation of the Biblical account of the Creation and of Original Sin; condemnation of polytheism; and a demonstration that the prophets were prior to the pagan writers, to refute those who claim that the Christian religion was a recent invention. The condemnation of classical culture is total and he gives much more space than his predecessors to the message of *Scripture*; in fact, the text is more protreptic than apologetic in character. His other writings are lost.

Melito of Sardis. We should note also Melito of Sardis, who lived in the mid-second century and whom we have already mentioned as the author of a homily. Only a fragment survives of his apologia: it confronts the problem of the relations between the empire and the Church, ultimately affirming the need for an organic link between these two institutions, as willed by the divine providential design.

Anonymus ad Diognetum. The apologia that is most admirable from the stylistic point of view is certainly the anonymous work addressed *To Diognetus*, the dating of which ranges between 140 and 200. The author is responding to a question about the faith of the Christians that has been posed by a certain Diognetus, a pagan who seems to be an educated person and someone of some importance. The usual accusations against the Christians are presented and refuted, but a paraenetic tone predominates over an apologetic one, though there is no lack of polemical attacks on the traditional religion or on Judaism, underlining the total difference of the new religion from these. The author intelligently reworks themes drawn from the letters of Paul and presents his arguments with a clearly superior organisation compared to the other apologists. With infectious enthusiasm and skilful use of rhetoric, a justly famous passage explains the position of the Christians in the world ("in the world but not of the world"): like the soul is in the body but does not form part of it, so the Christians are in the world and apparently their customs can be assimilated to those of other people (i.e. they play a full part in social life), but their eyes and their vocation are turned elsewhere.

Irrisio Ermiae. It is customary to include along with the group of apologetic writings also a work known as the *Irrisio Ermiae*, the full title of which is Διασυρμὸς τῶν ἔξω φιλοσόφων, i.e. *Mockery of the Pagan Philosophers* (οἱ ἔξω, literally "the outsiders"). It is a very violent invective against pagan philosophy, about which, however, the author can often be seen to be badly informed. The text is not cited by other ancient authors and the dating proposals range from 200 to even as late as 600.

1.4 Acts and Passions of the Martyrs

1.4.1 Dying for the faith

Among the earliest Christian texts, we should record a series of writings, characterised by forms that often differed sharply among themselves, which recounted and celebrated the deaths of the Martyrs, i.e. "witnesses" (μάρτυρες, *martyres*) to their faith even to the point of sacrificing their lives.

In their earliest and simplest form, these accounts are called the *Acts of the Martyrs*, which offer a narrative that is stripped to the bare essentials. These are probably simple reproductions of the interrogations after which the Christians, having refused to recant, were condemned to death. Sometimes the bare account is supplemented and completed by short additional notices. Despite the total lack of literary elaboration of some texts, it is also easy to find in them passages that are deeply moving.

These simple documentations subsequently tended to be accompanied by accounts that became ever richer and more extensive, generally called *Passions*. These contain reflection in various tenors, for example parallels between the martyr and scriptural figures are explicitly suggested. The literary form is more elaborate and the dialogue between the martyr and the accusers is richer, to the point that, in a later period, they at times turned into wholly fantastic accounts.

Martyrdom is an imitation of Christ and the literary model for these narratives is obviously the *Scriptures* themselves. Scholars have sometimes wanted to see literary precedents for these writings in pagan works that praise the lives of philosophers or celebrate victims of imperial cruelty, yet it cannot be denied that, while not a new genre in an absolute sense, in the Christian sphere these works take on notably original characteristics and lay the groundwork for major developments, also in very different directions.

These writings arose in the first place out of the need to inform the community through the example of Christian heroism offered by the martyrs. Over time, they became a standard tool for reflection and catechesis on the topic of martyrdom, through the commemoration of the anniversary of the event, which was considered to be the martyr's *dies natalis* (i.e. their day of birth into true life), and the recollection of the sufferings endured in the name of faith.

1.4.2 The *Acts of Justin* and the *Martyrdom of Polycarp*

A quite important document, also on account of its early date, is the *Acts of Justin and of his Companions*, which narrate the martyrdom of the apologetic writer Justin, of whom we have already spoken (see above).

The *Martyrdom of Polycarp* is the earliest preserved testimony of the martyrdom of a single figure. Polycarp died on 22 February 156. The account of his passion has been transmitted in the form of a letter signed by a certain Marcion, who can be identified with one of the addressees of the letters of Ignatius. The form is plain and direct, but we can clearly see here a greater level of elaboration than the sparse *Acts of Justin*. For example, in polemic against those who voluntarily suffered martyrdom by denouncing themselves, the editor dwells on details that tend to distinguish Polycarp from these voluntary martyrs. The dialogues and final prayer of the martyr also reveal a greater attention to the literary effect of the text.

1.5 Internal polemic: the struggle against heresy

1.5.1 Heresy and heresiarchs
Quite different positions on various aspects of religious conceptions and theology were simultaneously present in the Christian communities right from the start, beginning from the differences between Paul and the Judaising currents, and there are clear traces even of different conceptions about the nature of Christ. However, these disagreements, although important, were initially tolerated within the Christian community, which had to present a united front against the attacks from outside. With the steady growth of the communities and the systematisation and deepening of Christian thought, it became ever more obvious that there was a need to defend the assemblage of doctrines considered to be right thinking ("orthodoxy") against discordant interpretations that threatened its message in different ways.

1.5.2 Gnosticism
An important position in Christian culture of the first centuries is occupied by a movement known as *gnosticism* or more simply *gnosis* (from the Greek γνῶσις, "knowledge"). We do not know much about this movement, or, to put it better, of this collection of innumerable small-scale movements, which was widely diffused across the entire Mediterranean area in the second and third centuries, since the condemnation of these religious conceptions has led to the complete loss of gnostic literature. Although much remains obscure, our knowledge has been improved thanks to the discovery, in a jar buried near the cemetery of Nag Hammadi in Upper Egypt, of a series of gnostic writings in Coptic, and new papyrus discoveries are helping to improve our understanding of this phenomenon. On this topic, it is worth mentioning the *Gospel of Judas* recently discovered in a papyrus codex of 66 pages (which has been a subject also of media attention), which contains, as well as the *Gospel of Judas*, also the *First Apocalypse of James*, the *Letter* of Peter to Philip and a fragment of text provisionally known as the *Book of Allogenes*, a heresiarch of the third century A.D.

Various scholars hold that gnosticism, rather than being a Christian heresy, had originally emerged as a pre-Christian pagan religion of syncretistic type, imbued in particular with Neoplatonic concepts; others suppose it had an origin in Jewish circles. However, the testimonies that are available to us at present make clear that this spiritual conception, while it does have strongly syncretistic characteristics, spread widely within a Christian setting from the second century onwards. At any rate, both the Christians themselves and the pagans engaged in anti-Christian polemic considered the gnostic sects to be a movement within Christianity.

The basis of gnostic beliefs was the idea that the world is the fruit of the creation by a divine entity that, after a primordial sin, fell and wrongly came into contact with matter. The *gnosis* or knowledge preached by the gnostics is one obtained via a revelation. This revelation concerns the ways in which the Redeemer permits the Spirit, the divine substance that has fallen and has therefore become imprisoned in matter, to recover its primitive state of integrity. The gnostic Saviour does not come to redeem humanity by expiating its sins through his own suffering, but instead comes only to awaken knowledge within the portion of humanity made up of those endowed with the Spirit or divine *Pneuma* within themselves (who are for that reason called "pneumatics"); this knowledge is already present within them but is obscured by the decay that arises from matter. Hence the idea of a real incarnation of the Redeemer is unacceptable to them, since his resulting material aspect would be entirely apparent. The rest of humanity is divided between people of pure matter, who therefore cannot be saved, and others not endowed with Spirit but only with Anima or *Psyche* ("psychics"), who are in an intermediate condition and whose status varies among the different orientations of gnostic thought. The revelation is transmitted in esoteric form within groups consisting only of pneumatics, who are predestined to salvation. Individual schools of thought were then characterised by approaches which, as far as we know, differed notably among themselves. Among the more important gnostics we may cite the names of Basilides, Valentinus and Heracleon.

A special position in the history of the gnostic heresy is occupied by Marcion, a Christian who believed that it was necessary to reject the *Old Testament* totally, since its Creator God, distinct from God the Father of the *New Testament*, was a figuration of the divine fall into contact with matter. Condemned in 144 by the church of Rome, Marcion abandoned it and founded a well organised alternative church of his own, which had a wide diffusion (unlike other gnostic sects). In particular he established, on the basis of his own theological vision, a canon that included only some of the writings traditionally considered to belong to the *New Testament*, eliminating the passages that underline the continuity between the Christian revelation and the *Old Testament*. This was among the reasons why orthodox Christianity felt the need to fix a definite canon that could oppose the Marcionite one (and other similar initiatives).

1.5.3 Writers against heresy

The birth and spread of heresies prompted and promoted an anti-heretical literature. The first author cited as combatting heresies is Irenaeus, bishop of Lyons. Born in Asia Minor, he moved to Gaul around 177, where he spent a long time engaged in the difficult work of evangelisation. Of his five books known as *Against Heresies* (the original title is Ἔλεγχος καὶ ἀνατροπὴ τῆς ψευδωνύμου γνώσεως, *A Refutation and Overthrow of Knowledge [gnosis] Falsely So-Called*) all that remains is fragments of the Greek original and a Latin translation (perhaps third century), which seems to be literal. The text is particularly useful for knowledge of gnosticism, thanks to the analysis of gnosis provided in the first part. A work of apologetic character, the

Proof of the Apostolic Preaching (Ἐπίδειξις τοῦ ἀποστολικοῦ κηρύγματος), survives only in an Armenian version. In the preface to the *Against Heresies* the author declares that he is ignorant of rhetoric, and his style, although not without some happy moments, seems in fact to be quite uneducated.

Composed later than 222, a work by an unknown author, known as the *Philosophumena* (Φιλοσοφούμενα) and whose complete title translated into English is *Refutation of All Heresies*, in ten books (the second and third books are lost), aims to refute the various heresies, starting from the idea that they have all emerged through the damaging influence of philosophy and the pagan mysteries. The work is therefore an expression of a complete closing off against pagan culture and is interesting as a source of knowledge about gnostic doctrines. From the text one can deduce that the author was a Roman priest of eastern origin who, in the name of greater rigour, had opposed Pope Callistus, accusing him of laxness towards penitents. He has been identified with a writer by the name of Hippolytus mentioned by numerous sources, though with some divergences between them.

The ancient sources also attribute to a Hippolytus another group of works that have been transmitted in partial translations into Georgian, Armenian and Old Slavonic and only partly in the original Greek. In particular, a group of exegetical works represents the oldest example of systematic and continuous exegesis of *Scripture*. These include a *Commentary on the Song of Songs*, in which the typological interpretation (i.e. an approach that aims to interpret the *Old Testament* as a prefiguration of the events in the *New Testament*) appears for the first time in a Christian context, with the identification of the Bridegroom with Christ and the Bride with the Church. We then also have: a *Commentary on Daniel,* probably in homily form; a *Commentary on the Benedictions of Isaac, Jacob and Moses* and a homily on *Kings* I 17, known as the *Story of David and Goliath*. The significant differences in the level of doctrinal thought rules out an attribution of all these works to the same author as of the *Philosophumena*, and many different theories have been proposed, including that the work of two different authors, both called Hippolytus, have been united in this corpus.

Also transmitted in Greek under his name is a work *On the Antichrist,* whose coming is not seen as imminent, despite the persecution of the Christians. Finally, also attributed to Hippolytus are a *Paschal Canon,* i.e. a table for establishing the date of Easter, and the *Apostolic Tradition*, an ancient witness, together with the *Didachē*, to the liturgy and organisation of the Church, which has survived in small fragments quoted in later works.

1.6 The school of Alexandria

1.6.1 The rational study of revelation
In the Imperial Era Alexandria remained one of the most important cities of the Roman empire after the capital and, as we said when discussing the *Septuagint Bible* translation (cf. *The Hellenistic Age* IX 1), it was the seat of a large and lively Jewish community. Eusebius of Caesarea and others speak of the creation in Alexandria of a true school of religious studies, called the *Didaskaleion*, under the authority of the local bishop, which was founded by a certain Pantaenus. The school probably started in a private form on the model of the pagan philosophical schools of the period and was not, at least at the beginning, an official structure with a place in the ecclesiastical order, as the tradition claims. It is no surprise, however, that a school of this type would have been born in a centre with such a great and ancient philosophical culture and one that was open to different influences.

The new step taken by the thinkers of Alexandria was important. With notable intellectual force, they went in search of a more elaborate theoretical and rational systematisation of the Christian revelation, drawing also on tools of thought from ancient philosophy (in particular Plato), which were therefore re-evaluated in a constructive way. As regards exegesis, above all in opposition to Judaism, the school worked out complex allegorical interpretations, applying to *Scripture* the pagan tradition's ancient method of allegoresis.

1.6.2 Clement of Alexandria
The first author of the Alexandrian school from whom we have writings is Titus Flavius Clement, a person of vast and deep culture. Probably of Athenian origin and of pagan family, Clement was born around 150. He converted to Christianity after following various philosophical currents and, it seems, after being initiated into the pagan mysteries. He settled at Alexandria, where he was a pupil of Pantaenus, succeeding him as director of the *Didaskaleion* around 200. He abandoned Alexandria two years later, probably to escape the persecution of Septimius Severus, and around 211 he moved to Cappadocia. He died a little before 215.

In the first of his works, the *Exhortation to the Greeks* (*Protreptikos pros Hellenas*), Clement picks up polemical motifs against pagan religion from the apologetic writings, but in a positive form, as an invitation to convert to the true wisdom constituted by Christianity. To capture the attention of learned pagans, Clement deployed an elaborate style full of quotations from classical poets and pieces of rhetorical bravura. The resources of philosophy are used as a tool for discovering the truth in Christ, the divine *Logos*, and even the title of the work connects to the ancient practice of exhortations to philosophy.

The *Paedagogus*, composed by Clement after he had left Alexandria, is a work in three books that in a certain sense continues the previous work, as the author himself seems to indicate at the start, where he describes how the divine Logos acts on the faithful in three phases: exhortation to salvation; a first education; and finally deeper instruction (the Logos is thus a *paedagogus* or "teacher"). Matching the different content, this work has a less elaborate style than that of the *Exhortation*, but the phrasing is always elegant and the language pure and there is no shortage of moments of great rhetorical sophistication.

> The first book has general content and presents the *Logos* as a teacher full of love but also of severity, in order to direct the faithful properly (in evident polemic with gnostic-Marcionite thought, which attributed severity only to the God of the *Old Testament*). The two following books present specific moral precepts and norms of behaviour, inspired by principles of moderation in part shared also by ancient philosophy. The author addresses, at times with unusual frankness, many problems concerning the behaviour to be maintained in relation to consumption (food, drinks, luxurious living), dance and music, leisure pursuits, the practice of bathing and conjugal life. The themes are treated with explicit firmness, but the stated norms resist a rigid asceticism. The work closes with a hymn to Logos in anapaests.

Scholars have tried to identify the *Stromateis* (the title Στρωματεῖς means "rug, mat, tapestry," a metaphor for a miscellaneous work) with the third level of action of the *Logos*, but without success. The work is an eight-book collection of material and thoughts on disparate topics. The general intention is to find arguments to demonstrate that Christianity is the true philosophy. Despite the fact that it is an unordered collection of sketches of differing character, perhaps not intended for publication, and the formal workmanship is certainly inferior to that of the other works and is unequal within the work, it is the richest and most original of Clement's writings.

A work with the character of a homily is *The Rich Man's Salvation* (Τίς ὁ σωζόμενος πλούσιος;), which comments on a passage of the *Gospel of Mark* (10:17–31), interpreting the invitation to poverty in a moral-spiritual sense, an example of Clement's moderation and his tendency to harmonise the harsher points of Christian teaching with the values of the traditional culture.

1.6.3 Origen of Alexandria
The important figure of Clement was surpassed by that of another authoritative member of the Alexandrian school, Origen, with the byname *Adamantios*, i.e. "as hard as steel." Born around 185 at Alexandria to a Christian family (his father died a martyr), at just eighteen he was summoned by the bishop of the city to direct the catechetic school, with the task of preparing those who were to receive baptism. It is in this period that, to satisfy an aspiration to radical ascesis, he subjected himself to castration. Encouraged by the demands of the more educated faithful and pagans and heretics who attended his lectures, he entrusted to others the training of the catechumens and devoted himself to courses at a higher level. He attended the lectures of Ammonius Saccas, teacher of the Neoplatonic Plotinus (cf. *The Roman Imperial Period* VII 1.4.2), in order to deepen his own knowledge in the field of pagan

philosophy. In his theological thought Platonic influences can in fact be recognised. He undertook numerous voyages, in the course of which he preached at Caesarea and Jerusalem, although he was a layman, for which reason he was harshly reprimanded by his bishop and recalled to Alexandria. Around 230, during a stay at Caesarea in Palestine on another journey, he was ordained priest, again provoking the anger of the bishop of Alexandria, who banned him from his diocese and in 231 made him renounce his priesthood. Origen then definitively retired to Caesarea, where at the invitation of the local bishop he opened a school modelled on the programme of the one in Alexandria. During the harsh persecution of Decius (250–251) he was imprisoned and tortured. He died in 253.

Origen's literary output was immense. In the ancient world some thousands of works were attributed to him and the tradition represents his indefatigable activity as a writer by stating that he composed by simultaneously dictating to seven different stenographers. Certain ideas (for example that of the eternity of the world and of the total redemption or apocatastasis), and a theological terminology that was still imprecise and embryonic, caused his writings to be condemned as heretical in the following centuries, which led to the loss of a large part of them. Yet the importance of his work was enormous and it is easy to trace the enduring influence of his thought among Christian thinkers (if only because they opposed it). It should be noted that in very recent times (in 2012) a sensational discovery has led to the recovery of 29 unpublished homilies by Origen on the *Psalms*, only some of which were already known through a Latin translation. The new works cast an unforeseen light on Origen's homiletic texts and, through the comparison with the Latin translations, on the character of the latter.

Composed in the years between 246 and 248 is *Against Celsus* (*Contra Celsum*), an apologia that is sharply superior to the previous ones in its intellectual force. In it Origen refutes *The True Doctrine* of the pagan philosopher Celsus, which had been composed in 178 with an anti-Christian intent. Celsus' work is lost and we know it only through the extensive extracts quoted by Origen in his refutation.

The work that best allows us to grasp the originality of Origen's theological thought is the four-book *On Principles* (Περὶ ἀρχῶν, *De Principiis*), which has survived entire only in the Latin translation of Rufinus (who sometimes intervenes in the text to correct its less orthodox aspects). Origen begins by stating that, although some aspects of dogma are explicitly defined in *Scriptures*, others need to be derived from it by means of a speculative effort. One may attempt to summarise the content of the work by distinguishing in the four books treatments respectively on God, the created world, man and his characteristic of liberty, from which it comes to treat the Revelation. This is the first grand attempt to give a global theological-philosophical systematisation of the revealed truth, though the strong influence of Neoplatonic philosophy often leads Origen to depart from the testimony of *Scriptures*. Interpreting some biblical expressions in a Platonic sense, Origen came to envision a double level of the real: material reality is the image and symbol of a supernatural spiritual reality. This first attempt to make organic use of the tools of reason (and in particular of Platonic philosophy) in working out the content of the revelation is a fundamental step in the history of Christian thought. In 1941 the Egyptian desert at Tura (near Cairo) restored to us a papyrus codex containing the *Dialogue of Origen with Heraclides and his Companions the Bishops*, the report of a public theological discussion held in 245 in Arabia on the relations between Father and Son and on immortality. Among the paraenetic works we should record the text *On Prayer* (*De Oratione*).

The largest part of Origen's work (of which much has been lost, unfortunately) is formed by his exegetical work, which is conventionally divided into scholia (simple, brief notes of commentary), homilies (many of which are preserved in Latin translation) and true commentaries (which have often survived in fragmentary form within the so-called catenae, which consist of exegetical collections edited in the form of scholia to the biblical text). Origen works out complex allegorical exegeses of the *Old Testament*, but in reality he did not altogether refuse to acknowledge the literal and historical sense of these writings, and his own interpretation is in some cases typological, i.e. it aims to find in the *Old Testament* the prefiguration of events that then occurred with the coming of the Messiah. In the work *On Principles* Origen maintains, however, that three levels can be identified in *Scriptures*: one is yielded by the literal interpretation, which is therefore not derecognised but considered to be elementary; the second yields the moral interpretation, which teaches norms of behaviour; the third and most important is the spiritual level, in which we see in the narrated facts teachings concerning the spiritual sphere, the dimension of the divine. Also important was the philological work on the biblical text, which demonstrates Origen's attention to textual aspects of the *Bible*. An epochal contribution in this context was his *Hexapla*, a colossal work preserved only in brief parts: a "sixfold" edition (this is what the title means) of the *Old Testament*, which reports side by side in six columns the Hebrew text, its transliteration into Greek characters and four translations into Greek, i.e. the *Septuagint* and those of Aquila, Symmachus and Theodotion.

The works of Origen, unlike those of Clement, present little of interest in their stylistic elaboration or their compositional aspects. The argumentation is often disorderly, as is fair to expect with such a massive output, which, inspired by intentions not literary in character, must have left the author little time to add formal polish to his writings.

1.6.4 *Cohortatio ad gentiles*

In this section we should also briefly record the *Cohortatio ad Gentiles* (also referred to as *Cohortatio ad Graecos*), a violent anti-pagan invective that presents Platonic philosophy as a misunderstanding of Jewish wisdom. It is a text of uncertain date, but perhaps we may see in it polemical references against the way in which the first Alexandrians had exploited Neoplatonism.

2 Christian literature after Constantine

2.1 Christianity as the religion of the empire

With the edict issued by Constantine in 313 the Christian religion, which up to that point had been illegal, began to become the religion of state. This was completed definitively in 380 under Theodosius, who tried to use Christianity as a unifying element in the empire.

This recognition of Christianity led to a rapid growth in the number of faithful, with consequences of various kinds. The ecclesiastical community took on the appearance, in an ever more marked way, of small cells within a system that was institutionally organised and dependent on the central community of Rome. The perception of a problem of internal unity became more acute and the struggle against heresy took on systematic form, also via the official instrument of the ecumenical council, which was an occasion for collegial debate among the bishops and for the formulation of Christian dogmas. In parallel, the position of the Church in relation to the empire became more complex, since the Church took on a role of great social and political influence and the emperors began to rely on the ecclesiastical organisation to reinforce or restore the unity of the empire itself.

On the other hand, the fourth century was also the era that saw the resurgence of profane literature, which was committed to faithfully following the models of the past, alongside the new face of Christian literature, which had now become the expression of an official religion. The competition between the two cultures reached a critical point and a pivotal moment: paganism attempted a final tenacious resistance (above all through the pagan restoration of the emperor Julian: cf. *The Roman Imperial Period* XI 5), but the Christians were no longer prepared to be outshone by the traditional culture, which they were beginning to replace.

In the exposition that follows, we cannot adopt a rigidly chronological criterion, but must take into account above all the geographical area to which the various authors belonged. The reason for this is that the different churches were situated in different political, social and cultural circumstances in the different areas, and Christianity spread in different ways and forms within these different realities. For example, the social circumstances of the members of the Christian communities varied notably, for historical reasons, from one place to another. This gave rise to a differentiation among the interests and problems addressed by authors, whose writings constantly reflect the concrete reality of their churches.

2.2 The Alexandrian area: the Arian controversy

2.2.1 Arianism

A phenomenon of special importance that arose and spread in this period is the Arian heresy. Arius, born in Libya in 256, was a priest of the church of Alexandria in Egypt. In his Christological theology he maintained that the Son did not participate in the substance of the Father and was not co-eternal with the Father, but was simply the principal among his creatures. Arius formulated his doctrine in opposition to Sabellianism, a heresy which, to the contrary, did not distinguish the divine persons, considering Jesus to be simply a manifestation of the Father.

After the excommunication of Arius (which occurred at Alexandria around 318), the heresy spread above all in the East and in 325 Constantine himself summoned a council at Nicaea to resolve the controversy, which was threatening the unity of the Church and, in some respects, also that of the empire. However, the condemnation of the Arian doctrine and the proclamation of the consubstantiality of the Son to the Father (the Son, according to the definition of the council, is ὁμοούσιος, "of the same substance" as the Father) did not end the question and the controversy continued to go back and forth. Other councils that followed, promoted by the emperor Constantius II and held at Rimini and Seleucia, adopted a version of the *Apostolic Creed* (i.e. the text containing the profession of faith and hence the fundamental truths of the Christian religion, commonly known as the *Credo* in Latin, from which the English word "creed" derives) in which the Son was not said to have the same substance as the Father (ὁμοούσιος), but to be of similar substance (ὁμοιούσιος). By this the Arian doctrine was in fact given some credit. The definitive defeat of Arianism occurred only much later and ensured the near-total disappearance of the literature of the Arian party.

2.2.2 Athanasius of Alexandria

The principal opponent of Arianism was Athanasius, he too belonging to the Alexandrian cultural climate. Born at Alexandria in 295, he was present at the Council of Nicaea of 325 in his capacity as a priest in the entourage of the bishop of Alexandria, whom he succeeded in 328. Between 335 and 366, a period in which the Arians succeeded in obtaining imperial support, he was exiled first within Egypt and then to Rome and Trier. He was able to return to Alexandria only in 373. He died a few years later.

From the period before the Arian controversy there survive two orations of a polemical and apologetic character, one *Against the Greeks* and one *On the Incarnation of the Word*. The first picks up the traditional polemic against pagan polytheism with arguments drawn for the most part from Greek philosophy, the second is concerned with the Incarnation, in polemic both against the pagans and against the

Jews. The style of these writings, the fruit of carefully polished workmanship, is often rather cold.

A very different tone, which reveals Athanasius' impassioned involvement in the controversy, is found in the works composed to refute Arius' heresy, among which we should recall first of all the three *Speeches Against the Arians* (a fourth speech is probably spurious). In a rather disordered exposition, the theories of the Arians and their interpretations of *Scriptures* are refuted. Of particular interest are the three apologetic works: *Against the Arians*, *To Constantius* and a third composed to defend himself from the accusation of having evaded the Arian persecution by fleeing. In these works Athanasius, embroiled in defamatory accusations prompted by his adversaries, exploits his youthful studies of rhetoric, achieving moments of great expressive effectiveness.

While forced away from the see of Alexandria, Athanasius was long in contact with the Egyptian monks, about whom he wrote numerous works. It is worth recalling in particular the work that is considered his greatest success from the literary point of view, the *History of the Arians Addressed to the Monks*, which has survived in mutilated form, in which he reconstructs the birth and spread of the Arian heresy; and the *Life of Antony*, a hermit who lived from the mid-third to the mid-fourth century and who is regarded as the founder of Egyptian monasticism. The *Life*, which we possess also in the form of reworkings and Latin translations, narrates in simple language, and indulging the miraculous element (the story of the temptations to which the Devil subjected the saint is famous), the life of this figure, whom Athanasius knew personally. The first part tells of the saint's youth and monastic vocation; the large central section reports a long speech with moral and anti-Arian content, addressed by Antony to other monks; other episodes follow from his life and miracles. There has been much discussion about which literary models were followed by Athanasius in this work, which can clearly be traced in general to the ancient biographical tradition. What is certain is that Athanasius accomplished a composition that is able to include elements that are fresh and popular, enlivening a text that was a notable success and was adopted by later hagiographers as a model for composing lives of the saints in both the Greek and the Latin worlds.

Quite important from a historical and dogmatic point of view are Athanasius' letters. Then there are works, complete or fragmentary, that are exegetical in character, including a short work that briefly explicates the *Apostolic Creed*. Also under the name of Athanasius, who was universally recognised as the champion of Nicene anti-Arian orthodoxy, there have survived numerous spurious works of various character, attributed to him due to his authority.

2.3 Eusebius of Caesarea

Born at Caesarea in Palestine between 263 and 265, Eusebius studied with a follower of Origen named Pamphilus, with whom he was perhaps imprisoned during the persecution of Diocletian (303–304). Together they collaborated in composing an *Apologia for Origen* first in five books, to which Eusebius added a sixth after the death of his teacher. Eusebius was bishop of Caesarea from 313 to 315 and participated in the Arian controversy, taking an intermediate stance between the opposing positions, which earned him excommunication in 324. He was rehabilitated after the Council of Nicaea, when he accepted the *Nicene Creed*, but he never fully matched his position to that of Nicene orthodoxy. He was a personal friend of the emperor Constantine, to whom he was bound by a strong friendship, high esteem and admiration. Testimony to this is the enthusiastic speech he delivered on the occasion of the thirtieth anniversary of the emperor's reign and the encomiastic work in four books *On the Life of the Blessed Emperor Constantine*. Eusebius' attitude in these works seems clearly that of a courtier, but his unconditional admiration for Constantine can be understood in someone who had experienced the last great persecution pursued by Diocletian. He died before 340.

Some of Eusebius's works pick up the apologetic tradition. The contents are the usual topics in such writings, but they are clearly superior in their breadth and in the effort made towards exhaustivity and coherence in treating the individual themes. Leaving aside the works that have survived only in fragments, we may record the *Preparation for the Gospel*, in 15 books, which aims to demonstrate the superiority of Jewish wisdom over pagan knowledge, and the *Proof of the Gospel* in 20 books (the first ten and part of the fifteenth survive), which responds to accusations from the Jews by demonstrating the purely temporary value of the Mosaic law. Dating to a later period are two polemical works on the trinitarian question: the two books *Against Marcellus* and the three *On Ecclesiastical Theology*, the only works by Eusebius on theological controversy.

From his vast exegetical output there remain fragments of commentary on *Isaiah*, the *Psalms* and the *Gospel of Luke*. But more than an exegete or commentator, Eusebius was a learned scholar of the sacred texts. This is attested for example by a work of biblical geography of great thoroughness, from which the *Onomasticon* has survived, or by the *Canones evangelici*, a complex concordance of the *Gospels*. We should also recall the *Evangelical Questions* and *Evangelical Solutions*, which have survived in the Latin translation of Jerome, in which individual problems of interpretation are addressed.

Eusebius is best known for his *Ecclesiastical History*, which in its definitive version consists of 10 books and tells the story of the Church from its origins to 324, the year in which the empire was reunified under Constantine. We have already observed (cf. *The Roman Imperial Period* III 2.2) how a great trove of official documents and erudite materials weighs down the reading of this work, but on the other hand constitutes a precious source about people and events in Church and empire in the first three centuries. With the *Ecclesiastical History* Eusebius inaugurated a new genre, namely ecclesiastical historiography, indicating that it was a necessity of the times that the Church be given a historical narration from its particular point of view. Between the fourth and sixth century the history found a fair number of imitators and continuators: Philostorgius, Socrates, Sozomen, Theodoret and Evagrius Scholasticus (cf. *The Roman Imperial Period* III 2.5).

Also of great historiographical importance are the two works, mentioned above, that centre on the figure of Constantine: the speech celebrating the thirtieth anniversary of the emperor's reign and the four books *On the Life of the Blessed Emperor Constantine*. Both of them have survived in a version partially reworked at a later date, with an often rather pompous tone. The *Life* is accompanied by a *Speech to the Assembly of the Saints* attributed to Constantine himself, in which the emperor defends the Christian faith against pagan belief, attributing to Christ the merit for achieving the emperor's own military successes. However, the *Speech*, if it is not a total invention, has certainly been reworked thoroughly by Eusebius. Although in the past doubts have been raised about the authenticity of the *Life*, the dominant view now attributes it to Eusebius.

Among the historical works we may cite, finally, the *Chronicle*, of which significant remnants in indirect testimonies survive, versions that are in their turn based on a non-original version expanded with additions and reworked. This is a pared-down chronicle beginning from the birth of Abraham (placed in 2016 B.C.), accompanied by chronological tables.

2.4 Authors from the Syrian-Palestinian area

2.4.1 Cyril of Jerusalem

Cyril was bishop of Jerusalem from 348 until his death in 387. We know that, before the death of the emperor Valens (378), who had pro-Arian tendencies, Cyril was removed from his see three times because of his hostility to the Arians. Nonetheless, the events of his life are in part obscure. It seems, in fact, that he had initially become bishop with the support of the Arians. He belonged to the homoeousian theological current, which was very successful in the Palestinian area. They were opposed to Arianism, but nor did they accept consubstantiality, i.e. the attribution of the same substance to the Father and the Son, as affirmed in the *Nicene Creed*, and instead maintained that Father and Son are of similar substance.

From Cyril we have 24 sermons, known by the collective title *Catechesis*, since they were addressed to catechumens as instruction preceding baptism, and to the newly baptised. These writings are a stenographic report of the address delivered by Cyril and therefore they exhibit a modest level of formal sophistication. Often the direct and colloquial tone of the text is quite engaging.

2.4.2 Epiphanius

Epiphanius was born around 315 near Eleutheropolis in Palestine, south of Jerusalem. He spent a period in Egypt as a monk until, returning to his homeland, he founded a monastery. In 367 he became bishop of Constantia (the ancient Salamis). He died in 403.

Epiphanius was a stern opponent of the application of classical speculative methods to Christian thought and hence to theological reflection, opposing a tendency that had had one of its boldest supporters in Origen (a pioneer of Christian theology whose enthusiasm and boldness had moved him to hardly acceptable extremes and to real misrepresentations of the apostolic message). Further, the culture diffused in the area of Syria and Palestine was traditionally resistant to spiritualism of Platonic-Origenian stamp. This does not alter the fact that Epiphanius' refusal was anachronistic: the spread of Christianity in a world that until then had been imbued with pagan culture made it impossible to limit oneself by rejecting or ignoring the traditional culture in blind opposition.

He was also firm in rejecting allegorical exegesis, although in the short work *On the Twelve Gems* (*De gemmis*) he attributed a symbolic value to the ornaments on the priest's pectoral described in *Scriptures*. In *Ancoratus* (the title is a metaphorical reference to the safe anchorage of the true faith), Epiphanius presents a synthesis of Christian doctrine based exclusively on the *Scriptures* and on tradition. The polemical attacks present in *Ancoratus* are amplified in the *Panarion* ("medicine chest"), an immense work in which 80 Christian heresies and pagan philosophical schools are refuted. Attention to *Scriptures* is attested also in the treatise *On Biblical Weights and Measures* (*De mensuris et ponderibus*), an encyclopaedia that collects antiquarian notices of various kinds, which has survived whole in Syriac and in part in the original Greek. The style of Epiphanius is in general rather plodding and the structure of his works is not very linear and is full of repetitions.

2.4.3 Apollinaris of Laodicea

Also deserving mention is Apollinaris, who lived between 310 and the end of the fourth century. He was a friend of Athanasius and bishop of the community of Laodicea in Syria, and was faithful to the *Nicene Creed*. In 381 he was condemned for his Christological conception (he maintained that in Christ both a body and a sensible soul can be recognised, while the rational soul, the *nous*, is substituted by the divine *Logos*). For this reason his vast literary output suffered condemnation by the Church and has in large part been lost.

Apollinaris' importance in the history of Christian literature lies above all in the attempt, in collaboration with his father, to react to the decree by which the emperor Julian prohibited Christian teachers from commenting on pagan authors by preparing a series of writings of Christian content but formally inserted into the classical literary tradition. For example he paraphrased the *Pentateuch* into hexameters and the historical books of the *Bible* into tragic or epic verse and rewrote the *New Testament* in the form of Platonic dialogues. All that survives of this experiment is a *Paraphrase of the Psalms* in hexameters on the Homeric model, although serious doubts remain about its authorship. It exhibits good technical skills but little literary value. The significance of his experience lies in how he accorded to pagan literature the role of irreplaceable formal model.

2.5 The Cappadocian Fathers

2.5.1 Saints at the frontier

Among the most important Christian authors of this period, three were born and pursued their careers simultaneously in a region of Asia Minor that had in recent times been converted to the new religion, and hence was lacking in a cultural and religious tradition that could rival places like Alexandria of Egypt, namely Cappadocia.

Two of them, Basil, bishop of Caesarea in Cappadocia, and Gregory, bishop of Nyssa, were brothers. Their family, in good economic circumstances, had deep Christian roots. Their mother was the daughter of a martyr; their paternal grandmother Macrina had been a student of Gregory the Thaumaturge, the evangeliser of Cappadocia, and during a persecution, since she would not recant, she had been deprived of all her goods and forced to flee. Of the nine or ten children born from the union of these two families, maternal and paternal, four were declared saints by the Church: as well as Basil and Gregory, also Peter, bishop of Sebaste, and the nun Macrina, who bore her grandmother's name.

2.5.2 Basil of Caesarea

Born around 330 at Caesarea in Cappadocia, Basil studied at Constantinople and Athens, as was the tradition for young men of good family, and at Athens he met another young student: Gregory of Nazianzus, the third of the Cappadocian Fathers, with whom he was linked by an intimate friendship. He returned to his homeland in 326 and devoted himself to rhetorical activity, like his father, a famed rhetor. However, he was unsatisfied and, after a journey to various countries to meet teachers of the ascetic life, he retired to a hermitage near Neocaesarea in Pontus, where he was joined by his friend from his studies, Gregory. However, he was subsequently recalled to Caesarea by the bishop Eusebius, so that he could assist him. In 364 he was ordained priest and in 370 he took up the office of bishop. In this new role, Basil was both an ascetic and a man of action, to the point that, on account of his stature as a pastor, he gained the byname "the Great." A capable organiser, he set up an imposing complex at the gates of Caesarea of works of assistance to the poor, sick, elderly and pilgrims. He sternly defended the *Nicene Creed* against the Arians supported by the emperor Valens and was able to operate with diplomacy and decision in the complex internal politics of the Church. He died on January 1, 379.

Despite the onerous duties connected to his role as bishop, Basil's literary output was quite enormous. We may note here at least works such as the *Moralia*, a collection of texts that aim to constitute a guide to monastic life and containing, among other things, after two exhortations of a general character, 80 norms of Christian life inspired by the biblical texts, composed during Basil's monastic period at Neocaesarea, and, from a later period, 55 *Long Rules* and 313 *Short Rules* (in the form of a manual of questions and answers). The monastic model advanced by Basil is cenobitic (i.e. organised communities consisting of a number of monks), as opposed to the total isolation of the anchorites.

Together with Gregory of Nazianzus, in his monastic period Basil composed an anthology of Origen's writings, the *Philocalia*, which has made possible the preservation of texts that would otherwise in all likelihood have been lost, given the condemnation of Origen's doctrines (see above). Among the dogmatic writings we may record: *Against Eunomius*, a work of anti-Arian polemic; the treatise *On the Holy Spirit*, on the definition of the third person of the Trinity, a problem that was open and particularly thorny in the fourth century; and the treatise *On Baptism*, of contested authorship.

His exegetical work consists in practice only of his homiletic activity. Among the very many sermons, some of which are not authentic, we should note the *Homilies on the Hexameron* (i.e. on the account of the six days of the Creation), in an elevated tone, in which the bishop demonstrates his vast erudition also in the field of profane sciences and his love of culture. In a different tone are the *Homilies on the Psalms*, which contain simple exhortations of a moral character. Among the themes of these homilies we should note his particular insistence on moral themes linked to social necessities, such as assistance to the needy, the use of riches or the immorality of usury. In these exhortations Basil is in many cases indebted to the tradition of Cynic-Stoic diatribe, but they correspond to precise responsibilities that the bishop took up in his own person, as we have seen.

His beautiful correspondence consists of over 300 letters of various content, which are interesting both as a historical document and witness to the figure of Basil, and also from the stylistic point of view.

Finally we may record a short treatise of special interest for cultural and literary history and which gained later fame: the *Address to Young Men on How They Might Derive Benefit from Greek Literature*. Addressing the children of his sister, Basil addresses the thorny problem of the relations of Christians to pagan literature, which in this period still remained a formal model and basis of culture. The bishop maintains that in reality the literature of the Christian world, and *Scriptures* in particular, is clearly superior to the literature of the pagans, but at the same time that traditional literature should not be entirely ruled out for the Christian reader: there too, in both prose and poetry, one can find content inspired by high moral values, messages that ought to be appreciated even in a pagan text. Obviously we are a long way from attributing an autonomous value to pagan literature and thought and Basil's invitation is for a restricted and utilitarian use of the classical texts. Nonetheless, this affirmation of the paedagogic and propaedeutic value of pagan literature is important. Basil's position is quite open and balanced for this period, even though it is necessary to specify that in this work he is not addressing the theme of the relation to pagan literature in general, but speaking of it from the point of view of the education of the young.

Basil is certainly, in the common judgement of both ancients and moderns, one of the best of the Christian authors. A man of vast culture and a lover of knowledge, he is inspired by the language of pure Atticism, and his profound rhetorical training guides his style with a sure hand. However, this was a man of action whose literary output is always inspired by practical motives and by sincere passion, without slipping into dryness or the affectation of some professional rhetors.

2.5.3 Gregory of Nazianzus

The character of Gregory of Nazianzus is very different from that of his friend Basil. As is attested by the complex events of his life, he was not drawn to organisation or action: a sensitive and passionate man, quick to enthusiasm and disappointment, he did not have the temperament to devote himself to the government of a diocese or to cope with complex ecclesiastical politics.

A son of Christian parents (his father had converted to Christianity after a period belonging to a Jewish-pagan sect), he was born at Arianzus, a suburb of Nazianzus, around 329–330. He received a thorough education, going to study at Alexandria and Athens, among other places; at Athens he met Basil, whom he had already known at Caesarea in Cappadocia. Enthusiastic about rhetorical and philosophical studies, Gregory stayed at Athens longer than his friend, but then joined him in the monastic community that he had founded near Neocaesarea. In 361–362 his father, who had become bishop of Nazianzus, wanted him at his side as a priest, but Gregory accepted this unwillingly and even ran away in order to return to his hermitage. From that moment his life was an alternation of pastoral duties and flights to the monastic life, which was more congenial to him. In 371 Basil named him bishop of Sasima, in order to confirm his own authority as metropolitan over the entire territory of Cappadocia against his pro-Arian opponents. But Gregory soon regretted his acquiescence to his friend's wishes and never went to his diocese. In 374, when his father was dead, he became bishop of Nazianzus, but after a short time he fled, again retiring to the monastic life, at Seleucia.

In 379 he accepted the task of leading the small community of Nicene believers at Constantinople, a city where the community of Arian believers was at that time by far the majority and still had control over all the places of worship in the city. This time Gregory showed himself to be equal to his tough task and, thanks to his constant effort, the small Nicene community revived. An element of this success was due to the fame that was quickly won by Gregory's eloquence. The five orations delivered in this period (called *Theologica* or *On the Incarnation of the Word*) are perhaps his most outstanding works. In 380 the emperor Theodosius entered Constantinople in triumph, reversing the situation in favour of the Nicene community and the following year a council, summoned to resolve the Christological controversy definitively, solemnly installed Gregory as bishop of Constantinople and chose him as presider. Once again, however, having found himself at the centre of opposing interests and complex conflicts, he showed little diplomatic ability. In brief, the situation deteriorated, the council opposed him and he dismissed himself from his role. He retired first to Nazianzus and then definitively to Arianzus, where he died in 390.

A man of deep culture and sophisticated rhetorical education, actively committed to the ideals of the Second Sophistic, Gregory is not only an excellent writer, able to exploit the possibilities of rhetoric excellently without falling into empty repetition of literary models. He was also a particularly significant figure for his way of exploiting the resources of traditional culture in the Christian sphere. With a sure hand he utilised elements of philosophical and literary culture that were very often regarded with suspicion by Christian authors, even though in his works he did not address the theme of the relation between pagan civilisation and Christianity in a systematic or in-depth way.

Preserved from Gregory's vast oratorical output (in which the exegetical element is rarely present) are 45 *Speeches* or *Orations*, including the five *Theological Orations* already mentioned, which earned him the byname of "Theologian" (the "Second Theologian," with reference to the evangelist John, the "First Theologian"). In reality the theological thought expressed in these orations does not present particularly original traits. He is indebted to previous thought and also to Stoic philosophical speculation. Clearly superior, on the other hand, is the order, precision and coherence with which these themes are treated, revealing great compositional artistry. Among the other orations, on various topics, we may note the apologia for his own flight from Nazianzus in 361 and the speech with which he took his leave from the community of Constantinople, in which his highly sophisticated oratorical artistry excellently expresses this passionate figure's touching emotion. In his two *Invectives against Julian*, composed after the emperor's death, Gregory vented with unprecedented vehemence all his own resentment at the recent attempt at a pagan restoration. Among the funeral orations we note the one on the death of Basil. Another group of orations is formed by the panegyrics for religious festivals or in praise of the saints. His correspondence also has strongly literary intentions, with 245 letters on various topics organised by the author himself with a view to publication (letter 51 is a sort of short treatise on letter-writing).

Aside from works in prose, Gregory has left a poetic output that amounts to around 18,000 lines, for the most part composed in the period of retirement following his return from Constantinople. Despite some happy moments, his poetic work presents more coldness and artificiality than his prose. The metres used are very varied and traditional (dactylic hexameter, iambic trimeter, elegiac distich) and there are also unprecedented juxtapositions, trying out new strophic forms. In two poems of debated attribution Gregory even seems to be open to new metrical influences, no longer based on the traditional quantitative prosody. A collection of his epigrams forms Book VIII of the *Palatine Anthology*. The topics are as varied as the metres and range from strictly religious themes (prayer, biblical paraphrase, dogmatic and moral reflection) to historical and biographical ones. The most engaging lines are those that are autobiographical in character, inspired by personal circumstances, in which he addresses with a more sincere poetic sensibility the themes of friendship and, unusually for a Christian author, the inexorable passage of time.

In the past also attributed to Gregory is the *Christus patiens*, a cento in the form of a "tragedy" in which Euripidean hemistichs are adapted to represent the passion of Christ (and which is important also as a witness to lines of Euripides that are lost or corrupt). Today this tends to be considered a later work.

2.5.4 Gregory of Nyssa

The younger brother of Basil, born around 335, Gregory of Nyssa reveals a very different nature from that of the bishop of Caesarea. As we have said, Basil was a man of action and his spirit in this respect is reflected in his literary work. Gregory, to the contrary, was essentially a profound thinker.

He studied at Caesarea and, it seems, did not complete his training through travel like the other Cappadocians. It can be seen that he was equally well instructed in rhetorical material and above all in philosophy. His good knowledge of Plato, Aristotle, the Stoics and Neoplatonics not only provided him with sound methodological and speculative foundations, but is also at the basis of his deep and original theological reflection. At first he did not follow the ascetic example of his brother: he married and became a teacher of rhetoric, but after a certain period he too followed Basil and Gregory of Nazianzus. In 371 Basil appointed him bishop of Nyssa, just as he had appointed Gregory of Nazianzus to Sasima, to ensure that there were friendly bishops in strategic sees during the Arian controversy. Like Gregory of Nazianzus, however, Gregory of Nyssa, too, revealed that he had little inclination for the task and Basil himself chastises him in two letters for his lack of political sense and his naivety: in the course of a few years he was accused of embezzlement on a pretext and condemned to exile by a synod of Arian bishops. He returned to his see in 378, after the death of the pro-Arian emperor Valens, and from that point onward his prestige grew notably and his career was more successful. He was highly regarded by the emperor Theodosius, who conferred various official duties on him. After the death of Basil, he took over his position as defender of the Nicene faith. He participated in important councils, including the Council of Constantinople in 381, in which the *Nicene Creed* was confirmed. In 380 he was elevated as bishop of Sebaste, but remained there for only a few months before returning to Nyssa. He died after 394.

Gregory's literary output is copious and varied, and its speculative depth is adorned by a style that is skilful and full of brilliant rhetorical devices, testimony to a deep knowledge of the classics. Here we must limit ourselves to mentioning the principal works.

His first work is the treatise *On Virginity* (370–371), with a complex structure, written at the invitation of his brother at a time when Basil was opposing the ascetic model of Eustathius of Sebaste, whom he accused of excessive rigour. Dating to 379 are the dialogues *On the Soul and on the Resurrection*, in which he interweaves the model of Plato's *Phaedo* and the emotional recollection of his sister Macrina (whose *Life* he also wrote). The dialogue between Gregory himself and his sister at the point of her death treats the soul and its destiny of purification and rejoining God after death.

Dating to around 385 is the *Catechetical Discourse*, an attempt at global systematisation of dogma (on the model of Origen's *Principles*), intended to provide assistance to anyone engaged in catechesis. The manner of proceeding is Platonic in approach: he attempts to provide effective arguments by beginning from commonly accepted concepts, then working back from them to the truths of faith. Its orderly manner of proceeding, and the mastery and coherence with which dogma is addressed, set the *Catechetical Discourse* among Gregory's most successful works.

To be placed in the period between 380 and 383 are four treatises that have been transmitted under the title *Against Eunomius*, which use subtle analysis to continue the polemic already undertaken by Basil: the texts of the opponent are analysed and refuted in their tiniest details, down to every single expression. A similar manner of proceeding is found in the *Antirrheticus*, in which he replies to a work by Apollinaris.

In the sphere of biblical exegesis we should note the treatise *On the Making of Man* and the *Apology on the Hexameron*, both linked to Basil's work. The former proposes to complete the work of Basil and the latter is a defence of the *Hexameron*, although it corrects some of its theses. There is a clear influence of allegorical exegesis in the spirit of Origen, aiming to give an interpretation of the biblical text that is in harmony with the information provided by reason and "scientific knowledge." Dating to the final years of Gregory's life is a quite original work, which can in part be assigned to the genre of exegesis: *The Life of Moses*. The Hebrew lawgiver is presented as a spiritual model and his life story is read as an image of the path of the soul towards perfection. First the events of the life of Moses are presented by paraphrasing the account in *Exodus*; this lays the foundations for the spiritual interpretation, which is developed in the second part.

2.6 The school of Antioch

2.6.1 Historical and literal biblical exegesis

The Alexandrian tradition, championing an exegesis of spiritual type and the use of allegory, stood opposed to the historical and literal interpretation of the sacred text, which aimed rather to discover moral teachings and was preferred by scholars in another cultural centre of the first importance, Antioch in Syria. The city was also the seat of the famous rhetorical school of Libanius (cf. *The Roman Imperial Period* XI 4) and in it a Greek foundation was joined with different cultures (both Greek and Syriac were commonly spoken there).

A large part of the rich literary output linked to the Antiochene school has been lost. Of authors such as Diodorus of Tarsus and Theodore of Mopsuestia only a small number of texts have survived. We limit ourselves here to a brief mention of what remains of Theodore's commentary on the *Psalms*, a significant example of some aspects of Antiochene exegesis. Every expression is commented upon, always taking careful account of the context, even when this means denying the interpretation of many expressions as messianic prophecies, in favour of a reading that better matches the historicity and the letter of the text.

Beyond the loss of much of this literature, it should be said that the influence of Antiochene thought can be seen in the exegetic practice of figures working in other geographical areas, such as Cyril of Jerusalem and Epiphanius of Salamis.

2.6.2 John Chrysostom

Much has been preserved of the later figure of John, called Chrysostom ("golden mouth") for his extraordinary eloquence. Born at Antioch to a wealthy family in 345, he received a careful education and was, among other things, a pupil of Libanius. Health problems obliged him to renounce the ascetic life, which he had undertaken at first with other hermits, then in total solitude. In 386 he became a priest and his bishop gave him the duty of preaching. His eloquence soon achieved great fame, to the point that, it was said, even Jews and pagans came in great numbers to hear him. Dating to this period are 21 speeches *On Statues* (*De statuis*), delivered during Lent of 387, while the populace was living in an atmosphere of terror after the statues of the imperial family were knocked down during a revolt against taxes and Theodosius' revenge was feared.

In 397, thanks to his great prestige as a preacher, Chrysostom was elevated to the position of bishop of Constantinople at the wish of the emperor Arcadius, despite the opposition of the see of Alexandria, the traditional adversary of Antioch. Chrysostom's personality was not suited to life in the atmosphere of Constantinople, where a large role was played by the corrupt entourage at court. The bishop's moral uprightness, his commitment to denouncing the gulf between the rich and the mass of the poor and his outspokenness in combatting the vices of the court earned him the deep affection of the people, but it soon made him hated by powerful figures. First he drew the anger of the powerful minister Eutropius, and in 403 he felt the hostility of the empress Eudoxia herself, whom Chrysostom had rebuked for greed. With her help the Alexandrian bishop Theophilus, who was hostile to the Antiochene Chrysostom, had him deposed by the Synod of the Oak, held at Chalcedon. The people rebelled against this decision and John was restored to his see, but after a few months he was again deposed at the initiative of the empress. He did not submit to this prohibition and at Easter 404 soldiers broke into the church during the ceremony of baptism. The disturbances that followed led the empress to send him into exile at Cucusus, a remote town in Cilicia.

John nonetheless continued to take an interest in events at Constantinople and was in contact with many people who had remained loyal to him. His opponents were once again preoccupied with his popularity and in 407 they succeeded in achieving his transfer to Pityus, a desert region on the eastern shore of the Black Sea. He died at Comana, in Pontus, during the journey transferring him. Not until 438 was his body solemnly brought to Constantinople.

Chrysostom's extremely copious output consists almost entirely of homilies and sermons, over 500 of which have been transmitted under his name. Some of these orations have been preserved for us by the work of stenographers present when they were delivered at liturgical occasions. Many are exegetical homilies on the *New* and *Old Testament* (250 concern the letters of Paul), in which Chrysostom presents an exegesis on the Antiochene pattern, based on the literal meaning, but in which he does not hesitate to accept the typological value of *Scriptures* if the text offers an opportunity for it without excessive strain. Other sermons are dedicated to liturgical feasts and many had a catechetical role (i.e. in preparation for those about to be baptised). There are also sermons of a polemical character, panegyrics to saints and figures from the *Old Testament* and speeches of moral content. Among the most beautiful sermons we may record those in which the echo of current events can be heard: the speeches *On the Statues* and the two addressed to the minister Eutropius. In many texts the lack of a phase of polishing after delivery can be felt, but the bishop's ability to improvise, along with his vehemence and enthusiasm as a preacher, make these among his most engaging and effective works. Particularly significant in this respect is the speech on the transience of human goods, which was improvised when the powerful imperial minister Eutropius, who had always opposed Chrysostom, had fallen into disgrace and sought refuge in the church during a service in order to escape arrest. The theological themes are often treated in a way that is not very organic, but this is due to the character of the author, who was not a theorist of dogma, but a pastor attentive to the needs of his flock.

The non-homiletic texts belong above all to the period prior to taking office at Constantinople. We may note above all the dialogue *On Priesthood* (*De sacerdotio*) in six books, the most polished of his works and considered by many also to be the most successful, in which he praises the priestly vocation and debates with a friend whom he had encouraged to accept the episcopate although he himself had then run away to avoid it. He also wrote a book *On Virginity*, one *On Vainglory and on the Education of Children*, letters and treatises on the monastic life. Some consider spurious two works with a different interest, a *Panegyric of St Babylas*, in which the author opposes the emperor Julian the Apostate, and a work *Against the Jews and Gentiles on the Divinity of Christ*. Finally, we should recall his correspondence, which almost all dates to the period of his exile.

Traditionally Chrysostom is remembered with the byname of the "Christian Demosthenes." Labels of this kind do not mean a lot, of course, but it is true that, in the manner of the famous Athenian orator, he matched his refined rhetorical training with a sincere commitment and a vehemence that made his words particularly effective.

2.6.3 Theodoret of Cyrrhus and the Christological controversy

We will end this section by briefly recording the figure of Theodoret, born at Antioch in 393 and bishop of the small city of Cyrrhus (in Asia Minor). He was the last great theorist of the school of Antioch and played a role of primary importance in the Nestorian controversy.

Theodoret was involved in complex Christological controversies, which set in opposition the church of Antioch and that of Alexandria. Nestorius, a bishop of Constantinople of the Antiochene school, while accentuating the humanity of the figure of Christ had, among other things, denied that Mary could be called the Mother of God, which provoked a violent reaction from Bishop Cyril of Alexandria (cf. next section). Theodoret opposed Cyril's theses, refusing to subscribe to the condemnation of Nestorius. To the contrary, he condemned the monophysite theses of Eutyches, who saw in Christ a single divine nature and not two natures, divine and human, united but distinct. The position adopted by Theodoret within the Christological controversies earned him dismissal from his position. He returned to his career only after he was ready to openly condemn the position of Nestorius, though with some specifications that preserved the fundamental essence of Antiochene Christology.

Theodoret was a man of immense culture and enormously wide interests. His multifaceted work, which can be appreciated also for the clarity with which he addressed topics, has in large part been lost, the result also of a posthumous condemnation inflicted on him in 553 (he had died around 466). Despite this, the surviving texts are quite numerous. We have already mentioned the *Ecclesiastical History* (cf. above 2.3.2), which aimed to continue the history of Eusebius of Caesarea and drew on those of Socrates and Sozomen, covering the period from 323 to 428. We note here the value that the *History* assumes also as a source for the Antiochene point of view on the Arian controversy (though the Nestorian controversy remains excluded).

Among the works of theological polemic, his refutation of the *Twelve Anathemas* of Cyril of Alexandria, which we will discuss shortly, has reached us thanks to the extracts that Cyril makes from it in his response. We may then also recall the *Eranistes*, in which he combats the monophysite doctrine that was spread at Constantinople by Eutyches. As well as its strictly theological value, the work deserves attention for the presence of hundreds of passages from earlier authors, which are cited as authorities to confirm the theses presented, forming a useful testimony to the authoritative status achieved by the writings of the Church Fathers, as well as an example of a new way of arguing, which is found in part also in the writings of his adversary Cyril. His exegetical work is vast: we have continuous commentaries on the *Psalms*, the *Song of Songs*, the books of the prophets and the letters of Paul, and also some exegetical works structured as questions and answers. Theodoret's exegesis is clearly inspired by Antiochene principles, i.e. with particular interest in the literal interpretation of the text, but does not entirely rule out the approach of typological interpretation, though without indulging in strained readings. The orderly structure of a manual of questions and answers may be the inspiration for the form of an apologetic work by Theodoret: twelve speeches collected under the title *Cure of the Sicknesses of the Greeks* (*Graecarum Affectionum Curatio*) or *Demonstration of the Truth of the Gospels by Means of Greek Philosophy*. The work sets out to provide members of the faithful who are less well instructed in the faith with answers to questions and objections that might be made to them by pagans. It is therefore subdivided in a systematic way, by individual questions.

2.7 Africa: the end of the Alexandrian school

2.7.1 Cyril of Alexandria

Born around 370 and a nephew of Bishop Theophilus of Alexandria (the opponent of Chrysostom), Cyril succeeded him in 412, after having briefly been a monk. During his episcopate he found himself in continuous struggles involving dogmatic polemic. During the Nestorian controversy he at first succeeded in having his opponent condemned, then he was condemned in his turn and imprisoned, until, after the exiling of Nestorius, he reached a final accord with the Nestorians. This was not the only controversy in which he was involved: he always dealt with the incessant struggles with extreme decisiveness and harshness against heretics and personal enemies, demonstrating a hard and at times aggressive nature.

As regards his imposing literary activity, which is in large part lost, Cyril was not a skilful writer at all. The violence of his invective sometimes enlivens his style, though it is in most cases clumsy and barely effective.

A large part of his output is linked to doctrinal polemics. The *Book of Treasures Concerning the Holy and Consubstantial Trinity*, the seven dialogues *Concerning the Holy and Consubstantial Trinity* and a brief explanation of the *Nicene Creed* are connected to the controversy over the Arians. Numerous works are opposed to the Nestorians: the *Refutation of the Blasphemies of Nestorius*, the treatise *Against those who will not confess the divine maternity of the Holy Virgin* and the dialogue *That Christ is One*. Addressed to the emperor Theodosius II and members of the imperial family are the *Addresses Concerning the True Faith*, an *Apologetic Discourse* and an explanation of the *Twelve Anathemas* (ἀνάθεμα meaning "curse, excommunication") issued by Cyril against Nestorius. With the work *Against the Synousiasts* he combatted the Apollinarist heresy (from Apollinaris of Laodicea, cf. above 2.4.3) and in the *Letter to the Monks of Phua* he launches polemics against Origenism. He also wrote a long apologia, of which 10 books survive.

As regards Cyril's exegetical work, we should mention the dialogue in 17 books *On Adoration and Cult in Spirit and Truth* and the *Glaphyra* in 12 books (the title alludes metaphorically to the "chiselled, well polished" character of the interpretations), in which Cyril employs historical and typological exegesis to demonstrate that the *Old Testament* is a preparation and prefiguration of the *New*. His commentaries work along the same lines: for example, in the commentary on *Isaiah* and the twelve minor prophets, the author aims to seek both the literal and the spiritual meaning of the text. We may recall finally the 29 encyclical *Festive Letters*, by which the bishop communicated the date of Easter, which are devoted to moral exhortation.

Cyril is the last exponent of the prestigious Alexandrian tradition in the Greek language. A few years after his death, the church of Alexandria set off on a new path, which led it to detach itself from the catholic church and to profess monophysitism, the theology of Eutyches that saw in Christ only a divine nature and not a human one, and in parallel it adopted Coptic as its official language. The role of the final heir to Alexandrian culture seems a little paradoxical for a figure such as Cyril: lacking philosophical education, he saw philosophy as the cause of Origen's aberrations in thought, and in general he regarded the influence of philosophy as negative and the cause of heresies.

2.7.2 Synesius of Cyrene

We have already spoken of the Cyrenaican Synesius (370–413) in the chapter on rhetoric in Late Antiquity (cf. *The Roman Imperial Period* XI 7), to which we refer for notices on his life and works. Here we return to emphasise only the syncretistic character of his cultural profile, which achieved an original synthesis of Neoplatonic and Christian thought. He was educated at Alexandria at the school of Hypatia (cf. *The Roman Imperial Period* VII 1.4.7) and had lived in the heated climate of Christological polemics that inflamed the Christian community of that city. A particularly emblematic meaning is borne also by his election as bishop of Ptolemais, which took place through wild popular demand, despite the fact that he was still a pagan and did not want to renounce his own particular philosophical conceptions (for example the idea of the pre-existence of souls and the eternity of the world), which were hardly to be reconciled to traditional orthodoxy. The episode is an eloquent sign of the political role that had already been assumed by the office of bishop: Synesius, a son of the traditional aristocracy, was seen as the defender of his city, rather than its spiritual guide.

Bibliography of Translations (by Elena Squeri)

Aeschines

Carey, Christopher (ed.), *Aeschines*, The Oratory of Classical Greece 3, Austin, TX: University of
    Texas Press, 2000.

Aeschylus

Sommerstein, Alan H. (ed.), *Aeschylus: Persians. Seven against Thebes. Suppliants. Prometheus
    Bound*, Loeb Classical Library 145, Cambridge, MA: Harvard University Press, 2009.
Sommerstein, Alan H. (ed.), *Aeschylus: Oresteia: Agamemnon. Libation-Bearers. Eumenides*, Loeb
    Classical Library 146, Cambridge, MA: Harvard University Press, 2009.
Testimonia: sepulchral epigram
Olson, Douglas S. (ed.), *Athenaeus: The Learned Banqueters: Books XIII.594b-XIV*, Loeb Classical
    Library 345, Cambridge, MA: Harvard University Press, 2011, pp. 172–173.

Aesop

Temple, Olivia & Temple, Robert (transl.), *Aesop: The Complete Fables*, Penguin Classics, London:
    Penguin Books, 1998.*

Alcaeus of Mytilene

Campbell, David A. (ed.), *Greek Lyric I: Sappho and Alcaeus*, Loeb Classical Library 142, Cambridge,
    MA: Harvard University Press, 1982.

Alcidamas

Muir, John V. (ed.), *Alcidamas: the Works & Fragments*, Greek Texts, London: Bristol Classical Press,
    2001.

Alcman of Sardis

Campbell, David A. (ed.), *Greek Lyric II: Anacreon. Anacreontea. Choral Lyric from Olympus to Alc-
    man*, Loeb Classical Library 143, Cambridge, MA: Harvard University Press, 1988.

Alcmaeon of Croton

Laks, André & Most, Glenn W. (eds.), *Early Greek Philosophy V: Western Greek Thinkers (Part 2)*,
    Loeb Classical Library 528, Cambridge, MA: Harvard University Press, 2016, pp. 740–741.

Anacreon of Teos

Campbell, David A. (ed.), *Greek Lyric II: Anacreon. Anacreontea. Choral Lyric from Olympus to Alc-
    man*, Loeb Classical Library 143, Cambridge, MA: Harvard University Press, 1988.*

The presence of an asterisk at the end of a bibliographic item indicates that the quotation to which
it refers has been slightly altered, in order to better suit the argumentation and the syntactic structure of the surrounding text.
All quotations for which there is no related bibliographic item were provided either by the author or
the translator of the text.

https://doi.org/10.1515/9783110426328-043

Anaxagoras of Clazomenae

Laks, André & Most, Glenn W. (eds.), *Early Greek Philosophy VI: Later Ionian and Athenian Thinkers (Part 1)*, Loeb Classical Library 529, Cambridge, MA: Harvard University Press, 2016.

Antiochus of Syracuse (fr. 2 Jacoby)

Luraghi, Nino, *Antiochos of Syracuse* (555), in Worthington, Ian (ed.), *Brill's New Jacoby* (Online), 2016.

Antiphanes (fr. 189 Kassel-Austin):

Olson, Douglas S. (ed.), *Athenaeus: The Learned Banqueters: Books VI-VII*, Loeb Classical Library 224, Cambridge, MA: Harvard University Press, 2008, pp. 2–5.*

Antisthenes

Prince, Susan (ed.), *Antisthenes of Athens: texts, translations, and commentary*, Ann Arbor, MI: University of Michigan Press, 2015.

Archilochus of Paros

Gerber, Douglas E. (ed.), *Greek Iambic Poetry: From the Seventh to the Fifth Centuries BC*, Loeb Classical Library 259, Cambridge, MA: Harvard University Press, 1999.

fragment on Telephus

West, Martin L., *Archilochus and Telephos*, ZPE 156 (2006), pp. 11–17.

Aristarchus of Samos

Thomas, Ivor (transl.), *Greek Mathematical Works II: Aristarchus to Pappus*, Loeb Classical Library 362, Cambridge, MA: Harvard University Press, 1941.

Aristophanes

Henderson, Jeffrey (ed.), *Aristophanes: Acharnians. Knights*, Loeb Classical Library 178, Cambridge, MA: Harvard University Press, 1998.

Henderson, Jeffrey (ed.), *Aristophanes: Clouds. Wasps. Peace*, Loeb Classical Library 488, Cambridge, MA: Harvard University Press, 1998.

Henderson, Jeffrey (ed.), *Aristophanes: Frogs. Assemblywomen. Wealth*, Loeb Classical Library 180, Cambridge, MA: Harvard University Press, 2002.

Aristotle

Halliwell, Stephen (transl.), *Aristotle: Poetic*, in Halliwell, Stephen & Fyfe, Hamilton W. & Innes, Doreen C. & Roberts, William, R. (transl.), *Aristotle: Poetic. Longinus: On the Sublime. Demetrius: On Style*, revised by Russell, Donald A., Loeb Classical Library 199, Cambridge, MA: Harvard University Press, 1995.

Freese, John H. (ed.), *Aristotle: Art of Rhetoric*, revised by Striker, Gisela, Loeb Classical Library 193, Cambridge, MA: Harvard University Press, 2020.

Bacchylides of Ceos

Campbell, David A. (ed.), *Greek Lyric IV: Bacchylides. Corinna and Others*, Loeb Classical Library 461, Cambridge, MA: Harvard University Press, 1992.

Callimachus

Mair, Alexander W. (transl.), *Callimachus: Hymns and Epigrams*, in Mair, Alexander W. & Mair, Gilbert R. (transl.), *Callimachus: Hymns and Epigrams. Lycophron: Alexandra. Aratus: Phaenomena*, Loeb Classical Library 129, Cambridge, MA, 1921.

Hollis, Adrian S. (ed.), *Callimachus: Hecale*, Oxford/New York: Oxford University Press, 2009.

Harder, Annette M. (ed.), *Callimachus: Aetia*, Oxford/New York: Oxford University Press, 2012.

Stephens, Susan A. (ed.), *Callimachus: The Hymns*, Oxford/New York: Oxford University Press, 2015.

Callinus of Ephesus

Gerber, Douglas E. (ed.), *Greek Elegiac Poetry: From the Seventh to the Fifth Centuries BC*, Loeb Classical Library 258, Cambridge, MA: Harvard University Press, 1999.

Chariton of Aphrodisias

Goold, George P. (ed.), *Chariton: Callirhoe*, Loeb Classical Library 481, Cambridge, MA: Harvard University Press, 1995.*

Choerilus of Samos

Fr. 1 Bernabé

Freese, John H. (ed.), *Aristotle. Art of Rhetoric*, revised by Striker, Gisela, Loeb Classical Library 193, Cambridge, MA: Harvard University Press, 2020, pp. 430–431.

Cicero

Kaster, Robert A. (transl.), *Cicero: Brutus and Orator*, New York: Oxford University Press, 2020.

Demosthenes

Waterfield, Robin & Carey, Chris (eds.), *Demosthenes: Selected speeches,* Oxford World's Classics, Oxford/New York: Oxford University Press, 2014.

Diogenes Laertius

Miller, James (ed.) & Mensch, Pamela (transl.), *Diogenes Laertius: Lives of the Eminent philosophers*, New York: Oxford University Press, 2018.

Dio of Prusa, said Chrysostom

Cohoon, James W. (ed.), *Dio Chrysostom: Discourses* 1–11, Loeb Classical Library 257, Cambridge, MA: Harvard University Press, 1932.

Cohoon, James W. (ed.), *Dio Chrysostom: Discourses* 12–30, Loeb Classical Library 339, Cambridge, MA: Harvard University Press, 1939.

Dionysus of Halicarnassus

Usher, Stephen (transl.), *Dionysius of Halicarnassus: Critical Essays I: Ancient Orators*, Loeb Classical Library 465, Cambridge, MA: Harvard University Press, 1974.

Usher, Stephen (transl.), *Dionysius of Halicarnassus. Critical Essays, II: On Literary Composition. Dinarchus. Letters to Ammaeus and Pompeius*, Loeb Classical Library 466, Cambridge, MA: Harvard University Press, 1985.

Empedocles of Acragas

Laks, André & Most, Glenn W. (eds.), *Early Greek Philosophy V: Western Greek Thinkers (Part 2)*, Loeb Classical Library 528, Cambridge, MA: Harvard University Press, 2016.

Euripides
Kovacs, David (ed.), *Euripides: Helen. Phoenician Women. Orestes*, Loeb Classical Library 11, Cambridge, MA: Harvard University Press, 2002.
Kovacs, David (ed.), *Euripides: Bacchae. Iphigenia at Aulis. Rhesus*, Loeb Classical Library 495, Cambridge, MA: Harvard University Press, 2003.

Eusebius of Caesarea
Gifford, Edwin H. (ed.), *Eusebius Caesariensis, Preparation for the Gospel*, Oxford: Clarendon Press, 1903, p. 497.*

Flavius Philostratus
Wright, Wilmer C. (transl.), *Philostratus: Lives of the Sophists. Eunapius: Lives of the Philosophers and Sophists*, Loeb Classical Library 134, Cambridge, MA: Harvard University Press, 1921.

Gorgias of Leontini
Laks, André & Most, Glenn W. (eds.), *Early Greek Philosophy VIII: Sophists (Part 1)*, Loeb Classical Library 531, Cambridge, MA: Harvard University Press, 2016.

Hecataeus of Miletus
Fr. 1a Jacoby
Innes, Doreen C. (transl.), *Demetrius: On Style* in Halliwell, Stephen & Fyfe, Hamilton W. & Innes, Doreen C. & Roberts, William, R. (transl.), *Aristotle: Poetic. Longinus: On the Sublime. Demetrius: On Style*, revised by Russell, Donald A., Loeb Classical Library 199, Cambridge, MA: Harvard University Press, 1995, p. 357.

Heraclitus of Ephesus
Laks, André & Most, Glenn W., *Early Greek Philosophy III: Early Ionian Thinkers (Part 2)*, Loeb Classical Library 526, Cambridge, MA: Harvard University Press, 2016.

Herodotus
De Sélincourt, Aubrey (transl.), *Herodotus: The Histories*, revised with Introduction and Notes by Marincola, John, Penguin Classics, London: Penguin Books, 2003.*

Hesiod
West, Martin L. (ed.), *Hesiod: Theogony and Works and Days*, Oxford World's Classics, Oxford: Oxford University Press, 1988.
Testimonia
Most, Glenn W. (ed.), *Hesiod. Theogony. Works and Days. Testimonia*, Loeb Classical Library 57, Cambridge, MA: Harvard University Press, 2018.*

Hippias of Elis
Laks, André & Most, Glenn W. (eds.), *Early Greek Philosophy VIII: Sophists (Part 1)*, Loeb Classical Library 531, Cambridge, MA: Harvard University Press, 2016.*

Hippocrates
Jones, William H.S. (transl.), *Hippocrates: Ancient Medicine. Airs, Waters, Places. Epidemics 1 and 3. The Oath. Precepts. Nutriment*, Loeb Classical Library 147, Cambridge, MA: Harvard University Press, 1923.

Jones, William H.S. (transl.), *Hippocrates: Prognostic. Regimen in Acute Diseases. The Sacred Disease. The Art. Breaths. Law. Decorum. Physician (Ch. 1). Dentition*, Loeb Classical Library 148, Cambridge, MA: Harvard University Press, 1923.

Jones, William H.S. (transl.), *Hippocrates: Nature of Man. Regimen in Health. Humours. Aphorisms. Regimen 1–3. Dreams; Heracleitus: On the Universe*, Loeb Classical Library 150, Cambridge, MA: Harvard University Press, 1931.

Smith, Wesley D. (ed.), *Hippocrates: Epidemics 2, 4–7*, Loeb Classical Library 477, Cambridge, MA: Harvard University Press, 1994.

Hipponax of Ephesus

Gerber, Douglas E. (ed.), *Greek Iambic Poetry: From the Seventh to the Fifth Centuries BC*, Loeb Classical Library 259, Cambridge, MA: Harvard University Press, 1999.*

Homer

Verity, Anthony (transl.), *Homer: The Iliad*, with an Introduction and Notes by Graziosi, Barbara, Oxford World's Classics, Oxford/New York: Oxford University Press, 2011.*

Verity, Anthony (transl.), *Homer: The Odyssey*, with an Introduction and Notes by Allan, William, Oxford World's Classics, Oxford/New York: Oxford University Press, 2016.

Horace

Russell, Donald A. & Winterbottom, Michael (eds.), *Ancient Literary Criticism. The Principal Texts in New Translations*, Oxford: Clarendon Press, 1972.

Ibycus of Rhegium

Campbell, David A. (ed.), *Greek Lyric III: Stesichorus. Ibycus. Simonides and Others*, Loeb Classical Library 476, Cambridge, MA: Harvard University Press, 1991.

Isocrates

Papillon, Terry L. (ed.), *Isocrates II*, The Oratory of Classical Greece 7, Austin, TX: University of Texas Press, 2004.

Lucian of Samosata

A True Story

Costa, Charles D.N. (ed.), *Lucian: Selected dialogues*, Oxford World's Classics, Oxford/New York: Oxford University Press, 2005.

The Double Indictment

Harmon, Austin M. (transl.), *Lucian: The Dead Come to Life or The Fisherman. The Double Indictment or Trials by Jury. On Sacrifices. The Ignorant Book Collector. The Dream or Lucian's Career. The Parasite. The Lover of Lies. The Judgement of the Goddesses. On Salaried Posts in Great Houses*, Loeb Classical Library 130, Cambridge, MA: Harvard University Press, 1921.

Lysias

Todd, Stephen C. (ed.), *Lysias*, The Oratory of Classical Greece 2, Austin, TX: University of Texas Press, 2000.

Meleager of Gadara

Paton, William R. (transl.), *The Greek Anthology II: Book 7: Sepulchral Epigrams. Book 8: The Epigrams of St. Gregory the Theologian*, Loeb Classical Library 68, Cambridge, MA: Harvard University Press, 1917.

Mimnermus of Colophon
Gerber, Douglas E. (ed.), *Greek Elegiac Poetry: From the Seventh to the Fifth Centuries BC*, Loeb
    Classical Library 258, Cambridge, MA: Harvard University Press, 1999.

Palladas of Alexandria
Paton, William R. (transl.), *The Greek Anthology IV: Book 10: The Hortatory and Admonitory Epi-*
    grams. Book 11: The Convivial and Satirical Epigrams. Book 12: Strato's Musa Puerilis, Loeb
    Classical Library 85, Cambridge, MA: Harvard University Press, 1918.

Parmenides of Elea
Laks, André & Most, Glenn W., *Early Greek Philosophy V: Western Greek Thinkers (Part 2)*, Loeb
    Classical Library 528, Cambridge, MA: Harvard University Press, 2016.

Paulus Silentiarius
Paton, William R. (transl.), *Greek Anthology I: Book 1: Christian Epigrams. Book 2: Description of the*
    Statues in the Gymnasium of Zeuxippus. Book 3: Epigrams in the Temple of Apollonis at Cyzi-
    cus. Book 4: Prefaces to the Various Anthologies. Book 5: Erotic Epigrams, Revised by Tueller,
    Michael A., Loeb Classical Library 67, Cambridge, MA: Harvard University Press, 2014.

Pausanias
Jones, William H.S. (transl.), *Pausanias. Description of Greece: Books I-II*, Loeb Classical Library 93,
    Cambridge, MA: Harvard University Press, 1918.
Jones, William H.S. (transl.), *Pausanias. Description of Greece: Books VIII.22-X*, Loeb Classical Li-
    brary 297, Cambridge, MA: Harvard University Press, 1935.

Phrynichus (comic poet)
Storey, Ian C. (ed.), *Fragments of Old Comedy III: Philonicus to Xenophon. Adespota*, Loeb Classical
    Library 515, Cambridge, MA: Harvard University Press, 2011.

Pindar of Cynoscephalae
Race, William H. (ed.), *Pindar: Olympian Odes. Pythian Odes*, Loeb Classical Library 56, Cambridge,
    MA: Harvard University Press, 1997.
Race, William H. (ed.), *Pindar: Nemean Odes. Isthmian Odes. Fragments*, Loeb Classical Library 485,
    Cambridge, MA: Harvard University Press, 1997.

Plutarch of Chaeronea
Life of Theseus
Perrin, Bernadotte (transl.), *Plutarch. Lives I: Theseus and Romulus. Lycurgus and Numa. Solon and*
    Publicola, Loeb Classical Library 46, Cambridge, MA: Harvard University Press, 1914.
Life of Alexander & Life of Nicias
Waterfield, Robin & Stadter, Philip A. (eds.), *Plutarch: Greek Lives*, Oxford World's Classics, Oxford/
    New York: Oxford University Press, 1998.*
Life of Demosthenes
Lintott, Andrew W. (ed.), *Plutarch: Demosthenes and Cicero*, Clarendon Ancient History Series,
    Oxford: Oxford University Press, 2013.

Protagoras of Abdera
Laks, André & Most, Glenn W. (eds.), *Early Greek Philosophy VIII: Sophists (Part 1)*, Loeb Classical
    Library 531, Cambridge, MA: Harvard University Press, 2016.

Pseudo-Plutarch
Keaney, John J. & Lamberton, Robert (eds.), *Essay on the Life and Poetry of Homer*, American Philo-
    logical Association, American Classical Studies 40, Atlanta, GA: Scholars Press, 1996.

Sappho
The monodic fragments and the choral fragments
Campbell, David A. (ed.), *Greek Lyric I: Sappho and Alcaeus*, Loeb Classical Library 142, Cambridge,
    MA: Harvard University Press, 1982.
Old Age Poem (fr. 58 Voigt)
Obbink, Dirk, *Sappho Fragments 58–59: Text, Apparatus Criticus, and Translation*, in Greene, Ellen
    & Skinner, Marilyn (eds.), *The New Sappho on Old Age. Textual and Philosophical Issues*, Hel-
    lenic Studies 38, Cambridge, MA: Harvard University Press, 2009.
Tithonos Song of Sappho in P.Oxy. 1787
Nagy, Gregory, *The Tithonos Song of Sappho*, Classical Inquiries, 2015 (online: https://classical-
    inquiries.chs.harvard.edu/the-tithonos-song-of-sappho/).
Kypris Song
West, Martin L., *Nine poems of Sappho*, ZPE 191 (2014), pp. 1–12.

Semonides of Amorgos
Gerber, Douglas E. (ed.), *Greek Iambic Poetry: From the Seventh to the Fifth Centuries BC*, Loeb
    Classical Library 259, Cambridge, MA: Harvard University Press, 1999.

Simonides of Ceos
Campbell, David A. (ed.), *Greek Lyric III: Stesichorus. Ibycus. Simonides and Others*, Loeb Classical
    Library 476, Cambridge, MA: Harvard University Press, 1991.

Solon of Athens
Gerber, Douglas E. (ed.), *Greek Elegiac Poetry: From the Seventh to the Fifth Centuries BC*, Loeb
    Classical Library 258, Cambridge, MA: Harvard University Press, 1999.*

Sophocles
Lloyd-Jones, Hugh (ed.), *Sophocles: Antigone. The Women of Trachis. Philoctetes. Oedipus at Colo-
    nus*, Loeb Classical Library 21, Cambridge, MA: Harvard University Press, 1994.
Lloyd-Jones, Hugh (ed.), *Sophocles: Ajax. Electra. Oedipus Tyrannus*, Loeb Classical Library 20,
    Cambridge, MA: Harvard University Press, 1994.

Stesichorus
Campbell, David A. (ed.), *Greek Lyric III: Stesichorus. Ibycus. Simonides and Others*, Loeb Classical
    Library 476, Cambridge, MA: Harvard University Press, 1991.

On the Sublime
Fyfe, Hamilton W. (transl.), *Longinus: On the Sublime*, in Halliwell, Stephen & Fyfe, Hamilton W. &
    Innes, Doreen C. & Roberts, William, R. (transl.), *Aristotle: Poetic. Longinus: On the Sublime.
    Demetrius: On Style*, revised by Russell, Donald A., Loeb Classical Library 199, Cambridge, MA:
    Harvard University Press, 1995.

Theocritus of Syracuse
Hopkinson, Neil (ed.), *Theocritus. Moschus. Bion*, Loeb Classical Library 28, Cambridge, MA, 2015.

Theognis of Megara
Gerber, Douglas E. (ed.), *Greek Elegiac Poetry: From the Seventh to the Fifth Centuries BC*, Loeb
    Classical Library 258, Cambridge, MA: Harvard University Press, 1999.

Theophrastus
Rusten, Jeffrey (ed.), *Theophrastus: Characters*, in Rusten, Jeffrey & Cunningham, Ian C. (eds.),
    Theophrastus: Characters. Herodas: Mimes. Sophron and Other Mime Fragments, Loeb Classi-
    cal Library 225, Cambridge, MA: Harvard University Press, 2003.

Thrasymachus of Chalcedon
Laks, André & Most, Glenn W. (eds.), *Early Greek Philosophy VIII: Sophists (Part 1)*, Loeb Classical
    Library 531, Cambridge, MA: Harvard University Press, 2016.

Thucydides
Hammond, Martin & Rhodes, Peter J. (eds.), *Thucydides: The Peloponnesian War*, Oxford World's
    Classics, Oxford/New York: Oxford University Press, 2009.

Tyrtaeus
Gerber, Douglas E. (ed.), *Greek Elegiac Poetry: From the Seventh to the Fifth Centuries BC*, Loeb
    Classical Library 258, Cambridge, MA: Harvard University Press, 1999.

Xenophanes of Colophon
The elegies and *The Founding of Colophon*
Gerber, Douglas E. (ed.), *Greek Elegiac Poetry: From the Seventh to the Fifth Centuries BC*, Loeb
    Classical Library 258, Cambridge, MA: Harvard University Press, 1999.
Silloi
Laks, André & Most, Glenn W. (ed.), *Early Greek Philosophy III: Early Ionian Thinkers (Part 2)*, Loeb
    Classical Library 526, Cambridge, MA: Harvard University Press, 2016.

Xenophon of Ephesus
Henderson, Jeffrey (ed.), *Longus: Daphnis and Chloe. Xenophon of Ephesus: Anthia and Habro-
    comes*, Loeb Classical Library 69. Cambridge, MA: Harvard University Press, 2009.

Index of Authors (by Elena Squeri)

Abaris 144–145

Ablabes 880

Achaeus I of Eretria 482

Achilles Tatius 1057, 1063, **1065–1068**, 1071, 1075–1076, 1111

Acilius, Caius 910

Acts and Passions of the Martyrs **1123–1124**

Acts of the Apostles 737, 1010–1011, **1013– 1017**

Acts of Justin and of his Companions 1121, **1124**

Acusilaus of Argo 144, 286–287, **546–547**

Aeantides 765

Aelian 1044–1045, **1048**, 1079, 1089

Aelius Aristides 128, 770, 936, 938, 952, 955, 1023, 1040, **1046–1048**

Aelius Herodianus 785, 1081, **1083–1084**

Aelius Tubero, Quintus 945

Aeneas Tacticus **642–643**, 966

Aeneas, rhetor **1100**

Aenesidemus of Cnossus 1025

Aeschines, Athenian orator 12, 305, 322, 595, 654, 659–662, 664–665, 667, **668– 671**, 676, 770, 881, 885, 947, 1049, 1086, 1093

Aeschines of Sphettus 419, 425

Aeschylus 11–12, 24, 161, 236, 256, 277, 315, 321, 323, 327, 330, 331, 333, 349– 352, 359–363, 365, 370, 375, 378–379, **380–403**, 430–432, 437, 445–447, 449– 450, 452–455, 465, 468–469, 471–472, 474, 480, 482, 484, 487, 490–492, 506– 508, 514, 515, 517, 523, 525, 534, 567, 569, 676, 678, 723, 763, 770, 780, 946, 985, 1043

– *Oresteia* 333, 359, 383, 384, 388, 389– 390, **393–400**, 402, 446

– *Persians* 333, 351, 375, 379, 383, **384– 387**, 388, 401, 517, 523, 525, 567

– *Prometheus Bound* 227, 384, **391–393**

– *Seven against Thebes* 380, 384, **387– 389**, 393, 401–402, 437, 468–469

– *Suppliants* 278, 333, 383–384, **389–391**, 402

Aesop **315–317**, 733, 1078

Aetius 1089

Agatharchides of Cnidus **904**, 961

Agathias Scholasticus 802, 974, 1101, **1103**

Agathinus Lacedaemonius 879–880

Agathocles of Cyzicus 903

Agathon 407, **481**, 505, 693–694

Alcaeus, Comic poet 515

Alcaeus of Mytilene 8–9, 11, 43, 171, 176, 213, 215, 225, **233–238**, 246, 250, 302, 780, 806, 947, 1093

Alcaeus of Messene 800

Alcidamas 52, 407, 644–645, 654, **672– 673**, 675, 883

Alciphron **1079–1080**

Alcinous, Middle Platonist philosopher **1024**

Alcman of Sardis 9, 11, 43, 176, 214, 216, **218–222**, 243, 780, 784, 806

Alcmaeon of Croton 295, **537–538**

Alexander, son of Numenius 951

Alexander of Aphrodisias 709, 854, 1025

Alexander of Cotiaeum 1046

Alexander "the Aetolian" 764, 777, **794**, 799

Alexander Romance (see also Pseudo-Callis-thenes) 889, 891, **896–897**, 1057

Alexion 785, 1082

Alexis 519, **520–521**, 753

Alfieri, Vittorio 1000

Ameipsias 489, 495

Ammianus Marcellinus 955, 970, 1096

Ammonius Saccas 989, **1029–1030**, 1034, 1129

Anacharsis 187, 556

Anacreon of Teos 9, 11, 43, 171, 176, 215, 244, **246–251**, 252, 776, 780, 836, 1093

Anaxagoras of Clazomenae 12, 24, 321– 322, 333, 337–338, **341–344**, 345, 376, 410, 417, 453, 496, 574, 585, 775, 1091

Anaxandrides 515, 519, **521**

Anaxarchus of Abdera 856, 1091

Anaximander of Miletus 43, 209, 287, **289**, 290–291, 295, 308, 311, 1091

Anaximenes of Lampsacus 597, 635, 720, 889, **895–896**

Anaximenes of Miletus 287, **289–290**, 344, 1074, 1091

https://doi.org/10.1515/9783110426328-044

Anonymus ad Diognetum 1123

Aphareus 517

Aphthonius of Antioch 951, 953, 1079

Apocalypse of James 1125

Apocalypse of John (see John the Evangelist)

Apocalypse of Peter 1009

Apocrypha, New Testament 1009

Apocrypha, Old Testament 1021

Andocides 595, **607–609**, 1086

Andronicus of Rhodes 25, 708–709, 714, 716–717, 728, 784, 854, 1025

Androtion 575, 639, **640**, 642

Annibale Caro 1071

Anonymus Seguerianus 951

Antagoras of Rhodes 824

Anticleides of Athens 896

Antigonus of Carystus 780

Antimachus of Colophon 143, 147, 522–523, **527–529**, 775, 778, 791, 823, 826, 828, 946

Antimachus of Teos 140

Antiochus of Ascalon 858, 1024–1025

Antiochus of Syracuse **547–548**, 901

Antipater, Rhetor of the second to third century 1041

Antipater, Methodist doctor 879

Antipater of Sidon 800–801, 1101

Antipater of Thessalonica 1101

Antiphanes 353, 519, **520**, 521

Antiphon the Sophist (see also Antiphon of Rhamnus) 286, 332, **414–415**

Antiphon of Rhamnus 574, 593–595, **598–600**, 625, 946, 1086

Antisthenes 407, 419, **425–426**, 428–429, 619, 648, 684, 855, 1026, 1091

Antoninus Liberalis 822

Antonius Diogenes 1075

Antyllus 880

Anyte of Tegea 798

Apellicon of Teos 25, 708

Apion 786, 1085

Apollinaris of Laodicea **1137–1138**, 1143, 1148

Apollodorus of Athens 554, 573, 680, 783–784, 904, 917, 918, 921

Apollodorus of Carystus 752

Apollodorus of Pergamum **944–945**

Apollonides, Methodist doctor 879

Apollonius *eidographos* **779**

Apollonius of Perge 870–871, **874**

Apollonius of Tyana 1028, 1033

Apollonius Dyscolus **1081–1082**, 1083

Apollonius Molon 885–886

Apollonius Rhodius 13, 143, 160, 574, 744–745, 770, 777–778, 785, 788–789, 803–804, 816, 818, 823–824, **824–833**, 835, 839, 842, 903, 985, 1108

– *Argonautica* 778, 818, 823, 825, 826–833, 839

Apollonius Sophista 786, 1085

Appian of Alexandria 958–959

Apuleius 932, 1024, 1055, 1059, 1078

Aquila 926, 1131

Ararotes 495

Aratus of Soli 161–163, 745, 770, 782, 785, 789, 799, 819, **820–821**, 843, 997

Arcesilaus of Pitane 684, 854, 857

Archelaus of Athens (or of Miletus) 341, 343, 1091

Archias of Antioch 801

Archigenes of Apamea 880

Archilochus of Paros 9, 11, 43, 125, 172, 176, 178, **179–184**, 185–187, 189, 191–192, 199, 237, 315, 512, 778, 780, 791, 795, 812, 826, 840

Archimedes 674, 870–871, **872–874**, 875

Archippus, Pythagorean 295

Archippus, Comic poet 514

Arctinus of Miletus 140

Archytas of Tarentum 681, 683, 711, 732

Arend, Walter 104

Aretaeus of Cappadocia 879, 1036

Arion of Methymna 215, 217, **218**, 276–277, 369, 371, 378, 549

Aristaenetus 1079–1080

Aristarchus of Samos 853, 868, 870

Aristarchus of Samothrace 25, 51, 74, 109–110, 160–161, 556, 773, 776, 778, **779–780**, 781–785, 793, 841, 904, 1081, 1083, 1085

Aristarchus of Tegea 482

Aristeas of Proconnesus 144–145, 985

Aristeas (see *Letter of Aristeas to Philocrates*)

Aristias 379–380

Aristides of Miletus 1078

Aristides Quintilianus **1089**

Aristides, Athenian philosopher and Christian apologist 1121
Aristippus of Cyrene 428, 681, 684
Aristobulus, Alexander historian 889, **893–894**, 895, 960
Aristobulus, Biblical exegete **926**, 1002
Aristophanes 12, 23, 161–162, 321, 326, 331–332, 344, 349, 353–354, 361, 364–365, 367, 372–374, 376–378, 382, 403, 407, 411–412, 416, 419–420, 432, 453–454, 455, 477, 481–482, 485–491, **492–514**, 516–519, 533, 555, 588, 600, 694, 723, 751, 757, 770, 775, 780, 1055, 1072, 1104
– Acharnians 493–494, 496, **497–498**, 505, 510
– Assemblywomen 486, 496, 502–503, 508, **509**, 512
– Birds 354, 377, 496, 502, **503–504**, 511
– Clouds 344, 407, 411–412, 416, 419–420
– Frogs 23, 161–162, 354, 382, 403, 432, 453–454, 477
– Knights 378, 486, 488, 489, 490, 494, 496–497, **498–499**, 510
– Lysistrata 354, 496, 502, **504–505**, 509, 511
– Peace 496–497, **501–502**, 510, 513–514
– Women at the Thesmophoria 453, 481, 496, 502, 503, **505–506**, 511
– Wealth 495–496, 502–503, 508, **509–510**, 512, 518
– Wasps 354, 486, 496–497, **500–501**, 510
Aristophanes of Byzantium 25, 109–110, 160, 262, 363, 430, 684, 752, 756, 773–774, **778–779**, 780, 782, 876, 1081, 1085, 1088
Aristonicus 110, 785
Aristoxenus of Tarentum 420, 530–531, 533, **731–732**, 1035, 1089
Aristotle 9, 12, 24–25, 47, 62–63, 126, 130–131, 137–141, 163, 177, 199, 203, 240, 279, 286, 288, 296–297, 300, 315, 322, 332, 338, 342, 344, 346, 352, 363, 366, 368, 369, 371–373, 405, 407–408, 412, 416, 419–420, 477, 481, 483–484, 486–487, 516–518, 531, 553, 570, 591–592, 594–595, 597, 622, 634, 638, 652, 657, 672, 675, 678–679, 681, 688, 699–700, 702–704, **704–729**, 730–733, 743–745, 751, 771, 773, 775, 784, 805, 816, 818, 834, 853, 860, 868, 870, 873, 881, 891, 901, 994, 1022, 1025, 1032–1033, 1037, 1039, 1043, 1089–1091, 1142
– Categories 714, 873, 1034, 1037
– Metaphysics 712, 717–718, 727, 730
– Nicomachean Ethics 517, 718
– Physics 688, 712, 716, 727, 1034, 1095
– Poetics 47, 62, 126, 131, 137, 138, 141, 163, 177, 279, 366, 368–369, 372, 416, 477, 481, 483, 484, 486–487, 517, 712, 720, **722**, 724, 726–728, 751, 771–772, 818–819, 824, 834, 899
– Politics 288, 713, 719, 911
– Posterior Analytics 715, 1093
– Prior Analytics 715, 1093
– Rhetoric 240, 315, 408, 517, 553, 570, 591, 595, 597, 657, 672, 712, **720**, 727, 953
–The Athenian Constitution 622, 709, 728
Aristus of Salamis 896
Arius 967, 1133–1134
Arnobius of Sicca I 350
Arrian of Nicomedia 889–890, 892–897, **959–962**, 962, 1027, 1113
Arrianus, author of the Alexandrias 1112
Artemidorus of Daldis 1039
Artemidorus of Ephesus 977
Artemidorus of Tarsus 835, 841
Asclepiades of Myrlea 785
Asclepiades of Prusa 878
Asclepiades of Samos 790, 799–800
Asius of Samos 144, 984
Astydamas 517
Astydamas the Younger 516
Athanasius of Alexandria **1133–1134**, 1137
Athanis 629
Athenaeus, follower of Hermagoras 886
Athenaeus of Attaleia 879
Athenaeus of Naucratis 128, 131, 373, 486, 846, 894, 915, 1045, 1074, **1090**
Athenagoras 1122
Atthidographers **637–639**, 641
Aulus Gellius 453, 932, 1045
Avienus 112
Babrius 939, 1079
Bacchylides of Ceos 9, 11–12, 176, 214, 216, 247, 252–254, 261, 271, **272–280**, 321, 323, 327, 330, 369–370, 383, 533, 754, 780, 806, 810, 832

– *Dithyrambs* 273, **276–279**, 369
– *Epinicia* 272, **273–276**, 277
Bacchius 876–877
Barnes, Joshua 111
Basil of Caesarea 1093–1094, 1138, **1138–1140**, 1140–1143
Basilides 1126
Bentley, Richard 112, 1079
Beros(s)us 900
Besantinus 842
Bible (see also *Old Testament*) 10, 27, 113, 741, 923–927, 1001–1002, 1008, 1128, 1131, 1138
– *Pentateuch* 742, 926, 1001–1002, 1137
Bion of Smyrna 834–835, 841–843
Bion of Borysthenes 428
Blegen, Carl William 65–66
Boccaccio 28, 111, 840
Boethus of Sidon 978
Book of Allogenes 1125
Brutus 884
Caecilius of Caleacte 884, 886, 922, 937, 944–945, **948**, 948–949
Caesar 749, 884, 917, 921, 932, 959, 963–964, 1004, 1095, 1097, 1001
Caesius Bassus 1089
Callias, Comic poet 376, 486, **487**
Callimachus of Cyrene 13, 127, 141, 161, 638, 744–745, 775, 777, 785, 788–790, 792, 794, 799–800, **803–818**, 823, 825–826, 832–833, 835, 838–842, 844–846, 850, 871, 1034, 1084, 1102
– *Aetia* 161, 792, 794, 804–806, **808–811**, 811, 815–818, 832
– *Epigrams* 141, 803, 805–806, **813–814**, 816
– *Hecale* 805, 810, **814–815**, 817, 839
– *Hymns* 770, 789, 805–806, **806–808**, 817, 1034
– *Iambi* 790, 805, 809, **811–813**, 815, 817–818
Callinus of Ephesus 11, 43, 140, 176, 191, **192**, 196, 204, 302, 523
Callisthenes 707, 889–890, **891**, 894–896, 1057
Callistus 1112
Canfora, Luciano 583, 614
Canon Muratori 1009–1010, 1118
Carcinus I 482, 500

Carcinus II 516
Cassius Dio **962–964**, 1007
Cassius Longinus 949, 1029–1030
Castor of Rhodes **921**
Cato 910, 957
Catullus 228, 808, 811, 818, 871
Carneades 857
Celsus, philosopher 1096, 1130
Cercidas of Megalopolis **846**, 854
Chadwick, John 2
Chaeremon 517
Chaldaean Oracles 939, 1029, 1033, **1106**
Chamaeleon 712, 773
Chares **894**
Chariton of Aphrodisias 1056–1057, **1059–1063**, 1063, 1067, 1074–1075, 1111
Charon of Lampsacus 544–545
Chionides 486
Choerilus of Athens 379, 383
Choerilus of Samos 147, 523, **525–527**
Choricius of Gaza 1100
Chreophylus of Samos 141–142, 524
Christodorus of Coptus 1112
Christus patiens 1142
Chrysoloras, Manuel 28
Chrysippus of Soli 772–773, 782, 863–864, 879, 1091
Cicero 47, 109, 161, 163, 345, 412, 571, 592, 593, 602, 629, 639, 659, 699, 710, 728, 732, 801, 820–821, 858, 867, 881, 885, 895, 902, 915–916, 947
– *Brutus* 47, 602, 885
– *Letters to Atticus* 732, 916
– *On the Nature of the Gods* 161
– *Orator* 571
Cinaethon of Lacedaemon 140, 142, 144
Cinesias of Athens 503, 514, 532
Ciris 818
Claudianus 1112
Claudius Quadrigarius 964
Claudius Ptolemaeus 871, 961, 977, 980, **987**, 1032, 1035, 1089
Cleanthes of Assos 863–864, 866
Clearchus of Soli 712, 773
Cleidemus **639–640**, 640
Cleitarchus **894–895**, 895
Clement of Alexandria 903, 926, **1128–1129**, 1129, 1131
Clement of Rome 1013, **1116**, 1117–1118

Cleon of Curium 824, 828
Cleophon, Tragic poet 516
Cohortatio ad gentiles 1131–1132
Colluthus **1108**, 1110
Colotes of Lampsacus 862
Comoedia Florentina 754
Conon of Samos 811, **871**, 872, 874
Constantine Cephalas 802
Constantine Manasses 1066
Constantine VII Porphyrogenitus vd. *Excerpta Constantiniana*
Contest of Homer and Hesiod 51–52, 128, 131, 140, 155, 161–162
Corax 407, 591–593, 597
Corinna of Tanagra 261, **280**
Cornelius Gallus 794, 978
Cornelius Nepos 993–994
Cornelius Sisenna 1078
Corpus Hermeticum **1038–1039**
Crates of Athens, Platonist philosopher 702–703, 854, 857
Crates, Comic poet 376, 484, **486–487**, 487, 723
Crates of Mallus 161, 781–783, 785
Crates of Thebes, Cynic Philosopher 425, 427, 855, 863
Cratinus 376–377, 486, **487–489**, 492, 495, 519
Crinagoras of Mytilene 1101
Critias of Athens 24, **413–414**, 418, **481–482**, 611, 625, 680, 692, 698, 713
Ctesias of Cnidus **630–631**, 637
Ctesibius of Alexandria **874**
Curtius Rufus, Quintus 889, 895
Cycle of Heracles 132, 141
Cynaethus of Chios 128, 142
Cyprian 932
Cyril, Lexicographer (author of the *Cyril Lexicon*) 772, 1087
Cyril of Alexandria 1096, 1146–1147, **1147–1148**
Cyril of Jerusalem **1136**, 1144
Damastes of Sigeum **548–550**
Damon of Oa 530–532, 1089
Dante 111, 137
Dares of Phrygia 1059, 1077
De Sanctis, Gaetano 564
Decem oratorum vitae (see *Lives of the Ten Orators*)

Della Valle, Niccolò 162
Delphic Oracles 1105
Demades 660, 666, **675**, 676
Demetrius (author of the treatise *On Style*) 352, 667, 946, **950**, 952
Demetrius Chalcondyles 111
Demetrius Lacon 862
Demetrius of Phaleron 287, 642, **732–733**, 738, 746, 753, 776, 854, 868, 923, 950
Demetrius of Scepsis 780–781, 784, 903
Demo 781
Democritus 12, 321, 337, 344, **345–346**, 410, 539, 711, 771–772, 775, 856, 859, 860, 1091
Demon 639, **641**, 642, 773
Demosthenes 12, 305, 322, 329, 332, 334, 595, 640, 651, 653–654, 656, **657–667**, 668–677, 706, 745, 770, 895, 947–950, 952–953, 957, 970, 1042, 1044, 1047–1048, 1086, 1093, 1095
– *Philippics* 661–663, **664–665**
– *Olynthiacs* 661, 664, **665–666**
Demosthenes of Bithynia 824
Dexippus **966**, 976
Dicaearchus of Messana 731, **732**, 869
Dictys Cretensis 1059, 1077
Didachē **1188**, 1127
Didymus Chalcenterus 110, 575, 598, 774, 785, 895, 1085
Dinarchus 595, 660, 663, 676, **677**, 947, 1086
Dinon 895
Dio Cocceianus (see Dio of Prusa)
Diodorus Cronus 429
Diodorus Siculus 310, 547, 606, 615, 629–631, 633–634, 745, 887, 889, 895, 897, 900–901, 915, **916–920**, 920, 968, 973, 1060, 1076
Diodorus of Tarsus 1144
Diodorus of Tyre 854
Diogenes Laertius 109, 292, 294, 420, 425–426, 484, 537, 680–681, 684, 704–705, 856, 859, 864, 892, 1045, **1090–1091**
Diogenes of Apollonia 344, 453
Diogenes of Babylon 781, 783, 904
Diogenes of Oenoanda 859, 862, 1028
Diogenes of Sinope or "the Cynic" **425–427**, 854–856, 891, 895, 1023, 1026, 1043, 1054

Diogenianus of Heraclea 1086
Diomedes, Latin grammarian 163
Dionysiades of Mallus 765
Dionysius Longinus (see *On the Sublime*)
Dionysius, Methodist doctor 879
Dionysius of Halicarnassus 258–259, 404,
    524, 547, 570, 589, 607, 635, 637–639,
    645, 667–668, 671, 728, 882–884, 885,
    895–897, 902, 913, 915, 922, 936–937,
    939, 943–944, **945–947**, 948–949, 952,
    954, **956–957**, 964, 980, 1007
Dionysius of Miletus 544–545, 1061
Dionysius Periegetes 770, 978, 1112
Dionysius Thrax 708, 770, 773, 783–785,
    885, 1081
Dio of Prusa, said Chrysostom 94, 936,
    938, 955, 962, 1023, 1026, 1040–1042,
    1042–1044, 1045, 1093, 1098–1099
Diophantus 1036
Dioscorides of Alexandria 800
Diotimus of Adramyttium 824
Diphilus 752
Dissoi Logoi (δισσοὶ λόγοι) 411
Dörpfeld, Wilhelm 65–66
Dosiadas 842
Droysen, Johann Gustav 737
Duris **897–899**, 912
Ecphantides 486
Empedocles of Acragas 43, 163, 286, 296,
    337, **338–341**, 342–344, 404, 407, 542,
    591–593, 679, 723, 818, 821, 946, 998,
    1091
Ennius 818
Ephippus, Comic poet 519
Ephippus of Olynthus 890, **894**
Ephorus of Cyme 332, 546, 615, 627–628,
    631–633, 635–636, 646, 889, 899, 901–
    902, 913, 918–919, 977, 981
Epicharmus 9, 323, 327, 373, **483–484**,
    484–486, 492, 512, 723, 784, 850
Epicrates 519
Epictetus of Hierapolis 863, 959–960,
    1027, 1034
Epicurus of Samos 13, 742, 745, 753, 855,
    857, **858–862**, 863, 878, 996, 1028, 1039,
    1090–1091
Epimenides of Crete 144–145
Epiphanius of Eleutheropolis **1137**
Epiphanius of Salamis 1144

Erasistratus of Ceos 876–877
Eratosthenes of Cyrene 74, 82, 547, **778**,
    783–784, 825, 870, 872, 901, 903–904,
    910, 917, 961, 987
Eratosthenes Scholasticus 1103
Erinna 535
Etymologica 772, 1087
Eubulus, Comic poet 519, **521**
Euclid 869, **871**, 872, 875
Euclides of Megara 419, **429**, 681, 684
Eudemus of Rhodes 718, 885
Eudorus 1028
Eudoxus of Cnidus **703–704**, 820, 869, **870**
Euhemerus of Messana 917
Eugammon of Cyrene 139–141
Eumelus of Corinth 140, 143
Eumenes of Cardia 746, 891, 897
Eunapius of Sardis 966, 969–970, 976,
    1098
Euphorion, Tragic poet 363, 383, 482
Euphorion of Chalcis 742, 795, **844–845**,
    985
Euphronius of Chersonesus 765
Eupolis 376, 489, **490**, 495, 507, 517
Euripides 12, 23–24, 133, 293, 321, 330–
    331, 341–342, 349, 350, 352, 361–365,
    375, 379, 382, 387, 394, 400, 431–433,
    443, 445, **450–480**, 480–482, 484, 491–
    492, 498, 501, 505–507, 514, 517–518,
    520–521, 530, 533, 676, 732, 755, 763,
    766, 770, 779–780, 796, 831, 844, 939,
    946, 970, 997, 1043–1044, 1055, 1064–
    1065, 1072, 1074, 1104, 1109, 1142
– *Alcestis* 433, 443, 455, **456–457**
– *Andromache* 433, 455, 462, 464, **465–**
    466
– *Bacchae* 387, 455, 468, **470–471**, 479,
    482, 1109
– *Cyclops* 349, 352, 365, 455–456, **476**
– *Children of Heracles* 443, 455–456, **457–**
    458, 468, 479
– *Electra* 394, 455, **471–473**, 474
– *Hecuba* 433, 455, 462, 464, **465**, 470, 473
– *Helen* 350, 433, 455, 462, **466–467**, 473,
    479, 505
– *Heracles* 443, 455–456, **458**
– *Hippolytus* 455, **461–462**, 1064–1065,
    1072, 1074

– *Iphigenia among the Taurians* 394, 455, 472–473
– *Iphigenia at Aulis* 433, 455, **462–464**, 479
– *Ion* 350, 455, **475–476**, 479
– *Medea* 363, 455, **459–461**, 473, 482, 520–521, 831
– *Orestes* 394, 455, 472, **474**, 530
– *Phoenician Women* 361, 387, 455, 468, **469–470**
– *Rhesus* (Pseudo-Euripides) 365, 455, **477**, 516
– *Suppliant Women* 455, **468–469**
– *Trojan Women* 433, 455, 458, 462, **464–466**, 482
Euripides the Younger 454–455, 482
Eusebius of Caesarea 272, 281, 312, 921, 926–927, **967–968**, 970, 1006, 1128, **1135–1136**, 1138, 1146
Eustathius (or Eumathius) Macrembolites 1066
Eustathius of Antioch 1066
Eustathius of Thessalonica 781, 1079
Euthydemus, Collector of texts 24
Eutocius 874
Evagrius Scholasticus 968, 1136
Exagōgē **926–927**
Excerpta Constantiniana 907, 963, 968
Ezekiel vd. *Exagōgē*
Fabius Pictor 908, 914, 957
Favorinus of Arles 1023, 1040, 1043, **1045**, 1046, 1048, 1089
Ficino, Marsilio 1033
Finley, Moses Israel 74, 78
Flavius Josephus 936, 954, **1004–1008**, 1085
Flavius Philostratus (see Philostratus II)
Foscolo, Ugo 1000
Fronto 932, 958, 1027
Freud, Sigmund 1039
Galen 162, 412, 543, 783, 876, 878, **1036–1038**, 1084
Glycon 790
Gnomologium Vaticanum 859
Golden Verses 1028
Gorgias of Leontini 12, 321–323, 338, 389, 406, **407–409**, 425, 539, 592–594, 607, 619, 646, 648–649, 656–657, 672, 692, 710, 771–772, 883, 1040, 1049

Gospels 27, 1009–1010, **1013–1018**, 1019, 1021, 1109, 1118, 1121–1122, 1135
– *Gospel of John* 1010, **1017–1018**, 1109
– *Gospel of Judas* 1125
– *Gospel of Luke* 1010, 1014, **1016–1017**, 1135
– *Gospel of Mark* 1010, 1013–1015, **1015–1016**, 1021, 1129
– *Gospel of Matthew* 1010, 1014, **1014–1015**, 1021
Greek Anthology 803
Gregory of Nazianzus 1093–1094, 1096, 1138–1139, **1140–1142**, 1142
Gregory of Nyssa 1138, **1142–1143**
Gregory the Thaumaturge 1138
Hagias of Troezen 140
Harpocration, Valerius 1086
Havelock, Eric Alfred 107–108
Hecataeus of Abdera 900, 919
Hecataeus of Miletus 9, **309–313**, 545–546, 550, 556, 558–559, 564, 567, 570, 961, 977
–The *Geographic Map* **311–312**
–*Genealogies or Histories* **310**, 312
–*Periēgēsis of the Earth* **311–312**
Hédelin abate d'Aubignac, François 111
Hedylus of Samos 799
Hegesianax of Alexandria 903
Hegesias of Magnesia **883–884**, 884, **896**
Hegesippus 1008
Heliodorus, Pneumatist doctor 880
Heliodorus, Grammarian 1088
Heliodorus of Emesa 1057, 1063, 1065–1066, 1069, **1071–1073**, 1075–1076
Hellanicus of Mytilene **548–550**, 577, 637–639
Hellenica of Oxyrhynchus **627–628**, 888
Helvius Cinna 818
Hephaestion 483, 770, **1088–1089**
Heracleon 1126
Heraclides Lembus 712, 904, 1091
Heraclides of Miletus 1083
Heraclides of Tarentum 877
Heraclides Ponticus 527, **704**
Heraclitus, Author of the *Homeric Problems* 782
Heraclitus of Ephesus 290, **290–293**, 678, 681, 1091
Hermagoras of Temnos 886, 950

Hermann, Gottfried 98, 114
Hermarchus 862
Hermas 1009, **1118–1119**
Hermesianax of Colophon **793**, 793–794
Hermes Trismegistos 1028, 1038–1039
Hermetic Writings 1028, 1033, 1038–1039
Hermippus, Comic poet 376, 489, **489**
Hermogenes of Tarsus 570, 770, 886, 951,
  952–953
Herodas 485, 790, 838, 846, **847–851**
Herodes Atticus 983, 1027, 1040–1042,
  1045 **1046**, 1046
Herodian, Historian 965–966
Herodotus, Eclectic doctor 880
Herodotus 9, 12, 17, 41, 47, 51, 73, 84, 140,
  162, 218, 224, 275–276, 288, 305, 307–
  312, 315, 321–323, 332–333, 338, 369–
  370, 379, 385, 405, 431–432, 523, 525–
  526, 536, 544–546, 548–549, **550–571**,
  571–572, 576, 580, 585, 587–588, 613,
  630, 634, 657, 685, 721, 765, 769–770,
  780, 844, 888, 898, 900, 911, 919, 945,
  947, 956, 959, 961, 966, 970, 977, 982,
  984–986, 1053, 1055, 1078, 1105
– *The Histories* 41, 47, 333, 369–370, 379,
  544, 551–552, 554–556, **556–563**, 563,
  565–567, 571, 576, 765, 844, 1078
Heron of Alexandria 874, **875**
Herophilus of Chalcedon 876–877
Hesiod 11, 20, 43, 47–48, 51–52, 84, 89,
  93, 103, 125, 129, 132, 142, **147–163**, 173,
  183, 191, 202, 261, 269, 283, 302, 310,
  314, 330, 339, 392, 404, 523, 596, 770,
  776, 778–780, 782, 784–785, 793, 807,
  816, 818–821, 826, 838, 850, 905, 985,
  997, 1044, 1067, 1072, 1108
– *Theogony* 132, 147–148, **148–150**, 150–
  162, 167, 269, 283, 302, 807, 809, 838.
– *Works and Days* 51, 147–148, **150–151**,
  152–153, 156, 158, 160–162, 185, 201,
  283, 314, 819
Hesychius of Alexandria 244, 771, 1086
Heyne, Christian Gottlob 111
Hierocles 1034
Hieronymus of Cardia 888, **897**, 902, 919,
  984
Himerius of Prusa 1092, **1093**, 1093–1094,
  1098

Hippocrates of Cos and the *Hippocratic Cor-
  pus* 9, 12, 322, 332, 536, **538–543**, 583–
  585
Historia Augusta 1088
History of Apollonius King of Tyre (*Historia
  Apollonii regis Tyrii*) **1077–1078**
Hipparchus of Nicaea **870–871**, 981
Hippias of Elis 406, **413**, 692, 883, 901
Hippolytus 1127
Hipponax of Ephesus 9, 11, 43, 131, 176–
  179, 184, **187–189**, 512, 766, 780, 790,
  798, 812–813, 840, 846, 848–849, 851,
  1079
Hippys of Rhegium **547–548**
Homer 5, 11–12, 28, 41, 43, **47–132**, 133,
  138–144, 147–148, 154–155, 157–158,
  161–164, 167, 190, 210, 228, 240–242,
  258, 279, 283, 301, 330, 396, 398, 404,
  426, 442, 522–523, 526, 528–530, 547,
  571, 607, 632, 700, 723–724, 753, 769,
  771, 775–780, 782, 784–785, 795, 798,
  808, 815–816, 818, 826, 828, 830, 833,
  846, 947, 949–950, 953, 980–981, 984,
  998, 1032, 1044, 1047, 1054–1055, 1062–
  1063, 1072, 1082, 1105, 1107–1108, 1110–
  1111, 1115
– *Iliad* 8, 18, 20, 43, 48–50, 52, **53–56**, 57–
  65, 67, 72, 76–80, 82–87, 89–93, 98,
  108–121, 124–128, 131–134, 136–141, 143,
  159–160, 167, 283, 301–302, 306, 477,
  536, 539, 596, 711, 723, 770, 775, 777,
  779, 781, 783, 790, 827–830, 834, 846,
  903, 949, 1063, 1072, 1077, 1083–1084,
  1107–1109, 1112
– *Odyssey* 8, 20, 43, 47–53, **57–59**, 59–65,
  77–80, 83, 85, 87–93, 98, 108–111, 113–
  119, 124–127, 129, 131, 133–134, 136–141,
  167, 239, 275, 283, 395–398, 463, 525–
  526, 536, 711, 723, 770, 775, 779, 820,
  828, 830, 834, 893, 949, 1032, 1056,
  1063, 1072, 1075, 1083–1084, 1107–1109
Homer "Minor" **126–132**
– *Batrachomyomachia* **130–131**, 810
– *Homeric Epigrams* **131–132**
– *Homeric Hymns* 103, **127–129**, 141–142,
  170, 237, 806, 808, 815, 1034
– *Margites* **130**
Homerus of Byzantium 764
Horace 234–236, 378, 801, 812, 1103

Hypatia 1034, 1098, 1148
Hyperides 595, 646, 654, 661, 663, **673–675**, 676–677, 745, 873, 885, 947, 1086
Iamblichus, Neoplatonist philosopher 294, **1033**, 1097, 1106
Iamblicus, Novelist 1075, **1076**
Iambulus 1054, **1076–1077**
Ibycus of Rhegium 9, 11, 43, 176, 216, **243–246**, 247–248
Ignatius of Antioch **1116–1117**, 1124
Introductio sive medicus 878
Iophon 432, 461, 482
Ion, Rhapsode 103, 143, 692
Ion of Chios 306, 461, **480–481**, 482, 523, 765, 813
Irenaeus of Lyons 1016, 1126
Irrisio Ermiae **1123**
Isaeus 595, 659, 667, **671–672**, 947, 1086
Isocrates 12, 322, 332, 335, 404, 407, 517, 594–595, 616, 621, 625, 627, 631, 633–635, 637, 640, **644–657**, 657, 659–660, 667, 671–673, 676, 682–683, 710, 744, 770, 885, 891, 921, 946–947, 957, 1047, 1086
Istrus 902
Iustus of Tiberias 1006
Jacoby, Felix 563–564, 639
James, Apostle 1010, 1021
Johannes Xiphilinus 963
John Chrysostom 1094, **1144–1146**, 1147
John of Gaza 1112
John of Stobi 185, 287, 1039, 1091
John the Evangelist 1010, 1017–1020, 1117, 1141
– Apocalypse 1010, **1019–1020**, 1118
– Letters 1010, **1019**
– Gospel (see *Gospel of John*)
Jordanes 1043
Joseph and Aseneth, Novel of 927
Juba 991
Jude, author of the *Letter* of Jude 1010, 1021
Julius Africanus 921
Julius Vestinus 1086
Julian "the Chaldaean" 1106
Julian the Egyptian 1103
Julian the Emperor, or "the Apostate" 934, 942, 969, 976, 1023, 1038, 1092–1094, **1095–1098**, 1112, 1132, 1137, 1141, 1146
Julian "the Theurge" 1106

Justin (see also *Acts of Justin and of his Companions*) 1016, **1121–1122**
Kirchhoff, Adolf 114
Korfmann, Manfred 65, 67
Lachmann, Karl 113
Lamprias 988–989, 997–998
Lasus of Hermione 260, 276, 533
Leonidas of Alexandria, Eclectic doctor 880
Leonidas of Alexandria, Epigrammatist 1102
Leonidas of Tarentum 798, 1103
Leopardi, Giacomo 131, 960, 1000
Lesches of Mytilene 140
Letter of Aristeas to Philocrates 923–924, 926
Letter of James 1010, 1021
Letter of Jude (see Jude)
Letters of Peter 1010, 1021
Letter of Peter to Philip 1125
Letters of Phalaris 1079
Letters of the Apostles (see also John, Jude, Paul of Tarsus, *Letter* of James, *Letters* of Peter) 27
Letter to the Hebrews 1009–1010, **1013**
Leucippus 344–345, 1091
Leucon 489
Libanius of Antioch 659, 1092, **1094–1095**, 1096, 1098, 1144
Licinius Calvus 818, 884
Linus 48
Lives of Homer (see also Pseudo-Plutarch: *On the Life and Poetry of Homer*) 51, 131, 556
Lives of the Ten Orators 602, 645, 659, 668, 998
Livy 956, 963–964
Lollianus **1076**
Longus ("Sophistes") 1057, **1068–1071**
Lord, Albert Bates 102, 105, 122–123
Luke the Evangelist (see also: *Gospel of Luke* and *Acts of the Apostles*) 1014–1017
Lucian of Samosata 6, 428, 571, 770, 936, 938, 1023, 1040, 1044, 1048, **1050–1055**, 1059, 1075, 1080
– The dialogues **1053–1054**, 1055, 1070
– *A True Story* 1052, **1054**, 1075 (see also *Lucius or The Ass*)
Lucillius 1102
Lucius of Patras 1055, 1075

Lucius or The Ass 1052, **1054–1055**, 1058–1059

Lucius Septimius 1077

Lucretius 163, 858–862

Lutatius Catulus 801

Lycophron of Chalcis 13, 745, 764, 770, **777**, **843–844**, 1108

Lycurgus, Athenian orator and politician 24, 336, 357, 362, 517, 595, 641, 646, 661, **676**, 752, 1086

Lydiaca **544–546**

Lysias 12, 305, 322–323, 332, 595, **600–607**, 646, 649, 659, 667, 672–674, 695, 697, 884, 947–948, 1086

Macedonius of Thessalonica 1103

Machon 752

Magical Hymns 1103, **1105**

Magnes 486

Magnus 879

Malchus of Philadelphia 976

Manetho 900

Marcellus of Side 1112

Marcion, heretical 1117, 1126

Marcion (see *Martyrdom of Polycarp*)

Marcus Argentarius 1101

Marcus Aurelius Antoninus 863, 934, 941, 960, 962, 964–966, 982, 1022, **1027**, 1027, 1028, 1037, 1041, 1046, 1048, 1051, 1076, 1083, 1096–1097, 1106, 1113, 1121–1122

Mark the Evangelist (see *Gospel of Mark*)

Marmor Parium 382, 431, 453, 486

Marsyas **894**

Martial 1102

Martyrdom of Polycarp (Martyrium Polycarpi) **1124**

Matthew the Evangelist (see *Gospel of Matthew*)

Maximus Planudes (see also Planudean Anthology or *Appendix Planudea*) 802, 994

Maximus of Ephesus 1096

Maximus of Tyre 1024, 1042, **1044–1045**

Medius 889

Megacleides 160

Megasthenes 901, 961

Melanippides of Melos 533

Melanthius, Tragic poet 482

Melanthius, Atthidographer 639, **641**

Meleager of Gadara 800–802, 1102

Meletus 418, 516

Melinno **846–847**

Melissus of Samos 297, **299–300**, 344, 1091

Melito of Sardis 1120, **1123**

Menaechmus of Sicyon 896

Menander 12–13, 322, 332, 349, 365, 475, 518, 520, 742–743, 745, 750–752, **752–763**, 789, 859, 1054–1055, 1062, 1080
– *Aspis* (*The Shield*) 754–755, **759**, 762
– *Dyskolos* (*The Peevish Fellow*) 496, 753–755, **758**, 759, 761, 762
– *Epitrepontes* (*Men at Arbitration*) 754–755, **760**, 761–763
– *Herōs* (*Guardian Spirit*) 754, 758, **760–761**
– *Misoumenos* (*The Hated Man*) 755, **761**, 1062
– *Perikeiromenē* (*The Girl with Her Hair Cut Short*) 754, **758**, 759, 762
– *Samia* (*Woman from Samos*) 754–755, **759**, 761–762
– *Sicyōnios* or *Sicyōnioi* (*The Sicyonians*) 754, **761**

Menander Rhetor 951–952

Menelaus of Aegae 824

Menemachus 879

Menippus of Gadara 428, 546, 801, 1053–1054

Mesomedes of Crete 939, 1102

Metagenes 514

Metiochus and Parthenope 1056, 1062, **1074**

Metrodorus of Lampsacus 862

Mimnermus of Colophon 11, 43, 190–191, **196–199**, 202, 205, 209, 250, 302, 442, 523, 529, 780, 791, 816

Minucianus of Athens 951–952

Mnasalces of Sicyon 798

Mnaseas 879

Mnesimachus 519

Morsimus 482

Morychus 482

Moschion 517

Moschus 834–835, **841–842**, 843

Muratori, Ludovico Antonio (see also *Canon Muratori*) 1009

Musaeus, *Grammatikos* 1107, **1110–1111**

Musaeus, Legendary epic poet 47, 49, 145, 162, 284, 404, 793, 1107
Musaeus of Ephesus 824
Musti, Domenico 6
Nagy, Gregory 124
Nearchus 870, 889, 891–892, **893**, 961
Neleus of Scepsis 24–25, 708
Neoptolemus of Parium 824
Nestor of Laranda 1107–1108
New Testament 10, 27, 742, 940, **1008–1021**, 1116–1117, 1126–1127, 1138
Nicander of Colophon 161, 745, 770, 785, 789, 819, **821–822**, 843, 997
Nicanor 1084
Nicetes of Smyrna 881, 1041, 1049
Nicholas of Myra 951
Nicolaus of Damascus 633, 709, **920–921**, 955, 1007
Nicomachus of Gerasa 1028, 1033
Nicophon 514
Nicostratus 519
Ninus Novel 1056–1057, 1062, 1073, **1073**, 1074, 1077
Nonnus of Panopolis 143, 1107, **1109–1110**, 1110
Nossis of Locri 766, 798
Novel of Calligone **1077**
Novel of Chione 1056, 1062, **1074–1075**
Novel of Sesonchosis **1077**
Numenius of Apamea 1028, 1106
Odes of Solomon 1119
Old Testament (see also *Bible*) 26, 303, 737, 887, 925, 940, 1002, 1008–1009, 1012, 1014–1015, 1021, 1117, 1119, 1122, 1126–1127, 1129, 1131, 1145, 1148
Olympic discourses 596, 649
Olympicus 879
Olympiodorus, Neoplatonist 681
Olympiodorus of Thebes 969, 976
Onesicritus 889–890, **891–892**, 895, 961
On the Sublime 63, 259, 480, 571, 667, 674, 782, 895, 944, 946–948, **948–950**
Oppian of Anazarbus 770
Oppian of Apamea 1112–1113
Oracles (see *Chaldaean Oracles, Delphic Oracles* and *Sibylline Oracles*)
Oribasius of Pergamum 1038
Origen "the Pagan" 1030

Origen of Alexandria 926, 1029–1030, **1129–1131**, 1135, 1137, 1143
Orpheus 47–48, 127, 145–146, 162, 283–284, 404, 530, 534, 793–794, 827–828, 1103–1104
Orphic Argonautica 146, 284, 1103
Orphic Hymns 1103, **1104**, 1105
Orus of Alexandria 1086
Ovid 792, 794–795, 801, 808, 811, 821, 1103
Palatine Anthology 535, 669, 684, 801–803, 813, 820, 836, 840–841, 1036, 1066, 1102–1103, 1112, 1142
Palladas of Alexandria 1101–1102
Pamphilus of Alexandria 1086
Panaetius of Rhodes 863, 866–867, 915, 1026
Panya(s)sis of Halicarnassus 147, 523, **523–524**, 525, 527, 552, 898, 985
Papias of Hierapolis **1118**
Pappus of Alexandria 875, 1036
Parmenides of Elea 43, 163, 209, 294, 296–297, **297–299**, 299–300, 337, 339, 343, 404, 429, 678, 681, 698, 818, 821, 1091
Parry, Milman 99–101, 103–106, 121–123
Parthenius of Nicaea **794–795**
Passions (see *Acts and Passions of the Martyrs*)
Paul of Tarsus 1009–1013, 1015–1017, 1021, 1116–1117, 1123, 1125, 1145, 1147
Paulus Silentiarius 1101, **1103**, 1112
Pausanias of Damascus 819, 904
Pausanias 109, 128, 141, 160, 381, 547, 573, 575, 639, 897, 978, **982–986**, 993
Pearson, Lionel 639
Pedanius Dioscorides 1036
Persica **544–546**, 549, 630, 895
Petrarch 28, 111
Petronius 428, 1078
Peter, Apostle 1009–1010, 1015, 1017, 1021, 1116
Phaedimus of Bisanthe 824
Phalaecus 790
Phalaris (see *Letters of Phalaris*)
Phanocles **793–794**
Phanodemus 639, **641**, 642
Pherecrates 376, 486, **487**, 491, 533, 790
Pherecydes of Athens **546–547**
Pherecydes of Syros 9, 144, **308–309**

Philarchus 897, **898–899**, 899, 908, 912, 914
Philemon 752
Philetaerus 519
Philicus of Corcyra 764
Philinus of Acragas 908, 914
Philinus of Cos 875–876
Philippus, Pneumatist doctor 880
Philippus of Opus 684, 704
Philippus of Thessalonica 802, 1102
Philiscus, Comic poet 519
Philiscus of Miletus 901
Philistus of Syracuse 548, 575, **628–630**, 901–902
Philitas of Cos **776**, 776, 789, **792–793**, 793–794, 814, 816, 818, 835, 837, 843, 1070, 1085
Philocles I 482
Philochorus 639, 641, **641–642**, 814
Philodemus of Gadara 706, 800–801, 862, 1103
Philon of Byzantium 874–875
Philon of Larissa 858, 1025
Philonides 489, 494, 500
Philo of Alexandria 924, 926, 955, **1001– 1004**, 1023
Philosophumena (see *Refutation of All Heresies*)
Philostorgius 968, 1136
Philostratus I 1049
Philostratus II (Flavius Philostratus) 881, 1028, 1040–1042, 1046–1048, **1049– 1050**, 1050, 1080, 1098
Philostratus III **1050**
Philostratus IV **1050**
Philoxenus of Alexandria 785, 1081, 1088
Philoxenus of Cythera 533
Phocylides of Miletus **208**, 249
Phoenix of Colophon 790, **846**
Phormis 483, 723
Photius 570, 602–603, 607, 634, 645, 659, 667–669, 772, 958, 966, 968–970, 976, 1034, 1055, 1075–1076, 1087, 1093, 1099–1100
Phrynichus Arabius, Atticist 1085–1086
Phrynichus, Comic poet 377, 432, 489, **491**, 495

Phrynichus of Athens, Tragic poet 351, **379**, 380, 384, 465, 514, 523, 525, 765, 253– 254, **259**
Phrynis of Mytilene 533–534
Pigres of Halicarnassus 130–131
Pindar of Cynoscephalae 9, 11–12, 128, 176, 204, 214, 216, 247, 252, **259–272**, 272– 274, 276, 279–280, 321, 323, 327, 330, 383, 396–398, 404, 533, 769–770, 776, 779–780, 785, 798, 806, 810, 832, 905, 946, 949, 984
– *Epinicia* 252–254, 260–263, **265–270**, 271, 810
Pisander of Camirus 144, 523–524
Pytheas of Massalia 869, 910
Planudean Anthology or *Appendix Planudea* (see also Maximus Planudes) 802–803
Plato 9, 12, 24, 143, 162–163, 205, 257, 277, 285, 288, 296–297, 299, 305, 322, 328, 332, 335, 342, 345–346, 374, 404– 405, 408, 413, 418–421, 424–425, 481, 483–484, 495, 500, 521–522, 527, 532, 576, 597, 602–603, 607, 610, 616–619, 625, 644, 648, 652, 673, 676, 678–679, **680–702**, 703–705, 710, 715, 721, 725, 728, 730, 732, 772, 775, 796, 847, 853– 854, 870, 885, 911, 926, 947, 949, 953, 989, 999, 1022, 1030, 1032–1034, 1037, 1044–1045, 1047, 1072, 1079–1080, 1090–1091, 1096, 1104, 1128, 1142
– *Apology* 24, 412, 418, 421, 500, 684, 686, 691, 694
– *Crito* 691, 694
– *Epistles* 684, 686, **699–700**
– *Hippias Major* 413, 692
– *Ion* 103, 143, 522, 691, 775
– *Phaedo* 24, 418, 693–694, 701, 710, 1042, 1143
– *Phaedrus* 419, 597, 602–603, 686, 688, 693, 697, 700–701, 710, 775
– *Protagoras* 257, 406, 481, 685, 692, 701
– *Republic* 277, 285, 415, 594, 602, 622, 682, 689, 693, **695–697**, 699–701, 703, 713, 775, 1033
– *Symposium* 481, 495, 619, 685, 693, 701, 710, 1070
– *Theaetetus* 288, 483, 618, 685, 698
Plato, Comic poet 489, **491**
Plautus 491, 519, 752–753, 762

"Pleiad", Group of poets 764, 794, 843
Pliny the Elder 22, 961, 980
Pliny the Younger 850, 1043
Plotinus 1024, 1029–1032, 1034, 1098,
    1129
Plutarch of Athens 1033–1034
Plutarch of Chaeronea 51, 155, 162, 199–
    200, 229, 273, 489, 525, 553–554, 570,
    601, 628, 659, 662, 666, 668, 675, 680,
    708, 770, 800, 814, 889–891, 895, 897,
    921, 936, 938, 948, 966, 979, 984, **988–
    1000**, 1023–1024, 1045, 1074, 1078, 1090,
    1105
– Moralia 990, **994–999**, 1000, 1024
– Lives 659, 814, 936, **990–994**, 999–1000
Polemon of Laodicea 1040–1041, 1046
Polemon, Academic scholarch 703, 854
Polemon of Ilium 780, 802, 902
Poliziano, Angelo 162, 960
Pollux, Iulius 1085
Polus of Acragas 323, 594
Polyaenus **966**
Polybius 572, 632–633, 637, 643, 699, 745,
    748, 887–888, 891, 898, 899, 901–902,
    904, **904–915**, 915, 917, 920–921, 939,
    945, 955–957, 964, 969–970, 973, 977,
    979, 981–982, 993
Polycarp of Smyrna 1116, **1117**, 1124
Polycrates of Athens 416, 617, 646, 648
Polycrates of Mende 824
Polyphrasmon **379–380**
Polyzelus 514
Pomponius Mela 961
Porphyry of Tyre 294, 312, 730, 782, 1030,
    1032, 1033, 1035, 1075, 1084, 1089, 1096,
    1106
Posidippus of Pella 799
Posidonius of Apamea 745, 863, 866, 879,
    885, 888, **915–916**, 921, 956, 978–979,
    981–982, 987, 1026
Postumius Albinus, Aulus 910
Potamon of Mytilene 896
Pratinas of Phlius **379–380**, 383, 533
Praxagoras, Late Antique historian 976
Praxagoras of Cos, Doctor 876
Praxilla of Sicyon 281
Praxiphanes of Mytilene 161, 775, 816, 885
Priscian 1082, 1113

Priscus of Epirus, Neoplatonist philosopher
    1096
Priscus of Panion 976
Proclus, Author of the Chrestomathy 134–
    135, 138
Proclus, Neoplatonist philosopher 127,
    806, 1033–1034, 1100, 1103–1104, 1106
Procopius of Caesarea 967, **970–975**
Procopius of Gaza 968, 1100, 1110
Prodicus of Ceos **412–413**, 413, 453, 531,
    646, 692, 775
Propertius 792, 801
Protagoras of Abdera 257, 338, 404–405,
    410–412, 412, 453, 692, 775, 1091
Psellus, Michael 1070, 1099, 1106
Pseudo-Apollodorus 1089
Pseudo-Barnabas 1117–1118
Pseudo-Callisthenes (see also Alexander Ro-
    mance) 889, **896–897**, 1057
Pseudo-Longinus (see On the Sublime)
Pseudo-Lucian 1055, 1059
Pseudo-Plutarch 94, 645, 659, 668
– On the Life and Poetry of Homer 51, 94,
    998
Pseudo-Scymnus 820
Pseudo-Xenophon 622, **625–626**
Pseudo-Zonaras 772, 1088
Ptolemaeus of Ascalon 785, 1081
Pyrrhon of Elis **855–857**, 857, 900, 1025,
    1091
Pythagoras 39, 43, 45, 286, 290, 293, 294,
    294–295, 404, 483, 732, 926, 998, 1028,
    1032, 1035, 1075, 1091
Quadratus 1121
Quintilian 162, 239, 524, 593, 881, 885–
    886, 895, 951
Quintus Smyrnaeus 143, **1107–1108**
Ravel, Maurice 1071
Refutation of All Heresies 1127
Rhetoric to Alexander 591, **597–598**, 700
Rhianus of Crete or of Bene 142, **777**, 824
Rhinthon 765, **766**, 847
Romilly, Jacqueline Worms de 582
Royal Ephemerides **890–891**
Rufinus, Epigrammatist 1102
Rufinus, Latin translator of Origen 1130
Rufus of Ephesus 1036
Sallust 916
Sannazaro, Jacopo 840, 1070

Sappho of Eresus 8–9, 11–12, 43, 171, 176,
 213, 215, **223–233**, 233, 237–238, 246,
 250–251, 315, 491, 798, 800, 946, 1093
Satyrus, Doctor 1037
Satyrus, Peripatetic philosopher 453
Schadewaldt, Wolfgang 116
Schliemann, Heinrich 1, **64–68**, 72, 122
Scopelianus 1040, 1046
Scylax of Caryanda 307–308, 961
Scymnus of Chios 820, 904
Second Letter of Clement 1120
Séguier, Nicolas, marquis de St. Brisson
 951
Seleucus of Seleucia 870
Semonides of Amorgos 9, 11, 43, 173, 178–
 179, **184–186**, 208, 249, 315, 442, 780
Seneca, Lucius Annaeus 428, 863, 866,
 1026
Seneca the Rhetor 882
Septuagint 10, 26–27, 742, **923–924**, 925–
 926, 940, 1001, 1079, 1128, 1131
Seven Sages 200, 234, **286–287**, 288, 316,
 733, 773, 813, 1091
Sextus Empiricus 785, 856, 880, 1025
Shakespeare, William 1000
Sibylline Books 1105
Sibylline Oracles 1029, 1105, 1119
Simmias of Rhodes **794**, 798, 835, 841–842
Simonides of Ceos 9, 11, 43, 176, 184, 214,
 216, 247, 253, **254–259**, 261, 264, 266,
 271–272, 276, 323, 327, 383, 404, 533,
 624, 795–796
– The encomia 257–258
– *Lament of Danae* 258–259
Simonides of Magnesia 824
Simplicius, Peripatetic philosopher 1025
Socrates of Athens 12, 24, 163, 257, 285,
 293, 297, 322, 335, 337, 341, 343, 407,
 412–413, **415–424**, 424–425, 428–429,
 453, 480, 491, 499–500, 506, 531, 575,
 602–603, 611–612, 616–619, 646, 678–
 681, 684–695, 697–700, 703, 715–716,
 732, 853–857, 926, 968, 996, 1023, 1029,
 1071, 1079, 1091
Socrates, Ecclesiastical historian 1136,
 1146
Solon of Athens 11, 24, 36–38, 43, 45, 109,
 161, 176, 190–191, **199–204**, 205–206,
 286–287, 404, 413, 490, 498, 556–557,

 569, 573, 595, 640, 642, 650, 680, 685,
 698, 771, 818, 1096
Song of Songs 1127, 1147
Sophocles 12, 24, 133, 161, 236, 321, 330–
 331, 349, 352, 360–361, 363, 365, 381–
 383, 387–388, 390, 394, 400, 402, **430–
 450,** 452–456, 461–462, 468–469, 471–
 472, 475, 478, 480, 482, 484, 491, 506,
 516, 521, 552–553, 569, 676, 678, 723,
 726, 732, 763, 765, 770, 779–780, 947,
 949, 1043
– *Ajax* 361, 433, **433–436**, 438, 441, 447–
 449, 462
– *Antigone* 387–388, 430–433, 437, **437–
 439**, 448–449, 552
– *Electra* 394, 433, 445–446, 448
– *Oedipus at Colonus* 402, 432, 433, 437,
 441–442, 447, 468
– *Oedipus Tyrannus* 433, 437, **439–441**,
 447–448, 480, 482, 726
– *Philoctetes* 432–433, **433–436**, 441, 447–
 448, 462, 1043
– *The Women of Trachis* 433, **442–444**,
 447–448
Sophron 323, 483, **484–485**, 512, 784, 838,
 847–848, 850
Soranus of Ephesus 879, 1036
Sosibius of Sparta 373
Sosiphanes of Syracuse 765
Sositheus 764, **845–846**
Sotades 790
Sozomen 968, 1136, 1146
Speusippus of Athens 630, 682, 702–706,
 854
Stasinus of Cyprus 140
Stephanus, Henricus 111
Stephanus of Byzantium 311, 766, 983,
 986, 1086
Stesichorus 9, 11, 43, 133, 160, 176, 214,
 216, 222, 228, **238–243**, 243–246, 258,
 281, 396, 409, 467, 528, 947
Stesimbrotus of Thasos 50
Stilpon 429
Stobaeus (see John of Stobi)
Strabo 545, 547, 633, 708, 770, 846, 858,
 890, 892, 895, 915, 961, 977, **978–982**,
 987
– *Geography* 708, 977–979, **980–982**

Straton of Lampsacus 24, 731, 776, 853–854, 868, 870
Straton of Sardis 1102
Strattis 514
Sublime (see *On the Sublime*)
Suda, Lexicon 51, 131, 240, 260, 308, 369, 378, 380, 382–383, 425, 430–431, 453, 455, 480, 485–487, 494, 514, 521, 524, 545, 547, 549, 551, 554, 573, 602, 641, 645, 659, 731, 766, 772, 803–805, 811, 816, 824–825, 841, 845, 894, 896, 948, 953, 989, 1039, 1048–1049, 1051, 1063, 1065, 1076, 1087, 1108, 1112
Suetonius 1007
Symmachus 1131
Synesius of Cyrene 1023, 1034, 1043, **1098–1099**, 1103–1104. 1106, 1148–1149
Synagogē 1086
Syrianus 1033
Tacitus 916, 955, 964, 1007
Tasso, Torquato 840, 1066
Tatian 1122
Teleclides 376, 486, **487**
Telephus, Pergamene philologist 783
Telesilla of Argos **281**
Terence 752–753, 762
Terpander of Antissa 9, 215–216, **217–218**, 218, 534
Tertullian 932
Thaletas of Gortyn 216
Thestorides of Phocaea 140
Thales of Miletus 286–288, **288**, 289, 312, 404, 813, 1090
Theagenes of Rhegium 50, 143, 775
Theban Cycle 49, 133–134, 140, 242, 387, 433, 436, 468, 527, 824
Themison of Laodicea 878
Themistius 371, **1093–1094**, 1096–1098
Theocritus of Syracuse 9, 13, 485, 754, 770, 785, 789–790, 792–793, **833–841**, 841–842, 844–845, 848, 850, 1105
– *Idylls* 835, **836–839**
Theodectes of Phaselis 517, 635
Theodore of Mopsuestia 1144
Theodoret of Cyrrhus 968, 1136, **1146–1147**
Theodorus, Pneumatist doctor 879
Theodorus of Byzantium 594, 597, 602
Theodorus of Gadara **944–945**
Theodotion 926, 1131

Theognis, Tragic Poet 482
Theognis of Megara 11, 43, 176, 190, 191, **204–207**, 208, 236, 818
Theolytus of Methymna 824, 828
Theon, Grammarian 785, 834, 841, 1085
Theon, Aelius 886, 950–951
Theon of Alexandria, Philosopher and mathematician 868
Theophilus of Antioch **1122–1123**
Theophrastus 24–25, 675, 677, 706–708, 712, **729–731**, 731–732, 751, 753, 773, 775–776, 821, 853–854, 868, 897, 899, 1091
Theopompus, Comic poet 514, 519
Theopompus of Chios 308, 332, 628, 631, 633, **634–637**, 646, 888, 891, 895, 899, 909, 913–914, 957, 993
Thespis of Athens 371, **378–379**
Thessalus of Tralles 878
Thrasyllus 684
Thrasymachus of Chalcedon **414–415**, 593–594, 597, 695
Thucydides 9, 12, 24, 73–74, 128, 161, 304, 321–322, 332, 333, 334, 490, 496–497, 544, 548–549, 551, 517, **571–590**, 595, 598–600, 607, 611–614, 625, 627–632, 634–635, 637, 640, 643–644, 657, 678, 685, 770, 888, 907–908, 911–914, 916, 946–947, 955, 957, 959, 964, 966, 970, 974–975, 984–985, 992, 1047
– *The History of the Peloponnesian War* 544, **576–580**
Timaeus of Tauromenium 548, 575, 745, 844, 887–888, **901–903**, 909, 912–914, 919, 992
Timagenes of Alexandria 633, 922
Timonides of Leucas 630
Timon of Phlius 856–857, 1091
Timotheus of Miletus 20–21, 533, **534**
Tisias of Syracuse 323, 407, 591, 593–594, 597, 602
Tractatus Coislinianus de comoedia 163
Triphiodorus 1108
Trojan Cycle 56, 133–134, 137–140, 241, 400, 408, 433, 461, 464, 1059, 1077
Tryphon of Alexandria 785, 1081
Tyrannio 25, 784, 978, 1081
Tyrtaeus 11, 43, 176, 191, **193–196**, 201, 204–205, 210, 215, 218, 302, 523

Tzetzes, Johannes 844, 1080
Ullrich, Franz W. 581
Valentinus 1126
Valerius Antias 964
Valerius Flaccus 833
Varro Atacinus 821, 833
Varro, Marcus Terentius 22, 428, 782, 784,
   921, 956–957, 991, 1089
Vega, Lope de 1070
Ventris, Michael 2
Vettori, Piero 597
Vico, Giambattista 111–112
Villoison, Jean Baptiste Gaspard d'Ansse de
   112–113
Virgil 56, 111, 136, 161–163
West, Martin Litchfield 124
Wilamowitz–Moellendorff, Ulrich von 114,
   638–639
Wolf, Friedrich August 99, 111, 113, 122
Wood, Robert 112
Xanthus of Lydia (or of Sardis) 545–546
Xenarchus of Seleucia 978
Xenocles 482
Xenocrates of Chalcedon 682, 703, 854
Xenophanes of Colophon 43, 84, 130, 143,
   147, 161–163, 176, 191, 195, **208–212**,
   269, 284, 290, 294, **295–296**, 297, 302,
   305, 311, 339, 523, 818, 857, 1091
– Elegies 209–210
– Silloi 210–211, 296
Xenophon 9, 12, 24, 321, 332, 373, 412,
   418–420, 575–576, 583, **611–625**, 625–
   626, 628, 630, 635, 643, 685, 710, 713,
   770, 888, 892, 921, 950, 959–960, 962,
   970, 984, 993, 1044–1045, 1072, 1113
– Agesilaus 612, **616**, 624, 921, 962, 993
– Anabasis of Cyrus 373, 612, **614–615**,
   624, 960

– Apology of Socrates 418, **619**
– Constitution of the Lacedaemonians 612,
   622–623, 625, 713
– Cyropaedia 610, 612, **615–616**, 624
– Hellenica 583, 612, **613–614**, 624, 628,
   635, 888
– Hieron **624**
– Memorabilia 24, 412, 612, **617–618**, 624
– Oeconomicus 612, **618–619**, 623, 643
– On the Art of Horsemanship 612, **620–
   621**, 643
– On Hunting 612, 618, **621–622**, 623
– Symposium 612, **619**
– The Cavalry Commander 612, **620**, 643
– Ways and Means 610, **623–624**, 630
Xenophon of Ephesus 1057, **1063–1065**,
   1069, 1074
Zacharias Scholasticus 1100
Zenobius 774, 1087
Zenodotus of Ephesus 25, 110, **776–777**,
   777–779, 792, 803, 825, 843, 903, 1085
Zeno of Citium 13, 141, 161, 425, 742, 745,
   820, 855, 857, 863, **863–866**, 1091
Zeno of Elea 297, **299–300**, 429, 698, 711
Zeuxis 877
Zonaras, Johannes 963
Zosimus 659, 967, **968–970**, 970, 976

γνῶμαι μονόστιχοι 754
δισσοὶ λόγοι (see Dissoi Logoî)
Εἰσαγωγὴ ἢ Ἰατρός (see Introductio sive
   medicus)
Συναγωγὴ λέξεων χρησίμων (Collection of
   Useful Expressions, see Synagogē)
Φιλοσοφούμενα, see Refutation of All Here-
   sies